SEISTAN

A MEMOIR ON THE HISTORY, TOPOGRAPHY, RUINS, AND PEOPLE OF THE COUNTRY

IN FOUR PARTS

PARTS I TO III

Agents for the Sale of Books

PUBLISHED BY

The Superintendent of Government Printing, India, Calcutta.

In England.

- E. A. Arnold, 41 & 43, Maddox Street, Bond Street, London, W.
- Constable & Co., 10, Orange Street, Leicester Square, W.C.
- P. S. King & Sons, 2 & 4, Great Smith Street, Westminster, London, S.W.
- Henry S. King & Co., 65, Cornhill, and 9, Pall Mall, London.
- Kegan Paul, Trench, Trübner & Co., 43, Gerrard Street, Soho, London, W.
- Grindlay & Co., 54, Parliament Street, London, S.W.
- Bernard Quaritch, 11, Grafton Street, New Bond Street, W.
- Deighton, Bell & Co., Cambridge.
- B. H. Blackwell, 50 & 51, Broad Street, Oxford.
- T. Fisher Unwin, 1 Adelphi Terrace, London, W.C.
- W. Thacker & Co., 2, Creed Lane, London, E.C.
- Luzac & Co., 46, Great Russell Street, London, W.C.

On the Continent.

- R. Friedlander & Sohn, Berlin, W.N., Carlstrasse, 11.
- Otto Harrassowitz, Leipzig.
- Karl W. Hiersemann, Leipzig.
- Ernest Leroux, 28, Rue Bonaparte, Paris.
- Martinus Nijhoff, The Hague, Holland.
- Rudolf Haupt, 1, Dorrienstrasse, Leipzig, Germany.

In India.

- Thacker, Spink & Co., Calcutta and Simla.
- Newman & Co., Calcutta.
- S. K. Lahiri & Co., Calcutta.
- R. Cambray & Co., Calcutta.
- B. Banerjee & Co., Calcutta.
- Higginbotham & Co., Madras.
- V. Kalyanarama Aiyar & Co., Madras.
- G. A. Natesan & Co., Madras.
- S. Murthy & Co., Madras.
- Thompson & Co., Madras.
- Temple & Co., Madras.
- Combridge & Co., Madras.
- P. R. Rama Iyer & Co., Madras.
- Thacker & Co., Ld., Bombay.
- A. J. Combridge & Co., Bombay.
- D. B. Taraporevala Sons & Co., Bombay.
- Radhabai Atmaram Sagoon, Bombay.
- Sunder Pandurang, Bombay.
- Gopal Narayan & Co., Bombay.
- N. B. Mathur, Superintendent, Nazair Kanun Hind Press, Allahabad.
- A. Chand & Co., Punjab.
- Rai Sahib M. Gulab Singh and Sons, Mufid-i-Am Press, Lahore and Calcutta.
- Superintendent, American Baptist Mission Press, Rangoon.
- A. M. & J. Ferguson, Ceylon.
- S. C. Talukdar, Proprietor, Students and Company, Cooch Behar.

SEISTAN

A MEMOIR ON THE HISTORY, TOPOGRAPHY, RUINS, AND PEOPLE OF THE COUNTRY

IN FOUR PARTS

By Mr. G. P. TATE, M.R.A.S., F.R.G.S.
SURVEY OF INDIA
Author of
Kalat : a Memoir of the Country and Family of the
Ahmadzai Khans of Kala

PARTS I TO III

CALCUTTA
SUPERINTENDENT GOVERNMENT PRINTING, INDIA

PREFACE

THE account of Seistan contained in the following pages has been based on actual observation and on information collected in that country during the sojourn of the Boundary Commission, under Sir Arthur McMahon, together with the result of many years of close study of the History of Khurassan. The object that has been carefully kept in view is to record information and the result has been that the report is longer than is usually considered to be necessary, as it was believed to be advisable to preserve information rather than to aim at literary effect.

The traditions of the past are in danger of being lost, as there were in 1905 only one or two very old men who knew anything at all of these matters or who cared to preserve the knowledge. The population of Seistan is largely composed of tribes, or odd sections of tribes, who have migrated at a comparatively recent date into the country. These persons know nothing of the past history of the country and their struggle for a livelihood has rendered them indifferent to all but the problems of their daily existence.

This report has been revised during odd moments of leisure from official duties—and extensive emendations have been impossible. I hope all shortcomings will, for this reason, be regarded with leniency.

G. P. TATE.

PART I.
THE HISTORY OF SEISTAN.

Trakun, where a celebrated Fire-temple once existed.

(Part I Frontispiece.)

THE HISTORY OF SEISTAN.

CHAPTER I.

THE oases of Central Asia—those favoured and celebrated districts round Samarkand, Merv, Balkh, and the fertile valley of Herat—have been the homes of an agricultural population for many centuries before their names appear in History. The delta of Seistan nourished by the Helmand was on an equality in all respects but area, with those more widely known tracts. The former, however, passed in course of time into the possession of rulers of an alien race, and the ancient races have been overlaid by the influx of foreigners. Seistan on the other hand owing to its remote position, surrounded as it has always been by wide spreading deserts or semi-deserted tracts, has remained the patrimony of a family of ruling princes up to a century ago—the Kaiāni Maliks; who claim to be the descendants of the most ancient dynasty of Monarchs who ruled over the Persian Empire before the existence of History.

This claim was put forward many centuries ago, and it has been allowed to stand presumably in the absence of evidence to the contrary. It cannot be challenged now. The Kaiānis of Seistan are not, however, even in these days the only family which claims the Legendary Monarchs of Persia for its ancestors. It is understood that among the Zoroastrian Community so long domiciled in India, there are families styled Kaiāni who advance such a claim, and whose pretensions are tolerated or assented to by that Community. Oriental writers who treat of the various dynasties which have from time to time ruled over the Ancient Persian Empire, generally represent the purely native dynasties as being of one stock or race: the descendants of earlier dynasties which were overthrown, and for a season relegated to a position of obscurity by the inroads and consequent predominance of foreigners.

The Parsis believe the most ancient dynasty of Persian Monarchs, to have been the Kaianian. To it belonged Gushtasp, the father of Isfandiyar, and grandfather of Bahman. Their capital was Balkh,[1] oldest of all the cities of Khurassan.

The Akhœmenean Dynasty is said to be a continuation, and possibly may have been founded by a descendant of the Kaiânis. The capital of this family was Pasargadœ and Shustar. Between these dynasties intervened a long period when Iran is believed to have been overrun by the Assyrians, and after them to have been in a condition of servitude to the Medes. Such a condition of affairs would be sufficient to account for a change of capital; and the relations that had grown up in course of time with the states of the Mediterranean littoral would have rendered the change of capital in a westward direction very necessary.

The Court of the Monarch and the headquarters of the administration was any pleasant locality where the Royal Pavilions happened to be placed. But the archives of the dynasty and the centre of religion must have been located in some city, more favoured than others, which was honoured by the actual residence of the Monarch during some portion of the year. This became the capital city of the dynasty which happened to be in power. The Empire itself was an unweildy fabric, composed of Great Provinces, each of which was ruled by a Satrap appointed by the central Government. In many instances these Governors were undoubtedly members of territorial families which by reason of their numerous adherents and the following they were able to bring into the field under their banners, were more powerful than any other sections of the people inhabiting the province.

The loyalty, or disaffection, of these great families rendered the Great King powerful and victorious; or led him to supplicate the co-operation, and fealty which he had perhaps alienated, or weakened.

The personal qualities of the Supreme Ruler was the bond that drew together the discordant elements of his vast kingdom. A great soldier—himself an accomplished man-at-arms and a wise statesman, would be able to

---

[1] Balkh; the ancient Bakhdi mentioned in the Avesta, has not been often described by travellers; and the more recent of these descriptions are probably contained in narratives that are not available to the public. The following notices are taken from the notes made by Dr. Gerard Burnes' travelling companion who accompanied the latter to Bokhara. The latter wrote that the modern inhabitants will inform you that "the country between the Balkh and Kabul has the name of Bakhtar Zamin" (Journal of Asiatic Society, Bengal, Volume II, page 307). This name extended further to the south of Kabul, and both in the Malfuzat-i-Sahib Kiran and the Rauzat-ul-Jannat it is stated that the country to the south of, and around the modern town of, Kandahar was known as Bakhtar Zamin. Dr. Gerard writes of Balkh:—"The ruins which are mostly of mud, are very extensive: but they only mark the modern site of the city. The insalubrity of Balkh is proverbial * * * The eighteen beautiful acqueducts (Karezes), by which it was irrigated, no longer guided by the art of the husbandman have spread their waters over the face of the country, and transformed its fair landscape into a stagnant marsh." (Ibid, page 15.) Burnes and Gerard visited the graves of Moorcroft, and his travelling companions Trebeck and Guthrie at that place. After this city had for many generations been exposed to the vicissitudes of war, during the struggles that took place for the possession of the Empire of Timur, among the numerous descendants of the Great Amir, the ruin of Balkh according to the author of the Rauzt-us-Sata, was completed by Shaibani Khan the Uzbek, who besieged and took Balkh in the winter of $\frac{909\ A.\ H.}{1503\text{-}04\ A.D.}$.

compel the obedience, and stifle the personal and diversified interests of his subjects; and render his influence predominant over the neighbouring kingdoms. Under a weaker successor the racial animosities and personal jealousies and ambitions of the great feudal chiefs might at any time break and the kingdom lately feared and respected would be at the mercy of a numerically weaker enemy at the head of a homogeneous force acting under a well recognised central authority.

This condition of the political fabric of the ancient Persian Empire is portrayed most vividly in the Shahnameh. Only when he was aided by the personal prowess and the armed strength of the Prince of Khurassan, could the Great King make head against the Scythian invaders.

Faridun the mythical sovereign portioned the Empire he had built up among his three sons; assigning according to some authorities, the province of Khurassan to his son Iraj together with portions of Hind and Sind.

In his turn Zuhak the Tazi was overcome and a number of his descendants fled into the district of Ghur where they found a refuge. They became subjects of Faridun.

Karshasp, ancestor of Rustam, held Kabul, Zabul and Sijistan for Faridun; and the descendants of Zuhak would in this case have been subject to Karshasp. His nephew Nariman had a son Sam, who in turn became the father of Zal. Sam is said to have held Zabul and Kabul, as far as Hind in feudal sovereignty from the Rulers of Iran. Zal having succeeded to his father's fief went to Zabul from Zaranj (founded by Karshasp) and Mihrab Shah of the race of Zuhak, the Tazi, the tributary ruler, came forth to meet Zal and acknowledge his supremacy. Mihrab Shah also gave his daughter in marriage to Zal, and she was the mother of Rustam.

The same Mihrab Shah is said to have afterwards led the right wing of the army of Kaikubad I the first of the Kaianian Dynasty in the campaign against Afrasiyab and the Turk.

In the Jami-ut-Tawarik however it is stated, that when this invader crossed the Jaihun into Khurassan, he detached a force to intercept Sam or keep him in check. At this time Mihrab Shah is said to have held the city and fortress of Zabul as deputy for Zal; and when the invaders reached the Hirmend, the former tried to delude the enemy by means of a message to the commander, stating that he was neither Zabuli nor Irani, but of the race of Zuhak (an alien in fact), and consequently loyally inclined towards Afrasiyab.

The appanage of Zal was the territory included within the limits of Khurassan. The author of the Rauzat-ul-Jannat-fi-ausaf-i-Madinati-il-Herat has preserved some notices regarding the cities of that great province. He wrote in the year 898 H.; and though not an early author he has in very many instances recorded the statements of those who lived and wrote centuries before his time as well as traditions existing in the country in his day relating to the founding of the great cities of Khurassan.

There had been in existence in or close to Balkh a celebrated Fire Temple, named Bahar, reverenced by all Fire Worshippers on the face of the earth. The ruins of this pyrœum were said to be existing as late as the time when the author wrote; and he mentions that a legend was in existence to the effect that under its ruins vast treasures had been buried.

This city has already been mentioned as being according to the traditions of the Parsis, the capital of Gushtap. The famous city of Herat celebrated as the latter capital of Khurassan was built in comparatively recent times compared with the foundation of both Shamiran, Khuhanduz; Khiaban; or Aobah; all of which it outgrew. In course of time those towns, villages, or districts became the suburbs or were dependant on, the city of Herat.

Mulla Muin preserves a quatrain which was current in his day containing another version again of the building of Herat.

"Lohrasp had laid the foundations of Heri."

"Gushtasp, on them raised a superstructure."

"After him Bahman constructed the buildings and Alexander of Rum completed all."

Zābul or Zāwul however appears to have been the chief city of Khurassan while Balkh was the capital of the empire. Together with Kabul, and Zaranj, there seem to have existed three chief towns of as many provinces which formed the appanage of Zal, son of Sam; and after the former of his son the hero Rustom.

As late as the period of Mulla Muin the name of Zābul or Zāwal still survived. It was at that time one of the districts of Isfirār or Sabzawār, the native place of that author. Zāwul is also entered in the map drawn up by Connolly to illustrate his account of Seistan, which appeared during the year 1840, in the journal of the Asiatic Society of Bengal. The name probably still exists. According to Mulla Muin, in his day the district of Zāwul was 3 farsakhs across. In it there were no less than 80 karezes, none of which discharged less than enough to turn one watermill, while others contained so much water that it was not possible to repair or cleanse them; for if the flow of water was stopped the waters rose at once to the tops of the wells above the obstacle and overflowed, spreading over the land.

With regard to the city of Isfirār or Sabzawār, he states that it was universally believed in the country to be older than Herat; having been built 2,000 years before the time in which he wrote. This was 425 years ago.

He also describes a very ancient fortress, a place of very great strength in its day, which was called the Shahristān of Queen Belkis. The walls rest upon an outcrop of rock which rises to the height of a yard or so above the surface of the soil. Around the fort are verdant meadows and water is no more than a yard below the surface. Owing to this, and to the rock on which the walls were founded, it was impossible to undermine the defences. The city of Isfirār was situated between this fortress and another which crowned a height called Mozaffar Koh. The latter was however a modern work as its foundation was attributed to Alb-i-Ghazi [1]; whereas the Fort of Queen Belkis dated from prehistoric times. According to Connolly's map the town of Isfirār or Sabzawâr is situated in the western portion of the Zāwul District. It was built at the junction of the Rud-i-Bojzghanan with the Adraskan, a stream which there encircled the town on three sides. The place was very famous for its sweet water, and the salubrity of its climate. The extent of its meadows (Ulang), its beautiful trees, and splendid kanats : and, in consequence, the fruit raised there was celebrated throughout Khurassan.

Colonel Yate who visited Sabzawâr in April 1893 mentions the fact that the ruins of the capital were almost concealed by the gardens which surrounded it. There was abundance of water and much cultivation. Writing of the view from the top of the Governor's quarters, he states that "the whole ground below the town as I saw it that May evening, was one sheet of * * green the air was cool and pleasant after the heat of Farah." This author also mentions the old fortress of Muzaffar Koh, some three miles to the south of the town. The name of this place was given to him as being Kala-i-Dukhtar : but as his description agrees with the information recorded to by Mulla Muin, there can be no doubt that the fortress of Muzaffar Koh [2] and the Kala-i-Dukhtar are identical.

---

[1] Alb-i-Ghazi was Governor of Herat in 600 A. H. (1203-4) and surrendered the City to Sultan Shihab-ud-dīn, Ghuri. He was the nephew (sister's son) to the two Princes Gheiath-ud-din and Shihab-ud-din, Ghuri : Tabak-i-Nas, page 257, by Major Raverty, Alb-i-Ghazi may have been the builder of the Fortress of Muzaffar Koh, but it was perhaps merely restored by him, and had been used as a stronghold from prehistoric times.

Mulla Muin of Sabzawâr, writing 425 years ago, gave the following account of this well known stronghold. Built of baked brick and clay mortar upon an offshoot of the hills, composed of an extremely hard rock, very high and striking in appearance, and nearly one farsakh (about 4 miles) in circumference.

"The gate is situated at the foot of the hill on the banks of the river of Isfirār, while the citadel crowns the summit of the hill, and is extremely lofty and imposing in appearance. Within the fort there is a Jami-Masjid, Bazar, containing lofty buildings, and caravan serais, without exception plastered with Gach and Saruj. The width of the walls was such that seven horsemen could ride along them side by side and inside the gate there was a spring, the water of which used to flow out through the entrance and fall into the river. It is now choked with rubbish and the water has disappeared inside the citadel, also, there are reservoirs of great size constructed with baked brick and lime mortar, which used to be filled with rain water. On no side of that fort can a horseman reach the foot of the walls, except where the gate is situated on the bank of the river. On two sides there are places where man on foot can reach the foot of the walls. On the other two sides not even a bird can fly up to them (!!) from the gateway to the citadel is a distance of a mile or more, and the path for half the distance is practicable for a horse. The walls are so constructed that for the greater part of their circuit horsemen could ride along their summit.

"The place where the clay had been excavated to make the bricks and clay mortar used in the building of the walls is about one farsakh distant from them.

"There was a tradition that the fortress built by persons who had been brought for that purpose from Bagdad."

Colonel Yate also mentioned that on the other side of the river " were the mud walls of some ancient city, and in the hills beyond there was said to have been another fortress " either of these may have been the Shahristān-i-Belkis.

Farah is also one of the ancient sites of Khurassan. The author from whose work the description of Sabzawār is taken mentions it as such. He also alludes to its fertility and states that this district produced (then) wheat and barley in great abundance. Also, that in the district there were many strong fortresses. The town of Farah itself was also a place of great strength.

M. Ferrier in 1846 visited Farah and describes it as a parallelogram oriented due north and south. The Herat gate was placed in the middle of the north face and that of Kandahar in the middle of the southern face. The citadel occupied the north angle of the place. The walls were enormously thick and stood on a bank some 35 to 40 feet in height; apparently of pisé work; which in the course of time had become so hard that a pickaxe could make no impression on it. A covered way on the outside surrounded the fortifications, and beyond it again there was a broad and deep ditch which could be flooded at pleasure.

Yate, who visited Farah in 1893, entered the town by the Kandahar gate. " Farah," he writes, " is a square walled place standing out in the middle of the plain something like Kandahar, but with the ramparts of Herat. It is no longer a town."

He also mentions another conspicuous mound close to which he halted, having marched from Farah. It is called the Kala-i-Sām " or the fort of Sām, grand-father of Rustam, the hero of Seistan, a high square mound with a swamp all round, is the remains apparently of the ancient moat."

Localities such as those already described where good soil and water existed have undoubtedly been inhabited from the earliest ages; a space of time of which no record exists. For many centuries in historical times they have continued to be fertile and populous centres, and the tale of their decline and ruin will be unfolded in the course of this narrative. They were intimately connected with Seistan. Their rulers were members of Tajik families, and in the case of the maliks of Farah, connected by ties of relationship and alliance, if not ethnologically of the same stock, as the Kaiānis of the latter country.

Whether of this particular family or not, they belonged to the ancient Iranian race that formed the bulk of the population of this Great Province of Khurassan, from whence also sprung the Kaiānis, who for many centuries ruled over Iran.

The dates recorded by Mulla Muin of Sabzawār of the founding of his native town and Herat and other places are of very great interest. He does not state, and probably he could not learn from his authorities, how they had

been arrived at. A few, a very few dates of a similar character exist in Seistani legends.[1]   *   *   *   *   *   *
*   One of these, however, still remains to be noticed. It refers to the hero Rustam. He is said to have lived and flourished 1,000 years "before the Prophet Mohamed." The terms are vague; but if they mean that the 1,000 years was prior to the birth of Mohamed, then the period of Rustam, according to this tradition was the 5th century before the commencement of our era; and only some 100 years prior to the expedition of Alexander. The date, however, is based on no known authority, but it is an interesting piece of information, and as such is well worth preserving, though of course reliance cannot be placed on it, as being accurate, or even approximately correct.[1]

It seems strange, that if this great hero, the Champion of the Arians, and the bulwark of his country against the inroads of Turanian hordes, had lived only some 4 or 5 generations previous to the expedition of Alexander, no notice of him and his achievements should have reached the latter, for whom the martial fame and prowess of the Prince of Khurassan would have possessed a peculiar interest; and it seems improbable in that case that mention of him should not have been preserved in the accounts from which the historian Arian compiled his history. They however were incomplete. The sensation caused by the ingratitude and treachery of Bessus, the Bactrian satrap, towards his unfortunate Sovereign Darius may have been strengthened by the contrast between his conduct and the loyalty shown by Rustam towards his master.

This loyalty is emphasized in the accounts preserved in the Shahnameh of the relations that existed between the hero and his unworthy sovereign.

Zäwul the capital of fief handed down to Rustam by his father was probably Sabzawār (of later ages); and which was held by Mihrab Shah the Tazi. Thus early in the history of Khurassan the Ghuris (for the descendants of Zuhak settled in that mountainous district) had begun to take that prominent part in the affairs of Khurassan which they continued to do during subsequent ages. The inroads also of hordes from the country beyond the Oxus, or from High Asia, which in subsequent ages changed the face of the countries of the nearer east, had been recurring from time immemorial. The great invasion of the Turks under Afrasiyab was a foreshadowing of the irruption of the similar hordes under Tamurchi, the Chingiz Khan, during comparatively recent historical times.

The Samnameh which with the Gershasp (Karshasp) nameh was an older romance on which Firdausi built up his famous epic, treated (according

[1] According to a Seistani tradition, the town or fortress of Sar-o-Tar was abandoned once 1,702 years ago. This will be referred to again in the archaeological chapter, where other dates will be dealt with.

to the late Sir Henry Rawlinson) of the three expeditions of Sam against the Sakasaran (a Scythian race) by order of Faridun.

"The Greeks had a very early tradition, acquired in the country apparently at the time of Alexander's expedition, that Cyrus being reduced to great straits in his Scythian was received from a tribe named Agriaspœ, or Ariaspœ residing in the southern part of Drangiana ; in acknowledgment of which aid he gave them the honorary title of Euergetœ or the benefactors."

Drangiana was the Grœcised form of the name Zaranj by which the Arabs in later times knew Seistan. The limits of ancient Seistan were very much wider than they are at the present day, or even were as late as 100 years ago. In modern Seistan there are living the impoverished remnants of a family, all that is left of a once powerful community, to whom in past ages certain privileges are said to have been assigned by a former "King of Persia" in return for the very effective assistance they rendered him, when sore pressed by his enemies. The Reis[1] were once powerful in the south of the delta of Seistan, and in the adjoining districts of Sarhad ; but they have now almost entirely disappeared. They were Farsiwan, that is, they belonged to the ancient Iranian population, though modified to a certain extent in recent times by an admixture of Arab blood due to the influx to bands of Arab soldiers who settled among them.

The legends about the Reis is that they were "Ru-Shinas" admitted, that is, to the presence of the Monarch, and they had privileges of self-

---

[1] The Reis at one time were a well known and influential race in the south-eastern district of Sarhad, to the north of Pampur. Some part of the Ghuz tribes settled among and intermarried with the Reis whose descendants calling themselves by their name, say they are the descendants of the Ghuz. The Reis of Seistan were the head of this race. After that the Helmand left the southern delta the head of the tribe clung to Hauzdar hoping against hope that the river would change or that the canal from the Helmand would be revived and protected against the Afghans. They eventually had to abandon Hauzdar and emigrated to Sehkoha which had been the boundary between their possessions and those of the Kaiānis. Muhammad Reza Khan Sarbandi had then possession of Sehkoha, and owing to kinship with the Reis chief gave land to the latter at that place. On the downfall of all rule and order in Seistan some of the Reises emigrated to Kabul where their descendants still exist.

In ancient times they say, that the Kaiānis on the north, and the Reises on the south were the "Lords of the Soil" in Seistan and all other tribes held their property subject to these two families.

The following is the Reis genealogy, so far back as information is available of the family of the chief :—

Reis Muhammad Ali.
|
Reis Ghulam Muhammad.   Reis Muhammad.   Reis Nakh Muhammad Ali.
|
Reis Akbar.
|
Reis Husena (no brothers, left an orphan at an early age).
|
Reis Hasan   Haji
(Sons deceased)   (Sons deceased)
(without issue). (without issue).

Reis Ghulam Shah held on to Hauzdar, but had in the end to abandon it, and died shortly after. The Ramrodis belong to this tribe, but are perhaps a servile section of the tribe. They also are a very few in number. In the old days a gang of 400 men were always on hand to maintain and repair the canals of Ramrod and Hauzdar.

government, it is said, which rendered them independent of Kaiāni and other rulers of Seistan. These privileges were granted a very long time ago—it is not known by what king or to what particular dynasty he belonged, but they were bestowed, in return for the service rendered by the Reis to that Monarch, in his warfare with enemies who were bearing hard upon him.

It is impossible to say definitely that the Reis is the representative of that ancient tribe who aided Cyrus; but the geographical position of this (practically extinct) tribe and the stories of the privileges that were given them agree very closely with the tradition referring to the Euergetœ.

Some families very few in number of the Reis, or their servile tribes, are still to be found in Seistan. Sunk in utter poverty, they drag on an existence, as agriculturists in a small way.

The northern districts of Khurassan lay in the path of invaders from beyond the Oxus, and these inroads must in the course of time result in portions of Scythian tribes being left behind in the districts which had been overrun. The population of this great province therefore from prehistoric times must have been replenished by these inclusions of tribes from beyond the others; and so the infusion of foreign blood has been a long continued process.

The Expedition of Alexander overthrew the whole political and social fabric which the ancestors of Darius had built up. Persian, Mede, Scythian and Arian, alike succumbed to the genius and interpidity of the son of Phillip of Macedon; and for a short space of time the eastern world and its nations lay helpless and subdued at his feet.

Seistan must have formed a subsidiary base for the army of Krateras on his march from Upper Sind into Karamania. This country however lay too far from the great lines of communication between Babylon and India to have ever been worth holding by means of a Colony. The coins of the Grœco Bactrian Kings that are found from time to time, were therefore probably brought into Seistan in the course of trade.

As the Grœco Bactrian kingdom yielded to the pressure of Parthian and Scythian enemies, the barrier to the advance of the latter into Khurassan was no longer effective; and those nomad and equestrian tribes which the ancient writers classed as Scythians overflowed unchecked into Seistan, to such an extent as to give their name to the country, Sakastane, which in a corrupted form it bears at the present day.

In the 5th century of our era the Armenian historian Moses of Chorene alluding to Rustam as the chief figure in the heroic poetry, of Persia, gives him " the title of Sakjik or the Sacan." " This shows that the local nomenclature had displaced the ethnic distinction " as early as that date. At the present day there is a well known tribe occupying the country to the north of the Hamun, around Lash and Juwein, and in Kala-i-Kah and also in the oasis of Khash; to the east of the Hamun which calls itself Sak-zi. They are "Afghans," that is, they are included among the tribes of various races which are grouped under that general term. The tribe is called Ishakzai[1] by foreigners; but the people themselves do not call themselves Ishakzai, but very distinctly Sak-zi. They may possibly represent the vestiges at the present of the Sakas who overflowed into Seistan. The Jat element is also present in Seistan at the present day. A very small portion of the people call themselves Jat. There is probably also a large proportion of the so-called Farsiwan population of the country who are ethnologically the descendants of tribes who migrated from beyond the Oxus and made their home in Seistan some 2,000 years or so ago.

Ardeshar-i-Babak who overthrew the declining power of the Parthians and founded the last dynasty of Monarch in Persia, claimed to be a descendant of the more ancient native Royal Families who had previously ruled over that Empire, but their successors established their authority over not nearly the same extent of territory as those earlier Monarchs had governed. Mulla Muin of Sabzawar, the author of the Rauzat-ul-Jannat, gives the following derivation of the name by which the famous city of Nishapur, in Khurassan was called:—

"They say it was built by Shapur, son of Ardeshir; and in the old Persian Language a city was called Neh. Thus the city of Shapur was called Neh Shapur, which in the course of time was abbreviated into Nishapur."

It became one of the great cities[2] of the Empire founded by Ardeshir.

There was a tradition which has been alluded to, that during the period of the Parthian Empire, Herat was a capital of a governor or prince called Ashg. Seistan also was probably governed by a family or rulers or princes of the same race whose seat, or capital, was in Sar-o-Tar.

---

[1] Ishak Zai that is the descendants (sons of—used as in the Bible) of Ishak, son of Abraham, The Friend of God." The conversion to Islam of aboriginal, or tribes who had been long settled in the countries brought under the influence of that faith, upset all the old Ethnological distinctions, and the tribal or racial names that very often perhaps afforded an indication to the Ethnology of those who bore them.

These tribes, in course of time, claimed descent from the first converts to Islam.

[2] Istakhr was the capital of this Dynasty, but the seat of government was afterwards transferred to Madain in the plains that are watered by the Euphrates. Istakhr, however, is said to have held the Royal Archives, and to have been the head-quarters of the later form of the Zoroastrian religion. It occupied very nearly the same position as Pasargadœ probably designedly, as the Sassanians claimed to be a continuation of the older Dynasty was thrown by Alexander.

Istakhr was a city till comparatively recent years. Yakub-ibn-ul Leith is said to have occupied it and to have collected the Mubids and ordered them to compile a history of his ancestor prior to the Conquest of Persia by the Arabs.

Abu Ishak, al-Istakhari, the famous geographer who wrote in the early years of the 4th century of the Hezira or a little over 1,000 years ago, was a native of this place.

The descendants of Ardeshir-i-Babak completed the task which he had taken in hand. The Eastern provinces of the Parthian Empire had probably fallen away from the allegiance due to the latter kings of that race; and the territories up to the watershed of the valley of the Indus towards the East were included in the Kingdom ruled by the Sassanian Monarchs. Seistan was governed by satraps who were perhaps local princes, belonging to a family native to Seistan, or to one which had obtained precedence, in Khurassan, over the other chiefs of that Province.

The successors of Ardeshir-i-Babak had always to guard their kingdom against the successive hordes of nomadic tribes which advanced westwards from the eastern confines of Central Asia; until they found their progress barred by the arms of the Persian Monarch.

The history of the Sassanide Dynasty is a chronicle of expeditions against these hordes of nomads. At times the latter proved too strong for the forces of the Great King; and at other times the latter were victorious and the nomads were pushed back. These struggles must have taken place in the northern portions of the province of Khurassan; as the Sassanides never held any of the districts beyond the Oxus which had become the home of Turkish and Tarter tribes. About the commencement of the Christian Era the Kushans were settled in Bactria and the Romans condescended to enter into diplomatic relations with their chiefs in order to obtain assistance from the latter against the Parthians to whom Rome was then hostile. The inroads of the nomadic tribes during the period of the Sassanian Dynasty was also a very welcome diversion in favour of the latter Romans under the Eastern or Byzantine Empire, which was constantly embroiled with the Persian Monarchs; and had experienced frequent defeats at the hands of the Great King. Dissension among the members of the Royal family also helped the foreign enemies of Persia. The nomads took up the cause of one of the grandsons of Bahram Gur who disputed the throne with his brother; and these civil wars reduced Persia to a position of extreme insecurity; a condition of affairs which lasted until Khasrau I, better known as Anushirwan the Just, ascended the throne. More than half of his long reign was taken up with the task of restoring the supremacy of Persia which had before his time been seriously threatened by the Turkish hordes that had taken part in the struggle for power between Hurmuz III and his brother Piruz the sons of Yezdigird III.

The Turks were at last pushed back into the country beyond the Oxus and the Persians extended their authority over the districts of Tokharistan and Balkh. The Great King married the daughter of the Chief of the Turkish hordes and the successor of Anushirwan was his son by this marriage. 18th September 531 to March 579 A.D.

THE HISTORY OF SEISTAN.

579-590 A.D.

In the next generation the latter was embroiled with the Romans, and a horde of Turks made a diversion in their favour by advancing into the districts of Badghis and Herat; while the Khazars and two Arab Chieftains added their hostility to the difficulties that beset Hormuz the Fourth, the son of Anushirwan.

The scene of the operations which resulted in the rout of the Turks was far removed from Seistan. The portion of the Sakas which remained in that country had doubtless—long before this time—settled down as peaceful cultivators; and not being of the same stock and race with the Turks, the inroads of the latter probably never disturbed the prosperity of Seistan.

In the 7th century of our era the Districts of Kej were subject to the Hindu Kings of Sind, and one of the latter lost his life in a battle fought with the Satrap of Nimruz who had invaded Kej. This Satrap also must have had jurisdiction up to the limits of the country ruled from Sind, in those days, in the direction of the modern city of Kandahar.[1]

The direct line of communication between Seistan and those eastern districts under the jurisdiction of the Satrap of that country, followed the river to the Oasis of Khāsh: where the town of Khisht was then in existence.

This district was undoubtedly reckoned as a part of Seistan. It is a fertile locality: possessing an important area of cultivable soil, watered by the floods of the Khāsh Rud by means of canals. Large crops of wheat and barley are raised. The population is Tājik of the same stock, and allied to the Arbābs of the Helmand Valley, and the headmen of this family still administer the government of their small district notwithstanding a large influx of "Afghan" tribes, who have settled in the country. It was in the early history of Khāsh that the country as far as Bāsrig was occupied by a Tajik population, traces of whom exist to this day in the shape of ruined karezes which form a conspicuous feature on the route from Khash to Bakwa, on which Basrig (a small district on the left bank of the Khuspast Rud) is situated about midway between those two districts.

It is through the descendants of Ardeshir-i-Babak that the families which style themselves Kaiānis, or those which in recent historical times have claimed to be the descendants of the Royal Family of Persia (prior to the spread of Islam) derive their descent.

590-628 A.D.

Khasrau Parvez was the last of the Sassanian Dynasty of Kings who occupied the throne of Persia with authority. After him there followed a succession of puppets male and female members of the Royal family, who were advanced to the throne and deposed by a succession of Palace Intrigues.

---

[1] According to the Chachnama this event is said to have taken place previous to the revolution in the year 1 A. H. (622-23 A.D.) which caused in a change of dynasty in Sind.

The decline of the Race had been hastened by massacres of those members who were regarded as dangerous, being too near to the succession, and the country demoralised and harassed by successive revolutions, and split up into factions became unable in the course of a very few years to withstand the impetuous onslaught of the Arabs.

To Khasrau Parvez is said to have been addressed the admonition exhorting him to embrace the religion of Muhammed; and by him it was publicly contemned and the envoys dismissed with ignominy.

The bad fortunes of the Kaiānis of Seistan are attributed to these impious acts. "Barakat na dārand"—they have no luck. No blessing attends their efforts, or crowns them with success, is a common saying in Seistan, and this is believed to be the judgment on this race consequent on the rejection of Islam by their ancestor Khasrau the 2nd.

The details of the Conquest of Persia by the Arabs need not be recapitulated here. They are well known. But after the defeat of Yazdigerd a scion of the Royal Family named Kaikhasrau at the head of his immediate followers and the members of his family, took refuge in Seistan where for only a very short space of time, they found a refuge from their conquerors.

In the Caliphate of Uthman the Government of Khurassan was the prize offered to whomsoever of the Arab Commanders first entered it. Abdullah-ibn-ul Amir was the first who reached the goal. He was guided from Basrah, of which he was the Ruler by the more direct route through the Kirman desert; and when he had conquered the Kuhistan and overthrew all opposition to his progress, he summoned the Governor of Herat to acknowledge the supremacy of the Caliph. The latter said there would be time enough to do so when the Arab Commander had taken Nishapur. Abdullah-iban-ul Amir accordingly marched against this place.

Tus and Abivard were at that time dependencies of Nishapur and they were overrun. For the space of one month severe fighting took place round that city; until the severity of the winter compelled the Arabs to resort to a blockade. For this purpose, 4,000 men were detailed under Abdullah Jarim to cut off communications between the city and the surrounding country. At last Kanaz, the chief and Kad Khuda of Nishapur, made his submission, and agreed to pay 700,000 dinars in money in addition to a great variety of other valuables: and held himself responsible for both Tus and Abivard. The Ruler of Herat made his peace with the victorious Commander accepting the usual terms as to tribute, and the agreement drawn up in writing was dated the 14th of Ramzan 31 A. H. 2nd April 652 A.D.

The last Province of the Persian Empire was, within a very few years, brought into subjection. Seistan also was invaded, and conquered by expeditions despatched from Kirman; the ancient political fabric and religion of Persia was altogether overthrown, and the old Iranian names gave place to others derived from the language and religion of the conquerors.

In the third step from Kaikhasrau the Iranian names disappear from the genealogical tree of the Kaiânis of Seistan.

CHAPTER II.

The account taken from "Beladheri" by Sir H. Rawlinson, of the first invasion of Seistan by the Arabs gives some interesting information regarding the country. "A detachment under Rabi' was sent from Sirjan of Kirman against Sejestan in A. H. 30. They first came to Fohrij whence they crossed the desert 75 farsakhs (230 miles, English, according to Rawlinson,) to a district called Zalik, 5 farsakhs from Sejestan. This place was attacked and plundered on the feast of Mehrjan. Then they came to a village called Karkuyieh, 5 miles from Zalik, which submitted without resistance. Afterwards they reached a district called Hisun, the people of which also remained quiet and submitted: then they returned to Zalik and took guides (?) for Zaranj, going on till they reached the Hindmend, and crossing a canal named Nuk which was filled from it, then at last arriving at Rusht which was only one-third of a mile from Zaranj. The inhabitants came out and fought a great battle and inflicted some loss on the Moslems; but Rabi' turned again and fought till he conquered and drove the enemy in the city * * *. Then Rabi' went on to the village of Nashrud where he gained a victory, * * and afterwards passes on to Shirwadh which he took, * * * and then killing a great number of the people, he laid siege to the city of Zaranj, the Marzbān of which a Abarwizh by name at length yielded and was admitted to terms, giving as tribute 1,000 slaves each with a golden goblet. Rabi' then entered the city, and afterwards went on to the canal of the Sena Rud and passed over it, and came to Karnein where was the manager of the horse of Rustam. There he gained another victory and then returned to Zaranj where he remained two years." The operations of the Arab forces in Seistan were almost repeated 750 years later by Timur. His light cavalry drove the inhabitants from the open country into the forts, and the capital. To the latter he then laid siege and captured it, after some hard fighting within a very short space of time.

The positions of Sirjân of Kirman, and of Fohrij are known. The latter is 157 miles measured along the Trade Route, from the head of the Shela in Seistan. From this point another 58 miles would have brought the invaders to the country around the village of Warmāl, or Kala-i Nau. Another march of 15 miles in a northerly direction would have brought the Arabs to the part of Seistan in which the modern villages of Bunjar and Kasimābād are situated. Karkuyieh will be described; and Hisun may have been, perhaps, the Hisanik of Ibn-i-Rustah. The Arabs overran the districts and collected supplies after their long march across the desert. Their expedition was undoubtedly planned and carried out in the spring when the crops of Seistan would provide forage for their horses and camels. The invasion of Sind by

Muhammad Ibn-i-Kāsam also took place in the spring. In recent years, the extensive forays organised by the late Sardar Azâd Khan of Khārān took place in the spring, because at that season he could feed his animals on the young crops. The water of the Helmand at this time of the year is generally at a high level and the reason why the Arabs retired from Hisun may be due to the lands around that place, which was probably close to the mouth of the river being already more or less under water. Guides would also be necessary to point out fords and hence the retreat to Zalik for that purpose. The Helmand, that is, the living or working river lay between him and Zaranj. Noken-ju and its equivalent Naubur is still used to designate recently constructed canals. Both are purely Persian in their derivation and it is not too much to suppose that when Rabi' crossed the main river he had also to cross a wide canal that took off close to the ford of the river itself. A large city like Zaranj would require a constant supply of water, and canals would therefore have been kept up and renewed between every season of flood.

The villages mentioned were no doubt just beyond the suburbs of the capital. Having cleared the immediate neighbourhood of the city of enemies he attacked the latter and captured it. After this had been done he marched against Karnein, or (Karyetein), and to do this had to cross the Sena Rud which is called a canal. It was probably a Shela, that is, a former bed of the Helmand which at that period of time, nearly 1,300 years ago, was in the northern delta and on the west of the barrier between the modern delta and the districts of Ghulghula and Sâr-o-Tar. The two channels could only have separated close to the hamlet of Khwâbgâh. The older channel following the line of dasht passed the site of the modern hamlet of Shoru and onwards to the Āshkinak, entering the latter close to the site of the modern hamlet of Memo while the Helmand itself probably occupied a bed not far from that in which the Hamdar canal and channel afterwards flowed. The Shela would have been about 6 miles east of the Capital and the Helmand to the west of the latter, and probably not far from the more outlying suburbs and gardens which must have surrounded the city.

The next allusion to the Sena Rud is also translated from the same authors by Sir Henry Rawlinson. "Oba'd ibn Ziyad was sent against the Frontier of Sind from Sejestan. First he came to the Sena Rud and then he took his road by the old stream (Jui Kohneh) as far as Rudbar of Sejestan on the Hindmend, and came to Kish and further on:—

"Rabi' was succeeded by Ibn Samurah, who after conquering the Marzban of Zaranj and obliging him to pay 1,000,000 dirhems and 1,000 slaves, reduced all the country between Zaranj and Kish belonging to India and also subdued the districts along the road to Arrokhaj as far as the land of Dāwar and he afterwards reduced Bist and Zābil."

The Kish mentioned in both those extracts is not Kej, but Kisht in the Khāsh oasis. It was at that time, as it is now again, a district of Kandahar, which was always regarded by the Arabs as belonging to India, of which Sind was the most western Kingdom, and one with which the Arabs were most familiar.

The author was no doubt misled between Kisht of the oasis of Khash and Kech, or Kej of Makran.

It cannot be supposed for a moment that Obad ibn Ziyad or Ibn-i-Samurah would invade Kala-i-Bist by way of Kej in Makran. It must be, that the place Kish, named by that author is Kisht of the district of Khāsh. It is also altogether unlikely that Obad ibn Ziyad would have proceeded to Rudbār on the Helmand from Zaranj in order to reach Kisht, when the shortest route lay up the course of the Khāsh Rud. Rudbār is a name applied to any valley drained by a river which contains flowing water. The district in Persian Irak in which the Ismailians (Assassins) held some of their famous strongholds is called Rudbār, it is drained by the Shāh Rud, one of the many affluents of the Safed Rud. There is also a Rudbār near Bāmpur to the south-east of Kirman.

The Shela (to use a modern expression in vogue in Seistan) of the Sena Rud had first to be crossed, and from what is known to be the case now the allusion to the Helmand contained in the foregoing notices of events in Seistan prove that in the latter end of the 7th century A.D. the Helmand was established in that part of the northern delta where it is now to be found. It also at that date had two branches, one maintained as a canal (though it had been a natural channel once), and the main stream as well.

In Ibn-i-Rustah alternative route from Juwein to the city of Seistan he speaks of the Helmand lying to the east of the capital. The Helmand of his account and the Sena Rud of the Beladheri are no doubt the same stream.

Both the Istakhri and Ibn-i-Rustah wrote in about the first half of the 10th century A.D. And at that time there does not seem to have been the great changes in the course of the river which are proved to have occurred within the last 100 or 125 years. With a great city like Bina-i-Kai surrounded by suburbs and gardens, the centre of trade and well-populated with a civilized people who had all the desires for comfort and luxury that civilization brings in its train, the river could never have been permitted to oscillate uncontrolled. At one time threatening to ford out the capital at another allowed to threaten it with draught. The history of Seistan has always been an unrecorded struggle between the river and mankind; and although at times the river has been victorious, yet the balance of success has ever been greatly in favour of the people of Seistan. This has in course of time been altered. As the people grew exhausted by invasions and their spirit broken by frequent massacres and domestic turmoils they became unable to maintain the never ending struggle with the river. They have instead adapted their small requirements to the caprice of the river, instead of subduing it, and the result of this will be described further on.

The conquest of Persia by the Arabs differed from the destructive ravages of succeeding invaders from Central Asia, who left behind them a broad track of ruin and desolation. Where resistance was met with, or where the subject people proved contumacious, the Arab leaders did not hesitate to make an example; but as a rule their conquest was marked by a breadth of view and a wise tolerance which is remarkable.

With reference to Seistan this policy of toleration must have interfered very little with the existing state of things in the country, when it was subdued by the Arabs. There was in course of time continuous influx of Arabs into the country, but it was probably not large, until the absence of fresh fields of conquest caused those later religious dissensions to make their appearance, which were speedily rendered more bitter by the claims advanced to the office of Caliph by contending families.

Political adversaries and religious schismatics were alike involved in one general persecution and were compelled to take refuge on the outermost limits of the Empire of the Caliphs of the House of Ommeya. In these remote districts they were able to obtain some respite from persecution, as their valour was a valuable reinforcement to the forces available for the maintenance of the prestige of Islam against inroads of unbelieving Indian or Turkish tribes. But parties of Arab irreconcileables, urged by the bitter hatred which religious and political intolerance had engendered, sometimes went so far as to abandon the standard of Islam; and these found an asylum in Sind and in Kabul, where native dynasties for a time maintained their independence.

It was this persecuting zeal which drove the descendants of Abbas into Khurassan, and which peopled Seistan and the fastnesses of Kirman and the Kuhistan with crowds of Khariji schismatics, and which eventually led to a junction between them.

When the Arabs first took possession of Seistan, they probably garrisoned the capital, and destroyed the more prominent fire temples which were replaced by Masjids. Arab Governors collected the poll-tax and land revenue, but, as far as the latter was concerned, the administrative machinery in force at the conquest was allowed to continue. Towns and villages continued to exist as before, and to be supported by their system of irrigation. In the valley of the Tigris and Euphrates, on the banks of the Oxus and in Seistan, the Arabs found a system of revenue administration and an agricultural population living in villages under their ancient office holders, and dependant on a system of irrigation, in all essential particulars the same. These were doubtless preserved and maintained by the conquerors who fully appreciated their value, while unfamiliar with such institutions which did not exist in their native lands. The religion of Zoroaster no doubt lingered for a considerable time among the people at large. The edict of the Caliph Omar admitted the Persian Gabar to the benefits of the poll-tax, imposed on both Christian and Jew, who acknowledged the political supremacy of Islam, but determined to follow their religious observances. Towns and villages in existence at the conquest, with a few exceptions, must have continued to exist for a long time afterwards; and others sprang up as time went on. There can be but few, if any, of all the ruins in Seistan, now visible, which date from that time; although the sites that are mentioned as being in existence then and which were perhaps even at that time ancient, are in many cases occupied by remains of buildings which took the place of the ancient buildings as the latter fell into decay. In almost every case the older forms of the names of sites have disappeared, but yet there are a very few of the ancient names which have survived, and which are still to be found attached to localities where barely a trace of ruins exists at the present time.

The history of Seistan for many generations is a record of frequent outbreaks on the part of the Kharijis who had settled in great numbers in that country and in Khurassan. A famous battle was fought close to the city of Herat between a great body of these sectarians and the Governor of Nishapur. This place called Kārzārgāh, or the "Battle Field" became in after years a famous cemetery where the remains of many eminent divines and Holy Persons were committed to the Earth. In after years the name was corrupted into Kazargah and probably is still so called.

In 125 A. H. (742 A.D.) the Caliph Hisham of the house of Ommeya died and his successors, three in number, were in no way fitted, or found it possible, to deal with the events that paved the way for the revolution that brought the house of Abbas to power.

Khurassan had been thoroughly canvassed by the emissaries of the Family of Abbas, and the suffrages of the people in the various districts had been recorded in favour of the representative of that Family The rivalry between the Arab tribes of Modhar and Yemen also broke out in open hostility and in addition to this an obscure prophecy began to be put into circulation regarding the downfall of the House of Ommeya. In 130 A. H. Abu Muslim 747-48 A.D. raised the black banner of the House of Abbas in Merv and caused the public prayers to be read in the name of the representative of the Abbasides. But shortly before he had declared himself, there had been a serious rising in Seistan, of Kharijis; which at first sight seemed to be the fulfilment of the prophecy regarding the termination of the dynasty of the Bani Ommeya.[1]

---

[1] The prophecy was a prediction that the Bani Ommeya would be dispossessed of power by an individual named Abdur Rahman, and when a serious rising of the Kharijis of Seistan took place under the leadership of Abdur Rahman Ibn-ul-Muhammad Al Athath, it was deemed to be the fulfilment of the prophecy. This rising however was put down. It was followed within a short time by that of Abdur Rahman Abu Muslim of Merv, which did terminate the power of the Bani Ommeya.

None of these turmoils appear to have given the Kaiänis of Seistan (now of course converted to Islam), a chance for distinction. And none of them are mentioned in history till the rise of the great Provincial Families to the status of Ruling Princes that took place in the 3rd century of the Hegira, corresponding to the 9th and 10th centuries of our era.

This century saw the rise of the House of Sāmān to the position of Ruling Princes in the countries beyond the Oxus, and the sons of Leith, the Kaiâni known in history as the Coppersmith (in Arabic Saffär); from the occupation he followed. This term Saffär gave its name to that dynasty, and it has always been the appellation by which it has been known in history. There have been many coppersmiths in Seistan since the days of Leith, the Kaiâni. The ruins of ancient towns and habitations yield great quantities of ornaments and also articles of domestic use which are invariably made of copper either pure or in an alloyed state, the profession of a coppersmith must have been most lucrative, and there are many at this present time who follow it, but the term Saffär has remained the peculiar appellation of the sons of Leith, and the shortlived dynasty they founded.

865 A.D.
23rd June 875 A.D.

In the year 251 A. H. Yakub, son of Leith, established himself as the Ruler of Seistan, and on the 14th of Shawal in the year 265 A. H. he died at Jandi Shahpur, a town in Ahwaz, where he was buried. In the space of 15 years he had built up a vast kingdom that extended from Irak to the confines of Hindustan; which he bequeathed to his brother Umro. The Caliph with whom he had become embroiled played off the House of Sāmān against the Saffārides, while treating this family with distinction, and bestowing on its representative patents confirming him in the Government of Khurassan, Fars, Ispahan, Kirman and Sind. In addition to this a banner was sent by the Caliph to Umro, who hoisted it on the summit of the Citadel of Zaranj for three days as a sign to all the surrounding country of the honour conferred on him.

But notwithstanding his personal qualities the empire so hastily put together by his brother and afterwards by his own efforts, contained within it the elements of weakness. His own ambition, also, brought him very soon into collision with the Sāmānide Prince of Trans-Oxiana. Under the walls of Balkh, Umro was completely defeated by Ismail Sāmāni and made prisoner thirteen years after he had succeeded to his brother's possessions. He was sent to Baghdad by the Conqueror and died in the prison of the Caliph. Two years afterwards his brother's son and his own descendants made many attempts to assert their independence but one by one they were overthrown and were forwarded to Baghdad where they languished in the prisons of the Caliph.

Thus terminated what was no doubt the elder branch of the Kaiân. Family and their country became subject to the House of Sāmān and was ruled by a Governor appointed by that dynasty.

Safedik-the white mound, probable ruins of a palace: at Nád 'Ali Zaranj.

Part I to face page 26.

The family was, however, by no means extinct; and in 309 A. H. Ahmad, 921-22 A.D. son of Muhammad, son of Khalaf, son of Abu J'afar, son of Leith (a grandson probably of Leith the Coppersmith), who was living in great poverty in Herat, by some chance attracted the notice of Amir Abu-l-Hasan i-Nāsr, son of Ahmad, the fifth Prince of the House of Sāmān. The latter bestowed on Ahmad the Government of Seistan.

In 311 A. H. Shah Malik, son of Yakub-i-Leith, with a body of Sanjaris, 923-24 A.D. attempted to gain possession of Herat, but after a time he went off to Foshanj. He returned again and invested Herat for 4 months, but was compelled to retire discomfited. Ahmad was succeeded by his son Khalaf; probably in 344 A. H. In 353 A. H. Khalaf set out for Mekka leaving his 955-956 A.D. son-in-law Tāhir, the son of Al Husen, to act as regent in his absence. On 964 A.D. Khalaf's return, Tāhir refused to allow him to resume the Government, and the latter was compelled to seek for aid in person from the Amir Mansur, son of Nuh; the 8th of the Sāmāni Princes. Khalaf was reinstated and the troops returned to Bukhara. Tāhir, however, returned again and dispossessed Khalaf. Amir Mansur Sāmāni once more sent troops to aid Khalaf. By the time the troops arrived in Seistan, Tāhir was dead but his son Husen maintained his father's cause and shut himself up in one of the strongholds of Seistan and was besieged in it. He sent an envoy to the Sāmāni Prince and was ordered to attend at Court; and Husen was allowed to proceed to Bukhara.

At this period the power of the Sāmānis had become very much weakened, and in 395 A. H. the last Prince Abu Ibrahim was murdered and with him 1004-5 A.D. terminated the dynasty which had existed for 150 years. Nothing is known of the acts of Khalaf except his rebellion against Nuh Sāmāni and the seven years' investment of his capital.

Under this Prince Seistan appears to have been a flourishing state. Both Khalaf and his father, Ahmad, son of Muhammad, struck coins in their own name. Gold and copper coins of the latter have been found in Seistan and are described (in the journal of the Asiatic Society for July 1905). The descent of the Prince is given, in the former as Ahmad bin Muhammed bin Khalaf, also the fact of their having been struck in Sijistan.

A gold coin of Khalaf, son of the former, has also been described in that number of the Journal, and the date is probably 379 H. As the coins have no 989-90 A.D. mention of the Suzerain Prince of the House of Sāmān it would appear that the Princes of Seistan were independent rulers, and that even as early as those dates, the power of the Suzerain Princes was on the wane, and that Seistan was to all intents and purposes, an independent state. In the reign of Khalaf-ibn-ul-Ahmad, the Capital was, also, probably changed from Zaranj to Zāhidān. So much can be gathered from the writings of historians. They, however, do not mention the name of the new city, but the transference of the seat of government is clearly indicated.

The family of the hereditary Mujtahids of Seistan has been for very many centuries settled in that country, and as long as the Kaiâni Maliks ruled in the country, some member of this family enjoyed that dignity; and in the family was fixed the charge of educating the sons of the Princes, and of the leading men. They had the charge of the State College or Madrassah, the ruins of the two of the latest of these establishments can yet be recognised.

Mulla Khasrau, one of the descendants, of a younger branch of this priestly family, stated that his forebears came into Seistan when Zâhidân was first built and the prosperity of Seistan restored. The country had no men of learning at that period, and his ancestors had been invited to migrate to it from Shiraz. These first arrivals built the Masjid and Madrassah, to the north of Zâhidân the ruins of which are still to be seen around the Mil-i-Kasamâbâd, the larger mound to the north of the minaret having been the Masjid. The smaller chambers, the remains of which adjoin the minaret, mark the site of the Madrassah, and the traces of the court to the North and East and South of the minaret, the extent or precincts of this religious and educational foundation.

Khalaf-ibn-ul-Ahmad is known, from historical sources, to have been a zealous professor of Islam. He encouraged learned divines to settle in his country, and he was a great patron of learning, and many works on the exegesis of the Korân were attributed to him which were the work of the learned men whom he gathered round him.

It does not seem, therefore, to be an unwarrantable assumption to ascribe the foundation of the religious establishment the ruins of which have been just described to his reign. And nowhere else could a more appropriate place have been chosen than close to the new town he built. Situated upon the elevated tongue of land (or Lurg) these buildings would have been beyond the reach of floods; a contingency which is the first consideration in a deltaic tract of country. These facts also account for the similarity between the ruins that exist around the minaret (afterwards built there) and the ruins of building of similar size within the area of Zâhidân.

998-9 A.D. As the power of the Sâmâni Princes declined, their patrimony to the South of the Oxus was absorbed by the Ghaznavide Sultan Mahmud famed for his conquests in India. In 389 H. he defeated the last prince of the Sâmânides who was able to take the field in support of his pretensions, and in the same year the Caliph-Al Kâdir B'illah sent Amir Mahmud a dress of honour and bestowed on him titles of honour. Balkh at this time became his capital for a season. In 390 A. H. Mahmud made a dash on Nishapur which he took possession of and Bak Tuzun, the slave of the Sâmâni Princes, fled from there.

In this year Khalaf-ibn-ul-Ahmad also made an attempt to increase his dominions, probably in the belief that he would be able to take possession of some of the territory of his late suzerain. This brought him into competition

Mîl-i-Kâsimâbâd (ruined minaret).

(Part I to face page 22.)

with the power of Mahmud, and in 390 H. Tāhir, the eldest son of Khalaf, slew 1000 A.D. Bughrajak, the uncle of Mahmud, at Fushanj. This accident (for some say that Bughrajak, who was under the influence of wine fell off his horse and was killed in that way) drew down the wrath Mahmud on Khalaf. Seistan was invaded and Khalaf was beseiged in the fortress of Tāk. Some arrangement was doubtless made as the Ghaznavide troops were withdrawn ; very probably Khalaf was induced to recognise Mahmud as his suzerain.

In 393 H. Khalaf abdicated in favour of his son Tāhir, but soon after he 1002-93 A.D. regretted this step and resumed the authority ; putting his son to death. By some authorities he is accused of having put both his sons, Tāhir and Umro, to death, with his own hand. They were buried outside the walls of Tāk. This act apparently completed his downfall. He had become unpopular, and after the murder of his son, the chief men of Seistan including no doubt the greater part of his own kinsmen discarded their allegiance to him and invested him in the city he had made his capital, and read the public prayers and struck coin in the name of Mahmud of Ghazni.

As the rebels were probably unable to effect anything against Khalaf, Mahmud in person invaded Seistan, and Khalaf was forced to shut himself up again in the fortress of Tāk. After a long seige he was forced to surrender and was brought before Mahmud ; this occasion is famous in history as having been seized by Khalaf to address the conqueror by the title of Sultan which so pleased the latter that he spared the life of the Prince of Seistan ; and merely deported him with his family and effects to Juzjanān which was assigned for his maintenance. Khalaf left Seistan for good.

In 398 A. H. he was detected in correspondence with Ilak Khan, Ruler of 1007-8 A.D. Turkestan, against Mahmud ; and in consequence he was sent to the fortress of Juzdez where he was placed in confinement. He died there in 399 A. H. and 1008-9 A.D. Mahmud directed that his property should be made over to his youngest son Abu-l-Hifs, from whom the later Kaiānis derive their descent, according to the Shijrat-ul-Muluk, a copy of which was found in Seistan in 1903.

Notwithstanding his cruelty and his evidently bloodthirsty and cruel disposition, Khalaf like the Italian Princes of the Renaissance was a great patron of learning, as it was understood in his day. By his command and at his expense, the learned men of his time compiled a commentary on the Korān in one hundred volumes, which cost him, it is said, the enormous sum of 100,000 dinars—taking into consideration the value of money at that period.

Mahmud of Ghazni bestowed Seistan on his brother Nāsr and this country continued as an appandage of the Sultans of Ghazni until in course of time their power declined, and the Saljuks made their appearance on the Political stage of Khurassān.

Sultan Mahamud of Ghazni reigned for a period of 33 or 34 years, and after his death none of his successors occupied his throne for more than 10 years. The throne was filled in rapid succession by members of his family, and descendants, whose power gradually waned as that of the Seljuks increased. At last with the support of the Sultans Alb Arsalan, and Malik Shah, a great grandson of Khalaf, Tāhir son of Muhammad, son of Tāhir, son of Khalaf, obtained the government of his native country. Alb Arsalan, son of Daud Beg, was assassinated in 465 A. H., in the month of Rabi-ul-awal ; and was succeeded by Malik Shah.

<small>November-December 1072 A.D.</small>

Tahir bin Muhammad, bin Tahir, son of Khalaf was restored to his native land in 460 H. and ruled over it as the vassal of the Saljuk Sultans Alb Arsalan and Malik Shah for a period of 20 years (460—480 A. H. or 1067-68 A.D.—1087-8 A.D.O.S.). "After the assassination of Alb Arsalan, several rival pretenders were in the field, *viz*. :—

<small>1067-68 A. D.</small>

"Baha-ud-Daulah Tāhir bin Nāsr bin Ahmad, Badr-ul-daulah Shams-ul-Muluk Amir Abu-l'Abbas Arab, Abbas and Amir Shahinshah." There have been two families of Arab descent settled in Seistan from a very early date in its history. One of these enjoyed great influence in that country and have been known as the Mirs of Seistan. Their descendants are still living in Seistan where the family is represented by the sons of the late Mir Abbas of Iskil. The fact of the pretender Amir Abu-l-'Abbas being styled Arab shows that he was not a member of the Kaiāni family but belonged to an Arab family domiciled in Seistan.

The other family was that of the Mir-i-'Arab of Chakānsur ; and it is possible that a member of either of these powerful families may have attempted to seize the government of Seistan after the murder of Sultan Alb Arsalan.

Amir Shahinshah was doubtless a member of the Kaiāni family ; and he "having got possession of Zaranj and there assumed sovereignty, finally seized the City of Seistan in the year 480 H. Tahir bin Mahammad died in 480 H. according to the Jannat-al Firdaus, and Baha-ud-Daulah Tāhir bin Nāsr, bin Ahmad obtained the sovereignty of Seistan as vassal of Malik Shah, towards the end of the latter's reign." He died in 481 A. H.

<small>1087-88 A.D.</small>

<small>1088 A D.</small>

The government however was confirmed to the posterity of Tāhir bin Muhammad, in the person of his son ; who is styled Tāj-ud-din, abul Fazl-i-Nāsr, son of Tāhir by some writers. He succeeded to the sovereignty in 480 A. H. This is the date obtained by Major Raverty, and it is possible that the period of the power of the pretender Baha-ud-Daulah, who ruled for about a year, may have been ignored or was unknown to the authorities consulted by that learned translator.

<small>1087-88 A.D.</small>

Before however proceeding with the account of the son of Tāhir, son of Muhammad, the Malik Tāj-ud-Din, it will be useful to give some details of the condition of the country at the time of the restoration of Tāhir, the great-grandson of Khalaf-ibn-ul-Ahmad.

The citadel of Zaranj; ruins crowned by an Afghan fortified post.   Nād' Ali.

(Part I to face page 24.)

"In the time of Tahir restoration of the fortresses and other buildings of Seistan took place, and the Royal palace which he built in the castle (Ark) became known as the Palace of Tāhir. From the ruins thereof the munificence of his House is evident."

This is the fortified palace within the citadel of Zāhidān, the remains of which still form a very prominent landmark in that country; and this palace became the keep or citadel itself; within the Ark or citadel of the town.

During the tenure of Seistan by the Ghaznavide Sultans the country was doubtless governed by Deputies of the Sultans. And all fortifications were probably more or less dismantled or allowed to fall into disrepair, in order to render their seizure and occupation by insurgents a matter of little importance, or of avail to the latter. Tāhir with an insecure seat on the throne would naturally wish to provide himself with a place of refuge in which he could defy all those who might revolt and attempt to overthrow his government.

The pretender the "Amir Shahinshah caused the Khutbah to be in his own name in Zaranj. During several years a struggle was carried on between the King and nobles of that place on the one side, assisted by the people of Uk, and the Amirs of Seistan on the other. Finally in 480 H. the city was surrendered to Amir Shahinshah." He probably obtained possession of Zāhidān on the death of Tāhir and held it for a short time. There seems to have been therefore two cities, both of the first importance, at that period in Seistan, that they were Zāhidān and Bina-i-Kai, there can be but little doubt. The population of large cities in the east have always been factions and turbulent, and it was no doubt owing to this that Khalaf-ibn-ul-Ahmad transferred the seat of his government to another city which he built for himself and peopled with his adherents.

With reference to Zaranj or Bina-i-Kai; Abu Ishak, Al Istakhri (cir 305 H.) 917-18 A.D. notices its wet ditch, the water in which flowed from natural springs in its bed. In the low-lying tract of land in which the city of Zaranj was situated, water would be found at no great depth from the surface, and there a deep fosses rounding the walls would become filled by the percolation of subsoil water, which was very likely also (unknown to him)—replenished by spill water from canals. No great exercise of the imagination is needed to picture the deep (and also wide) ditch with its stagnant water, fringed with reeds wherever the people allowed these to spring up; not at all unlike the ditch to be seen round the fort of Nasirabad, the modern capital of Seistan, at the present day.

The factions existing in Seistan during the reign of Tāhir bin Muhammad from whom the five pretenders derived support is also a touch of local colour which is true to nature. This factious spirit, and the divided counsels consequent thereon, was a direct heritage from the Khariji element, for ages powerful in Seistan; and at every stage in its history when foreign invasions or other causes have weakened the influence of the Ruler, this factious, and turbulent spirit has repeatedly made itself apparent. The numerous branches of the Kaiānis have always produced individuals willing to fill the part of pretenders, or to be puppets in the hands of designing persons to the ruin of the true interests of the family in general and of the country as well.

1039-40 A.D.

Malik Tājud-din Abul Fath succeeded his father Tāhir, the son of Muhammad. His was a long and prosperous reign. As the vassal of the Saljuk Monarchs, he marched at the head of the armed forces of Seistan to serve under the standard of Sultan Sanjar in his campaign against the Kara Khitai. This was in 534 H. Sultan Sanjar was defeated, but at the head of 300 horse effected his escape from the battlefield; the Malik of Nimroz (as the country of Seistan is now beginning to be called) on the contrary maintained his ground, and was made prisoner together with Turkan Khatun, the consort of Sultan Sanjar. This battle was fought on the Dasht-i-Katrān on the frontier of Samarkand; and the defeated Monarch fled to the fortress of Tirmiz where he found a refuge.

After a considerable time spent in of captivity Malik Tāj-ud-din returned to Seistan. The lower inscription on the ruins of the great minaret now called the Mili-Kasimabad, because it is not far from that village, contains the name of this ruler; and it is not assuming too much to say that this work was probably commenced and nearly completed by him as a mark of gratitude for Divine Aid in effecting his escape or release from the bonds of the infidel Kāra Khitais. It was a work which a pious follower of Islam might well undertake, as an embellishment to the religious foundation that existed at that spot, and it was probably in the Masjid at that place that Maik Tāj-ud-din, hung up the fetters which he had worn during his captivity in the hands of the nomands; and which the author of the Tabakat-i-Nasiri saw when he visited Seistan. Events also were taking place in Khurassan towards the end of the reign of Tāj-ud-din which rendered him independent of the Saljucks. The westward movement

1053-4 A.D.

of the Turkish horde of the Ghuz had begun, and in 548 A. H. Sultan Sanjar having attacked them, suffered a complete defeat and was made prisoner with

1056 A.D.
1057 A.D.

his Consort Turkan Khatun. In 551 H. Sultan Sanjar made his escape from the hands of his captors; but in 552 A. H. he died at Merv. Sultan Sanjar was the last of the great sovereigns of the Saljuk family or tribe, but that empire lasted for 32 years after his death. A branch of the same tribe estab-

1073-74 A.D.

lished itself in Kirman. In 466 H. Takish, brother of Sultan Malik Shah, rebelled in Herat, he was taken prisoner and confined in Isfahan. In the same year Kāward Shah rebelled in Kirman, but fell in battle. The successors of Kāward Shah however ruled as independent princes till 607 A. H. when Kirman was annexed to the Empire of Khwarazam, after the family of Kāward had become extinct: but before the annexation of Kirman; the Ghuz[1] tribes had settled in that Province under Malik Dīnār, and his subordinate chiefs; and had destroyed the prosperity of the country. The great tribes of Sarhad, the eastern districts of Kirman, such as the Gamshādzais, Yār Ahmadzais, Nāhruis, and others probably represent the Ghuz. Their habits, mode of life, and turbulence, and the low scale of civilization generally which characterizes these tribes and the so-called "Brahui" tribes, also render it probable that they are the representatives of the Ghuz, modified however, by association and intermarriage with people of other origin among whom they dwell.

Malik Tāj-ud-din died in 559 A. H. and was succeeded by his eldest son Malik Shams-ud-din; known as the "Executioner." This Prince, who built the Sarai-i-Siāsati (the Royal Palace), was known by his nickname of the Malik us-Sais. He however maintained his principality against the inroads of the Ghuz who had by that time overrun Khurassan and Ghazni; and he on one occasion extended his hospitality to the brothers Gheiath-ud-din and Muiz-ud-din, Princes of Ghur, the latter being the future conqueror of Hindustan. 1163-64 A. D.

Malik Shams-ud-din had deprived his brother Izz-ul-Muluk of sight; and put to death 18 other sons of his father, as well as many of the leading men of Seistan. His sanguinary disposition and tyranny led to conspiracy being formed, and he was put to death by his own officers.

Malik Tāj-ud-din Harab was raised to the dignity of Malik of Seistan. He was the son of the blind Izz-ul-Muluk who was still living. Being however

---

[1] The following brief notice on the Ghaz or Ghuz tribes has been principally compiled from the valuable notes by Major Raverty to his translation of the Tabakat-i-Nasiri.

Shash is the name of a district, river and city in the country beyond the Oxus: on the frontiers of Turks. It was also known as Fanakat, and corresponds to the Modern Tashkand. It was also called Chato and Jaj. Its inhabitants were Musulmans of the tribes of Ghuz and Khalaj.

The Ghuz took Ghazni in 545 H. which was retaken in 569 H. (1173-4 A.D.) by Sultan Gheiath-ud-din who made it over to his brother (and successor) Muiz-ud-din. Sultan Muiz-ud-din Ghuri defeated a horde of the Sankuran, a sept of the Ghuz in 571 H. (1175-6 A.D.).

A horde of the Ghuz advanced from Khutlan and Khandan and defeated Sultan, Sanjar the Suljuk, in 548 H. (20th March 1056 A.D.). The Ghuz laid waste Khurassan and it is said upwards of 100,000 persons not including women and children were massacred by the invaders. The Khwarazm Rulers were compelled to seek the aid of the Khan of the Khitais to free Khurassan from the Ghuz. With this aid he attacked Malik Dinar, who held Sarakhs; and drove the latter and his tribe into Kirman, in 570-6 H. he reached Kirman in 581 H. (1174-1181 A.D. and 1185 A.D.). He established his authority there in the month of Rajab in the year 583 H. (August 1187 A.D.) and ruled 8 years. He was succeeded by his son.

The Ghuz were converted during the Caliphate of Mahdi the Abbassid. They became followers of Mokanna, the veiled prophet of Khurassan deserted him and retired to the country beyond the Oxus.

This tribe owned great herds of sheep, annually used to pay 24,000 sheep to the Suljuk Monarch and it was a dispute with them about an increase of this tribute that led to his defeat and downfall.

The Ghuz streamed over the Zamin-i-Dawar, Merve, Sarakhs and Balkh, the country around Kala-i-Bist and the Garmsir; and had taken possession even of Herat. Nishapur was sacked by them and they broke up and carried away on their camels, the famous copper lamp which was suspended by a chain from the dome of the Jami Masjid. This lamp had 400 lights. The great copper reservoir in front of the Masjid was also broken into pieces by them and removed. The Ghuz who had flowed into the Zamin-i-Dawar and the Garmsir were subdued by Sultan Muiz-ud-din of Ghur.

These tribes were thus gradually pushed down towards the South, where their descendants now are to be found among the Brahui and their kindred tribe, who are regarded in Baluchistan as new-comers.

blind, the latter would have been debarred from the succession, after the murder of his brother. According to the MS. of the Ihya-ul-Muluk, Malik Táj-ud-din "assumed the Insignia of Royalty on this father's death." Also according to the author of the Tabakat-i-Nāsiri, Malik Táj-ud-din Harab, "entered into communication with the Sultans of Ghur and Khurassan, and became feudatory to them." In 571 A. H. according to the same author Sultan Gheiath-ud-din of Ghur obtained possession of Herat ; which, however, was probably only a temporary success and the town was evacuated by them not long after. There were probably indications of the supremacy of the Ghuris being about to be established over the western districts of Khurassan and this induced the Malik Taj-ud-din to enter into relations with the Sultan of Ghur, as being the only powerful ruler of that period and one who was a neighbour also. Moreover even in his predecessor's reign relations between Seistan and Ghur had been established.

1175-76 A.D.

The accession of Táj-ud-din Harab of Seistan took place probably, therefore, prior to 571 H. This date would give a period of 12 years for the reign of the Malik-ul-Sais ; which is probably too long a time for such a bloodthirsty tyrant to have oppressed his family and subjects generally. The title Harab borne by Malik Táj-ud-din and his successors may have been due to his prowess as a warrior, and an equivalent to the title of Mono Machus ; in use in the Byzantine Empire.[1] This Prince completed the Minaret commenced by his grandfather, already described ; as the name "Táj-ud-din, Abu-l-Fath, Harb bin Muhammad" is to be found in the upper inscription on the Mil-i-Kasimabad.

1175-76 A.D.

There is no doubt that his reign was a long and a prosperous one, but the statement that it lasted for 60 years, contained in the Tabakat-i-Nāsiri (at page 193 of Major Raverty's translation), is manifestly absurd. Fifty years would however be not improbable, allowing only 4 years for the reign of his tyrannical Uncle the Malik-ul-Sais.

Eventually becoming blind Malik Táj-ud-din Abu-l-Fath, Harab, appointed his eldest son Nasir-ud-din Uthman as regent. The latter was married to a daughter of the Malik of Khurassan, Umr-i-Maraghāni. The author of the Rauzat-ul-Jannat calls him Izz-ud-din Umar, Maraghāni, and states that he was the All Powerful Vizier of Sultan Gheiath-ud-din of Ghur. By this marriage of Malik Nasr-ud-din Uthman, the Maliks of Seistan became connected with the Maliks of the Al-i-Kurt who afterwards played a great part in the history of Khurassan : this family being descended from Malik Táj-ud-din Uthman, the brother of Izz-ud-din Maraghāni.

[1] Mono Machus, the single combatant, the title of Constantine X, 1034-56 A.D., Emperor of Byzantium, who lived about a century and a quarter earlier than the Malik of Seistan who bore the title of Harab.

THE HISTORY OF SEISTAN.

Malik Táj-ud-din Uthman of Seistan served under the banners of the Sultan of Ghur (already named) at the taking of Nishapur in 597 A. H. The author of the Tabakát-i-Násiri mentions that he founded a large and noble palace outside the City of Seistan, on the banks of the Hirmend. He died in his father's lifetime. [1200-1 A.D.]

The latter was succeeded in 612 A. H. by the eldest son of Nasír-ud-din Uthman, who is called in the Ihya-ul-Muluk, Shams-ud-din, but in the Tabakát-i-Násiri, Malik-ul-Gházi Yamin-ud-daulah wa-ud-din Baharam Shah. A just and strong ruler, he became embroiled with the Mulahidah of the Kuhistan,[1] and was assassinated by four emissaries sent to remove him, while passing through the Bazar on his way to the Masjid, where he was to have performed his devotions on a Friday. [1215-16 A.D.]

It was during the reign of this Malik that the author of the Tabakát-i-Násiri visited Seistan in 613 A. H. His description of the City is most vague and he does not appear to have observed much. His mind being occupied with the high affairs of kingdoms and of their rulers, he does not seem to have paid attention to details of topography. It is not at all easy to do so when the time that is available is taken up with state visits, and ceremonious interviews with recurring crowds of visitors; such as a person of his standing would have to undergo. The ruins of the ancient city mentioned by him where the conspirators assembled to mature their designs [1216-17 A.D.]

---

[1] The Mulahidah were the followers of Hasan-i-Sabah, and were known to Europeans as the assassins. Hasan-i-Sabah was a school fellow of Umar Khayam (the tent maker) in Nishapur. The followers of Hasan who held many fortresses of strength (besides Alamut) in the west, brought into contract with Europeans (during the crusades) have thus become more celebrated than their fellows who held the Kuhistan, the country to the South of Meshed now known as the Káinát. In this tract they held 7 forts and when the hordes of Changíz Khan broke into Khurassan, the Mulahidah gave shelter to crowds of refugees (Ullmah and others included) who fled before the Infidel Moghols.

The Head of the Mulahidah of the Kuhistan was styled the Muhtashim (leader of the Congregation, hashm being the root of this word). He was appointed from Alamut.

A ruined fort is still pointed out as the birth place of Hasan-i-Sabah, it is called Mir-Ismailee. It is a historical fact that Hasan was born in these parts.

At the time of the Moghol invasion, the Mulahidah besides the town of Kain, held possession of the forts of Sar-i-Takhot, Takht, Sowarsher, and Farmandih. The head or Muhtashim, of the sect was Shiháb-i-Mansur, Abul Fath.

Mominábád, the town of Karah, Tun, and Tabas were also in their hands, in 622 H. (1225 A.D.).

The author of the Rauzat-ul-Jannat mentions that the doctrines of Hasan-i-Sabáh were held by the inhabitants of certain district in his time; 425 years ago.

Hulaku Khan who captured Alamut and broke the power of the western branch of this sect summoned the Muhtashim Násir-ud-din, one of the chief Dá-is of the Ismailians; whose head-quarters were then in the town of Tun. The fortress of Sar-i-Takht was in the neighbourhood of that place. Násir-ud-din, the Ismailian appeared before Hulaku on the 17 Jámadi-ul-awwal in the year 614 H. (26th July 1217 A.D.).

425 years ago the author of the Rauzat-ul-jannat mentioned that the Kuhistan was divided into (9) nine districts Tun, Tabas, Masita, Dasht-i-Biaz (the white plain ?), Naharján, Mominábád, Shákhim, Fasharud, Janábad, Zerkuh, and Bushish. Tun and Maharján were chiefly populated by people of the Ismailian sect.

A severe earthquake was felt in the country on the evening of the 21st Rabi I in the year 898 H. (6th December 1492 A.D.O.S.). In the villages of Nauzád and Mask, in the Baluk of Mominábád much damage was wrought, houses were levelled with the ground and a very large number of human beings lost their lives. The inhabitants of these villages were suspected of being followers of Hasan Sabah. Between Mask and Nauzád a fissure appeared in the earth, several miles in length, the traces of which are still visible in a narrow long glen or ravine.

against the Malik-ul-Sais, outside the City was no doubt the ancient site of Rām Shahristān; although the author calls it Hashnu. The mound of Shahristān is only 4 miles in a direct line from the southern end of the ruined town of Zāhidān; a convenient distance; and a spot to which the conspirators could easily make their way without the fear of detection. These ancient mounds are still the resort of idlers, and the play-grounds of children and it is not at all unlikely that the mounds of Shahristān was also the resort of the Sons of Leith and their companions; where the ambitious plans of the former were formulated. This great mound is clearly visible from Zāhidān, and at the present day all the names of intervening places are given in reply to a question as to the name of any prominent landmark at a distance.

The Shahristān Mound is due S. of Zāhidān. The city having been built in the direction of the wind of 120 days or on a bearing of 30 to the W. of N. and as dwellings extended along this bearing for many miles; the term N. and S. or E. and W. are not so exactly applicable to it as they would to a place truly oriented.

At the eastern angle of the town walls, there are ruins of windmills, and other buildings which formed a group by themselves, in advance of the town walls. The Dar-i-Ta'am would be a very natural appellation for the south or south-eastern gate of the town for the grain that was ground in these windmills would have to be taken to them through that gate. These windmills were of considerable size and were probably maintained by the Government.

To the N. W. of the Sarai-i-Siasati, which is most likely to have been the extramural palace described in the preceding paragraph; there are still existing the ruins of a reservoir, covered over with a dome and close to it the ruins of a Masjid adjoining which there are ruins of other buildings. But the place where Minhaj-i-Saraj alighted was probably the group of ruins to the south-east of the windmills and the town. These are now in ruins, but it is evident that they are the remains of some establishment, which may have been that which is mentioned by the author of the Tabakāt-i-Nāsiri.

The latter must have journeyed from Bist to Seistan by the direct route through Khāsh and he would in that case have entered the Delta at Chakānsur. Where the Gumbaz-i-Baluch is situated is not now known, but it could not have been far from the town, as he was met there by a deputation who brought him to his destination. The ruins at Milak may be the remains of the Gumbaz of the Baluchis.

The fortress of Shāhin Shāhi, mentioned in the Tabakāt-i-Nāsiri, as being the cause of the quarrel between the Mulahidah of Kuhistan and Malik Bāhrām Shah on account of which the latter was assassinated, is said to have been situated in the confines of Neh in the territory of Nimroz that is Seistan. There is little doubt but that it is the fortress now called Shāhduz, the ruins of which crown an isolated hill not far from the town of Neh. The name it now goes by, is most probably a corruption of Shahdiz: the word duz or diz in the old Persian language meant a fort, and the name would therefore signify the fort of the Shah of Seistan which is the same in effect as the " fortress of Shahin shahi " mentioned by Minhaj-i-Saraj. The ruins include those of reservoirs in which rain water collected. Vestiges of houses and fortifications are still plainly visible. A steep path leads to the summit.

Neh is of course the Old Persian word for town; as in Nishapur. It was, and is still the only town in the district to the west of the Hâmun and south of the Kainât.

Malik Bâhrâm Shah reigned for a period about 7 years from 612 to 618 H. or 1215—1221 A. D.

Malik Nusrat-ud-din, the middle son of the late Malik Bâhrâm Shah, succeeded the latter, but he was involved in a civil war with his eldest brother Malik Rukn-ud-din who had been imprisoned by his father for gross misconduct. The latter had the support of the heretical party of the people of Seistan while the orthodox Section favoured his brother. After a struggle in which fortune favoured first one and then another; both claimants were slain by an invading force of Mongols. In this way passed the year 618 H. 1221-22 A.D.

Malik Shihab-ud-din Mahmud, son of the late Malik Nasir-ud-din, came out of concealment and assumed the Government of Seistan, in 619 H.; after 1222-23 A.D. the Moghols retired. His claims were opposed by the heretics of Seistan who again brought forward their man, in the person of Uthman, the grandson of Nasir-ud-din, Uthman-i-Tâj-ud-din Harab, as a rival claimant.

The latter asked for help from Kirman, at that time held by Burâk Hâjib; the Kara Khitai, who despatched Taj-ud-din, Niâl Tigin, a cousin of Mahmud Khwârazm Shah, and his own vassal, to help the pretender. Niâl Tigin joined the latter at Neh in the year 622 H. whence he was invited to Seistan, after that Malik Shihab-ud-din had been killed. Niâl Tigin, thereupon ignored the grandson of Nasir-u-din-i-Tâj-ud-din, Harab; and seized the partimony of the latter for himself.

Malik Taj-ud-din Niâl Tigin was embroiled with the Mulahidah of the Kuhistân, as well as the Khariji element in Seistan, but he proved victorious and even took the fortress of Tulak and Isfirâr. In 625 H. an army of Moghols 1227-28 A.D. invaded Seistan, and besieged him in the fortress of Arg and after a defence of 19 months, or perhaps of two years, he was forced to surrender in 627 H. 1 29-30 A.D. He was afterwards executed before the walls Safed Koh.

This fortress of Arg was not in the delta but to the N. E. of the Sharistân. This term Sharistân refers to the area in that country in which there exist permanent villages and it is still in use.

At this period both Kal-i-Kâh and Farah were included in Seistan, and though it seems more than probable that Lâsh was the fortress of Arg alluded to, still it is not impossible that either the former or another fort in the territory of Farah may have been the fortress so long defended by Táj-ud-din, Niäl Tigin. The Moghols also suffered heavy losses before the fortress of Arg was surrendered, as it is recorded that the leader of their host was slain, or died, during the course of the siege; and that his place was taken by the Bahädur Tair: a name that figures prominently in the annals of Khurassan in after years. There are also discrepancies in the account of the siege of the fortress of Arg (it is also called the fortress of Uk): the latter being the name of the District of Hokat, or Aukat. According to some authorities the siege of this fortress lasted for two years; and this shows how very strong the place must have been. No city or fortress, attacked by the Moghols of Chingiz Khan ever made such a prolonged resistance and it was the outbreak of scurvy and the wound and capture of the gallant commander, Táj-ud-din Niäl Tigin, that at last compelled the survivors of the garrison to surrender.

1205-1206 A.D.

The unwieldy Empire of the Khwārazm Shāhi Dynasty had been built upon the neighbouring kingdom as the latter decayed and broke up. Province had been added to Province, and the death of Sultan Shihāb-ud-din Ghuri (the conqueror of India) in 602 A. H. enabled Sultan Muhammad of Khwārazm to turn his attention towards the countries beyond the Oxus. In course of time his ambitious designs in this direction brought him into collision with the rising power of Chingiz Khan. It is indeed stated that, owing to the deadly hostility that existed between the family of Sultan Muhammad and the Caliphs, the Caliph An Nāsr despatched an agent to Chingiz Khan inciting him to take war upon Sultan Muhammad who was then contemplating his expedition into 'Irak. Seistan was a feudatory state of the Empire of the Sultan of Khwārazm. During the lifetime of Malik Bāhräm Shah, a mandate was sent to him from Sultan Muhammad of Khwārazm, commanding him to mobilize the armed forces of Seistan, and to despatch them to the aid of his Suzerain. This force marched under the command of Malik Ruknud-din, eldest son of the Malik of Seistan, but when he had arrived at Foshang the young Malik while engaged in drinking wine slew the envoy of Khwārazm. Alarmed at this, Malik Rukn-ud-din returned to Seistan where his father put him into confinement; and despatched another force to join Sultan Muhammad. On their arrival the troops of Seistan were detailed for duty to the frontier fortress of Tirmid, and when Chingiz Khan advanced against that place, and had taken it and massacred the garrison, the troops of Seistan perished with the rest.

1221-1222 A.D.

In the last month of the year 617 or early in the year 618 H. Chingiz Khan crossed the Oxus, and his armies overran Khurassan. In the course of a short period of time the Moghol hordes had penetrated into Persia, and had captured most of the strong places in Khurassan.

THE HISTORY OF SEISTAN.

"In three months the world-seizing Tuli"
"Captured these all to the Gates of Seistan."
"He razed and he slew, and he swept and he seized."
"Not a person remained, neither of great nor small."

It was on this occasion that the Moghols first entered Seistan and the rival claimants to the government, Malik Nusrat Uddin and his brother Rukn-ud-din, were slain. The first inroads of these fierce warriors, however, did not result in the appalling massacres and destruction of the great cities which took place later on. There was a great deal of very hard fighting; but once a city had surrendered, it received good treatment. This was notably the case with regard to Herat. According to the history of Asif (or Seifi) the Hirawi, quoted by the author of the Rauzat-ul Jannat, the enemy appeared first opposite the gateway of Firuzabad; and for 7 days there was all round the city much hard fighting. After this Tuli Khan and his officers rode up to the edge of the great ditch and summoned the town to surrender promising quarter; and stating that no more tribute would be demanded than the revenue which the town had paid to the Sultan Jallaludin Khwārazm Shah. These terms he swore with solemn oaths to observe. The city opened its gates, and a formal submission was made. Twelve thousand men, adherents of Prince Jallaludin were put to death, but not a single other person was molested. Malik Abu Bakr Marjaki was appointed to be Governor of the city and one of Tuli Khan's Moghols named Mangutae was left there to represent Chingiz Khan's interests. So lenient was the government, that it took no heed of the warlike preparations made by the populace to resist further demands, especially if the Tajiks were to be ordered to furnish their quota of troops to aid the Moghols in their further conquests.

Nishapur also submitted on terms; and all the conditions were observed by the conquerors; until the short-lived success obtained by Prince Jallaludin over the Moghols in the battle of Parwān caused a general rising, in very many parts of Khurassan against the Moghols. The populace of Herat took part in the movement and slew both Malik Abu Bakr, and Mangutae, the Moghol Intendant. The author of the History of Herat states that the people entered into a compact with the garrison of Kaliyun, better known afterwards as Nar-Tu in Badghis; and a body of men from that place made for Herat, which they entered as merchants, by different gates, and having stirred up the people of Herat put the Malik to death in the Chahar Su; while Mangutae was slain outside the citadel. Malik Mubāriz-ud-din was chosen as the leader of the movement—he had come to Herat from Firuzkuh, with the Khwājah Fakkhr-ud-din, Abdur Rahman Ghairāni, as the head of his administrative staff.

Iljikdae Nuyin was appointed to conduct the operations against Herat, and in the month of Shawal of the year 618 H. he appeared in front of Herat — December 1221 A.D.

and placed his camp on the Herat Rud, having advanced from Ghazni for the purpose of punishing the insurgents.

July 1222 A.D.

The defence was stubborn and 6 months and 18 days had passed, and the Moghols had obtained no distinct success. In the 7th month of the year 619 H. Iljikdae made a general assault on the defences which cost him nearly 5,000 men in killed alone, and directing his principal attack on the tower of Kharlak, he obtained a footing on the bank at the foot of the walls with a large body of miners. The wall was pierced in several places and this resulted in bringing down 50 yards of the lofty curtain, burying 400 Moghols, warriors of fame, under the débris.

The people of the city were by this time reduced to very great straits; and a division took place among them, one party being in favour of a surrender, while the opposite faction were for holding out to the last.

2rd July 1222 A.D.

The decision, however, rested with Iljikdae Nuyin; and on a Friday in the month of Jamādi-As-Sāni of the same year, he assaulted the city in the direction of the tower of Khāk, and having captured the tower, he effected an entrance into Herat. In the general massacre that took place, it is said 1,600,000 persons were slain. He stayed 8 days at Herat: and having demolished the town, he set out to reduce the fortress of Nar Tu; but from Aobah he sent back 2,000 horse to kill those who had been able to conceal themselves and thus escape the general massacre. Two thousand persons were accounted for by this detachment. In the end only 16 persons, who had found a refuge on the summit and the steeper declivities of the hills, survived the massacre. They were eventually joined by others until their numbers were brought up to 40, and these refugees took up their abode in the Jami Masjid built by Sultan Gheiath-ud-din-us-Ghuri, by the side of which that monarch's remains had been laid to rest.[1]

Ten thousand Kankulis, belonging to the army of Prince Jallaludin of Khwārazm, had drawn to ahead under three leaders, Karācha, Tughan, and Sikur, among the hills of Nishapur and Tus. They infested the roads passing through those districts, and slew certain of Chingiz Khan's envoys.

The Moghol leader Jurmaghun sent from Khwārazm a force to disperse them, and the Kankulis were defeated in three engagements. The latter, however, re-assembled again and were again attacked and compelled to fight a battle on the border of the Sabzawār, and a second time the Kankulis were put to flight, but with a loss of 2,000 men on the part of the Moghols. Karācha fled into Seistan and Tughan into the Kuhistan. Sikur is not alluded to again. Three thousand Kankulis fled to Herat, and 4,000 Moghol horse were sent in pursuit of them. The fugitives took post in the Jami Masjid where they were

---

The author of the Rauzat-ul-Jannat states that over the arch of the great entrance to the Masjid a Kufic inscription existed, in his day, stating that that monarch built the Masjid, and the date 597 H. was given as that of the building (597 A.H.—1200 I A.D.).

brought to bay, and massacred to a man after a desperate struggle lasting for three days, in which they inflicted great losses on their assailants.

The refugees were at this time dwelling in Azab and Shafilan, during the period of 15 years in which Herat lay in ruins, and at other times among the hills.

Kaliyun or Nar-Tu was taken by the Moghols, and completely destroyed; and Nishapur and Shādyāk were also captured and razed to the ground.

The invasion of Seistan a second time in 625 A. H. may possibly have been due to the flight of the Kankuli chief Karācha in that direction; but it was more likely to have been due to the fact that Prince Jallaludin had returned from India, and had collected troops once more in Fars; perhaps to the attempt made by his kinsman Niāl Tigin in Seistan and Farah to establish himself as an independent ruler; as well as his ambitions with regard to Tulak and Isfirar. He was in addition a member of the Royal Family of Khwārazm, and as such, an object of suspicion to Chingiz Khan. A great army of Moghols wintered in the confines of Panjgur during the cold weather of 619-20 H. (1222-23 A.D.). The name of the district is given in a corrupt form in the Jami-ut-Tawārikh, but the last syllable of the name is distinctly "gur": and there are existing to this day very distinct traditions of a large force of Moghols having passed a winter in the country around Dizak, a well-known tract of country bordering on the Panjgur district; the latter being situated in that portion of Makran which belongs to the Kalat State. *1227-1228 A.D.*

As long as Prince Jallaludin of Khwārazm was alive, and able to collect troops, and indulge in an irreconcilable hostility towards the Moghols, the ambitions of his kinsman Niāl Tigin must have been looked on with grave suspicion by the Prince of the Moghols; and so it was that another expedition was undertaken against the former which resulted in his being wounded, taken prisoner, and then put to death.

CHAPTER III.

Many of the dynasties which had risen in Khurassan to sovereign power previous to the Moghol invasion, and who in turn had extended their power over the Provinces of Modern Persia on one hand and into Hindustan on the other, were founded by persons belonging to the Tajik or Farsiwān race. The Tāhiri Maliks who arose in Khurassan, and afterwards were famous during the most glorious period of the Abbasid Caliphs, derived their descent from Minuchihr of the earliest race of Persian kings from which the Kaiānis of Seistan also claim to be descended. It was the last of that family whom Yakub, the son of Leith, dispossessed of the government, first of Seistan, and afterwards of Khurassan.

The house of Sāmān which rose to great power beyond the Oxus claimed to be descendants of that Bāhrām Chubin, who, in the reign of Hurmuz, son of Naushirwan, overthrew the son of the Khākān of Turkestan (at the head of an immense army) under the walls of Balkh. Having been insulted by Hurmuz, Chubin afterwards rebelled and dethroned the former, setting up another in his stead.

The ancestor of the Āl-i-Buwiah was said to have been a fisherman of Dilem; he belonged probably to a family native to that district. The last of this family died in 487 H., a dependant of the Saljuks.

The ancestor of the Yaminiah dynasty whose capital was Ghazni and to which the famous Mahmud Ghaznawi belonged is also said to have been a descendant of Yazdigerd, the last of the sovereigns of Persia.

The Ghuri Sultans, to whom Shihāb-ud-din, the conqueror of Hindustan belonged, were of the stock of the Tājiks (also written Tāzik) of Ghur, and claimed to be the descendants of Zuhak the Tāzi.

The Khwārazm Shāhi dynasty, overthrown by Chingiz, were Turks who had migrated from the tribes of Kipchak and Kankulis; but these had merely taken possession of the patrimony of an earlier race. Khwārazm is said to have been acquired by a kinsman of Bāhrām Gur, the famous monarch of the Sassanian dynasty; and the title of Khwārazm Shah belonged to the earlier race of its rulers who were probably Tājiks.

After the first severities of the Moghols gradually became mitigated, the whole of Khurassan once more came under the rule of a Tājik family of Ghur who claimed to be the representatives of that family of Ghuri Monarchs to which Shihāb-ud-din, of Indian fame, belonged.

This family is known as the Āl-i-Kurt. A Tājik family also ruled over Isfirar and another of the same race over Farah. These two families of local rulers were always recognised as being subordinate to the Al-i-Kurt, but frequently were in a state of opposition to the latter.

The Maliks of Farah are said by the author of the Rauzat-ul-Jannat to have been related to the Kaiānis of Seistan, and to have been an ancient and distinguished race. In the transactions of this family with the Al-i-Kurt the name borne by many members of the former is said to have been Niāl Tigin, which was evidently a family name. Farah and Kala-i-Kah were in ancient times portions of Seistan; and when Tāj-ud-din Niāl Tigin had seized the patrimony of the Malik of Seistan to whose aid he had been sent by Burak Hajib, from Kirman, he evidently had made Farah his head-quarters, for it was at this place that the author of the Tabakāt-i-Nasīri met Niāl Tigin in 623 H.

Having usurped the government of Seistan Tāj-ud-din Niāl Tigin very probably married a female member of Malik Uthmān's family, and in this way became a member of that family himself. The later Maliks of Farah are very probably descended from this Niāl Tigin, which would account for the name recurring in their family.

Chingiz Khan died on the 4th of the month of Ramzan 624 H. (or the 16th of August 1227 A.D.). He was born in the year 549 H., following that in which Sultan Sanjar the Saljuk was overthrown and taken prisoner by the Ghuzz. In the year 626 A. H. and the month of Rabi-ul-awal (February 1228 A.D.), Uktāe was proclaimed the successor of the late chieftain according to the last wishes of his father. Uktāe was the second son of the late Chingiz Khan, and in character he was the reverse of his elder brother Chagatai, the latter being specially inimical to the faith of Islam and its professors. In 634 A. H. a decree of Uktāe was promulgated regarding the restoration of cities destroyed during his father's lifetime, and Herat was one of the places selected for restoration owing to its climate.

Amir Izz-ud-din, the provost of the guild of weavers of fine cloths, who with 1,000 families had been transported to Beshbaligh after the destruction of Herat, was ordered to take 100 families with him and proceed to Herat and settle there, with a view to commence the restoration of the city. In 637 A. H. 200 other families were sent to Herat. In this year the canals of Herat were divided among the inhabitants and the canals of Sikur, the Jui-Malāni, and some of the Anjil canals were cleaned and restored. 1239-1240 A.D.

In 638 H. Malik Mujd-ud-din Kaliyuni became Governor of Herat. In conjunction with Karlugh, the Moghol Intendent, this Governor restored the system of the Anjil canals to their former condition, as well as that of the Alinjan canals. 1240-1241 A.D.

In 640 H. this Governor fell a victim to an intrigue and was put to death. 1242-1243 A.D. In 641 his son, Malik Shams-ud-din, was appointed by Batu Khan, Governor 1243-1244 A.D. of Herat, and in 649 was poisoned by one of his confidential servants, suborned 1251-1252 A.D.

for this purpose, by Shams-ud-din Lachin, who had been acting as the deputy of his master, whom he caused to be murdered.

Shams-ud-din Lachin fled from Herat and the administration of the country passed into the hands of the Āl-i-Kurt.

1240-1241 A.D. In 638 H. Malik Mujd-ud-din Kaliyuni had caused an enumeration to be made of the population of Herat, and it was found to number 6,000 families. This was due to the influx of people into Herat, owing in great measure to the character of this Governor. He was the son of the chief of all the headmen of Badghis who, with his family and fellow townsmen, was cut off in the calamity that befell Kaliyun or Nar-Tu, following upon the destruction of Herat. Mujd-ud-din had been carried away as a child and preserved by a certain Amir named Arsalan in the service of Chingiz Khan.

1245-1246 A.D. At the time of the predominance of the Moghols when the Provinces of Khurassan had been overrun by the various hordes despatched by Chingiz Khan, Malik Rukn-ud-din Kurt had shut himself up in the fortress of Khaesār where he was besieged, but the Moghols despairing of reducing the place accepted his submission and recognized him as the Governor of Ghur by virtue of which his descendants claimed to hold that country. Malik Rukn-ud-din was the son of Malik Tāj-ud-din Uthman, the brother of Izz-ud-din Umar Maraghani already alluded to as the Vizier of Sultan Gheiath-ud-din of Ghur. The Vizier placed each of his sons and relatives in charge of a Province, and to his brother Tāj-ud-din Uthman was assigned the stronghold of Khaesār,

1246-1247 A.D. which his son Malik Rukn-ud-din inherited. The latter died in the year 643 H.

According to the history of Wassāf, Malik Shams-ud-din was the descendant of Kurt who had been the Leader-in-Chief of the armed forces of that district at the Court of Sultan Maudud; and was himself related to Sultan Shihāb-ud-din, the rival of Sultan Muhammed, of Khwārazm. In the year 644 H. Malik Shams-ud-din is said to have accompanied Sali Nuyin into Hindustan, but owing to the jealousy of his rivals he abandoned that leader with the intention of making his way to the camp of Tair Bahādur in Khurassan. Having joined this chief he stayed in the camp till the latter

1247-1248 A.D. died in the year 645 H.

The son of Tair Bahādur was not well disposed towards the Malik who thereupon made his way to the Court of Mangu Khan, who at that time occupied the throne of Chingiz Khan.

Mangu Khan bestowed on Malik Shams-ud-din the government of Herat with all its dependencies, such as Jām, Bakhārz, Kuhsuiāh, Firuzkuh, Gharjistan, Murghab, Maruchak, and Faryab, up to the Oxus; Isfirar, Farah, Sijistan, Takyan, Kabul, Tirah of Afghanistan up to the Frontiers of Sind. In addition to the usual dresses of honour, choice weapons and 10,000 dinars in cash were bestowed on him and an order was issued on Arghūn Āka to make over to the Malik 50 tomans (bodies) of troops.

Malik Shams-ud-din arrived at Herat and took over the government. 1254-1255 A.D. In the year 652 H. Malik Shams-ud-din besieged the town of Mastung, a dependency of the Garmsir, and conducted an expedition into the country of the Afghans, taking the forts of Piri, Kuhpura, Daki and Saji. In 656 Malik Shams-ud-din returned to Herat. 1258 A.D. In the meantime intrigues had been set on foot against the Tajik ruler of Herat, in consequence of which Prince Batu sent orders to the Prince Bulghā, his nephew, to seize Malik Shams-ud-din. Prince Bulghā, who had by that time moved from Khurassan into Mazenderān, despatched an agent who was to arrest the Malik and, placing him in strict custody, to forward the latter to his camp. While these matters were being set on foot Malik Shams-ud-din had set out for Seistan in order to settle the affairs of that country. On the way he was met by Malik Ali-i-Mas'ud who was ruler of Seistan. The latter was on his way to the camp of Katbuga Nuyin (to whom the order for the arrest of Malik Shams-ud-din had been intrusted for execution). The Malik of Seistan informed Malik Shams-ud-din that he would be back again in the course of a month, when he would present himself again before the ruler of Herat, and in the meantime letters were written to his kinsmen in Seistan to place the fortress of Malik Ali at the disposal of Malik Shams-ud-din; and to do everything in their power, to show due respect and honour towards him. Malik Shams-ud-din set out towards Seistan, but sent an agent, the Amir Shams-ud-din of Isfirār, to follow Malik Ali Seistani to the camp of Kitbuga Nuyin. There the matter of the arrest of Malik Shams-ud-din was made known to the Chief of Seistān, and the messengers of Prince Bulghā were ordered to proceed with the Malik to Seistan and execute their warrant.

News of the danger that threatened him was brought to Malik Shams-ud-din Kurt to Seistan, so that he was prepared to act by the time that Malik Ali-i-Mas'ud arrived with the emissaries of the Moghol Prince. Negotiations were opened with the Malik of Herat, and each side endeavoured to outwit the other, till at last Malik Ali-i-Mas'ud accepted an invitation to enter the fortress for the purpose of conferring with the former, hoping to find an opportunity of slaying him. Malik Shams-ud-din had also made a similar plan; and as soon as Malik Ali set foot within the place, the former, who was standing behind the door, with his own sabre struck off the head of the Chief of Seistan. This untoward event dispersed Malik Ali's retinue and the armed men he had collected; and Malik Shams-ud-din was able to leave Seistan, and made straight for the Court of the Ilkhan, after putting to death three of the leading men of Seistan; distributing alms and largesses on the learned and religious community as well as conferring dresses of honour on 1,700 of the chief men of the country. Arrived at the Court of the Ilkhan both Malik Shams-ud-din and his detractors were able to state their respective cases, and the former having succeeded in convincing the Ilkhan of his loyalty received fresh patent restoring to him the government of Herat.

1258-1259 A.D. — In the year 657 H. Malik Shams-ud-din reduced the fortress of Bakar in the country of the Afghans which was built on a plateau in a wide river. The Governor agreed to pay tribute. Fifty Kharwars of fine cloth were given to the conqueror with 50 slaves, 10,000 dinars in money, five Arab horses, and a variety of other rarities and valuables were likewise tendered.

From thence Malik Shams-ud-din entered the country of the Zamin-i-Dawar where he captured Malik Mirān Shah who was on this occasion put to death.

1264-1265 A.D. — In the year 663 Malik Tāj-ud-din Khar, a relation of Malik Shams-ud-din, was put to death by him.

1266-1267 A.D. — In the year 665 H. the latter proceeded to Irak to the Court of Abāka Khan and served under his standards in the struggle between him and his rival Barka Khan, after which the Malik returned to Herat.

1276-1277 A.D. — In the year 675 H. the latter again proceeded to the Court of the Ilkhan, but the great influence he had built up in Khurassan and the countries under his sway had not been without its effect on the mind of his Suzerain. The Malik was kept in attendance in the camp of the Ilkhan, and his son Rukn-ud-din and his brother were sent off to Darband-i-Bāku. Eventually Malik Shams-ud-din died from the effects of poison administered in a water melon by order of Abākā Khan in a Hamman in Tabriz. This took place during

1277-1278 A.D. — the month of Shawal of the year 676 H.

So much did Abākā Khan fear the deceased, and his wily nature, that a special messenger, a Moghol named Halkato, was sent from Court to verify the circumstance by a personal examination of the corpse.

1278-1279 A.D. — In the year 677 H. Abākā Khan visited Herat and finding it in a condition of decline appointed Malik Rukn-ud-din as Governor of the city and its dependencies, bestowing on the latter the title of Shams-ud-din enjoyed by his father. And he is known in the History of the Kurts as Shams-ud-din the Less.

1281-1282 A.D. — In 680 A. H. he took Kandahar after 13 days' hard fighting by assault, the ruler having disregarded his appointment to Herat.

1283-1284 A.D. — In the year 682 Shams-ud-din the Less installed his son Ala-ud-din as his deputy in Herat and retired to Khaesār. Bands of Moghols under leaders of lower rank, and hordes under Princes of the Blood of Chingiz, wandered at will through the more Eastern and Northern Provinces under the government of the Ilkhan, the member of the Royal Family, who filled the throne of Chingiz. These Princes of the Blood exercised sovereign powers, and their mandates could only be overruled by the Ilkhan. Moreover, the position of rulers of Tājik race was one of extreme difficulty as they were exposed to unceasing misrepresentations at the hands of the Moghol Chiefs as well as the Princes of the Blood. Owing to the exactions of a rebel leader of Moghols, both Malik Shams-ud-din and his son Ala-ud-din abandoned Herat and retired to the fortress of Khaesār; the population of Herat migrated to other districts and the city was almost depopulated. The general disorder was heightened by the raid of Ayāji, the Nikudari leader who plundered the city and its districts, making prisoners of the inhabitants and their families.

In the year 690 H. a decree of Ghazan Khan was promulgated by which Malik Hisam-ud-din of Sabzawār (Isfirar), Malik Jallaludin of Farah, and Malik Nasīr-ud-dīn of Sejistan were commanded to send all people of Herat who had migrated to those districts under the sway of the Maliks back to that city. 1291 A.D.

The Amir Nauroz was sent by the Ilkhan with 5,000 horse to protect the city and Province; and no one, Moghol or Moslem, was permitted to levy any revenue or make other demands on the inhabitants. In this way it came to pass that prosperity again was restored to the city, and all the people blessed the Amir Nauroz for his benevolence and the protection he afforded them. Malik Shams-ud-din had imprisoned his eldest son Fakhr-ud-din for seven years, but the Amir Nauroz obtained the youth's release, and took the latter into his care, educated and disciplined him, and used him as occasion offered against the enemies of the Ilkhan. Among other appointments Malik Fakhr-ud-din was entrusted with the command of the expedition against Malik Niāl Tigin of Farah. The latter had rebelled because, while he was absent in Irak, the Amir Nauroz had seized his brother Malik Jallaluddin and imprisoned him in a fortress of Gharjistān. When Malik Niāl Tigin returned from Irak he took possession of all the forts held by Amir Nauroz's men, and put to death the members of the party in his Province who had come to an understanding with that leader. Malik Fakhr-ud-din entered into communication with Niāl Tigin, and induced him to surrender, promising to intercede for him and his brother Jallaluddin as well.

The Maliks of Farah had very probably attempted to assert their independence during the period of the disturbances that had taken place in Khurassan, owing to which the population of the city of Herat had been forced to emigrate. About the same time, Prince Dua, son of Barak (Barka ?), entered Khurassan at the head of 100,000 men, and attempted open communications with Malik Fakhr-ud-din. The latter refused to deal with Prince Dua, and Amir Nauroz taking his *protégé* with him, retired to the Court of Ghazan Khan in Irak.

The Ilkhan bestowed the government of Herat on Malik Fakhr-ud-din, 10,000 dinars in ready money and a number of other valuable presents, and gave him in addition a body of 1,000 Moghols to be his personal escort.

In course of time, it came to pass that the Amir Nauroz fell out with Ghazan Khan, and eventually was driven to seek refuge in the citadel of Herat. The Amir Kutlugh at the head of 70,000 soldiers appeared before Herat which was invested for 18 days. In this quandary Malik Fakhr-ud-din decided to be loyal to the Ilkhan, rather than to his benefactor, he therefore seized the latter and delivered him over to his enemy by whom he was at once put to death,—10th August 1297.

1298-1299 A.D. In the year 698 H. the Amir-i-Nikudar arrived from Irak at the head of 3,000 men, and were allotted lands round Herat. They were an impudent and low minded race; and the havoc they wrought by their raids in Kuhistan, Farah, Sijistan, and Jazruan, and the excesses they committed, earned them universal reprobation.

At length Ghazan Khan ordered his brother Khudabanda to disperse the Nikudaris, Sanjaris, and Ghurians whom the Malik had allowed to settle around Herat.

Malik Fakhr-ud-din refused to consent to this and Khudabanda marched on Herat, but when he had reached the Herat Rud, the Malik abandoned the city and fled to the fortress of Āmān Koh,[1] known later as Ispakalacheh.

Khudabanda laid siege to it for four days without avail, after which a great battle took place in which the besiegers lost 2,000 men killed as well as 2,000 wounded. The following night the Malik sallied out, at the head of a body of picked men, cut his way through the investing force, and entered Herat; but leaving the city the same night, he took the road towards Ghur. Khudabanda laid siege to Herat for 18 days, but the Sheikh-ul-Islam represented that Malik Fakhr-ud-din was not there; and induced Khudabanda to draw off his forces. Malik Fakhr-ud-din immediately returned to the city, and after distributing alms, he set about to strengthen the fortification of Herat. The whole population of the city was set to labour on this task which **1301-1302 A.D.** was completed in 699 A. H. In 701 A. H. Malik Fakhr-ud-din set out to subdue Malik Hisam-ud-din of Sabzawār and his brother Malik Rukn-ud-din neither of whom recognised the supremacy of the Malik of Herat. Malik Hisam-ud-din died in the meantime, but his brother met the invasion in arms, and after severe fighting shut himself in the fortress of Robah, and Malik Fakhr-ud-din retreated to Herat.

A second time the latter having raised a large army of Moghols and Muhammadan warriors attacked Isfirar (Sabzawār), but was compelled again to retire.

A third time did Malik Fakhr-ud-din invade Sabzawār (Isfirar) at the head of a vast force composed of Heratis, Tulakis, Bakharzis, Khafis, Ghuris and Nikudaris, while his brother Ala-ud-din marched to his aid from Ghur at the head of 3,000 men of the hilly country. After seven days' desperate fighting the capital town of Isfirar was taken and a great slaughter took place; while a large number of the inhabitants were carried away to Herat and compelled to work at making bricks and kneading clay.

---

[1] Aman Koh lay to the south-west and not far from Herat. It is almost certain that it occupied a position close to the modern Ghurian. This name signifies "the people of Ghur" and Aman Koh was a military post held by Ghurians.

After this lesson Malik Rukn-ud-din submitted and visited Malik Fakhr-ud-din in Herat, but becoming apprehensive of treachery he fled away. Afterwards his son Malik Izz-ud-din visited Herat, where in course of time he was arrested and placed in confinement.

In the year 703 H. Khudabanda succeeded his brother Ghazan Khan, and assumed the title and style of Uljaitu Sultan. On Panj Shamba, the 12th of the month of Safar, in 705 A. H., Malik Shams-ud-din Muhammad, the Kurt, died at Khaesar and his funeral service was performed in the Jami Masjid of Herat. In 706 A. H. hostilities broke out between Malik Fakhr-ud-din and his Suzerain, and Danishmand Bahadur was detailed with 10,000 horse to capture Malik Fakhr-ud-din and the Nikudaris and bring them to the presence of Uljaitu Sultan. Malik Fakhr-ud-din had shut himself up in Āmān Koh, and his son Jamāl-ud-din Muhammad Sām held the citadel of Herat, called the Fort of Ikhtiyār-ud-din, with a selected garrison. After some desultory operations on the part of the Moghol leader he was inveigled into the citadel with a party of followers, where all were massacred to a man by Malik Jamāl-ud-din. Malik Niāl Tigin of Farah with an escort of Danishmand's troops were waiting for the latter without the citadel, when a certain Sanjari, an acquaintance of the Malik of Farah, came out from the fortress and, in reply to a question put by the latter, said that Danishmand had partaken of the meal which Amir Nauroz had tasted. Alarmed by this intelligence the Malik Niāl Tigin, who knew what was the full import of the statement, mounted his horse and with the rest of the escort fled away in a state of terror. When the fugitives arrived at the gate of Firuzabad, the southern gateway of the city, they found it closed, but one of their number, named Umar, hewed the lock and the chains that fastened the gates into pieces with his battle-axe, and the party made their escape. *[margin: 1303-1304 A.D. · 4th September 1305. · 1306-1307 A.D.]*

The murder of Danishmand Bahadur was avenged by his son Bujae, and during his siege of Herat, Malik Fakhr-ud-din fell ill and died on the 24th of Sha'aban in the year 706 H., Malik Jamal-ud-din Muhammad Sām having at length surrendered was eventually put to death by Amir Bujae. *[margin: Sunday, 16th January 1307 A.D.]*

Malik Gheiath-ul-Hak-wa-ud-din, brother of Malik Fakhr-ud-din, succeeded to the government of Herat in the year 707 H. under Uljaitu Sultan, and in 708 A. H. he visited Ghur and Isfirar to establish his authority. *[margin: 1307-1308 A.D. · 1308-1309 A.D.]*

In consequence of intrigues set on foot by the Moghols who were in Khurassan, Malik Gheiath-ud-din was summoned to the presence of his Suzerain Uljaitu Sultan in the year 711 H. He was detained there till the year 715 H. In this year he was reinstated in the government of Herat, with extraordinary marks of the Sultan's favour. *[margin: 1311-1312 A.D. · 1315-1316 A.D.]*

In the year 716 H. Malik Gheiath-ud-din visited Isfirar and defeated and dispersed a great body of the Nikudaris. *[margin: 1316-1317 A.D.]*

44   THE HISTORY OF SEISTAN.

1317-1318 A.D. In this year Prince Yasur of the Blood Royal of the Moghols overran the Province of Khurassan, and the next year 717 H. was passed in conflicts with these marauders. In this same year Sultan Uljaitu died and was succeeded by his son Abu Said Sultan. The latter confirmed Malik Gheiath-ud-din in the government of Herat and its dependencies.

1319 A.D. The Prince Yasur ravaged Khurassan till the year 719 H. when he drew off his horde towards the Garmsir.

The districts of Sabzawâr (Isfirar), Farah, and Seistan were subject to Malik Gheiath-ud-din, but during the inroads of the Moghol hordes under Prince Yasur the Maliks of Sabzawâr and Farah had made friends with that errant Prince, who had won them over from their allegiance to Malik Gheiath-ud-din. Malik Kutb-ud-din of Sabzawâr made an attempt to sieze the fortress of 'Ikil, but Amir Ali Khat-tai, who was the Governor left by Malik Gheiath-ud-din, collected all those who were well disposed to his master and blockaded Malik Kutb-ud-din in the citadel of Isfirar. Malik Gheiath-ud-din collected a strong force and marched to the aid of his adherents; while Malik Niâl Tigin of Farah from the south, at the head of 10,000 men, set out to the rescue of his ally of Sabzawâr. He arrived at the plain of Shâkân when he heard of the presence of Malik Gheith-ud-din. This news so alarmed Niâl Tigin that he fled away abandoning his men to their fate, and returned by way of the desert to Farah. The troops of Niâl Tigin were attacked by Malik Gheiath-ud-din in their camp at Shâkân, and, without leaders to direct them, were overthrown and dispersed, leaving 2,000 prisoners in the hands of their assailants. In consequence of this Malik Kutb-ud-din and his son Malik Khasrau were compelled to render themselves up to the Malik of Herat and were carried away prisoners to that place when the former was publicly beaten in the Chaharsu of the city. News of all that had taken place was sent to the Court of Abu Said Sultan who was well satisfied by the way in which Malik Gheiath-ud-din had maintained the interests of his Suzerain in Khurassan against all comers. The fiefs of Malik Kutb-ud-din of Isfirar, the Malik of Farah, and of all those who had joined Prince Yasur were declared to be forfeited, and they, with all the leaders of the Nikudaris, were ordered to recognise the Malik as their feudal overlord. Malik Gheiath-ud-din restored the Jam'i Masjid of Herat built by his namesake, the Sultan of Ghur. Most of the precincts of this building had by this time fallen into disrepair, while the eastern and southern cloisters had become altogether ruinous. These were all restored by this Malik, who in person, with the leading men of the city, encamped on the spot for a space of 50 days while the restoration was in progress. Many other buildings also did he construct, both in Herat itself and in outlying towns of the districts under his jurisdiction.

1320 A.D. In the year 720 H. he conquered the district of Bakharz, and in this year also, his inveterate and powerful antagonist, Prince Yasur, fell in a battle against the forces of the Malik aided by the Moghols of Prince Kipak from beyond the Oxus.

In the year 720 H. Malik Gheiath-ud-din accompanied by a great retinue set out to make the pilgrimage to Mecca; having made over his government to his son Malik Shams-ud-din Muhammad. 1320 A.D.

In 721 A. H. Amir Husen who commanded in chief in Khurassan, on behalf of Abu Said Sultan, sent an official order to Malik Niâl Tigin of Farah to forward 5,000 Kharwars of grain to his Suzerain the Malik of Herat. Niâl Tigin utterly refused to comply with this request, and declared that as in the past all dealings with Herat would be referred to the arbitration of the sword. 1321-1322 A.D.

Malik Shams-ud-din Muhammad Kurt accordingly overran the districts of Farah and having collected much booty he returned to Herat.

Malik Gheiath-ud-din Kurt died in the year 729 H., leaving four sons, Malik Shams-ud-din Muhammad, Malik Hafiz Malik Muiz-ud-din, and Malik Bakr. 1328-1329 A.D.

Under their father the fortunes of the Al-i-Kurt had reached their zenith. The whole of Khurassan was subject to him, and Seistan nominally so. Although nothing is clearly stated as to the relations existing between the Kaiâni Maliks and their nominal Suzerain, there seems to be but little doubt that the former were in close alliance with Malik Niâl Tigin of Farah, and co-operated with him in his opposition to the Maliks of Herat. The author of the Rauzat-ul-Jannat has recorded a satirical verse referring to the abortive attempt to relieve Isfirar, when Malik Kutb-ud-din was besieged therein by the Heratis.

It is also expressly stated that Malik Kutb-ud-din was warned against expecting to be relieved by the troops of Farah and Seistan.

During the troubles consequent on the inroads of Prince Yasur, and previously also, the Maliks of Seistan, there can be but little doubt, ruled as independent Princes.

Seistan never seems to have been entered by the Maliks of the Al-i-Kurt after the occasion in which Malik Ali-i-Masud lost his life.

Malik Shams-ud-din Muhammad succeeded his father in the government of Herat, and proved himself to be a wise and just ruler. But the period of his life, like a day of rejoicing and happiness, came all too quickly to a close as he died only two months after his accession.

Malik Hafiz succeeded his deceased brother. He was a weak Prince and in his day the Ghuris did what they pleased, as he could not restrain their ferocity.

At this time also, in the year 736 H., Abu Said Sultan died. This Prince was the last and greatest of the descendants of Chingiz Khan, and after him there was left no one to occupy the throne bequeathed by the Great 1335-1336 A.D.

Conqueror. In all directions there sprang up tumults, and on every side there arose those who asserted their pretensions to sovereignty. Iran, owing to these disturbances, became unsettled and desolate.

In these gloomy times the justice of Malik Muiz-ud-din Husen of Herat formed a brilliant exception. He was a strong barrier to injustice and violence; the dispenser of justice and benevolence; and he was the refuge of all who were oppressed.

The Al-i-Muzaffar rose to power in Fars, while in Sabzawār (Nishapur) the Sarbadāris represented by Amir Abdur Rahman, one of the great men of Baihak, claimed the position of an independent state. He was murdered by his brother Wajih-ud-din on the 12th of the month Rajab, in the year 738 H., and the latter became the head of the government.

6th January 1338 A.D.

Amir Wajih-ud-din at last made war against Herat and Malik Muiz-ud-din Husen advanced to meet him at the head of a great array of Ghuris, men Khaesār, Sanjaris, Baluch, and Nikudaris. Both parties came into collision in the district of Zawah on the 13th of Safar 743 A.H. and after a hard struggle victory declared at last for the Malik of Herat owing to his personal valour and presence of mind.

1342-1343 A.D.

After this decisive victory Malik Muiz-ud-din Husen subdued parts of the Kuhistan, and set up as an independent ruler. He turned his attention towards Badghis, and led a force in the directions of Balkh, Shibarghan and Andikhud. He laid waste those districts and defeated the tribes of Arlat and Abivard with great slaughter, and made two pillars of the heads of the slain.

In those days the countries beyond the Oxus were in a condition of anarchy, and no one cared what happened in Khurassan in consequence of which Malik Muiz-ud-din Husen found himself at liberty to set up as an independent ruler. His state music was played five times a day, and he prepared all the usual regulations and insignia of an independent sovereign. He greatly strengthened the existing defences of Herat, and added an outer line of extremely strong and massive fortifications which enclosed a very wide area. The author of the Rauzat-ul-Jannat describes their ruins as follows: "They extended from the bridge over the Jui Anjil to the gate (Darband) of Shaikh Khuram and from the confines of Malasian to the bridge of the tent makers, a distance of nearly one farsakh." His ambitious projects brought him into collision with the Kāiāni Maliks of Seistan, who had for some time past been ruling as an independent dynasty of Princes, a point on which their coins afford clear evidence.

"Malik Qutb-ud-din bin Shah Rukn succeeded his uncle Shah Nusrat on the throne of Seistan in A. H. 731, having been duly elected at the votes of the princes of the royal house and great men of the State. His investiture with the sovereignty of Nimruz took place on Monday, Rabi I. 8., on which occasion much largess was judiciously distributed. Qutb ud din was an excellent ruler, firm, politic, just, liberal, brave, devout, a patron of

1330-1331 A.D.

13th January 1331 A.D.

learning, genius and piety, an enemy of vice and profligacy. He was wont to encourage worth by conferring of stipends, and every day there used to issue from his kitchens thirty ass loads of bread and ten of meat, with other necessaries in proportion which were distributed to strangers and poor. All Seistan acknowledged his sway. When he had completed the organisation of his kingdom, certain traitorous persons incited Malik Husain Ghuri, Ruler of Herat, to invade Seistan, who in consequence in A. H. 734 led an army 1333-1334 A.D. more numerous than ants or locusts against the King. When the news of this invasion reached Malik Qutb-ud-din he gathered a force of 80,000 veteran troops, foot and horse, together with elephants, and set out from the city of Seistan to meet the army of Khurassan. When the troops of Seistan had reached Chargewak (?), the army of Khurassan being encamped by the stream of Panjdeh, Amir Iqbal Sabiq,[1] one of the trusted adherents of Shaik Ala-ud-daulah Seistani, came to Malik Qutb-ud-din and besought him to halt his army that he might go to the King of Herat and dissuade him from this enterprise, attacking Moslems, without just cause. The King said, Go and tell him that I have no fear or dread of him, but that I am loth to shed the blood of Moslems. If he will not relinquish this enterprise our dispute must be settled on the field of battle. Mir Iqbal delivered this message to Malik Husain, and showed him the overwhelming superiority of the army of Seistan. Malik Husain accepted his advice, and at once returned to Herat by double marches. Thus the two Kings returned home without fighting."

The geographical position of Seistan favoured the independence of the Kaiāni Princes. While various claimants were striving for power in the countries to the north, the ambitions of the Kaiānis would necessarily be unable to find expression in the acquisition of territory in that direction.

In the opposite direction, however, towards the south there lay the districts which are now called Baluchistan and in these tracts the expansion of authority of the Kaiāni family probably found unchecked scope.

There is evidence to show that after the decease of Abu Said Sultan, Malik Kutb-ud-din probably took advantage of the condition of anarchy which ensued to extend his authority over Kirman. A gold coin bearing the title of Kutb-ul-Hak Waūd-dunya-wa-ud-din was examined in Seistan which bore, as mint town, the name Kirman. It was also dated 74 x, the last figure being illegible.

The Al-i-Muzaffar who obtained possession of Fars, and Kirman in the course of a few years after the demise of Abu Said Sultan was a very short-lived dynasty and it did not gain possession of Kirman until after the year 754 H., 1353 A. D. or 18 years after the death of the last sovereign of the House of Chingiz Khan; while Malik Kutb-ud-din alluded to in the extract from the Ihya-ul-Mulukas having repulsed Malik Husen Kurt, of Herat, was raised to the government

---

[1] It is probable that Sabiq was his father's name, following a well established custom in Seistan at the present day.

The shrine of Mir Iqbal near the ruins of Peshawaran also was probably established at the residence of this holy person whose tomb it probably is that exists inside the building, where after his death and canonization the people of the country have resorted to invoke his aid and perform their vows.

of Seistan in 731 A. H. It would therefore not have been impossible for Malik Kutb-ud-din to have gained possession of Kirman after the death of Abu Said Sultan.

To return to the account of the affairs of Seistan, it is apparent that after the retreat of Malik Husen Kurt, of Herat, the Kaiānis continued to rule as independent Princes in Seistan for some time until they in their turn came into collision with Timur.

This great conqueror, who had revived the supremacy of the Turks and who emulated the achievements of the Chingiz Khan, was born in the year in which had died Abu Said, the last Sultan of the family of Chingiz Khan. He was born in Kesh in the country beyond the Oxus on the 25th of the month of Shab'an in the year 736 H.

In his early years he was involved in the struggles that were taking place in the Provinces beyond the Oxus, and in this period of his career he was brought into contact with the Kaiānis of Seistan and the Maliks of Herat, both of whom he subdued at a later date.

Just before the turning point in his career he was compelled to retire into the country to the south of the Oxus, and in company with his ally, the Amir Husen (a descendant of Chingiz Khan), he retreated into the district of Kirmiz in the direction of Kandahar, and the district of Bakhtar Zamin. His intention was to wait for an opportunity to take possession of Kandahar, then in the possession of the Ghuris, and to make it his capital. While he was waiting for a chance to effect this, a revolution or insurrection had taken place in Seistan, and the Prince of Seistan having been worsted by his enemies asked for help from Timur (who was at that time in his 29th year). This took place in the year 764 H.

Timur and his ally, Amir Husen, marched to the assistance of the Kaiāni, and the latter, who is named Jallal-ud-din Mahmud, received them well expressing his everlasting gratitude and bestowing valuable presents on his allies. Suitable provision was also made for the 1,000 men at arms who formed the retinue of Timur.

At this time seven forts were in the hands of the faction opposed to Malik Jallal-ud-din Mahmud; and three of these were quickly taken by Timur. This so alarmed the Seistanis that they made their submission to the Malik and pointed out that if Timur captured the rest of the strongholds the country would be at his mercy. Malik Jallal-ud-din Mahmud also saw the danger and without informing his allies withdrew to his own territory, where his subjects rallied round him, and he raised a large force, of both horse and foot, at the head of which he marched against Timur and Amir Husen. Timur divided his force into three bodies, Amir Husen faced the right wing of the Seistanis, the second body under one of Timur's chiefs was opposed to their left wing, and Timur himself commanded the third body of his troops and the

Palace of a Kaiāni noble (circ. 14th century A.D.) in ruins; S. E. of Chakānsur.

(Part I to face page 48.)

advanced guard in person fronting the centre of the array of the men of Seistan. A fierce struggle took place and the troops of Timur and Amir Husen were being pushed back by the Seistanis; seeing this Timur, at the head of his personal escort, entered the battle and after a severe struggle broke through the army of Seistan. In this struggle Timur received two wounds, one on his arm and another at the back of his foot, both of which were inflicted by arrows discharged by one of the enemy. The wound in his foot left permanent effects, and it was owing to it that Timur was lame for the rest of his life, and was ever afterwards called "Timur-lang," "the lame Timur," which has been corrupted into Tamerlane by European writers.

In the list of Princes translated by A. G. Ellis, Esq., from the Ihya-ul-Muluk, there is no Prince of that name reigning in 764 H. But Sultan Mahmud bin Shah, Ali bin Nasr-ud-din (Kaiāni) appears in that list as having reigned from 751 to 753 H. Either the latter date is wrong, or he was deposed in favour of his successor 'Izz-ud-din bin Rukn-ud-din Mahmud. If the date is wrong then 'Izz-ud-din was the pretender or rival candidate whose successor brought Timur into Seistan to the aid of Jallal-ud-din Mahmud. It is impossible to suppose that Timur did not know which of the two was the rightful ruler, and it is still less probable that he made a mistake as to his name, and the date given for the transaction is too precise to admit of a mistake being possible with respect to it. It can be shown that another date in the same list is also very probably incorrect, so that the probabilities in favour of the date given in the History of the Maliks being in this case doubtful are very great.

A revolution therefore appears to have taken place during the lifetime of Sultan Mahmud Kaiāni, and after his death Malik 'Izz-ud-din succeeded to the government of Seistan.

The state of affairs that prevailed in Seistan is very apparent from a reference to the genealogical scheme in Plate III. The office of ruler was not fixed and hereditary in one branch of this family, but the individual was elected by his kinsmen to hold the office, and he was in consequence at the mercy of those who raised him to that position which he could only hold while he kept friends with them. The stories of Arbab Seif-ud-din are borne out by the genealogical scheme, as he was full of the existence of Kaiāni nobles, men of position and great power; and his statement that the ruined palaces were the abodes of those persons is no doubt correct, or as close to the truth as it is possible to attain at this distance of time.

The period of 50 years following the death of Abu Said Sultan was one of great prosperity for the Tājik Rulers in Khurassan. The Maliks of the Al-i-Kurt, ruling in Herat, held the eastern districts round Kandahar which in 764 H. was held by the Ghuris. The Kaiānis had extended their power 1362-1363 A.D. probably over Kirman, and to the south over Baluchistan.

Trade must have been briskly maintained with India, for if Malik Kutb-ud-din actually did possess elephants, as stated in the account taken from the Ihya-ul-Muluk, he could only have obtained them from India through Kandahar. From this place to Seistan there were two routes, one by way of Khisht in the oasis of Khāsh, and the second down the valley of the Helmand. But these routes were not always open and generally unsafe owing to the encampments of the Nikudari tomāns on the upper reaches of the Helmand. These were almost all non-Moslem tribes, professing the ancient pagan religion which their forefathers had brought with them from the steppes of High Asia. There were frequent complaints about the excesses of these predatory tribes, and it was this conduct that in the end drew upon them the wrath of the Great Amir Timur.

Some of these tribes were doubtless subject to Seistan; or at all events in the service of the Princes of that country. It was one of these tribal Maliks, or the headman of a tomān serving in the Seistan army, who discharged the arrows at Timur in the engagement already alluded to, by which the latter was severely injured; but it was also to the encampment of the Nikudaris that he repaired for treatment, and where he rested until his wounds had healed.

Elephants are not mentioned in the war with Timur on the first occasion or later. Either there were no longer elephants in Seistan, owing to the facilities for trade having disappeared, through the growing insecurity of the trade route, or the author of the Ihya-ul-Muluk was desirous of exalting the past glories of his family, in the eyes of the Persian Monarch, at whose Court he resided, by fanciful details of the resources of his ancestors.

Malik Muiz-ud-din Husen Kurt, as has already been mentioned, extended his jurisdiction over the tribes of Turkish origin settled in Badghis. These carried the complaints to the Amir Aziz, a chieftain of the Yurt of Chingiz Khan who had established supremacy for a time in the country beyond the Oxus. This chieftain thereupon resolved to put down the pretensions of the Tājik Ruler of Herat. He collected troops from all the districts between Kashghar on the east, and Andikhud on the west, and appointed their rendezvous at Balkh. The outposts of Malik Muiz-ud-din Kurt brought in intelligence of the advance of this great army towards Herat; and that chief determined to confine himself to a strong position under the walls of Herat; and he drew up intrenchments for this purpose which extended from the meadows of Kuhdastan, on the east and north side of the city of Herat, up to the village of Yumurgh (?) and the force he mustered to hold this line amounted to 4,000 horse and from 10,000 to 12,000 foot soldiers. The issue was, however, unfavourable for the Malik, and after a strenuous resistance he was compelled to obtain terms of surrender through the good offices of the heads of the religious establishments in Herat. Malik Muiz-ud-din promised to regard the ruler of trans-Oxiana as his Suzerain.

These events took place in the year 752 H. A conspiracy among the Ghuris in Herat drove him from the city to the fortress of Amān Koh, and his youngest brother Malik Bākir was raised to the seat of authority in Herat.   1352 A.D.

In the year 753 Malik Muiz-ud-din set out for the country beyond the Oxus. He was well received, and was permitted to return to Herat where he seized Malik Bākir and re-established his own authority.

In the year 759 H. he was involved in a struggle with the Amir Sitalmish 1358 A.D. who held the Kuhistān and with Amir Muhammad Khwājah, two Turkish Chiefs, each of whom were at the head of a large body of followers. Both these chieftains were, however, slain in battle.

During the early period of his career, Timur was on terms of friendship with Malik Husen, and when the former moved across the Oxus to attempt the conquest of the country beyond that river, he left his family and those of his followers in the charge of the Malik.

When Malik Muiz-ud-din Husen discerned that he had not much longer to live, he nominated his eldest son Malik Gheiath-ud-din Pir Ali to be his successor, and he willed the fort of Sarakhs and the surrounding country to his next son Malik Muhamad, better known as the Amir-i-Khurd, and to his own widow, of the Arlat tribe. Malik Muiz-ud-din Husen, the Kurt, died on the 5th of Zil-Kadeh in the year 772 H. 20th May 1371 A.D.

Malik Gheiath-ud-din Pir Ali succeeded his father, and he strengthened the walls of Herat and built a new line of fortifications, included within them many buildings and gardens, which before that time had been beyond the walls of the city. His attitude, however, towards Timur was not particularly friendly, and he was much too powerful to be neglected; so that eventually Timur decided to march against him and reduce him to a position of subserviency; and to this end, having given orders for the mobilisation of his forces, he crossed the Oxus in the last days of the year 782 H. at the head of 1386 A.D. a very numerous force.

Malik Muhammad, the brother of the Malik Gheiath-ud-din, submitted to the invader. The latter was at Nishāpur operating against the Sarbadāris, and Timur at once entered Jām and the Kohsuieh in order to prevent the fighting men of those districts joining the Malik.

Before, however, advancing on Herat, Timur attacked and took the stronghold of Foshanj, and then marched on the city itself. The gateway of Ansāri, one of the exits in the new fortifications, was the scene of the principal attack, but two days afterwards a party of Timur's soldiers effected an entrance by means of the passage, close to the Kushk-i-Maraghāni, through which the Anjil canal entered the defences and which had apparently been left unguarded. The outer line of his defences having been pierced, the Malik, who had been fighting bravely at the gate which opened on the bridge over the Anjil canal, was forced to retire within the city walls. Further resistance was rendered impossible by Timur having promised quarter to all those who desisted from strife, and the Malik was compelled to surrender, and the next day he advanced from the citadel of Ikhtiyār-ud-din and made his formal submission to Timur, in the Bagh-i-Zāghān where that chief had placed his headquarters.

The outer walls of Herat were demolished. A sum of money was imposed as a ransom on the city. It was paid within four days. The treasury and store-houses containing the hoards of the house of Kurt, which had been amassed during many generations, were taken possession of and removed by Timur, who in addition ordered Maulānā Nizām-ud-din with 200 families to remove to Shahr-i-Sābz, with all their dependants and clients.

The fortress of Āmān Koh which was held by the younger son of Malik Gheiath-ud-din, the Amir-i-Ghuri, was also rendered up to Timur.

1382-1383 A.D.

In 784 A. H. after the capture of the fortress of Turshiz and the reduction of the famous stronghold of Kallat, Malik Gheiath-ud-din Kurt was carried to Samarkand [1] with other captives of rank by Timur.

The sons of Malik Fakhr-ud-din Muhammad and of his brother complained in person to Timur that during the lifetime of Malik Husen and his son Gheiath-ud-din Pir Ali, they had been deprived of their inheritance they were well received and the government of Ghur was conferred on the elder of the brothers, named Muhammad.

1382-1383 A.D.

At the close of the year 784 H. a revolution took place in Herat, the moving spirit being a certain man of Ghur named Abu Said-i-Ispahbad. This man, also known as the "Ghuri Bacha," had been imprisoned for ten years by Malik Gheiath-ud-din, but was released by Timur when he took Herat.

---

[1] Samarkand, the traditionary capital of that leader of the Turkish horde, whom the Persians call Afrasyab. Principal E. Denison Ross in Part I of the Heart of Asia, in a footnote to page 115, states that "Tradition has it that Afrasiyab flourished about B.C. 580"; he does not, however, mention the source from whence he derived his information. According to this tradition he must have been a contemporary of Kyaxares, the Median King who died in 584 B.C. according to some authorities.

A dynasty of Princes who are called the Afrasiyabi Maliks flourished in the countries beyond the Oxus, whose capital city was Samarkand until just previous to the invasion of the Moghols when the overgrown Empire of Khwārazm absorbed their principality. But their power had previously been reduced by the encroachments of the Kara Khitais and other tribes whose westward movement heralded the advent of the Chingiz Khan.

These Afrasiyabi Maliks were Turks, but they had long been professors of Islam and their titles and names are derived from Arabic sources. After capture of Bokhara, the Chingiz Khan advanced against Samarkand before which he appeared at the end of the month of Zib.—Haj 616 A. H. (end of February 1220 A.D.); after the siege had continued for a few days, varying in different authorities from the 5th to the 9th day, the Kazi of the city, the Sheikh-ul-Islam, and a body of the ecclesiastical class and profession, who were old officials of the Afrasiyabi Maliks, went out and made their submission to Chingiz Khan and having returned to the city seized an opportunity and opened the gate, either of the Namazgah or Idgah, and admitted the Moghols.

The citadel garrisoned by troops of Sultan Muhammad Khwārazm Shah was invested and assaulted. It was taken and the garrison put to the sword. This took place on the 4th of April 1220 A.D. A Moghol Intendent was left at Samarkand and a native of the place, a Muhammadan, was placed in charge of the city under him. The latter, therefore, was not destroyed by the Moghols; although the walls and the works of the citadel were doubtless, to a great extent, dismantled.

There is at this day close to the modern city of Samarkand the ancient site called "Afrosiab." This site was examined in 1903, in a very cursory manner, by the American Expedition under the

Malik Muhammad advanced on the city from Ghur, at the head of an array of the turbulent inhabitants of that country, more foolish than he; and the "Ghuri Bacha" having joined him they drove Timur's officials into the citadel of Ikhtiyār-ud-din; and their bands spreading over the city committed all sorts of excesses. A portion of these desperadoes approached the gates of that fortress, and having piled the faggots of wood against the doors set them on fire. A body of Turks hoping to escape let themselves down from the walls, but they were intercepted and massacred to a man by these villains.

Prince Mirān Shāh, son of Timur, was, however, in winter quarters at Panjdeh (commonly known as Pandi), and when he heard of the state of affairs in the city, he forthwith despatched troops under Amir Hāji Seif-ud-din, and Amir Ak Bughā, to Herat, following in person with the rest of his forces. When those leaders arrived on the scene, they were met in the streets of Khiabān by the Ghuris, where a desperate struggle took place. The Ghuris were defeated and some of them fled into the city. Having dispersed during the night they wandered about the country. When, however, the Prince arrived in Herat, he made search for the fugitives, of whom his troops slew a great number and made a pillar of their heads as a warning to others.

This foolish and ill-timed outbreak sealed the fate of the captive Malik and his family; for, on news of the occurrence having reached Timur, he issued orders for the execution of Malik Gheiāth-ud-din Pir 'Ali who was imprisoned in the citadel in Samarkand, and his brother Malik Muhammad, the Amir Ghuri, and Ali Beg, the Chief of the Jun Ghurbānis, who had held out in Kallat against Timur were likewise put to death in Andijan where they had been detained. The eldest son of the Malik, Pir Muhammad, however, still languished in prison, but the family of the Kurt Maliks of Herat ceased from this time forth to be of any importance.

---

direction of Mr. Raphael Pumpelly. The following description is from his published report:— "This is a plateau of made earth, the débris of ruins, standing on the 'loess' plain. It is covered to a great extent with Muhammadan cemeteries, with some traces of Mussulman occupation and with fragments of pottery and bricks. The loess plain is deeply dissected by a stream, and several gullies have been cut in both the plateau of the ruins and the loess. It is difficult to distinguish between the made earth of the plateau and the underlying loess, except through the presence of fragments of pottery, charcoal and bones.

"We found such fragments down to a depth of about 40 feet below the general surface in the gullies, and it is not improbable that the thickness of débris is still greater."

"Above this general surface rises the citadel mound to an additional height of 30 to 40 feet, or 170 feet above stream at its base."

* * * * * * * * * * *

"The former walls of the city are represented now by ridges rising 20 or 30 feet above the surface within. Where the walls are cut by gullies old galleries are exposed which seem to have been continuous with the wall. * * (pages 11 and 12). The circumference of these remains is about 3 miles."

The town of Samarkand as it existed after the conquest by Chingiz, even to so late a date as the early years of Timur's career, possessed no walls nor a ditch. It was an open town or large village and was doubtless founded by those of the inhabitants of the older city whose lives had been spared by Chingiz Khan. Timur made Samarkand his capital, fortified it and raised those buildings whose decaying remains are still to be classed among the wonders of the world.

There now remained only the Kaiāni Maliks of Seistan; and they were destined to feel the force of Timur's power very shortly. The Sarbadāris continued to rule in Sabzawār, where Khwājah 'Ali Mu'wid held authority in subordinate to Timur, whereas the Maliks of Seistan were independent rulers, though they had doubtless before this recognized Timur as their Suzerain.

1338-1384 A.D.

In the year 785 H. Timur lost his elder sister Kutlugh Turkān Agha; and in addition to his private grief he was involved in hostilities in the direction of the Jattah. In the autumn of the same year he was, however, once more at liberty to turn his attention towards Māzenderān; but when he had reached the Murghāb news was brought to him that Sheikh Daud had broken out in open rebellion in Sabzawār. That Tābān Bahādur had been slain, and the Sheikh had shut himself up in the fortress of Badarābād, which is a stronghold situated on the summit of a hill. The Nikudaris of the Garmsir were also exhibiting signs of disaffection, as well as the people of Seistan. On learning of the state of affairs in Khurassan Timur gave up his plan for the invasion of Māzenderān, merely despatching a force to watch the movements of Amir Wali, and to safeguard his own frontier, and at the head of his troops he turned aside to deal with the movement in Khurassan.

The fort of Badarābād was of great strength. It was one of the ancient strongholds in the hills of Isfirār (Sabzawār). Tābān Bahādur was slain at Farmakān by an arrow and the Sheikh Daud, or as he is styled in the Rauzat-ul-Jannat, Sheikh Ali, Khat-tai, fled to Badarābād because he considered that the responsibility for this deed would be thrown on him. A general tumult had evidently arisen in the district; for Farmakān is one of the fortress in it. It is said to have been of exceeding great strength and its construction is attributed to Sultan Masud Ghaznawi.

The Government of Sabzawār had been conferred on Sheikh Daud, while Tābān Bahādur was the Intendent or Resident at his Court to watch over Timur's interests. The operations in Sabzawār were intrusted to an expeditionary force, while Timur himself proceeded to Herat. After he had settled the affairs of Herat Timur set out for Sabzawār. Badarābād was reduced and the garrison numbering 6,000 men were put to the sword. After this place had been reduced Timur continued his march towards Seistan.

Shah Jallaludin, the Malik of Farah, hastened to make his submission and was rewarded with gifts.

"And from Farah I set my face towards Seistan and sent on in advance Ak Timur Bahādur, at the head of a force of my devoted and valiant soldiers and leaders of squadrons and I ordered him to lay waste the country of Seistan. They having set forth, overran the whole country up to the very gates of (the city of) Seistan and rejoined me with a great store of wheat, flocks of sheep, cattle and slaves without number. Having disposed of the affairs of Uk I arrived before the fortress of Zirreh. The men within closed the gates and opposed me. I thereupon ordered my commanders and the leaders of my troops to advance against the fort at once, to give the garrison no rest, and to carry it by assault. In accordance with my orders my devoted soldiers attacked the place like swarms of ants and locusts upon every side. Having gained the bank and the foot of the walls they made breaches in the defences and entered the place. They commenced slaying and spoiling the enemy within it. But within the citadel fortress there were 5,000 men of war who, renouncing all hope of existence, offered a brave resistance until they fell under the weapon of my soldiers. By the assistance of Divine Providence the capture of this fortress was effected in the first day of the operations. Having captured the fortress of Zirreh I mounted my charger and set out with the intention of taking the fortress of Seistan itself, and when I had approached that place I halted my troops at some distance from it; and accompanied by a detachment, I advanced to make a personal reconnaissance of the fortress of Seistan and its approaches and the points open to attack. I made towards a gate, and when only a short distance away I ascended a "tappa" (mound) which is called Kutluk and halted upon the summit. I placed as a precautionary measure 2,000 men at arms in complete armour, in an ambush. When the people of the country saw me come to a stand upon the summit of the "tappa" they recognised whom they had to deal with, and Shah Kutb-ud-din, the Prince of Seistan, despatched to my presence Shāh-i-Shāhān and Tāj-ud-din Seistan[1] who were the chief of all his leaders. When they had been admitted to my presence and had bent their knees in homage they gave me the message entrusted to them by Malik Kutb-ud-din, to the effect that if my benevolence and favour would be directed to the affairs of Seistan and the people of that country any tribute which my officials might fix would be accepted by him and no delay in its payment would be allowed to occur."

A reference to the plan of Zāhidān, which the traditions of Seistan represent as having been the city which Timur captured and which was the capital at that period, will show the natural mound that exists at the present day not far from the southern angle of the ruins of the town wall of Zāhidān. The word "tappa" used in the record from which the foregoing account has been taken is in ordinary use to this day in Seistan, and it is applied either to the natural outlying mounds of "dasht" formation, such as is the isolated mound close to Zāhidān, or to those formed by the débris of ruined buildings. In the account of Sharaf-ud-din Ali, Yazdi, it is stated that Timur ascended a sandhill, or dune. It, however, is certain that Timur must have had in attendance on him a considerable staff of officers of high rank, as well as his own personal escort of horsemen; and it would have been a very large sandhill which would have afforded room for this body of horsemen on its summit and its slopes. It does not seem to be likely that in the immediate vicinity of the city there should be such a group of sandhills of such a height as would afford a favour-

---

[1] Tāj-ud-din Seistani who is mentioned here was not a member of the family of the Maliks of Seistan. There are some grounds for believing him to have been the head of the family of the Mirs of Seistan, whose descendants are now Kad-Khudas of the circle of villages for which Iskil is the centre, and this is also the residence of the family; the eldest son of the late Mir Abbas is the Kad-Khuda of that circle; of his younger brothers two hold the same office in other circles. This family of the Mirs, the descendants of Mir Barid, is one of undoubted and great antiquity.

able position for reconnoitring. Timur must have ridden round the whole of the town which he proposed to attack, and as his course would be just beyond the walls of the gardens that surrounded Zāhidān he would come upon the natural "tappa," or pass, so close to it as at once to see the advantages it offered for a general view of the positions held by the Seistanis. To the east of the ruins, wherever the sands have been moved by the summer winds, extending up to the deposit of recent alluvium in the direction of Khadang (a modern village), there are revealed the traces of ancient canals, watercourses and their distributaries, and the time-worn mounds formed by the walls of enclosures, evidently once upon a time gardens, each having been surrounded by a mud wall. In the direction of Khadang these gardens (among which there were also pleasure houses and residences of rich men and the people employed in the care of the gardens) extended for at least half a mile beyond the city. To the north-west beyond the Maidan that stretches between the Extra Mural Palace (the Sarai-i-Siasati), and the Masjid, the surface of the country is strewn with débris, the remains of humble tenements occupied by agriculturists, who lived on the banks of the canals that irrigated the land which they tilled. To the east, gardens and residences must have extended up very nearly to the foot of the natural mound alluded to and up to the string of loosely linked but striking sandhills which at this day shut out the view of the country towards the west from the ruins of Zāhidān.

The gardens were irrigated by means of the distributaries from the canals which existed at that time. To the south-east of Zāhidān these canals entered the city through passages left in the walls of the town, just such as that by which the Anjil canal entered the new defences of Herat (the neglect of which led to the fall of that city) already alluded to. Beyond the city walls of Zāhidān towards the south-east there is a trace of the fosse that cut through the Lurg, or rise in the ground on which the city stood; an ancient canal comes up to the outer edge of this fosse, and there it ends; there were no doubt aqueducts which admitted the canal water into the city. To the south-east of Zāhidān the ground is however so torn by the wind and overlaid by sand that at a very short distance from the ruined walls all traces of ancient canals or gardens and their enclosing walls have disappeared. But there is no doubt that the old windmills and the remains of buildings to the south-east of the former, which are situated at the east angle of the ruined city, were well within the suburbs and gardens that surrounded Zāhidān.

No trees could have shut out the view of the city walls on that afternoon when Timur rode up to the summit of the mound to view the defences he was about to assail. The high walls of the gardens, as they do now, sheltered orchards of pomegranates and also vines. A few mulberry, cypress or Kora Gaz trees must alone have broken the flat lines of the mud walls, and the round outlines of the smaller trees appearing over them.

The entrances of the narrow lanes that were bounded by the gardens and which pursued a devious course between their walls towards the city probably had been closed and their openings in the direction of the country beyond probably fortified by banks and ditches, and they were full of armed men.

Behind the outlying gardens, rose the walls and towers of Zāhidān, doubtless crowded with deeply interested spectators, and further away to the left hand there stood the yet loftier battlements of the Sarai-i-Tāhiri with its massive outer fortifications. On the highest tower of this pile of buildings, where now is pointed out the so-called bower of Malik Kutb-ud-din's fair daughter, the insignia of the Kaiānis and their banners must have been displayed on that day.

The declining rays of a winter sun cast its pale light, on that fateful afternoon, upon the scene, illuminating the walls of gardens, city and palace alike, and its rays were reflected back from the weapons and armour of the crowds that lined the walls to view that group of chieftains gathered on the summit and slopes of the mound beyond the outlying gardens.

From the ramparts, and from the city itself, there must have arisen a confused murmur of human voices, mingled with the cries of animals, from the crowds of fugitives who had streamed for days into the space within the town walls, driven to shelter within their protective sweep by the bands of fierce riders of the advanced screen of Timur's light horsemen.

The fate of Zirreh might well be guessed from the presence of that group of chiefs of the invading force who had reined up their chargers on the summit of that mound.

There must have been many persons that day among that crowd of anxious spectators who had seen Timur previously, and these could have pointed out to their more ignorant brethren that figure, the centre of the group of chieftains, mounted on a war horse, the best of all the studs of conquered provinces; as the Great Amir whose fame even then as a leader and as an intrepid man-at-arms himself had rendered him the idol of his followers and the great exemplar of the Champion of Islam and the Holy Warrior, through all succeeding ages of the History of the Nearer East.

Concealed from the view of the crowds which lined the ramparts stood the serried ranks of the 2,000 men-at-arms, armed cap-a-pie after the oriental fashion. These men were drawn up out of sight of the garrison of Zāhidān ready for any emergency.

Their services were soon required.

While negotiations were being instituted and Timur was listening to the petition of the deputation from the Malik, the Seistanis seeing him on the mound with apparently only a few men around him, with one accord issued from the shelter of the walls, and regardless of the chiefs who were in Timur's presence, and unmindful of the orders of their ruler Malik Kutb-ud-din, they advanced in warlike array with the obvious intention of referring matters to the arbitration of the sword.

"When a breach of the negotiations became apparent," to continue the narrative of the Malfuzāt-i-Sahib Kiran, "I detailed Muhammad Sultan at the head of a small body of men to attract the Seistanis in the direction of the open country and by engaging the enemy to entice them into a position in which my troops hidden in ambush could act effectually. In accordance with my orders, Muhammad Sultan advanced and engaging the enemy commenced gradually to give way before their attack until at last the enemy were drawn towards those 2,000 horsemen. The Seistanis thinking Muhammad Sultan's retirement to be real became greatly emboldened and fiercer in their efforts, and advanced into the open country. Then the 2,000 horsemen (emerging from their concealment) suddenly charged the men of Seistan and cut off their retreat. A desperate conflict took place and on both sides a very great number of men were laid low upon that field of death. At this crisis I ordered my personal escort to advance and they riding to the aid of their comrades completely overthrew the Seistanis. A very great number of these were killed and wounded, and the remainder fled in a sad plight and entered their defences closing the gate behind them."

The Seistanis were almost all foot soldiers and with their daggers brought down the chargers of Timur's horsemen.

Timur thereupon returned to the main body of his troops, who had encamped for the night, and during the hours of darkness a vigilant guard was maintained.

The next day Timur arrayed his forces for the attack on Zāhidān, and his divisions advanced to take up their respective positions with their warlike music playing and shouting their war cries, in order to overawe the garrison. On this day there was no fighting and the troops returned to their lines, which as a precautionary measure had been entrenched.

The night being dark, 10,000 Seistanis stole out of Zāhidān to make a night attack on the besiegers; and perceiving that the position occupied by Amir Shams-ud-din, the son of Mir 'Abbās, and Birāt Khwājah, was not vigilantly guarded, they fell upon it, and those officers failing to repulse the attack, the enemy entered the entrenchments and penetrated to the camp itself; and there they destroyed and injured many transport and other animals such as camels and horses. When the assailants got among the tents, the troops now thoroughly roused assembled from all sides, and poured volleys of arrows into the ranks of the enemy who were at length driven back with the loss of a very great number who fell under the lances and swords of Timur's men, and only a small proportion of the attacking force retired wounded and disheartened to their positions.

The next morning at dawn Timur drew up his forces in the order assigned to them the day previous, and a general attack was maintained on the works the whole of that day. In the midst of the struggle the Amir Zādah Ali at the head of 500 horse charged a body of the enemy who were drawn up before the gate opposite him, and compelling them to retire entered the place with the fugitives. The Seistanis from all sides rushed upon this devoted band, and a desperate battle took place, the enemy succeeding in cutting off the retreat of this band of their enemies. Amir Zādah Ali, however, at the head of the few men at his disposal maintained a valiant attitude inflicting great loss on the enemy, but of his men there was hardly one left alive who was not wounded. Ak Timur, Bahādur, had in the meantime come to their rescue at the head of 1,000 horse, and having dispersed the body of the enemy who were keeping the gate, entered it, and brought away Amir Zādah Ali and his own men. Returning after this feat of arms to the presence of Timur who commanded the centre in person, these officers received prompt reward and his congratulations on their conduct. At this juncture, having made trial of his fortune, and perceiving he was not at all likely to oppose Timur with any prospect of success, Shāh Kutb-ud-din consulted with his chieftains as to whether he ought not to repair to the presence of Timur and contrive to avert the calamity which threatened to overwhelm his state. Some of his nobles agreed with him, while others were all for continuing the struggle. Shāh Kutb-ud-din, however, cut short all further discussion by coming out of the fortress and lowering his banners.

"My commanders having reported the circumstances to me, taking the lowering of the standards of Seistan as a sign of the enemy having submitted, while I was discussing the subject the envoy of Shāh Kutb-ud-din relying on my benevolence came into my presence, and making a humble obeisance asked for a cessation of hostilities. I accordingly ordered my troops to refrain from further strife and despatched Amir Zādah Ali to bring Shāh Kutb-ud-din to me. When Shāh Kutb-ud-din rode up he alighted from his horse and bent his knee in token of submission, but I desired him to mount his horse again. He then broached the subject at issue, and asked pardon for his faults and misdeed. I replied that as he had shown his sincerity by coming in person to me, I bestowed on him again the country of Seistan, and with deep obeisance he expressed his gratitude for my clemency. My officers and soldiers thereupon entered into conversation with him and offered their congratulations on his conduct throughout (the operations)."

Timur now laid aside his armour, and retained only the quilted jacket worn under it, and mounting a palfrey and attended only by 15 men-at-arms he set out to visit the left division of his forces. On his way 20,000 or 30,000 Seistanis let themselves down from the battlements and set upon Timur and his small escort. He thereupon was compelled to retire to the centre, but before he got out of range of the arrows, shot by the enemy, his horse was wounded by one of these missiles.

Orders were at once issued that Shāh Kutb-ud-din was to be forthwith put into confinement and orders were also issued to recommence hostilities.

Zāhidān was taken; and the garrison that remained was put to the sword and a general massacre took place. The assailants obtained much booty.

"I issued orders that the fortress and city of Seistan should be destroyed and that the treasures and buried hoards laid up by the Maliks and sovereigns of past ages should be collected and brought into my presence.

"Arab horses, pacing mules, Backtrian camels, and other valuable booty without end were seized and reserved as my personal property."

Timur rested several days in Seistan and then set out up the valley of the Helmand for Kala-i-Bist. The destruction of Tak and of the Band-i-Rustam, and the consequent alteration of the scheme in existence and balance of population followed.

Although the name of the city of Seistan was not mentioned in the narrative of its destruction, there does not seem, however, any probability that the statement of the Shijrat-ul-Muluk and the traditions that Zāhidān was the city is incorrect. The interior of the ruined city is full of decaying human skeletons, which occur also beyond the north-east wall of the town and in front of the Darwāza-i-Bakhtiāri.[1] These are the remains of corpses hastily buried under fallen walls and which now after the course of centuries have been uncovered by erosion due to wind action. The high and dry situation of Zāhidān has preserved these remains, which are probably the lowest layer of the buried corpses of the victims of their own rashness, put to the sword by Timur's orders.

The government of Seistan was made over to Shāh-i-Shahān, a member of the Princely Family to which Shāh Kutb-ud-din belonged, and the latter with his family was deputed to Samark, while the Ulema, men of the religious profession and Kāzis of the country, were ordered to betake themselves to Farah, there to dwell. Seistan was conquered in the month of Shawal in the year 785 H. *December 1353 A.D.*

It henceforward ceased to exist as an independent state, and although its rulers (of the Kaiāni family) were afterwards reinstated, they held the country of the descendants of Timur. It required, however, another massacre and invasion to bring them completely under the sway of the Timurid Princes, after the great Amir Timur had departed from this transitory world.

According to the Ihya-ul-Muluk, Shāh Kutb-ud-din was executed by Timur, and this is also the account preserved in a very confused and manifestly inaccurate legend in which Timur and his son Shāh Rukh are interchanged, and both are made to play a part in the sack of Zāhidān. Neither the Malfuzāt-i-Sahib Kiran, nor the Zafarnāmah, makes any mention of Malik Kutb-ud-din having been executed.

---

[1] The Darwāza-i-Bahhtiāri, to judge from the ruins, was the principal entrance to Zāhidān. Why it should have been such is not obvious. None of the remains of the other gates are anything like as massive. Indeed with the exception of the gates of the citadel, the entrances to the town other than the gate of the Bakhtiaris, are merely gaps in the circuit of the ruined walls.

Ruins of Zāhidān, destroyed by Timur (Tamerlane), Decr.-Jany. 1384 A.D.

(Part I to face page 60.)

THE HISTORY OF SEISTAN.

The Malik Gheiāth-ud-din of Herat was put to death, but his death was due to the tumult and sedition raised by the Ghuri Bacha and Malik Muhammad, the Kurt.

Seistan after the terrible fate of Zāhidān remained quiescent, if not loyal, under the government of the Shāh-i-Shahān, and the troops of Seistan saw much service under the banners of the Great Amir, notably 5 years after the episode of Zāhidān, when the Shāh-i-Shahān commanded in person with the troops of his country aided by other contingents of Timur's troops, at the prolonged siege of Sirjān, in which Gudarz, the Mamluk of Abu Ishak of the Āl-i-Muzzaffar, held out for a long time. There was therefore no reason why Shāh Kutb-ud-din should have been put to death by Timur, nor is the fact of his having died in Samarkand alluded to. As he was, in all probability, a young man when Zāhidān was taken, it is not improbable that he returned to Seistan and resumed the government on the death of Timur in 807 H. The author of the Ihya-ul-Muluk appears to have had a very convenient memory, and he never alludes to the fate of Malik Husen, Shahīd, the Malik Muiz-ud-din Husen of the Rauzat-ul-Jannat.[1] This Prince is styled Shahīd, or the Martyr, to this day, and his end and reign are altogether omitted by the author of the Ihya-ul-Muluk; he does not appear among the Princes of Seistan in the genealogical scheme nor in the list of Princes. Moreover, the legends and the Shijrat-ul-Muluk distinctly mention the building of Kala-i-Fath by Malik Kutb-ud-din, and the latter mentions his release by Shāh Rukh, and his re-appointment to Seistan, and his subsequent rebellion against that Prince.

1288 A.D.

---

[1] A good example of the partiality of the Ihya-ul-Muluk is to be found in his versions of the position of Malik Kutb-ud-din with reference to Malik Husen of Herat, and the account of the same in the Rauzat-us-Safa. Malik Kutb-ud-din, bin Shah Rukn, is represented by the author of the Ihya-ul-Muluk as being a most puissant chieftain, and to have possessed elephants, and a veteran army at his command. The following account is taken from the Rauzat-us-Safa:—In the month of Muharram of the year 741 H. the Muzzaffarides invaded Kirman and took possession of it.

Malik Kutb-ud-din of Nimroz asked for aid to capture Kirman of Malik Husen of Herat. The latter despatched Malik Daud in command of a body of Ghuris to effect the capture of Kirman, who marched with Malik Kutb-ud-din.

This body of troops, by marching at night and hiding among the hills by day, succeeded in concealing their movements, and arrived all unperceived to a distance of 4 farsakhs of Kirman. One of the officials of the Amir Mubāriz discovered their presence in the village of Khash Khak and fled to Kirman with the news. After consulting with his adherents the Amir Mubāriz evacuated Kirman, and Malik Daud and his men took possession of it. Amir Mubāriz returned, however, with troops to Kirman and laid siege to it and, notwithstanding the sorties made by the Ghuris, reduced the garrison to great straits. Malik Kutb-ud-din left the city on the pretence of going to bring reinforcements to raise the siege, and Malik Daud and his son, after prolonging their resistance for some time longer, eventually were forced to make terms, and in the month of Jamādi-ul-Akhir in the year 741 H. (November 1340 A.D.) he was permitted to march away in the direction of Khurassan. This Malik Kutb-ud-din of Nimroz is the same person as he who is mentioned in the Ihya-ul-Muluk as having successfully "bluffed" Malik Husen of Herat in 734 A. H. (1333-1334 A.D.). Unless a pestilence had killed his elephants and swept away his veterans in the space of seven years that had elapsed, it appears inexplicable, that he was compelled to ask for assistance from his former antagonist.

The Muzaffarides, however, dispossessed the Shirwānid Maliks, some two or three of whom followed the last of the Kara Khitai Rulers of Kirman. This dynasty founded by Burāk Hājib in 610 A. H. (1213-1214 A.D.) is said by the author of the Habib-us-Siyār to have lasted 80 years.

The last of the Maliks of the Shirwan family was named Kutb-ud-din, Nekroz, and abandoned Kirman to the Amir Mubāriz-ud-din in 741 A. H.

The same author just alluded to mentioned that one of the rulers of the Shirwānid family introduced a large body of Hazara and "Avghan" tribes whom he settled on his frontiers as a protective measure; but as these rulers had no means at their disposal to overawe these guardians of the peace, the latter, waxing bold and defying the local rulers, committed great depredations in Abar Koh and Fārs.

CHAPTER IV.

After he had completed the subjugation of the country, and destroyed the dam, or weir, in the Helmand, Timur continued his journey towards Kala-i-Bist, along the banks of the Helmand. It is not possible to identify any of the localities mentioned in his route. Though the names exist, the sites have long ago been obliterated partially or altogether. Arbab Seif-ud-din, whose stories and information as to the legends, and old sites of Seistan, were of very great interest, was not with the Mission when it marched down the valley of the Helmand in the winter of 1903. The names of Kala-i-Kakah and Kala-i-Surkh exist, but which of the crumbling ruins through which the Mission passed on its journey along the banks of the Helmand should bear those names it is not possible to decide.

At Kala-i-Kakah information reached Timur that the Nikudaris who were encamped in the valley of the Helmand, their usual resort in the winter, had broken up their encampments and were on the move towards Kej and Makran. A strong force under the Amir Zādah Mirānshah was despatched in pursuit of those fugitives, and after travelling day and night across the waterless desert, the Nikudaris were discovered in the pasture lands of Karan.[1] The latter, true to their traditions, elected to fight rather than submit tamely; and probably the recollections of past misdemeanours weighed heavily upon their conscience; at any rate they fought, and were defeated and the head of their leader taken back as a voucher of the complete fulfilment of his orders to Timur. In the meantime Timur had met the Malik Mamakatū who had wounded him so grievously many years previously in Seistan. The bearing of the Malik was regarded as suspicious, notwithstanding the submission he had made, and the presents he had placed before the Great Amir. Upon a sign from the latter, as soon as Malik Mamakatū had left the presence, he was seized, and volleys of arrows were discharged at him, which soon put him out of the world.

Nothing of importance is heard of Seistan during the lifetime of Timur; and it undoubtedly continued as a district subject to the Governor of Khurassan who held his Court in Herat.

18th February 1405.   The Great Amir died in the year 807 H. and the usual scramble for power took place among the 36 descendants whom he left behind him. The only surviving son of the Great Conqueror Shāh Rukh Mirza, however, very shortly afterwards succeeded in gaining possession of his father's empire; and in

---

[1] Karan is spelled both in the Zafar Namah and Malfuzat-i-Sahib Karani with a hard K; from its general direction from the Helmand it probably was the district in which Chagai is situated, or the delta of the Māshkel river.

808 H. there was a Shāh Kutb-ud-din reigning in Seistan, as a feudatory of that Prince who held his court in Herat.[1]

In that year the Prince of Seistan (according to the Rauzat-us-Safa) reported that the brothers 'Ali Shāh and Gheiāth-ud-din Shāh, sons of the late Jallal-ud-din Shāh of Farah, were becoming restive, and were not amenable to authority. Shāh Rukh accordingly despatched an expedition to Farah and the refractory brothers having been made prisoners were duly punished.

According to the Ihya-ul Muluk, there are two Maliks of Seistan of the name of Kutb-ud-din, but it does not appear to be improbable that there was in reality only one of that name who was taken prisoner by Timur and released, or who made his escape, after the death of the conqueror. The author of the Rauzat-ul-Jannat mentions the fact of Malik Kutb-ud-din Muhammad having on more than one occasion proved refractory, and to have actively opposed Shāh Rukh's demands for money and help; no dates are given in that account; but the Rauzat-us-Safa mentions that in 819 A. H. Shāh Rukh, marched from Fārs to Kirman to put down local disturbances, and that he continued his march towards Herat from Kirmān, by way of the desert, that is to say, by way of Gurg and Nasirabad, along the ancient Trade Route. He would in this case have passed through Seistan, and probably it was on this occasion that the intercession of the Famous Divine, styled the Zain-ul-Millat Wa-ud-din, saved, Malik Kutb-ud-din from experiencing the wrath of his Suzerain.[2] *1416 A.D.*

According to the "Ihya-ul-Muluk," in 825-826 A. H. the city "having become largely invaded by the moving sands, Malik Ali decided to build a new city. For this purpose he selected a locality (called Mirak), the property of Mirān Mir-Abd-Allah, and acquired it by purchase. The spot thus chosen was removed from the sands and close to the Helmand." This perhaps refers to the building of the town which grew up round the citadel of Kala-i-Fath. The ruins from which the fragments of tile bearing the date 831 A. H. was brought are now submerged by great drifts of sand, and the temporary capital after the sack and destruction of Zāhidān probably occupied that site. The position of Kala-i-Fath is even now removed from the encroachments of sand and at that time it was also close to the Helmand. *1421-1422 A.D.*

Kala-i-Mir, Deh Mirak and Mirabad are names that still linger in the country closely adjoining the ruins of Kala-i-Fath, and the district in which the latter stands may have been called Mirak as it was held by the Mir family *1427-1428 A.D.*

---

[1] Malik Kutb-ud-din Kaiāni apparently escaped during the confusion which followed on the death of Timur, and made his way to Herat and threw himself on the clemency of Shāh Rukh.

[2] Shāh Rukh did invade Seistan in force (Matl'a-us-Sa'adain), but the capital Kala Fath held out successfully and on the intervention of the Chief Priest of Seistan Shāh Rukh withdrew to Herat after laying waste the country and destroying the three weirs in the Helmand River

of which Abdullah was the chief. In course of time Sultan Shāh Rukh passed away. He had seven sons born to him, of whom six had died during his own lifetime. His eldest and sole surviving son was secure in his government of the provinces beyond the Oxus, but the wide dominion of the late monarch to the south of that river was the scene of the struggles for their possession that took place between the progeny of the six sons who had predeceased their father. Seistan had for many years been recovering from the effects of the conquest of the country by Timur; and to such an extent that the Prince of Seistan was able to take advantage of the state of anarchy that prevailed to set up as an independent ruler.

1447-1448 A.D.

In 851 A. H. Prince Bābar Mirza, son of Baisanghar Mirza son of Shāh Rukh, established himself in Herat, and the pretensions of the Kaiāni Prince of Seistan towards independence brought the latter very soon into collision with that Prince. Malik Mu'i'z-ud-din Husen, "Husen Shahid" as he is called in the local traditions, is a historical personage and he is mentioned in the Rauzat-ul-Jannat as having set up as an independent Prince in Seistan where he had coined money and had caused the public prayers to be read in his own name omitting all mention of his Suzerain in both. He had in addition greatly strengthened his city (Kala-i-Fath). He had, however, become unpopular. He was a tyrant and had alienated the regard of his subjects by undue severity, and a too close regard for humiliating observances on the part of his chief men and nobles. He is also accused of having put to death many of the latter, and had also slain many of his subjects, who were not deserving of death. This description reads very much like the account of a revolution, in which the defeated side had suffered greatly from the vindictive nature of the successful claimant to supreme authority. He also inaugurated changes in the currency and the money coined by him had been increased to a weight of 2½ Mith Kals.

None of his coins have, however, been discovered.

The first expedition undertaken by Prince Bābar in person was not very successful. Amir Khalil Hindukah, his chief supporter, was away in Badghis, to watch the movements of Ilagh Beg and his son Abdul Latif, who were massing troops on their frontier. Malik Husen was induced to make a nominal surrender. He promised to behave in a proper manner in the future, and he also sent presents to the Prince, who was in all probability only too glad to have saved his face, and was thus set free to act against his more formidable enemies who were drawing to a head in the north. Malik Husen evidently did not fulfil his promises of amendment, and continued to ignore the rights of the Lord Paramount over him and his state.

When Prince Bābar had placed his own affairs on a more stable footing for the time being and had returned to Herat in 859 A. H., he despatched a force under the command of Amir Khalil Hindukah to reduce the Prince of

Seistan to a state of complete obedience. Malik Husen seems, however, to have been a match for this force, and the commander was obliged to ask for reinforcements. These were despatched under the Amirs Aweis Tarkhān, Husen, Jāndār, and others to assist Amir Khalil Hindukah, who drove Malik Husen into his city, which was thereupon blockaded.

The Seistanis issued from the place and fought an action in the open field in which they were defeated with heavy loss. Malik Husen finding himself hard pressed, and that his subjects also were tired of him, fled from the capital to the island in the Zirreh, where he took shelter among the jungle (reed beds). This place was undoubtedly the Koh-i-Khwājah and the city (now in ruins) upon its slopes. Seistan was bestowed on the successful leader by Prince Bābar to be held as a fief under the latter; and all the Sardars of Seistan and Zābulistān submitted to their new master. Malik Husen, however, still possessed influence in Seistan for he again collected a force and attempted to regain possession of his capital. He was unsuccessful, and in the end he was routed and his followers dispersed. Then at last, after a short time had lapsed, his head was brought in to Amir Khalil Hindukah who was freed from all further anxiety with reference to this energetic but unfortunate Prince.

The Rauzat-us-Safa contains details as to the manner in which the death of Malik Husen was compassed which were gathered from the accounts that existed in the country.

After that their cause had become desperate and they had been completely overthrown by the Royal troops, Shāh Husen and his elder (or eldest) brother, Shāh Kutb-ud-din, abandoned Seistan and at the head of only 3 or 4 attendants set out towards Kej and Makrān. In the course of the journey Shāh Husen dismounted one of his attendants, a rash and vindictive person; and gave his horse to another who was his master's favourite. The man deprived of his horse was grievously offended; and he pondered over this injustice as he followed on foot after the cavalcade. It was midnight when this man reached the camp, where everybody, worn out with fatigue and the hardships of the march, were in deep slumber. Under cover of the darkness the servant took advantage of there being no one on watch, to sever the heads of both Shāh Kutb-ud-din and Shāh Husen from their bodies; and taking to flight brought them both to Amir Khalil Hindukah as an acceptable offering.

The various fiefs held by this great noble extended up to Kabul itself and included the districts dependent upon Kandahar up to the very confines of Hindustan. In Seistan, however, the Kaiani family were still numerous and they had a following; so in order to completely break the spirit of the people Amir Khalil gave free vent to his naturally fierce and bloodthirsty nature. He caused a great slaughter in Seistan. Chiefs as well as the common people were put to death until the country became depopulated and fell into an utterly disorganized condition. Irrigation was neglected as numbers of the people must have fled into other districts to preserve their lives.

Both the districts of Farah and Sabzawār were included in this destruction. The Maliks of Sabzawār had probably ceased to exist, for they are not again mentioned as a ruling family after that Malik Fakhr-ud-din Kurt removed Malik Kutb-ud-din from Sabzawār, and imprisoned his son in Herat. But their country continued in a condition of prosperity, and its downfall and ruin is attributed to Amir Khalil Hindukah. He raided it on many occasions, either in person or by his officers and members of his family, and sacked the town nine times.

The citadel within the town was always kept in repair until at last, driven to despair, the people of the country, taking advantage of an occasion when it was unoccupied, came together and with one accord dismantled it themselves. The author of the Rauzat-ul-Jannat (writing in 898 H.) states that he had heard that in former times in the main bazaar of Sabzawār itself there were 1,200 shops, not counting those which existed in the various quarters of the town or in the surrounding districts. The desolation that prevailed in his day was the result of the violence and excesses committed by the chief and his followers.

1492-1493 A. D.

Like the people of Seistan, the inhabitants of Farah were strongly attached to the family of their local chiefs; and did not prove amenable to the severe and oppressive rule of the Amir Hindukah and his companions. Amir Husen Jāndār was the Governor of Farah after the desolation of Seistan and he "perceived that as long as there were any representatives of the family of the Shāhs alive, the people of the country would not respect his authority as Governor. He therefore formed a plan by which to extirpate the whole family. For this purpose he inveigled the members of this family to an assembly, and when they had all come together, he caused them to be put to the sword thereby overthrowing at one stroke a dynasty that had endured for many ages."

"It is stated that after the massacre of the Shāhs, Amir Aweis, the Tarkhān, summoned the notables of Farah to his presence, and after he had pacified their fears, he signified his willingness to make them all Tarkháns;[1] but Maulāna Muhammad Shāh of Farah, who was present, declined this honour on behalf of his fellow countrymen."

At the time of writing (898 A. H.) the above, the author stated that a member of this family was still alive; he was named Shāh Sikandar and he was living in a state of great poverty.

---

[1] Tarkhān was a title which distinguished a grade, or class, of nobles among the tribes beyond the Oxus. Certain privileges were attached to this title.

The representative of this family who was contemporary with Shāh Rukh the son of Timur, was named Shāh Sikandar Niāl Tigin. He was frequently at variance with his Suzerain.

The Maulānā Muhammad Shāh alluded to was perhaps the representative of a branch of this same family the founder of which resigned his right to the succession (he was the eldest son) and adopted a religious life.

Amir Aweis, the Tarkhān noble, was himself involved in a catastrophe similar to that which resulted in the downfall of the Maliks of Farah. After the death of Prince Bābar Mirza on the 25th of the month of Rabi-us-Sāni in the year 861 H., his 11-year-old son was proclaimed his successor, and the chief supporter of the youthful Prince, the Amir Sheikh Hājī, found it necessary to curb the insolence and break the strength of the Tarkhān nobles, who had become, by reason of their possessions, so powerful, that their good will or opposition was of supreme importance and decided the fate and fortune of any Prince who aspired to possess Herat. That noble accordingly, upon the 1st of Jamadi-ul-Akhir of the same year, invited all the Tarkhāns to an entertainment in the Bagh-i-Zāghān close to Herat where certain matters were also to be discussed. When they had all gathered together, a general massacre took place. With the exception of Amir Aweis Tarkhān, who had a small dagger by him, no one of them was armed, but he succeeded in reaching Amir Sheikh Hājī and wounded the latter severely. Both Amir Aweis and his son were, however, put to death. *(11th March 1457 A.D.)* *(15th May 1457 A.D.)*

The family of the Maliks of Farah still exists. No longer possessed of authority, they, however, hold some land and are thus somewhat more favourably situated than the Kaiāni Maliks of Seistan with whom they have so long been allied.

Malik Bahā-ud-din (or Ma-ud-din), son of Malik Zainalo (Zain-ul-'Abidin), and his nephew returned to Farah from Kabul in 1904-05, and came into Seistan with the Governor of Farah in 1905. A nephew of the Malik, named Seif-ud-din, accompanied him.

It is said, but with what amount of truth it is not possible to state, that the lands of Farah were originally divided between the Maliks, the Arbābs, and Aghāzādah. The Maliks were the rulers, but the leaders of the two other tribes, or races, had a voice in affairs. Indeed it is said that the Aghāzādah were considered the most illustrious of these three groups.

The Maliks at the present day are of course quite subordinate to the Afghans, the extent of their holdings is also said to be small; whereas the Arbābs hold the villages and forts of Chīn and Sāj; also Basta close to Farah itself.

Kala-i-Kah is a district which in older times was included within the limits of Farah. It is divided into two parts by two ranges of hills, the strike of which is from north-east to south-west. They are not continuous. The part to the south of these hills is known as the Sheb-i-Koh and the district of Kala-i-Kah to the north of the hills is called Pusht-i-Koh.

The inhabitants are very mixed. "Afghans" naturally predominate, but there is a large leaven of Tājiks, Arabs, Khwājahs (or Khojas), and Mirs also to be found. In the Sheb-i-Koh district there is the famous shrine of Imām Zeid. The tomb or ziarat is on the summit of a flat-topped hill and there are two great drifts of sand on the slopes. The custodians of the shrine are Sheikhs who are believed to have been the original inhabitants of this tract in pre-Islamitic times. The Imām Zeid, it is said, was made a prisoner by these unbelievers in the early days of Islam, and taken to the summit of this hill to be put to death. Imām Zeid prayed fervently for divine aid, and he was concealed by the sand. Finding their victim had eluded them the enemies of that holy person went to their homes, leaving a party to watch for the re-appearance of the fugitives. Their descendants still continue the watch; no longer as enemies do they await the advent of the Holy Imām, but as the custodians of his shrine. Such is the legend.

The sand drifts are famous for certain sounds that issue from them or from the hills, which are attributed to supernatural agency. The author of the Rauzat-ul-Jannat wrote that pilgrims ascend the hill and casting themselves down on the slope of the sand-drift slide down to the bottom, and the sound continues to be heard till they reach the bottom.

The following account is taken from the account of Sir Frederick Goldsmidt's Mission of 1872:—

"Captain Lovett, who was fortunate enough to hear it, describes its effect upon him as like the wailing of an olion harp or the sound occasioned by the vibration of several telegraph wires * * * It should be remarked * * * that the sound is often heard in perfectly still weather and when nobody is near the hill, and it is singular also that the limit of sand at the bottom seems never to be encroached upon by falling sand from the summit, though the face of the hill and sand drift is very steep."

The circumstance is also mentioned by the author of the Rauzat-ul-Jannat who believed that the sand that descended was miraculously conveyed back to the summit.[1]

The Sheb-i-Koh district is watered by a large canal, said to be a natural drainage line, which takes off from the Farāh Rud just below the village of Kūk-i-Sheb. This canal or old river bed flows past the shrine dedicated to Sheikh Mahmud. There is an ancient superstition attaching to this water-course. It is said never to require any cleaning; and whenever any cleansing is necessary, the earth at the bottom ought merely to be scraped and allowed to be carried away by the water, and the spoil should never be cast out upon

---

[1] There is a similar hill, to which a similar legend attaches, in the district of Parwān, about 40 miles to the north of Kabul City.

the banks. The supply of water is very plentiful and it irrigates, or helps to irrigate, almost all the villages in the district. It terminates at, or close to, the village of Jurg, 5 farsakhs (about 20 miles) from its source, where it breaks up into many channels and forms a meadow or Ulang.

The ziarat of Sheikh Mahmud is a very celebrated shrine, the custodians of which are Tājiks. There is, it is said, at this place a grove of about 100 large trees of the "Kora Gaz" variety of tamarisk. The trunks are said to be about 15 feet in circumference and the height of the trees to be greater than that of the cypress trees of Darg.

"Within a farsakh distance of Farah," wrote the author of the Rauzat-ul-Jannat, "there is a certain hill called Barandak where there is a shallow recess from which water issues in drops. This is resorted to as a shrine by those who have any desires they wish gratified. Below this recess they take up their position, and stretching forth their hands in prayer make mention of their needs. If the dropping of the water increases they go away satisfied that their desires will be fulfilled; but if there is no increase in the flow it is looked upon as a sign that their requests will not be gratified. During the petitions offered up by some people the dropping of the water increases so much as to make a continuous flow. I have seen many people who have witnessed this occurrence. And at the petitions of certain persons which it is not lawful should be fulfilled the water ceases to drop."

* * * * * * *

The ancient site of Kala-i-Kah is at present almost deserted. The remains of the ancient fort are still traceable, but the former populous character of the place can be judged by the fact that 18 karezes are at this day out of work and only 10 are utilized for cultivation.

The devastation wrought by the inroads of Chingiz Khan and Timur wrought but little damage compared to that which took place after they had died, and their degenerate successors fought over the Empires built up by them.

In the case of the Timurides this period of anarchy was greatly prolonged. The great-grandsons of Shāh Rukh became mere puppets in the hands of one or other of the Commanders, or Chiefs, who found an opportunity in the turmoil for their ambitions.

Sultan Said, the Timuride, a great-grandson of Shāh Rukh Mirza, advanced on Khurassan from the country beyond the Oxus, and eventually established his authority in that province, and Irāk and Māzenderān as well.

In the year 864 H. that sovereign turned his attention towards Seistan 1460 A.D. and Shāh Yāhyāh (called in the Rauzat-ul-Jannat, Nizām-ud-din Yāhyāh), who was distinguished above all his countrymen and family for valour and generosity, was invested with Seistan as a fief. In addition to this the sovereign issued orders that certain of his chiefs should march to Seistan at the head of a powerful force, and wrest that country from the control of Amir Khalil Hindukah. Having proceeded some distance these leaders consulted together, and decided to send one of their number to Amir Khalil to try and induce him to yield to the sovereign's wishes, by means of threats on the one hand, and by means of promises on the other of benefits that he might expect from his sovereign's good pleasure. In the meantime, however, the latter found himself compelled to march towards Māzenderān and he recalled the expedition he had despatched towards Seistan.

Amir Khalil finding that Sultan Said had left Herat considered it to be a favourable opportunity of asserting his independence, and even of taking possession of that city itself. He collected a force of armed men and advanced on the city which he reached on the 12th of Ramzan of the same year. The inhabitants of the outlying districts had fled before him into the city, abandoning their crops which were at the time fit to be reaped. The Amir Khalil was only able to blockade the gate of Irāk and Firuzābād and Khush, as he had not men enough to completely surround the walls, and his attempts to storm the city were also defeated. An alarm of the return of Sultan Said from Māzenderān so terrified Amir Khalil that he fled from Herat, and never halted until he had reached the boundary of Seistan.

<small>4th May 1460 A.D.</small>

Sultan Said was actually on his march towards Herat, and at Jām he heard of the events that had taken place, and of the retirement of that ambitious chief.

From Herat the sovereign detailed a force to reduce Amir Khalil Hindukah which overran the outlying districts of Seistan, but as the leader of this force was an old friend of the refractory noble he induced the latter to submit himself to the Royal authority. Amir Khalil was received by the sovereign who overlooked his past conduct, and again enrolled him among the servants of the state, but he was sent away to Balkh to govern the frontier districts in that direction, and in this way Seistan and the countries adjoining it were freed from his grasp. The havoc wrought was, however, very lasting in its effect, and the country as late as 898 was still in ruinous and desolate condition, while the dearth of water, alluded to by the author of the Rauzat-ul-Jannat, must have been due to the fact that canals and weirs had been neglected and the river passed down in its undiminished volume into the southern end of the Hamun, and into the Shela.

<small>1492-1493 A.D.</small>

<small>1492 1493 A.D.</small>

Notwithstanding the bestowal of Seistan as his appanage upon Malik Nizām-ud-din Yāhyāh, the status of the Maliks was very far removed from that enjoyed by their forefathers.

During the reign of Sultan Husen, Baikāra, Seistan was held by Amir Sultan Arghūn who is styled in the Rauzat-ul-Safa, the Hākim of Seistan, and who was the Ruler or Governor of that territory. It was reported that this person had manifested signs of disloyalty, and the Prince Ibn-ul-Husen was accordingly despatched with 2,000 horse to reduce the Governor to obedience. This raised the ire of all the members of the family of Arghūn. Zulnun Beg from the Zamin-i-Dāwar and Shujā Beg from Kandahar mustered their fighting men and proceeded to the help of their kinsman. The Arghūns were too strong for the Prince, and attacking the latter when his forces were dispersed in his quarters in the Hokāt, drove him out of the country to Herat, wounded and unsuccessful. The status of the Kaiāni Princes of Seistan is clearly evidenced by the absence of coins bearing their own names or titles. With the exception of the ill-fated Malik Husen, none of the Maliks coined money in their own name after the capture of Zāhidān. At least none of their coins have been found. Copper coins were struck by Malik Jallāl-ud-din later on, but they are very rare, and he does not appear to have coined money in gold or silver.

As the descendants of the Great Amir grew more and more effete, and as their fortunes waned before the rise of the Uzbek power under Shaibāni Khān, their hold over Seistan weakened. The Arghūns abandoned Khurassan. They were eventually forced to relinquish Kandahar and to retire to Sind where they founded a short-lived dynasty. Shaibāni Khān overthrew the sons of Sultan Husen Baikara in 912 H. (1507 A.D.) ; and on the other side of Seistan Shāh Ismāil Saffavi was consolidating his power in the Western Provinces. These two ambitious chiefs very soon came into collision and the Uzbek suffered a decisive overthrow and was slain in battle in the vicinity of Merv in 916 A. H. (1510). 1506-1507 A.D.

The decisive victory won by Shāh Ismāil over Shaibāni Khān and the death of that chief for a time relieved Khurassan of the depredations of the Uzbeks. Herat once more was the capital of the Province which was annexed to the Empire of the Saffavis ; and Meshed, the Holy City, began to obtain that pre-eminence which is now its due in the sight of all those who follow the faith of Islam according to the doctrines of the Shiah persuasion. Relatives of the ruling family of the Saffavis received in fief districts in Khurassan, over which their deputies held authority in the name of the particular Prince. Seistan had been the personal appanage of Prince Badi-uz-Zamān Mirza, Saffavi, whose deputy, and the actual Governor of that country, was an Afshār noble named Timur Khān, of the tribe of Istājlū. His harshness, together with the violence and rapacity of his fellow tribesmen, alienated the hearts of the people, who led by their own chiefs rose up with one accord, and turned the Afshārs out of Seistan. For a long time that country was free from the presence of Persian officials and their troops. After this had been effected, the Seistanis led by the Mirs of Seistan, desired to raise one of the family of their ancient Princes to the chiefside of that country ; and after some discussion the office 986 A.H 1578-1579 A. D.

of ruler was offered to Malik Mahmud and accepted by him. He was elected as their Prince; but before he consolidated his power, J'afir Sultan, who had been appointed Governor of Seistan by the Persian Government, appeared on the scene. The greater part of the Seistanis, with the Mirs, and the more cautious element among the people abandoned Malik Mahmud and gave the newly appointed Governor a fitting reception and inducted him to his residence in the capital, Kala-i-Fath. But Malik Mahmud and his party had betaken themselves to the island and the other strongholds they possessed and dwelt therein for a season.

J'afir Sultan possessed no means by which to enforce his authority; and being suspicious also of the sincerity of the welcome he had received, treated all those that came to him, without distinction, with uniform kindness and courtesy. After his installation he retained by his side a representative of the Maliks, the Malik Gheiāth-ud-din Muhammad; and of the Mirs, Mir Ali; and dismissed all the rest of the people to their own homes. He made friends with the Arbābs, the inhabitants of land to the north of the city, while the districts between the canals furnished him with supplies.

After six months had passed Malik Gheiāth-ud-din died; and his companions and followers asked for leave to visit their tribesmen and the members of their family. The party of Malik Mahmud now cast aside all restraint and incited a feeling of hostility towards the Persian Governor, and day by day the disloyal faction waxing bolder, they began at last to commit acts of overt hostility, extending their depredations up to the very city itself. J'afir Sultan had in the meantime been joined by 'Ubād Sultan from the Garmsir at the head of 2,000 well appointed troops; and the two leaders advanced from the city to punish the disloyal section of the people of Seistan whose depredations had exceeded all bounds and could no longer be tolerated. In addition to the troops of his colleague, the Governor was aided by a contingent of about 1,000 men drawn from his supporters in the country, who joined him as auxiliaries.

Malik Mahmud with all his kinsmen and the Amirs of Seistan took the field against the Persians and their allies, and having crossed the Hirmend, the two parties met in combat on the banks of that river. J'afir Sultan had his charger shot under him, and falling heavily was unable to rise, and in this condition he was put to death by one of his enemies.

The Persians fled to Kala-i-Fath; but Malik Mahmud with a rare foresight strictly held back his men from pursuing them, and in addition allowed the Persians to evacuate Kala-i-Fath and march away with all their property, unmolested. Malik Mahmud thereupon took possession of the city with great pomp, and assumed the government; and the fame of his exploit was noised abroad throughout Khurassan. He, however, did not allow this success to

Ruined mausoleum-near Kala Fath, materials baked brick and tempered clay mortar.

(Part I to face page 72.)

inflame his ambition, but despatched an envoy to the Court of the Shah to make known his sincerity, and plead his case.

Muhammad Khān, the Turkmān, who had been the Deputy Governor of Seistan in the lifetime of Badī-uz-Zamān Mirza, was at this time in high office at the Shah's Court. Interest was made with this powerful noble, and by means of his efforts on behalf of Malik Mahmud, the actions of the latter were condoned, and the government of Seistan conferred upon him by the Shah.

His reign was prosperous and beneficial to his country on the whole, but the times were unfavourable to the arts of peace; and it needed all the talents which this Malik undoubtedly possessed to maintain his hold on the government. He was evidently a strong ruler, as in course of time there grew up a party opposed to him among his subjects which eventually compassed his death. The grand-nephews of the late Prince Badī-uz-Zamān had divided the appanage of their father Sultan Husen Mirza, after the latter died. The eldest son of the late Sultan, Muzaffar Ḥusen Mirza, obtained possession of Kandahar, while to Rustām Mirza was assigned the Zamin-i-Dāwar; and the two youngest sons of the late Sultan, who were by the same mother as the second son, continued to dwell with him in his portion of his father's appanage. Both Muzaffar Ḥusen Mirza and his brother Rustām Mirza were deficient in ability and those qualities which the times demanded of all who aspired to fill exalted positions. Muzaffar Ḥusen Mirza was Prince only in name; all real authority being exercised by his deputy, a person named Hamza Beg, who had received this office directly from the Shah of Persia. This person, with a view to add Seistan to the territory of the sons of his late master Sultan Husen Mirza, and unaware of the resources at the disposal of the Malik Mahmud Kaiāni, entered that country at the head of a body of troops.

"When he had reached the ancient city of Seistan and had established his camp at a distance of two farsakhs to the north of the Zirreh, which was the refuge and stronghold of Malik Mahmud, the Malik Zadāhs and Amirs of Seistan, he perceived the strength of the islands and the number of valiant men of that country."

Hamza Beg was compelled to rest satisfied with the treaty which was drawn up with the consent of his master and Malik Mahmud. It was also agreed upon that Muzaffar Ḥusen Mirza should marry the daughter of Malik Mahmud; and that Malik Jallāl-ud-din, the eldest son of the Malik, should marry the daughter of Hamza Beg. The Mirzas thereupon returned to Kandahar. Soon afterwards, Muzaffar Ḥusen Mirza become discontented with his position and connived at a plot to murder Hamza Beg. The latter having obtained information of this, fled to Zamin-i-Dāwar and returned with Rustām Mirza whom he proposed to set up in place of his ungrateful brother. Muzaffar Husen was defeated in a battle fought on the banks of the Arghand Āb River, and fled to Kandahar. By the good offices of the leaders of the Persian element in that place, Muzaffar Ḥusen Mirza was reconciled to his deputy; and peace having been ostensibly restored, the latter resumed his office.

Three years after, and in consequence of another plot against his life, Hamza Beg deposed his master in favour of his brother Rustām Mirza, and the former was placed as a prisoner at large in the fortress of Kallāt under the care of Muhammad Beg, the chief of the Biyāt tribe, and also son-in-law of Hamza Beg; the revenues of the Hazārajāt being assigned for the maintenance of the captive prince.

Six months later, the latter having won over his jailor and the garrison of Kallāt, effected his escape, and escorted by a body of 300 Biyāts from that garrison, made his way to Seistan, by the route through the desert. Malik Mahmud received the fugitive most hospitably, and showed him every attention, making over to the Prince his affianced wife. For the space of six months Muzaffar Ḥusen Mirza dwelt in Seistan in amity with its ruler. At last, however, a party of the Mirs of Seistan, who were always exciting strife and replenishing the fires of discord, estranged the fickle tempered Mirza from his host, and one day the Prince, on the pretence of hunting, left his quarters and made his way to the north of the Zirreh to the fort of Tāhzūn (or Tāhazwun) which was the residence of these chiefs and Mirza of Seistan who were disaffected towards the Malik. In the course of one week he was joined by all the Nakibs and Mirs of Zirreh, Rūāmrod,[1] and the headmen of the lower classes also flocked to his side. Parties of Kizzilbashes had moreover joined him from Farāh, and at the head of this gathering he laid siege to the fort of Chārūnak (or Jārūnak), the residence of Malik Nāsr-ud-din, the uncle of Malik Mahmud.

When this outbreak took place Malik Mahmud was in residence in the village or town of Rāsalik[2] on the bank of the Helmand, and at the time when the Mirza left him, the Malik was quite unattended by any of his adherents. By great exertions he, however, raised a large force to put down this movement. He despatched in advance his son Jallāl-ud-din together with his cousins, the Maliks Mahmud, and Malik Shāh Ḥusen in command of a force of his own tribesmen, following in person at the head of his main army. On the forenoon of 6th March 1582 A.D. a great battle was fought before the fort of Jārūnak in which the malcontents were defeated and the Mirs retreated towards the jungles and the islands. Malik Mahmud at the

---

[1] This is the only name about which there seems to be little or any doubt. It must be Ramrod. The other names are, however, doubtful to a degree. Tahzūn may possibly stand for Trakun, and probably does. The Zirah is the Gaud-i-Zireh.

[2] This is called "Mouzah-i-Rasalik": it is possible to translate it as the "cultivated lands on the bank"; in this case Rasalik would not be a proper name.

No help is obtained from the Shijrat-ul-Muluk, as the orthography of the names in the manuscript found in Seistan is a great deal worse than in the copy of the Alam Ara used for this part of the narrative.

end of a week deputed a party of Seiads to the Mirza and they reconciled the Prince to his father-in-law.

At the same time Hamza Beg invited the former to return to Kandahar, and the Prince set out for his capital escorted by 3,000 fighting men of Seistan (under command of one of Malik Mahmud's kinsmen), who returned from Kandahar.

Six months later, the Malik again had to support his son-in-law with another detachment of 3,000 men, commanded by his cousin Malik Izzat, from Seistan.

A short time after this Muzaffar Husen Mirza was once more a fugitive in Seistan, where he again listened to the promptings of the malcontents, and headed another rising against the Malik. The rebels again attacked Jārūnak, and Malik Jallāl-ud-din who was entrusted with the task of putting down the insurrection was on the first day defeated near the village of Deh 'Ali and forced to take shelter within the village behind the houses and the walls of its garden. The same afternoon, however, he was reinforced by Malik Mahmud in person, and early in the next day Nāsr-ud-din sallied out of Jārūnak at the head of about 1,000 men and the rebels attacked from two directions were utterly defeated and the Mirs were compelled to seek refuge in the mountains and jungles. In this engagement about 300 men of the Malik's adherents and about 1,000 of the enemy were slain. The Mirza was a second time reconciled to Malik Mahmud, and two months later proceeded to Kandahar. Muhammad Beg, the Biyāt, assassin and successor of Hamza Beg, was in his turn removed, having fallen a victim to a plot against his life instituted by his master. Muzaffar Husen Mirza now assumed the control of affairs, and the grudge he entertained against his benefactor Malik Mahmud increased, but he was only restrained by the predominance in Khurassan of the Uzbeks, and his own dangerous position in consequence of their supremacy.

Khurassan had for many years been the exercising ground of the Uzbek horsemen, and the whole of this great province was reduced to a state of chaos.

Herat and Meshed had in turn been occupied and bands of marauding horsemen had penetrated even as far as Yazd.

In this state of affairs the Afshārs of Farah invited Rustām Mirza to assume the government of that district. The Prince eagerly availed himself of this invitation and was accorded a most cordial reception. Two days after he put to death Yakān Khān, chief of the Afshārs, who had invited him, and shortly afterwards took possession of that chief's wealth and the common property of his tribesmen. Threatened by the Uzbeks the latter were compelled to submit to this harsh usage; and on his part the tyrant they themselves introduced proved himself victorious over the Uzbeks, and on one occasion he defeated them with the loss of 800 of their most approved warriors.

Rustām Mirza also was casting coveteous glances in the direction of Seistan. Malik Mahmud aware of this had raised an array of nearly 10,000 men and had established himself in the fort of Chap (or Chin?).[1] Here he continued for the space of six months when a pestilence broke out, caused by the concourse of such a large number of human beings; and his forces were dispersed.

Rustām Mirza by means of his favourite and tool, Malik Abdullah, one of the Malik family of Farah, who were related to the Kaiānis, succeeded in seducing from his allegiance one Malik Zarif, son of that Malik Nāsr-ud-din Kaiāni already mentioned. This youth, although destitute of wisdom and ability, was very ambitious; and he was led away by promises to betray his kinsman and chieftain, Malik Mahmud, to the Mirza.

Malik Zarif had invited his chief to the fort of Jārūnak[2] for a change of air while the pestilence was raging; and the Malik, against the advice of his son Jallāl-ud-din and his own relations, accepted this invitation, to give pleasure to his young kinsman; and proceeded to Jārūnak.

News was sent to Rustām Mirza, who at the head of a force of Afshārs and others hastened towards that place. Malik Zarif, urged by a feeling of shame, held out for 16 days, but at last he and his followers went over to the enemy. Malik Mahmud was thereupon also compelled to surrender. The traitors met with a fitting recompense as they were put into restraint and two days later Malik Nāsr-ud-din, his son Malik Zarif, and his family were put to death by the Prince; but Malik Mahmud with one or two companions continued in prison.

Malik Jallāl-ud-din had before this retired to Kala-i-Fath, where he was blockaded by a body of troops detailed for the purpose of Rustām Mirza, until he was relieved.

Malik Shāh Husen with his brother and Malik Ali, however, broke their bonds and escaped from prison. Those persons fell in with a band of Seistanis who were searching for them in the vicinity of the scene of their imprisonment. The refugees thereupon went off to their homes in Zirreh and raised the country against the invaders and very soon found themselves at the head of nearly 10,000 men. A thousand men relieved Kala-i-Fath, and enabled Malik

---

[1] This name is taken from the Shijrat-ul-Muluk. The Alam Ara merely states it to have been a stronghold fortified on the right and left. I am inclined to think it may have been meant for Juwein. But it is not possible to speak with any certainty on this point.

[2] This place from the narrative appears to have been at some distance from Kala-i-Fath. I am inclined to think it was Chakansur. But this is only a conjecture on my part. If it was Chakansur then the direct *route* from this place to Zamin Dāwar would be through Khash. Moreover, it is possible for a force of cavalry to have reached the vicinity of Chakansur from Farah in two days. Jārūnak must have been a place of some size to have held enough men for Malik Nāsr-ud-din to have brought 1,000 men to the help of Malik Jallāl-ud-din, as mentioned in the narrative, previous to this present allusion. The river crossed by Rustām Mirza must therefore have been the Khash and not the Helmand if this place was Chakansur. On the other hand Jārūnak may have occupied the site covered by the ruins of Chargewak about 3 or 4 miles to the north of Juwein.

Jallāl-ud-din to join his kinsmen and the fighting men of Zirreh; and the whole array with one accord then marched against Rustām Mirza.

This Prince obtaining news of the impending attack put Malik Mahmud to death and, crossing the Hirmend, retired in the direction of Sarayān (or Sarabān?) intending to retire into Zamin Dāwar. Malik Jallāl-ud-din and the men of Seistan followed hard on his tracks, and in the neighbourhood of Pusht-i-Zāwah the Prince was brought to bay and compelled to fight. Defeated in the engagement, he was again forced to make a stand the next day in Sarayān (or Sarabān) and was completely routed and forced to retire in disorder to the Zamin Dāwar. According to the Shijrat-ul-Muluk, Malik Mahmud was murdered in the year 995 H. The foregoing account is, however, taken from 1587 A.D. the Ālam Ārā-i-Ābbāsi. No date is given in the latter with reference to this event, and the orthography also of some of the names in the manuscript is very doubtful.

After the expulsion of Rustām Mirza, Saffavi, from Seistan, Malik Jallāl-ud-din was declared successor to the late Malik Mahmud by the unanimous decision of his family and the chief men of Seistan.

The opening years of the reign of this ruler were full of troubles. The Uzbeks were everywhere in great strength, and there seems to have been a design to annex Khurassan to the kingdom of Ābdullah Khan II, the last but one of the family of Abdul Khair (who was the father of the famous Muhammad Shaibāni Khan) who ruled the country beyond the Oxus.

Seistan was exposed to the raids of these invaders and for a long time there was continuous fighting between the Uzbeks and the subjects of Malik Jallāl-ud-din. While the Maliks maintained their grasp on the forts and towns in which they held out against the attacks of the Uzbeks, the latter had acquired possession of many of the districts of the open country, and had even attempted to capture Kala-i-Fath itself. Malik Jallāl-ud-din was not uniformly unsuccessful in his endeavours to stem the tide of invasion, but the general balance of success was greatly in favour of the invaders, and despairing of effecting any permanent result unaided, he placed his family in the charge of his retainers inside the fort of Kala-i-Fath, and by way of Kirman made his way to the Court of the Shah, which he reached during its stay in Isfahān, in the year 1005 H. He met with a distinguished reception, and many signal marks of his 1596-1597 A.D. Suzerain's favour were bestowed on him; and he continued to dwell at the Court of the Shah for some time. Seized at last with a great desire to see his family and country again, he received permission to leave the Court and set out for Seistan. Arrived in that country he discovered that the descendants of Sāni Beg Sultan, who had been appointed by Abdullah Khan II of Bokhara to the government of Seistan, and entrusted with the conquest of Nimroz, had obtained a complete mastery over that country. Malik Jallāl-ud-din found himself unable to cope with the Uzbeks; and he was also unable to submit to their predominance, until such time as the Shah would put into effect his intention of moving towards Khurassan to restore his authority. Under these circumstances the Malik collected his retainers and gathering up his family and effects he made his way into Kandahar where he resided for some time. He had even entertained the idea of following these old enemies of his house, the Prince Muzaffar Husen and his brother Rustām Mirza, into India; when the rumour of the Shah's march towards Khurassan reached him and after that Khurassan had been rid of the presence of the Uzbeks, Malik Jallāl-ud-din who had hastened to join the Shah was raised to the dignity of Khān, and in 1006 or 1007 A. H. he was also rewarded with the government of Seistan.

1597-98 or 1598-99 A.D.

The Princes Muzaffar Husen and Rustām had been compelled to retire into India before the continued advance eastwards of the Uzbeks. The purely Kizzilbash or Persian element among the followers had been greatly reduced in numbers, owing to casualties in the fighting that had taken place regularly for so many years. Both brothers found an honourable asylum at the Court of the Great Akbar, who despatched Shāhi Beg Khān, Kabuli, to take possession of Kandahar from Muzaffar Husen Mirza, and that Province passed in this manner into the hands of the Emperors of India with the Zamin-i-Dāwar and the Hazārājat.

In the struggle that took place periodically for the possession of Kandahar between the Emperors of Delhi and the Sovereigns of Persia, Seistan owing to its position became a base of operations, and for this reason the movements of Malik Jallāl-ud-din, the ruler of that country, were reported in India and his name appears in the chronicles of the Timuride Sovereigns of Delhi. Malik Jallāl-ud-din was succeeded by his second son Malik Hamza. Malik Hamza was a benevolent ruler and his name is mentioned with respect in the traditions which still exist in Seistan. His tomb inside the central building of the Gumbaz-i-Surkh, the State College (the remains of which exist just beyond the ruined walls of Kala-i-Fath), was for a long time a place of pilgrimage as a ziārat. Here in course of time the *ex voto* offerings placed by pilgrims increased to such an extent that the interior of the building was filled with great stacks and sheaves of tamarisk rods, on which the pilgrims suspended handkerchiefs and strips of cloth torn from their garments. The usual offerings of strangely shaped stones, fragments of old sculptures, and slabs of travertine formed a great pile, until about 25 or 30 years ago the legends of treasure concealed among the remains of the buildings excited the cupidity of a certain Fakir called Sartor, a Sheikh by descent, who was greatly reverenced by the Afghans who had swarmed into the valley of the Helmand. Malik Hamza was a Shiah; and the Fakir Sartor, carried away by his zeal as a Sunni, and by his avarice as well, set fire to the great sheaves of tamarisk rods over Malik Hamza's tomb; and aided by his followers he dug up the ground, and threw down walls in the search for the two Kharwars of gold and silver said to have

Ruins of the Government College, Kala Fath; endowed by Malik Hamza (17th century A.D.).

(Part I to face page 78.)

been buried somewhere on the premises. He found nothing; but his efforts completed the ruin of the buildings.

Malik Hamza Khan died without male issue. His tenure of office lasted from about 1028 to 1055 H. He was succeeded by his nephew Malik Nusrat Khan, who held the reins of authority from 1055 to 1085 H. This Prince was succeeded by the younger of his two sons Malik J'afir Khān who ruled over Seistan from 1085-1104 H. The mother of this Prince was a Lady of the Household of the Shah, and her son took precedence of his brother Malik Fath Ali Khān. On his brother's death, however, the latter was raised to the seat of authority and ruled from 1104-1134 H. In his reign Kala-i-Fath was finally abandoned and the capital transferred to Kundrak in the northern delta of the Helmand. 1619-1645 A.D. 1645-1674 A.D. 1674-1692 A.D. 1692-1721-22 A.D.

Malik J'afir left a son named Asadullah Khān, who eventually, after asserting himself ineffectually in support of his pretensions, retired to the Court of the Shah.

NOTE.—After the surrender of Kandahar by Ali Mardan Khan, to the Indian Government, on the 22nd of March 1638, Malik Hamza Khan appears to have entered into communication with Kitij Khan, the Subahdār, or Viceroy, of the Kandahar Province, who was probably very anxious to extend his sovereign's authority over Seistan; for at this period in Indian history a revival of energy had taken place, and the tyranny of Shah Sefi which had estranged the Governor of Kandahar had probably a similar effect on Provincial Rulers in other directions, and the time was favourable for a forward policy on the part of the Indian Government to find expression, and with a prospect of success.

At this time the limits of the Kandahar Province certainly extended as far as Khwaja Ali on the Helmand, and Khānshi (the modern Khānishin) appears to have been the frontier district in this direction. This district was under Izat Khan, who held the lands dependant on Kala Bist as a military fief. At this time also, Khānshi was in the hands of Abdal (probably meant for the Chief of the Abdalis) whose authority extended over half of the lands in the Province of Kandahar; and who resided in the fort at Khānsi (probably the ruined fort at Landi Muhammad Amin Khan). This person had been inciting Malik Hamza to take possession of the Khānshi district, and also, while the Subahdār had repaired to the Emperor's presence, to make an attempt on the fort of Kala Bist. Malik Hamza like a wise man turned a deaf ear to the instigation of the Abdali Chief; until a friend at the Persian Court gave him warning that the Shah had become aware of his relations with the Indian Governor of Kandahar, and that, if he wished to avert the Shah's wrath, he ought to take prompt action to propitiate the tyrant by declaring himself loyal. Malik Hamza thereupon availed himself of the Abdali's invitation and took possession of Khānshi.

This at once provoked a retaliatory expedition, and the Indian troops, 1,500 strong, recovered Khānshi, and drove the Seistanis down the Helmand. Following up this success the Indian troops entered Seistan. They laid waste many townships, and destroyed the band, or weir, in the Helmand, by means of which the prosperity of the country had been restored, and on which its continuance depended. All the water (of the river) flowed towards the districts lower down and the upper part of Seistan was rendered desolate and waterless.

Malik Hamza shut himself up in Kala Fath, which was his capital, and the Indian expeditionary force having worked their will on the country in its vicinity, retreated to Kandahar. This expedition took place late in the autumn of 1639: and the report of the result of the operations was placed before the Emperor Shah Jahan on the 23rd December 1639. The Abdali who was at the bottom of this trouble was punished (with death ?).

Badshahnāmah, Bibliotheca Indica, pages 170—173.

In 1715 Mir Weis, the Ghilzai, after he had thrown off the Persian yoke, overran Seistan and took possession of Farah. In 1718-19 a Malik Jafar Kaiāni was in detention in Kandahar. The great difference in the dates makes it very improbable that he was the Malik Jafar of the text, son of Malik Musrat Khan. The predominance of the Afghans in Seistan was probably the cause of Maliks Husen and Mahmud (page 80) and Asadullah, son of Malik Jafar (and grandson of Nusrat Khan), abandoning Seistan. The former retired to the district of Tun, and the latter to Isfahan. The enmity between the Ghilzais and Abdalis in Herat, and the intrusion into Seistan of the Ghilzais (who were rebels also against the Persian Government), probably decided Malik Mahmud in after years to keep friends with his neighbours the Abdalis.

CHAPTER IV.

In the stormy period succeeding the conquest of Seistan by Timur, the Kaiānis had become greatly weakened, and the representatives or chiefs of tribes settled in Seistan had gradually obtained influence in the country and they were destined eventually to reduce the family of their Princes to a condition inferior to that which they hold themselves.

Two sons survived Malik Fath Ali Khān, Muhammad Husen Khān and Mahmud. The former was confirmed as his father's successor and he proceeded to Court where he stayed for some time. According to the Shijrat-ul-Muluk from which these details are taken, the Shah, for some reason best known to his Ministers, bestowed Seistan, including the territory from Kala-i-Bist to the Khushk Rud, Uk (that is the modern district of Lāsh and Juwein) as well as the Province of Tun and Khiābād, on Assadullah Khān, with a variety of other gifts of value, and he became ruler of Seistan.

The sons of Malik Fath Ali, Muhammad Husen Khān and Malik Mahmud, with a party of the chiefs of their country abandoned their native land, and made for Kirman. From that place they proceeded to Tun. Here they were joined by the chiefs of the tribes of Nakhe, Lalue, and Hamdin; while the leaders of the inhabitants of Tun and Khiābād also gathered round the Kaiāni Princes.

The following they had collected soon attracted the attention of the Persian Government who regarded the matter as being too serious to be neglected. For this reason, therefore, the Beglar Begi of Meshed, Fath Ali Khān, Afshār, was ordered by Shah Husen Saffavi to crush this movement, and at the head of 12,000 men (according to the Shijrat-ul-Muluk) he set out to put these orders into effect. Having marched to within two farsakhs of Tun, where the gardens of that town were situated, the Beglar Begi commenced to lay waste the country and eventually invested the town itself. The fighting strength at the disposal of the Maliks did not exceed 300 men, but at the head of these Malik Mahmud sallied out and attacked the Persian troops and having slain the Commander put his men to flight.

The account of the Shijrat-ul-Muluk is corroborated by the notice of this event contained in the Tarikh-i-Jahān Kushā-i-Nādiri. The latter makes it evident that Muhammad Husen Khān was more or less of a nonentity; perhaps the stronger character of his brother Malik Mahmud, and his subsequent brilliant career, contributed to place his elder brother in the background. According to the Tarikh-i-Jahān Kushā-i-Nādiri, Malik Mahmud was enabled to take the offensive against the Shah's troops owing to the defection of Pir Muhammad, an Afghan leader in the Persian Army, who went over to Malik Mahmud.

This victory put Malik Mahmud on the footing of an independent ruler, and he maintained himself as such in Tun.

The dynasty of the Saffavis was now in its death throes. The Afghan, Mahmud Ghilzai, had invaded Persia and was threatening the capital at that time (Isfahan). Shah Husen, the last of the Saffavis, had been a devoted follower of the arts of peace. His time was taken up wholly in designing buildings and erecting palaces, in literature and self-indulgence; and the warlike resources of Persia improved under the superintendence of Europeans in the reign of Shah Abbās the Great, had by his successors been neglected until in the reign of Shah Husen no effectual means could be taken to defend even the capital from the attack of the undisciplined levies composed of Afghan and Baluch adventurers led by Mahmud. According to the Shijrat-ul-Muluk, Malik Mahmud raised an army and volunteered his services to aid in repelling the invasion. He had reached Yazd with this object in view, and had despatched an envoy to the Shah informing him of his advance; and asking to be forgiven for his action in opposing the Royal troops and for having been the cause of the death of the Beglar Begi. The Shah's Commanders advised their master that he had nothing to fear from the rabble under Mahmud; but that the movement of the Kaiānis were open to very grave suspicion. Orders were accordingly issued, instructing Malik Mahmud to return, by the same road by which he advanced, to his own territory, and that he should maintain a close watch over affairs in Khurassan.

From this point in his career, the account of the doings of Malik Mahmud is taken from the Tarikh-i-Jahān Kushā-i-Nādiri. Disturbances had broken out in all the outlying Provinces of the Empire. In Kandahar the Ghilzais had set up as independent rulers, and the Abdālis had taken possession of Herat and Farah. In Kirman, Saiyad Ahmad, the grandson of Mirza Da'ud, was in rebellion; and in Baluchistan towards Banādir (that is, the ports on the Persian Gulf) Sultan Muhammad, better known as the Khar Sawār ("donkey rider"), was committing depredations.

Many attempts were made to reduce the Abdālis of Herat to obedience by the Shah's Government, but these had failed. The Ghilzais had in the meantime attacked the Abdālis and in an engagement fought at Dilārām between Farah and Kandahar, Asadullah, the Abdāli chief, had been slain. This event was reported to the Shah's Government, then at Kazvin, and the title of Husen Kuli had been conferred on Mahmud who had commanded the Ghilzais in that action.

After this Zamān Khān having declared himself to be the heir, took possession of Herat and placed Abdullah, the father of the late Asad Khān, in confinement, while J'afir Khān and the other Kazzilbash prisoners were put to death by him in the garden of Naubarreh at the head (or commencement) of Khaibān. Zamān Khān then assumed the reins of authority. While the Ghilzais and Abdālis were engaged with one another and Mahmud Ghilzai had been rewarded for his so-called loyalty. Sufi Kuli Khān Turkmān Oghli, was appointed Sardar of Herat and despatched at the head of a number of efficient troops and with warlike stores in abundance to take possession of that city. In the plains around Kāfir Kal'a he was met by Zamān Khān, and in the action that took place the Sardar was slain. This event was the chief reason of the future predominance of the Afghans, as after it they obtained a complete control over the country around Herat, and held it for many years until they were driven thence by Nādir.

1719-1720 A.D.

In the year 1132 H. when news of the death of Sufi Kuli Khān reached the Court, Ismail Khān, Ghulam, was advanced to the position of Commander-in-Chief, and ordered to re-take Herat. He, however, loitered in Meshed on his way to Herat.

The expedition had subsequently been undertaken against Malik Mahmud which resulted in the death and overthrow of the Beglar Begi, and the predominance of the Malik. After the death of the Beglar Begi, the office of Commander-in-Chief, and Governor in Meshed, was conferred upon Ali Kuli Khān Shāmlu, at that time Beglar Begi of Merv, but who resided in Meshed. Dissensions sprang up between Ali Kuli Khān and Ismail Khān, and the former deputed a gang of bad characters, who were devoted to his interests, to proceed to the residence of the latter, and drag him from his private apartments and, through the Khaibān, to prison. This event took place on the 11th of the month of Muharram in the year 1135 H., the date on which the Afghans took Isfahan.[1]

12th October 1722 A.D.

March 1723 A.D.

The bad characters of the town gradually obtained complete control over the city of Meshed, until in the month of Jamadi-ul-Awal they invaded the privacy of Ali Kuli's dwelling and put him to death, and taking Ismail Khān out of prison, they set him up as Governor. His authority was only nominal, as he was in the hands of the lower orders who did as they pleased, and carried on the administration; he was therefore compelled to send letters to Malik Mahmud, and invite him to Meshed.

Malik Mahmud, who had been waiting for such an opportunity to take place, hastened to that city with the utmost speed, and on his arrival he took measures to suppress the seditious and rebellious sections among the population. Ismail Khān was made away with, and Malik Mahmud took full possession of the city.

His elder brother resigned his claims in favour of Mahmud, and shortly after he had given place to his younger brother he died.[2] He left four sons—Lutf Ali Khān, Fath Ali Khān, Suleman, and Muhammad.

---

[1] A gold coin struck by Mahmud Shah, as he is called after the capture of Isfahan and his conquest of Persia, was examined by me in Seistan. It bore the following legend on the obverse :— "Zarab Kāshān." Sikah Mahmud Shāh Alam dar-Sīnat 113 (5). The last figure was much worn and might have stood for a five or an eight as the lower half was illegible.

[2] He was taken ill in Farah.

Malik Mahmud built a palace for himself, and prepared a crown fashioned after that of the Kaiānis of ancient times; this head-dress was decked with gems; and, having sought out skilful Mobids, he ordered them to select an auspicious hour for his ascending the throne. The latter was placed in a lofty Aiwān, or hall, also planned after the traditions relating to Faridun and Kai Khasrau.

This event took place in the year 1135 H., and the Kaiāni Prince styled himself Shah-i-Meshed. He is said to have struck money, but no coins issued by him have so far been discovered, though search has been made, especially, for this issue. 1722 A.D.

Among his troops it is said that Nādir Kuli, the Afshār, was himself enrolled. The future Conqueror of India and the middle east, who was himself to overthrow Malik Mahmud's power, is said to have continued for a year in the service of the latter. Nādir Kuli then deserted the Malik and set up for himself in Ābivard, and the knowledge he gained in the Malik's service no doubt proved most useful; for Malik Mahmud soon was at the head of a disciplined force, and he had armed his infantry with matchlocks, and possessed a large number of guns. In after years these very musketeers and the artillery in Malik Mahmud's army foiled the attacks of Nādir's cavalry in many an engagement.

Malik Mahmud seems to have avoided a collision with the Abdālis who had taken possession of Farah and Sabzawār, as he never seemed to direct his attention towards these districts, but he led his armies towards the western districts of Khurassan. During the early period of Nādir's career, when he commenced to establish his authority among the Afshārs of Ābivard and Kallāt, along the edge of the Great Plain towards the north, there was a party in those tribes and also among the Kurds, who were opposed to his pretensions; and these joined themselves to Malik Mahmud. The latter also had received the submission of the leaders of the Iliyat tribes in Khurassan, including Kilich Khān, Pā-Pālu and Imām Kuli, Irlu, of the Afshārs. Nādir visited Malik Mahmud in Meshed with treacherous designs against the latter which, however, he was unable to put into execution. He won over Kilich Khān and Imām Kuli, and while the Kaiāni Prince was away on a hunting expedition Nādir carried away both these leaders with him to Ābivard. This showed the attitude of Nādir towards the Malik; and not long after open hostilities resulted.

The rival chieftains first came into hostile contact in Khabushān (Kuchān) where the Malik had proceeded with 5,000 or 6,000 men to put down an outbreak that had taken place. Nādir had marched to the aid of the rebellious Kurds, and within a distance of two farsakhs of Kuchān had cut up a detachment of the Malik's troops. Mahmud upon this retired towards Meshed protecting his rear with his artillery and musketeers against whom Nādir refused to adventure his horsemen.

In the meantime Shah Thāmāsp (son of the late Shah Husen Safavi) had determined to proceed to Khurassan. Nādir also advanced from Kuchān and took up a position at a place called Mirkahrez, one farsakh distant from Meshed in the direction of Khiabān Alia. Here he was attacked by the Malik, who was repulsed with heavy loss and forced to retire behind the walls of the city. Nādir thereupon took possession of the fort of Tus called Haji Turāb, 3 farsakhs to the west of Meshed, from whence he harassed the communications of the Malik.

Shah Thāmāsp in the meantime had despatched Reza Kuli Khan, one of his nobles, to represent his interests in Khurassan, and the latter having raised a force among the Kurds of Kuchān, directed his march towards Meshed. He was beaten off by the Malik, and was driven back on Tus; where he sank into a condition of careless repose and allowed his levies to disperse.

The inhabitants of Meshed had been prepared to open the gates to Reza Kuli; and, disappointed at his retreat, had raised bands of armed men, and shut the gates of the city against the Malik. The citadel, however, was held by Mahdi, the Meshedi, for the Malik; and the latter was admitted into the place with all his ordnance and artillery. He very speedily regained his hold over the city and for the future he treated the populace with severity being convinced of their faithlessness.

Nādir becoming convinced that no good result would accrue to him from his alliance with the Sardar, Reza Kuli, marched back to Ābivard, and the latter retired to Kuchān. He made another attempt on Meshed, but was defeated by Malik Mahmud, and driven back to Kuchān. News of these occurrences reached Shah Thāmāsp in Azarbāijān where he held his Court; and he appointed Muhammad Khan, Turkomān to the Sardāri of Khurassan. Before, however, the latter could arrive, Malik Mahmud had declared his independence and had seized Nishāpur, having deputed his brother's son, Malik Ishāk, to carry out this project. The Biyāts of Nishāpur appealed to Nādir for aid; and the latter having raised a force from among the Afshārs and Kurds of Kallat, the Darah-i-Juz [1] and Abivard, he set out for Nishāpur. The Kurds of Kuchān, threw in their lot, also with Nādir, and by means of their aid Malik Ishāk was driven out of Nishāpur with great loss; and compelled to intrench himself in a garden on the outskirts of the town.

He, however, through the efforts of Mulla Muhammad Rafi-ai, one of the celebrated divines of the day, obtained terms enabling him to march with all his forces back to Meshed. Some of the savage and bestial Kurds resented this and attempted to seize the baggage and effects of the Malik on account of an

---

[1] The modern form is Derehgez

old standing grudge against him. But before they could act Malik Mahmud arrived in person from Meshed having marched with all haste to his nephew's assistance; and he took up a position at the Kadamgāh in the neighbourhood of Nishāpur. Nādir issued from the town and attacked the Malik but was repulsed with loss, his brother having been wounded. The turbulent Kurds, unaccustomed to restraint, and continuous exertion, seeing the firm attitude of the Malik, made off to their homes with such plunder as they had obtained. Malik Mahmud thereupon laid seige to the city of Nishāpur, and the populace seeing that they had been abandoned by Nādir made their submission to the former. He reinstated the former Governor Fath Ali Khan, Biyāt, and returned to Meshed.

According to the Tarikh-i-Jahān Kushā-i-Nādiri, it was after this event that Malik Mahmud caused himself to be crowned. The fact that he had struck money in his own name is also mentioned.

The people of Bu Kamij situated between Meshed and Ābivard having proved refractory Malik Mahmud deputed his nephew to reduce them to obedience. The Bu Kamij called in Nādir to help them, but before he could reach them Malik Ishāk had compelled the Bu Kamij to submit and had retired to Meshed. In order to effect a diversion in favour of the Bu Kamij Nādir advanced on Meshed by way of Rādkān, and Malik Mahmud issuing from the city in order to oppose that advance marched in the direction of Kuchān. The two forces came into contact at Ashtarpi, one of the villages of Meshed and in the battle that took place, Nādir was defeated with great loss in killed and wounded; his forces dispersed to their own homes, while he himself reached Kallat with only two companions. Malik Mahmud next marched to Kuchān to punish the inhabitants of that district. Nādir at this crisis was called upon to take measures to put down a serious rising against him on the part of the Afshārs who called in the Turkomāns of Darun to their aid. Nādir marched from Kallat to Ābivard and in front of the fort at that place inflicted a severe defeat on the malcontents. Having freed himself from this danger he set out for Kuchān, but by that time Malik Mahmud had plundered the Kurds and scattered their levies of armed men, and had retired to Meshed, and Nādir finding he was too late also returned to Ābivard.

At this juncture Muhammad Khan, the Turkomān whom Shah Thāmāsp had appointed to be the Sardar of Khurassan, reached the Province, and Fath Ali Khan, the Biyāt whom Malik Mahmud had appointed Governor of Nishāpur, immediately cast off his allegiance to the Kaiāni and declared for the representative of the Shah. The Malik a second time marched on the city by the right hand route, the rebellious Governor came out to fight him, but was defeated, captured, and beheaded. Malik Mahmud having gained possession of the city installed his nephew Malik Ishāk as his representative and returned to Meshed. Nādir was advancing against Meshed and the Malik in order to oppose him, after the reduction of Nishāpur, summoned Malik Ishāk from that place with his troops, while he himself at the head of a great array, marched in state to the gardens without the City of Meshed. When Nādir reached Janābād, he found it to be held by that same Pir Muhammad, who had deserted to Malik Mahmud at Tun some years before. This Chief opposed Nādir's advance, but was defeated and compelled to take refuge within the fort, after which Nādir continued his march towards Meshed. At Koshk-i-Mahdi he learnt of the Malik's movements. This place was two farsakhs from Meshed and Nādir marched from it to the Koh-i-Sangin, distant one farsakh from the city.

Malik Ishāk had that same day arrived at Turuk, 2 farsakhs from Meshed. In the afternoon Malik Ishāk from the direction of Bābākudrat and Malik Mahmud from his position among the gardens led their forces against the position taken up by Nādir. Victory, however, declared for the latter on this occasion and the Maliks were defeated with heavy losses. The kettle drums and guns of Malik Mahmud fell into the hands of Nādir and the Kaiānis fled into the city. Such of his prisoners who were natives of Meshed were released and kindly treated by the victor; while the men of distinction belonging to the party of the Malik were sent away to Kallat, and Nādir himself retired to that place.

After this defeat Malik Mahmud instigated by the party adverse to Nādir among the Afshārs, who were well disposed towards his rival, despatched agents to the Turkomāns of Darūn and Nisā, and to the Kurds of Kuchān to effect a diversion in his favour by taking the field against Nādir Kuli. This plan was successful, but Nādir obtaining exact information with regard to this intrigue, marched with the utmost speed against Meshed where his rendezvous was the fort of Behār. Malik Mahmud sallied out to attack him, but owing to the severe weather, all operations were stopped by heavy falls of snow and rain. The Kaiāni Prince was compelled to retreat into the city, and Nādir retired to Abivard. From this place he was compelled to proceed to Merv where a movement had taken place in favour of Malik Mahmud. The latter relieved from immediate danger took advantage of this respite to march in the direction of Juwein and Isfarain in the hope of obtaining a victory over Shah Thāmāsp before the latter was joined by Nādir Kuli. The Prince was at that time in Shāhrud-i-Bustām and hearing of the movements of the Malik, marched by way of Jājurm and Isfarain to effect a junction with Nādir, and despatched in advance Husen 'Ali Beg the Muiar-ul-Mamālik to Nādir's camp.

Malik Mahmud at this time had reduced the fortress of Juwein and was busied in taking possession of the whole country along the Shah's proposed route, but having heard that Nādir had moved out of Merv and was marching upon Meshed, he was compelled to relinquish his recent acquisitions and fall back to protect the city.

Husen 'Ali Beg having reached Nādir, and informed him of the Shah's advance, the latter renounced his intention of attacking Meshed and marched to join the Royal Cortege in Kuchān. Nādir was suspicious of the intrigues of the Kurds, but on his arrival he happily found that they had quarrelled with the Shah, and were hard pressed by the Royal Troops. The Kurds were thus compelled to ask Nādir to make their peace with the Shah, and having obtained an audience he was successful in his efforts on behalf of the rebels, and on his advice the Shah appointed Muhammad Husen Beg, son of Sām Beg, Vakil, to act as Governor of Kuchān, and promoted him to the Chieftainship of the tribes.

Upon the 2nd of the month of Muharram in the year 1139 H. the Royal Forces marched from Kuchān to lay siege to Meshed, where Malik Mahmud had shut himself up in the citadel, and, having closed the gates of the city, prepared for a siege. *27th August 1726 A.D.*

The Royal Forces reached Meshed on the 2nd of the month of Safar; and passing by the citadel under fire of the guns mounted on the walls, took up a position at the Zāwiyeh of Khwājah Rabi. There was fighting every day with the enemy who held the outworks of the place.

On the 14th of the same month, Fath 'Ali Khan, Chief of the Kājārs of Astarābād, was put to death; and Malik Mahmud having obtained intelligence of this event, hoping that the Kājārs would abandon the cause of Shah Thāmāsp, sallied out of Meshed in great strength to attack the Royal Camp. Nādir Kuli led the Shah's troops against the assailants, and half a farsakh from the city a desperate battle took place, in which Malik Mahmud was completely defeated. A number of his leading men fell on the field, among whom was Ibrahim Khan, the Commander of his artillery. Malik Mahmud retreated into the city, and never again issued beyond the walls. The siege continued after this for two months, and as it had then become evident that the fortunes of the Kaiānis were in a desperate condition, his adherents began to desert to his enemies. *20th September.*

Pir Muhammad, the Commander of the Malik's troops, again was ready to change sides; and he despatched a messenger to Nādir, to say that if he received a perfect assurance of safety he would undertake to overpower the guards at the gateway in the direction of Mir 'Ali Amuyiah and admit the troops of Nādir who was to advance at night and lie in wait beyond the gate, in readiness to enter the city. After dark on the night of the 16th of the month of Rabi-us-Sāni 1139 A. H. Nādir set out from Khwājah Rab'i at the head of 12,000 men, and Pir Muhammad opened the gate and admitted the enemy. Nādir immediately took possession of the city up to the Sacred Area and the Chahār Bāgh, and the troops of the Malik who were holding the city walls fled into the citadel. *Night of 30th November 1726 A.D.*

The next morning Malik Macmud sallied out in great strength to clear the city, from two directions; one column advanced towards the Khaibān-i-

Chahār Bagh and another column advanced towards the Khaibān-i-Sifli and with the utmost valour assaulted the enemy who were holding the city. Nādir in person led his men against this attack and after a severe struggle drove the Malik into the citadel. That day the whole of the city was occupied by the Shah's troops; and the Prince himself visited the shrine and returned to his camp after having performed his devotions. The next day Malik Mahmud laid aside the Insignia of Royalty; and having obtained quarter for himself, his family and partisans, he betook himself, as a fugitive to the shrine of Imam Reza.

Pir Muhammad was rewarded with the government of Jām.

Malik Mahmud remained for some time a fugitive within the precincts of the shrine. The times were, however, full of danger. Shah Thāmāsp jealous of Nādir's power, intrigued against him, inciting Malik Mahmud and Malik Ishāk and even the leaders of Nādir's own troops to rise against that Chieftain. Mahmud and his nephew were, however, loyal to Nādir, and disclosed the intrigue to him. On the 26th of the month of Rajab the Kurds of Kallat and Darah-i-Juz made a hostile demonstration. The Tatars also of Merv rebelled and proclaimed Malik Mahmud as their Chief. Nādir in person put down the movements among the Kurds, and his brother marched against Merv. He destroyed the Band-i-Sultāni at that place and reduced the Tatars to subjection by depriving them of water. Letters written to the Tatars by Malik Mahmud were discovered, and as he was possessed of great influence his continued existence was felt to be an ever present source of danger.

8th February 1727 A.D.

By order of Nādir, Muhammad Khan Chuleh put both Malik Mahmud and Malik Ishāk to death, in retaliation for the execution of Muhammad Beg, the Min Bāshi of the Chulehs who had been slain by order of the Malik. Muhammad Ali, younger brother of the latter, was sent to Bira Ma'ali Khan, the Biyāt, and was put to death in retaliation for the execution of Fath Ali Khan, the brother of Bira Ma'ali Khan. "These three persons each of whom was worthy of wearing a Crown, had thus to bow their heads to the decree of Fate."

Probably in March 1727 A.D.

After their death Malik Asadullah Khan, the former ruler of Seistan, who had arrived in Nādir's Camp from that country, was sent away to his government in charge of the children, women, and relations of Malik Mahmud.

While these events were taking place at Meshed, Husen Sultan, one of the leading men of Seistan, who was in the country of Kāin by order of Malik Mahmud, had set on foot a rebellion against Nādir, and had defeated a force sent to reduce him to obedience.

26th June 1727 A.D.

As it had become necessary to subdue the Afghans of Khāf upon the 16th of the month Zi-i-Haj in the year 1139 H.; in company with the Shah, Nādir Kuli set out from Meshed at the head of 8,000 well equipped troops. This movement on Nādir's part threw the people of Kāin into a state of consternation, and Malik Kalb 'Ali, a son of the late Malik Mahmud, Lutf 'Ali, the son of his brother, with the Chiefs of Seistan, fled to Isfahān and joined themselves to Ashraf, the Ghilzai. Husen Sultan, however, shut himself up in the fort of Kāin, and when Nādir arrived before that place Husen surrendered the place, and found favour in the sight of the conqueror.

From this point in the narrative the Tarikh-i-Jahān Kushā-i-Nādiri contains no further allusions to Seistan, and for the remainder of this narrative we shall have to depend altogether on the Shijrat-ul-Muluk.

The narrative of the eventful career of Malik Mahmud who set up as an independent ruler in Khurassan, contained in the latter, and that found in the Tarikhi-Jahān Kushā, differs only in unimportant details. Instead of Malik Ishāk, in the account of the Shijrat-ul-Muluk, Lutf 'Ali Khan appears as the commander of his uncle's forces. But the son of Malik Husen Khan the elder brother of Malik Mahmud could hardly have been of sufficient age, to take a very prominent part in the events that took place during his uncle's short tenure of power.

Seven sons survived Malik Mahmud and one daughter also is known to have existed. The names of the sons were 'Abbas Khan, J'afir Khan, Kalb 'Ali, Malik Rustam, Husen Khan, Muhammad and Ahmad. Most of these are represented at this present date, and the descendents of these seven sons are to be found at this day in Tabas of the Kuhistān, in Persia; and in the Kohāt District of the Punjab in India.

Malik Lutf 'Ali is said to have been received with honour, at first by Ashraf the Ghilzai, but to have been subsequently placed in confinement by the Afghan Chief in Isfahān, and on the capture of the place by Nādir he was set free with the other captives.

Lutf 'Ali is said to have received the government of Seistan from Nādir and the Malik Asadullah retired to Persia where he died shortly afterwards. Malik Lutf 'Ali served with the contingent of fighting men supplied by Seistan against Farah. He also is said to have served under Nādir's standards in the campaign against the Turks, in which Nādir was wounded in the battle fought with Topāl Othmān, the Turkish Pasha of Baghdad.

Nādir Shah passed through Seistan on his way to the seige of Kandahar (he left Isfahan on the 17th of the month of Rajab in the year 1149 H). He left his family with those of his men, under a strong escort of musketeers and on the 2nd of the month of Shawal of the same year he set out for Girishk by way of Dalkhak and Dilārām. He, at the same time, ordered Malik Lutf 'Ali Khan to proceed to Makrān and subdue the turbulent tribesmen of that district. The Chief of Sarbāz hastily collected the fighting men of the hilly country and offered what resistance he was able. The Malik however overpowered the opposition of the tribes and defeating them had compelled them to submit. The camp of the invaders was set up in the vicinity of Sarbāz, and hostilities against the Rinds had ceased. There arrived, however, to their aid

13th October 1736 A.D.
24th January 1737 A.D.

a contingent of armed men, all of whom were bent on fighting and too late to participate in the quarrel that had been adjusted; they induced the Chief to break the agreement arrived at and to recommence hostilities. Malik Lutf 'Ali was unaware of the reinforcements that had joined the Chief of Sarbāz until the latter attacked him; and in leading his men to the encounter, he was shot down by one of the enemy who had singled him out and waited for him. The expedition to Makrān broke up after the death of their leader.

When news of the death of Malik Lutf 'Ali Khan reached Nādir, the latter summoned the brother of the deceased Chieftain to his presence and bestowed on him the government of Seistan. Malik Fath 'Ali Khan served under Nādir's orders in Afghanistan, the forcing of the Khyber Pass, and the subsequent operations in Hindustan. He also took part in the campaign against the Ruler of Bokhara, and rendered good service. After this last campaign Malik Fath 'Ali appears to have returned to Seistan and taken up the government of that country. The country of Seistan, in common with the other provinces of Nādir Shāh's empire, experienced the oppression of the last years of his life and reign. The taxes were increased to such an extent that (to quote again from the Tarikh-i-Jahān Kushā-i-Nādiri) it would have been impossible to make up the tenth part of the amount assessed even if the leaves of the trees had been of gold.

The money revenue at which Seistan had been assessed had been fixed at four "Alifs" and from the work already quoted, it appears that each "Alif" represented 5,000 tomans; and according to this calculation the four Alifs were equivalent to 20,000 tomans. Under the later régime of violence and oppression, each of those Alifs was increased fivefold and 100,000 tomans therefore were demanded from the Governor of Seistan.

The people of that country resolved to resist the imposition or the realization of the enhanced contribution to the Imperial Exchequer, and even if it was necessary, to do so with arms in their hands. Before however, he resorted to desperate measures, Malik Fath Ali Khan (according to the Shijrat-ul-Muluk) represented the inability of the Seistanis to raise such a contribution. Having obtained no relief by means of this submissive line of conduct, Malik Fath Ali Khan took up arms and threw off his allegiance to Nādir. The people of Uk and Kala-i-Kah flocked to his standard, and he advanced against Farah where a similar course of tyranny had estranged the population of that district. In consequence of this when Malik Fath 'Ali Khan reached Farah he was welcomed by all ranks of the population, who laid hold of the Governor and brought him to the presence of the Malik; but this unfortunate man had merely obeyed the instructions he had received, and he was released after a time.

Seistan became the refuge to which the inhabitants of Uk, Kala-'i-Kah, and Farah fled from the oppression of Nādir Shāh; and on all sides there took place tumults and risings against his tyranny.

When Nādir Shah heard of the rising in Seistan, he laid hold of the brother of Fath Ali Khan, named Muhammad, who represented the Malik at the Court of the Shah, and had him made away with in private, cutting him off in the bloom of his youth. The task of putting down the rising was made over to Muhammad Reza Khan, Farklu, Afshār.

Malik Fath Ali Khan, on his part, selected a commander whom he intended to despatch into the Garmsir, to raid that flourishing district. His choice fell on the Amir Seif-ud-din, Chief of the Shāhrakis. This raid was successful and followed by the Malik in person; Amir Seif-ud-din defeated the officer of Nādir Shah who was detailed to protect the district of the Garmsir with 6,000 men. The men of Seistan returned to their homes with much spoil.

After the raid on the Garmsir, Malik Fath 'Ali Khan marched on Farah to meet the invading force under the command of Muhammad Reza Khan Afshār. The whole of the Kalāntars of Seistan followed the Malik into the field, but evidently the result of the campaign was disastrous to Seistan, or the Malik was foolish and credulous; for, it is said, that after much fighting, Malik Fath 'Ali accompanied by his Commander-in-Chief Mir Kambar and Muhammad Reza Khan, the Kalāntar (of the Sarbandis), were induced to accompany the Persian General to the Court of Nādir where the Malik and his two companions were condemned to have their sight destroyed. The former, after enduring agonies for two days, was eventually put to death. This event took place in the year 1160 H.

1747 A.D.

There were, however, still living two other sons of Malik Muhammad Husen Khan; the elder brother of Malik Mahmud the "Shah of Meshed."

They were Suleimān (the elder of the two) and Husen Khan-i-Sāni. Both were at the Court of Nādir Shah in Kuchān. On the death of Malik Fath 'Ali, the Shah appointed Husen Khan-i-Sāni to be ruler of Seistan. On his way to take up the government, this Prince was waylaid by a party of Afghans of Farah, who had been incensed by the disturbances caused in that district, and by them he was put to death.

Malik Sulemān Khan, and his uncle's son, J'afir Khan (son of Malik Mahmud), continued to reside on Persian soil. The former had been sent to Kāshān as Governor of that place (Shijrat-ul-Muluk), where he served for 4 months. After the overthrow of Nādir's nephew and also (the instigator of his murder) Adil Shah, and when it came to pass that the grandson of Nādir Shah, Shah Rukh Mirza, was raised to the throne in Meshed, the latter recalled the Kaiāni Princes to his Court.

Sulemān Khan was appointed Malik of Seistan, and his brother J'afir Khan Governor of Herat. With him went his younger brother Rustam Khan from whom the Indian Branch of the Kaiāni Family are descended.

When Ahmad Shah the Durrāni captured Herat he took away with him on his return to Kandahar, the Kaiāni Princes sons of Malik Mahmud, Abbās Khan, J'afir Khan and Rustam Khan.

The power of the Durrāni Chieftain being in the ascendant, Malik Sulemān Khan visited Kandahar and on his return he begged that his cousins might be allowed to accompany him to their native land. Ahmad Shah permitted both J'afir Khan and Rustam Khan to return to Seistan, but 'Abbās Khan he retained at his court.

Sulemān Khan, Kaiāni, Malik of Seistan, was ordered to march at the head of the levies of his subject to aid his Suzerain, Ahmad Shah, in his expedition against Kāin. The Malik was absent for a year or more, and the chief men among the population of Seistan seized the opportunity to raise a tumult, and a civil war broke out in that country. Malik Sulemān Khan returned to Seistan, where for some years he had difficulty in asserting his authority; there were frequent rebellions and the country remained in a disturbed condition; but eventually he succeeded in establishing his power in his native land.

1756-57 A.D.

In the year 1170 H. a son was born to him by the daughter of Malik Mahmud (his principal wife). This child was named Muhammad Nasīr Khan. After the child had attained a certain age, Ahmad Shah Durrāni bestowed on him the districts of Khiābād and Kākh, an extensive and fertile tract of country. Malik Sulemān Khan then proceeded to take possession of this appanage and at Khiābād he was welcomed by Muhammad Husen Khan, another son of Malik Mahmud, "Shah of Meshed," with the headmen of the place, and this valuable possession remained in the family of the Maliks for a long period of time.

Ahmad Shah Durrāni next ordered Malik Sulemān to take possession of Kirman. For this purpose he raised a force of armed men in Khiābād and Khusf enrolling many of the Nakhè tribe under his banner. The people of Seistan again proving turbulent, the Malik used this force to restore order in his native country before proceeding to Kirman.

1772-3 A.D.

In the year 1185 H. Timur Shah succeeded his father Ahmad Shah as Ruler over Afghanistan and this monarch confirmed Malik Nasīr Khan in all his honours and possessions. Malik Sulemān Khan died in 1196 A.H. at the age of 66 years, and was succeeded by his eldest son. The latter and his brother Bāhrām Khan observed the funeral rites of their father with great pomp, as was the custom in their family; and the period of mourning was 40 days. The corpse of the deceased Prince was sent for interment to Najaf.

1781-2 A.D.

Malik Nasīr-ud-din Khan was confirmed by his suzerain in his father's possessions, and gifts were in due course forwarded to him by Timur Shah.

1787-8 A.D.

A son was born to him in the year 1202 who was named Sulemān Khan after his grandfather, according to the Shijrat-ul-Muluk; but in other records, discovered in the country, this child is named as Khan Jahān Khan.

In 1207 A. H. Timur Shah Durrāni also died and his successor continued 1792-3 A.D. to show favour to the Ruler of Seistan. The latter had some years previously received the government of Kirman, and had advanced at the head of an army to assert his authority in that quarter and to take effective possession of his appanage.

When Malik Muhammad Nasir Khan died in 1208 A. H. the chiefs and 1793-4 A.D. headmen of the Nakhè and of the people of Seistan urged Malik Bāhrām Khan to take possession of the country as his brother's successor, but the latter, with a rare and commendable generosity, refused to do this, and was content to act as the tutor and regent of his nephew.

Malik Sulemān Khan (or Khan Jahān Khan) died while in his minority 1802-3 A.D. from the effects of a fall from his horse while hunting in 1217 A. H. He had, however, received the Royal Letters Patent conferring on him this office of Malik of Seistan, and also Sardār of Kirman; while his uncle had also been appointed as the Deputy of the young Chieftain.

According to certain MS. records alluded to, even after the death of his nephew, Malik Bāhrām preferred to act as the deputy of the daughter of Malik Mahmud, "Shah of Meshed," who lived, it is said, for two years after the untimely death of her grandson. All real power was, however, vested in the hands of Malik Bāhrām Khan; and all his acts, and the public works he constructed, and the reputation he enjoyed need not be repeated here.

Malik Bāhrām Khan was the last Prince of his race who possessed authority in Seistan.

His eldest son Malik Muhammad Jallal-ud-din Khan was born in 1210 1795-6 A.D. A. H., Malik Hamza Khan, his second son, was born in about 1211 or 12 A. H., 1796-7 or 8 A.D. and two years after the latter a third son, named Ali Akbar Khan, who however 1800 A.D. is never alluded to again and probably died young.

The great influx of Baluch tribes into Seistan came about in the reign of this Malik. The Shijrat-ul-Muluk states that from the skirts of the mountains to the tower of Ilumdār the country was covered with the tents of these nomads. Bam was the last place in Persia which afforded a refuge to the representative of the Zend Family which for a short time had ruled over Persia; having seized the reins of authority as they fell from the nerveless grasp of the last degenerate representative of the shortlived dynasty founded by Nādir Shah. Luft 'Ali, the last Zend Prince, had very many adherents among the Baluch tribes of the Kirman Province. He was seized and put to death, having been betrayed while attempting to escape from Bam [1] in the fortress of 1795 Circ. which he was surrounded by the forces of the Kajar Chieftain who had disputed his claim to the sovereignty of Persia. After that the fortress had been

---

[1] The headmen of Bam who were instrumental in surrendering the Zend Prince to Aga Muhammad Khan Kajar were Shaharkis from Seistan.

delivered up to the latter, a most fearful vengeance was wreaked on the people of the surrounding country.

The Province of Kirman could have been no dwelling place at that time for those who had favoured the losing cause, as the Baluchis had done ; so the emigration into Seistan of these nomads must have taken place shortly before the time in which Christie passed through the country. In this country the adherents of Luft 'Ali Khan, Zend, were assured a refuge ; for Seistan was a part of the dominions of the Afghan Kings ; and it lay therefore beyond the scope of any pursuit by the victorious troops of the Kajar Chief ; as the great achievements of Ahmad Shah, Durrāni, still shed a glamour over his degenerate successors.

Alam Khan, the Nāhrui Chief, a nephew of Mir Mehrab, the head of that clan domiciled in the country around Bāmpur, migrated about the same time to Seistan, where he received permission to settle in the lands around Kala-i-Nau. In that district the Chief built the village of Burj-i-Mir Alam Khan, now called Kala-i-Kohna.

Malik Jallal-ud-din Khān, the son of Malik Bāhrām Khān, was a voluptuary, immoderately addicted to wine, narcotics and debauchery in general ; he was turned out of Seistan by a combination of the Sarbandi and Shāhraki Chiefs. He was reinstated in (about) 1835 A.D. by Shah Kamrān, Sadozai, who ruled in Herāt, but was, shortly after, again deprived of his power. He lived in exile in the Hokāt, and died there attended in his last hours by his grandson (now alive) Malik Muhammad Azim Khan.

1854-55 or 1856-57 A.D.   This event took place in either 1271 or 3 A. H.

The Sarbandi and Shāhraki Chiefs raised Malik Hamza to a position of nominal power after that Malik Jallal-ud-din had been turned out of Seistan for good.

Malik Hamza was also a voluptuary ; but, though addicted to the same evil habits as his elder brother, he did not carry them to the same pitch of excess. He, however, possessed no real authority.

1847 A.D.   Malik Hamza died in 1263 A. H.

Malik Jallal-ud-din married into the family of Ibrahim Khān Sanjārāni, the Chief of Chakānsur ; and Hamza Khan into that of the Sarbandi Chief of Sehkoha. These opposing factions played off these young Chiefs against each other, using their names as a warrant for all the wrong that was committed by their partisans.

Jallal-ud-din[1] proving worthless, and being also of bad uncertain temper and desirous of asserting his claim as Ruler of the country, was discarded and thrust forth into exile.

---

[1] Major Abbott who saw this person in Herat in 1838, describes him as an extraordinarly fine looking man. Such was his distinguished bearing and appearance that people of the city suspended the business, or work, on which they might be engaged when he passed by, to look at him in admiration. Pity of it was that his debauched habits rendered him unable to hold his own in Seistan.

By the time that Connolly visited Seistan in 1839, the Kaiānis had lost all authority. Seistan of that time was partitioned between the Chiefs of the Sarbandis, Sanjarānis, Nāhruis and the Shāhrakis. The Kaiānis are not alluded to by that observant traveller in the account published in the journal of the Asiatic Society of Bengal in 1840; and in his map of Seistan attached to that account the country is shown to be divided between those tribal Chiefs.

For a space of a generation or a little more they misused their power, and the country became the scene of raids and reprisals until the Persians took advantage of the Civil War that had raged in Afghanistan after the death of Dost Muhammad, the Bārakzai Ruler, between his descendants; and of its after effects, to extend their frontier to the east including within it almost the whole extent of Seistan as it existed in the days of later Maliks of that country when that family held effectual possession of their patrimony.

Before concluding this Memoir a brief notice of the so-called Baluch tribes who attained to such notoriety in the recent history of Seistan may not be amiss. No reference at any length is necessary as to the ethnology, or origin, of these tribes as that has formed the subject of a separate note.

The Mir Kambar, who was the Commander-in-Chief of Malik Fath Ali's forces in his campaign against Nādir Shah, belonged to the Sarbandi family of whom he was the Chief, and the Kalāntar Muhammad Reza Khan alluded to in the account of that ill-fated expedition was, there can be little doubt, the second son of Mir Kambar. The usually accepted story about the family is that they have been settled in Seistan for not less than 300 years, and in course of time gradually obtained the predominance they attained afterwards in its affairs. They are reputed to be (and are considered so by the people of Seistan) the descendants of the famous Malik Ul Ashtar, the general of Ali the rival of Moaviyah, the Calif of the Bani Ommeya.

The elder son of Mir Kambar, named Kuchak, was killed in Kirman, perhaps during the reign of Sulemān Khan Kaiāni. The Sarbandis and Shāhrakis took their share in the troubles that that Malik had to put down.

Muhammad Reza Khan, the grandson of the Chief, who was blinded by the orders of Nadir Shah, is said to have been the eldest of five sons. He took a prominent part in expelling Malik Jallal-ud-din Khan. He died at a good old age it is said, and, according to Sir Frederik Goldsmidt, this event took place in 1848. This Muhammad Reza Khan is said to have dug the wells which bear his name, at the present time, to the south of Sehkoha. He is revered as a wise and benevolent ruler, and his grave was regarded as a ziārat by the people of Seistan; after his remains had been removed to Karbala.

Lutf 'Ali, eldest son of the deceased Chief, succeeded to his father's honours and property, but his uncle Ali Khan conspired against the young Chief, and he was seized and his sight destroyed. Ali Khan then became Chief.

This revolution was effected by means of a force of Afghans as Ali Khan had obtained help from the Sardar of Kandahar.

Ali Khan afterwards looked to the Persians for help to retain the power he had thus obtained, and he proceeded to Teheran and received a Princess of Royal Blood in marriage. After a stay of some time in the Capital, Ali Khan returned to Seistan. He built or enlarged the northern square tower of Seh-koha, which he called Burj-i-Falak-Sar, as a residence for his bride. But his tenure of power was destined to be short. Even as he had conspired against his nephew, two years or so after his return, he became the victim of a plot. The conspirators obtained entrance to his dwelling and put him to death before the eyes of the Princess, his wife, who returned to Persia after this event had taken place.

Strangely enough the murder of Ali Khan is reprobated very strongly by the common people of the country, who one and all declare that with the murder of Ali Khan the prosperity of Seistan departed for ever. They also attribute this deed to Tāj Muhammad, a nephew of the murdered Chief, who was raised to that position in his uncle's stead and thus directly benefited by the crime.

A daughter of Mir Khan, son of the Muhammad Reza Khan, whose sight was destroyed by Nādir Shah, was given in marriage to Malik Hamza Khan, the second son of Malik Bāhrām Khan.

The Nāhruis entered Seistan during the lifetime of Malik Bāhrām Khan.

Alam Khan was given the lands where now the villages of Aliābād, Kala-i-Kuhna and Kala-i-Nan exist, Burj-i-Alam or Kala-i-Alam Khan occupied the now deserted site of the last named village. The gradual reclamation of these lands has already been noticed, but as late as 1839 when Connolly visited Seistan, the reclamation was not completed, and he mentions that Burj-i-Alam as it seems always to have been called was situated on the edge of a Hamun. It was at that time regarded as being the principal town in the country.

Mir Alam Khan left many sons, but the commanding talents of his second son Sharif Khan raised him to the position of head of the family. Sharif Khan was the perfect type of a Sardār after the Baluch idea. He was lavish and profuse when he was in funds or property. Reputed to be a good swordsman and marksman; although he was more than a trifle given to ostentation; and full of words, he led the Baluch faction in Seistan, and became a power in the land.

The son of the Amir of Kāin of that day married the daughter of Sharif Khan, and Mir Māsum Khan, the present Deputy Governor of Seistan, is the son of this marriage. Always favourably disposed towards the Persians, his friendship enabled that power to take possession of Seistan; in his later years, however, Sharif Khan turned against the Persians, and caused a tumult in the country, which resulted, if anything, in the Persians getting a firmer grip on the country. This took place in or about 1896. Shortly after this, Sharif Khan died and his eldest son succeeded to his father's position, but not to the property of the latter, the greater part of which the Hashmat-ul-Mulk, his son-in-law, took possession of.

Said Khan, the successor of Sharif Khan, lived in the small village of Khwāja Ahmad on the Rud-i-Seistan. In 1904 after the Hashmat-ul-Mulk was called to Teheran to render an account of his stewardship, Said Khan himself went to the Court of the Shah.

Six villages which belonged to his father were, it was said, restored to Said Khan, and the latter was on his way back to Seistan when the report of his death was received in that country in April 1905.

His son succeeds to his property.

The Shāhrakis are said to have immigrated into Seistan some 900 years ago from Irāk. They are probably a remnant or the descendants of the old Khāriji element so strong at one time in Seistan and Kirman.

In the recent history of Seistan, the Shāhrakis have generally been in alliance with the Sarbandis as a counterpoise to the "Baluch" party formed by the Nāhruis and Sanjarānis.

The Shāhrakis have ever been noted for their courage, bodily strength and want of acuteness; and this has been well exemplified in the course of events in recent history. They have generally pulled the nuts out of the fire for the Sarbandis; the Chief of this clan or family having reaped the rewards such as they are.

The Shāhrakis once held a great extent of land along the Helmand, but they seem to have shared in the decadence of their country and to have declined with it. At one time the leaders of the population, or at any rate possessing more influence than any other section of the population, they are now inferior in influence to the Sarbandis or Nāhruis.

The Shāhraki holdings lie to the south of the Husenki system of canals; and to the north of the Rud-i-Seistan. Within this area are situated the greater portion of the lands they still own. The head-quarters of their Chiefs is in the village of Dashtak, a collection of ruinous houses, built on an outlying block of the dasht to the south of that place. Hence the name—the little dasht. In the seasons of flood, this village occupies an island and at low river an embankment leads up to the place from the mainland to the south of the village.

Muhammad Ali Khan, the Chief of this tribe or race, has not much influence; he leads the usual self-indulgent life of notables in Seistan. They are sunk in poverty. They have no ambitions, and they can do nothing. Petty intrigues at the small court of the Deputy Governor or the Kārguzār afford the only outlet for such ability these men possess.

The Sanjarānis are a much older tribe than their so-called genealogies cause them to appear. In comparison with other and neighbouring tribes whether in Seistan or in the Chāgai District, the men of this tribe contrast very unfavourably whether on the score of intelligence or energy.

Compared with either the Sarbandi or Nāhrui Chiefs, the present representative Khan Jahān Khan Sanjarāni is a boor, a semi-savage Baluch. His father Sardar Ibrahim Khan (who murdered Dr. Forbes)[1] ruled over the tribe for over 50 years. Forbes was murdered in 1840 or 1841, and Ibrahim Khan died as recently as the autumn of 1892.

Khan Jahān Khan, the father of Ibrahim Khan, had, it is said, four sons, Muin, Ali Khan, Ibrahim Khan, and Jān Beg. Each of the two elder sons came to a violent end. Muin, it is said, was murdered by his brother Ali Khan, and the latter was also murdered or killed in a skirmish, with his Naib, a Baluch of the Jamālzai tribe. This man had acquired a great deal of influence, and though he had served Ali Khan and his father before him for many years, the young Sardar fell out with him and is said to have attempted his life.

According to Sir Frederik Goldsmidt, Ali Khan is supposed to have died in 1840. He built the fortalice on the summit of the citadel mound at Bina-i-Kai, since when the site has been known as Nād Ali—so the story goes. It was at this place that 'Ali Khan was either murdered or wounded in a skirmish in the immediate vicinity of the mound.

Ibrahim Khan who possessed the Jahānābād property of the Sanjarānis, then became the head of this tribe.

At the death of Malik Bāhrām Khān the patrimony of the Kaiānis, the lands held by the members of that family formed but a narrow strip to the west of what is now the Pariun branch of the River Helmand. A straight line connecting the villages of Hamzabād and Sharifābād, and another straight line parallel to the first, passing through Jallālābād would include the greatest part of the possessions of that ancient family. This formed the prize on which the Sarbandis aided by the Shāhrakis on the one side and the Sanjarānis on the other were casting covetous glances. When Malik Jallāl-ud-din, the son and heir of the late Malik Bāhrām Khan, had succeeded in alienating all classes of his subjects, and his presence in Seistan was no longer necessary to anyone, but proved likely to be a hinderance, he was summarily ejected. Thereupon smaller villages along the western edge of the present Pariun area were seized by the Sanjarāni Sardar who also coveted Jallālābād, at that time a most valuable and desirable property. Jallālābād was also wanted badly by the Sarbandi Chief, Tāj Muhamad, and from all accounts the Sanjarānis

---

[1] Dr. Frederick Forbes, a Surgeon in the Hon'ble East India Company's Service, visited Seistan with the intention of passing through to Kandahar during our first occupation of that country. Dr. Forbes had previously travelled in Kurdistan. He was an enterprising officer and apparently a very close observer. His paper on his travels in Kurdistan is published in the Royal Geographical Society's Journal, Volume IX.

were proving too strong for him, and so he called in the Persians. This event took place in 1866 according to Sir Frederik Goldsmidt, and the Persians then gained the hold over Seistan which they continue to keep. Khān Jahān Khān, son of Ibrahim Khān, returned to Seistan in March 1903. He seemed to be in very poor circumstances. A few Ghulams and a few women formed his retinue. He was given the village of Siādak in the Mian Kangi and a few small hamlets in the vicinity of that village; and these form his appanage at the present time (1904).

Under a boorish and rough manner he conceals a considerable amount of shrewdness, but his manners are those of an ordinary Baluch nomad.

The Kaiāni family is however by no means extinct, as the geneological schemes in Plates IV and V will prove.

The representatives of the family, in Seistan, are however very unpromising. Pride will not allow them to give their daughters in marriage to other Chiefs in that country; and they are too poor and uninfluential to be able now to marry their daughters into great territorial families in the surrounding country, and it seems to be possible that the mortality of female infants is very considerable among the family. The daughters of this house are given in marriage to the members of the family in Seistan, Tabas, or Meshed, but even the money needed for a journey to the last two places is rarely forthcoming.

The best of all the rising generation of the Kaiānis is the young son of Malik Muhammad 'Azim Khān, Ḥaidar Ḳuli, who as yet has not taken to the use of opium or other narcotics; under the influence of which the descendants of this princely family forget the sordid details of their poverty and their fallen estate.

The late Governor, the Ḥashmat-ul-Mulk, is said to have nourished a grievance against the Kaiānis, and to have pressed heavily on them, either as a matter of policy or to satisfy a private grudge. It was whispered that the Kaiānis had rejected proposals for the hand of one of the daughters of the family made by the Governor.

The late Malik Gulzār Khān Kaiāni was compelled by the Ḥashmat-ul-Mulk to give one of his daughters in marriage to Kad Khuda, Tāj Muḥammad. This man belonged to the servile race or class called "Kul," and the blow thus inflicted on the pride of the Malik is said to have helped greatly to shorten his life. As far as it is possible to judge of such matters the Kaiānis have no prospect of ever rising to any position in their own country. This is due first of all not to a glaring deficiency of talent, but to their pride and the tenacity with which they cling to the memory of their former status. But, though they cannot or will not work, they do not beg in quite the same shameless and very open manner which is the prevailing custom even among the higher ranks of society in Seistan.

APPENDIX I.

Genealogy of the Kaiani Princes of Seistan from original sources 1904.

Plate I.

GENEALOGY OF THE KAIÁNI PRINCES OF SEISTAN.

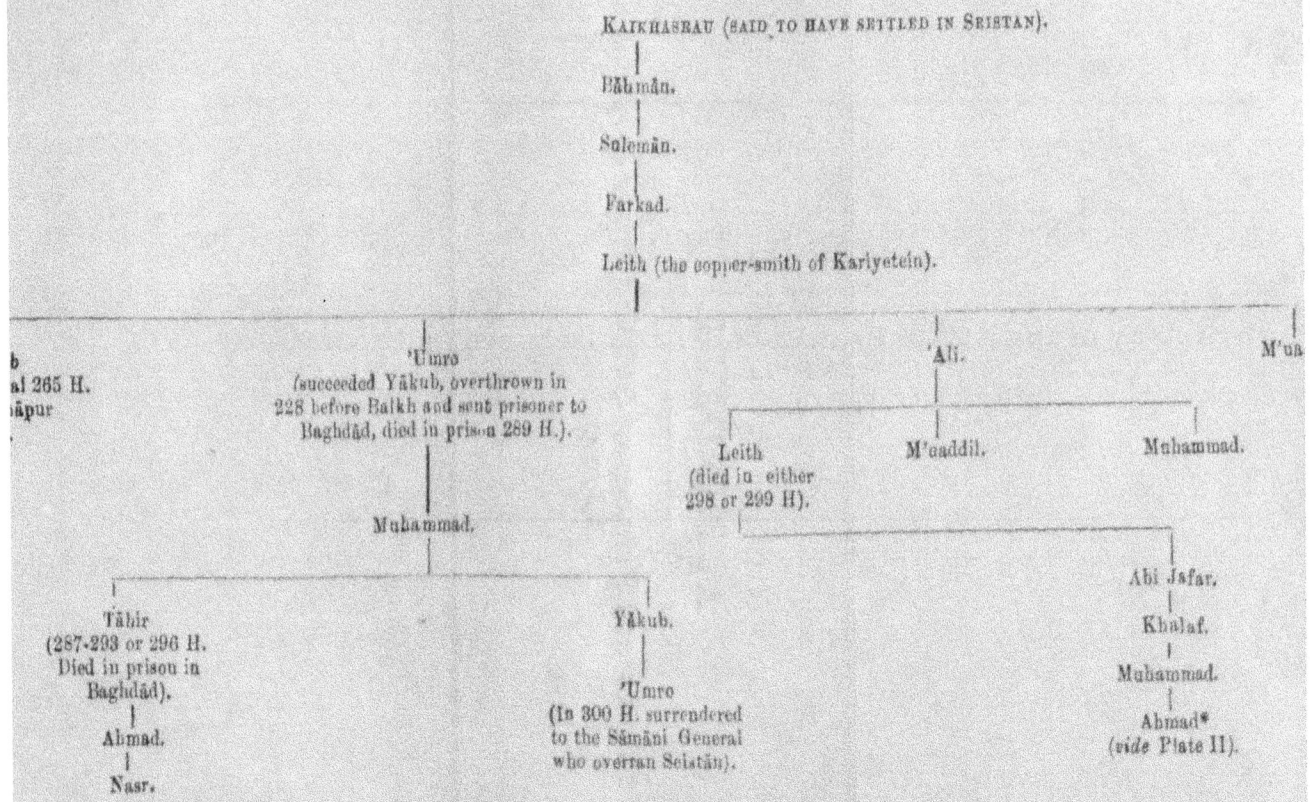

* In the Tarikh-e-Guzidah is said to have been the grandson of Táhir. This Prince heads the genealogy in Plate II.

(From notes by Major Raverty to his translation of the Tabakāt-i-Nāsiri and also from the Shijrat-ul-Mulūk.)

G. P. TATE

Plate II.

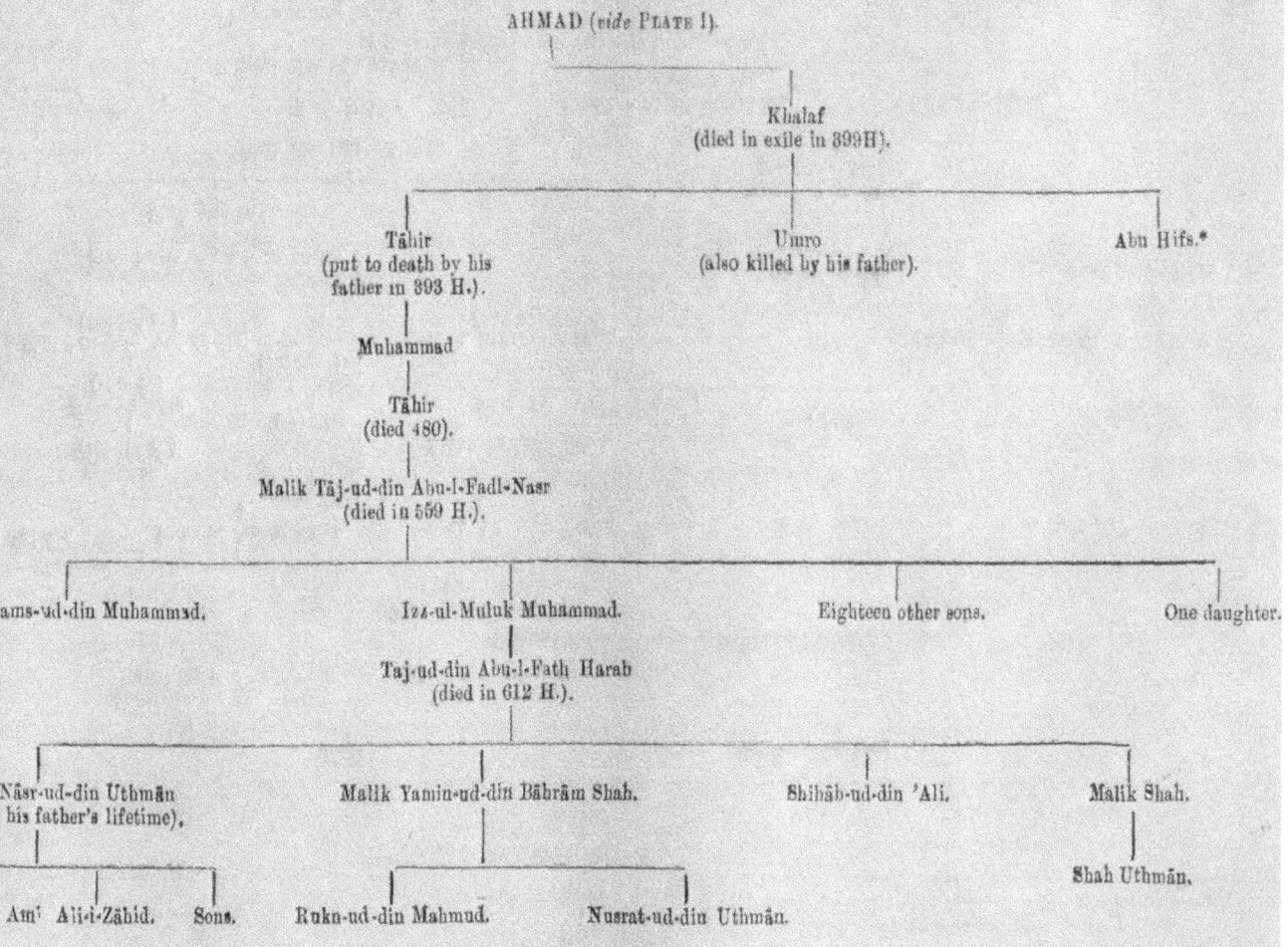

* This person heads the genealogy in Plate III.

Plate III.

E MS. IHYA-UL-MULUK TRANSLATED (AND ENTERED WITH HIS PERMISSION) BY C. A. ELLIS, ESQ., OF THE BRITISH MUSEUM.

ABU HIFS (vide PLATE II).

Ahmad.

Nasr.

Bahā-ud-daula Tāhir (died 481 H.).

Mihirbān (Shahryár).

Khalaf.

Ma'sud. — Shujā-ud-din Nasr.

Shams-ud-din Ali. (639-652 H.).

Mubāriz-ud-din Abu-l-Fath (died 641).

Nāsr-ud-din Muhammad. (652-728 H.).

'Ala-ud-Din.

Bahrām. Rukn-ud-din Mahmud. Shah Ali. Shah Nusrat. (728-731 H.). Shah Mirānshah. Shah Jahāngir. Shah Arsa

Izz-ud-din. (753-784 H.).

Kutb-ud-din Muhammad. (731-747).

Shahzada Muhammad.

Sultan Mahmud. (731-753 H.).

Kutub-ud-din. (784-788).

Taj-ud-din. (747-751 H.).

Shah Ali.

Shah-i-Shabān, Tāj-ud-din. (788-805 H.).

Shah Mahmud-al Hāji, died 854 H.

Kutb-ud-din, 806-822 H.

Shah Nasrat Shah Nasr-ud-din.

Shah-i-Shabán Shams-ud-din 'Ali (822-842-852 ?).

Shah Jalal-ud-din

Shah Abu Sa'id.

Nazim-ud-din Yāhyā. (842-852 ? 885 H.).

h Mahmud.

Shah Abu Ishāk, died 937.

Shah Ali Shams-ud-din Muhammad, 885.

Sultan Mahmud.

Ghiyās-ud-din uhammad.

Shah Haidar.

ah Husen.

* Malik Mahmud, 986-995 A. H. (Author of the Ihya-ul-Muluk Ser.: 1028 H.).

* (Vide Plate IV) as Ruling Prince.
† His tombstone was found in the shrine of the 44 Recluses in Zāhidān in Seistan in 1903.—G. P. T.

G. P. TATE,
M.R.A.S

PLATE IV.

MALIK MAHMUD, DIED 995 H. (*VIDE* PLATE III).

Jallalud-din-Mahmud Khan (995-1028 H).

Abu-l-Fath   *Malik Hamza, 1028-1055 (no issue besides one daughter).

Nusrat Khan, 1055-1085 H.

Fath Ali Khan, 1104-34 H.   *J'afir Khan, 1085-1104 H.

Assad Ullah Khan 1124-1139, as a pretender and subsequently as

Muhamad Husen Khan.   Shah Mahmud.

tf Ali   Fath Ali   Suleman Khan   Husen Khan   Muhammad Husen   Malik J'afir.   Abbas Khan.   Malik Rustan Khan.   Daughter Suleman
led in   (executed by   (born 1130,   (Sáni killed by   Khan.   Khan.
kran).   Nadir Shah).   died 1196 H.).   Afghans, 1160. H).

descendants said to be living in Tabas.

Muhammad Nasîr Khan   Bâhrâm Khan 1213-1217 H.   Daughter   Mahmud Khan.   Mahammad Kha
(1196-1212 H).   (as regent and afterwards   Ahmad Shah Durrâni.
                 as Ruler).   Sikandar Khan.   Malik Khan
Khan Jahan Khan   Ghulâm Haider Khan   (Deh Kahnum Bra
(killed in 1217 H. by   (decendants in India   see Plate V).
a fall from his horse).   see Plate V).

Malik Jalallud-din   Malik Hamza Khan   Ali Akbar (died in non-age).
(born 1210 H.   (born and died 1263 H.).
died 1274 H.).

Nasir Khan.   Husen Khan.   Abbas   Malik Gulzar—   Fath Ali Khan
                                                           (died 1313 H.), 1894-5 A. D.   (died 1322 H.)   (said to have gone to
hammad Azîm Khan   Lohrasp.   Malik Ali   1903 A. D.   India).
                                                                      deported to Sarakhs
dar Kuli   Ali Kuli   Daughters also   Nasir Khan.   Reza Khan.   Khan Jahan.   Aghâ Khan.   Husen Khan.   Abba
Seistan   in Seistan, 1904.   Issue.
1904.   Living at Daulatabad in the Miau Kangi in 1904.

Darwesh Khan.   Suleman Khan.   Amir Khan

Two daughters   Aghâ Khan   Seid Khan
(in 1904).   (Imbecile 1904).   (1904).

This plate has been drawn up on the authority of the Shijât-ul-Muluk and from information derived from members of this family now living in
ther of Malik Hamza and Jâfir Khan were princesses of Persia, their sons took precedence of the issue of a previous marriage. See text.—G. P. T.

G. P. TAT

M.

Plate V.

INDIAN BRANCH (KOHAT, PUNJAB).

GHULĀM HAIDAR (descended from Rustam, a son of Shah Mahmud—*vide* Plate IV).

- Khan Bahādar, Malik Jān Khān.
  - Ghulam Hasan Khān.
    - Sardar Ali Khān.
    - Murād Ali Khān.
    - Ramzān Ali Khān.
- Sher Muhammad Khān.
  - Zakriya Khān.
  - Zabardast Khān.
  - Sikandar Khān.
  - Faridum Khān.
  - Muhammad Yusuf Khān.
  - Sher Ali Khān.
  - 'Abdus Samad Khān.
    - Rustam Khan.
    - Abdur Rahman Khan.
      - 'Abdul 'Aziz.
      - 'Abdul Mahdud.
      - Abdul Mohin.
      - Abdul Wahāb.
      - Ghulam Ahmed Khān.
      - 'Abdul Gha— Khān.
  - 'Abdulla Khān.

…M (SEISTAN) FAMILY OF KAIANIS; ALSO DESCENDED FROM A SON OF RUSTAM, A SON OF SHAH MAHMUD—*vide* PLATE IV.

Malik Khān.
- Muhammad Amir Khān.
- Muhammad 'Ali Khān.
- Mansur Khān.

…MABAD FAMILY (SEISTAN) ARE DESCENDED FROM FATH 'ALI KHAN, THIRD SON OF MALIK HAMZA—*vide* PLATE IV.

Fath 'Ali Khān.
- Bahram Khān.
  - Issue.

These descents are entered from information supplied by members of the family now alive.

G. P. TATE,
M.R.A.S.

Part II.
THE TOPOGRAPHY OF SEISTAN.

The second line of walls, Sār-o-tār, from the outside.

(Frontis piece to part II.)

THE TOPOGRAPHY OF SEISTAN.

CHAPTER I.

THE physical record is the only source of information regarding the changes that have taken place in this country. These have left scars. Some of these scars have now faded and need very close observation before they can be recognised, as they have been so overlaid by traces of subsequent changes that it is a very difficult matter to arrive at any conclusion regarding the sequence of the geographical changes, which have left evidences on the face of the country. The ruins of Seistan do not (except in a very few instances) afford very much help in working out the history of the country; and local traditions and even the legends of later events need to be very carefully analysed, before they can be finally accepted. *General.*

Modern Seistan is one of that series of inland lake basins which form such a conspicuous feature in Central Asian geography, and of which the Caspian and Aral Seas are the most important. In Baluchistan and Persia, these inland lake basins occur in the tracts that lie to the north of the watershed of the Persian Gulf. The streams which take their rise in the southern slopes of the ranges that form that watershed reach the sea. The streams that flow from those ranges to the north, discharge into Hāmuns or landlocked basins. In Baluchistan there are the Hāmuns of the Lora and Māshkel. These are however, generally dry, clayey expanses, with here and there deposits rich in salt. The volume of water brought down by the Lora and Māshkel Rivers is not large enough to replenish the moisture that is lost by evaporation. The Hāmun-i-Seistan receives the discharge of three rivers, each of which drains a large tract of country, as their wide catchment areas are situated on the southern slopes of the great Hindu Kush Range, where the climate is favourable, and the springs are replenished yearly by snow and rain. These rivers in consequence fertilize large tracts of country along their banks, and save, in very exceptional years, discharge their surplus water into the Hāmun. The volume of these floods is not constant: as it varies from year to year, a larger or smaller area of the Hāmun is flooded; and in consequence of this the outline of the Hāmun basin (except in those places where cliffs form the shore) is subject to great alterations. *Inland Basins.*

There are, roughly speaking, four pockets or basins. The Hāmun-i-Puza to the east of the Sāwari; the Hāmun-i-Sāwari itself, in the north-west angle of the basin. Another to the north of the Koh-i-Khwājah, and between it *The four pockets basins or Hāmuns.*

and the Sāwari; and lastly the Daryā-i-Singi to the south of Koh-i-Khwājah. As water enters these great basins, it spreads into the smaller saucer-like depressions or *Chungs* within them.

Deltas.

For an unknown number of centuries the Helmand, the Farah Rud and the Khāsh Rud have deposited silt and built up, each of them, its delta. From the west, a wide glacis or talus descends from the hills. The deltas built up by the various channels of the Helmand and the other rivers have been thrust forward and have formed a contact with the small deltas which exist at the embouchure of each of the *wadis* that discharge the rarely occurring floods which run down from the western hills into the Hāmun.

Ridges forming roads across the Hāmun.

Where these opposite deltas touch, a ridge or Lurg is formed. There are three of these. The first is formed by the contact of ancient silt deposits formed by old channels of the Helmand and Farah Rud. The high road from Seistan to Juwein follows this ridge. Next is the ridge called the Kucha-i-Afzalābād. This has been formed by the ancient silt deposit of the Helmand on the east and the much smaller delta formed by the River of Bandān on the west. The latter only occasionally contains water. The third is the deposit of silt formed by a very ancient channel of the Helmand, and thrust out against the smaller delta formed by the streams that issue from the Baloch-ap and Trushpap Passes, in the western hills.

These ridges are gently swelling, and it is not possible to detect them with the naked eye; but they are the last dry land that is covered by highest floods and they are first to appear when the level of the water decreases.

The high road between Seistan and Birjand or Meshed crosses the Hāmun Basin by the Kucha-i-Afzalābād, and this is also followed by the Persian telegraph line. When this Lurg is submerged, travellers and their effects have to be ferried across on rafts of reeds. The third, and southernmost of the three ridges, forms a barrier between the Hāmun-i-Seistan and the Gaud-i-Zireh, which can only be surmounted by the water in the former, in seasons of highest floods and of the strongest wind.

The opposite deltas meet in undulating lines of contact and there, where the lowest levels would probably be found, exist a series of lateral communications between Hāmun and Hāmun, and one chung and another.

As the volume of water brought down in flood by the Helmand is greater than that contributed by the rivers of Farah and Khāsh, and much more so than the contributions of the *wadis* that descend from the west; their undulating lines of contact and the channels they form, are closer to the western and northern shore of the Hāmun.

Chung.

The re-entrant angles of these deltaic fans enclose saucer-like basins forming *chungs*, and where a number of these run into one another they form large expanses of clear water called *Hāmun*. Both Chung and Hāmuns being fringed by dense growths of reeds and bulrushes where the soil is congenial to the growth of aquatic plants.

While the reeds grow in the shallows, those tracts along the edge of the Hāmun which are subject to annual inundation, but are not always under water, are called *Āshkin* and are covered with a species of that coarse grass. This is an excellent fodder for cattle. Āshkin.

The Hāmun-i-Seistan hitherto considered is merely that portion of the great basin which is situated within the present limits of that country. This occupies only a part of a great tract of hollow land, whose southern shores are formed by the edge of the northern glacis of the Koh-i-Sultan and of the Kacha Koh hills. The western limit of the extensive tract is the glacis of the Palangān hills, and the long slope that descends eastwards from the Bandān hills. The Hāmun-i-Seistan.

If we take the delta of the Helmand in the widest sense of the term we find that it fills a very large area of this depression. The Gaud-i-Zireh to which allusion has been made is nothing more than a large pocket, situated at the extreme eastern part or end of this great depression. Gaud-i-Zireh.

The deepest channel of the Shela (which is a continuation of the Helmand) affords a passage in favourable years for water to reach the Gaud, and it marks the undulating line of contact between the south edge of the great Helmand Talus or delta and the opposite slope of the depression. The Shela.

This great Talus of the Helmand is Seistan proper. It consists of alluvial soil and "dasht" or a gravelly plateau, in the proportions about two-thirds to one-third of the latter.

We have seen what the southern and western limits of this tract are. Its eastern one is the scarp of the great Talus which descends towards the south from the skirts of the mountainous districts of Zamin-i-Dāwar and Ghur.

This Talus is drained by the Khāsh and Farah Rud, as well as by other streams of less importance, such as the Khuspās Rud, which interposes between the basins of the rivers of Farah and Khāsh. The Hārut Rud, to the west of the former, receives a small portion of the drainage from these extensive steppes. But the Hārut Rud is not replenished by the streams, that rise in the hills to the west of its course, and only in years of good rainfall do more than one or two floods make their way through its channel to the Sāwari pocket of the Seistan Hāmun. Khāsh, Farah, Hārut and Khuspās Rud.

The Khāsh Rud emerges from the hills at a place called Dilārām. This is a small district containing several villages. Between Dilārām and Seistan, equidistant from both, there is the small fertile district of Khāsh. Between the latter and Seistan, although there is a certain amount of cultivable soil, on either bank of the river, there is no place of importance, below Khāsh. The cultivable land lies in loops or bays between the Dasht and the bed of the stream, each of which has its distinctive name.

A series of fertile districts, Kala-i-Kah, Farah, Sabzawār (the ancient Isfirār) connect Seistan with the great and fertile areas within the Herat district; and to the west of this lie the districts of Khaf, and further away country around Meshed.

Owing to its situation Seistan has always possessed a permanent supply of water which could be diverted for purposes of irrigation. It was, therefore, and still is, a much more prosperous and fertile country than any of the intermediate links that connected it with the more extensive countries to the north and east.

In a direct line, a strip of waterless desert some 50 miles wide, divided the district of Khāsh from the fertile districts on the Helmand around Girishk, or Kala-i-Bist and Kandahar.

Tracts to south and south-west of Seistan. To the south and south-west expanses of desert or semi-desert tracts interpose between the fertile districts of Bām, and Makran and Seistan.

To the west, there is the mountainous country of Kuhistan, and the Kāināt.

Isolated situation of Seistan. By reason of its geographical situation, Seistan has always been isolated, to a great extent, from neighbouring countries, and this has influenced its history and civilization. These geographical conditions have prevailed from the earliest ages. At various times the course of the Helmand within the delta had been subject to change, and these alterations of its course have affected various parts of the delta modifying the conditions of human existence in each; but these changes have been purely local, and have not influenced the general configuration of the country to any great appreciable extent.

Progressive dessication in ancient lake. A mental survey of the country of Seistan shows very clearly the process of dessication that has taken place. That the lake basin was at one time filled to a greater depth with water is clearly indicated, and the present extent of water in the Hāmun covers barely a third part of the area of the ancient lake.

This is no doubt the reason of the fable that the ancient lake of Seistan was filled by genii acting according to the orders of the celebrated Pir Khizr: as this task occupied but half a day, the country was called Nimroz. All the legends of saints after whom the highest summits of mountains are named in the country to the south of Seistan are associated with earth movements.

Ramadthan Ghaibi and Pulchota disappeared in chasms that opened in the earth's surface and closed after those mythical personages had been received within. Pir Sultan vanished into the Koh-i-Sultan in an outburst of flame. Sheikh Husen was also swallowed by the earth opening; and this is supposed to have taken place on the peak now called after him. These ancient legends become significant when we find them associated with localities

THE TOPOGRAPHY OF SEISTAN.

which are either close to or actually show traces of having been centres of volcanic activity.

The alluvial deltas which form the greater part of this country, were undoubtedly at one time under water. The volume of water contributed by the rivers which drained into the lake must have been very much greater. As the discharge of these rivers diminished the lake would naturally contract and in the course of countless centuries the present stage in the process of dessication has been arrived at.

Long lines of shingly beaches are found at the head of deep bays and gulfs which the ancient lake had eaten into the gravelly plateau which represent, perhaps, the delta of the Helmand during geological periods of time. These beaches can now best be seen on the bays that indent the shores of the Sāwari-Hāmun, in the process of formation. At the present embouchure of the Farah Rud to the north of the river's channel a beach of shingle has been piled up to a height of fully 10 feet above the present level of water in the Hāmun. *Ancient beaches.*

Beaches of gravel and coarse shingle are overlaid by the alluvial soil in the northern delta and here and there where the latter has been removed by the action of water or by the efforts of man, portions of the long buried beaches are exposed to view, and gravel and shingle are found to exist many feet below the alluvial surface. One such beach was found close to the mound of ancient Shahristan; what was probably a continuation of this beach was exposed by the cutting made by the Afghans in 1902 immediately above the bifurcation of the Pariun and Nād Ali channels of the river. One of the surveyors attached to the mission brought a stone 1 lb. avoir. in weight from a beach about 6 or 7 miles to the south of Khwābgāh. The latter being about 8 miles higher up stream than the first named beach, it is only to be expected that the boulders and stones would be coarse and heavier in the higher beach. The water worn stones which are so common in the country around Sar-o-Tar are probably from some ancient each overlaid by silt, and have been turned up by the plough. The succession of those beaches or banks of water worn gravel and shingle prove that there has been at a very ancient period a subsidence of the waters of the lake as each of these beaches marks a stage in that subsidence. This was apparently followed by an increase in the water and in the discharge of the rivers during which the present alluvium has been laid down. This was followed by the dessication which has reduced the lake to its present size.

These beaches have been formed, as they are now being formed, by the action of the water under the influence of the strong gales that prevail in this country during the summer. The shingle is derived to a great extent from the cap of conglomerate which covers the clay formation of the Dasht; as the water eats into the clay, masses of the latter subside and the conglomerate is broken up by the fall and speedily disintegrated by the water acting on the coarse matrix. The fine water-worn pebbles are released and distributed gradually by the unceasing wash of the waves as they enter the bays and indentations. Shingle is then in course of time washed inwards from the headlands and piled in orderly and regular curves on the shelving slopes at the head of the bays. Then alluvial soil collects behind these bars of shingle, and the latter become the lakeward face of a small natural reclamation or plateau.

In succeeding ages, after the water had receded to its present comparatively restricted area, the scour of the wind has removed the alluvial soil and the beach of shingle stands by itself, with beautifully dressed sides some 10 or more feet, perhaps, above the level of the ground in its neighbourhood. In some of the indentations of the geological delta of the Helmand, these shingle beaches are very remarkable. They invariably merge into the general slope of the enclosing head-lands and extend in a perfectly regular curve round the head of the indentations.

The ridges are slightly troughed and this lends the appearance to the shingle bars of having been constructed artificially, to serve as an acqueduct. The natives of the country in consequence regard these as the works of men's hands, and say, they were built by Rustam, for purposes of irrigation, or to act as dams.

The clays of Seistan.

The clays of Seistan are well worth studying. Even in the alluvial delta of the present day there is a great diversity. Tracts of loam or sandy soil are bounded by tracts where the soil is hard, stiff, white clay. The former is always clothed with vegetation, dwarf kahur, camel thorn, tamarisk, and salt bush. The latter is often almost destitute of vegetation. Except in a wind scoured rift in its surface, where sand has collected, or where some slight obstacle has enabled sand to gather round it, the hard smooth surface of the stiff clay does not allow wind born seeds to find a resting place upon it and to germinate. The clay is of two sorts. A friable variety containing large traces of gypsum, and a stiff variety, which is almost as hard as stone. The inhabitants call the latter *Sir* or *Kim*. It is laid in horizontal beds. A pale reddish brown alternating with a pale greenish grey. The strata are sometimes so thin as to be measured in inches, brown succeeding grey, a series of thin lamine of either, followed by strata several feet in depth. That part of the great Talus which forms the eastern and northern boundary of the Seistan Basin, is formed very extensively of this hard Kim or Sir. The action of water appears to harden this particular variety of clay. In many parts of the Basin of Seistan bordering on the Hāmun, there are isolated bluffs of Kim, which seem to have resisted the general subsidence that appears to have taken place all round them when the depression of Seistan was formed.

Some of these isolated bluffs are very nearly the same height above sea-level, and quite as high relatively as the scarp of the Talus to the east of the alluvial delta of the country.

The isolated hills of the Koh-i-Khwājah, and Koh-i-Chako[1] appear, so far as it is possible for an untrained observer to judge, to be formed of a lava cap, very nearly horizontal, resting on horizontal (or nearly so) strata of Kim. The stratum of the latter immediately below the lava cap, in the case of the Koh-i-Chako, is of a bright red or orange colour, as though it had been baked. At the western extremity of the Koh-i-Khwājah, there is a subsidence of the lava cap apparently caused by the partial settling of the clay (Kim) on which it rests. The clays of the dasht are however covered with a cap of conglomerate comprised, generally, of fine water-worn pebbles set in a coarse matrix, which disintegrates very readily.

This cap covers a layer of friable clay. The order in the descending scale seems to be friable clay, then Kim. And below the surface of the ground in wells, the water bearing stratum is a bed of either very sandy loam, or an almost pure sand about 6 to 8 feet thick underlying a stratum of hard clay the impermeable stratum below, again, being Kim of the densest and hardest variety. This alternation of extremely hard, with a softer stratum cause wells to fall in after a time unless they are lined with tamarisk boughs, and wattles. The same sequence of strata of varying densities is found on the plateaux themselves. The wind scours out the more friable clay, and scores deep grooves in the stratum where it is most exposed to the force of the gales; giving a water-worn appearance to the cliffs, and in course of time causing heavy falls of clay blocks on the under cut faces. The line of springs high up on the scarp of the dasht, overlooking the bay, at the foot of Koh-i-Chako, is due to a softer stratum existing between a hard and dense upper and lower layer of Kim. This dasht slopes gradually down towards the Hāmun, and the subsoil water oozing through the more permeable stratum finally makes its appearance on the face of the cliff, where the bluffs of Kim below the softer stratum are moistened by the dripping of water which finally reaches the beach below, and forms shallow puddles. A growth of reeds and tamarisk bushes find nourishment on the outer face of the water-sodden stratum of clay; and where ravines have cut back into the dasht, there is a tiny flow of water in their beds, which collects in the hollows and forms miniature pools and rivulets among the tamarisk bushes and clumps of reeds, which grow in the watercourses and along their banks. This water is too saline to be of use, animals even refuse to touch it.

Action of the strong prevailing wind.— In parts of Seistan the power of the wind is very well illustrated. Over large areas almost the whole of the upper layer of friable clay apparently has been eroded, exposing the level floor of Kim that lay beneath it. In certain areas the upper strata has not been removed altogether. Where layers or

---

[1] Similar lava capped hills exist in the hills to the west of the Hāmun, and in the direction of Neti, and also to the west of the Palangān Mountains. These table-topped hills are invariably called Sam-Kuh by the Baluchis. *Cf.*—The Sam-Kuh to the north of Amir Chah wells (Koh-i-Sultan) examined in 1899 by E. Vredenburg, Esq.

bands of harder material have existed, they have offered a resistance to the action of the wind, and patches of unequal density have been worn into long mounds whose strike is the same as the direction from which the wind blows at the present day. The windward ends of these mounds are bluff and comparatively rounded while their leeward extremities taper off to a fine point decreasing in height, as well as in thickness very rapidly.[1] As the softer clay between is scoured away by the wind, these mounds act as bench marks, such as are left by railway engineers in excavations in order to enable the latter to be measured up. Where such mounds are numerous, the tract looks exactly like an enormous cemetery filled to overflowing with the graves of giants. Many of these mounds are fully 15 to 40 feet in height, so that to remove the softer clay, by a process of erosion, and by wind action alone, must have required very many centuries of time. The regular direction of these bench marks proves that for unknown ages of time, the direction of the strong summer gales has been unchanged, and they have blown exactly from the quarter from which the wind sets in now.

Plains of hard white clay or Kim.

The floor of Kim thus exposed to view is so hard that it is a very difficult matter to drive wooden tent pegs to any depth at all. The latter unless made of very hard wood split or lose their points. The hard white clay, of which mention has been made as existing in the modern delta of the Helmand, is also of very nearly the same density.

The plain thus formed is a very striking feature in the country, as it is almost destitute of vegetation. In some of the deserted canals that traverse its expanse, sand has collected, and in these a struggling growth of Tā gaz, the desert tamarisk, or Salsola, manages to find nourishment. With such exceptions there is nothing to break the monotony of the expanse of white clay. Almost truly level, its white hard surface reflects the rays of the sun almost like a mirror. The action of the climate produces a small "crackle" such as is seen on the surface of white porcelain. It is the existence of the underlying stratum of Kim that makes the wells which the Baluchis dig hard and almost impervious to water. The subsoil water collects in the slight undulations that exist in its surface, and wherever a well hits off one of these pockets, a fairly permanent supply is obtained, as water drains into the hollow from all sides, percolating through the permeable stratum which overlies the Kim. An examination of dry wells, reveals the impermeable stratum in all its strength, and any attempt to pierce it shows at once the difference between it and the stratum above. Flakes and chips are all that come up in the basket, instead of loose material.

Method by which waters of lake are dispersed.

The bed of the Hāmun Basin, also, has in the course of centuries become very thoroughly puddled, and with the lower stratum of impermeable Kim

---

[1] Shaped like a fish viewed from above its back.

has rendered absorption almost non-existent. The diminution of water in the lake area is due perhaps so very nearly altogether to evaporation that the loss by absorption may be regarded almost as a negligible quantity. Evaporation owing to the heat of summer, and the strong north-westerly gales, goes on very rapidly. The lake presents a large surface to the influence of these agents, and as the average depth of water is not great, the loss of moisture is very rapid. Unless replenished by floods, the fall in the level of water is rapid, and by August the "Lurg" or ridges are practicable and can be used to cross the lake. Then the smaller depressions in the floor begin to dry, and this process once set on foot goes on very rapidly, as the depth of water decreases until at length, only the deeper and larger areas have any water at all in their basins. Fish die in shoals, and the edges of the dried Chungs are fringed with the remains of thousands of small fish.

In 1902 the Helmand ran dry. For a space of about 62 days there was no water at all in its bed, and the Hāmun including the Sāwari basin (which is the deepest of all the basins in the Hāmun) was perfectly dry. Not only did the inhabitants of Seistan flock to this drying basin for the fish, which had collected therein and died in thousands as the water gradually evaporated, but they were able also to ransack the ancient town of Sāwari, whose foundations are ordinarily several feet under water. Coins, copper seals—all highly oxidised, were obtained for sale, having been picked up among the débris of ruined walls, and crumbling brick work. Those who have seen these remains declare them to represent a town of considerable size, burnt bricks having been used very largely in the construction of the walls and foundations. In other parts of the Hāmun area, traces of wells, lined with burnt bricks, have been found to exist when the water has receded and exposed the floor of the basin to view. Brick kilns also have been discovered, well within the annual flood limits. Owing to long submersion the bricks have disintegrated and exist only as dust or by small fragments, much worn and softened by water. Only vitrified portions of the kilns preserve any coherence. These ancient kilns are recognisable very clearly by the russet colour of the crumbled bricks, and the existence of masses of vitrified clay, some of which closely resembles the refuse of smelting furnaces.

Description of Hāmun when dry in 1907.

A margin on the east and southern shores of the Hāmun contains the debateable area which is liable to inundation when the level of the water rises above a certain height; or is dry, or nearly dry, land when the general level of the floods fall short of that standard. In the case of the period of the highest known flood, and that of low or moderate flood, the area between the extreme limits can be expressed in square miles. Within this debateable area, ruins of ancient forts, canals, and dwellings, and tombs abound. Shapeless though they be, worn by the action of damp, and of water itself in seasons

Area of inundation.

of high floods, with their salient angles ground away by the action of the wind, yet the original purpose they were intended to fulfil is very clearly indicated. Burnt brick or Pise work and sundried brick are alike covered with a thick coating of saline efflorescence which gives a curious winter-like appearance to the landscape. The white and glittering expanses of saline flats are fringed with salsola and tamarisk, the dark coloring of their foliage giving greater prominence to the white crust of saline matter, and they bear undeniable traces of man's handiwork and of his occupation.

Works of man in inundated area and inference therefrom.

It is impossible to suppose that human beings could have placed their dwellings, or made permanent works like the system of canals, the remains of which can now be traced, in a situation where they would be exposed to inundation. The presence of such remains as those just described proves that the localities which are now subject to the variations of flood level in bad and good years, were at one time safe from the effects of floods.

The ancient canals were not open ditches, almost obliterated with débris, but regular and well established works of considerable magnitude, with their channels, and spoil bank above the level of the lands they at one time irrigated. As the volume of water discharged by the Helmand, and the rivers of Farah and Khāsh cannot have decreased appreciably within the past 1,000 years, and perhaps not for many an equal period, previous to that time, the inference is that the rivers themselves have altered their embouchures and an attempt will be made to prove this with respect to the Helmand and the Farah Rud.

NOTE.—The Basin of Seistan has been formed by a succession of subsidences of the earth's crust there. In the lowest part of all, the Koh-i-Khwajah stands as a bench mark ; its summit level with the lofty dasht to the east of the Basin. The chimney, and alteration of the underlying Kim by heat, etc., has rendered the lower strata stable. The lines of cliff surrounding the Basin, are the original lines of fracture, modified of course by climatic influences. The cap of friable conglomerate covering plateaus of varying altitudes is the same everywhere, and its differences of position can only be due to subsidences, one after another, that have taken place. The exposed faces of the cliffs show only one stratum of conglomerate at the top of the most recent of all the strata composing the Dashts. No fossils were discovered. In parts the strata contain nodules of a coarse calcareous lime.—G. TATE.

CHAPTER II.

The Deltas of the Farah and Khāsh Rud, and a description of the Lake.

More interesting, and of much greater importance than any attempt to identify ancient sites and locate places named by ancient authors, is the investigation of changes that have taken place in the country of Seistan, that in course of time have been brought about by the rivers themselves which feed the great Lake. <small>Alterations in river beds.</small>

The Helmand having the largest discharge has been responsible to a much greater degree for such changes, and as its effects have been considerable, affecting the balance of population, they can better be considered last and at leisure.

The Khāsh Rud almost ceases to exist as a river before it reaches the easternmost end of the Seistan Lake Basin. As soon as it emerges from the control of the dashts below Khāsh, its bed dwindles away in the midst of a wide clay plain which it has itself, in past ages of time, helped very materially to build up. Its flood waters spread over this plain, and fertilize it. The surplus flows into a depression where it lodges until evaporation dissipates its accumulated volume after the season of floods has passed. The tract then subjected to annual inundation is known as the Āshkin. It affords pasture for herds of cattle as the water evaporates. At its southern end there is a saucer like basin the Chung-i-Darāzgu into which several canals from the Helmand empty their surplus water. Owing to this there is generally water in this *Chung* when the remainder of the Āshkin is dry. From the earliest ages of which there is any information available the discharge of the River of Khāsh has been diverted very largely for cultivation, and as it has no continuous flow of water its delta presents no features which claim especial notice. <small>The Delta of the Khāsh Rud.</small>

The case of the Farah Rud is very different. In the course of ages it has cut a passage through the broad talus that forms the glacis of the hills towards the north, and emerges beyond the last scarp of that talus which overlooks the basin of the Seistan depression. This scarp is a well-defined and prominent feature in the country, and it represents the southern limit of the high talus. South of it there are merely islands, and under features of the higher plateau, forming an intermediate step between it and the lower levels in which the lake is placed. This intermediate terrace extends in a wedge whose greatest length is about 16 miles, and the river of Farah emerges on the delta in the re-entrant angle formed by the eastern edge of the wedge of lower dasht where it merges into the higher. <small>The Delta of the Farah Rud.</small>

At this point the Farah Rud leaves the shelter of the higher glacis, and emerges from a gorge, about half a mile wide. The eastern dasht immediately above the riverbed, is low, and is a step or underfeature of the higher ground further to the east; which forms an angle or bay, whose limit is a line of well marked cliffs, recognisable from afar. The western side of the gorge is a line of perpendicular cliffs some 200 feet high, formed by a huge block of dasht, capped with gravel at the foot of which the river flows. Upon the south-eastern corner of the plateau is placed the fortress of Lāsh, while the town of Juwein, the headquarters of the civil administration of the district, is situated to the east of the river upon the lower dasht the under feature already alluded to.

To the south of the gorge, there is a small extent of alluvial soil beyond which there is a tongue of slightly higher ground formed of a low gravel-topped plateaux. Originally these, no doubt, extended up to the lower dasht terraces that exist further to the west, and from which they are now separated by a narrow strip of alluvium. The low plateau has in course of time been cut up by the ancient channels of the Farah Rud of which there appear to have been three. All of these in turn discharged their waters into the Hāmun-i-Puza. The first of these ancient channels, close to the modern village of Lāftān, turns almost due east, and its course is now distinguished by a broad belt of alluvium in which there are ruins and several very large cypress trees, both of which, and more especially the latter, show that at one time this old bed of the Farah Rud, after it ceased to be a river, was occupied and cultivated by means of a canal. The second of the ancient riverbeds takes off from almost abreast of the ancient site of Dārg; and in its lower end is the hamlet of Zāhak, inhabited temporarily by Sārunis, whose dwellings are concealed from view by the group of ruins which show that it had also been a village in past ages.

The third ancient bed also takes off from the patch of alluvial soil to the east of Dārg; and makes its way through the low dasht issuing forth on the east in the midst of ruins; the remains of a more considerable and older collection of alluvial lands around the village of Sālihān. This is a modern hamlet.

These ancient river beds are marked by bands of alluvial soil which, whether bare or sparsely covered with coarse grass, are very easily recognised by the difference of colour between the soil in them, and that of the gravelly plateau[1] through which they had made their way, and which form a low but marked bank on either side of the alluvial.

The largest of these beds is the first. It is wider, and the soil is not clothed with the coarse grass, which springs up so readily in the light clay of the district. The bare appearance of the clay in this ancient bed, shows that the river when it flowed in that direction, deposited a finely divided alluvium, and that the silt was chiefly composed of the scour from strata of hard clay

---

[1] These mark the lowest stage in the subsidence of the country in which the gravel or conglomerate cap of the dasht formation can be recognised. The Farah Rud and its ancient channels (like the Helmand) follows lines of fracture.

or Kim. The absence of vegetation on this older clay has already been noticed and accounted for. Below the southernmost of these ancient channels, the low gravel-covered plateau sinks down and disappears under the loam which forms the delta of the river in the more recent stages of its existence. A small patch of gravel a short distance to the north of the ruins of Kolmārut, is the last appearance of the low plateau.

The Farah Rud of the present day flows rather more towards the wedge of dasht that forms the under feature of the higher plateau, and projects beyond it towards the south. The course of the stream is a little to the west of south. To within a distance of about 5 or 6 miles above its more recent delta, the shallow bed of the river deepens, and in its final length of 5 or 6 miles, it attains to a depth of about 40 feet. Here it is deeper than the Hāmun-i-Sāwari into which its flood waters discharge, and, in consequence, the last 6 miles of the Farah Rud is one deep pool of standing water, fringed with a growth of poplar, willow, and tamarisk; the long reaches of clear, still water, set in a mass of foliage, combined with the width of the river, appear all the more beautiful by the commonplace nature of the surrounding country— either wind scoured and bleak plains of alluvial soil, or the still more unhappy expanses of saline flats, or beds of reeds.

In the last 7 or 8 miles the Farah Rud doubles back upon its former course; to such an extent is this the case, that if the axes of these beds were prolonged so that they might meet, the angle enclosed between them would fall short of a right angle by as much as 20 degrees or more. The direction of the last portion is towards the northwest. Unlike the opposite shore of the delta of the Helmand the alluvial delta of the Farah Rud has a well-defined limit, beyond which no flood has probably ever been known to encroach. Even in 1885, the last of the "years of Noah," the waters of the Hāmun did not rise above this coastline. Beyond this, that is, to the east, and south there is no defined limit which any one can point to and say that it is the edge of the Hāmun. A succession of saline flats shelve away into the "Naizar." The flats are covered with the vestiges of ancient civilization. Weatherworn tumuli of various sizes mark where in olden days there stood the dwellings of mankind.

There is a reason that will account for the traces of human handwork that exist on the floor of the Hāmun and which are now only revealed when the water in it fails completely. The deltaic fan, that has been thrust forward by the Helmand till it met and overlaid the lower portion of the delta of the Farah Rud, was formed when the former discharged its full volume of water, or the greater part of it, directly to the northern portion of the Hāmun. And when this discharge ceased, the delta would at once be laid bare, and exist as an ordinary expanse of dry land, available for occupation by human beings. It is quite clear that this occupation did take place, and as the traces of it are

Work of man on the floors of the Hāmun.

now covered either annually, or always, with water, the inference is very clear that there must have been some great changes (within the delta area) of the channels by which the flood waters of the Helmand found an outlet into the Hāmun. These changes must have been sufficiently great to allow of a large portion of the present Hāmun, existing for many generations, and probably for many centuries, as dry land. There is evidence to show that this change occurred more than once in historical times.

The Delta of the Farah Rud.

Before, however, the discussion of the changes in the course of the Helmand (within its delta) is taken up, it will be more convenient to finish the description of the Farah Rud and its delta.

The banks of the Farah Rud, close to its mouth form a perceptible lip, sloping away from the river, and this is rendered all the more prominent by the fact that a line of sand dunes now stationary, and covered with a thick growth of small tamarisk, extends along the banks from the point where the stream leaves the comparatively defined line of the coast up to about 2 miles short of its actual mouth.

The sand dunes that are heaped up on the right bank are higher than those along the opposite bank. They form a low ridge which is recognisable from a distance of several miles. The sand is coarser, and of a darker colour than the usual desert sand, but it is so thickly covered with small tamarisk that the material is concealed by this growth, and the light reddish brown of their twigs and stems gives an appearance to the dunes of being mounds of gravel or of brick débris. Many modern spill-water channels break through the lip of the stream bed, and lose themselves in the low-lying ground along the Hāmun Basin. One of these passes by the ruins of Peshāwarān and is lost in the Hāmun area, not far from the Tapa (mound) of Khārān. A second spill-water channel takes off from the elbow, where the change of direction takes place in the last reaches of the stream, and this channel dies away among the low-lying saline flats and hollows which form the Hāmun area to the west of the mound of Khārān. The third spill-water channel is much smaller and disappears also in the Hamun area. The raised edge along the banks continue up to the present mouth of the Farah Rud, and is thickly wooded with tamarisk jungle and poplar willows. The top of the bank above the level of the standing water in the bed is some 130 feet in places.

Between the mouth of the Farah Rud and the permanent coastline to the east of the former, there is an expanse of alluvial soil which rests against a high gravel beach. The latter is some 10 feet above the winter water level (in 1904) of the Hāmun-i-Sāwari; and acts like a revetment behind which an accumulation of soil has taken place. There seems at one time to have been a spill channel that took off at the elbow of the Farah Rud and followed the toe of the coast (which here becomes more pronounced) in the direction of the Hāmun. This channel is now almost entirely obliterated. The crest of the beach just alluded to is some 5 feet above the soil behind it, and the plateau thus formed, close to the beach is covered with Bannu grass; while tamarisk thickets line the junction beween alluvial soil and the shingle. This beach curves round in an irregular curve, and becoming less marked as it extends southwards, finally disappears under the alluvial soil some half a mile from the left bank of the stream. The Farah Rud has cut a passage through it, and owing to this the river, in winter at least, is easily fordable at its mouth, although a very short distance upstream of this ford the depth is too great to admit of this being done. On the left or west of the river, to trace the continuation of the old beach is not at all easy, but on the opposite bank it slopes down in steps to the present beach of the Hāmun, and there are faint indications of a second old beach, or bar of shingle in the rear again of that just described.

The Farah Rud appears to have flowed in its present course for very many centuries. The older channels probably date to periods of which there is no record. The ancient canals of which so many traces exist, among other mounds within the present Hāmun area, evidently were fed by the river as it now exists. The canals which are to be found among the later ruins also take off from the river as it was found to exist in 1904. *Ancient canals in the Delta of the Farah Rud.*

Watercourses no doubt followed the course of the three ancient river beds and distributed the water in the tract along the east shore of the Hāmun-i-Puza. The only difference between this very ancient canal system and that in use when Peshāwarān was an inhabited town is that the latter appear to have taken off from the river lower down than did the former. The more ancient canals were not only much more numerous, but they seem to have been more elaborate and carefully made. Their distributaries carried the water in a bold curve eastward to irrigate the lands close to Sālihān. The Zahak, and part of the Sālihān, lands were undoubtedly fed by means of canals following the old beds that debouched upon those tracks.

There is a very great space of time separating the oldest ruins of canals and mounds, and the later ruins which are now thickly studded over the plain above the level of the flood of 1885. The canals belonging to the latter stages of civilization seem to have been more numerous and to have had, in some of them at least, a continuous supply of water, because over the water-way of two, there still exist culverts constructed of burnt brick. These would hardly have been found to be necessary unless the canals had a larger supply of water than is contained in the present canals of Dārg and Kairābād. The lands of Sālihān are still apparently irrigated by a canal that closely follows one of the older beds of the Farah Rud.

The oldest system of canals almost appear to suggest a much greater supply of water in the river than is to be found in it now.

Hokāt and Juwein.

The name of the District is Hokāt. The exact significance of the name cannot be ascertained. As it is now pronounced, the word differs from the form in which it is met with in the writings of ancient historians and geographers. In their works it is written as though it was pronounced Uk. Another form in vogue at the present day in Seistan is Auk and the inhabitants are called Aukātis; this is very much closer to the ancient form of the name than the first.

The name of Juwein is also found in old records; but whether the modern town occupies the site of one that was older, it is impossible to say. Looking at it from a distance of several miles, there appear to be many ruins around the fort, and the small town outside of the walls of the latter. These ruins were, however, said to belong to another town or village called Chargewak.

The name Juwein is said to be given to the town because it is the centre of a tract famous for its crops of barley. It is said that the soil is especially congenial to this cereal. Barley is said to yield a hundredfold on the seed that is sown, whereas wheat returns about a third of that amount. The barley also is said to be very fine. The name of Juwein occurs in itineraries which were compiled 1,000 years ago. The fort of Juwein, the modern town, is imposing in its extent, but whether it is in repair or not it was impossible to see from a distance.

Description of the Hāmun-i-Seistan by ancient writers 903—952 A.D.

The description of the Hāmun-i-Seistan contained in the translation made from Istākhri's work is as true now as it was when he wrote. Both his and Ibn-i-Rusteh's narrative gives a most faithful outline picture of the country, and contains touches of local colour, which stamp their record as having been carefully compiled from reliable information.

The period in which they were wrote, was one closely following that in which the fortunes of the House of Leis, the coppersmith, had reached their height. Seistan bulked largely in the field of Oriental Politics at that time, and thus the country, its people, and its geography must have attracted a very great deal of attention. Reliable information was no doubt easily obtained, as the rise of a native dynasty of rulers brought Seistan into contact with the surrounding principalities, as well as with the supreme head of Islam, in Baghdad.

Istākhri states, regarding the Lake of Seistan, that its extreme length is about 30 farsakhs from " the district of Kuring road to Kushistan, to the bridge of Kirman on the road to Fars, and its breadth throughout is about the distance of one stage. Its water is sweet and it produces fish in abundance and reeds, and there are villages all round it except on the side which faces the desert. He had previously mentioned that the Hindmend * * * finishes in Seistan (Sejestan, he calls it) where it falls into the lake of Zireh, and this lake of Zireh increases or diminishes in size according as a greater or less quantity of water falls into it."

The bridge of Kirman, according to the same author, was no bridge at all, but a rabāt built by Amru, son of Leis, about 4 stages west of the capital of Seistan. This crossing must have been practically at nearly the same spot where the old trail from Hurmuk to Seistan crossed the Shela at its head or close to it. The distance between this point and the site of Kurun, or Kuring,[1] is 88 miles measured in a direct line down the middle of the lake area. Sir Henry Rawlinson allowed a little over 3 miles, as the equivalent for the farsakh of the oriental geographers whom he quotes; the exact equivalent worked from his figures give 3·1 miles to each farsakh and at this average the length of the lake area would be 93 miles, or five miles in excess of the truth. This is a sufficiently close approximation, and it shows that the author must have exercised great care in collecting his material, and had access to reliable sources of knowledge. The breadth of the Hāmun varies, but whatever the actual distance in miles may be, it always forms one stage. Both when the waters are out and cover the surface of the floor from shore to shore, and when it is perfectly dry, it is equally impossible to divide the stages and to camp midway.

The years of flood and of drought cause the volume of water in the lake to increase or to shrink. The conditions when Istākhri wrote were the same in their general aspect as they are now. Ibn-i-Rusteh mentions that there was sometimes water to be crossed in the stage beyond Kurung, deep enough, and therefore wide enough, to compel the use of boats; and on such occasions the alternative route might be used by travellers. The flooded areas of the Hāmun depended on the situation of the working channel of the Helmand and of its actual mouth, and were also due to the discharge of superfluous water through the canals that tailed off into the lake basin; and the depth of the water in the latter depended on the volume of the discharge from the river as well as canals.

In order therefore to allow of boats (or tutins) being used for the crossing of the lake the depth of water must have been fairly great, and it could only have been great if the Helmand had emptied its waters directly into the northern section of the Hāmun basin. Ibn-i-Rusteh states that Hisanik on the southern shore was a distance of 4 farsakhs. At present the direct distance across the Hāmun from the centre of the Kuring district measures about 9 miles, taking as the southern shore of the lake the watermark of 1903. This is an arbitrary shore line and on the occasion of a "year of Noah," when the Helmand comes down in its might, this arbitrary coastline would be greatly changed. The low-lying tracts of the Miān Kangi have been built up by annual deposits of silt, and this may have thrust out the deltaic fan quite 2 or 3 miles in 1,000 years. That the northern shore of the Miān Kangi has been pushed forward in the course of centuries of time, is sufficiently indicated by

---

[1] The position of this place will be discussed later on. It was about 2 or 3 miles to the north-west of the Tapa-i-Khārān.

the absence of very ancient sites near the present coastline. The ridge or lurg on which the modern village of Burj-i-Mirgul stands is composed largely of the harder (and older) clays, and it is probably a more ancient deposit than the softer and friable clay around it. The mounds around Takht-i-Shâh and others to the east were probably islands in the Naizâr, as they can be proved to have again been within the memory of persons who are now alive in Seistan.

Description of the life of the people inhabiting the Hâmun at the present day. Fishing.

The Hâmun abounds with fish. From the neighbouring villages gangs of men may be seen going towards the Hâmun with nets for the purpose of fishing. Whatever portion of their take is not required for their own food, finds ready sale in the villages around their homes. These fishermen are quite distinct from the regular Seiâd folk, who live in collections of huts formed of mats and sheaves of reeds and bulrushes whose principal means of livelihood is the fish and game they take in the Hâmun.

Grazing.

The naizârs, or reed beds, mentioned by Al Istâkhri, still afford pasture to herds of cattle which browse on the leaves. As the water recedes, the reeds dry; and in the winter the greater part of the growth in the beds is of a dull yellow hue. They are set fire to about the end of January, and by the end of February, there are clearings of burnt reeds all over the lake area. The basins fill gradually, as the Helmand begins to rise in January; and as the water creeps in among the charred stumps where the growth of reeds have been fired a fresh growth of tender leaves makes its appearance; and by the end of April the fresh reeds have attained to their full size. The seeds of both reeds and bulrushes are distributed by the strong winds, which blow for some days at a time during the winter. As the wind shakes the stems the sheaths containing the seed of the bulrushes burst and set free a white down not unlike thistledown, and the country and all that is on it to the leeward of a bed of reeds and bulrushes is covered with a coating of the fluffy seeds that escape from the bursting sheaths.

Homes of Seiâds and cattle owners.

The summer huts of the Seiâds and cattle graziers are formed of mats stretched over hoops of wood, the latter being the branches and stems of tamarisk. The winter huts are built of sheaves of bulrushes placed on end, and the roof formed of the same material.

Reeds and bulrushes.

The wild reeds of the Naizâr are not used for any other purposes than those already enumerated. The reed from which oriental scribes fashion their pens, and from which flageolets are made, and which also is used for pipe stems, is grown in gardens, and is a cultivated variety. The latter may be seen in some corner of any garden of considerable size, growing in thickets. The wild reed will grow anywhere where its roots can obtain the smallest amount of moisture that will nourish it. The bulrush on the contrary will only thrive when there is a depth of water and a fairly constant supply.

Seiâds.

The lake area is portioned out among the Seiâds, each community of whom must conform to the limits of their allotment. Within these they fish and snare game. The cattleherds also, who are in the habit of taking the village cattle into the reed beds and who live with their charges in huts or shelters made of sheaves of bulrushes and reeds, have likewise their own well established runs. As the waters recede, the cattle shelters and huts of the herds are moved down into the beds of reeds where they are renewed within the protection of low banks of earth. By the end of December, when the first rise in the level of the water may be expected, the cattle and their herds with their families move up to higher levels which are above the reach of all but the highest floods. Here are set up their winter huts, each group being surrounded by a low embankment and outer trench to keep the water out of their huts. When the sheaves of reeds and bulrushes are no longer needed for the winter quarters they are carefully stacked within the enclosure of the embankment, and there they remain until needed again the next winter. The cattleherds settlement and the stacks of sheaves not in use, are a very prominent feature in the basin of the Hāmun.

The basin of the Hāmun is in this way parcelled out among communities each living under its own headman who is responsible to the Government for the annual payment of revenue. The organisation of these communities resembles those which exist among the agricultural population. The latter make a living out of the land, while the Seiād makes his from the produce of the water, and the herdsman from the reeds and bulrushes that grow therein. The basin of the Hāmun is, therefore, by no means a waste or unproductive area. And so it has come to pass that as the streets and squares of a great city need to be named for the convenience of the inhabitants thereof, the chungs and reed beds and shelas of the Hāmun have each of them their appropriate names by which they are known to those who frequent the lake. So it ever must of necessity have been. No useful purpose would be served by giving a list of these names. To describe and locate the Chung-i-Aruna[1] or the Chung-i-Reg-i-Zaruni, or to specify which of these various basins receive their water in the first instance through the Shela-i-Ghulām Shah, or those others which are served by the Shela-i-Meshkushi, would be a profitless task and is better omitted.

The productive value of the basin of the Hāmun.

---

[1] The Chung or basin of the female camel.

CHAPTER III.

The new Helmand and its Deltas.

ANCIENT AND RECENT.

The alluvial soils of Seistan like a Palimpset.

The statement contained in the writings of Al Istākhri that there were villages all round the lake, except on the side which faces the desert, is quite applicable to the country at the present day. To the east and south of the lake basin the country has always been inhabited, and in this tract are to be found the traces of successive ages of human occupation. In this area, the centres of Political and Religious authority have always been placed. In it are the sites of the various towns which have at different times been the seat of the Government of the country. The modern record which is borne on the face of the delta overlies that of more ancient times, and in this way Seistan resembles a Palimpset, for while the more evident and recent characters are being examined, others reveal themselves partially erased and in most cases barely intelligible, which carry the record back to periods of time lying very far beyond those of which any historical information exists. These ancient characters, so far as they can be deciphered, prove the antiquity of the general scheme of human existence as it is found to exist at the present day. The system of irrigation has been the same as it now is, excepting that in past ages it was more efficiently carried out, perhaps, than it is in the present time of decadence of skill and energy on the part of the present inhabitants.

Before, however, any attempt is made to work out problems of the ancient topography of the He'mand and its deltas, it is necessary to describe the country as it exists. The main features of the topography of Seistan cannot have altered very appreciably since the first appearance of life and of human beings in the country. It will therefore be useful first to obtain a general idea of these existing conditions, and to complete the description of the geographical record which the forces of nature have engraved in indelible characters upon the face of the country, and which in point of antiquity take precedence over the earliest traces of man's handiwork which are to be found on those portions of the delta which have always been the scene of his existence and his work.

Comparison of the Helmand with the Nile.

The author of a recent work, treating of his travels in Persia, describes incidentally the relation of fertile Seistan to the surrounding less favoured tracts adjoining it, as resembling that of ancient Egypt with the countries that lay to the east and west of the fertile lands of that delta. The resemblance is even closer in the case of the Nile and the Helmand. A considerable extent of desert is traversed by these rivers, both of which have furrowed narrow channels for themselves through the inhospitable tracts which separate their catchment areas from their deltas. The loss of fluid by evaporation while traversing the intervening desert must in both cases be enormous. In the case of the Helmand, it is an unknown quantity, and affects the supply of water that is finally delivered in the delta to a very great extent. Here the resemblance ceases. In one case the catchment area is greater and the nature of the vast forest-clad regions comprised within the area, the drainage from which feeds the River of Egypt, ensures the flow of water therein against failure.

The catchment of the Helmand comprises a tract of country less in area and of a very different character to that of the Nile. The snows of winter and the modest autumn and spring rainfall is the source whence the springs that feed the Helmand draw their supplies, and any diminution of the latter results in a great decrease of the supply in the delta which is only the excess over the quantity lost by evaporation and requirements of the country above the desert area. Hence the Helmand sometimes fails altogether, and in its periods of highest possible flood, it can barely be comparable with the Nile at its season of low river.

At Kala-i-Bist the Arghandāb joins the Helmand, and below that junction the river receives no other tributaries. The remainder of the course of the river is a "single channel" as described about 1,000 years ago by Al Istākhri. This bed forms a great curve, its termination in the Hāmun being on the same latitude as Kala-i-Bist. The river lies within well defined limits in a narrow trough at the southern end of the great talus which slopes towards the south from the last of the foot-hills of the tract of country called Zamindāwar. *The valley of the Helmand from Kala-i-Bist.*

Between Kala-i-Bist and the elbow at the village of Landi Wali Muhammed, the country to the east of the river is low and covered with sand hills, but from a point a short distance below that village the river enters a very narrow valley, confined by a line of rugged cliffs, formed by the talus to the north and by a similar plateau to the south. From this point to another, about 36 or 40 miles above the delta of Seistan, the valley of the Helmand is a narrow trough lying at the foot of the northern talus. Below the village and district of Khāwajah Ali, this trough is separated by a very narrow terrace of dasht from the extensive depression in which the lake of Seistan and the Gaud-i-Zireh are situated, and which has already been described.[1]

At the point where the Helmand emerges beyond the control of the cliffs which up to that place have formed the sides of the trough, a bifurcation takes place, raised above the level of the modern delta of Seistan. It is formed by a plateau, very much broken, whose apex is thrust like a wedge *The Helmand at Bandār-i-Kamāl Khan.*

---

[1] At Rudbār (on the Helmand) the trough of the river is 320 feet above the floor of the Gaud-i-Zireh to the south of that district. The springs at Urak on the banks above the floor of the great depression are probably due to leakage from the Helmand allowed by a softer stratum.—G. P. T.

into the jaws of the valley where the cliffs on either side open out and finally come to an abrupt end. Close to this apex, but on the alluvial floor of the valley, is an insignificant hamlet and also the remains of a small fortalice built by one Kamāl Khan, a Baluch of the Sanjarāni tribe, who took possession of the lands at that place in an unsettled period of modern Seistani history. It is widely known as it used to be the point to which caravans from the hilly tracts of Sarhad and around Jālk, and even from Makran, directed their steps when they journeyed to the Helmand and Seistan for the purpose of buying grain and exchanging the produce of their flocks and herds for wheat and barley grown in those more favoured districts. It was owing to its being the rendezvous of caravans that it obtained the name of Bandar. It is an important point in the geography of the country. The terrace that forms the southern edge of the trough of the Helmand ends abruptly abreast of that place in a bold cliff some 200 feet in height above the talus and the river bed.

The northern band of the river. From Deshu and Malakhān, above Khwāja Ali, the northern edge of the trough of the Helmand is formed by the cliffs of the southern scarp of the Dasht-i-Mārgo. The latter forms an unbroken line up to Bandar, and just a little to the east of that place the cliffs swing away towards the north and finally terminate in a bold headline above the town of Kala-i-Fath from whence the edge of the plateau retreats towards the east, rejoining the eastern scarp of Seistan. This outlier of the eastern plateau is known as the Dasht-i-Meski and rises to over 200 feet above the valley of the Helmand at Bandar.

Northern channel to Khwābgāh. From Bandar-i-Kamāl Khan the present channel of the Helmand turns abruptly to the north[1] and hugs the eastern edge of the western dasht to which it clings for a distance of about 35 miles where it emerges on the plain of Seistan which is the modern recent delta. This embouchure of the Helmand is another very important point, and it so happens that at it there is an insignificant hamlet called "Khwābgāh" perched upon a block of dasht, or clay plateau, some 34 feet above the river and beyond the reach of its highest floods. At this point the dasht just described, curves away towards the west and south-west.

Rud-i-Sina. Midway between Bandar and Khwābgāh there is a third channel and the most ancient of all the channels which the Helmand has occupied at one time or another of its existence. It is called the Sana Rud, also the Rud-i-Sina. This ancient bed of the river enters the south-western portion of the northern of the two modern deltas. Its embouchure is situated at the eastern end of a deep bay where its ancient delta has been obliterated by more recent deposits of silt.[2]

The northern and southern delta. There are two deltas in Seistan. The northern, where all the cultivation and population of the country is located at the present time (and always

---

[1] Following an evident line of fracture or dislocation.
[2] Also following a fracture of the dasht.

has been located), and the southern, which is separated from the former by the plateau, projects towards the west, ending in a well marked headland about 3 miles to the south of the modern village of Warmāl.

The eastern limit of both the northern and southern deltas is the water-mark in any year of the Hāmun. The head of the northern delta is where the Helmand enters it at the village of Khwābgāh. The southern delta lies at the tail of that ancient bed of the river which runs straight away in a direction almost due west from Bandar-i-Kamāl Khan.

This old bed of the Helmand is called the Rud-i-Biyabān (the river of the desert) in a manuscript which was found in Seistan. A shorter and more convenient name for it is the Trākun channel from some remarkable ruins that exist in the deserted bed of this stream. *Rud-i-Biyabān or Trākun channel.*

All the old channels of the Helmand are at a higher level than the present course of the river.

The southern delta has been always a separate district from the northern delta. It is smaller than the latter. These deltas are treated of as geographical features, without any regard to the political divisions of Persian and Afghan territory. There is evidence to show that in past ages both of these deltas existed as inhabited tracts at the same period, and this presupposes a division of the water in the Helmand river. *The two deltas.*

The Trākun channel is not the only course the Helmand has ever adopted in the southern delta. A smaller channel (and an older one exists on the gravelly plain that forms the left bank of the ancient channel. This was probably a spill-water channel and took off from the main channel below, that is, to the west of Bandar-i-Kamāl Khan. From close to the same point, some 5 or 6 miles to the west of Bandar, another spill-water channel descends the eastern edge of the fan in a south-easterly direction into the Gaud-i-Zireh following the line where the lower western plateau touches the foot of the cliffs that form the southern scarp (overlooking the Gaud-i-Zireh) of the terrace that separates the Helmand valley from that depression.[1] *Spill channels from the Trākun channel.*

The whole of this area bears ample evidence of having been at one time well populated. The banks of the Trākun channel were at that time graced by the presence of man, and the remains of human dwellings and other structures raised by human hands exist in great profusion along the low cliffs that form the banks of this channel. The actual ribbon of alluvial soil inside these limits varies much in width. The dasht on either hand encloses well marked loops, and within the bold curves of the cliffs on either side in these places there may be as much as 1 or 2 square miles of alluvial soil. The limit between one loop and the next is formed by the cliffs of the dasht closing in and pinch- *Evidence of previous populations on Trākun channel and description of the soil thereof.*

---

[1] Here the fact of the subsidence of the western and now lower plateau is vividly presented to the observer. The line of fracture also is emphasized by the existence of the spill-water channel. The face of the higher plateau is very much sculptured by wind action.

ing the strip of alluvial between opposing headlands of gravel-capped clay. Each of these loops formed a small district, and the whole of the cultivable soil was thus divided by nature into districts with separate names which distinguish one from another. Within the limits imposed by the low plateau on each bank, the ancient Helmand must have flowed in bold curves, crossing the wider reaches of soil within the loops as its course changed in its periodical oscillations.

The floor of this narrow valley between the low cliffs that form its banks on either hand is composed of the finely divided silt that forms the hard white plains in the delta. But by reason of the channel having been deserted by the river, and abandoned by the inhabitants, the alluvial floor has suffered very greatly from the force of the wind. The latter has torn up the soil into deep rifts and caused the floor to resemble in places a network of shallow ravines sometimes as much as 5 or 6 feet in depth. Wherever this has not taken place in some of the loops within this old channel, the floor is almost level from one cliff across to the opposite, the white hard clay that forms it being scantily clothed with the desert tamarisk or Tagaz.

Plateau of the desert to the north of the Trākun channel.

The desert plateau to the north of the channel, whose cliffs form its bank in that direction, is higher than the desert plateau to the south of this old bed of the Helmand.[1] This difference of level is, however, most noticeable to the west of Trākun and takes place at a point almost abreast of that place. This rise in the ground is due to the presence upon the surface of the plateau of isolated bocks of a similar formation, and covered with a cap of gravel which form higher plateaus rising some 15 or 20 feet above the level of the lower terrace. Then again the eastern portion rises in low steps from the present river bed towards the west. Examined closely these steps appear as beaches and as if their low cliffs had been eaten away by the water lapping at their feet. And each line of cliffs marks (apparently) a stage or period in the subsidence of the plateau. The last stage of this progressive subsidence being the present low cliff which overlooks the valley, and at the foot of which the Helmand of the present day is to be found. To the west of the village of Khwābgāh, upon the low plateau overlooking the plain of Seistan, it is possible to follow indications of these higher terraces and islands and by their means to trace the course of what look like more than one ancient channel of the Helmand upon the terraces of the dasht which evidently took off from the modern valley of the river 5 or 6 miles above Khwābgāh, and which ultimately fell into the lake 4 or 5 miles to the west of that hamlet.

The Plateau between the Helmand and the Gaud-i-Zireh.

The successive fall of the river bed in the trough of the Helmand is also very marked. The present river hugs the foot of the Dasht-i-Mārgo whose cliffs rise sheer from the bed, the current during the months of flood sometimes

---

[1] The Rūd-i-Biyabān also follows a line of fracture, like the spill-water channel alluded to already so does the northern and modern, or working channel, of the Helmand River.

bears towards these steep slopes and has increased their declivity by undercutting the clay and thereby causing land slides. Upon these slopes the lines of former levels are not very easily followed, but on the opposite side of the trough they are so clearly indicated as to arrest attention. In addition to other signs the track which descends the trough of the Helmand itself crosses these changes of levels; at first almost unnoticeable, they soon attract attention owing to the necessity of descending a few feet from a low gravel terrace to a lower plain. The low terrace thus left behind runs into and forms an under terrace of the south cliff immediately overlooking the narrow valley. These successive changes of level are about four in number, and as one climbs towards the summit of the southern terrace from the river valley, they rise towards the south in a succession of low terraces with marked bluffs and cliffs. The highest terrace of all is a flat expanse covered with a dark brown gravel, and upon this stand low isolated island-like blocks of the same formation. This southern terrace is not more than 100 feet above the river valley close to Bandar-i-Kamāl Khan.

Its southern face overlooking the Gaud-i-Zireh is quite different. It ends abruptly in a line of frowning cliffs overlooking a tangle of ravines and outlying and isolated bluffs of clay; the yellow and red clays comprising these are for the most part naked, scoured and smoothed by wind action and devoid of their gravel cap, of which only portions may be found crowning the larger sized isolated blocks of Kim. This belt of broken ground at the foot of the cliffs is intersected by an almost unintelligible system of ravines, but which as they descend towards the Gaud-i-Zireh become more defined and develop ultimately into "wādis" which end in the expanse of clay which forms the floor or bottom of the Hollow of Zireh.

The edges of terraces on the dasht described in the foregoing paragraphs resemble contours graven on the surface of the country, and although altered by subsequent exposure to climatic influences and the unequal weathering of the material of which they are composed, if they are carefully followed, they reveal a history of changes that have taken place at a period very far back from the present.

The scarp of the Dasht-i-Margo exhibits Kim in horizontal strata. There is the same alternation of pale reddish clay with the pale green or almost white deposit. The cap of friable conglomerate that covers the deposits is thick. The terrace to the south of the river is also composed of the same material, and at intervals, barriers of Kim stretch across the bed of the river and form rapids. This stiff clay consolidates and hardens under water, and the existence of these bars of Kim has been taken advantage of, in past ages of the history of Seistan, to build weirs or regulators by means of which a system of irrigation was maintained by which very nearly all the arable soil in the deltas was at one time or another brought under cultivation. The

Sites of ancient weirs in the bed of the river.

unequal density of the material results in inequalities in the outline of the Dasht-i-Margo. Bluffs or headlands project beyond the crest of the steep slope towards the river, and these form well known landmarks. The natives call such a headland "Puz" or nose. At a considerable distance above Bandar-i-Kamāl Khan there is a very prominent headland, well known for a considerable distance down stream. It is called the Puz-i-Māshi, and below this headland there is a bar of Kim which extends across the river bed and forms a rapid when the water in the river is at a low level.

Mouths of the Trākun channel. The Trākun channel, or Rud-i-Biyabān, discharged its water in times past through 5 or 6 mouths into the Hāmun. These channels are still very clearly defined as they have cut their way through the outer talus to the level of the lake. This outer talus is also covered with gravel, though the pebbles are much smaller than the shingle which covers the plateau on either banks of the old channel. The channels which the water had cut through this outer talus are now ribbons of alluvium, of the same kind as the floor of the main stream bed and thus are clearly traceable up to the point where they leave the gravel talus and enter the alluvial tract to the west. This district is, however, so torn by the action of the wind that it is not easy to trace the continuation of the 5 or 6 mouths of the Trākun channel once they leave the low undulating talus with its covering of fine dark coloured gravel and enter the region of deep fissures and wind scours.

The Shela and moving sand on its bank. The western face of the lower plateau between the Trākun channel and the working river presents most interesting evidences of the sculpture of the exposed cliff faces by the wind alone—for the rainfall and its effect is a negligible quantity in Seistan. On the surface of this plateau also may be seen the same operation also in progress as that which has broken and altered the original level outline of the lower plateau, which faces the west. One great bay is here full of the bench marks alluded to which gives the locality the appearance of a vast cemetery. The southern edge of the southern plateau forms a line of low cliffs overlooking a strip of alluvial soil some 15 or 16 miles wide; the opposite limit of this tract being the north glacis of the Kacha Koh mountains to the south of the depression. In this strip of alluvial and lying closer to its southern edge is the Shela, the channel through which any overflows of the Seistan lake may find its way into the Gaud-i-Zireh. The alluvial soil is however covered with barkhans or mounds of drift sand, and it is only occasionally in the open spaces between the great heaps of loose sand that the alluvial floor is to be seen.

Bay near Surh Dagāl. The distributaries of the Trākun channel in the days when it was a river, discharged their overflow into the Hāmun, and also directly into the Shela, which at that time was a continuation of the Helmand. At the point where this delta recurves back to the plateau, there is a deep bay, similar to that

The Surh-dagāl; example of the erosive action of the "Wind of-120-days."

(Part II to face page 132.)

of the Surh Dagāl[1] and separated from the latter by a narrow projecting ridge of Kim, which is widely known as the Puzh-i-Surh Dagāl. This bay adjoining the talus at the mouth of the Trākun channel, presents the same effects of wind scour which exists in the more northern bay. The basins on the plateaux also exhibit the same effect of wind's erosive action. This has gone on, until a hard substratum of Kim has been exposed, or until gravel loosened from the enclosing banks have slid down into the hollows, and thus afforded protection to the clay floor. In all of these depressions there are bench marks left to show what extent of material has been removed.

But the country to the south of the Trākun channel has been inhabited at a very early period—how long ago it is impossible to say, but from the appearance of the canals which once irrigated this tract,[2] now a waterless desert, it is conclusively proved that in this tract at least the erosion of soil in the basins has taken place subsequently to the existence of human beings in this country. In more than one instance in the course of a cursory examination of the tract there were found remains of canals by which some of these basins had been irrigated. That section of the canal which passed through the plateau dividing the basins can be clearly followed by means of the permanent scar left by the excavation upon the dasht, while both ends may be now some 8 or 10 feet above the present floor of the adjacent basins. *Signs of human habitations.*

The erosion that has taken place can be thus clearly estimated, and this is open to confirmation by the existence of bench marks, a mound or two, perhaps, of clay where, owing to some accident, the material has been able to withstand the persistent removal of soil that has gone on around. These tracts, once deserted, were evidently never reoccupied, and thus the effects of the wind have never been retarded, nor has the material thus removed been replaced by later silt and an equilibrium maintained between erosion and accumulation by flood-borne alluvium. Upon this deserted plateau, lying to the south of the Rud-i-Biyabān, are thus to be seen the remains of a prehistoric civilization, dating back perhaps to legendary periods of time when those Princes of Seistan lived and ruled, whose mighty deeds are preserved in a Firdausi's great romance.

The Sana Rud differs greatly from the Rud-i-Biyabān. If appearances are to be trusted, it does not seem to have been an actual flowing river subsequent to geologically recent times, speaking, that is to say, under correction, and always as an untrained observer. Along its whole course, from its western embouchure to the point where its valley diverges from the present Helmand valley, there is not one single remain or sign that points to human occupation. It enters the bay in which the village of Aliābād is *Description of the Sana Rud.*

---

[1] Surh Dagāl the red earth; owing to the darker colour of the material of which the bench marks are composed, contrasted against the ivory white plain on which they stand.

[2] This is the plateau called the Dasht-i-Zireh and its western continuation, the surface of the latter was once commanded by water conveyed to it in canals.—G. P. T.

situated close to the modern hamlet of Shamsābād about 4 miles to the east of the former. In its course after that it diverges from the modern valley of the Helmand; there are no features that may be considered as abnormal. Its embouchure is interesting, and in some respects is not unlike the mouth of the Farah Rud. The stream of the Sana Rud entered the lake on a leeshore. When the Sana Rud entered the bay there must have been a depth of water in it, and there extends a bar of fine gravel across it from the southern cliffs overlooking the bay to the foot of the northern coastline. This gravel bar resembles that other one at the head of the Surh Dagāl bay. The former is however not so pronounced owing to later deposits of silt, which has replaced any loss which might have taken place by the erosive action of the wind. The height of the bar across the mouth of the Sana Rud is about 16 feet above the level of the plain on either side. It continues for a short distance only at this height which refers to that portion of it alone which retains its original condition. Two original outlets communicate between the hollows or depressions behind it with the open valley in the bay to the west. The deposit of modern silt, and still more recent additions of sand, have obscured the detail to a considerable extent.

About 2 miles above the hamlet of Shamsābād, the Sana Rud developed a third outlet which cut a way through a low plateau, evidently composed of débris, gravel, and clays, washed down from the higher ground, and this channel can still be traced through the gorge it had made for itself, and issued forth upon a small plateau of alluvial soil which rests against the gravel beach already described. This on a smaller scale is like the similar feature which was found in very much the same position to the north of the mouth of the Farah Rud, where there is a plain of alluvial deposit resting against a gravel beach which forms a revetment facing the Hāmun. This third outlet of the Sana Rud appears to have entered the Aliābād bay under the Sabz Kim bluff over a bar of fine gravel resting on a shingly beach below. The other outlet of the Sana Rud issues on the Shamsābād plain through a distinct gorge about a mile south of the hamlet. From this point and onwards there are indications of two channels, one of which to the right or east is followed by the modern canal, and the other which entered the bay about a mile to the south of the small village of Deh Khālkdād. Between these outlets the bar is very much broken, and with the exception of a section of about a third of a mile in length, midway between these outlets, it has almost disappeared, having been worn down to the level of the alluvial deposit which has overlaid its east and west slopes. Wherever there is a wind scour in the surface of the clay, the existence of fine gravel underneath is revealed, the deposit of clay deepening towards the west as it recedes from the bar.

The bar or beach of fine shingle can be traced from the east end of the slopes of the Sabz Kím mound up to the bluffs that overlook the plain up the south of the village of Kala-i-Nau. To the north-west of the Sabz Kim mound, there is a sloping beach of coarse shingle which follows the toe of the bluffs that form the coast of the Aliābād bay in this direction. It can be traced along the foot of these cliffs, up to the point where there is a large graveyard with a very conspicuous domed mausoleum built upon the dasht. Beyond this point the alluvial soil comes right up to the foot of the plateau, and the well defined shingly beach is not a prominent feature any longer. The shingle and gravel are now covered by a depth of alluvial deposit, ancient and modern, and it is probably owing to this subsoil of gravel which keeps the alluvial clays well drained that the fertility of the lands around Aliābād and the villages in its neighbourhood is due. Another very striking feature is the way in which the shingly beach is littered with bivalve shells of various sizes. The lands in the vicinity of Aliābād are also full of minute shells of this description. Acres of soil appear to be chiefly composed of these remains. They are not, however, to be referred to any but a quite modern period, as will be demonstrated further on.

At the back of the hamlet of Shamsābād, between it and the cliffs of the dasht to the east, there is a large depression or Nāwar called Bandik. At first sight it appears as if an outlet of the Sana Rud flowed into it, but if this was ever the case a low bar or ridge had formed and opposed a barrier to the ingress of water. Two low ridges of rounded summits separates the Bandik from the lowlying plain around the hamlet of Shamsābād. These ridges are separated by a narrow gorge or passage through which an irrigation channel enters the Bandik depression, and by means of which some cultivation is carried on in the latter. This water is derived from the canals that are supplied by the main canal which takes off from the modern or present channel of the Helmand, close to Khwābgāh.

The ground at the outlet of the Sana Rud is broken, and the recent additions of alluvial deposit have modified the older features of this part of the country to such an extent that to arrive at any definite conclusions as to what may have been the ancient condition of the head of the Aliābād bay is now impossible. The separation of the Sana Rud from the Helmand takes place almost under a tall pinnacle of Kim, which rises in narrow terraces and ledges to a height of quite 150 feet above the level of the Helmand at its foot. A miniature fortress stands on the ledges and the peak of this hill of Kim. The towers and walls are of necessity small and low, which lend an air of unreality to it, as if it was a model of a mountain stronghold. There is a companion hill, also of Kim, but the latter is smaller and steeper with no room on it for building. It is also a good deal lower than the fortified peak.

The fortalice is called Dik-i-Dela, or Dela's Peak. Dela, they say, was an official of Naushirwān, the Just, and the fortalice was constructed to hold a garrison to whose care the weir or regulator, which existed in the Helmand

Dik-i-Dela at the head of the Sana Rud.

below this point, was entrusted. This place is about 12 miles to the north of Bandar-i-Kamāl Khan. This section of the present channel of the Helmand is common to both the present river and also to the Sana Rud or Rud-i-Sina. Kala-i-Fath, the last capital of the Kaiāni Maliks of Seistan, before that family lost their independence, lies about 8 miles below Dik-i-Dela. It will be necessary to refer to that place frequently later on.

The plateau at the valley of Chahas buyah.

To the east of Bandar-i-Kamāl Khan, on the right bank of the river, there is a low plateau covered with shingle, the eastern cliff of which is some 2 miles distant from Chahārburjak. The latter, a modern village, is about 10 miles to the east of Bandar-i-Kamāl Khan. About 2 miles to the north of the latter, and upon the opposite bank of the Helmand, there is situated the modern village of Deh Ghulām Haidar. The low plateau lies immediately to the east of this village, and about a mile to the north of it, there is a deep cutting through a narrow part of the dasht through which the tail of the Chahārburjak canal is able to irrigate some land belonging to the village. Further north of this cutting the dasht is intact, and it continues for a distance of about 2 miles beyond it and then finally breaks up. Its continuation to the north is a series of broken clay knolls and sand dunes, and the plateau of Kim opposite to Dik-i-Dela is a part of this dislocated series of mounds of Kim. Upon this plateau is a very ancient enclosure, the walls of which are now in heaps, dissolving under the action of the weather. Between this place and Kala-i-Fath the sand dunes and clay knolls finally disappear almost completely, the former reappearing at intervals until they again form a continuous line of dunes along the river bank to the north of Kala-i-Fath. Between the detached plateau above and to the east of Deh Ghulām Haidar, and the line of low cliffs which form the toe of the lofty Meski plateau, there is a wide channel, capacious enough to contain the Helmand, the eastern end of which opens on the alluvial soil to the west of and around Chahārburjak. This channel continues along the foot of the lofty plateau until the clay knolls and broken ground which lie between it and the Helmand disappear. Here the channel is practically lost in the sandy soil, but the under-features of the plateau to the east continue to end in a water and wind-worn line of cliffs, which are further on separated from the great block of kim, on which the citadel of Kala-i-Fath is built, by a continuation of that channel.

T rkoh pla eaux.

The plateau upon which the ancient fortified enclosure of Tirkoh stands is also a block of kim. Along the Helmand, the term "Sirr" is used to distinguish this hard clay. A bar of this material extends across the bed of the Helmand from the Tirkoh plateau, forming a rapid over which the current during low river makes a distinct ripple. The kim formation upon which the fortalice of Dik-i-Dela stands together with its companion mound is a part of this ledge of kim which has withstood the action of weather and the inroads of the river. About $1\frac{1}{4}$ miles to the north-east of the Dik-i-Dela crag, there is

The aiwan-or hall in the ruined palace of Machi, near Hauzdār, on the Trade Route.

(Part II to face page 136.)

a detached plateau rising to a height of about 50 feet above the level of the ground at its foot. This is also a block of kim. This outcrop of the hard clay extends in a north-westerly direction from Tirkoh. On the north-east and east faces this isolated plateau is very broken, and a subordinate ledge or plateau extends beyond the highest part for nearly ¾ mile, and that part of this lower terrace which meets the river forms a low but marked cliff. Between this cliff on the western and Tirkoh cliff on the opposite side of the river, the latter issues forth as out of a gate on the open valley in which the town of Kala-i-Fath is situated. To the south and west of that isolated block of kim, there is alluvial soil and at this end of the Sana Rud the canal that follows its course as far as the western limit of the Kemāri district is very distinct. It is said that this canal originally took off a considerable distance above Dik-i-Dela. In years of very high river, it still receives a supply of water which, however, does not reach to any great distance down its bed. It is also said that in the days when Kala-i-Fath was in the height of its prosperity, this canal was used to cultivate the eastern end of the valley of the Sana Rud. There appears to be very little doubt that the Helmand did, once upon a time, flow to the west of the Dik-i-Dela mound and turned the western end of the high isolated plateau to the north-west of that little fortress, and regained the valley where it now flows about 3 or 4 miles further down.

The Sana Rud does not appear ever to have possessed any practical value as a river. There are along its course many places where by means of irrigation crops could have been raised. The floor of the valley along which it flowed, although covered now with a layer of dark brown gravel, contains in many places good soil not far from the channel of the stream which could easily have been irrigated and brought into cultivation. No attempt seems ever to have been made, nor are there the faintest indications of habitation along its banks. Nomad shepherds occasionally enter its valley and traces of their encampments are here and there to be met with. Fragments of pottery, so common on the present waterless dasht along the channel of the Rud-i-Biyabān, are non-existent along the banks of the Sana Rud. *Traces of human habitation in the Sana Rud.*

It appears also from the direction of the old canal that it was constructed with a view to conduct water from the Helmand into the districts in which the ruins of Machi and Hauzdār are situated, for the purpose of irrigating the very excellent land around those places. The task evidently was abandoned, as proving too difficult, or was cut short by some commotion in the country, or the death of the person to whose energy and foresight it had owed its inception. It was undoubtedly constructed many centuries ago. The only branches of the Helmand that seem to have possessed any value whatever and to have affected the condition of the country are the Rud-i-Biyabān and the present working river. *Ancient canal was probably never completed.*

DESCRIPTION OF DELTA TO THE EAST OF KALA-I-FATH.

The promontory of Kala-i-Fath.

When the river issues out of the gorge immediately below Dik-i-Dela, it is practically freed from all control except towards the west where the dasht forms a defined bank, and prevents any attempt at a change of course in that direction. On the east the toe of the slope of the Meski plateau forms a line of low cliffs which are situated about a mile from the bank of the Helmand, and within these narrow limits only it is possible for the river to oscillate. At a point some 2½ miles to the north of Kala-i-Fath, this restricted opposition ceases. At this point the slope from the plateau of Meski follows the course of that plateau which recedes towards the east and rejoins the Dasht-i-Margo of which it is an outlying portion. The point where this change of direction in the under-features takes place is a fairly conspicuous promontory of the last low series of cliffs which overlook the alluvial plain. Beyond this point towards the east the orderly termination of the lower slope ceases after a short distance, and further on, the slope of the plateau descends in a steady incline to the alluvial deposit that rests upon it, but its junction with the latter is obscured by an untidy jumble of broken mounds of naked clay, interspersed here and there with small plateaux of insignificant elevation covered with gravel and the all-pervading sand. The promontory had evidently been fortified at one time, and the position was divided into two separate strongholds by a channel which it is very evident is artificial (constructed to admit of a canal some 50 feet wide) cut through the kim to the level of the alluvial tract on each side. The southern fort was connected with the slope that descends from the lofty plateau, but the block of kim thus cut through rises to a height above the ground near it.

Sargāh-i-Seistan or Damb-i-Rustam.

The northern block rises in a cliff some 15 or 20 feet in height above the alluvial lands on its three sides. This site is known as the Sargāh-i-Seistan, and it is also called Damb-i-Rustam, or Rustam's mound. This latter term merely denoted the fact that the remains are of very great age, and their origin is unknown. The two fortalices separated by the canal are only some 300 feet in length, but their position is important for many reasons.

These ruins stand at the head of the great area of alluvial soil which formed the heart of Seistan lying at the termination of the Helmand. To the east of the promontory there extends the great district, now a waterless tract, which at one time was the seat of an ancient and advanced condition of civilization. This tract is limited towards the east by the under-features of the Dasht-i-Margo plateau. To the north the delta extends for a distance of about 50 miles, gradually sloping down to the lake which occupies the lowest level in the country.

Old channels of the Helmand to the east of the Sargāh-i-Seistan.

Standing on the mound to the north of this artificial cutting that separates the two fortified positions at Sargāh, and looking at the alluvial plain towards the north and east, there are visible to the eye very clear indications that the Helmand at one time swung to the east under the promontory on which Sargāh is situated and flowed in a parallel direction to the foot of the slope that descends from the summit of the Meski plateau to the north. This faint trace of the ancient bed of the Helmand continues in this direction until past the ruins known as Paisai, where it forsakes its hitherto easterly course and turns towards the north gradually becoming fainter. It is finally lost among the sand hills, but long before the ruins are reached it completely disappears in the level plain of hard alluvium upon which the barkhans (moving sand hills) stand.

To the north the present Helmand continues its course, past Sargāh, and past the modern village of Arbab Dost Muhammad. This village is about $3\frac{1}{2}$ miles to the north of Sargāh and about $\frac{1}{2}$ mile from the right bank of the river. This bank of the Helmand is fringed with a chain of fairly high sand dunes such as were found on the banks of the Farah Rud. *Description of the present valley of the Helmand to the north of Kala-i-Fath.*

For a space of about 2 miles to the north of the Sargāh promontory the alluvial plain continues at the same level as that of the ground immediately to the west of that place, and along the bank of the river. To the north of this plain the ground commences to rise very gently at first, but by the time that the village of Dost Muhammad is reached there is a marked gravel covered rise, a little to the north-west of the Paisai ruins, and closer to the village there are patches of soil covered with gravel which point to the existence of a gravel covered undulation overlaid by alluvium. The latter in places has worn away and the summit of the undulation having been but lightly covered are laid bare by the erosion that has taken place in the course of time. The more eastern mounds apparently take the form of low detached plateaux of gravel, the spaces between being covered with alluvial, but the system of detached blocks is very soon lost to sight under a great height of drift sand which stands on the terraces and forms a barrier which effectually shuts off any view of the great collection of ruins that exist to the east of them. They extend up to the latitude of Nād Ali, a modern fort, which exists below the bifurcation of the two working branches of the Helmand. The ruins that lie choked with drifts of sand in the tract to the east of this barrier are many of them large and important masses of sundried brick work, which the dry air of the desert has to a great extent preserved from utter decay. So marked, however, is the barrier that lies between them and the present delta of the Helmand that, even from the lofty mound of the Safedik, 90 feet above ground level, it is not possible to get a glimpse of the ruins that lie beyond the barriers, some of the ruins being not more than 16 miles distant and the intervening country covered for a short distance only beyond Nād Ali with low tamarisk. From abreast of this place the height of this barrier decreases rapidly, and it finally ends in several low gravel covered terraces that stand some 5 or 6 miles to the south-west of the modern hamlet of Meno on the southern end of the Āshkin, the eastern termination of the Hāmun.

Abreast of the hamlet of Khwābgāh and to the east of it there are some isolated blocks of dasht, outliers of the barrier just described. They are separated one from another by strips of alluvial soil of varying width.

In the direction of this barrier the area affected by the annual floods of the Helmand is very limited. Whether by canals or by simple inundation there is merely a narrow strip of land that is nourished by water from the Helmand. This is due to the existence of the higher ground that separates the district of Sār-o-Tār and Ghulghula from the working delta.

GENERAL DESCRIPTION OF THE SĀR-O-TĀR TRACT AND HOW IT WAS IRRIGATED.

The districts of Sār-o-Tār and Ghulghula were dependent on canals taking their water from the river above Kala-i-Fath or in the vicinity of that place.

Canal systems. These works would naturally demand great care and attention to be maintained in working order. It is evident that such was the case. The remains of old canals prove this. Some of these were constructed to pass through the opening towards the east along which the Helmand once made its way, below the Sargāh promontory. Others radiated from a centre or focus close to the ruins which are now known as Kala-i-Gāwak. Upon these canals the prosperity of the districts of Sār-o-Tār and Ghulghula was dependent. Any calamity which destroyed the head of this extensive system of irrigation would at once render those districts uninhabitable. Circumstances rendered it impossible to thoroughly explore those tracts, but they were visited by members of the Indian Staff and a good general idea obtained as to the undoubtedly populous condition of these tracts in past ages.

Nature of the ruins. They abound in ruins (massive structures), fortified manor houses and defensive posts, domed mausolea and the remains of the dwellings of the more wealthy classes.

Ruins of gardens, traces of cultivation, are laid bare at each movement of the drifts of soft loose sand, under the impulse of the wind of 120 days as it hurries the barkhans in their march across that tract towards their final destination in the wadis of the Dasht-i-Mārgo and that dreadful tract called by the natives "Jehanam" or "Hell." This great scour, which forms a deep indentation in the western face of the Dasht-i-Mārgo, is the dustbin of the country. There are to be found, piled high against the steep scarps that enclose that hollow, vast drifts of loose sands. Among the ruins there are traces of canals and innumerable watercourses. Drain pipes were used to carry water underneath garden paths, and syphon bridges also have been discovered. The division of water in canals and watercourses are affected by means of permanent structures, masonry distributaries with baked earthen drain pipes set in the brickwork to allow of the water passing through. Lime mortar was

Ruin near Sar-o-tar, materials Béton-Pisé below, & sun-dried bricks above.

(Part II to face page 140.)

used in all places where the action of water had to be resisted. Human skeletons, whole and in fragments, are laid bare by the action of the wind which tears away and removes the tombs under which these remains had been laid to rest. The tales which the Baluchis tell of this country having been depopulated by a great pestilence or by a general massacre are due to the skeleton which they see lying on the surface of the wind scoured ground.

It is from these ruins that the treasure seekers bring back coins of Parthian and Sassanian monarchs, mixed with the early Muhammadan mintages, intaglios, seals, some bearing representations of human heads, others inscriptions alone, some in ancient characters and others in Arabic, beads of cornelians, agate and crystal and a variety of relics, all of which prove that the people who inhabited those districts in ancient time were civilized and cultured persons. Those districts which are now deserts were the seat, perhaps, of the most ancient of all the various stages of civilization through which Seistan has passed. The knowledge that is available of the past history of this country covers an extent of only some 1,100 or 1,200 years. Everything before the Arab conquest of Seistan is legendary and uncertain to a very great degree. But it seems to be clearly established that never since that conquest has the river Helmand passed to the east of the barrier between those districts of Seistan and the present northern delta. And it was owing to this that the relics of the old civilization of the country are still above ground.

In the northern delta the silt distributed over the face of the country by the various changes in the channels of the Helmand for centuries past has buried the evidences of a corresponding period of history below the present level of the country. The northern delta of the Helmand has been the location of the population of the country and subject to cultivation, and this also combined with other causes alluded to, has effaced nearly all traces of former periods of civilization. *Corresponding period of history buried in northern delta.*

That the population of the ancient districts to the east of the barrier were dependent on canal irrigation alone, and not on water from any channel of the Helmand situated in those districts, can be deduced from the disposition of the ruins. They are most numerous where the old canals enter that district, and as these watercourses tail off towards the Dasht-i-Margo, and in the direction of the delta of the Khash Rud, the ruins themselves become less numerous and there is a great deal of open ground between the more important blocks of ruins. *No river went to the east of the barrier.*

Before proceeding with the task of reconstructing the delta of the Helmand as it probably existed subsequent to the conquest by the Arabs, it will be useful to complete the account of the topographical features which now exist and which cannot have altered to any appreciable extent since that period. The reconstruction of the ancient topography must of course conform to those features, for any hypothesis that are contradicted by them would naturally be unsupportable by any arguments that could be produced in their favour.

The plateau near Shahristān with its basins or fissures.

From a point abreast of the hamlet of Khwābgāh the western plateau sheers off from the river, and continues for about 7 miles to a point a mile or so below the site of the modern village of Shahristān. From this most northerly point the dasht turns abruptly towards the south-west, making less than a right angle with its former course with a greater angle than 270 degrees facing the plain of the delta. This change of course in the line of cliffs forms one limit of the Aliābād bay. Between the most northerly point and the mouth of the Sana Rud, the line of cliffs is not continuous; great rents exist on the terrace of the dasht, and one of these forms an irregular shaped valley that extends in a south-east direction towards the Helmand. The bottom of this valley is a succession of basins or "nāwars," those towards the eastern end being raised above the western floor of the valley. Other smaller fissures exist to the south of this great rent. In addition to the fissures which communicate in a measure with the Aliābād bay, there extends, further to the south-west and closer to the Helmand, a succession of smaller and land-locked basins. As these extend further towards the Helmand they decrease in area as well as in depth, until about 6 or 7 miles from the isolated plateau at Dik-i-Dela the series of basins come to an end. Whatever may have been their origin at an early stage of their formation, there can be no doubt whatever that their further excavation is almost due to the wind. Signs of wind sculpture is plainly visible in the cliffs that form their banks and in the isolated mounds that stand in places upon their floors like bench marks. Their direction also is the same as that of the wind of 120 days.

Chah Nima depression.

The Chah Nima depression is at the present time being put under cultivation. Irrigation is carried on by means of a canal which is supplied by water from the main artery of the Rud-i-Seistan that derives its existence from the Helmand at a point about a mile to the north of Khwābgāh. This irrigation cut is carried back almost to the head of the main depression only some $2\frac{1}{2}$ miles to the west of the river banks under Khwābgāh.

The karez to the Chah Nima depression.

A most ancient karez was once constructed with a view to bring water directly from the ancient bed of the Helmand into the Chah Nima depression. The course of this karez is still plainly visible upon the surface of the dasht by little heaps of white clay, which are all that remains of the earth, excavated from the shafts which also exist, though more or less filled up with wind-borne débris. This karez never was completed. It did not reach the head of the depression it was intended to irrigate. The last shaft is nearly a mile from the eastern and highest part of the depression which at this point is very shallow. Between the last shaft of the karez and the depression there is no other shaft, nor even a cutting to allow of the water to flow out into the lower ground. Had this ever taken place, and had the karez been completed and worked, there would have resulted a scar on the surface of the ground which the lapse of centuries of time could not have completely effaced. The cutting would have been too deep to allow of this, and it would have extended for several hundreds of yards beyond the last shaft upon the dasht. This karez, as far as it is possible to judge at present from indications, took off from the canal which was constructed at the toe of this low plateau and which in its turn must have taken off from the river fully 7 miles above the present head of the Seistan canal system. The actual point where the karez across the dasht to the Chah Nima depression branched off from that ancient canal is about 3 miles above Khwābgāh.

The only reason for abandoning the canal could have been the fact that the levels at that time did not admit of its being worked successfully. A very short distance only separates the last shaft from the head of the depression, and if the levels had been favourable a very little more work would have carried the scheme through to completion. There must be therefore a considerable difference in level between the delta now and what it was at the time when the karez was planned. There has always been a canal upon which the lower or southern districts of the modern delta is dependent for its water supply. The head of the cultivable area in the Chah Nima valley could not have been commanded by it, because if such had been the case there would have been no reason for the karez being put in hand. The difference in level between now and then must amount to several feet, and how many centuries were required to raise the present level it is impossible to say, especially as the water of the Helmand is so lightly burdened with silt as to enable a minimum of annual clearing being sufficient to keep the modern canals working satisfactorily. A similar attempt was made lower down to irrigate a portion of land at the mouth of the Chah Nima depression. This also was abandoned. If appearances are of any value, both these abortive undertakings look as they belonged to one and the same period of time, or that very many years cannot separate their dates. These karezes are the only irrigation works whose traces remain on the face of the dasht to the north of the Trākun channel.

Deductions to be made from Chah Nima karez.

The entrance to the Chah Nima depression gives no clue to the configuration of the valley beyond. It is a narrow channel, half shela or old branch of the river, and half canal. The portion under the modern hamlet of Chah Nima partakes of the nature of a canal, while further to the west this channel is, in all respects and appearance, an offshoot of the river which at the commencement of the 19th century can be proved to have flowed in a southerly direction into the Aliābād valley on its course towards the Hāmun. At the village of Chah Nima is a broad embankment thrown across the canal which arrests the progress of the water contained in it. Otherwise as the valley immediately

Depression.

to the east of this embankment begins to descend and forms further on an extensive depression, the water admitted by the canal would fill the hollow and form a lake. A supply of water is admitted by means of a small irrigation channel by means of which crops are grown in one part of the depression, and in another part a little further on the admission of water forms a shallow pool, where after evaporation had taken place and the water dried up, the floor of the pool is coated with a thick deposit of impure salt. This the natives collect; they separate the earthy matter from the salt and use the latter.

The depression near the Ziarat-i-Murtaza Ali.

There is another "Nāwar" or depression a short distance to the south of the valley of Chah Nima where there is salt deposit. This is not far from the shrine of Murtaza Ali, and is under the protection of the Patron Saint, in this case the son-in-law of the Prophet of Islam. It was a very wise precaution placing the source whence this necessary article is obtained under the protection of Ali, as it is practically rendered neutral territory and free to all adherents of contending factions, and it is not long since Seistan was divided into three parties at deadly feud with one another.

With the Bandik depressions, the two just described compose the greatest of all the basins into which this dasht is broken, and all of these at one time no doubt communicated with the Aliābād bay when the latter was a part of the older lake of Seistan.

These tedious descriptive paragraphs are necessary to allow of the changes which have taken place in the northern delta being described with any degree of certainty. There now remain only a few minor points which it is useful to describe before proceeding with the following chapters.

The plateau near Kinmak and Kala-i-Nau.

The north-western promontory of the dasht overlooks the alluvial delta of the Helmand, and about $2\frac{1}{2}$ miles further in this direction in the midst of a low-lying alluvial tract there is a triangular patch of isolated and low plateaux covered with ruins, and separated from one another by stretches of alluvial soil. Between the promontory and the mouth of the valley of Chah Nima the ground is broken, but through the mounds and detached and covered plateaux a strip of low-lying alluvial soil can be traced in broad curves, immediately at the foot of the detached block of dasht on which stands the modern village of Kimak (the little Kim), and further to the south it enters the Aliābād plain. In this direction the isolated lofty bluff of clay on whose eastern slopes the village of Kala-i-Nau stood, till it was overwhelmed by drifting sand, forms a very conspicuous land-mark. To the north of this bluff there is a similar isolated plateau barely a mile to the west of Kimmak, on whose summit there are some very ancient ruins. These are called the ruins of Atishkada or the Temple of the Sacred Fire. These complete the description of the salient feature of the modern delta of Seistan.

CHAPTER IV.

The following extract is taken from Sir H. Rawlinson's memoir. It is from Al Istākhri who gives a sketch of the hydrography of Seistan which contains many very realistic touches. He writes : " The largest river of this region is the Hindmend, which rises at the back of the country of Ghur, and comes out on the border of Arrokhaj and the district of Date wor. Then it goes on to Bist, and finishes in Sejestan, where it falls into the Lake of Zirreh." Istākhri's account of the hydrography of Seistan.

"The Hindmend flows in one single bed from Bist until it arrives within one stage of Sejestan where canals begin to be taken off from it. The first canal which is derived from the river is the Te'am which waters several districts till it arrives at the borders of Nishk. The second canal is the Nashrud which also irrigates many districts. Then is taken off the Sena Rud which flows to within a farsakh of Sejestan, and this is the stream on which boats ply from Bist to Sejestan, when the river is in flood, for at that season only is the river practical to boats ; and all the streams of the city of Sejestan are derived from this canal of Sena Rud. This as the Hindmend descends, the canal of Shabeh is taken off from it, which waters some 30 villages and after that the canal of Mili branches off which irrigates many districts. Lower down the canal of Zalik is also taken off, which furnishes water to a large tract of country ; and what remains of the Hindmend goes on in a river bed which is named the Karak and here there is a band or dam to prevent the residue falling into the Lake of Zirreh, except in the time of flood, for when that arrives the dam is of course broken down and the overflow falls into the lake."

The current of the Helmand in flood is about 4 miles an hour. That boats can descend it at that time is also certain, provided their draught is small. In the winter during the period of low river the stream is too shallow to allow of navigation, and that season there probably existed, in older times, weirs in the river bed in order to keep a good level of water in the canals. There is no mention made of a permanent weir or regulator such as evidently existed later on. Had any work of this nature been in existence it would have put an end to all navigation, even by the smallest of craft.

If the ruins of Sargāh-i-Seistan (Damb-i-Rustan it is also called) are regarded as the point from which Seistan was generally reckoned to commence, as the name certainly implies it did, a stage above that point would place the head of the first canal mentioned by Al Istākhri close to the position of the modern village of Chahārburjak. Near that place a very large canal some 200 feet in width can yet be traced, although it is much broken up and partially erased by more recent canals. This would have given the Te'am canal suffi- The Te'am canal.

cient command over the districts it was intended to water, and this ancient and wide canal bed is perhaps the remains of that work. It would in this case have passed down the old river bed between the foot of the Meski plateau and the low dasht which separates the present river from that old bed.

In the immediate vicinity of Kala-i-Fath a wisp of modern canals of no very great size, and now also in ruins, took off from the river, and they have obliterated all traces of the ancient alignment of the Te'am canal except in places where the latter was carried through a dasht or rise in the ground. The cutting which divides the ruins of Sargeh into two distinct forts must have been made to allow of a canal to pass through and hug the toe of the dasht, at a high level, to carry water from the parent stream to the lands around the ruins of Paisai and Tikāla, towards the ruins now called Sār-o-Tār.

The Zorkan and Zarkan canals.

The ancient canals called in tradition the Zorkan and Zarkan and ascribed to Nushirwān the Just, also bifurcated either under the ruins of Sargāh or more probably above the ancient site marked by a mound known as Damb-i-Kalān. The exact spot of this parting of the waters cannot now be recognised as the vestiges of the old canal have been overlaid and effaced by recent silt deposits. But tradition states, and the general statement may be accepted, that both the sites were fortified posts to keep watch over a regulator where the waters of the canals were distributed to the various districts they nourished. These canals of Zorkan or Zarkan are said to have been made during the early years of the reign of Naushirwan, and a detailed account of the various weirs that have at one time or another been made across the Helmand will include another of these ancient works. From the description of the Te'am canal recorded by Istākhri, and the traces of the Zorkan and Zarkan canals followed up carefully to their final termination in the lands around Nishk, there seems to be no room for doubting that they were part of the great Te'am canal. The Zorkan kept to the west of the barrier alluded to and passed the now ruined fort of Kurdo at a short distance to its west. The Zarkan, a much larger canal judged by the scars it has left, trended towards the north-east and was carried, by means of a deep cutting with very high spoil banks both of which still exist, through the barrier to the south-east of Kala-i-Gāwak and thence by alternate deep cuttings through dasht and ordinary channels in the alluvial tracts it distributed its fertilizing waters over the district of Ghulghula and further to the north-east around the sites to the north-east of Chahilburj. At a point some 5 or 6 miles to the north of the Ziarat of Amirān the Zorkan canal turned back towards the Zarkan, and onwards from this point the two canals flowed side by side with merely the thickness of their spoil banks between their channels. The reason for this sudden change of course was the ancient deltaic fan of the ancient and

Sand buried ruins, inside second line of walls-Sar-o-tar.

(Part II to face page 146.)

now deserted river bed called the Dor[1] which enters the Seistan delta to the north-east of Ziarat-i-Amirān, and which lay beyond the command of the Zarkan canal to a very great extent.

The continuity of the beds of these twin canals has been broken up by the Khāsh Rud in the course of time. This was however a contingency which was always foreseen and guarded against. There is yet a well-known place to the south of Chakansur, a locality called Dahana, or the embouchure of the river, to which its waters were confined artificially, for there are signs at this place still existing of an acqueduct by which the waters of the canals were carried over the river channel thereby safeguarding them from being breached and interrupted by floods. The traces of the brick flooring and other remains of baked brick still exist, and the river of Khāsh was probably kept to this, as an escape for its flood water, by artificial means.

The remains of the Zorkan and Zarkan fulfil all the conditions of Istākhri's description. From what little is known of the districts of Ghulghula and Sār-o-Tār, and of the soil now covered with sand drifts, there seems to be room for very little doubt that it was these districts which were known as the Rasalik and which were the granary of ancient Seistan. The twin canals have been laboriously followed for purposes of identification to their very end, and the lie of their channels and their situation generally fulfils so closely all the conditions laid down in their description as to render the identification complete up to the last point. The Te'am canal, therefore, which separated from the Helmand close to Chaharburjak was the parent stream of these as well as the canal which flowed eastward through the cutting through the Sargāh headland.

A length of about 300 feet of the ancient Zarkan canal can be still seen about a mile to the north of the village of Arbāb Dost Muhammad, and further on in places where its spoil banks, or a portion of one of them, is weathered into all the appearance of a natural mound there stands a cairn called after one Ghulam, a Baluch. Further to the north and from a point almost abreast of the Kurdo fort (ruined) the course of this branch of the Te'am can be followed up to its termination, as this tract of country seems not to have been overrun by the Helmand and no recent silt has in consequence been deposited.

---

[1] The Iudai or Dor is wider than the Rud i-Biyaban and its bed is defined by low cliffs of dasht. The floor is a hard and ivory white surface of alluvium. The famous wells at Shand and further to the east are all situated in the bed of this ancient river, which, however, so far above its termination is full of shingle, covered with wind borne deposits. The water bearing stratum is shingle—Shand in Baluchi. I am inclined to believe that this ancient river bed was occupied at one time by the Helmand before the river turned aside from it, abreast of Girishk. How can it be possible on other grounds to account for this wide river bed in a notoriously waterless tract. The latter is as yet, however, absolutely unknown. How is it possible on other grounds to account for the gravel, the water bearing stratum, or the presence of water, unless it is fed by moisture that oozes into the old line of drainage through the Chaman, or low meadow on which Girishk is located. The deep bed of the Khash Rud intercepts subsoil drainage from the Zamindawar foot hills. With a small and uncertain rainfall the water in the bed of the Dor cannot be attributed to local springs replenished by the annual rainfall.—G. P. T.

There is a modern hamlet called Deh Niāz Khan close to the remains of this canal, and abreast of this place there are two masonry abutments of baked brick which line both banks for about 40 feet in length. They give a waterway of 15 feet to the canal, which at this point is some 8 feet deep now. These masonry abutments are partly exposed and partly buried under a mound which marks the site of an ancient village, or buildings, and upon this mound are perched the group of squalid huts which form the hamlet. From this point onwards nothing of a similar nature was discovered until the remains of the acqueduct were reached which have already been described.

The Nash Rud.

The next canal on the list is that of the Nash Rud which probably took off on the left bank, for there would not have been room for two large canals on the right bank of the river. It is also quite natural to suppose that some effort was made to keep the southern delta supplied with water.

At present, on a low cliff of a terrace, some 3 miles above Chahārburjak, there stands a ruined fort called Chahilimirez, built it is said to safeguard 40 distributaries, or a canal whose share of water were distributed into 40 parts of 24 hours each. "Mi" is the same word as "Shabānaruz," and used to describe a share of water flowing for 24 hours, or a "day and night." The ancient Nash Rud would probably not have needed to take off as high up river as this. It perhaps did so, not very far above Bandar-i-Kamāl Khan; and in the remains of the great canal of the Jui Gershasp we may perhaps find the canal mentioned by Al Istākhri. There seemed to have existed a number of canals at this point, so that while the canal named the Nash Rud fed the lands at the end of the Rud-i-Biyabān, the others may have irrigated the lands on the terrace of dasht to the south of the channel. The name of the Nash Rud probably lingers in the form of Rud-i-Nasru which is the name given to a much later bed of the Helmand. With the Sena Rud this is the only name of an ancient canal which survives.

The Sena Rud.

The next in order is the Sena Rud, and the statement that it flowed (lower down) within a farsakh of the Capital[1] disposes of any claim the present Sena Rud may be considered to possess as being the representative of this ancient river bed. From indications on the face of the country the point of bifurcation between this branch of the river and the Helmand may be located with a very great deal of probability near the ruins known as the Haftār Kund, about 7 miles up stream of Khwābgāh. The Sena Rud flowed to the east of the detached block of dasht 2¼ miles to the south-east of that hamlet and thence past the modern hamlet of Dantanu, past the site where Kala-i-Mahmud stands, and into the depression near the other modern hamlet of Diwālak through which its waters reached the Chung-i-Darāzgu. The whole of this tract through which the Sona Rud passed is now a marshy bottom, and with the

---

[1] The ruin of Bina-i-kair, the City of the Khosroes at Nad Ali, was the capital of Seistan at the time in which Al Istākhri wrote, *vide* Part III.

suburbs and gardens which existed then, it must have been a very short 6 miles from the outskirts of that City. If the Sena Rud did not take off close to Haftār Kund, it must have done so near Khwābgāh, following the western toe of the isolated dasht terraces about 2½ miles to the east of that place. On the western cliffs of these terraces there are most ancient ruins which may have overlooked the waters of the Sena Rud. This alternative channel would join the first above Dantanu, and thence onwards, as already indicated. The Helmand probably occupied its present bed as far as the modern fort of Kuhak, and thence wheeling towards the west or left, past the (now) ruined fort Khwājah Ahmad, it must have occupied very nearly the same channel, or course, which the Ilamdar River held for some time about 60 years ago, and passing to the west and not far from the capital.

Below Bandar-i-Kamāl Khan no canal could have taken off to the west from the river except through a very deep cutting through the dasht. This would have left a scar which the lapse of centuries could not have healed. No such scar exists until abreast of Māshi on the present Helmand.

The Sha'abeh canal was the next in order on the list and it was the forerunner of the modern Rud-i-Seistan. The word Sha'abeh may be taken to mean the lower or southern canal, and it watered the same tracts which are now served by the Rud-i-Seistan. This district, to the left of the main canal, is called Sheb-i-Āb (south of the water), and the district probably gave its name to the ancient canal which irrigated it. Or the latter may have been named from the fact that it served the southern districts of Seistan. The Sha'abeh canal differed considerably from the usual type. Its actual take off from the Helmand when Istakhri wrote was at a point opposite the ruins of Gāwak at the locality now called Māshi. It crosses the dasht immediately to the west by a karez, the spoil heaps of which form a series of tumuli of considerable height. This plateau is separated from the tableland to the west by a depression, once no doubt a bed of the Helmand. The northern end of this small valley is filled with alluvium, and as soon as the karez comes up to this narrow plain, it is succeeded by an open canal now some 15 feet wide, which crosses the alluvial soil up to the foot of the western dasht. From this point where the open canal ceased, it was carried through the western dasht by a tunnel with vertical shafts at intervals, a karez in fact, up to a point abreast of the hamlet of Khwābgāh where a deep cutting exists at the point where the karez was again succeeded by an open channel. About 1½ miles further on the open channel again ceased and a promontory of the dasht was tunnelled as a karez to carry the water through it, instead of round the toe of the promontory, and once more on the north of this dasht the karez gave place to an open channel. This succession of open channel and karez in the first 10 or 12 miles of the Sha'abeh canal is very remarkable. This canal was evidently kept at as high a level as was possible in order to obtain greater com-

The Sha'abeh canal.

y 2

n and for its water. The labour in constructing it must have been very considerable. There is, however, another point of very great interest attaching to the karez portions of this canal. The shafts at the present time are of course filled up, but their spoil mounds are still in existence, and though much reduced in size, they afford a certain guide to the alignment of the tunnel below. They are however so very close to the present edge of the dasht, as to render them useless. Many of them have disappeared in the course of time. Ravines have cut back into the dasht, and the latter has been gradually eroded. The fact that it had been considered worth while to make certain sections of the canal as karezes, and not to carry an open channel round those projections which the karezes crossed, shows that at the time of construction the dasht undoubtedly extended very much further to the east and north-east and that the karezes at that time gave a better alignment. The karez that had been made with a view to irrigate the Chah Nima depression and then abandoned within a short distance of its south-east end was a branch of the second karez section of this ancient Sha'abeh canal. A continuation of the ancient canal may have been carried through the promontory to the south of Warmāl by a karez (signs of which exist) and so reached the northern portion of the southern delta of Seistan. The fact of certain sections of the Sha'abeh canal having been carried across projections of the dasht either in an open channel or by means of karezes has preserved those portions, and enabled some idea to be formed of the magnitude of the work and its alignment, after the lapse of 1,000 years. To the north-west of the site of the Mission camp at Kuhak, this ancient canal enters a nawar or depression in the dasht called Ja-i-surkh owing to the red colour of the soil through which it passed. There exists a great cutting through the dasht forming the north bank of this basin, and it may have been that this depression was used as a reservoir whence the water was distributed into more than one channel beyond it. The depression is still filled by the overflow of the Rud-i-Seistan.

Inside the course of the present Khwābgāh canal it is said that the abutments of an ancient bridge or regulator were found embedded in the banks on each side of the waterway. These were constructed with baked bricks, and as the arch is absent it was not possible to say to what particular class of public work it at one time belonged. It was in this part of the country that wind scours have revealed the existence of certainly a most ancient system of irrigation, the canals or watercourses of which have been buried $2\frac{1}{2}$ feet below the present level of the ground.

The canals of Zalik. The canals of Zalik are next in order in Al Istākhri's list. The district of Zalik was probably the tract of country between Bunjār and Kasamābād (both old villages) on the west, with Jallālābād and Kārku on the north and east. The limits of this sub-division may have extended a great deal further than Jallālābād towards the north, and it probably included the country as far as the Kohlak mound, in the direction of Sāwari Shah. The Zalik canal probably took off not very far from where the modern village of Sharifābād stands. Beyond this point the course of the canal was probably towards the north-west where now the Pariun channels lie, and it probably had very much the same alignment as the old Mārgo canal, a work of some age and importance in its time, the remains of which are traceable here and there between Jallālā-bād and Karku, but closer to the latter. The remains called Chahārdari, a group of strange ruins about 6 miles south-west of the Karku mound, were built along the course of the old canal of Mārgo. The ruins of Chahārdari belong, as far as it is now possible to judge by their appearance, to the period of Zāhidān, but whether the old canal in their neighbourhood belongs also to that period or not, it is impossible to say. To the north and east of the Tappa-i-Kohlak there are traces of a great canal which extended towards the north-west and which must have irrigated the lands around the ancient town of Sāwari Shah. The course of this canal can still be traced by a line of mounds, the fragments of its lofty spoil banks, which, when the waters are out over this low-lying tract, stand up as islands whose outline the tall reeds cannot conceal. The considerable mound of Akbarābad and innumerable fragments of walls (and brick kilns) mark the course of this great canal and are the remains of ancient dwellings which once graced its banks. The furthest mound formed by this old spoil banks is the Tappa-i-Beringak which stands in the Chung of that name, the greatest of all the reed beds of the Hāmun. All round Tapa-i-Kohlak the ground is full of traces of canals and buildings, all of course nearly obliterated by the annual submersion of this tract by the Pariun. These remains or rather the mounds formed by the spoil banks of old canals and dèbris of buildings form little islands in the swamp that surrounds the mound of Kohlak for 8 or 9 months in every year. Many of the remains in the vicinity of the Kohlak mound are, however, of quite modern date.

Another point has to be borne in mind when dealing with the ancient hydrography of Seistan. That is—the entrance of the river on the northern delta has always been a fixed point or moveable only within certain narrow limits that do not allow of much scope for change.[1] Whenever the river, in the centuries that have passed since Istākhri lived and wrote, has entered the present delta it has done so at this point; and whenever its course has approximated nearly to that which it occupied 1,000 years ago, the alignment of the canals necessary to maintain the population has also gone back of necessity almost to the actual alignment of the older canals, that is to say as long as any pretence has been kept up with regard to a control of the water supply and of the river. So that canals, the traces of which exist in a more or less legible condition now, are possibly either occupying almost the same alignment of

The entrance of the river into the delta—a fixed point.

---

[1] The limits within which the change can now (or ever could) have taken place, is represented by the area of an isoceles triangle, each side of which is about 6 miles long and base (to the north of the apex) not more than 4 miles wide.

much older works, or are existing over the latter buried under 2 or 3 feet and perhaps more of silt. The modern alignment of canals under the conditions prevailing at present bear the same relation to the river as the older canals bore to the Helmand 1,000 years ago.

The Mili canal. The Mili canal took off perhaps not very far from the site of the modern Kuhak fort. Its course was also in a north-west direction and it irrigated probably a good deal of the present lands of Kasamābād and Bunjar, if not the whole of the tract further on in the direction of Kachiān, a modern village. The Mili canal and its distributaries did the work which now falls to the share of the modern Husenki canal system. The name is very curious: Mili—or belonging to the Mil. It almost presupposes the existence of the Mil-i-Kasamābād up to whose very foot the waters of the old Mili canal must have reached. If the great minaret had been then in existence it would account for the name given to the canal.

CHAPTER V.

The river being the source from which the canals were fed, it was necessary to adopt some means of maintaining a head of water in these channels. This has always been done by means of weirs, and a notice of these important works and at the same time of the great changes that have taken place in the course of the river itself will now be of interest.

First in order, being the most ancient was the weir attributed to Jamshid, the famous legendary and prehistoric monarch of the First Persian Dynasty. This work was built and kept up at such a remote period of time that its name has been almost forgotten. It is referred to as the Band-i-Koshk, because it spanned the river some four miles above Khwābgāh and two miles above a small ruin called Koshk. *Band-i-Koshk.*

This ruin stands on a mound of dasht at the mouth of a bay weathered out of a rectangular piece of dasht whose greater diagonal lay in an almost exactly north and south direction. The southern angle overlooks the present Helmand, and the eastern some modern ruins called Haftār Kund. It is not at all clear whether the dam, weir, or regulator existed across the channel when the river was in the bed where it now lies, or when it flowed past the eastern angle of the dasht. The tradition is vague in all essential particulars. But wherever the river may have been, there are to the north of the Haftār Kund ruins of the remains of at least four very old canals, the general alignment of which can be followed by the remains of their spoil banks; and two of these canals must have been large. They seemed to take off from the river when it was very much in its present position, and the point of divergence must have been about a mile-and-half above the Haftār Kund ruins.

The clay soil contains a considerable proportion of very fine water worn gravel, and when the spoil banks of a newly excavated canal are heaped up the stones are not noticeable. But in the revolution of centuries of time, the wind carries away the soil which has become loosened by the alternations of heat and of cold and the action of damp combined with the presence of saline matter. The shingle is left behind, and thus in course of ages the earth heaped up disappear and leaves a heap of shingle which overlies and protects from the wind a residuum of clay. The broken and worn spoil banks in this condition are very easily mistaken for natural mounds where they occur singly. But in the case of several ancient canals that have flowed parallel to one another, or whose courses have otherwise conformed to similar curves, the isolated mounds group themselves and lead the eye of a spectator to their original alignment. *How the shingle remains spoil banks of canals.*

Once the river turned into the northern delta its point of embouchure could not find much scope for change, and so it is that the present Helmand may very possibly occupy what is practically the same channel as it did when the dam or weir of Jamshed was in existence.

Dam of Naushirwān between Tirkoh and Dik-i-Dela.

The next in order is the Dam of Naushirwān. This was many miles higher up the river. It was built according to tradition on the reef of kim that stretches across the river bed from the mound or bluff overlooking the river on the right bank on which some ruins are situated. The bluff is called Tirkoh. The letters r and l are constantly and easily interchanged and Tirkoh is the same word as Tilgkoh, the g being silent or omitted before the k. Tilg is a very old word for a grave, and is used frequently in place of the more familiar Persian word Gur. The remains of this bluff are said to be those of a graveyard, and in the face of the low cliff there are ancient sepulchres excavated in the clay. The little fort of Dik-i-Dela was built by an official of Naushirwān to guard the dam, and to give timely notice of its needing repair. The tradition with reference to this dam and the purpose it served is very detailed. The ancient canals of Zorkan and Zarkan, already referred to, are said to have taken off in one channel from the right bank, or end of the weir, constructed with a view to maintain a head of water in these important canals and to keep the Rud-i-Sina or Sena Rud also supplied with water. The canal on the right bank nourished tracts of country now a desert and lands as far as their channels extended.

Explanation of words Zarkan and Zorkan.

The names Zarkan and Zorkan are thus accounted for. The Zorkan was first to be constructed. Forced labour was employed, and in consequence of this it was so called. The Zarkan was constructed after it, and the labourers received wages and in consequence worked more willingly, and this was the larger of the two canals.[1]

Both the Dam of Jamshid and that of Naushirwān are said to have been carried away by floods.

The traditions probably contain a proportion of truth, as it is for other reasons more than possible that weirs did exist at these points. The work attributed to Naushirwān being of a later date would need to be built higher up the stream, as the river kept piling up its delta below; and also in order to help the abandoned channel of the Rud-i-Sina. It is, however, more probable that instead of these weirs being swept away, when it would have been easy to rebuild them, the river itself changed its course either into the Rud-i-Biyabān or some one or other of the older and now almost obliterated channels on the terrace to the south of Trākun. By the time it came back again to the northern delta, a fresh alignment or a readjustment of the canals system would have become absolutely necessary, as several centuries must have separated the date of one change from that of another. Khusrau I, surnamed Naushirwān the Just, reigned for about 48 years, dying in the

---

[1] Zor—force; hence oppression. Zar—gold, i.e., wages.

year 579 A.D. Al Istākhri wrote about the middle of the 10th century A.D., or about 400 years after the death of that monarch. A longer period of time therefore has passed since the invasion of Seistan by Timur, which resulted in the sack of Zāhidān and the captivity of its Prince, Malik Kutb-ud-din, and the present day, than had separated the death of Naushirwān from the period in which Al Istākhri wrote. The account of the movements of the forces of the Arabs in 36 and 40 A.H. show that the Helmand river was at that time in the northern delta, and it is not impossible that the Dam of Naushirwān may really have been a much older structure and which tradition has assigned to him in default of exact knowledge. These same remarks would apply to the two celebrated canals. The presence of the capital renders it certain that the river must have been in the northern delta for a very long time before the Arabs crossed it on their way to the city.

This Band-i-Naushirwān is said to have been called also Band-i-Chash-makā.

The Jui Kohneh followed by Obad Ibn Ziyad, after he had crossed the Sena Rud on his march from Zaranj to Kish, was undoubtedly the Zorkan, the western of the two canals attributed to Naushirwān the Just. The information is taken from Sir Henry Rawlinson's memoir and translated by him from Beladhuri. In course of time when Istākhri obtained his information the Te'am canal had been constructed taking off higher up the river, and from his account it must have been brought down to the two older canals which it supplied with water. That these canals fertilized exactly the same tracts of country as that alluded to by the Istākhri, is clearly proved by their remains which exist at this present time. The Zarkan canal where it passes through the dasht must have had a waterway of nearly 100 feet when it was clean and in working order. In its ruined condition it appears to have been larger than the old Sha'abeh canal, of which the remains are still visible. Its spoil banks on the dasht also belong to two distinct periods, the upper and more recent resting on the older spoil banks.

The third weir in the Helmand was higher up again than the Band-i-Chashmakā. The tradition relating to its existence is more definite than the tale attached to the latter. It was a much more recent work and there are allusions to it in historical writings which prove that this great and useful work did actually exist. As the traditions deal with facts closer to the present time, they take definite form, and contain many interesting details that are likely to be true. The order in which these dams are said to have been in existence at various periods of time is also in agreement with geographical knowledge and the configuration of the country.

Bard i-Rustam.

The story of the Band-i-Rustam will be related in its proper place.

The destruction of Rām Shahristān alluded to by Al Istākhri probably took place owing to the sudden return of the Helmand into the northern delta.

It can be shewn to have done so at comparatively recent period, when Kala-i-Fath had to be vacated for the same reason and the seat of Government transferred to another site.

The dam across the Helmand described by Al Istakhri which prevented the water in the river running to waste in the Hāmun, during the season of low river, must have existed below or to the north-west of the Takht-i-Pul bridge. It was probably built with fascines of tamarisk branches, having been merely a temporary structure as that author is careful to explain. It enabled a great deal of cultivation to be carried on in tracts now overgrown with reeds, or submerged to the depths of several feet by the water of the Helmand, and the existence of the town of Sāwari Shah was rendered possible within the actual Hāmun. This ruin occupies undoubtedly a very ancient site, and its continuance was dependent on the control of the river which is indicated by the legends of the dams built and maintained by the mythical Persian Monarch Jamshid and the later and historical personage Naushirwān the Just. In the absence of the Helmand the superfluous waters that may have reached the Hāmun-i-Sāwari from the Farah Rud probably supported the agricultural population, and for the rest wells would have answered all demands for domestic use. The existence of the dam near the mouth of the Helmand, and probably within a couple of miles of the bridge, would account for the necessity of providing some means of crossing the channel, as above the band the flow of water having been arrested it would accumulate and attain a considerable depth. Between Kārku Shah and Nād Ali no other bridge has been found, although it is very possible that ruins may have been overlooked in that tract owing to the growth of tamarisk, or lie buried in silt.

The invasion of Seistan by Timur. The invasion of Seistan by Timur brought to an end the state of affairs which had lasted since the time when Al Istākhri wrote, and which had been in existence with perhaps very little modification from the time when the country was a province of the Persian kingdom under the Sassanians. Changes had of course taken place, but they were gradual and tended towards improvement. Some time long before the period of Malik Kutb-ud-din, the Helmand had altered its course from the northern to the southern delta, and flowed down the Rud-i-Biyabān into the Hamun.

The weir across the Helmand. The effects of this change were, however, modified by a great work which was constructed in the Helmand to give the districts of the northern delta sufficient water for cultivation. This was the great weir built in the river bed above Bandar-i-Kamāl Khan. When this change took place, and when

A. D. 1385. this weir was built it is impossible to say for certain. In 785 A. H. it is mentioned in history as the Band-i-Rustam, and this is sufficient to stamp it as having been at that time regarded as an ancient work. Zāhidān had been in existence then 430 years according to traditions, and the Band-i-Rustam must have been certainly as old as Zāhidān. Asiatics have long memories, and traditions of 200 or 300 years frequently contain facts, and are often replete with valuable information. So that if the Band had been a structure of merely two centuries, there would have existed some distinct tradition as to its age. It is, however, quite possible that when the change took place, a weir was built on an older site where an earlier work had once existed, and the modern structure being thus a revival of the older was merged into the legend attaching to the latter, and its later origin forgotten. The sites of the weirs attributed to Jamshid and to Naushirwân are still pointed out, and if it was necessary to reconstruct either in these days the latter would be looked on merely as a reconstruction of the ancient work by the country folk. The Band-i-Rustam which Timur destroyed may, therefore, have well been in existence for some 300 or more years previous to its destruction. The tradition regarding the irrigation system is explicit and most valuable. According to it, for nine months of the year the canals were kept full by the head of water that accumulated behind the weir. During the three months of floods the surplus water escaped over the weir down the Rud-i-Biyabān and into the Hamun, and also to the Gaud-i-Zireh. The Kaiānis may well be proud of their ancestry when among their forebears there were princes capable of constructing and maintaining such a great work, and of keeping up a fairly large and complex system of irrigation.

The last act of Timur in Seistan was to destroy the famous Band-i-Rustam. Tradition locates this great work in a portion of the river bed some 4 or 5 miles above Bandar-i-Kamāl Khan. Here the river bed narrowed and a bar of Kim stretched across the bed, the banks on either side being for this reason well marked and forming low cliffs. At this point a great weir had been built by some previous Ruler of Seistan when the Helmand had altered its course and flowed down the Rud-i-Biyabān. Such a work then became absolutely necessary in order to maintain the prosperity of the country around the capital. Tradition also states that the water that accumulated behind this band submerged a good portion of the alluvial soil that lies between Chahārburjak village and the low isolated plateau to the west of the former. The old channel of the Helmand that existed in the northern delta was in this way kept supplied with water which flowed in the old channel already described as existing between those limits.   *   *   *

*   *   *   *   *   This weir it is said was built with baked brick lime and saruj; along the summit of this structure there was a line of large earthenware pipes through which the flood water found an outlet towards the west. The name of the weir is said to have been Yakau, and it is as well known as the Band-i-Yakau as it is by the name of Band-i-Rustam. The ruins that grace the terraces overlooking the Rud-i-Biyabān evidently date from a period anterior to the destruction of

Destruction of the Band-i-Rustam.

Tradition regarding the Band-i-Rustam.

this great work, when in the summer the escape of the water down the bed of the western channel rendered it unsafe to build within reach of a sudden flood. The districts on the banks of the Shela were cultivated and inhabited tracts and whatever water escaped during the season of floods entered the Hāmun-i-Seistan south of the Koh-i-Khwāja, and formed a lake and Naizār in this direction.

The architect of this band is said to have been a person of the tribe of Kakāh, but his name unhappily has perished, as well as that of the ruler under whose auspices it was constructed. On either flanks of this weir there were two fortified posts established in which permanent garrisons were kept up to guard the weir against destruction and to give early notice of repairs becoming necessary.

Reference to the weir in ancient literature. Turning now to such works of reference as are available, the weir recorded by Sharafud-i-din Ali of Yazd and in the Malfuzat-i-Sahib Kiran are identical and a point of interest makes itself at once apparent. It is most important as it bears out the truth of the tradition. After the destruction of Tāk, Timur continued his march and when the camp was pitched on the Helmand the work of destruction was begun and carried on until not a vestige of the weir remained visible. The Helmand must have been at some distance from Tāk, and it had not been met with in the vicinity of the capital. Secondly it was necessary to form a camp so that the work of destruction could be carried out thoroughly. This shows that the work could not have been of a temporary nature, though it would not have been an easy task to remove any weir strong enough to withstand the weight and force of the water behind it, except when the river was almost quite dry. This revengeful act put an end to the irrigation system of the northern delta.

At this period the southern delta must have been the principal cultivated area, and all the population of the northern delta must have gravitated into the lands around the distributaries of the Rud-i-Biyabān, while a part of the present valley of the Helmand as low down perhaps as Kala-i-Fath was also probably cultivated by means of local canals.

Malik Kutb-ud-din remained in Samarkand for 21 years until the spring of 807 A. H. Timur had formed the intention of invading China where the founder of the Ming Dynasty had some time before dispossessed the descendants of Kubilai Khan of their throne. In order to succour the representative of the illustrious race of Chingiz and to curb the insolence of the heathen who had usurped their throne, the forces of Central Asia were mobilized and before the winter was well over the Royal pavilions were pitched beyond the walls of Otrār. But the spirit of the great soldier was stronger than the frail and warworn body which had housed it so long, and the progress of the expedition was put an end to by his illness. *   *

*   *   *   *   *   *   *   *

* * * * * * * *

Early news of his death was probably conveyed to Malik Kutb-ud-din who succeeded in escaping to Herat, where the son of the late Ruler of Asia was keeping his court. Shah Rukh Mirza restored to the Kaiāni his appanage of Seistan, which he was to govern as a feudatory of his benefactor. Malik Kutb-ud-din took over the Government and one of his first acts was apparently the building of Kala-i-Fath, which he made his capital, and the restoration of the prosperity of his country. Shortly after his return to Seistan, the oppressive demands for revenue made by the Suzerain to meet the charges entailed by the quarrel with his nephew, who had seized Trans-Oxiana and was setting himself up as an independent sovereign, drove Kutb-ud-din into rebellion. This entailed an invasion of Seistan by Shah Rukh, but as the Seistani declined to put their fortunes to the test of a battle, the Imperial troops effected nothing; peace was made, and Shah Rukh proceeded to Kandahar to consolidate his authority in that direction.[1] Merza Shah Rukh Shah's invasion of Seistan.

The fact that the capital was located at Kala-i-Fath proves the absence of the Helmand from the northern delta. Had the river been in this delta, there were many sites which Kutb-ud-din might have selected for that purpose. And it would not have been necessary to look for a strong position for his palace so high up the river. It is undoubtedly owing to the necessity of being close to the source from which the water for irrigation purposes was drawn that led Malik Kutb-ud-din to place his capital and residence at Kala-i-Fath. Although Timur had punished Seistan very severely, still he did not utterly destroy the country, and during the 21 years that Shah-i-Shāhān had governed it he had doubtless done something towards restoring the prosperity of the country. Reasons for saying the main river flowed at the Trākun channel.

It is to the period that was ushered in by the return of Malik Kutb-ud-din that the third Band-i-Seistan must be attributed. This was built on a bar of Kim that extends across the river bed below the Puz-i-Māshi. This dam is called in tradition the Band-i-Bul'baka. The architect of this is also said to have been a person belonging to the Kakāh tribe. This band though not quite a permanent structure was such in a great measure. It was carefully constructed. A row of tamarisk stakes was first placed in line across the river; then hurdles of tamarisk boughs bent to form cylinders were arranged against the stakes and touching one another. These were filled with shingle and boulders from the river bed, fascines of tamarisk boughs and trunks were made and placed against the line of gabions on the upper side, then shingle The Band-i-Bul'-baka.

---

[1] This invasion took place in 1407-1408 A. D. There were then three weirs or bands said by the historian to have dated from the time of Rustam ! (1) the Band-i-Raskak, (2) Band-i-Shahr (i.e., the weir at, or of, the City), (3) Band-i-Bulghān (Abu'l Ghani ?). This was the strongest (or largest of the three. All were destroyed, but the capital was not captured. Shah Rukh left Seistan 26th January 1408.

and boulders were piled on both sides of the latter. This band or weir remained in position during flood and low water and from above it there took off canals which not only supplied Kala-i-Fath with water, but which conveyed the latter almost as far as the "District of Nishk."

Proofs that the Zorkan and Zarkan or some such canals were restored.

Either the Zorkan and Zarkan canals were resuscitated, or some others were constructed by means of which water was carried into the lands to the east of the barrier as far as the ruins of Ghulghula. In March 1905 a fragment of a dedicatory tablet was brought in from a ruin between Ghulghula and the fort of Kurdo. This tablet was a coarsely glazed tile, the letters were written in a bad hand fluctuating between Arabic and Persian script.

1428-9 A.D.

This was only a fragment, but the date 831 A. H. was so well preserved as to be perfectly legible. The fragment with one or two others was found on a low mound on the north of a graveyard, and the mound may have been the ruins of a mausoleum. It is highly improbable that a corpse would have been taken into the desert for burial; and the deceased person must have lived near the place of his burial, and the place must have been rendered habitable by means of a canal.[1]

The country round Chakānsur was nourished by the Khāsh Rud and the district the southern delta, and the tract around Kala-i-Fath, were the localities where the bulk of the cultivation existed. In the northern delta to the west of the barrier there may have been cultivation as far north as the village of Malik Haidari or up to Zāhidān, but the lands beyond towards the present Hāmun must have been a desert.

Number of cultivators in the time of Malik Hamza Khan.

The Chigini ruins in this direction mark the furthest extent of the cultivation that was carried on by means of the Helmand canals in the time of Malik Hamza, and it is said that 2,000 pagaus or gangs of labourers were needed for the operations of agriculture and the maintenance of the canals and watercourses between the capital and that place. The lands in the direction of Post-i-Gau and to the north of that ruined town, in the direction of the site called Khwāja Surju, required another 1,000 pagaus to carry on the task of cultivation, the lands they tilled being watered from the Khāsh Rud.

Canals of Khāsh Rud at Kadah were in flow 300 years ago.

If this information is correct, it appears that the ancient canals that took off from the river of Khāsh near Kadah must have been working barely 300 years ago. It is possible, as the spoil banks of these cuttings, it is said, present a clayey surface and have not been worn down into heaps of gravel. The Hokāt was also cultivated and irrigated from the Farah Rud, so that the patrimony that descended to Malik Hamza was a valuable and flourishing possession.

Hauzdār tract was cultivated.

Those tracts of land, now a desert, around Trākun Rāmrod and Hauzdār, were at that time cultivated and populated. The Rud-i-Biyabān discharged

---

[1] This was in all probability the site of the capital founded after the destruction of Zāhidān, which was buried by drifts of sand, and had to be abandoned by its inhabitants.

The Windmill Chigini, or ornamented.   Materials Béton-Pisé, and clay plaster.

(Part II to face page 160.)

the water in separate outlets and one of these flowed into the deep bay to the south of the Puza-i-Surhdagāl, into which its course can yet be easily traced. These outlets could only have been very full during the season of floods, when the water escaped over the weir of Māshi. During the winter months the volume of water must have been considerably reduced, and the task of utilising and controlling it was therefore rendered much easier. That deserted region around Kala-i-Maksud and the Ziārat of Shah-i-Mardān was at that time also populated and under cultivation, and around that ruined fort and the Ziārat there are visible at the present day remains of watercourses which brought water from the southernmost of the outlets of the river. Then also, when the river came down in flood, and the superfluous water found its way into the Hāmun and into the Shela, the latter was a flowing stream of water and slowly made its way into the Gaud-i-Zireh. The bed of the Shela must have contained reeds in abundance, as these were to be found, even in 1896, growing in one or two small but luxuriant patches, in places near the pools of water that existed close to the Ziārat at Gudar-i-Shah. The Gaud-i-Zireh also, instead of being the inhospitable tract it now is, covered with saline efflorescence, was at that time a pasture for sheep and cattle in the spring and autumn after the Bunnu grass and reeds had sprung up wherever the flood water of the Hāmun had made its presence felt. It is said that there were in those days from 1,000 to 1,500 pagaus engaged in agriculture in the districts from Trākun westwards. These figures are of course not to be taken as being absolutely correct, but at any rate in the absence of all other information they are too valuable to be neglected.

Tract around Shah-i-Mardān and the Gaud-i-Zireh was cultivated.

Number of cultivators in the southern delta in the time of Malik Hamza.

Kala-i-Fath had been held to ransom one year before the death of Malik Hamza, and at the same time the Band-i-Bulbaka had been damaged if not destroyed by a column of Indian troops which had marched down the valley of the Helmand. Tradition however states that the period of prosperity of Kala-i-Fath lasted for about 230 years, while its decay set in about 240 years ago. These figures do not agree very closely with the dates and periods of time obtainable from these, which are to be found in history. There is however only a difference of 26 years in defect, and from historical dates it appears that the two periods of prosperity and decadence were probably almost equal making a total of 496 years. The period of its gradual descent in the scale of prosperity had now come about and in the time of Fath Ali Khan the Helmand changed its course from the Rud-i-Biyabān. The great change occurred, if tradition be correct, in his reign, but the river had probably for some time previously shown its liability to effect a change of course. The 6 or 7 outlets of the Rud-i-Biyabān, each of them narrow, had been gradually clogged by the accumulation of silt, and the bed of the channel itself had been raised by a similar process. In the reigns of previous Maliks the ancient Shela or bed which must have existed among the gardens and pleasant suburbs

Description of the change of course of the river from the southern to the northern delta.

1692·3 to 1721·2 A.D.

of Kala-i-Fath had probably been receiving gradually an increasing share of superfluous water from the river during seasons of flood, and in this insiduous manner was being gradually cleared for the reception of the Helmand. This channel it was which probably afforded an outlet to such water as it received and rendered possible the foundations by Malik Haidar of the village that bears his name in the lands to the south of Zāhidān.

NOTE.—A pagan, or pagau is an association usually of seven men who take up land for cultivation and share both the outlay and the profits. Each pago therefore represents 7 families, and taking as an average the family to consist of 4·5 souls, the pago represents about 30 souls—a modest estimate.—G. P. T.

CHAPTER VI.

It was in the reign of Malik Fath Ali, however, that the great change took place. According to an exceedingly precise and consistent tradition, the year when this occurred was a season of very great flood. The Helmand came down in its fullest strength. The waters it is said swept away the weir known as the Band-i-Bul'baka, and all other embankments also melted away before the rush of the furious torrent. The choked outlets of the Rud-i-Biyabān could not have been able to relieve the pressure of the water, which turned aside down the old and probably neglected channel to force its way into the northern delta. The river spread over both banks and as the dasht on the right of the west of the valley offered an impregnable barrier, the floods wreaked their fury on the suburbs of Kala-i-Fath which lay at their mercy and broke into the town itself; it became necessary to seek for a fresh site to which the seat of Government could be transferred. A site was taken up in the north delta 11 miles to the south-west of Zāhidān, and almost exactly the same distance from Rām Shahristān, and on a wide plain at some distance no doubt from the newly developed river the town of Kundarak was built.

To this period of change must also be referred those buildings which are now found to exist on the floor of the Rud-i-Biyabān. The newly formed channel within the course of a very short time, must have rapidly increased at the expense of the older, till at last it was found to be necessary to construct those canals, the traces of which are now to be seen following the course of the old river along its bed. When this came to pass, men abandoned their ancient dwellings on the terrace to the south of the riverbed, and moved down into the latter, erecting their new dwellings on the banks of, or very close to, the canals. Hence the ruins of old Gina are to be found on the terrace overlooking the Rud-i-Biyabān surrounded by the domed mausolea containing the tombs of past generations of its leading families of citizens. This place was abandoned, and the chief or headman built the modern fort of Gina for his own residence upon the floor of the ancient riverbed, while the cultivators spread themselves over the alluvial soil thus laid bare, dwelling in unpretending homes on the land they cultivated. They were secure from all apprehension of floods, and as long as the gangs assembled to keep the head of the canal open and the channel clear, they were equally safe from the calamities of bad seasons and drought. The change in the course of the Helmand was without doubt followed by a corresponding alteration in the distribution of population. The wider lands of the northern delta offered a great return to the agriculturist for his labour, and to them undoubtedly must have flocked the mass of the people, who left their narrow holdings around Kala-i-Fath,

Description of the canal and buildings in the Rud-i-Biyabān.

and the Helmand valley for the wide spreading lands of the northern delta. From the southern delta must have also migrated the bulk of its labouring population. The alteration in the river's course must have very nearly at one blow extinguished the cultivation in that direction, and the canal that was constructed to replace the river could have afforded but a scanty supply of water to those sunbaked and thirsty lands that fringe the Shela and those which the outlets of the Rud-i-Biyabān were wont to nourish when that was the Helmand.

Description of the channels in the northern delta that the river followed after the change—Rud-i-Nāseru.

The now almost forgotten channel called the Rud-i-Nāseru was the outlet which the Helmand made for its waters towards the north. The old channel to the east of Zāhidān had doubtless in the course of centuries of time become obliterated filled up with sand drifts and obstacles to the free course needed by the river. The latter however formed a small lagoon in the delta itself which covered a tract of land some 5 or 6 miles long and about 2 miles wide. This tract is still liable to inundation in the summer from the spill water of the canals, and there is a tradition that " in the time of the Kaiānis " it was a naizār.[1] The modern villages of Malik Haidari lies just to the south of this depression, and the village of Jalai, also of recent date, at about its northern end. The Rud-i-Nāseru emerges from this hollow and passing close to the western edge of the rising ground on which Zāhidān was built, reaches the present Hāmun to the south of the Kohlak mound close to the ruin called Adira.

After the river had become definitely fixed in the northern delta, the second branch must have formed. The latter also emerges from that depression out of which the Rud-i-Nāseru takes its origin, but while the latter took a north-westerly direction, the second branch swung almost directly away towards the west. The hollow alluded to thus became the head of the delta, and two branches enclosed a fairly large tract of land between them almost as large as the present Miān Kangi. Within this area there can now be traced a third channel which emerges from the low lying tract, and pursues a course almost midway between the two branches of the Helmand just alluded to, passing about a mile to the east of the village of Jalai, and about 2 miles to the south and again to the west of the equally modern village of Bunjār, and finally reaching the Hāmun area close to the modern village of Nasirābād. This intermediate bed is rather closer to the old southern branch of the Helmand than to the Rud-i-Nāseru, and it runs into a low lying arm of the Hāmun just to the N. of the ruins of the town of Allahābād-miyān-i-Shela. Lines of embankments encircled the depression between the villages of Jalai and Malik Haidari, and though these have to some extent been destroyed by subsequent water action, here and there are yet to be met the rapidly fading traces of these embankments. They were needed to prevent the water of the

---

A bed of reeds.

Helmand, which filled the depression in flood time, from spreading over the surrounding country. Similarly the southern of the two channels that emerged from that depression still shows the traces of embankments along its banks. These also were intended as protective works, as there was only a short distance intervening between this riverbed and the Capital, Kundarak, not only was it necessary to protect the cultivated lands but also that town itself. The set of the river was undoubtedly towards the west or the south of the delta. The need of maintaining the protective embankment was therefore imperative, and very shortly after the capital had been transferred and the town of Kundarak built, it must have made itself recognised.

The fate that befell Kala-i-Fath was one that has always hung over the Capital of Seistan. Bina-i-Kai in its low lying site must have been always threatened with destruction, and during the period of strife and confusion which prevailed after the downfall of Amru, son of Leis, it is probable that the city had suffered from the inroads of the river.

Kundarak continued to be the capital for a generation after Malik Fath Ali Khan's death, and a desperate struggle was maintained between the people and the river which was inclining towards it. The embankments to which allusion has been made date from this period and were raised to protect the capital from the inroads of the river.

Description of Kundarak.

In the time of Malik Muhammad Nasīr Khan, Kundarak having been ruined by floods as well as the town of Allahābād-miyān-i-Shela, the present fort of Nasīrabad was built closely adjoining the village of Husenābād. The latter had also been fortified but its walls have now almost disappeared. The Helmand in the process of moving from Rud-i-Nāseru into the extreme southern edge of the alluvial delta had built up the lands on which its waters debouched during this period of change, and owing to this increase in height, the site of Nasīrabad was rendered secure from floods. At the time when this place was built, probably between the years 1196 and 1200 A. H. the Helmand had reached its furthest southerly limit beyond which the dasht formed an impassable barrier. To the west of the new capital a lurg or plateau of hard wide clay also offered a barrier to any water reaching the town from the Hāmun. These conditions account for the site occupied by the present capital, built by Nasīr Khan Kaiāni which is by no means the best which might be chosen now-a-days. At the time in which Nasīrabad was built, the main river was several miles distant towards the south and there existed no doubt a very reasonable prospect for its continuance there and for the safety of the town from its floods. The name of the capital, by the way, is rightly Nasirabad and not Nasratabad.

Building of the present fort of Nasīrabad.

1782-1786 A. D.

By the end of the 12th century A. H. the Helmand was flowing practically at the toe of the dasht which separates the northern from the southern delta. Here it was destined to rest until the time came round to make, once more a move towards the east. The political conditions were such that no opposition worth mentioning could be offered to any change of course it might make, and hence it has come to pass that information regarding the changes that have taken place in the course of the Helmand during the 13th century A. H. is almost as scanty as to detail and lacking in precision as those which deal with similar occurrences which took place centuries earlier. Changes in the river's bed which have taken place within the lifetime of men now living cannot be described by them in detail, and seem to have failed to arrest the attention of the inhabitants of the districts affected by them.

There were very good reasons for this. The state of disorganisation that prevailed was such that it mattered but little to the unfortunate inhabitants whether they were ruined, by their stock being carried away by floods, or by the crews of brigands that formed the tail of each of the Chiefs who were quarrelling over the remains of the inheritance of the Kaiânis. The result was the same. Excepting in certain villages where the Saiads mustered strong, and owned the lands, security for life and property (once such a distinguishing feature in the government of the country), had practically ceased to exist. It mattered little to any one whether his kith and kin, and loved ones, perished in the swirling eddies of the Helmand or fell victims to some treacherous attack in overwhelming numbers by the caitiff retainers of Ibrahim Khan Sanjarâni, or the followers of the Sarbandi and Nâhrui Sardars. The changes in the river that took place in this period did so unopposed, and their occurrence passed unnoticed in the presence of other events that engaged to their utmost the powers of human observation to follow and to avoid.

As long, however, as Malik Bahram Khan was alive, some resemblance of order was preserved in Seistan. The Malik, the last of his House who retained any authority, undoubtedly possessed a great deal of ability and administrative talent. He made a great effort, shortly after his accession, to revive the prosperity of Seistan, and the Sadozai dynasty being then nominally his Suzerain and in the enjoyment of power, he was able to enforce his authority, and he would, no doubt, have succeeded in restoring the country to some degree of prosperity had he continued to be able to assert his authority over the discordant factions into which the country was at that time divided. Least of all did he receive any aid from his own family. The last pruning of the Kaiâni stock which had been carried out by the ruthless hand of Nâdir seems to have resulted in the destruction of its vitality. Instead of throwing out fresh vigorous shoots, that severe treatment appears to have killed the little remaining vigour that the race still possessed. Malik Bahrâm, therefore, was utterly dependant on such aid as his Suzerain could afford him, and as time went on and the dissensions between the Sadozais and their tribal Chiefs became acute, this source of help was gradually cut off or the supply from it was intermittent and feeble.

Bahrām Khan, however, began well. The Shijrat-ul-Muluk mentions three of his great works. One was the restoration of the canal in the Rud-i-Biyabān and the other revival of the Husenki canal. He also constructed the Dushāk canal so called from its two great branches, one of which the Ju-i-Ilamdār flowed in a northernly direction, while the other passed to the north-west. The former fertilized the lands in the direction of the Ziārat-i-Khwājah Rabāt and the mounds of Kurki, while the second nourished the country around Jallalābād and the Kohlak mound. These lands were for many years in the hands of the Malik himself, and at that time their condition was one of great prosperity. The Husenki canal fertilized the lands around Hamzabād (Kachiān) and Bunjar. The lands of Hamzabād formed the inheritance of his younger son after whom it was named. Bunjar was divided into equal shares between the family of the Mirs and that of Mulla Khasrau who it is said founded the religious establishment where in after years the piety of Malik Taj-ud-din the first, raised the minaret now called the Mil-i-Kāsamābād. *(margin: Irrigation work built by Malik Bahrām Khan.)*

The canal in the Rud-i-Biyabān had evidently fallen into disrepair and it was revived by Malik Bahrām, but its existence depended on a strong government which was able to protect its head from being damaged by the Afghan who were pressing down the Helmand valley, driving the Shāraki and Arbāb population before them towards the delta. The canalization of the deserted channel is said to have depended upon a weir built at some distance up the valley, and the canal which now can be followed along its bed conveyed water to the districts around Rāmrod and Hauzdār. It is to this work that the author of the Shijrat-ul-Muluk refers which he says that a tract of land extending for a distance of a two days' journey was once more rendered fertile. *(margin: The canal in the Trākun trough.)*

Small distributary channels nourished the districts of Gina and Burri, and the excellent alluvial soil that formed the floor of the various narrow outlets into which the Rud-i-Biyabān broke up just below Burri were cultivated by means of these watercourses. The two larger canals which irrigated the districts of Rāmrod and Hauzdār bifurcated at a point about two miles to the east of a conspicuous mausoleum which crowns an island of dasht surrounded by the old outlets of the Rud-i-Biyabān. This mausoleum is called Yak Gumbad or the "Solitary Domed Building." The two canals alluded to separated at a masonry regulator which had originally, no doubt, been constructed when the Helmand first altered its course, and by means of which a head of water was maintained in both of the canals. The existence of the regulator was discovered by the merest accident. The width of the old channel at that place is about 55 feet and there is a bar of Kim which afforded a reliable foundation for the masonry of the regulator. This work was 30 feet in length, and its width about 5 or 6 feet. The bricks were of two sizes, one of which was 12 inches square, and the smaller (12×6 inches), and both about 2 inches thick. The regulator was carefully laid bare to the depth of about 2 feet in order to allow of examination, as it was almost completely hidden by wind-borne deposits of sand which supported a growth of salsola bushes. The bricks composing this work were set in Saruj, of a very good quality, as the thin layers were quite as hard as the bricks they had held in position. The openings of the regulator had been heavily plastered with Saruj and there were traces of floors extending towards each side of the depression in which the work was situated. To the right and left canals took off. That on the left had a water-way of some 15 feet, and the other on the opposite bank was about 10 feet wide and these formed the source from which the districts of Rāmrod and Hauzdār derived their water. On the spoil banks of the Rāmrod canal there are yet to be seen the roots of the coarse "Drug" grass that at one time clothed the banks, as on this side the soil is of a lighter quality than that on the opposite bank which is the hard white clay so often alluded to, and along the spoil banks of the canal on this bank there are no traces of grass ever having grown. About 15 feet from the head of the right bank canal, the spoil banks of the latter widen, and the bank on the side towards the old channel, in which the regulator was built, had been strengthened with baked bricks. A distributary also took off at this point parallel to the main canal by means of which local cultivation was carried on in the alluvial lands to the north of the Yak Gumbad ruin. The Hauzdār canal has been followed up as its course is still quite legible, this being due to the harder soil of the country it traversed. It irrigated the Machi lands to the east of Hauzdār and those around Kundar and the City of Rustam (also called Zarnigār) to the south of the latter.

The Rāmrod canal followed the course of an outlet of the Rud-i-Biyabān called Hādāli, and distributaries took off down all the neighbouring outlets of that old river most of which partially under cultivation.

The size of these canals combined with evaporation precluded a very large and constant supply of water being delivered and the inhabitants must have been dependant to a great extent on wells. The area under cultivation also could not have been very extensive; but it was nevertheless a gallant attempt to keep up portions of the southern delta as a cultivated and inhabitated district, on the part of Malik Bahrām Khan. The effects were, however, not permanent and first Rāmrod, and then the northern district languished and were at last finally abandoned. Hauzdār and Machi being in the hands of the Chief of the Sarbandis were probably maintained after the Rāmrod District was abandoned.

Dushāk canal.   Malik Bahrām Khan's other great work, the canal of the Dushāk or Dahshākh, has also disappeared. The Jui Ilamdār, a branch of this canal was so called because it watered the lands around the tower of Ilamdār, close to the site now occupied by the modern village of Jān Muhammad, in Afghan territory.

Ferry at Burj-i-Sarband; Rud-i-Seistan Canal.

(Part II to face page 168.)

In the beginning of the 12th century A. H., corresponding with the last quarter of the 18th of our reckoning, the Helmand had attained its greatest southern declination and it occupied this position for many years. It turned to the south at a point close to the modern village of Burj-i-Sarband, and flowing in great loops it passed to the east of Kala-i-Nau where its bed can still be followed, hugging the cliffs of the dasht, which it turned close to the present village of Dashtak. From this point some two miles to the west of that village it swung towards the west, its main channel emptying its waters into the Hāmun immediately south of the Koh-i-Khwajah through the Shela-i-Kāfiri. In those days the lands around Aliābād were for the most part under water. The head of the delta was not far from the modern village of Muhammadabad. From a point close to this place one outlet trended towards the south-west passing the ancient fort of Kala-i-Sām and falling into the Hāmun near the modern village of Warmāl. Another outlet went away to the north-west and entered the Hāmun close to the village of Afzalābād. The area included between the extreme outlets was more or less a naizār and seiāds punted their rafts and pursued their avocations of fishermen over the lands which are now occupied by flourishing villages.

Around the villages of Kala-i-Kohna and Kala-i-Nau, the land which is now a bare plain, covered in parts with sand dunes, at that time was covered with a dense growth of tamarisk, and there are men alive now who mention the existence of tamarisk trees in that district whose girth could with difficulty be encircled by a man's arms extended to their fullest extent. The Husenk[1] canal took off close to the ruins of the old village of Kaud, while the head of the Dushākh canal was situated close to the modern hamlet of Kalukhi. The village of Burj-i-Sarband[1] was founded at some time early in the 19th century of the Christian era to safeguard the dam which was thrown across the river about half mile above the village, by means of which those canals were kept supplied with water.

In the month of April in the year 1810 Captain Christie arrived in Seistan on his way to Persia. That officer and his companion Lieutenant Pottinger had been deputed to explore the countries lying between Persia and the territories of the Khan of Kalat. They separated at Nushki, the former making for the Helmand which he reached in 10 marches striking the valley above Rudbār. The river was in flood and two attempts to cross it proved unsuccessful. A third attempt near Rudbār was, however, successful and he followed the right bank of the river into Seistan. He eventually reached a place which he called Ilamdār (10 miles from Jallālābād), and from this place he rode to Jallālābād to call on Malik Bahrām Khan. Christie describes the river at a place which he calls Poolgee (but which was no doubt Palangi) as being 400

---

[1] Burj-i-Sarband—the tower upon (or near) the dam. It is inhabited by the Sharakis who till the lands.

yards wide and very deep. "Poolgee" he describes as a "city in ruins," and it was, no doubt, the great mass of ruins near Palangi which he describes. Christie's Ilamdār was 32 miles from this place, and 10 from Jallālābād, and these distances show that it was Jahānābād, and not the tower of Ilamdār, that is meant, as the latter is much further from both of these places which are still existing and about the positions of which no doubt exists.

The Ju-i-Ilamdār passed close to Jahānābād and Christie's bivouac was probably on the banks of that great canal, close to that town, and owing to this he has confused the names giving to the town the name which belonged to the canal, the former being about a mile to the west of the canal.

In the same way he wrote of Jallālābād which according to the Shijrat-ul-Muluk was irrigated by the Dushākh canal. Christie gives this name to the very conspicuous ruins that are such a striking feature in the landscape, and which are close to that town.

Christie's itinerary appears among others in Kinneir's Geographical Memoir of the Persian Empire and in his introduction to the itineraries the compiler devotes 4½ pages to a description of Seistan. At page 192 of the Memoir it is stated that "the country in the vicinity of Dooshāk is open, well cultivated and produces wheat and barley in sufficient quantities to be exported to Herat. The pasturage is good and abundant",—a condition of things very different to the present state of the lands around Jallālābād. This town is described as being situated among the ruins of an ancient city, and it is described as being small but compact, but the ruins cover a vast extent of ground. It is populous, has a good bazar, and the inhabitants who dressed in the Persian manner had a more civilized appearance than the other "Patan or Balouche shepherds who live a wandering life and pitch their tents amidst the ruins of ancient palaces."

From "Dooshāk" Christie marched to Juwein, but he describes the country in only a very few words. He passed through the villages of Akbar and Daulatābād. Then over "a bare hard desert" he reached Peshāwarān (in ruins) and on to Juwein. The bare hard desert was undoubtedly the dry floor of the Hāmun, and it must have been free from water for many years previously as the reed beds had ceased to exist. The village of Akbar was probably a collection of temporary huts, and it has disappeared, but the site of Daulatābād exists. A mound of white clay marks the place and it is called the Tappa-i-Daulatābād. Upon this mound in a squalid building dwell the representatives of one branch of the Kiāni family, with a collection of mean hovels which house the agricultural families that till the lands. Jallālābād still exists and the lofty palace at that place, which Malik Bahrām Khan built for his eldest son, forms a very conspicuous landmark. From a distance it presents an imposing appearance, but a closer examination very soon dispels all illusions. It is a very modern building constructed in the usual slovenly manner. Both the palace and the small town nestling round its walls have been deserted for some 10 years and have suffered much from the inroads of floods which every year submerge a large tract of the adjoining lands. The remains of gardens still exist, and at one time Jallālābād was celebrated for its fruit. All the vines have been killed by the floods. Here and there a pomegranate tree still exists, but the only trees that are still alive are a few mulberries whose trunks are a veritable record of the depth of water that has at various times covered the land on which they grow.

The rich lands around Jallālābād show traces of having at one time been highly cultivated. Old watercourses and embankments can yet be traced, but the soil now nourishes a rank growth of camel thorn and salsola, and dense thickets of tamarisk clothe the land and fringe the channels which the flood waters have excavated in this district.

Even as late as 1872, when the Mission under Sir Frederick Goldsmit passed through the Seistan, the conditions were temporarily, however, nearly the same as those which Christie's itinerary show to have existed in his day. The Hāmun was quite dry, and so was the tract to the north of Jallālābād and around the Tapa-i-Kohlak. In the month of October 1903, in order to reach this mound it was necessary to wade across (very nearly) 7 miles of swamp, and the once cultivated lands around the town of Jallālābād are now the breeding grounds of the Seistan fly and myriads of other specimens of insect life.

Owing to that excusable error "Dushāk" has been regarded as the site of the ancient capital of Seistan, and has figured as such in all disquisitions on the history or topography of that country. The name of Dushāk or Dashāk occurs in the continuation of the Shijrat-ul-Muluk and it is applied to the canal which irrigated Jallālābād, and as such this name has been found to exist in the country at the present day. Malik Bahrām called the town after his eldest son Jallaluddin Khan. Malik Bahrām had succeeded to the Government of Seistan while the French Revolution was at its height, and when Captain Christie visited Jallālābād he had held authority for more than fifteen years and must have been then an old man, for he succeeded his elder brother and the son of the latter, a minor, and after this lad's death had allowed the mother of the deceased to figure as ruler of Seistan, having been himself content to act as the deputy of the lady and her son. She was a daughter of Malik Mahmud Khan Kaiāni, Shah of Mashad as he was called, and this no doubt promoted Malik Bahrām Khan in acting as he did, with a forbearance and self-denial rare in the annals of an Asiatic family of Princes.

Kinneir, at page 192 of his Memoir of the Persian Empire, states that the revenues of Malik Bahrām Khan amounted to "*no more than* 80,000 *rupees*." The italics are Kinneir's who goes on to say that the Chief of Seistan could bring into the field about 3,000 men. By rupees, no doubt, the Indian rupee of the Honourable East India Company is meant, the value of which at that

The revenue of Seistan in the time of Malik Bahrām Khan.

period was probably double that which prevails at the present time, so that the revenues of Seistan at that time would have been equal to about 1,70,000 rupees of the present day, or about 68,000 Tomans roughly in modern Persian coinage. It shows that notwithstanding the growth of the power of the factions headed by the Sanjarāni and Sarbandi chiefs, Malik Bahrām Khan had contrived to maintain authority to some extent over Seistan to the end of his lifetime, thus bearing out the tradition which states that this was the case.

Position of the river at the time of Christie's visit.

After describing the Helmand as he saw it close to "Pooljee" Christie only once again refers to it. The river itself lay at a distance from Jallālābād, though the Rud-i-Nāseru still continued to receive a little water when the Helmand was in flood. It is no doubt to this channel that Christie refers, in the statement that the river was 8 or 9 miles from Jallālābād, and he does not mention crossing it between his camp on the Hamdār canal and Jallālābād. The distance given by him agrees very well with the position of the Rud-i-Nāseru with respect to that town. That old bed of the Helmand did continue to receive water for many years after Christie's visit — there are men living now, whose parents dwelt on its banks, cultivating small patches of melons and grain, long after the death of Malik Bahrām Khan. To the north and west of the village of Aliābād, there can yet be traced the channel of the Helmand, restrained on either bank with protective embankments, the traces of which are clearly visible. The reclamation of the fertile lands around that prosperous village had been taken in hand, and to the south of the village of Burj-i-Sarband, there is still visible the strong embankment which barred the progress of the water further in that direction, and by means of which the Aliābād lands and others in the same direction were protected from inundation.

Other works of a like nature trained the river to flow in the old bed just alluded to. Mir Alam Khan had occupied the lands affected by their maintenance, and this accounts for the fact that these works were kept up efficiently. Between Khwābgāh and Burj-i-Sarband, the river was also controlled by similar works. Restrained within those narrow limits the annual deposits of silt took place over a restricted area, and the delta on which the towns of Chilling, Daulatabad and many another flourishing village now stand was rapidly built up.

Great change in the direction of the river in 1830.

In course of time the free course of water to the Lake was impeded, and the floods checked on all sides by embankments and their discharge by the formation of land sought out and found a weak spot in the embankment and broke through it, making a new channel by means of which access to the Hāmun was insured. This great change took place in 1830 according to Connolly. Whether there were any intermediate changes is not known. No information on the subject is forthcoming. The traditions that exist and the stories that old men tell of this period are wearisome recitals of bloodshed, and it is with the greatest difficulty that the narrators can be dissuaded from enumerating

Ruins in the area, near Jalálabad, subject to annual inundation.

(Part II to face page 172.)

the casualty lists of their kinsfolk who at various times met their deaths at the hands of the adherents of the opposite faction to which they themselves had belonged. At this time the Sarbandi and Sanjarāni Chiefs had each taken up the cause of a son of the late Malik and were ostensibly pushing the interests of their candidates from whom they used to hide their own personal ambitions and aims. Amidst the welter of bloodshed and intrigue such minor details as the position of the river were completely lost sight of except when either the river itself or an older channel happened to be the scene of some act of violence, when only it is possible to gather some slight and valuable indications of the Hydrography of the country. Connolly in 1839 learnt " that about nine years ago an unusually large inundation changed the whole face of the country. The main stream of the Helmand deserted its old bed, and cutting off for itself a wide channel out of that small branch which went off from Khwajah Ahmed, carried the greater part of its waters to the Dak-i-Tir." The position of Khwajah Ahmed mentioned by Connolly is well known. It is that mound of débris which marks the site of some ancient building, perhaps a fortified palace, or manor house, which is situated about two miles to the north of the fort at Kuhak and upon which in quite recent times, Bunyād Khan the Baluch built a modern enclosure, which in its turn has nearly disappeared. The " small branch " of the Helmand must have formed at a much earlier period, and it occupied very probably the depression in which the Jharoki canal in Afghan Seistan is situated. This low-lying tract receives water during floods from the surplus of the Sultāni canal and also from the river. This ancient bed in its lower part bifurcates into two branches both of which discharge into the Āshkin, the right or eastern outlet existing about two or three miles to the east of the modern hamlet of Meno, and the left hand mouth, immediately to the west of the hamlet of Diwālak. The last eight or ten miles of the tract probably represent the Shela of the Sena Rud, which figures so prominently in the old accounts of Seistan.

Abreast of Nād Ali the water it receives forms great lagoons and the course of this depression is clearly marked by the sombre tones of the Tamarisk thickets, dense growths of which outline the depression and fringe the margin of the narrow reaches. This river played an important part in Seistan history at one time during the invasion of that country by the Sadozai Prince Shah Kamrān, who continued to maintain himself in Herat for some time after the family to which he belonged had been driven from Kabul. The river at that time flowed where the modern hamlet of Deh Karimdād is situated, and its general direction was towards north-east and a lofty mound to the east of the hamlet is said at that time to have overlooked the river. In about the year 1835, Malik Jallaludin was driven out of Seistan by his subjects. He fled to Herat, and after a time persuaded Shah Kamrān to march into Seistan at the head of an army to reinstate him. The advance of the troops from

An account of Shah Kamrān's invasion of Seistan in 1835 A.D.

Herat having been noised abroad, the contending factions in Seistan agreed to suspend their differences for a time, and making common cause with one another, they collected their fighting men and took up a position on the bank of the river just alluded to. The forces of Shah Kamrān arrived at the river and perceiving it to be very broad and that the Seistanis were assembled on the off-bank to dispute the crossing, the Shah halted his men on the river and formed a camp. This camp was protected by works and a lofty mound was thrown up, or was already in existence, on which the pavilion of Shah Kamrān was placed. This mound still exists and is known as the Dik-i-Shah or the "mound of the Shah."

The river was then beginning to fail, and though it was broad and apparently a formidable obstacle it was in reality fordable, but the Afghans, it is said, had not discovered this fact and did not know of the existence of any fords. For some time the two forces were in position facing one another until at last the rashness of a young man named Asghar, son of Ghulām Shah, the headman of Shārak, betrayed the fact of the river being fordable. Tired of the undecided and inactive part which the leaders of the Seistanis had adopted, he determined to attack the Afghans accompanied by only a few others as impetuous as himself. He crossed the river and fell upon the Afghans, but the attack failed, as he was not supported, and the invaders perceiving what a delusive barrier the river was in reality, themselves crossed to the other bank and assailed the levies of Seistan, who immediately ran away.

On this occasion the river having played a part in the history of Seistan is dignified by being brought into the recital, and its position is approximately ascertained.

The Dik-i-Shah still exists, and by it the exact position of the channel as it existed in the year 1836 or thereabouts can be laid down, and the scars left on the surface of the ground by it can be assigned to their proper date with reference to similar marks of old rivers in the neighbouring districts. As this channel developed, it did so at the expense of the other that flowed towards the west, still however a river of some size. The lands hitherto covered with water at its embouchure began to be exposed and the town of Chilling was founded; one or two other settlements sprang up and land was gradually taken up and put under cultivation.

Changes in the main stream of the river about 1859.   At what time the branch of the Helmand which flowed past the Dik-i-Shah began to fail it is impossible to say, but it must have been some time after the invasion of Shah Kamrān just alluded to. When that channel had become clogged and failed to afford an outlet for the Helmand, the latter made a fresh channel towards the north. This change is said to have taken place at the spot where the modern hamlet of Kalukhi now stands, and the Helmand forced a way which coincided very closely with, or was drawn into, the Ju-i-Hamdār and discharged its waters directly into the Hāmun-i-Puza and into the Āshkin to the east of the village of Chakansur. The details regarding this channel are very precise. Three points are mentioned by which the course of this channel can be laid down. First its point of bifurcation at the site now occupied by the hamlet of Kalukhi. Deh Jahāngir, a modern hamlet also, is said to occupy a site which was in the very bed of the Ilamdār channel. The tower of Ilamdār already described under which the main channel flowed and where it divided into two branches. In after years, during the time of Ali Khan when the Dushāk or Dashāk Canal was revived, in order to put the lands around Jallalābād again under cultivation, it took off from a point close to the site of Deh Jahāngir where the Ilamdār Branch of the Helmand then flowed. At that place a weir was placed across the stream to keep up a head of water in the new canal. The old town of Jahānābād was about a mile west of the river to the south of the tower of Ilamdār; this stream flowed past the site now occupied by Deh Ido, and some traces of the river are still visible in the deep Shela or canalized and natural channel called the Shela-i-Rud-Gashta. This evidently natural, deep, and wide bed probably represents the deep water channel of the Ilamdār river at the last period of its existence. The head of the Delta, at that time, was a point somewhere in the vicinity of the present hamlet of Deh Luch. The exact position cannot be located with any degree of exactitude, but it could not have been very far from this village as the scars of its old channels all appear to converge on this place. Below this point the river broke up at once. There were four channels. The most western of all the four took off close to Deh Luch and is now represented by the Shela-i-Shamshiri. The next passed close to Deh Gul Shah. The third can still be recognised, when attention has been drawn to it, on the east of the modern village of Deh Bahlol. The fourth channel broke up into two branches close to the tower of Ilamdār, one of which was the Chung-i-Chori immediately to the west of the isolated plateau on which the ziārat dedicated to Khwājah Rabat is located.

Account of the murder and burial of Dr. Forbes. The other branch formed the Shela-i-Inglisi and lay immediately to the east of that isolated plateau. This branch was named the "Shela of the Englishman" from the fact that it was the scene of the murder of the ill-fated and foolhardy traveller Dr. Forbes by his host that demented Chieftain of the Sanjarānis, Ibrahim Khan.

This traveller had been repeatedly warned against visiting this Chief, both by the Chief of Lāsh, and again, it is said, by the notables of the town of Chilling to which he had made his way from Lāsh. His visit is remembered yet. Undeterred by these warnings he went on to Jahānābād where Ibrahim Khan resided. The latter was an enthusiastic sportsman, while his guest wished to collect specimens of water fowl, and they set out down the river in one tutin to Ibrahimābād. From that place they punted down into the Shela, both occupying the same raft, when in a sudden paroxysm of homicidal mania the savage Chieftain deliberately shot his guest. After this deed Ibrahim Khan returned to his dwelling, and when darkness had set in his henchman sought out two or three men on whom he could absolutely rely, and began to search for the body of their master's victim with the object of mitigating the scandal attaching to the deed by giving the remains a decent burial and hiding the traces of the crime. The body was recovered the next day, and it was committed to the earth somewhere on the outskirts of the cemetery around the ziārat of Khwājah Rabat. The spot has been forgotten as the pious act was performed by stealth, and those who carried it out have themselves passed away long ago.

In addition to the four outlets of this river, there was a fifth, a mere spill water channel, which passed close to Kārku; it is traceable up to that place and is now called the Khar Kushta.

The discharge from the Ilamdār channel filled the Hamun-i-Puza-i-Dak-i-Tir with water, and also the Āshkin lands to the west of the Chakānsur, and the Chung-i-Khargoshki. The naizār, or reed bed, extended as far as Kala-i-Kang, the low mound on which this fort was afterwards built having been at that time an island. The reed beds extended very nearly to within 2 or 3 miles of the modern village of Dost Muhammad Sāruni. The mounds at Takht-i-Shah were, it is said, islands surrounded by water and marshes,—as were also those other conspicuous mounds to the east of the former called Kurki and Shāraki, and Kaud-i-Gaz. The country in the direction of the modern settlements of Khāmak and Pulgi to the north-west of the Kārku mound, it is said, also supported beds of reeds.

In those days Ibrahim Khan Sanjarāni had built the fort of Ibrahimābād inside the limits of the naizār, selecting that site on account of its being near his favourite shooting ground and also because he looked on it as a more or less impregnable position, surrounded as it was by marshes and land subject to annual inundation by the river.

The mentions of the river by General Ferrier on his visit in 1845.

In 1845, General Ferrier, the well-known traveller, visited Jahánābād, and mentions the dispersal of the waters of the river at Burj-i-Ilamdār, and as he also crossed the other branch of the Helmand about a mile-and-a-half from the village of Aliābād which according to him was wide and a deep channel, the Ilamdār Branch of the Helmand had not at that time drawn to itself all the water supplied by the Helmand.

Rud Tāj Muhammad.

In course of a few years afterwards this did disappear. The western channel failed and in order to keep up the irrigation of the lands which it had hitherto nourished Tāj Muhammad Sarbandi constructed the great canal called after him the Rud-i-Tāj Muhammad utilizing older beds of the Helmand for this purpose. The Rud-i-Tāj Muhammad issued from the low-lying tract between the villages of Jalai and Malik Haidari and passing to the south of the former was continued towards the village of Bahrāmābād, the source from

Nād'Ali channel of the Helmand near Burj-i-Ās; showing causeway of tamarisk fascines.

(Part II to face page 176.)

which he derived the water being the Ilamdār Channel. At this time also water used on occasions to enter the Rud-i-Nāseru during the season of flood, by means of which a little cultivation was carried out in the lands adjoining its bed to the north of the village of Bolai.

The increased volume of the Ilamdār channel also resulted in an accelerated deposit of silt at its mouth and after some years had passed, this accumulation of soil prepared the way for another change of course. The change when it came about took place, it is said, towards the east. The river apparently for a short distance flowed not far from the course it had taken in 1830, and broke through the ruins of Bina-i-Kai[1] between the channel of that year and the Ilamdār bed. The time-worn ruins of the ancient Capital of Seistan up to this period had been practically buried under drifts of sand, but they were henceforward exposed to the direct action of water. At the point where now the modern garden of Rustam Khan is laid out, close to the south-east corner of the inner town, the newly developed channel divided into two branches. The right hand channel passed to the east of and under the great mound of Safed-dik, when the bed of the river can still be traced without difficulty. This was apparently the main branch and it entered the Āshkin lands near the hamlet of Diwālak. The other branch passed to the west of the Sorhdik mound and it also reached the Āshkin at the point where the present Charkh canal discharges its surplus waters. *The change to a channel.*

When the Muzaffaru-daulah entered Seistan at the head of a body of Persian troops to put an end to the anarchy that prevailed so long in Seistan, the river is said to have occupied this position. In 1866, a year of great floods, the river changed its course and reverted to the channel in which approximately it is now to be found. This was the Helmand of (the Boundary Commission of) 1872, and it had continued as such ever since. It now has two branches: the Siksar, which practically occupies the bed formed in 1866, and the Pariun, a comparatively recent development, and under the very altered circumstances which prevail in the country, with a settled Government on either side of the boundary, this condition of things will undoubtedly be carefully maintained as it is to the interest of all concerned to do so. *In 1866 A.D.*

---

[1] That is Nād Ali.

NOTE.—The development of the Ilamdār Channel, according to a very precise tradition delivered by Arbāb Seif-ud-din, probably took place 65 years previous to 1904, or in the spring or summer of 1840. Kala Fath was washed out. The whole of the western and north-western walls were ruined or washed away; and the houses about and inside the walls were destroyed, completing the desolation of the deserted capital. After this occurred the drying up of the Rud Māhi, Connolly's name for the eastern branch of the Helmand in 1839 (pages 173-4) must have been completed in a year or two—certainly before the adventurous traveller M. Ferrier visited the Seistan (page 176). This date for the flood which created the Ilamdār Channel depends on the tradition of Arbāb Seif-ud-din, and although undoubtedly correct generally cannot be regarded as final with regard to the date of the occurrence to within two or three years. Connolly's visit in 1839 however proves that this channel must have developed *after* 1839, so that the summer of 1840 as the date of the flood is probably not far from the truth; probably 1845, when M. Ferrier visited Seistan the Ilamdar Channel was well established.—G. P. T.

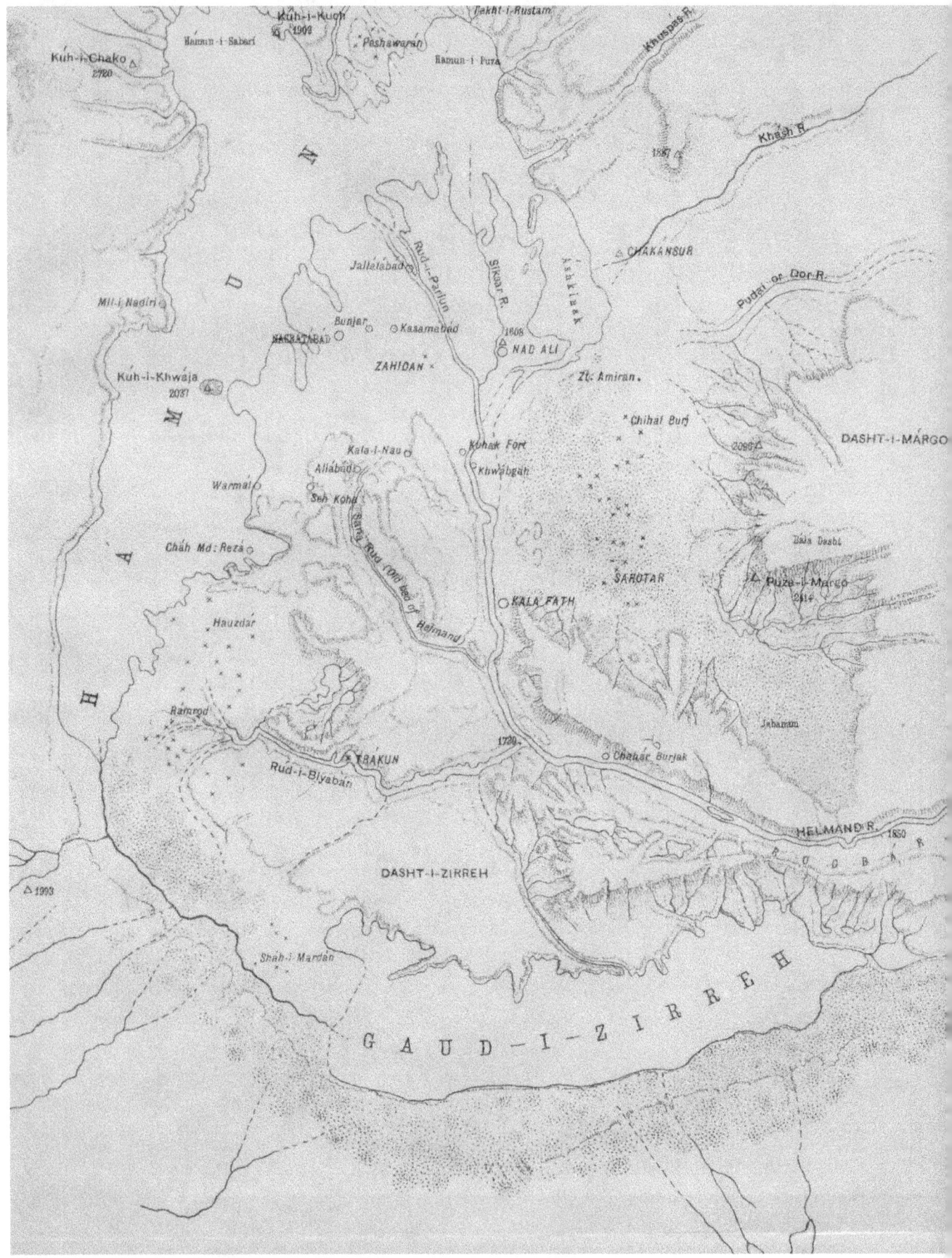

PART III.
THE RUINS IN SEISTAN.

Decorations carried out in clay plaster–Masjid near Deh Dost Muhammad.

NOTE—The interlaced triangles–a Masonic Symbol.

(Frontispiece to part III.)

THE RUINS IN SEISTAN.

CHAPTER I.

INTRODUCTION.

Sources of information.

FOR the subject of this section, we have to depend altogether on traditions. Vague though these be, yet they contain some facts, and in the absence of other information it is not possible to disregard the legends, and an attempt has been made to deal with them by the faint light of historical information that is available.

There were (in 1905) living in Seistan, actually only two persons who knew anything at all about the traditions relating to the past history of that country. The first of these, Arbāb Seif-ud-din, is the descendant of an ancient family, members of whom are said to have been the ministers and trusted officials of the Kaiāni rulers. As recently as the time of the famous Ahmad Shah, Abdali, he who founded the kingdom of Afghanistan, an ancestor of Seif-ud-din held the office of Yesāwal,—an executive office which it is not easy to define. This person, however, seems to have held the charge of the lands that formed the district of Garmsir, which began at or close to Kala-i-Bist, and extended down to the head of the delta of the Helmand, and a commission issued by the sovereign to him is still extant and was examined in 1904. Arbāb Seif-ud-din accompanied his father to Kandahar when that place was occupied by our troops in 1839, and it was from the former that Leech obtained his information regarding Seistan which he furnished to the Asiatic Society of Bengal, and which was published in the journal of that Society.

As long as the Kaiāni Maliks retained any semblance of authority over Seistan the Arbābs held the lands round Kala Fath where in the 16th and 17th centuries they formed a numerous and important community, and in those days could put 1,000 men into the field as their quota towards the territorial militia of their country. With the progressive decay of the family of the Princes of Seistan, the condition of the Arbāb community has gone from bad to worse, and, although they still cling tenaciously to the land, the hand of the Afghan rulers has despoiled them of their former privileges and of their patrimony as well. Notwithstanding his poverty Arbāb Seif-ud-

Arbāb Seif ud-din

din still retains some flavour of gentle birth and breeding which raises him above his neighbours and compatriots, a pathetic relic of better times.

Muhammad, Dādi. Muhammad Dādi, the other person who knows something about the past history of Seistan, is the descendant of a family the members of which have apparently always followed the profession of irrigation officers— held the appointments of engineers and water bailiffs, and it is not surprising that his knowledge of the past conditions of the country extends more in the direction of the ancient water systems, rather than in the direction of the ancient history of Seistan. In recent years the inherited knowledge of Muhammad Dādi was found most useful by the Afghan Governor of Chakānsur, the Akundzada, in his schemes of irrigating the land on the right bank of the Helmand. Like Arbāb Seif-ud-din, he is an old man and in the usual course of nature both must soon pass away, and with them will die out all knowledge relating to ancient Seistan. The traditions handed down to these aged persons have proved of the greatest value as they provide clues which we used in prosecuting enquiries into a condition of affairs that has passed away for ever. Independent enquiries in the direction indicated by the traditions have resulted, most unexpectedly—if not in actual confirmation in all details yet in showing that in the absence of direct proof or confirmation a strong probability exists in favour of the general truth of the traditions, and also that it would be most unsafe to ignore or despise such sources or information.

Both these persons belong to the Tajik or Farsi-wān (Farsi-khwān or Persian-speaking) races, which represent at the present day the ancient Iranian race that formed the bulk of the population down to the first quarter of the 13th century of our era when the irruption of the hordes of Chingiz Khan shattered and overthrew the civilization which Islam had crystallized into a form that had endured for over six centuries of time.

Ancient records. The Princes of Seistan have always been more distinguished for their high spirit than for prudence—and a spirited foreign policy beyond the resources at their disposal has exposed their country to the vicissitudes of foreign invasions that have periodically dyed the fields of Seistan with the blood of its people. Even after that this country enjoyed a degree of prosperity; as a province of the empire of the Safavis, it was always in a condition of unstable equilibrium, liable to foreign inroads and to domestic treason. During this period of some 300 years there must have accumulated masses of records, and survivals of earlier ages also are known to have existed from which the author of the Ihya-ul-Muluk wrote his account of the family of the Princes, of which he was himself a member. The ancestors of Arbāb Seif-ud-din, and of Muhammad Dādi (Dādi is the name of the tribe to which the latter belonged), had access to these records, and it is from these that the knowledge they possess has been derived. These records have unfortunately been destroyed in the turmoils of the last 75 or 80 years.

The last great destruction of records took place after the death of Malik Bahrām Khan. His heir Jallāl-ud-din was despoiled by Shah Kamrān of the last of the manuscripts, whether books or records, and of illuminated genealogical tables his ancestors had accumulated for about 200 years and more. This act of plunder disposed of the records of the ruling family. Any that escaped Shah Kamrān were probably afterwards sold by the voluptuaries Jallāl-ud-din and his younger brother Hamza Khan, or passed without their knowledge into other hands. Papers, documents, title deeds of other families were however destroyed at one fell blow when the Muzaffar-ud-daulah (on behalf of the Persian Government) took formal possession of Seistan about 1866. The representatives of the leading families in Seistan were called upon (by him) to produce all records in their possession, so as to enable him to ascertain the rights and privileges they had enjoyed in the past. This order was obeyed with alacrity. Every family of consequence was only too glad to submit these vouchers of their former position in the country, and bundles of original documents were delivered into the hands of the Muzaffar-ud-daulah. They were ruthlessly destroyed. It is said that the country to the leeward of the Persian camp was strewed with fragments of these ancient records. The Arbābs of the Helmand (the family of Arbāb Seif-ud-din) it is said, in this way lost the whole of their "daftar" or family papers. Any that escaped the hands of the Persian on this occasion were caught up later by Mir Alam Khan, Sardar of Birjand, when he became ruler over Seistan.

Destruction of records by the Persians, deliberately carried out.

A few memorial tablets with inscriptions that had survived the destruction had been collected at Kachiān by the Kaiāni headman of that village to whom they would naturally be of great interest. A large slab, said to have been the memorial tablet of Malik Kutb-ud-din, was set up at one of the entrances of that village. Just before the arrival of the Mission in Seistan, in February 1903, it is said that the Governor of Seistan, incited by the Persian officials, collected these tablets and caused them to be broken into pieces. The two which escaped, and which we found at the shrine of the 44 recluses in the Zāhidān ruins, owed their escape to the sanctity of that place. They were purely memorial tablets of little or no value. The inscriptions were photographed, and translated from prints of the latter by A. G. Ellis, Esq., of the British Museum.

Destruction of tablets, on approach of the Mission.

We were thus cut off from any sources of information other than the traditions which had been handed down to Arbāb Seif-ud-din and Muhammad Dādi. Examination of the more important sites covered with ruins gave interesting details connected with the architecture prevailing at evidently different periods, but as excavations were out of the question, owing to the

Excavations were not possible, owing to attitude of Afghans and Persians.

2 D 2

jealous attitude of the Afghan and Persian authorities, the examination of sites was confined to ruins above ground, and those which the accumulations of wind-impelled sand had not completely hidden. In that part of the basin of Seistan in which the Helmand is at present, the operations of agriculture have effaced ancient ruins, except in one narrow strip where the soil is not commanded by water. The remains in this strip are however exploited by the natives, who use them as quarries and extract baked bricks where these exist or use the nitre impregnated soil from the débris of mud walls as manure for their fields. One authentic and most interesting relic of ancient Seistan is the great minaret known as the Mil (or pillar) of Kasamābād, with its two bands of inscriptions, recording the names of father and son, two Princes who ruled over that country. Both of these are historical persons. It is, however, on account of the high degree of skill shown in its construction that this forlorn relic of mediæval times is of interest. It is a testimony to the state of civilization that at one time prevailed in Seistan, both as regards architecture and the perfection of the materials used. The minaret although 75 feet in height is only a fragment, and when in its perfect condition must have been quite 100 feet in height, if not more. An enterprising person had obtained permission from the local authorities to demolish this ruin, and to sell the bricks to any one who cared to buy them. Doubtless the permission had been paid for handsomely. The intervention of the British Commissioner, however, obtained a respite from the threatened danger for the remains of the minaret.

Apathy of oriental races towards their history.

The apathy shown by the present generation of Asiatic races for the past history of their country is a very curious feature in oriental character. It is the zeal of foreigners that has rescued the ancient history of Asia from oblivion, and the few remaining monuments at the present day from destruction, at the hands of those who might be regarded as having an interest in their preservation.

The meaning of the Rustam legends.

The older sites in Seistan are always connected with stories of Rustam— the members of his family, or his famous war horse. These fables are never assigned to any but genuinely ancient sites, and at these places experience has proved that the existence of Zoroastrian remains will reward a diligent search. A legend of Rustam coupled with such a place is, of course, another form of stating that the locality has (perhaps for centuries) been regarded as one of very great antiquity.

CHAPTER II.

The names by which Seistan has been known.

The name Seistan is a modern corruption of Sakastana, and the latter in its turn was altered to Sagastan by the change of the 'k' into a 'g,' both these letters being constantly interchanged at the present day. The Arabs again wrote the name Sajestan, as in Arabic a hard 'g' and 'j' are also interchangeable. The word jemal—a camel, in the Egyptian dialect of Arabic—is altered into gemal (or kemal), and our word camel was introduced probably by the crusaders from the pronounciation met with in Egypt and Palestine. There are however two other, and probably more ancient, names for this country of Seistan. One is Nimruz and the other Zarī. The latter again is more ancient than the first. From it was derived the form Drangiana used by Greek and Latin authors, and this form was introduced to the West by the writers whose records formed the basis of the detailed accounts which we possess of the expedition of Alexander. The Arab conquerors also found the name Zarī in existence when they added Seistan to the dominions of the Caliphs, but they altered the name into Zaranj and in this form the name appears in the early chronicles which mention this country. From Zarī we get Zireh, a form that is still in existence, but which is in common use in a restricted sense. The Gaud-i-Zirī, means the Hollow of Zireh, but while it would apply to the whole of Seistan its use is confined to the depression to the south of the Lake. This local application is in all probability due to the fact that for many centuries this particular depression has remained destitute of water, and where the saline matter that so strongly impregnates the soil of the floor renders it hostile to the presence or introduction of vegetable growth. The northern depression on the other hand appears more often to have been the receptacle of the waters of the Helmand and auxiliary rivers. Owing to the superior quality of the soil the floor of this depression, wherever it is not covered with water, has always been utilized in the service of mankind. Hence the northern basin has always been known as the Hāmun, or Lake.

Names by which Seistan has been known.

The antiquity of the name Zarī is established by the discovery, in the famous inscription of Darius Hystaspes, of the word Zranka (Jour., Royal As. Soc., 1906) as the name for Seistan. The word zrayah (zend) or draya (old Persian) has been regarded as applicable to the Hāmun Lake (*ibid.*). The well known word daryā or dariā is of course a descendant of the older word. When the Helmand is at its height the Lake may well be termed the Sea of Seistan. But the name continued to be used for the low-lying tracts certainly in the middle of the 12th century. Abu-l-Fazl Allami, of Baihak, wrote it Zaragān (plural of Zireh or Zarah) the Zirehs, and applied

Zarī, Zarah or Zireh.

184 — THE RUINS IN SEISTAN.

Allusions to Seistan by Abul-Fazl, all Baihaki in the 12th century A.D.

it with reference to the low-lying country south of Sabzawār. Incidentally he throws a light on the nature of the countries to the south of Nīshāpur and Herat. He describes a hunting expedition of Masaud, the son of the famous Muhammad of Ghazni. The Prince and his suite proceeded to Isfirār (Sabzawār), and from the jungles or forests on the Adraskan river the party went on towards Farah and the Zarahs. In the latter a male tiger was slain, and satisfied with the success of his expedition the Royal cortège made for Kala-Bist and returned to Ghazni. The forest or jungles on the banks of the Adraskan River and in the lower country adjoining the Zarah or Lake of Seistan have long since vanished and the tamarisk thickets in Seistan no longer harbour larger game than wild pig and jackals. The name Zireh or Zarah still lingers in the country. Besides the Gaud-i-Zireh, the plateau overlooking the Shela is known as the Dusht-i-Zireh, and a group of insignificant ruins to the south of the modern capital, Nasratabad, is still called Zaro or Zireh with great impartiality.

Allusions to the Lake of Seistan in the Avesta.

In the Avesta the Lake of Seistan is spoken of as Kānsu, and in the Bundahish this name has been transformed into Kyānsih, where the Lake is spoken of as a sea. At the present day the part of the Lake to the west of the Kuh-Khwāja is still called the Darya-i-Singi. The Lake Frazdān, also mentioned in the Bundahish, has been identified with the Āb-i-Istādah—the Lake southeast of Ghazni, but it is barely possible that the limits of Seistan—that is of the country and not the State—ever extended so far to the east. Rather it may be that the Māshkel and Tahlāb-Hāmuns may, under ancient conditions of climate, be the remains of the Lake Frazdān.

Moses of Khoren, the Armenian Chronicler.

Abu-l-Fazl of Baihak uses the name Nimruz when speaking of the administrative division, or province, of Seistan—as well as Sijistan. The Armenian monk, Moses, of Khoren, mentions that Fars (Persia proper) was called Chiustia Nimroz and enumerates the provinces of Persia or Nimruz, and among them appears Sagastan. The name which in the 5th century of our era was applied to the kingdom (according to the authority cited) has in course of time been restricted to the province of Sagastan. In poetry Seistan is spoken of as Nimruz, but this name was used for other purposes as well. The mintages of the Caliphs included the mint town of Zaranj—the capital of that country—but when the local Princes began to coin their own money, Zaranj gave way to Nimruz, and their coins bear the legend on the reverse—Struck in the town (or country) of Nimruz.

Another peculiarity is, that the name of the capital is never specified in ancient history. It is written either the city, or the city of Seistan—or simply Seistan; the ancient usage is followed by the modern custom.

CHAPTER III.

Coins, seals, intaglios, etc.

Sometimes the mattock or plough of a cultivator brings to light small hoards of coins in the inhabited area of Seistan, but all our finds of coins, seals, and intaglios were obtained from the ruin-covered area to the east of the present delta of the Helmand. In Seistan there are families who depend on treasure-seeking in a great measure for their support. They visit the ruins after heavy rain has fallen, when on the slopes of ancient mounds and in the heaps of débris the action of water lays bare these souvenirs of a bygone age. The coins which I collected were sent by me to the British Museum and have been described in the Journal of the Royal Asiatic Society. These coins were obtained from the treasure-seekers and are of interest, and of some value from a numismatic point of view. In every case I was careful to locate the sites of the finds. They vary from a very early archaic type to the more finished and known types of the Sassanian Græco-Bactrian and Parthian mintages. Considerable interest attached to the last, owing to their having been countermarked (and probably re-issued) by Indo-Parthian Kings. The intaglios were of various periods if the workmanship is to be relied on. Some were of an evidently earlier period than others. On the later the human form was conventionally and crudely represented, but the earlier types showed the influence of Greek art in the exquisite modelling of the figures and of the heads and torsos represented on pieces of cornelian and other stones. On one was the representation of a figure of a man, curiously Chinese, in the details.
_{Provenance of old coins, seals, intaglios, etc.}

Copper seems to have been largely used in those early days. Crude figures of human beings, animals and birds were very plentiful; and copper rings, some of which seemed to reveal the use of armorial bearings and devices, were also found in abundance. In the ruins of Sār-o-Tār I found a seal on which was the representation of two humped zebus, or Indian oxen, combined with characters resembling some form of Sanskrit. This was a curious confirmation of the legend, that at one time Sār-o-Tār was the seat of a Hindu king. This tradition will be alluded to when the site is described.
_{Copper largely used in olden times.}

No remains that could be said to be Buddhist were discovered, but to the east and south of the Sār-o-Tār mound and ruins, there were one or two that appeared at a distance as if they might have been small topes. It was impossible to excavate these, or to examine them in detail owing to their remote position, far from the river.
_{Absence of Buddhist remains.}

The Zoroastrian Religion lingered in Seistan.

Of the period when the religion of Zoroaster flourished in Seistan there are abundant traces, and there can be no doubt that this form of religious belief flourished in Seistan long after the country was conquered by the Arabs, and there must have been large communities of Gabrs (Fire worshippers—Parsees) in Seistan who were tolerated by the early conquerors, before the latter developed the bigotry that finally quenched the Sacred Fires and destroyed the altars on which they burned. There are traditions as to the sites of Fire Temples, one of which can be verified from the writings of Arab authors. The identification of these sites, and of the early capitals of Seistan destroyed and founded long before the day of Muhammad, depend on the notices of the authors mentioned, and they will be dealt with separately as the identifications depend on the scanty historical and other notices of the country contained in those writings.

CHAPTER IV.

The most ancient of all the time-worn remains in Seistan are the mounds or Tells which mark the site of the neighbouring towns of Post-i-Gau and Chapu. These extensive ruins are situated about six miles to the north of Chakānsur. The lands round them and to the north, around the equally old ruin called Khwājah Siah-posh by the Baluchis, were in days gone by irrigated by the wisp of four or five canals which took off from the right bank of the Khāsh Rud in the district of Kadah. These canals fertilised the country to the north of the Khāsh Rud and must have exhausted its supply of water, for to the south of the ruins the Zorkan and Zarkan canals die away before they reached Post-i-Gau and Chapu.

<small>Ruins of Post-i-Gau and of Chapu.</small>

These sites are said to date from the times of Rustam, and certainly the former in all probability may be referred to the 7th or 6th century B.C. The remains at Post-i-Gau consist of a very large enclosure with remains of lofty massive walls. The latter are now in ruins and form a chain of conspicuous mounds. These enclosed an area of about 500 yards square, and the mounds are now about thirty feet high and in places perhaps a little more. The angles face the cardinal points of the compass. Opposite the northern angle there was a fort (?) built on a solid plinth of pisé. The whole of the walls of this building having fallen in and they form a mound which is about fifty feet in height. Adjoining the north-western face of the enclosure are the remains of what must have been a goodly town in its day. These ruins extend fully a mile and-a-half in that direction; and beyond them again are the ruins of a smaller town or village, now called Kala-i-Bāiān (Bhāi-Khān) which is also said to be an ancient site. These remains contain no burnt bricks.

<small>Description of Post-i-Gau.</small>

Kala-i-Chapu is said to have been a town in times of antiquity. The citadel is irregular in its trace; the walls are in heaps; the gateway alone is standing. Unbaked bricks were extensively used in its construction. Baked bricks are rare. The keep or palace inside the citadel occupied the centre of the enclosed area. It has fallen and its débris forms a mound some fifty feet high. To the south of the citadel is another enclosure within which are the ruins of two handsome buildings, the plinths of which, and about five feet of the walls above it, had been constructed with baked bricks. The superstructure was of sundried brick. This enclosure is about one hundred and twenty feet square, and the ruins of its walls are now about twenty feet high. The entrance faced the citadel which is only some hundred feet away. On the west of the citadel there are the remains of two other buildings which still exhibit signs of very great care in their construction, and of having been elaborately decorated. The surrounding country is full of other ruins. The

<small>Description of Chapu.</small>

sites of Post-i-Gau and Chapu are practically continuous, as the short interval between them is covered with ruins.

Post-i-Gau probably derived from the name of the King Parshat Gau. Tora (or the Bull).

The name Post-i-Gau is at first sight unmeaning. It recalls the ancient devices of acquiring a hide of land, by cutting a bullock's hide into thin strips practised at the foundation of Carthage as described by Virgil. At the time when the name was obtained it seemed to be of modern date, but despite the absence of any obvious meaning its form was carefully preserved by me. But with more time at my disposal, and with increasing knowledge, it seems to be highly probable that Post-i-Gau is a modernised version (or corruption) of the Avestan Parshat-Gau, the king who, according to the Dinkard, dwelt at the end of Sagastan; and whose title was 'Tora' the bull. This royal person was not converted by Zoroaster's preaching. Here also the teacher is said to have cured a four-year old bull which had lost its virile power by means of the Hōm-water from the River Dāitī, the 'Iranian Jordan.' If the generally accepted date for the lifetime of Zoroaster can be regarded as correct, the native tradition places the opening of his ministry 258 years before Alexander, we can assign a very respectable antiquity to the site of Post-i-Gau—possibly the capital of the king who dwelt at the end of Seistan and also for the companion town of Chāpu. As a further coincidence—which however must not be strained in application—the reed beds of the Hāmun immediately to the west of this ruin-covered site are still the resort of large camps of graziers—cattle-owners pure and simple. One of the tribes to which these belong is the Abil, or Abir, who in their mode of life are the same in every respect as that of other Indian people who in the 1st century A.D. gave their name to a part of the Indian coast of the Arabian Sea—and who probably were immigrants from Seistan.

It is not unreasonable to regard these as the sites of early towns and as the only known places of great antiquity—as antiquity is reckoned in the East.

Cypress trees near Darg, in the Hokāt ascribed to Nau-Shirwān.

There are three other remains of well ascertained Zoroastrian antiquity. These are the cypress trees about 2 miles north of the modern village of Darg in the Hokat and about sixteen miles below the town of Juwein. According to tradition they were planted in the "days of Naushirwān." The cypress is a slow-growing tree—and for these to have attained their present size they must have been planted certainly not later than that period (some 1,500 years almost ago); and very probably at a much earlier date. Turning again to the life and teachings of Zoroaster, we see that a peculiar significance was attached to this species of the vegetable kingdom. There is, for instance, the legend regarding the planting of the cypress tree of Kishmar. This tree is said to have been planted by Zoroaster himself to commemorate the fact and its importance of the conversion of King Vishtaspa, by his teaching. The evergreen foliage and sturdy vitality of the cypress was probably intended to be symbolical of the endurance and increase of this form of belief, as well as a fitting memorial for all time of the especial event it was intended to mark. This tree existed till very nearly the ninth century of our era. Kishmar is situated in Khurassan, and the famous tree was cut down in A.D. 846 (232 A.H.) by the command of Mutawakkal, tenth Caliph of the family of Abbas. By that time probably the ancient tree had assumed a sacred aspect, and probably its destruction had a great deal to do with a desire to bring the people of the country into closer communion with Islam.[1]

A giant specimen of cypress was found by Colonel P. M. Sykes in 1899 at the village of Sangun, in the Sarhad district of Eastern Persia. "To our surprise we saw in this remote hamlet perhaps one of the largest cypresses in the world. Its girth at about 5 feet from the ground was 25 feet, and just above huge limbs like those of an oak branched off. From a distance it resembled a big Plane tree except for its colour, and it was quite worth a long journey to inspect it." *Cypress tree at Sangun, in Sarhad.*

The cypresses of Darg in Seistan were carefully measured by me. I also at first mistook them for Plane trees, but the dull and dark green colour of the foliage assured me of a mistake long before I reached them. The taller of the two trees is not a perfect specimen. Its crown has been broken off; nevertheless it was found to be 64 feet in height. At a height of six feet above the ground its girth was found to be 17 feet. It was in good leaf. From the roots of this tree another had sprung up which does not attain to quite half of the stature of the parent tree. At six feet above ground the sapling gave a measurement of 12 feet. About two hundred yards to the east stands the butt end of a much larger specimen. This imperfect tree at 5 feet above ground measured about 23 feet in girth, and its height is only 25 feet. It is a much older tree than the others. The latter stand on the banks of an old irrigation channel and as their roots conform to the spoil banks and bed of the latter the channel must have endured for innumerable centuries and the tree must have been originally planted where it now stands. *Measurement of the Cypresses of Dorg, in the Hokart.*

The villagers of Darg told me that this variety of cypress may be propagated by means of cuttings, and if so it is by no means impossible that both the cypresses of Darg in Seistan and of Sangun in Sarhad may have been in this way propagated from the famous tree of Kishmar, and may have both been planted to commemorate some event of importance in Sarhad and in *The Cypress tree of Kishmar*

---

[1] For a very interesting notice by General Houloum-Schindler on the Cypress of Zoroaster, see Jour. R. As. Soc. for January 1909. Kashmar or Kishmar is said to have been near Turshīz. According to the legend this tree was 1,450 years old when it was cut down by the Caliph's order and carried to Sāmarrā (north of Baghdad) to be used in the construction of the J'afariya palace. When the tree reached the station which is one day's march from Sāmarrā the Caliph was murdered by his son— 9th December, 861 A.D. This fixes the date of legend; but there is nothing in the early Arab chronicles to corroborate the story of the tree.

The omission of all allusion to the tree casts a doubt on the legend, but is not necessarily fatal to it.—G. P. T.

Seistan, connected with the spread of the doctrines of Zoroaster. A smaller and less perfect cypress exists in Seistan to the west of the Pariun, which I was told was once a cutting from the trees of Darg. These trees are undoubtedly regarded with respect if not veneration by the Seistanis who also hold the kora-gaz variety of the tamarisk family in a similar light. A grove of these trees exist round a shrine (now of a Muhammadan Saint). They are both numerous and of large size. It is said that when any calamity is about to befall the country, one of these trees always falls, and the country folk bring offerings to the shrine in order to avert or minimize the threatened disasters. The shrine and grove is situated in the Kala-i-Kāh district.

In the next chapter those Zoroastrian remains will be dealt with, which cannot be assigned to a period anterior to the spread of Islam.

Marginal note: Seistanis reverence the Kora-gaz trees. Lingering traces of tree worship.

CHAPTER V.

Zoroastrian remains of probably more recent date.

The remains of Dakhmas, or towers of silence, are so numerous and in some cases the remains are in such preservation as to clearly indicate their original purpose—that it seems quite probable that the religion of Zoroaster lingered in Seistan for many centuries after the conquest of the country by the Arabs and the promulgation of the doctrines of Muhammad. This was a condition of affairs that we know to have existed in parts of Persia not remote from Seistan. The Khariji sectarians embittered by their quarrel with the orthodox party in Islam, regarded the infidel Turk or Indian as less of an enemy than the orthodox community of their countrymen. The great schisms first of the Aliide sect which developed later into the Ismailian heresy took its rise in the eastern parts of the empire of the Caliphs, and were probably due to the imperfect conversion of the people of that territory. The extinction of the religion of Zoroaster was probably synchronous with the extermination of the Kharijite sectaries in Seistan, and Khurassan generally. It follows therefore that the existing remains such as those of towers of silence, of fire temples, by no means belong to a period prior to the promulgation of Islam. The fact of any traces existing at this time raises a presumption in favour of their comparatively recent date of abandonment. *Towers of silence, in ruins.*

The Seistanis call the ruins of towers of silences akhurs or mangers and assign them to the period of Rustam, for the use of whose fabulous charger they are believed to have been constructed. In Khurassan circular mangers are built—about 2 feet or 30 inches in diameter—in which is placed the feed of chopped straw for the use of horses, camels and cattle. The remains of the Dakhmas consist of the ruined inner or outer walls, which are circular. Hence the application of the term akhur. Wherever the people say that one of the mangers of Rustam's charger exists, there it is quite legitimate to suppose that a ruined Dakhma is to be found. These remains are most common in the tract on the left bank of the Helmand River. One notable example stood in 1905 on a mound by the side of the track that led from the Mission Camp to the capital Nasratabad. These ancient buildings are generally met with occupying such commanding sites. This is in agreement with the modern practice of the Parsees of India, whenever such sites are available. One of these ruins crowned a conspicuous height near the village of Kala-i-Nau. It was broken into and explored by the villagers, and out of the débris a much decayed bone was found which was pronounced to be a finger bone of a human being, thus the origin of these ruins was established beyond doubt. Owing to *Rustam legends attached to these ruins. Purposes to whih they were turned.*

their situation some of these ruins have been utilized in still more recent times as watch towers, on which beacon fires were lit in order to signal the approach of an enemy. One of these crowned the height immediately above the village of Kala-i-Nau. The story runs that when this method of disposing of the dead was discontinued, the people filled up the inner annulei of the Dakhmas with earth, and the building if not used as already has been mentioned, was allowed to fall into ruin. In many instances the ground in the vicinity of a ruined tower of silence has been in use as a cemetery where the dead are laid to rest in conformity with the tenets of Islam.

The Burj-i-Lār. About 8 miles to the east of the ruins of Chapu a very prominent promontory of the plateau is crowned with a tower, named Burj-i-Lār—the road tower. It commands an extensive view of the valley of the Khāsh River and was used to light a beacon fire in the troublous times, when this was the route by which Afghan or other invaders were in the habit of entering Seistan. This tower was originally a Dakhma, and used, when Post-i-Gau and Chapu were inhabited, by those who followed the religion of their ancestors.

Ruins most numerous, near Rām Shāhristān. These ruins are most numerous in the vicinity of the mound that marks the site of the ancient city of Rām Shāhristān, the oldest of the cities of Seistan of which any knowledge survives. This city was inhabited long before the time of Muhammad, and it is not surprising therefore that such ruins should be met with near the ancient site. Rām Shāhristān was a populous city, and the dead in those days were exposed in the Dakhmas, which must have been numerous in consequence—and at a distance from human abodes. When Rām Shāhristān was destroyed and abandoned, the towers of silence must have been used by the rural population until the use of these structures was discontinued in later times.

Ruins of the Fire Temple near Rām Shāhristān. In this area also was pointed out the remains of a building of very ancient date—and now almost formless, which is believed to have been a Pyrœum. It goes by the name of Atish Kadah—the fire temple. This is the only trace of such an institution met with in Seistan, though the existence of celebrated Pyrœa at Kārku Shah and Trākun is still known to the people. Here, however, the buildings have disappeared. The ruin named Atish Kadah is at the northern end of a block of Dasht about a mile or a little more to the west of the modern village of Kimmak, inside the flood limits of the Rud-i-Seistan canal, and it is generally surrounded with water and swampy ground. This building was constructed either of unbaked brick or of pisé—no baked bricks were found in it. A large hall or room originally covered with a domed roof can still be recognised. These remains should not be confounded with the domed buildings which crown the southern extremity of the island. These are of quite a recent date. They are mausolea, and in one of them is buried the Nāhrui Sardar, Ālam Khān. Although there is nothing to show that the ruins named Atish Kada are actually those of a fire temple, yet all the local traditions agree on this point. The remains are certainly very old—in appearance almost as old as the few ruins on the mound of Rām Shāhristān.

Local information was also forthcoming to the effect that the Atish Kada also marks the site of a place called Rāshak, which, like so many place-names, is the designation of a small district. This information was volunteered by the inhabitants of a modern hamlet, situated in the old Mahāl or sub-division, which it is said, at the time of the conquest of Seistan by Timur, was named Gulistān, or the Rose Gardens. This name is not in use now—and it is no longer applicable to the locality.

The small division or sub-division of Rāshak.

In the following chapters an attempt will be made to identify the sites of the earlier capitals of Seistan, and of the places mentioned by the authors Al Istakhri and Ibn-i-Rusteh, for the accounts of these writers contain all that can be discovered in the way of hints, rather than actual information regarding Seistan in the 9th and 10th centuries of our era.

Al Istakhri and Ibn-i-Rustāh.

CHAPTER VI.

Rām Shāhristān.

Description of Rām Shāhristān.

Although Bina-i-Kai was the chief city of Seistan over 1,000 years ago, there was another still more ancient, which had been the seat of government before that later capital came into existence. The site of this is still well known, and the name attaching to it, Rām Shāhristān, is the same as that contained in the authors alluded to. Like other places in Seistan the name exists, with nothing worthy of remark in the way of ruins to mark the position of the site.

Distance from Nad Ali.

The position of this more ancient city is about 12 miles in direct distance from Nād Ali, in a south-westerly direction, and some 8 miles in a north-westerly direction from the hamlet of Khwābgāh.

Description of the site.

Just short of the most northerly point of the plateau which overlooks the delta, there is an outlying fragment of dasht separated from the rest of the plateau by a narrow strip of alluvial soil some 200 or 300 yards wide. This detached bluff is about $\frac{1}{2}$ mile long and about 200 yards in width, and is surrounded on all sides by heavy deposits of alluvial soil. The strike of the island of dasht is towards the north-west and at its southern end is a great mound which rises about 100 feet above the plain. An ancient fosse or ditch separates the southern end from the rest, and this isolated position was evidently either a fortified palace or the keep of the citadel which at one time undoubtedly crowned the plateau. At present a few graves and a Baluch Ziarat occupy the centre of the mound, and at the north end overlooking the alluvial plain there stands the remains of a wind mill of comparatively recent date. The summit of the mound is covered with very little débris, as the bricks, burnt though they had been, have crumbled away to a reddish dust. There is a great quantity of ordinary red pottery; all in very small fragments. The southern mound or keep is a mass of shapeless ruins, in such an advanced stage of decay as to be quite undistinguishable from the natural surface of the mound itself. The débris of unbaked brick is streaked with the red dust of decayed burnt brick, and only a few pieces of vitrified brick, too hard to be dissolved, are to be found imbedded in the mass of clay or in the ravines and fissures cut by the action of the weather, which are full of broken pottery. None of the pieces show any signs of having been glazed.

Battlements and towers have long since lost all shape and distinction, but along the western edge of the mound it is possible to trace some resemblance to the outline of defensive works. The latter is much too broken to be easily recognised on the spot, but from the plateau to the west the detached fragments, divided by deep fissures and gaps, are grouped and a general effect is obtained of the ancient fortifications. In a small patch of cultivation to the east a mound some 20 yards in length is visible, and to the west about a mile away there is a worn and decaying enclosure just visible, in spite of the silt which has concealed everything, and drifts of sand which have hidden all that the silt could not cover up. This is all that remains of Rām Shāhristān, except the name, by which it is still well known.

The popular account of the desertion of Rām Shāhristān is that an ancient dam on the Helmand gave way and the river broke in upon the town flooding it out, and causing the inhabitants to fly for their lives. They founded another city, and Zāhidān (being the nearest and most obvious group of ruins) is said to have been built by the fugitives. *Tradition as to the destruction of the City.*

Al Istakhri's account of Rām Shāhristān has been translated by Sir H. Rawlinson; it is to this effect: "It is said that the ancient capital of the Province, in the time of the 1st Persian Dynasty, was on the high road from Sejestan to Kirman, as you go to Darek, opposite to Rasak, at the distance of three stages from Zaranj, its foundations and many of its buildings remaining to the present day. The name of the city was Rām Shāhristān, and the canal of Sejestan flowed to it; owing to the bursting of the dyke in the Helmand, the water of this canal was lowered and cut off from it; so that its prosperity diminished and the inhabitants removed from it and built Zaranj." *Istakhri's account of Rām Shāhristān and its destruction.*

The "canal of Sejestan"—the Rud-i-Seistan of the present day—still passes close to the ancient site, and all the details given by the Istakhri agree with the position assigned by the people of the country to their most ancient capital city, excepting the distance—three stages. If the position given by local tradition to the ancient site of Rāshak is correct, it places the identification of Rām Shāhristān beyond a doubt. The great mound of the latter may very correctly be said to lie opposite to Rāshak. But, not even with the most liberal allowance for detours can the 12 miles of direct distance be increased beyond fifteen. That section of the great Trade Route from the Persian Gulf ports to Herat which lies in Seistan has been clearly identified, and Rasak or Rāshak lies on it. The crossing of the "canal of Sejestan" mentioned in the foregoing account was at that time probably not far from Rāshak. The name of Darek, however, no trace can be discovered in the country. *Analysis of Al Istakhri's account.*

The trade route alluded to passed to the east of the modern fort of Sehkoha, leaving the latter some miles to the west. Where this track crosses the dasht that separates the northern from the southern delta, it was marked by a succession of low pillars constructed with baked brick, and lime was probably also used to render them durable. These pillars were placed by the side of the road, a certain number consecutively on the left and no doubt a corresponding sequence on the right of the track. The pillars have dissolved, but the red brick dust into which their materials have been reduced has stained the ground, where they stood, a dull orange colour which is indelible. In some of these spots tiny fragments of lime mortar can also be discovered. *Ancient trade route discovered.*

2 F

This portion of the ancient trade route is still the direct road from the eastern districts of the present delta towards the south. It is also, as far as Bam, the road to Kirman. The town of Darek must therefore have been situated on that trade route. It could not have occupied the site of modern Sehkoha. The trade route passes through the tract of country where the modern manor house of Machi and the equally recent fort of Hauzdār are to be found, both having lain empty and deserted only for the last 100 years or so.

The town (or district) of Darek.

South of Hauzdār fort there is a mound some 15 or 20 feet high and about 300 feet in diameter, and apparently not artificial, on the northern toe of which there stands an akhur or manger of Rustam's charger. To the north of this between it and Hauzdār is a fairly ancient ruin called the Pā'Kash-i-Rustam. Tradition assigns this as having been the peg to which the heel ropes of Rustam's charger used to be fastened. The akhur is the shell of an old tower of silence, and the existence of such a ruin, with the Rustam legend attached to it, marks the locality as having been the site of a settlement in days long past. This locality is over 50 miles from the ruins of Bina-i-Kai, which would make it three stages from Zarang, if that distance was intended to refer to Darek instead of to Rāshak (or Rām Shāhristān).

Description of Rāmrod. Impossible to have been the ancient capital of Seistan.

Sir H. Rawlinson was disposed to find the position of this more ancient capital in the ruins of Rāmrod. This place is modern though it probably occupies an ancient site. Nowhere in the vicinity of Rāmrod is there any trace of a large city or even a town ever having existed, nor is there any legend to this effect. The present fort at this place was a very small affair—moreover it is situated almost at the southern end of the Seistan basin and there are no signs of any towns of considerable size between it and the Shela.

Modern Rāmrod was deserted owing to the failure of Malik Bahrām Khān's canal which has been described in its appropriate place. Such a catastrophe would also have caused a city in its position to be deserted at any time previously. The bifurcation of the Rud-i-Biyabān from the present Helmand is some 60 miles to the east, and a change taking place here would render all the country to the west uninhabitable. In this respect alone does the site of Rāmrod appear to fulfil the conditions of the description of Rām Shāhristān given by Al Istakhri. Rāmrod is also 75 miles approximately from Bina-i-Kai.[1] The tradition that Rām Shāhristān had been rendered

---

[1] Seventy-five miles is too great a distance to be regarded as representing three stages. It was the general practice in the east and is still the common usage, to make the first stage from a large town or city a very short one. Travellers usually in such a case camp just outside the town for the night, and then make their ordinary day's stage from there. Twelve miles would not be too short a distance for traders to traverse in such marches through a cultivated, irrigated and populous district. At any rate it is impossible to ignore the existence of the name of the ancient capital, and the general consensus of local opinion, simply on the grounds of the short distance which separates the ruins at Nād Ali from those of Rām Shāhristān, especially when other conditions agree with Al Istakhri's description. A very great deal of the information collected by that writer and Ibn-i-Rusteh must have been hearsay; there is also very little difference between the Arabic numerals 2 and 3—and a bad or myopic copyist could originate an error that would easily be perpetrated. Two stages from Zaranj to Rasek would exactly agree with actual conditions.

uninhabitable by floods also appears to be more probable than that the water supply was cut off. It would in this case have been easier to restore or rebuild the dam rather than to found a new capital. Floods have always been the danger to which sites, ancient and modern, in the delta of Seistan have been liable.

CHAPTER VII.

Bina-i-Kai—the city of Kai Khasrau.

Bina-i-Kai, or Zaranj- ruins of : now called Nad Ali.

Before dealing with the remains that mark the site of this ancient city built after that Rām Shāhristan had been destroyed, it will be necessary to revert to the itinerary of Ibn Rusteh and Al Istakhri once more, using for the purpose of course the translations made by that eminent scholar—the late Sir Henry Rawlinson. We are only concerned now with that section of the itinerary from Juwein to Zaranj. The names of the stages differ. Ibn Rusteh gives them as follows—Kuring or Kurinj, Hisanik, Zaranj. According to Al Istakhri, the halting places were—Basher (Peshawarān); Karkuyeh; Zaranj. The place-name Hisanik of Ibn Rusteh and the Hisun of Beladheri's account of the invasion of Seistan by Rabi must be variants of the same name. According to the route of the invaders given by this writer it lay 5 miles from Karkuyieh, also mentioned by him. As the Arabs were advancing towards the north, Hisun or Hisanik must have been situated either north or north-west of Karkuyieh, and the ancient mounds in the locality now known as Takht-i-Shah or those further to the east towards Gaud-i-Gaz, now crowned by pillars of the boundary between Persia and Afghanistan, probably mark the position of the ancient sub-division of Hisun. Ibn Rusteh's route therefore lay to the east of that perpetuated by Al Istakhri, and probably it was an alternative route, which avoided the Helmand of that period and led to Zaranj without the necessity of crossing the channel of the river. The latter especially mentions the fact that between Basher and Karkuyieh the residue of the water of the Helmand was crossed by a bridge which can be no other than the ancient bridge of two arches which was discovered in the jungle of the Miān Kangi and which is now called Takht-i-Pul, to the north of the Kārku Shāh mound. The distance between this ancient site and the ruins at Nad Ali, according to Al Istakhri, was 3 farsangs or about 12 miles which agrees very well with the actual distance in a straight line from one site to another, at the present time.

Route to from Herat. Alternative route round the head of the Lake.

Ibn Rusteh however has recorded the fact that in order to get from Kurung to Hisanik, if there was water on the road (*i.e.*, if that part of the Hāmun was full), it was necessary to take boats (tutin or raft) to traverse the four farsakhs (16 miles). But if the traveller was not minded to make the tranship-ment of his property, or goods in the case of a merchant, it was possible to avoid doing so by following an alternative route called the desert route, to the left. He states (to quote Sir Henry Rawlinson's translation)—"You need not cross any river or water at all except the river of Nishk : for you leave the Serat (Straits or Hāmun) and the Hindmend to the right-hand and at a

Masjid in Peshawarān, distirct of Juwein: materials baked brick & clay mortār (17th century A.D.)

(Part III to face page 195.)

point below where you would come out below Hisanik, but two farsakhs before reaching the capital you cross the Hindmend and another river called the Wadi Abras and so on to Sejestan." This route can be clearly traced at the present time, for the site of the town and small district of Nishk has been identified, and the name is still in existence. From Juwein the alternative route followed the toe of the dasht, passing by the mound called Takht-i-Rustam, at the head of the Hāmun-i-Puzah, by the ruins of Khwajah Siahposh and Post-i-Gau to Chakānsur and so on to Nad Ali.

Nishk is a small district on the right bank of the Khâsh Rud and the "river of Nishk" mentioned by the author quoted must be the Khāsh Rud. At the present day there is the swampy tract between Meno and Nad Ali, filled by the spill water of the Jaroki canal which occupies the position of the Helmand in 1830 to 1839. The channel of the Helmand mentioned by Ibn Rusteh must therefore have been the Sena Rud channel mentioned by Beladheri as having been crossed first of all by 'Obād bin Ziyād when that leader marched by Kish (Khisht or Kisht to the east of Khāsh) on his way to conquer Kandahar. The Wadi Abras was in all likelihood a great canal that irrigated the country to the north of Kala-i-Kang—faint traces of the spoil banks of which were found by me further to the north of this modern fort. <small>Nishk and the Sena Rud; the Wadi Abras, probably a canal.</small>

The writers Al Istakhri and Ibn Rusteh appear to have recorded information obtained at two periods of time: the latter is the earlier author who lived at the end of the 9th and the early part of the 10th century—his work is supposed to have been compiled about 903 A.D.; while Al Istakhri wrote his account in about 951.[1] The route given by the former from Kurung to Hisanik and thence to the capital of Seistan was used probably before the construction of the bridge mentioned by the later author, which must have caused the earlier route to have been abandoned. Once the bridge was available the crossing of the tail of the Helmand river was obviated—and the crossing must have been notoriously difficult for the bridge to have been considered necessary. <small>Period of Al Istakhri and Ibn-i-Rusteh.</small>

The information that it has been possible to collect from independent sources with reference to the site of Zaranj, the capital city of Seistan in the 10th century of our era, as far as it goes, confirms the local tradition that the ruins which exist at Nad Ali are those of the great city founded by Kai Khasrau, when Rām Shāhristān had to be abandoned—known to the Arabs as Zaranj. <small>Information points to Nad Ali, as the site of Zaranj.</small>

It will be as well at this stage to describe the ruins as we found them to exist in 1903. The greater part of the ruins have been destroyed and effaced by the action of water and the silt deposited when the Helmand forced its way through the ruins. What is undoubtedly the vestiges of the inner town <small>Condition of the ruins in 1903-05.</small>

---

[1] The lands of the Eastern Caliphate—Guy Lestrange.

is all that is left. Encircled by the remains of massive walls which form a continuous line of mounds—showing here and there a fragment of the wall still erect—there is a formless mass of débris composed of broken pottery and baked brick, with the exception of the ruins of a minaret. The protecting walls and heaps of ruins have formed an island beyond the reach of all floods the recurrence of which can be recognised by the deposit of rich alluvial soil above which rise the vestiges of the walls that protected the inner city. The ruins of the latter are in a fair way of disappearing altogether. They form a quarry which is freely exploited for baked bricks by all who need materials for building. A contractor who has obtained the monopoly of the manufacture of gunpowder in the Chakansur district is helping the process of destruction as his workmen delve in the mounds of the walls and piles of débris searching for saltpetre which abounds in such localities and which is extracted largely from the ruins of Nad Ali.

Ruins exploited for bricks and making of saltpetre.

The trace of the walls can however be followed with ease. The trace is irregular as will be seen from a reference to the plan. A group of modern dwellings, and a garden laid out by one Rustam Khan, occupy the south-east angle of the defences, and here it is said that, when the ground was being cleared for building, the foundations of other remains—identified as those of a Madrassah or College—were laid bare.

Walls of the inner city can be easily traced.

Separated from the remains of the inner city by a moat (now silted up to a great extent) about 100 feet wide, there rises a huge mound some 90 feet above ground level. This is the site of the ancient citadel, and on its southern slope it is possible to recognise the vestiges of massive fortifications, especially one circular bastion which overlooks the angle formed by the moat towards the south-west. The silt that filled the latter now reaches up to the foot of the mound and the moat cannot be traced on the sides away from the ruins of the inner city. The sides of the mound are strewn with bricks, and of these Ali Khan, the Sanjarāni, built the modern fort that occupies the summit which is now held by a garrison of Afghan regular troops as an outpost. This post is called Nad Ali and has given a name to the ancient site.

The great citadel mound, divided by a broad moat from the inner city.

To the north-east of the inner city there are two lofty mounds, the remains of great piles of buildings, the summits of which are over 90 feet in height above the level of the plain of alluvium on which they stand. The northern one of these mounds is comprised of the débris of buildings constructed either altogether, or very largely of baked brick. This gives a russet colour to the slopes owing to which it is called the "Red hill" (Surhdik). About half mile to the south of this is an equally lofty mound, but the buildings, of the remains of which it is formed, were constructed with either unbaked brick or "pisé," owing to which the mound is of a pale grey colour. For this reason it is called the "white hill" (Safedik). These great mounds

The Surhdik and Safedik mounds at Nad Ali.

dominate every other feature in the landscape and are visible for a very long distance in every direction where there is no tamarisk jungle to obstruct the view. And the buildings of which they are the remains must have been huge piles of masonry and pisé work—either fortresses or well fortified palaces.

Safedik is fully a mile from the central or inner city, and Surhdik is three-fifths of a mile distant. These distances quite disprove the Baluch tradition that these mounds were raised by Nādir Shah upon which to plant his batteries when he captured and destroyed Nad Ali. None of Nādir's guns could have had such an effective range. The mounds are called Dam Damah, because they are attributed to Nādir Shah, the last great conqueror who arose in Asia before the influence of Europe extended into that continent and rendered for ever a similar occurrence impossible.[1] *Story of Nādir Shah, improbable.*

The space between these mounds and the inner city is now covered with an alluvial deposit which is at times even now renewed in every year of high river. But through this covering of silt remains of buildings, too large to be completely buried, here and there make their appearance as tumuli of bricks, with perhaps a small fragment of wall that has been able to resist the action of water and the more insidious ravages of damp.

To the north and east of Surhdik there is a long and low mound of white clay, the undoubted remains of the outer wall, about 400 yards in advance of that hill. At the northern end of this low ridge there is the undoubted site of a gateway, which was certainly the north gate of the outer city. About half mile of water-worn and saline soil separates the two mounds, and at the foot of Safedik facing the "Red hill" there are the remains of a Madrassa (college), or Court-house. The ends of the building face the north-west and south-east, and in each end there was a gateway. The centre was an open quadrangle, around which on either side there ran a colonnade which doubtless supported an upper row of cells. On either side of the south-east entrance is a group of ruined apartments, on an upper and lower story, which extend over the gateway or entrance arch. The method of building is very well illustrated in these remains. The foundations, and for 3 or 4 feet above ground the walls also, were built of baked brick, the superstructure being constructed of sundried brick. Tempered clay was used in place of mortar. *The Madrassa at Nad Ali.*

To the north-west of the inner city there are several low mounds of clay, and on one of these about a mile and-a-half distance from the ruins there stands a ruinous but very modern tower known as the "horse's tower" (Burj-i-Asp), because it is said to have been the stable in which Rustam's charger had been stalled. This particular mound is higher than others in its vicinity. Beyond the ruined walls the ground for upwards of a mile *Burj-i-Asp, near Nad Ali.*

---

[1] Needless to say that Nādir never had occasion to besiege or capture Nad Ali which was in ruins when he passed through Seistan.—G. P. T.

around shows everywhere traces of old buildings, the larger of which have formed low mounds composed of baked brick and débris. To the west of the principal ruins the land has been cultivated for several years, and for this reason the mounds are not as numerous as they are to the east of the ruins.

Extent of the ancient city of Bira-i-Kai. There is, however, evidence to show that the outer city must have extended towards the north as far as Deh Gul Muhammad. Thence to Burj-i-Ās, and in a southerly direction towards Jān Muhammad, the Tapa-i-Mari, Deh Khoja and Alam Khan, and towards the east up to the mound which represents the north-east face of the wall of the outer city. There are men still alive who have seen the ruins of Nad Ali when they were half covered with drifts of sand, extending for great distances on all sides. The inroads of the Helmand and the effects of damp have been, however, too powerful to be resisted, and to such potent influences the time-worn remains of the ancient city have at last succumbed. In the drought of 1902, when the Helmand remained dry for some time, it is said that the foundations of buildings constructed with baked bricks were laid bare in the channel near Burj-i-Ās, and even when the channel re-filled remains of walls and baked bricks have been seen projecting from the banks.

To the north a succession of low mounds extend for fully two miles and are at last concealed by sand dunes. These mounds are probably the sites of an old suburb.

Ruins inside the city. Within the city is a chaotic jumble of bricks, potsherds and other débris, spread over the ground and piled in high mounds. But within the walls of the inner city the remains are all of buildings (carefully constructed with burnt brick) closely packed. No remains of buildings of sundried brick or "pisé" ruins are to be found within this city. The walls were, however, composed of these materials, merely the lower courses having been built with baked brick.

Description of the octagonal form of Kheshk-i-Dukhtar. The only ruin inside the walls of any importance is the minaret, a mere fragment about 25 or 30 feet in height. It is surrounded by piles of fallen bricks. Octagonal in plan, each side, above the piles of débris, measures 10 feet. About 25 feet above the present ground level there are traces of a balcony having projected beyond the sides. Great baked bricks carved and fixed in the walls as brackets still retain their positions in places, and above this the upper part of the minaret evidently rose in a plain shaft much less in diameter than that portion below the balcony. In the middle of each face there is a semi-circular pilaster or buttress which was carried up to the balcony. The latter was reached by a flight of spiral steps which closed the centre of the shaft, the first turn of the spiral above ground forming a vaulted chamber.

The following description of this minaret is taken from the record of Sir F. Goldsmidt's Mission of 1872. It will be interesting to refer to, as it shows

Ruined minaret, of the great masjid of Zaranj-Nād'Ali.

(Part III to face page 202.)

very clearly the nature of the building to which the minaret belonged, and the progress of delapidation that has gone on since then. "The most interesting ruin still standing is that of a very massive brick-built octagonal shaped tower, with excellent mortar, situated at the south-west corner of the town walls, in the neighbourhood of which are the remains of a reservoir with enormous bricks and a very spacious gateway. This tower has a spiral vaulted staircase of 40 steps, about four feet broad, by which we ascended to the top. It was probably designed for the Muezzin, and has two rooms inside it. Between this minaret and the Safedik mound and Surhdik the members of that Mission described the ruins as a vast extent of ground from which crop up solid brick foundations of tenements, or on which are strewed detached baked bricks of large size and broken specimens of painted tiles and earthenware of past generations." *Sir F. Goldsmidt's description of the minaret, and ruins generally.*

The minaret stood at the north-east corner of a quadrangle, around which there were cells or chambers. The centre of the court is now a hollow silted up, and the remains of walls and piles of bricks which surround it form a bank some 8 or 10 feet high. Immediately to the north of the minaret there are high mounds of brick débris. The massive gateway and reservoir can no longer be traced.

The fragments of pottery are of the most varied description. Among the ordinary kinds of glazed earthenware are to be found pieces of coarse porcelain and earthenware covered with a white glaze and bearing a floral or scroll design in blue of not a bad colour. Ordinary red earthenware is most abundant, and among those fragments of finer porcelain are to be found covered with a smooth, hard and pale olive coloured glaze, underneath which is a white vitreous biscuit. *Pottery strewn mounds.*

There was also a story told of a great well, the shaft of which was lined with baked brick, somewhere among the ruins, which, it was said, is full of human bones. The position of this well could not be discovered.

In Sir H. Rawlinson's most valuable memoir on Seistan there is a list of the gates of Zaranj taken from the writings of Al Istakhri, whose descriptions have been copied by later authors. The inner city possessed five gates: the outer "thirteen entrances. The names of the latter commencing from the south, and circling round by the east to the north were as follows:—(1) Mina; (2) Jurjan; (3) Sizak (?); (4) Sarak; (5) Shuib; (6) Nuh Kih (?); (7) Alkam; (8) Nishk, (9) Karkuyieh; (10) Istris; (11) Ghanjerah; (12) Nustan; (13) Rudgeran." Also in another place that "the south-eastern gate of Zaranj leading to the grain district was called the Bab-et-Te'am." This was perhaps identical with the gate called Shuib, the latter is almost the very word now used in Seistan to denote the southern[1] or lower part of the inhabited country. *Istakhri's list of the gateways of Zaranj.*

---

[1] Sheb-lower is used to denote the south, i.e., Sheb-i-Ab—south of a river or canal. Bala upper is used for the north Pa'a-i-Ab—north of a river or canal. The word Pusht is also used for the north Pusht-i-Kuh—north of the hills or range —G. P. T.

According to the same authority, "the great buildings in the city were (1) the great Mosque at the southern or Fars gate of the inner town; (2) the Court-house in the outer town between the Te'am and the Fars gates; (3) the prison in the inner town near the Mosque; (4) another Court-house at the back of the Mosque near the prison; (5) between the Te'am and the Fars gates, the palaces of Yakub and of Amru, sons of Leis; and (6) inside the city between the Karkuyieh and the Nishk gates, the celebrated citadel called the Ark in which was the treasury built by Amru, son of Leis." Besides a description of the bazaars, mosques, hospitals, markets, interior canals and reservoirs, etc., the shapeless gaps which now exist in the ruins of the walls that once enclosed the inner town to the south and south-west of the ruined minaret, are probably the positions of the old gateways of Te'am and Fars. There seems not to be room for doubt, but that the great mounds of Surhdik and Safedik are the ruins of the Palaces of Yakub and Amru, sons of Leis.

Identification of the gateways and other buildings mentioned by Al Istakhri.

There is some confusion, however, between the capital of Seistan and the town which was the birthplace of the sons of the coppersmith. The statement that at this place there was to be seen the site of the manger of Rustam's charger probably referred to the capital, where still the people of the country point to Burj-i-Ās as the site of the manger of the celebrated Rakhsh, the charger which so often bore his master to victory, and which the genius of Firdusi has rendered as famous in story as the steed of Alexander the Great has been in subsequent ages.

That the palace of one of the sons of Leis should have been built of sundried brick or even of pisé is not at all surprising. The Seistanis have always been celebrated for the way in which they handled these materials. At the present time there are buildings not much more than 200 years old which contain handsome domed apartments 25 feet square and well built, even though they date from a period of decadence.

CHAPTER VIII.

Identification of other ancient remains and sites mentioned in the itineraries of Ibn Rusteh and Al Istakhri.

For this purpose it is again necessary to refer to the two itineraries translated and quoted by Sir H. Rawlinson. One is the route from Herat to Zaranj taken from the Istakhri, which has already been referred to with respect to the positions of Kuring and Basher. The second itinerary describes the route from Zaranj to Kala-i-Bist by way of Khash.

In the first it is stated that having passed Basher (Peshāwarān) the traveller will " pass on the way to Kar Kuyieh by a bridge, the residue of the Helmand water, 4 farsakhs to Kar Kuyieh and 3 farsakhs to Zaranj." That bridge still exists. It is known as Takht-i-Pul. It stands in its delapidated present condition on an alluvial plain surrounded by a fairly thick jungle of tall tamarisk. The broken roadway is about 8 feet above the level of the plain. There are only two brick-built relics of antiquity outside Bina-i-Kai in Seistan that still retain some of their original plan and shape. One is the Mil-i-Kasamabad, the other is this bridge, and the latter is certainly to all appearance the older structure. It is very massively built, a great deal more material having been used in its construction than was absolutely necessary to safely bear the strains of traffic. The architect evidently was not sure of his skill. Labour no doubt was abundant and material as well, and in order to be perfectly certain of the result he sacrificed appearances. *Description of the arched bridge Takht-i-Pul.*

In addition to the clumsy strength of this bridge it was not countersunk, and the approach at either end must have been an inclined plane, the ascent being relieved, perhaps, by the roadway being ramped to meet the slope of the bridge. There is no trace of baked bricks having been employed for this purpose.

The bridge has two arches separated by a pier 10 feet in width, the ends of which project beyond the sides of the bridge to a length of 6 feet, and both of the ends of the pier are brought to a point. The waterway of each arch is 13 feet and the abutments on either bank of the canal perhaps projected $1\frac{1}{2}$ to 2 feet. These dimensions make the width of the ancient channel or river which it must have spanned about 40 feet. The bricks forming the arches radiate from a centre as is usual, and the waterways themselves are practically intact. The bricks forming the roadway above have been torn up and removed, leaving barely anything more than the thickness of the bricks necessary to form the arches. *Vussoir arches.*

The width of the roadway must have been fully 22 feet, affording plenty of room for laden camels from opposite directions crossing on the bridge.

There was a parapet which was continued down to the ends of the bridge where they ended in an outward curve. These may possibly have been used to retain the earthen ramp at either end in its place. Excavations to the foundations of the bridge give a height of 18½ feet from the floor of the latter to the crown of the arches above the heaps of débris inside the old waterways.

Accumulation of silt in (about) 1,000 years, as exemplified by the ruined bridge, about ·012 of a foot per annum.

This gives an accumulation of silt or sand to a depth of about 12 feet above the masonry floor. The depth of water which it spanned must have been not less than 8 or 9 feet, and this channel must have been a serious obstacle. The great trade route through Seistan passed over this bridge. The merchandise in those remote periods was very costly in comparison with its bulk, and any accident to a camel which resulted in total destruction or damage to its load meant perhaps that the profits on the whole venture were at once lost. The bridge then was an important and valuable public work; hence the anxious care to make it strong enough. The abutments at either side are heavy blocks of masonry. The cement used is the celebrated Sārūj, still very extensively used in Persia for all works exposed to the action of water. The process of preparation at the present day is almost the same as to ingredients and process as described by Pedro Texeira in the 16th century. In this particular case, the Takht-i-Pul bridge, the thin layers of Sārūj between the bricks are as hard as the latter.

Direction or orientation of the roadway over the bridge.

The roadway over the bridge bears 329 degrees, or 31 degrees west of north. In this direction there are a group of mounds, evidently of old buildings, around the Ziārat of Shāh Ismail about 3 miles beyond the bridge. And as the general direction of the trade route must have determined the direction of the roadway over the bridge, the route must have entered the Hamun area not far from the ancient graveyard close to which the modern hamlet of Deh Surkh is situated. In the reverse direction, that is, on the bearing of 149 degrees, the sight of the prismatic compass intersected the mound of Kārku, or as it is often called Kārku Shāh. From this place towards Deh Surkh there is a low undulation or rise in the ground on which the modern village of Burj-i-Mir Gul is situated. The trade route followed this rise. From a few yards to the east of this bridge a system of old canals ran parallel to the old road or track. They pass to the west of Mir Gul and are still traceable by their spoil banks, though the latter are very much broken. Along the banks of these canals there were a very large number of brick kilns and fragments of walls as well, which are the remains of old buildings.

Description of Kārku Shāh.

Kārku Shāh is the most conspicuous landmark in the district of the Miān Kangi. It is a mound about 30 feet high, above which a splinter of a wall rises to the height of 25 feet. The lower part of this wall is built of very large baked bricks, and the part above this (which rises about 5 feet above ground) was built of either sundried brick or pisé.

Takht-i-Pul (ancient bridge), baked brick & "sāruj" mortar (9th-10th century A.D.).

Upon the summit of the mound is a platform, the lower part of a plinth of the ancient building of which the wall was a part. The remains of the walls forming the apartments, built of huge baked bricks, stand on a plinth some 3 or 4 feet in height, the interior of the rooms having been filled up to the level of the bricks with the débris of the decayed superstructure. The whole forms the platform, some 80 feet square, lying to the south of the upright fragment of wall. The plinth is formed entirely of baked bricks, and in order to make an ornamental design alternate course of bricks have been set up on edge, the dividing courses being laid in headers and stretchers. The largest sized bricks were used in the main building alone, the baked brick largely excavated in its vicinity being of the usual size 6″×12″. Judging from the great size of the bricks in the main building, it appears to have been built at a very early date, and nowhere else have such large bricks been excavated or seen in the other ruins of Seistan.[1] *Remains of an ancient building, laid bare by the people excavating for bricks.*

This mound is 750 feet long by 360 feet in width, and it slopes downwards to the ground towards the south-east. Along the north-west foot of the mound there are still left signs of towers and bastions of "pisé" or sun-dried brick which were without doubt a part of a fortification which once encircled the buildings that form the mound. *Dimensions and orientation of the mound.*

The whole of the country around Kārku Shāh has been subjected to the inroads of floods. On every side there are old channels scoured by the water. Dense thickets of tamarisk, some 25 feet high and more, flourish on the alluvial soil and render it not at all an easy matter to detect the existence of ruins. *Character of the country round the mound.*

Immediately to the north of the great mound there are a line of low mounds which look like the remains of a wall, but which can be traced only for a short distance. Between them and the former there are several tumuli or mounds composed of baked bricks, thickly coated with nitre. These are ruins of larger buildings which have not been concealed as yet by silt deposits. To the east of the central mounds there are other ruins, one of which was evidently a mausoleum. To the south of the central mound there are the remains of a building which may have been either a mausoleum or a gatehouse, and on each side of this there are low water-worn mounds which may perhaps be the remains of a wall. These ruins are about ½ mile from the central mound.

Hidden away among the jungle are mounds of brick, white with a coating of nitre, the remains of large sized buildings. About 3 miles to the east of Kārku, there is still to be seen the remains of a small out-lying fort, or defensive post, a place of refuge, or the residence of some person of consequence, and a outpost of Kārku Shāh. It is called the Kala Tapa or "fort mound," and it consists of an outer line of defences with a small keep or citadel nearer the north-west face. The jungle hides many more remains for which there was not time to make a search. *Remains of a town round the mound.*

---

[1] They were 30″×14″ and about 4″ thick—rough measurement.

THE RUINS IN SEISTAN.

There is no doubt that the mound at Kârku (or Kârku Shâh) represents the citadel of a town, which in olden days was the centre of a thickly populated little district. The settlement (as seemed to have been the case generally in Seistan) was no doubt composed of isolated manor houses and cultivators' homesteads, and at certain localities fortified centres existed to which the inhabitants could fly for safety on occasions of war and invasion. The vestiges of the former prosperity of this district are very few, and it will not be long perhaps before they fade away altogether in this part of Seistan. Kârku seems to have been the furthest place in the direction of the Hâmun where there were permanent habitations. Beyond it, that is to the north and southwest, there could not have been many settlements containing large buildings, for of these only two or three mounds have been found to exist and the lands in this direction were either cultivated from Kârku—the agriculturists living in temporary dwellings, or they were in the hands of graziers. There can be no doubt that the ruins in and around Kârku (or Kârku Shâh)[1] are those of Karkuyieh of the Istakhri, where in pre-Islamitic times there existed, according the Mas'udi, the third most ancient of the fire temples of Persia. The name has come down to us through all the many intervening centuries without suffering any change at all. In Sir Henry Rawlinson's memoir is the following translation from the work of the Kasvini,[2] a later author than Istakhri: "Karkuyieh is an ancient city of Seistan where there are two lofty cupolas about a mile apart, and each surmounted by a horn which resembles the horns of a bull. They are reported to belong to the age of Rustam and have remained from that time to the present as objects of wonder. And beneath the two cupolas is a fire temple of the Magi, which would seem to show that the king had built near his dwelling place a temple where he might worship. The fire of this Pyrœum has never been extinguished, for the servitors who are told off to the duty of keeping up the flame, sit down at the distance of 20 cubits from the fire, and covering their mouth and breath, take with silver tongs bits of tamarisk wood of the size of a span, and when the flame languishes and threatens to be extinguished, throw them upon the fire stick after stick; and this Pyrœum is one of the most celebrated of all the temples of the Magi." Further on it is stated that Mas'udi assigned the foundations of the temple to Bâhman, son of Isfandiâr, whose warlike exploits in Seistan are famous in story.

Kârku Shâh is undoubtedly the site of Karkuyieh. Al Kasvini's account of the Pyrœum at this place.

The ancient building laid bare is probably the temple.

Kârku is without doubt the site of that ancient Pyrœum—perhaps the plinth and walls that are laid bare on the summit of the mound may have

---

[1] The word Shâh is a term of respect applied to holy men much as the word "reverend" is used by Europeans. There are two ancient sites in Seistan, to the names of which this suffix is attached: one is Kârku, and the other is the ruined and submerged town of Sâwari Shâh. There is also a Ziârat overlooking the sheet of water which covers the latter, dedicated to Sâwari Shâh.

[2] He is believed to have compiled or finished his work in 1275 A.D. (The lands of the eastern Caliphate: Guy Lestrange).

themselves supported that temple. The name at any rate is applied exclusively to the mounds and the ruins on its summit where the fragments of wall as yet stands. And there is every probability that some lingering tradition of its having been holy ground at a remote period of the history of Seistan may have caused the place to be held in respect and spoken of in corresponding terms.[1]

Seistan was the refuge of the Kharijis who settled in the country in great numbers, and the history of Islam contains frequent references to disturbances in Seistan caused by some fanatical leader of that sect rebelling against the authority of the religious head of Islam, both with reference to his spiritual and temporal jurisdiction. The translation made by Sir Henry Rawlinson from oriental authors contains a strange reference to this sect as being weavers of cloth. This is a touch of local colour which even at this distance of time retains its distinctive effect, and it is a point which evidently struck the persons from whom ancient authors obtained their information. It is a very striking feature in Seistani villages at the present day where groups of men may be seen busily engaged in weaving the narrow coarse cloth of the country. A place is set apart for this, and there, on the leeward side of a high garden wall, a slight shelter from the sun is constructed under which there are shallow pits sunk where the weavers take their seats, the weft of the piece of cloth upon which they work being attached to a peg some 60 or 80 feet beyond the booths, a cross bar being used to keep the threads apart. Sometimes parties of as many as a dozen men may be seen engaged in this work, and a hum of conversation goes on as they ply their shuttles. After a time the process must become mechanical, and demand but the smallest amount of attention. The close association of the workers favours conversation, and it is very easy to imagine how the fierce sectarians of ancient Seistan, as they sat at work, could have discussed the religious and political shortcomings of any ruler who had made himself obnoxious to them. Karkuyieh was the seat of a Khariji community, who followed the profession of hand-loom weavers.

The life of a Khariji weaver revealed by the life of a modern weaver.

The itinerary of Ibn-i-Rusteh has also been noticed in reference to the sites of Kurun and Juwein. The tutins landed travellers at Hisanik on the southern edge of the Hamun. From Hisanik there was evidently a direct road to Zaranj, which did not pass through the district of Karkuyieh. Hisanik, therefore, was probably situated at the head of the Chung-i-Chahārshahr, or perhaps still further east. The road to Zaranj from either of those points at the present day leaves Kārku on the right.

The routes across the āmun given by Ibn-i-Rusteh.

---

[1] It is highly probable that the peculiar respect with which the ruins of Kārku Shāh and Sāwari Shāh are spoken of, and they are also regarded as dating from most ancient times, is due to there having existed in the pre-Islamitic period fire temples at both the sites.

Istakhri itinerary from Zaranj to Kala-i-Bist.

The second itinerary from Zaranj (or Sejestan) to Bist is given by the Istakhri. Sir Henry Rawlinson translates it as follows:—

(1) "Zanbuk (a very doubtful name)."
(2) "Suruwar, a large royal village."
(3) "Haruri, a flourishing place; in this stage you cross the Nishk river by an arched bridge of brick."
(4) "Dehak, halt at the Robat; desert from here."
(5 to 8) "Robats, posts or caravansarais," named in the itinerary, but it is not necessary to repeat the list of them here.
(9) "Bist; all desert from Robat-i-Dehak to within one farsakh of Bist."

Identification of Suruwar and description of Chakānsur and its modern history.

The story of the building of Chakānsur gives us the information that the mound on which it stands was known as Dik-i-Surh. This may mean the mound of Sur, or merely the "Red mound."

But Chakānsur is said to have been in existence for very many centuries. It was in the hands of a family who possessed the hereditary title of Mir, and the family was known as the Mir-i-Arab, or Mir Arab. Jān Beg, the cadet of the House of Chagai who emigrated into Seistan, promised allegiance to the Mirs of Chakānsur. The Sanjarāni paid grazing dues for the privilege of pasturing his flocks on the lands belonging to that family. In course of a generation the Sanjarāni Chief got possession of the Ark by stratagem, having married the daughter of the Mir of his day. Seistan had been drained so often of treasure and of human blood that all the old families were in a condition of instability, and in order to maintain some condition of equilibrium, they willingly allied themselves to any Chief of Baluchis who could muster a tail of armed men. After being dispossessed of their property the Mir-i-Arab family of Chakānsur fell upon evil days. The last known representative of the ancient family was a pensioner on the bounty of the late Mir Abbās Kaiāni, and lived in Jallālābād. After this place was abandoned that person took refuge in the hamlet of Mārgo, in the Miān Kangi. He still lives, it is said, but has fallen into a state of dotage. A family existing in obscurity in Chakānsur claim to be the ancient Mirs of that place, but they are not regarded as being of true descent. Chakānsur may be the royal village of Suruwar. There are wide and fertile lands around it which in olden times were irrigated, and the signs of the ancient canals still are both numerous and distinct. But although there are many other sites as old as Chakānsur, there are none that command anything like the same acreage of cultivated soil. If there is no water in the Āshinak, Chakānsur by the direct road or even by way of Kala-i-Kang is not more than 18 miles from Nād Ali, but if the water is out between those two places, it is necessary to turn the southern end of the basin which increases the distance to about 26 miles. Or the place

Suruwar may also have occupied the ancient site about 6 miles to the east of Chakānsur which is now called Irindās.[1]

The fourth stage was the post or caravansarai at Dehak. The present village of Khāsh is about 50 miles from Chakānsur, so that it could easily be reached from the latter in two stages.[2] *Identification of Dehak and Haruri.*

The intermediate stage was Haruri. This is undoubtedly the place called, at the present day, Aleli. The substitution of l for r being by no means uncommon. This direct road from Chakānsur to Bist is still well known and used by those who need to travel quickly.

With reference to Aleli, Connolly mentions the fact that it was at this point that the road to Khāsh town from Chakānsur crosses the Khāsh river and that it was known as Gudar or Guzar-i-Khāsh—both the name and the necessity for crossing the river at this point exist at this present day, and Connolly also heard of the tradition regarding a bridge over the Khāsh river at or close to the modern site of Aleli.

There remains another identification with which we will close this chapter. It is the town or city which was the home of the coppersmith Leis and his sons who formed the Suffari dynasty of Princes. This town was named Karnein. According to Sir Henry Rawlinson, who states that in the printed edition of Beladheri it is written Kariyetcin, the editor of the text, M. De Goeje, considered this name (Kariyetein) to be different from that of Karnein, whence sprung the Suffarians. In the Arabic character the difference between the two names lies in the number and position of the dots which represent the letters t and y and n. Kariyetein, the two villages—or towns, also makes sense, whereas Karnein—the two horns (or conjunctions), makes no sense. The mistake could very easily have been made by a weaksighted and not very painstaking copyist, or from using a badly written or a mutilated original; and once it was perpetrated it would be passed on, and be accepted by subsequent copyists. The word Karnein also would be regarded with favour by these persons, because in their minds it would associate the locality with the tradition of the Two Horned Alexander, Sikander Zul Karnein—one of the fabulous heroes of antiquity, whose exploits are based on a legendary knowledge of the Macedonian sovereign's famous campaigns in the East. Kariyetein, the two towns, was at first believed by me to have been the city whose ruins have been described at Nad Ali, especially as here also was one of the famous "Mangers" of Rustam's charger. In all the notices of the city which was the home of the Suffarians it is noted that the remains of the manger of Rustam's horse used to be pointed out close to that place. It would have not been unreasonable to suppose that the family of Leis the coppersmith dwelt at the *Identification of Karnein properly Kariyetein. Preliminary observations.*

---

[1] There is a lofty mound—or Tell, at Irindās, formed probably by the ruins of an ancient fortalice.
[2] There is a village or township of Dehak in the Khāsh District.—G. P. T.

capital, where the outer and inner cities each girt with a protecting wall might well have been known as the two towns. But there are definite statements regarding the position of the latter which at once shows that the birthplace of the Suffarians was not the capital.

Position of Kariyetein with respect to other known sites.

Turning to Sir Henry Rawlinson's Memoir on Seistan the following allusions to Karnein are to be found by means of which the position of the town can be determined:—" Yakut (1225 A. D.) in voce Karnein, says 'it "'is a village in the district of Nishk, in the Province of Sistan. Ahmad "'ibn Sahal al Balkhi reports that it is a small town with dependent villages "' and district, one stage from Sistan, to the left of the road leading to Bist; "' and distant 2 farsakhs from Suruwar.' ** Istakhri, and Ibn-Haukal (978 " A. D), have the very same words that are quoted from Al Balkhi by Yakut.

" In the same way Beladheri says, page 394, that 'Rabi crossed the Sinā " 'Rud from Zaranj and came to Karnein, where the traces are to be seen of " 'the manger of Rustam's horse '—again—Istakhri says, with respect to " position, 'that Khāsh is one stage from Karnein and a farsakh to the left of " ' the road leading from Zaranj to Bist; also that Farah is two stages from " 'Karnein, the intermediate stage being Jizeh ***.' The manuscripts " however vary much as to these distances, and the numbers are therefore " not much to be depended on."

The neighbouring ruined towns of Post-i-Gau and Chapu, undoubtedly represent Kariyetein.

Suruwar we have seen was either the site on which Chakānsur stand or Irindās, and from either of these sites Post-i-Gau and Chapu are distant about 8 miles, while both these groups of ruins are situated in the district of Nishk— and to the left of the route to Khāsh now in use—which has been identified ; and the name of which still exists. Horsemen carrying despatches reach Farah in two days from Chakānsur, and the name Jizeh still exists on the direct route between these places. Post-i-Gau and Chapu are therefore practically the same distance (measured in stages) from Farah, and as the direct route crosses a waterless plain, caravans also would cross it as rapidly as possible and would thus also make Farah on the second day. Khāsh however is fully 50 miles from either Post-i-Gau or Chapu, and in this direction the distance (in stages) is too long, unless the district of Khāsh is meant, for the boundary of this district is still a little above Kadah and the latter is a short march from Chapu. The statement that Rabi crossed the Sinā Rud on his march from Zaranj to Karnein is also in accordance with what can be gathered at this interval of time as to the position of the Helmand and its partially deserted branch at that period.

These indications point to the ruins of Post-i-Gau and Chapu as being the two towns which may claim to have been the home of Leis the coppersmith. Better evidence than that which has been offered cannot ever be expected to be forthcoming, and the strong presumption in favour of Post-i-Gau dating back to a remote antiquity tends to confirm the conclusion as to it and Chapu being the sites once upon a time known as the " two towns " or Kariyetein.

With regard to the remains of the manger of Rustam's charger—the Dakhma on the lofty promontory some 3 miles east of the ruins of Chapu, afterwards converted into a watch tower and place for a beacon, may very well have been the akhur or manger even then regarded as having been built for the use of the celebrated steed. The remains of the tower of silence on this bluff would have been clearly visible from either Post-i-Gau or Chapu—I have seen it with my unaided vision from the mounds at Nad Ali.

The Burj-i-Lar is the Manger of Rustam's charger.

The ruins which lie close to those of Post-i-Gau show that this town was surrounded by dependent villages, agreeing closely with the description of the place recorded by Al Balkhi.

In conclusion it may be stated that Chakānsur is still regarded as one stage from Nad Ali and the ruins of Post-i-Gau, which begin at about 5 miles from Chakānsur, and would therefore also be one stage from Zaranj—especially if the country between was full of small villages as the ruins show it to have been.

CHAPTER IX.

The ancient trade routes connecting Seistan with the Persian Gulf and the countries to the North, West and East.

Seistan the resort of merchants, bound from the Persian Gulf to Herat.

At the period when Zaranj was the capital of Seistan, that city must have witnessed a brisk trade carried on by the caravans that passed to and from the Perisan Gulf and Herat, and in a lesser degree between Kandahar on the east and Yazd on the west. The people of Seistan must have benefited by the passing of caravans and profited by the intercourse with countries richer and more civilized than it was. Owing to its position, surrounded on all sides by deserts or semi-deserted tracts Seistan lay in the direct track of merchants, and its capital must have been a house of call for traders from remote countries.

Restoration of the Trade Route by the first Saljuk Ruler of Kirmān, after ravages of the Ghazz.

From the ports of Tiz, or Sirāf, or from Hormuz in later times, the great trade route passed through Jiruft and Regān, and thence to Bām where the caravans probably rested before they attempted the passage across the semi-deserted tract that intervened before they could reach the fertile lands watered by the Helmand. The importance of this route can be estimated by the efforts made to restore it in the 12th century of our era, by the first Saljuk ruler of Kirman—Kaward Shāh; after that the country had been ravaged by the hordes of the barbarous Ghazz. At this period the pass on the route from Seistan to Bām, now named the Darband-i-Nādiri, was the boundary of Seistan in this direction.

Facilities for the passage of Caravans.

Kaward Shāh built caravansarais and out-posts to safeguard the progress of camel trains loaded with merchandise. He sunk wells, dug karezes to supply travellers with water. Then in addition he constructed lofty minarets to serve as land marks, and in order to further insure that travellers should run no risk of losing their way in darkness of night or in bad weather the trade route was marked by masonry pillars of the height of a man, so placed as to be mutually visible. In the pass alluded to he built a gateway of masonry and put up gates which was held by an outpost of troops in order to prevent irruptions of marauding bands from Seistan. This work was styled Darband-i-Seistan—the gate of Seistan—and it marked the boundary between his dominions and those of the Rulers of Seistan. To the north-west of this pass there were doubtless similar facilities for the comfort of travellers and merchants up to the capital of Seistan, the great City of Zaranj. The historian of the Saljuk Rulers of Kirmān ascribes all these works to Kaward Shāh, but there can hardly be a doubt that in many cases he must have restored earlier buildings, wells and *karezes* constructed in those earlier days

THE RUINS IN SEISTAN.   215

when the power of the Caliphs was felt in these outlying districts of their Empire.

At the present time across the wide plains to the north-west of Bām, the remains of the works restored or constructed by the Saljuk Ruler are still to be met with, and form a melancholy contrast with the impotence of the modern rulers of the country and their neglect to maintain these useful and important structures. When the telegraph line was in contemplation, which now links Seistan with Kirmān, many of the ancient wells along this route from Bām to Seistan were cleaned and were found to contain water and were once more rendered of service to the needs of man. These wells were lined with masonry, and the latter was found to be still in good repair after having been neglected for centuries. Kaward Shāh and his far-sighted policy has faded from the minds of the people, and the handiwork of this benevolent ruler is attributed to Nādir Shāh who used this route in the 18th century on his march to Kandahar. Faint traces of the masonry pillars which marked the route in Seistan were discovered by me, and these have been alluded to. *Ruins of these buildings still visible between Bam and Seistan.*

The itineraries of the Istakhri and Ibn Rusteh contain information regarding the trade route from Seistan to Herat which is of value, and both these narratives are almost as true now as they were at the time when they were compiled, and contain details which stamp their record as having been drawn up from reliable information. *Itineraries of Al Istakhri and Ibn-i-Rusteh can be traced.*

Both Istakhri and Ibn Rusteh state that there were sixteen stages from Herat to Zaranj, though the names of stages differ. At the 6th stage from Herat travellers entered Seistan territory according to the first named author and both mention Juwein as the 13th stage from Herat. The town which is now the capital of the Hokat is therefore a place of considerable antiquity. Across the river stands the fortress of Lāsh, also famous in times past for its great strength. It is mentioned in history as the fortress of Uk. The defence made by the garrison of this place against the Moghol troops of Chingiz Khan has already been described, but in the early part of the 15th century Lash again held out against the forces of Shāh Rukh, son of Tamerlane. At this time the fort is mentioned as being in the possession of the Sigzis, who acquitted themselves manfully in its defence. It seemingly held out successfully against all attacks, and the besiegers were compelled to drive galleries under the walls until the mines reached the wells on which garrison depended for water. These efforts were successful, and the water being cut off the defenders were compelled to yield the fortress. The caves which are mentioned by Connolly as existing at the foot of the cliffs on which the fortress stands, in 1839, are probably the entrances of Shāh Rukh's mines, and the fissures on the eastern face of the bluff which in his opinion threatened the stability of the walls in this direction were perhaps due to the partial *Number of stages from Seistan (Zaranj) to Herat.* *The Fortress of Uk-Lash.*

subsidence of the strata owing to the galleries which penetrated to the wells within the works of the fort. As the cliff on which Lash stands is about 200 feet in height above the river bed and the ground at their feet on the south, these wells must have been of very great depth and the task of raising water to their mouths must have been one of very great labour.

Basher-Peshāwarān. Basher, or Kuring, the next stage on the road to Zaranj, can also be identified. The former is the group of ruins that are known at the present day as Peshāwarān. At one time there was a town of some size here, and part of the south-west walls can be recognised. These ruins are however of recent date; but within the perimeter of the modern town there is an ancient mound which may have been composed of the débris of ancient Basher. To the north of the latter is a shrine dedicated to Mir Ikbāl, who very probably was the holy person despatched by Malik Kutb-ud-din of Seistan to carry his defiance to the Ruler of Herat, when the latter invaded Seistan, in the latter part of the 14th century. The town of Peshāwarān and the ruins that are such a prominent feature in the Hokat at the present time date probably from the 16th century or may be as late as the 17th century. The group of ruins called Kol Marut are also assignable to the same period. Both these groups of ruins were examined by Bellew in 1872, but the latter did not visit the ruins of a fine Masjid among the ruins of Peshāwarān.

Identification of Kuring or Kurun. Kuring was about four miles further to the south, and the name in a corrupted form still exists. There are five mounds of considerable size, named Masjidak, Tapa-i-Shagālak and Khārān which are evidently remains of forts. These mounds stand on the brink of the Hamun of Seistan, and owing to the damp they are coated with a thick outcrop of saline matter. Between them there are very many remains of canals and smaller mounds. The mound of Khārān owes its name, according to the modern inhabitants of the adjoining districts, to the fact that somebody's donkeys were drowned there or died there, or because some one else's sisters lived there. These people have never heard of the existence of Kuring—or according to other authors Kurun,—and when pressed to account for the existence of the name Khārān, they took refuge behind the puerile statement alluded to rather than own their ignorance. Ibn Rusteh mentions that at Juwein a river was crossed which must have been the Farah Rud; and that at Kuring also there was running water. One of the mouths by which the Farah Rud discharged into the Hamun passes through the ruins, and at the present day at times water from that river flows down the abandoned channel. The canals, the ruins of which have been alluded to, also took off from the Farah Rud and Kuring was thus supplied with flowing water from that river. Yakut thus alludes to this place which he calls Kurun according to some authorities. It is a pleasant and flourishing place, the inhabitants of which were all Khariji weavers. According to Ibn Rusteh, Kuring was the birthplace of Abu Auf, a Khariji leader, who evidently was famous, but of whom no mention survives in history.

In the Hokat we discovered two bridges crossing fairly large irrigation channels, both of these structures being well built of baked brick. They were evidently of a much recent date to the bridge at Takht-i-Pul. Both were skilfully constructed without superfluous material such as we found in the last named structure and both were countersunk, so that the arch of the bridge was level with the approaches at either end. One of these bridges, and evidently the older of the two, was at Kol Marut. It is in the direct line from Juwein to Kuring and must have been made for the convenience of traders on the ancient trade route. The other bridge lay to the east and carried a road from Kuring that went towards the east, perhaps the alternative route mentioned by Ibn Rusteh. Kuring is 20 miles south of Juwein and is a district containing perhaps 20 square miles covered with ancient mounds some of which, especially one facing Kol Marut, are of considerable area. It stood on the brink of the Hāmun and thus was eminently suited for a halting place when water was in that part of the lake, as goods could be at once put on the tutins. For this very reason however Kuring was never re-occupied in recent times as Basher has been. It lay below the highest flood level of the lake, and when the latter is full water even now surrounds many of the time-worn mounds. What may be called the coast line of the Hokat, the limit beyond which the water did not encroach in 1885, is about one mile to the north of the greater part of the remains which define the position of this Khariji settlement of the 10th century A.D. *Routes of Al Istakhri and Ibn-i-Rusteh confirmed by discovery of arched bridges of baked brick.*

The Hokat is in the hands of the Sakzi Afghans, usually called (but not by themselves) Ishakzai. Their chief resides at Juwein, the headquarters of the district. *The Sakzis of the Hokat.*

An ancient trade route connected the towns of Juwein and Neh. From the latter access to Kain and onwards to Yazd was by the desert route which as far as the former traversed the valleys of the southern portion of the Kuhistan—the home of the eastern and less known division of the sect of the Ismailians or Assassins. This road is now only used by migratory Baluch tribes. It passes close to the head of the Hāmun-i-Sāwari, and about half a mile from the shore of the latter are the faint traces of a tower (of course now called Nādir Shāh's tower) once undoubtedly a post or stage on the road, about 20 miles from Juwein (and about 16 from the village of Laftan) which was probably the first stage from Juwein on the Neh road. Where the latter crosses the plateau, which terminates in the Safed Kūh headland overlooking the Hāmun, the path is still well marked, ascending by well graded ascent on the east, and similarly descending on the west to the ruined tower. From this point the route made straight for the Tabar Kan Pass, crossing the northern *Trade Route from Juwein to Neh—discovery of remains.*

218 THE RUINS IN SEISTAN.

The Tabar Kan Pass.

prolongation of the range distinguished by the peaks named the Male and Female Antelope. The pass owes its name to the fact that it had been cut down to a depth of 20 or 25 feet, through hard rock, in order to make the gradient easier for laden camels—hence Tabar Kan or the "Axehewn" pass. To the east of the pass in the valley Tabasain and Zainulabad are situated; and on the side of this ancient road there are the remains of an artificial reservoir and of a tower marking a stage or halting place. This was the road which Minhaj-us-Saraj, the author of the Tabakāt-i-Nasiri, used when he visited the chieftains of the Ismailian sect at the beginning of the 13th century—at the bidding of Niāl-Tigin who had seized the government of Seistan.

Description of Kadāh and the family of its Arbābs.

The trade route from Zaranj to Bist, by way of Khāsh and Khisht, has been alluded to in several places in earlier chapters; there is no need therefore to allude to it here. Before however we bring this chapter to an end a short description of Kadāh will, perhaps, be not uninteresting. The district of that name is the last district of Seistan on the way to Khash. It was till not very long ago in the possession of a family who traced their descent back to the early ages of Islam. The dagger with which the miscreant Shimir is believed to have slain the holy Imam at Karbala was believed to have been handed down in this family. The Arbābs of Kadāh, the Mir Arab family of Chakānsur, and the Mirs of Seistan (the Iskil family) are supposed to have contributed 80 warriors who took part in that unhallowed war against the progeny of Ali. The two first named families are extinct and the Mirs of Seistan labour under a curse. None of this family may be interred in a cemetery with orthodox followers of Islam, for the earth is said to reject their unhallowed remains, and they must therefore bury their dead apart from true believers! Female members of this family labour under other bodily defects!

Discussion of alternative sites or Zaranj.

The site of Bina-i-Kai, or Nad Ali, fulfils all the conditions of those itineraries without difficulty. The discovery of the ancient site of Nishk, however, puts the fact of Nad Ali being the ancient capital of the country beyond a doubt.

There is Zāhidān of course. There are many points of similarity between the architecture of Zāhidān and of Nad Ali. But there can be no doubt that the former is of very much later date than the latter. In a timberless country like Seistan the style of architecture cannot vary to any considerable extent. Judging from the oldest ruins there is no striking change in the buildings of the present day, as far as design and construction are concerned; only in carrying out the latter, careless workmanship is very palpable in the more recent buildings.

The other places and geographical details by the various writers who have dealt with Seistan at once fall into what is known to be their probable proper relation to Nad Ali.

CHAPTER X.

Description of Zāhidān.

The ruins of Zāhidān are well known. Although the extent of the ruins is not nearly as large as some persons have reported them to be, they are yet considerable. The place is said to have been the capital of Seistan to which Timur laid siege, and which he destroyed. The ruins owe their preservation to the site they occupy on a Lurg (*i.e.*, ridge) of white hard clay which has saved them from the fate which befell the remains of Bina-i-Kai, when the Helmand broke through this place. The sand has been merciful to these frail remains of the past glory of Seistan and has sheltered them from the ravages of the wind. The state of the city wall of Zāhidān shows how the effects of the wind can be modified by the position of the objects exposed to its fury. The north and south walls of Zāhidān have practically ceased to exist; a line of mounds marks their position and direction. The walls to the east and west are in somewhat better condition, and their continuity is well preserved. The city is almost a rectangle, and its length is almost double its width: and it is placed in the direction from which the wind blows. The south-east and south-west angles of the rectangle are curtailed, and the reason for destroying the symmetry of the plan is not obvious. The great citadel with its triple line of defences occupies a position a little above the line that would divide the city into two equal parts. The bazar and a small town occupied a position abreast of the fort and separated from the latter by the outer moat. The remainder of the area included within the city walls was devoted to gardens and cultivation among which the chief men of the country had their town residences. This vacant space was necessary to allow of the people of the country taking refuge within the outer walls which the manhood of the country could defend while their families found shelter behind them. There were four gates, one in each face, and two gates to the fortress, both of the latter well protected by flanking towers; and roomy gatehouses or guard-rooms above, which with the towers would have held 200 to 300 men, whose duty it was exclusively to guard the entrance. Within the gate there were traverses built to force an enemy who might penetrate into the fort after having overpowered the defenders of the gate, to remain under fire as long as possible. In the north-west corner of the citadel there stood the palace where the Princes of Seistan dwelt. The dwellings within the two outer lines of defences of the citadel formed the precincts of the palace. Beyond the north-western wall of the town, and distant a quarter of a mile from it, there are the ruins of an extra-mural palace. This was situated in a garden, surrounded by a wall guarded by towers at short intervals. This enclosure was almost a square, its width from east to west being about 1,000 feet while its other dimension was a little less. Within this enclosure the remains of the palaces are yet standing. Each face of the garden wall possessed a gate; but the main entrance seemed to have been in the east wall where a handsome double storied building formed the gatehouse. In this building there were several handsome apartments. None to compare in size with the apartments of the palaces, but still sufficiently large to have been commodious and pleasant retreats.

Description of the extra-mural Palaces.

The palaces show quite a modern standard of comfort to have been attained in the interior arrangement, a central lofty hall of audience reaching to the domed roof, with smaller apartments around it on two floors. In the larger of the two palaces the western end of the hall ends in a bay. This was probably done, because the Prince, and his nobles-in-waiting, could turn their faces towards that direction at the stated times of prayer, and perform their devotions. A staircase placed on the outside of the larger palace gave access to the upper story. Offices for the menials were arranged in rear of this palace; just as in India they are arranged out of sight, behind an European dwelling. In fact the whole arrangement of the palace shows an almost modern appreciation of comfort and order.

The Citadel of Zāhidān.

In the fortress palace, or the citadel, within the town comfort, of course, had been sacrificed to considerations of defence. The whole is now in a state of ruin and only two domed rooms at the top of two lofty towers remain intact or nearly so. These are octagonal and 8 feet in diameter, each face having a window looking out over the country outside, above which there was an arched recess. The interior had been finished with stucco and plastered, and in one of the octagonal sides the window was replaced by a tiny fireplace with a chimney leading through the wall and having an exit on the side of the dome. These chambers must be 50 feet above the ground below, even in the present delapidated condition of the towers, the débris from which has formed a great heap at their foot. The citadel was most massively built. The bastions of its outer defences were built of pisé with a thick skin of unbaked brick over the pisé. Baked brick also was largely used for the lower portions of the walls, the harder material extending a long way above ground. The cores of archways were all formed with baked brick above and behind which were massive piles of pisé. The town walls were constructed on the same principle; but they lacked the massive strength of the citadel and its outworks; and they have consequently not worn as well as the latter.

Water supply from canals.

Zāhidān was watered by canals as the river was nowhere near it. The large canals, of which there were three, can be followed up for several miles, and the water was distributed in small cuts through the city: the gardens and cultivated lands. The environs of the city consisted of walled gardens

The bower of Malik Kutb-ud-din's daughter.

(Part III to face page 220.)

Kala-i-Timur-interior of audience-hall.

Kala-i-Timur, the extra-mural palace-Zahidan; from the north.

(Part III to face page 221.)

extending about half a mile perhaps on either side. On the east side of the city there are signs of gardens still visible where the sand has preserved them from being obliterated by cultivation. This part of the ground also seems to be a trifle above the command of the modern watercourses. Whatever may have been the reason for it, the traces of old garden enclosures, houses and canals have not been erased in this direction. On the west the plough has passed over the face of the country and all signs have been effaced. The ruins also are being placed under crops; small pieces of ground between the mounds are ploughed and irrigated; and as the citadel and mounds within the city wall abound in baked bricks they are freely drawn upon for building material. To the north there is the extra-mural palace; and there are other ruins to the east and north-east of it which may be those of garden-houses similarly enclosed within walls, forming in their day pleasant resorts. To the north-west of the palace beyond the walls, the most conspicuous remains are those of a Masjid, and close to it of a reservoir covered with a domed roof which of course has fallen in. A great canal passed to the west of these remains and trended away to the north-west. This canal is fringed with heaps of bricks and mounds where houses at one time stood close to its banks. Immediately to the north of the extra-mural palace there is a maidan that extends for almost a quarter of a square mile, and right up to the Masjid. This plain is covered with gravel and does not appear to have ever been built upon. Canals pass to the east and west of it, and there seems to be no doubt that it was the maidan of Zāhidān where the prayers of the Id that follows the Ramzan were held, also other functions which needed an open space. Beyond this space towards the north-west the country was covered with homesteads; the site of the latter being marked by piles of baked bricks. The plinths of even the more humble class of dwellings were apparently always made of baked bricks and the latter are all that mark the sites, because as these plinths get broken up their material forms heaps and mounds of bricks. These dwellings extended for miles. Up to and around the great minaret and beyond it ruins of humble dwellings and groups of more pretentious mansions extend for miles following the course of ancient canals until the area is reached which is affected by the annual floods. To the west of the modern and prosperous villages of Bolai, there stand the ruins of an old square fort, built of baked bricks and said by the people to have been the site of an older village of Bolai which had existed at the time of Timur's invasion and had been destroyed by his troops. To the south and south-east of Zāhidān the face of the country is scoured and torn to such an extent by the violence of the wind that all traces of ancient times have been erased, with the exception of old canals, and even these have been so broken and interrupted that it is impossible to distinguish them from the torn surface of the ground. Moreover, in this direction there are sand dunes piled over the wind

scours, and beyond these again is that triangle of country within which all the changes in the course of the Helmand have been initiated, and where these alterations of the river-bed have completely erased all remains of ancient days. The eastern gate of Zāhidān is the only object that rises above the undulating contours of the sandhills, with the exception of the ruins of the great windmills a little further to the south, where no doubt the revenue grain was converted into flour. This eastern gate, it is said, was the fighting station of the Chief of the Bakhtiāris, who, or a part of this tribe, at that time were inhabitants of Seistan and whose task was to man a length of the walls on either side of the gate where their chief took post. The other tribes of Seistan each had their own places assigned to them in the general scheme of defence.

The Darwāza-i-Bakhtiāri or Eastern gate of Zāhidān.

To the south-west of Zāhidān almost abreast of the south-west angle of the city walls, there is a low, isolated mound covered with gravel where there are a few very old graves, and a ziarat. This point is a little more than half a mile from the ruins of the city wall, but in the days when Timur invaded the country the gardens and suburbs must have extended to within a couple of hundred yards or so of that knoll. Within the walls of the town is a small ziarat dedicated to the 44 Pirs of Zāhidān. It is a tomb with a rude wall of baked bricks built recently, in isolated piers surrounding the tomb. The ground in the vicinity of the ziarat is used as a cemetery by the people of the surrounding country.

The natural mound.

Among a few odds and ends placed there as *ex voto* offerings, there are two inscribed tablets. The inscriptions date from the middle of the 9th century A. H. and are well executed. From translations made by A. G. Ellis, Esq., of the British Museum, it appears that one of these was a dedicatory tablet, commemorating the building of a Masjid by Shah Ali, a member of the princely family of Seistan : and the second the death of the head of the junior branch of the same family, Amir Gheiath-ud-din Muhammad, Kaiāni. The pious care of some members of this family, or dependent thereof, had saved these poor relics of the past status of the Princes of Seistan, and their relatives, from destruction, and in order to protect them from danger in the future had transferred them to a place of safety at the ziarat.

The inscribed tablets at the Ziarat.

Zāhidān is 6 miles in a direct line to the north of the mound of Rām Shāhristān, and about 12 miles to the south-west of Bina-i-Kai. Here within a small area are the ruins of the three capitals of Seistan each of which marks a distinct period in the history of that country. The question of precedence lies between the latter and Zāhidān : and there is no doubt whatever that the latter is the more recent city.

The close proximity of the three ancient capitals of Seistan.

A tradition exists, which states that this town had existed 420 years, when it was destroyed by Timur, and this would place the completion of the

Remains of a bye-gone age; at the shrine of the 44 recluses-ruins of Zāhidān.

(Part III to face page 222.)

capital in 365 A. H. or well within the reign of Khalaf-ibn-i-Ahmad who had Date of Foundation of Zāhidān.
been besieged for seven years in his capital, before he was finally subdued by
Sultan Mahmud of Ghazni.

There is nothing improbable in assigning the building of Zāhidān to Founded by Khalaf ibn Ahmad, Prince of Seistan.
Khalaf, son of Ahmad. The dates and other information taken from Major
Raverty's transalation of the Tabakāt-i-Nāsiri suggest the inference that the
city which Khalaf had made his capital was some place other than Zaranj
(or Bina-i-Kai), the former capital from which he had removed the seat of
government. There can be no doubt that Zāhidān is not the city described
by Al Istakhri as the capital of Seistan. The details given by that author,
as translated by Sir H. Rawlinson, do not fit Zāhidān. But the description
of the capital of Seistan, meagre though it be, given by the author of the
Tabakāt-i-Nāsiri, do apply with a great deal of appropriateness to Zāhidān.
The Sarai-i-Siasati is no doubt the extra-mural palace now called the Kala-i-
Taimur. The Masjid near the Hauz, or reservoir, is also existing close to this
palace. So that it may be taken as fairly well established that the frequent
sieges and the rebellions that led to them had caused the older capital to fall
into disrepair. And as the power of the Samāni Princes had commenced
to decline, Khalaf, the Prince of Seistan, probably thought he would be able
to maintain himself as an independent ruler. The time was one in which a
change of capital would naturally have suggested itself, and it probably saw
the rise of Zāhidān as such. The site was a good one. Built upon the low
ridge of hard clay, a good foundation for the fortress and town walls was
obtained, and the slight elevation of the ridge would promise safety from
the inroads of floods, an ever-present danger in Seistan at all times, which
also no doubt helped to reduce Zaranj to insignificance. According to the
traditions of the condition of the country when it was invaded by Timur, a
Shela—a great canal—existed to the east of Zāhidān and at a distance from
the city; and it was probably on the banks of this canal, which might very
well have been a Shela or the old canalized bed of the Helmand, that Timur
halted his army.

CHAPTER XI.

The ruins of Sār-o-Tār, or Tāk.

The fortress of Tāk.

Of all the ancient fortresses of Seistan, Tāk alone is mentioned in history.

999-1000 A.D.

The first appearance of Tāk, as a fortress, in history is the account of the siege of that place in 390 A. H. by Mahmud of Ghazni. Khalaf-ibn-Ahmad was the Prince of Seistan at that time. The ruler of Ghazni invaded the country; and Khalaf elected to stand a siege in Tāk. He probably was only able to muster a small party of adherents, on whom he could implicitly rely, too few to hold out in the capital against the invasion. Tāk being a comparatively small place he chose it, no doubt, as a refuge, as it was possible to defend it with those only of his followers upon whom he was thoroughly able to depend. In addition the place was an ancient and famous stronghold and in it no doubt he thought he would be able to wear out the constancy of his enemies; or at least obtain better terms.

Notices of Tāk.

"The standard notice of At Tāk, wrote Sir Henry Rawlinson, repeated by Istakhri-Ibn-i-Haukal, etc., is simply that it is a small city of Sejestan at the back of one who travels from Zaranj to Khurassan; one of its districts supplies grapes to all the people of the Province. It is also said in one passage to be a stage distant from Zaranj, and in another to be on the road from Zaranj to Kish, and at the distance of five farsakhs from the former place."

The author of the Rauzat-ul-Jannat-fi-l-ausaf-i-Madinat-l-Herat supplements the account of Tāk by some details which, although they be few, yet afford means of identifying the site of the fortress:—

"There is also the fort of Tāk which is celebrated throughout the universe * * * * This was a fort of great size. It had three lines of defences. The outer space was cultivated and contained gardens. That between the second and third lines of defences was inhabited by the populace, and within the last enclosure was the residence of an evil spirit, which had been built by the Magians. This is a malevolent demon which desired the death of all people * * and Khalaf-bin-Ahmad, who was the author of innumerable works dealing with the exegesis of the Holy Texts, was the master of the fortress. And it was here that he was besieged, and compelled to surrender the fortress, by Sultan Mahmud-i-Sabak Tigin."

Destruction of Tāk by Timur.

About 100 or 125 years before the author of the foregoing description wrote his account, Tāk had been destroyed, or at all events dismantled, by Timur on his departure from Seistan after the destruction of the capital city. As Timur marched towards the Helmand he must have passed through the valley where the present Helmand is to be found, below Bandar; Tāk, therefore, must have been some fortress that lay towards the south from Zāhidān.

No ruins of such a fortress exist anywhere within a radius of five farsakhs or 20 to 25 miles from either Zāhidān or Bina-i-Kai, so the record of the distance between the capital and it must be erroneous. Neither could it have been on the road to Kish, which has been shown to stand for Kisht in the oasis of Khāsh. The bearing assigned to it by Al Istakhri, that it lay at the back of one who travels from Zaranj to Khurasan, is correct. Any person going on such a journey at that time would have been travelling towards the north or to the west of north in a general direction. This would have placed the fortress of Tāk to the south or south-east of the capital. Moreover, Timur had a previous knowledge of Seistan acquired years before he became famous. It is not likely that any other but the actual fortress would have been called by that name. The site of Sār-o-Tār is offered for identification as being the fortress of Tāk. Of all the places of Seistan after Bina-i-Kai, Sār-o-Tār is said to be the most ancient, Rām Shāhristān being of course excepted. *Identification of Sār-o-Tār with Tāk.*

Sār-o-Tār has been visited, and although it was impossible to make a very exhaustive search of this district and the ruins that are visible from the walls of the ruined fort, yet that tract has been examined, and its more important details and ruins understood. A rough plan, also, of Sār-o-Tār has been made. The following details are from personal inspection of the site and its ruins. *Description of Sār-o-Tār.*

It is situated in what at one time was an alluvial plain, in a rather isolated position with reference to the bulk of the ruins in the Ghulghula district about 14 miles to the north-east of this ancient fortress. The site also is placed well back into the great re-entrant angle, where the western slopes of the Dasht-i-Margo are joined by Meski plateau, and at the entrance to that great scour in the former at the bottom of which the Lalla basin is set. There are no great or extensive ruins close to Sār-o-Tār. A little further to the east the watercourses, which all come in from the west and irrigated the land around it, commence to tail off towards the gravelly soil at the foot of the Margo plateau. Two ancient tracks cross the Dasht-i-Meski. One starting from a short distance below the Puz-i-Māshi headland on the Helmand traverses the narrow plateau of Meski; descends into the great scour alluded to; and crossing the low lip or edge of this depression reaches Sār-o-Tār. Upon the low ridge which forms the lip of that great depression to the east of the fort there is the ruin of a tower. It appears to be too tall and too narrow to have been a Dakhma, or tower of silence, and it was probably used as a watch tower, from which to signal the approach of any intruders by that route. The southern route is much shorter than the first named. *Position of the ruins of Sār-o-Tār.* *Routes from the Helmand to Sār-o-Tār.*

It starts directly from Chahārburjak on the Helmand and after crossing the Meski plateau descends by a valley into the plain and reaches Sār-o-Tār to the north of that plateau.

Distance of Sār-o-Tār from Nad Ali and Zāhidān.

When the canals were flowing and the ruins around the fort inhabited, the country must have been populous and very extensively cultivated. It is about 32 miles from Bina-i-Kai; and about the same from Zāhidān. In a direct line it is 17 or 18 miles from the present Helmand, but owing to the huge drifts of loose sand which have hidden both alluvial plain and ruins alike, in its soft mantle, the actual distance to be traversed from the river is increased to about 22 miles. Sār-o-Tār is situated at the tail of the old canal that entered this district under the Sargāh ruins; and a still more ancient river-bed can just be traced by most careful observation to a point about 6 or 7 miles to the south of the ruins of that place. It was a fortress pure and simple, which is said to have existed from time immemorial.

Fortifications of Sār-o-Tār.

Sār-o-Tār was defended by a double line of walls, or if the fortified palace or citadel be regarded as a separate position, which it undoubtedly has been, there are three lines of defences, all of which are in sufficient preservation to be able to present a very fair amount of material by means of which it is possible to reconstruct the fortress as it undoubtedly did exist. There is nothing in the description which cannot be supported by the evidence of the ruins.

The walls and moats.

The third and outer line of defences is in a very ruinous condition, and the sequence of the fragments of wall still standing is very much interrupted by great drifts of sand that are piled over them; but still the position of two gates can be recognised and the remains here and there of a tower (mere shells) can be also distinguished. This outer wall forms an irregular rhomboid. It is oriented in the direction of the wind and its north-eastern wall measures 4,300 feet, its north-western wall 3,500, and the south-western wall 3,000 feet. Between this line of walls and the second line, there are scarcely any ruins. The second line of defences is in very much better repair. They are enormously high and solid piles of sundried bricks and pisé, and form, in plan, an irregular circle, the diameter of which is about 1,800 feet. In the centre of this girdle of walls rises a lofty mound crowned with the remains of a fortress palace, which with its outer defences formed the citadel and in which the Prince, when in residence, took up his abode. All of the three lines of walls were protected by moats. The first beyond the outer wall originally must have been about 150 feet in width, the next about 120 feet, and the third which surrounded the citadel about 80 or 100 feet, in width. All three are now filled up by the washing down of the materials from the decaying walls; and they are now reduced to mere shallow depressions, easily overlooked in a casual examination. Twenty feet above the third moat, in vertical height, there are the remains of an outer wall behind which ran a covered way round the citadel. This work defended the ditch and the foot of the defences of the citadel. The existence of this outwork is still very clearly indicated, though the wall as such has almost disappeared. From the palace above a steep slope descends to this covered way, which is now littered with débris, bricks and decomposing clay from the works that crowned the summit of the mound.

A very strong gatehouse protected a narrow entrance to the covered way, and this fortified entrance was connected with the citadel by means of two parallel walls divided by traverses, which cut off all access to the covered way except through an opening to the left and right of the entrance. There was no doubt a sally port in the citadel walls by means of which reinforcements could be hurried down to make good the defences of the outer gate. Notwithstanding the zealous care with which the entrance was defended, the walls were not loopholed and in consequence there must have been a great deal of dead ground at their base. *Entrance to the outworks of the Citadel.*

From the outer gate an inclined road passing under the citadel walls ascended to the entrance of that work. The walls above are also singularly devoid of loopholes, and the missiles of the defenders must have been discharged from the summits alone of the walls. Everything about Sār-o-Tār points to a period when the art of war was in a very simple stage ; when the ranges were short, and individual strength and prowess was a very large factor in determining the success of an enterprise, and exercised in a combat either hand to hand or at very close ranges. *Entrance to the Citadel.*

The palace buildings are now almost formless ruins as to their upper chambers, and their débris covers up the entrances of those below. Through a hole in a wall it is possible to enter a vaulted chamber, evidently paved with large baked bricks, and the tale is possibly true that below the surface of the mound there are still lower tiers of chambers. The outer walls also have weathered badly and lost the crenelations that graced that summit. The plan of the citadel is a ploygon of six irregular sides. The outer walls are of sundried bricks or pisé, but below the crest there ran a moulding, the string course of baked bricks being still in its place here and there. *Plan of the Citadel.*

An outer skin of baked bricks may have covered the clay or sundried bricks, but the former has been stripped very nearly completely off, and the material composing it strews the steep slope of the mound down to the covered way itself. Among this litter of brick and pottery there are numerous waterworn boulders varying in size, some being about 2 lbs. and others as much as 4 lbs. in weight. These are also to be found in the surrounding country, but they do not appear to have been used for building purposes. Within the inner walls there is a great litter of baked bricks, and fragments of walls, broken arches and other traces of a closely packed, hive like mass of ruins *Materials used and character of the ruins.*

the whole of which now form an untidy and much decayed mass, the arrangement of which it is not possible to unravel. To add to the confusion great drifts of sand have occupied the deserted area of the inner fort and have very effectually concealed most of the ruined contents. Some of the ruins appear to have been larger buildings than the rest. Baked bricks were largely employed in those parts of the buildings which were exposed to great strains or inroads of damp as well as for purely decorative purposes.

Palace inside the second line of defences.

The remains of a handsome building of great size occupies a site in the inner fort adjoining the walls and overlooking the western angle of the third line of defences. This was, no doubt, a building of importance, as it had been very carefully constructed, decorated and plastered. It was two or three stories in height. On the north-east front, courses of baked bricks ran along the top of the wall or slightly below the summit. From the roof open drains descended, which were constructed in the wall with baked bricks set in lime mortar, and also heavily plastered with the same. Owing to the want of space, kitchens and bathrooms were no doubt placed upon the roof, and the drains led down from those offices; and also let rain water escape: for the roofs must have been flat. Below the string course of baked bricks there was a line of very shallow pilasters formed in the plaster, resembling very shallow machicolations. All the summits of the walls in Sār-o-Tār, where the wind has not stripped them of their original design, are thus ornamented. It is a very ancient style of decoration, and gives a curiously antiquated appearance to the structures. This design can be traced on the citadel walls away from the wind, and along the summit of the inner line of defences near the Takht-i-Pul opening.

Architectural details—arches.

This outer palace shows two distinct types of arches used for openings or entrances. In the lower story the bricks used to form the latter are all of them baked, and arranged, as usual, radiating from a centre. On the upper story arches are formed entirely with clay slabs, and only an inch or two thick, evidently moulded in a curve and then merely dried in the sun. These were set in clay mortar side by side and the arch was constructed in this way, the under surface of the slabs being heavily plastered. The latter has now peeled off, and laid bare the ribbed surface below, where the edges of the thin slabs are exposed, displaying this curious method of building. The archways on the upper story where it has been put into practice are large and handsome openings; and it has always been a favourite device of Seistani architects to construct such with these clay laminæ or tiles.

The walls of the inner fortress were originally lined with vaulted chambers and a narrow gallery extended throughout the circumference of the walls, affording lateral communication between each chamber. These were provided of course with openings, that on the inside being a low entrance, and on the outside a loophole.

The chambers in the round towers were provided with three of these apertures, one facing the front, and one on each side facing respectively to the left and right. In the wedge-shaped towers the chambers were provided with only the left and right apertures, one in each face of the wedge. These alternated with the round towers, as in the ruins of Chahilburj, which will be described. *Chambers provided with loop holes.*

The towers themselves were weak, possessing very little relief, and the amount of flanking defence afforded by them was quite inconsiderable. Owing to the great height of the walls (which even now attain to an elevation of some 50 feet), unless there had been lower tiers of chambers provided with loopholes, the area of dead ground at the foot must have been very large. The sand lies in great drifts against the ramparts, on the outside and on the inner, and owing to this it is impossible to say what other details originally existed for the defence of the walls. There must, however, have existed a covered way between the foot of each line of walls and the edge of the ditch outside. The wall of this out-work has long ago disappeared, or lies buried under great piles of loose sand which rest against the inner line of defences. *Weak flanking defence.*

The citadel itself seemed never to have possessed towers or bastions, and flat lofty walls crowned by a moulding of baked bricks with shallow and simulated machicolations, for some 2 or 3 feet down the walls, seem to have been all the protection deemed necessary. The expanse of the walls shows no signs of loopholes, and only in places is their surface broken by what, at the present time, look like mere holes, but which were no doubt arched embrasures or windows looking into the inner fort. The outer wall overlooking the ditch was probably the only protection besides its lofty wall that the citadel possessed. *Walls of the Citadel unprovided with towers.*

The great entrance was a projecting tower (also not loopholed), and it was very carefully planned. The entrance was some 10 or 12 feet wide. Ascending through a vaulted passage it reached a guard-room, which gave access to the courtyard on the right. The entrance to the palace itself was on the side away from the gatehouse, and the path which led to the former passed under the west and north walls of the palace, which was a square building two or more stories high, and with, it is said, three tiers of chambers under what is now the ground level. The arch of the main gate was lined with baked bricks, and the vaulting of the passage was probably also formed with the same material. Above the passage was a guard-room, and the gatehouse itself was two stories high. The vaulted roof of the ascending passage has fallen in, and the passage and rooms above are now open to the sky. Here and there a few bricks hold together in the pisé masonry which shows that the passage and gate was very carefully finished with burnt bricks. The passage was a curve of double flexure and the entrances of the guard-room were no *Description of the entrance to the Citadel.*

doubt low and narrow, capable of being barricaded and held successfully against an enemy.

The palace itself is of the ordinary style of Seistani architecture and was probably renewed at a later period, while the older fortifications probably were never altered. The arches in the palace are all formed with sundried bricks radiating from a centre.

There was apparently an uppermost tower or chamber, one wall of which still remains in its place. This was no doubt a pleasant retreat in time of peace from which an extensive view could be obtained over the surrounding country, and in times of war it was a post of observation from which a watchman might descry the approach of an enemy, or the commander of the fortress control the progress of the defence. The walls of the citadel were lined with chambers, and these looked upon a small courtyard in which it is said there was a well, which supplied the garrison and palace with water.

Entrance to the town beyond the Citadel not discovered.

No actual gateway to the inner fortress can be discovered, owing to the drifts of sand, but in the south-eastern segment of the girdle of walls there are the remains of a very large square tower of which the only eastern face remains in its place. This tower projected fully 30 feet from the walls and must have contained the entrance with posterns on either side communicating with the covered way to the right and left of the tower.

There are, however, two places in the north-west and south-east segments of the inner walls where the latter were cut down some 25 feet or more forming a platform or opening about the same height above ground, and measuring about 12 feet square.

Tradition as to existence of drawbridges.

Tradition states that in these openings drawbridges or other flying bridges existed. The western opening is in an utterly ruinous condition, but that opposite to it is in much better order. No masonry piers appear ever to have existed to which the tackle of a drawbridge could have been attached and which must have supported the pulleys by means of which the bridge was raised and lowered. The width of the moat would have forbidden the use of such a bridge. A large semi-circular tower immediately to the south of the platform guards the opening. The interior of this tower contains a set of six chambers communicating with each other and loopholed on the outside. Each of these were capable of holding 5 or 6 persons. These also had openings looking into the tower itself in which an ascending semi-circular ramp led to a guard-room some 12 feet square. This room afforded access to the five chambers, and, by means of a low brick-lined arch, to the platform in the opening of the walls. A handsome arched window flush with the present floor of the guard-room afforded a view of the ramp which led up to it. The outside of the opening faces lofty drifts of sand, so it is not possible to say whether there was any abutment, or pier, which would have rendered a flying bridge possible; but on the opposite opening in the western segment there are no drifts of sand, and here there are faint signs of such an abutment having been built. It is therefore hard to understand what purpose these openings served. Situated as they are on the direction of the wind they may have been intended to admit it to the inner fort which with its closely packed buildings within high walls must have needed ventilation very badly, or they may have also been used to shoot rubbish into the outermost area of the fort whence it would be carried away to manure gardens and the fields that existed within the latter. The guard-room may also, in time of war, have been the fighting quarters of officers to whose care the eastern and western halves of the walls were entrusted.

Close to the Takht-i-Pul and beyond the ditch are the remains of graves built with baked bricks as to the foundations and lower portion of the walls. The superstructure of the two ruined mausolea, which still lift up their shattered walls, was constructed with either sundried bricks, or pisé. These graves were the probable burial-places where the Prince Khalaf Ibn Ahmad buried the corpses of his murdered sons Tāhir and Amru, and where some of their descendants were also laid to rest. They are to the south of the walls. *Graves outside the second line of walls.*

The large palace inside the inner fort with its well proportioned and lofty halls on the upper floor no doubt contained the administrative staff under the various ministers of the State. The upper halls were used when the Prince himself gave audience, and below were the various departments of State where the scribes sat and drew up documents and carried on the clerical work of the Government under the general guidance of the prime minister. All the buildings adjoining this must have been built with a very great proportion of baked bricks, as the débris that is partially uncovered where the sand has moved on is composed largely of this material. Foundations and plinths of baked brick extend up to the edge of the moat. Fragments of walls lined or decorated with burnt bricks, or whose lower walls were built of the same, abound in the neighbourhood, and there must have been several tiers of buildings, or the latter must have been at least two stories high.

The alternation of round towers with others of a triangular or wedge shaped outline is very clearly exemplified in the fortifications of Chahilburj. This is a square fort, much smaller than Sār-o-Tār. Within the walls there is an open court 500 feet square. Round the walls were two storied buildings whose remains are some 50 feet wide, and which ran all round the open court. A passage also continued throughout the whole extent of the four walls, dividing the upper apartments into two sets. Those towards the right or outer side of the passage or gallery communicated with the chambers in the towers. Those on the opposite side, or left of the gallery, were larger and evidently used as ordinary dwellings. The roofs of these formed a wide platform upon which the defenders could assemble and stand to the embrasures *Description of Chahilburj probably contemporary with Sār-o-Tār.*

232   THE RUINS IN SEISTAN.

between the crenelations which undoubtedly formed the summit of the walls when called upon to defend the place against attack.

Comparison with Sär-o-Tär.

This was undoubtedly the arrangement of the buildings inside the inner fort of Sär-o-Tär, probably, however, on a larger scale. Between them and the outer edge of the citadel ditch were larger buildings with perhaps small open spaces and lanes. The citadel of Sär-o-Tär was represented in Chahilburj by a small house, a temple or the quarters of the Governor. Like Chahilburj, Sär-o-Tär was a fortress pure and simple. There may have been some permanent inhabitants in Sär-o-Tär, and the inner fort could thus have been called a town—and very rightly, a small town.

The people who built Sär-o-Tär and Chahilburj.

In Sär-o-Tär and Chahilburj probably are to be found the handiwork of the Parthian or Indo-Parthian race and the seat of their Government of Seistan was located at these centres. It is from the district around these ruins that most of the Sassanian and Parthian coins are brought for sale. And according to the legend of Khwājah Amirān, this district was inhabited by the Ashg-ka-Putr, the sons of Ashgk. Not only is this firmly believed by the people, but it is worthy of belief as there is a well-known tribe in Seistan who are said to be and themselves claim descent from that ancient ruling race who could have been no other than of Parthian stock.

Legend of Sish Päl.

There is a curious legend attaching to Sär-o-Tär. The story of Sish Päl which gives the reason why the fortress was abandoned may well be alluded to here. All of a sudden, 1,702 years ago,[1] for no assigned reason, an animal of the size of a fox made its appearance in the country. This animal had a tail, many yards in length, and wherever it went the crops were destroyed and the inhabitants lost their lives. The evil spirit who was responsible for this destruction of property and life took up its abode in Sär-o-Tär, and for forty years that place was rendered uninhabitable. At last the remnant of the inhabitants that had escaped out of that tract found a recluse celebrated for his piety and virtues. They returned bringing their newly discovered ally with them, who succeeded in exorcising the evil spirit and thus rendered both the fort and the country safe for human habitation. This figure of speech evidently refers to a pestilence or foreign invasion that swept the country and which is typified by the quickly moving little animal carrying destruction in its wake and which depopulated it. The period of 1,720 years would give as the date of the occurrence the year 203 A.D. A few years previous to this date, Ardashir-i-Bābak the founder of the Sassanian Dynasty, had defeated the last Parthian Monarch Ardavān in a battle which for ever put an end to the power of that long line of monarchs. It was a period in history when the founder of the Persian Empire was subjugating the districts which had been held so long by chiefs

---

[1] That is counting backwards from 1905.

who had yielded a nominal allegiance to the various Princes who had followed one another to the throne in the last days of the Parthian Empire.

Parthian or Indo-Parthian chiefs had during that period no doubt ruled over Seistan also, and here in this out-of-the-way position there are probably the ruins of towns and fortresses once held by them. Sär-o-Tár owing to its strength and the distance from the river was no doubt a stronghold which was always appreciated and maintained. The ramparts themselves are no doubt those which were constructed when first the fortress was laid out: and this would account for the difference in the greater part of the buildings of the palace and inside the inner fort, which are of the type and same descriptions as the remains inside Zähidän.

Another curious feature is the existence of drains; there can still be traced no less than four open drains, built of burnt brick and mortar, which are now almost completely destroyed, that led down to the covered way and on to the ditch from the usual offices in the palace. *The drains of Sär-o-Tár.*

The condition of damp, the alternations of cold and heat, aided by the wind, have prevailed from all time in Seistan. A certain type of building was found to be most suitable for the climate, and a certain method of construction was recognised to be best able to contend against the disintegrating action of those elements. In all ancient remains in Seistan the type of building and the amount of orientation, and the construction varied little in essential particulars. The only comparison that can be made is between the system of fortification when the latter are sufficiently preserved to make a comparison possible. The relief of the bastions of Zähidän and the great amount of protection they afford to the curtains and covered ways which they command at once imparts an air of modern science to the works, which is altogether absent in those which protect Sär-o-Tár. The enormous wall of Sär-o-Tár seems to have been constructed at a period when the art of war was in an undeveloped state and it was considered sufficient to oppose uneducated valour and brute force by raising, as physical obstacles to those qualities, enormous piles of solid masonry in the shape of walls. In its ruined condition the summit of the citadel is 80 feet above ground level and it can easily be seen even now from afar even though there are a succession of huge drifts of sand to obstruct the view. From any one of the mounds in the vicinity of the village of Arbab Deh Dost Muhammad it is possible to see Sär-o-Tár. *Discussion of the system of fortification that prevailed at Sär-o-Tár and Zähidän.*

In 785 A. H. after having destroyed Zähidän and made an end of removing the treasures of its Prince, the Amir Timur, Gurgän, marched towards the Helmand, and his army must of necessity have passed close to where the modern village of Deh Dost Muhammad stands. In those days, when the country was irrigated and cultivated, there could not have existed the *Concluding remarks—destruction of Sär-o Tár. December 1384 A.D.*

piles of sand that are now to be found around Sâr-o-Târ or Tâk. The great fortress therefore could have easily been seen and its existence must have been known to Timur from previous knowledge, or reported by his scouts. The conqueror turned aside to summon the place and its commander to surrender. The destruction of the capital and the captivity of the Prince of Seistan had rendered the defence of an outlying fortress of no practical value, and this celebrated stronghold which had long resisted the fierce valour of a succession of enemies was delivered up to Timur by whose order probably it was dismantled.

CHAPTER XII.

Ruins of the same probable date as those of Zāhidān.

The Shela on the east of Zāhidān passed on towards the north-west and upon it, or close to it, were built the long line of ruins which Christie believed to be the ruins of Dushak, an identification which has led to much confusion, as Dushak has ever since been taken as the name, and the ruins as being the site, of a great town. The whole of these ruins together with those of Chahārdari, the remains to the east of the modern village of Burji-Afghan, Old Bolai, and the ruins further to the north-west towards Tappa-i-Kohlak belong to the period of Zāhidān and were laid waste when that city was captured.

Ruins of the north Zāhidān.

The greater ruins are those of manor houses, and in a central position with reference to these there was a strongly fortified post to which the inhabitants could fly for refuge. The latter is represented by the ruins that surround the mound known as Rinda or Rindān; the mound itself having been the old citadel of the fort. The latter was rectangular, and enclosed by solid walls which now form mounds of considerable size. At each of the four corners there stood large flanking towers or bastions. The interior was divided by a wall, extending from the citadel to the eastern face of the square enclosure, into two unequal parts, and the mounds which are the remains of this wall are strewn with baked bricks and broken pottery; the former show signs of having been set in lime mortar and not either in Saruj or in clay. The northern and larger part of the square is full of shapeless mounds, the remains of isolated buildings, but the southern and smaller portion was laid out in three parallel streets, quite straight and unlike anything which is to be met with among other ruins, where regularity is the last thing that may be expected. The fort having been oriented on the same bearing as Zāhidān, or about 29 degrees west of north, the streets lie in this direction, and in each portion of the fort there was apparently a gate in the north-western face. Between these streets there are still recognisable the trace of small houses, and along the inside of the southern rampart there are still to be seen the distinct vestiges of chambers about 16 by 8 feet which extended all round the inner side of the fort walls. These gave shelter to the garrison, and their roofs formed a banquette on which the defenders could stand and defend the walls. This fort was square, 600 feet by 600 feet, and its trace is as yet quite distinct, though walls, buildings and citadels have been reduced to mounds of débris covered with a thick efflorescence of saline matter. To the south of this fort there is the remains of what may have been an outer line of defence, about 100 yards in advance of the main walls, or all that now remains of the latter. On the north is a large

Rindān.

outlying ruin, evidently of a fortified place, much smaller than the fort of Rindān; but the country has been for so many years regularly flooded every time that the Helmand rises, that it is not possible to do more than trace the extent of the fort itself; extensive and deep scours exist all over the land in the vicinity of the fort and the works of the latter must have been extremely solid to have withstood both time and the action of water.

A large canal which flowed immediately under the east wall of Zāhidān also passed this fort on the east, and another of the Zāhidān canals flowed past the fort on the west. Both these are now regularly filled by the Pariun and the fort is partially an island, and partly a succession of mounds surrounded by water of varying depth, or by marshy lands.

Ruins to the north of Rindān.

The ruins to the east of Rindān are built along what may have been a branch of the Shela or great canal alluded to as existing at a little distance from Zāhidān to the east of that town. The ruins occupy a spur of the Lurg on which that town is situated. They are, in consequence, above the reach of floods; and it is to this that they owe their escape from total destruction. Some three miles to the north-west of Rindān, these ruins come to an end, as beyond this the Lurg descends to the level of the alluvial plain, and the annual inundations have utterly wiped out the traces of all buildings that occupied the country around the Kohlak mound. These end in a large ruin composed of domed chambers, which surround an interior hall. This was a building of some size as the ruins are lofty and form a striking landmark. It is called Chahil Khana, owing to the cells or chambers having numbered 40, and it may very likely have been a Masjid and Madrassah combined.

Kohlak.

Kohlak was another small fort, and the mound that now marks the site of the keep is all that is left of the place, with the exception of a few low waterworn mounds which may be the remains of the outer wall. This place must have been half as large again almost as the fort at Rindān. But as it was the last fort in the direction of Peshāwarān and on what is now the southern edge of the Hamun area, it probably was built to hold a larger number of fugitives than Rindān could accommodate.

The great canal to Sāwari Shāh.

The great canal of which traces now exist, which passed Kohlak about two miles to the east and extended towards Sāwari Shāh irrigating lands now submerged, was probably the Shela, or canal, alluded to as having existed to the east of Zāhidān and at some distance from its walls.

Ruins to the west of Rindān.

To the west and south-west of the old Rindān fort, the country is strewn with ruins; but as in this direction the country has been regularly cultivated for the last 200 years, these relics of the civilization which Timur destroyed speedily disappear. Here and there an ancient brick kiln forms a mound and the agriculturists turn up old baked bricks as they break ground for their crops. The bricks are heaped together, and the first person who needs material for building brings a donkey or two, and carries them away. For this reason, to the east of Zāhidān remains that are of the same age as it have entirely disappeared. Further to the west there is situated the depressed tract of land which for a long time has been the playground of the Helmand, and where the rich deposits of recent silt lie thick. Also whatever the silt has been unable to completely hide, sand dunes have concealed. Most of the latter extend in lines, and probably have accumulated over ruins as their alignment is parallel to the general direction of the wind; these dunes are covered with tamarisk whose roots probably have penetrated to the ruins that exist below the sands, and the latter have been in this way rendered permanent, and anchored so to speak by the vegetation they support. Looking towards the east from Zāhidān a line of high dunes extends in a north-westerly direction, and as this is the axis of the Zāhidān canal systems, it is more than probable that they overlie some old canals, whose channels and spoil banks have afforded a resting place for the sand.

To the south of the city of Seistan of the present day there is an old ruin called Kala-i-Ziro, which is the last of ruins attributable to the period of Zāhidān. Further to the south the ruins around the mound which is now called "Chung-i-Marghun," and which are noticed by Colonel Yate in the account of his journey to Seistan, also belong to this period. The present representative of the Kaiāni family in Seistan stated that in the vicinity of the mound a small hoard of silver coins, struck in the reign of Malik Kutb-ud-din, was turned up in a field some few years ago shortly before the Mission arrived in Seistan. *Kala-i-Ziro.*

Seven and-a-half miles almost due south of the present day capital of this country there exists a small tract of land, much cut up by the wind, and covered with ruins of dwellings and canals. The most prominent being a mound of white clay formed by the débris of a ruined building. It is said that here stood a pleasure house in the days of Malik Kutb-ud-din which was a great pleasure resort, as the lands all round the buildings were laid out in gardens. Owing to this, the little sub-division, or mahal, was known as Gulistān (the rose garden). The gardens, they say, supplied annually 70 "mans" or bushels of rose leaves to the palace, which were used in distilling rose water. Anything more removed from that condition of things cannot be imagined than the present state of this once flourishing sub-division. It included the lands of the modern villages of Bahrāmābād and Bāgh-ak on the west, Jotegh on the north, and the flourishing village of Jazinak on the east; another southern limit of this district ends as far south as the modern village of Pulgi; in this direction it is overlaid by the barkhans that rest on the north bank of the Rud Seistan. The modern ruins of Kundarak and As-i-Ghāzi are situated within the ancient limits of the Mahal of Gulistān. These, however, are modern. The white mound of débris alluded to is called Tapa-i-Safed, and about two miles to the west of it there are some ruins *The ancient district of Gulistān near Zāhidān.*

of an old town, with gardens round it, the walls of some of the latter being quite distinguishable, though worn very thin by the grinding of the wind; and to the south of these again half buried in the sand drifts are the ruins of a domed building near which the fragments of arches are just visible. These are known as the Madrassah or College, and it is no doubt a correct explanation of the purpose for which the buildings were constructed. In 1903 in some mounds to the south-west of Bahrāmābād a labourer, who was exploring the sites for bricks, was fortunate enough to find a few gold coins which the Kaiāni Sardar, Malik Azim Khan, said bore Kutb-ud-din's name, and which weighed $2\frac{1}{2}$ miskals each, or about 170 grains. The ruins of the College, buried in the sand, are, however, comparatively modern.

Description of Kala-i-Sam.

In the Sheb-i-Āb district the post of refuge was no doubt the fort of Rāskak which very likely occupied the site on which the present town and castle of Sehkoha are situated. About $2\frac{1}{2}$ miles to north-west of the latter there is a very old fortified enclosure about 1,900 feet long and about 500 feet wide; a gateway in the eastern face can be still recognised, but on the other side, there is only a gap in the walls which gives access now to the interior. Whether this was originally a gate or a mere breach made by the action of wind and weather it is not possible to say. This fort is built on the edge of the dasht, but the block of dasht on which it stands is now separated from the terrace to the east by a narrow strip of alluvial deposit. In the commencement of the 19th century when the Helmand flowed into the Hamun below the Koh Khwajah, one outlet of that river undoubtedly flowed past this fort towards the village of Warmal. The orientation of the ancient walls differs from all other ruins in the northern delta; the four sides face the cardinal points of the compass. The walls must have been very massive, for they are now great mounds of clay, and they seem to have been built entirely of pisé. The orientation of this ruin is identical with that of the older ruins on the dasht terrace south of the Rud-i-Biyaban. The east and west walls face those points where the sun, in the summer, rises and sets. A moat was cut across the dasht to defend the south wall, and the place seems to have been built at a time when there was water below the other faces, either a Naizar, or the river which served to protect those faces from attack. In appearance the ruins seem only a little more recent than those of Rām Shāhristān, and it is probable that the Kala-i-Sam is a prehistoric site. In one or two places alone are there any vestiges of buildings, and the fort appears to have been a mere fortified enclosure to which people retired for shelter, and never to have enclosed a town within its walls.

The district irrigated by the Zarkan and Zorkan.

To the east of the Helmand there were no doubt similar places of refuge. But as this district was more or less hastily explored owing to circumstances, it is not possible to speak with certainty regarding it. The Zarkan and Zorkan canals must have long been maintained, and the districts of Ghulghual

Sohren-Kalat-'the red fort'-S.E. of Chakansur.

Noken-Kalat, the new fort-S.E. of Chakansur.

(Part III to face page 230.)

and Sār-o-Tār were of course inhabited. The fort of Chahilburj also was no doubt in repair and afforded protection to the population of the districts around it.

Six or seven miles to the east of the ruin of Chahilburj there is a detached fort which is in a very good state of preservation, owing to which it is called Noken Kalat, or the new fort. It is a rectangle measuring 220 feet in width and 300 feet in length. Four round towers stand at the angles and one in the centre of each curtain except that facing the east, where there is instead a gateway, lined with an arch of baked bricks; inside the four walls is a collection of partially ruined dwellings. The wall has no berm and merely forms an enclosure. The gateway is not flanked by towers, but a detached work 60 feet square and about 50 feet in advance of the gate evidently defended the entrance; a wall joins the outwork with the curtain of the fort. The detached tower is 70 feet high and the walls of the fort about 10 feet lower. The former was elaborately decorated. *Noken Kalat.*

To the east about 2 miles distant from Noken Kalat there is a ruin called Sohren Kalat from the reddish colour of the remains. It was at one time a fort 100 feet square, the walls were defended by eight towers and all round the inside there were quarters two stories high; a banquette formed by them afforded the garrison means of defending the wall. The entrance is on the eastern face, and is protected by an outer fortification. *Sohren Kalat.*

The name Ghulghula is applied both to a district and also to a group of ruins in it. The latter consists of a lofty ruined tower, and to the south of and close to it is a domed building, well constructed with baked bricks, the roof of which has however fallen in. There are very numerous traces of gardens, and the roads among the ruins crossed irrigation channels by means of syphon bridges, the drain pipes of the latter being still intact. The largest site is known merely as Shahr-i-Kalān, and is marked by two high mounds of unequal height. All around this site there are the remains of gardens and irrigation cuts. One of the mounds was a fort built on a plinth about 40 feet thick in their present ruined condition, and there were without doubt dwellings all round them on the inside. The summit of the ruined walls is about 50 or 60 feet above the ground outside. The masonry was exclusively sundried bricks set in clay; a few baked bricks, however, were found inside the enclosure, one of which measured 30 inches by 24 inches, and was 4 inches thick. This fort stands on the alluvial soil of the district, and the land in its neighbourhood shows signs of having once been highly cultivated. The divisions between fields and irrigation channels are still very clearly visible in many places. About two miles to the north and west of this site is a ruin of a Masjid which was constructed with baked bricks. To the north of this ruined Masjid between the Shahr-i-Kalān ruins and the fort of Kurdo, another deserted site, there *Ghulghula.*

stands an ancient icehouse, the dome of which has fallen in and the pit also has been choked with sand.

Kurdo.

Kurdo is a very well-known and ancient site; it stands on the western edge of the deserted tracts round Ghulghula; it is a fort built on a plinth about 15 feet above the ground, and it forms a square of 200 feet sides. It is built of unbaked bricks. The walls are about 40 feet above ground and many feet thick at the base. The entrance was merely a doorway in the southern curtain. Owing to its situation on the slopes of the barrier that divides the modern delta from the Sār-o-Tār and adjoining districts, the Kurdo Fort is a prominent landmark.

Seven forts mentioned in the time of Timur which existed in the southern delta.

In addition to the prosperity of the northern delta, the southern delta at the end of the Rud-i-Biyaban was also populated and well cultivated. This rests upon the testimony of Timur himself who entered Seistan as an ally of the Malik whom he calls Jallaludin Mahmud; in 764 A. H. a rebellion had broken out in Seistan and the malcontents had got the better of their ruler to some extent, and had obtained possession of several forts in the country. In his perplexity the Malik of Seistan called on Timur for assistance, as the latter had under his command a compact band of free lances, all of whom were staunch men-at-arms, and had seen much service under their leader in Turkestan. The details of this campaign and its unfortunate ending belong to the historical portion of this narrative, and has been treated in detail in it. Timur mentions seven forts as being in the hands of the malcontents. The seven forts, of which the enemies of this Prince were in possession, were, there is hardly room for doubt, situated in the Helmand valley and in the southern delta. This tract had always been in the hands of the Reises, who were more or less independent of the later Maliks of Seistan, and it is quite reasonable to suppose that the sedition arose first among this section of the population of Seistan, which drove the Malik to call in to his aid the great soldier who was fated to prove, 21 years after, the destroyer of the kingdom and of the independence of his family.

Trākun was one of the seven, without doubt; also the old fort at Rāmrod, parts of which are incorporated in the modern building; the ruined fort, now called by the Baluchis Girdi Kalat, and Kala Maksud on the Shela, about 20 miles to the west of the Gaud-i-Zireh. These were probably the forts, whose inhabitants and garrisons made common cause with the Malik when he determined to expel his allies from Seistan. The three forts, of which Timur and Amir Husen obtained possession, could not have been places of any size or strength as they were taken without trouble or delay with the help of 1,000 horsemen, which is all the force those two leaders could raise. These forts were garrisoned by Amir Husen, and they could not have been destroyed at this time, though they may have been dismantled after the conquest of Seistan which was carried out 21 years later. It is possible that the forts of Chahilmirez and Kala-i-Khārān may have been two of the three forts taken by the allies. The former is a ruin, about three miles above Chahārburjak, and the latter another ruin about four or five miles to the west of Bandar-i-Kamal Khan. The latter stands on the cliff of the low terrace some 30 feet above the old bed of the Rud-i-Biyaban. Kəla-i-Maksud, Rāmrod and Girdi Kalat are undoubtedly all three ancient sites, which stood in the same relation to the population of the southern delta, as that which the forts, now marked by the Kohlak and Rindān mounds, bore to the inhabitants of dwellings by which they were surrounded. The older portions of Rāmrod, though few, are exactly like portions of the Zāhidān ruins as to style of architecture and construction. The ruins of Girdi Kalat are also, on a small scale, like the ruins of that capital city and in very much the same stage of decay. This place seems never to have been rebuilt in modern times, as Rāmrod is about three and a half miles distant, and it was probably deemed sufficient to restore the latter as the place of refuge for the diminished population of that district.

CHAPTER XIII.

Trākun and neighbouring ruins.

Description of Trākun.

There is, therefore, only left for consideration the fort of Trākun. This is undoubtedly a very ancient site. It is universally believed to have been the birth-place of Rustam. According to the Shahnamah he was cut out of his mother's womb and the place where this operation was performed was named after this occurrence. It is an article of faith throughout the country that Trākun (or Trākan as it really ought to be written) is that place.

This place was deserted comparatively at a very recent date and must have always been inhabited and maintained as a stronghold, for which purpose its natural position has always been most suitable, especially in ancient days before the art of war had made much progress. The town is situated upon an isolated block of Kim which lies in a direction from north to south, far advanced from the northern terrace of the valley of the Rud-i-Biyaban, which abreast of this place widens out into the first of the loops or districts which continue towards the west. A plain about half a mile wide divides the isolated block of Kim from the northern terrace of dasht, and to the west about 400 yards of alluvial soil separates Trākun from a low mass of dasht, which forms a second and larger island; the western limit of the Trākun loop or district lying about a mile to the west again of this second island. The eastern face of the latter is scarped almost to the plain below, but the opposite slopes have been worn into deep ravines and narrow spurs which slope gradually towards the plain on the west. Between the island of Trākun and the northern terrace the old Rud-i-Biyaban apparently sent out a branch, as there is an unmistakable water-worn depression not far from the foot of the northern edge of that island; this channel formed the north-eastern end of the second isolated block of the dasht, and flowed past it on the west joining the main valley just to the east of the point where two projecting headlands of the dasht pinch the alluvial plain between them and divide in this way the Trākun loop or district from that of Gina—the next in the order and to the west of the former.

Site occupied by the remains.

The block of Kim on which Trākun is built is in round numbers about 1,000 feet in length and about 500 in width, and slopes down towards the east. Its height above the plain on the other sides is quite 150 feet above the plain, and on these sides it ends in a sheer precipice; the horizontal stratum of Kim forming here and there narrow ledges, the last of which, however, is fully 80 or 100 feet above the plain. The eastern front of the block of Kim ends in a cliff some 25 feet high above the ground, and it is on this side alone that Trākun had been fortified. The walls rise to a great height and are built in one or two places almost from the foot of the cliff, their trace naturally conformed to the outline of the latter; but on both the north and south flanks, as the cliffs increase in height, the walls decrease, till at last they cease altogether as a protection against enemies, and only a low parapet exists in open spaces between buildings as a safeguard against accidents. The gateway is ruined, but it probably existed nearer to the north end of the walls, and led up into a small courtyard about 100 feet square on all sides of which, like cells in a wasp's hive, the domed buildings of the town rose up tier above tier. Trākun must have been a veritable sun trap, and only less terrible to existence than the city of the Kakahs on the rocky slopes of the Koh-i-Khwaja, as only those dwellings on the ridge could have obtained the full benefit of the wind of Seistan. The dwellings are domed. The better class of houses show a trace of architectural decoration very much resembling that of the two octagonal chambers at the summit of the two western towers of Zāhidān. But as Trākun could have been finally deserted not more than two hundred years ago, if so long, the buildings are in much better repair than any in Zāhidān; many of the buildings indeed, especially some towards the north, appear to belong to the modern period of architectural design and construction of Seistan. The lower courses of the lofty northern walls were built with baked bricks, the latter being some 18 inches square. The superstructure and the inside chambers were all constructed with sundried bricks. The houses of the town are of this material also, baked bricks being very sparingly used almost and for decorative purposes alone. The only structure built exclusively of this harder material is the shaft of the great well which supplied the town with water. The opening of the shaft is 10 feet square and it must have been very deep; now, however, it is filled up to within about 50 feet of the mouth. About half-way down the slope there is a subterranean gallery that descends to the bowels of the earth, and ends after a length of some one hundred feet in a chamber about 15 feet square. This gallery was evidently vaulted and lined with baked bricks, but only a fragment of the latter exists near the entrance. The latter is, however, very probably not the original entrance, as it is partially choked with ashes, forming a huge kitchen midden full of bones and rags and other rubbish. Its appearance would almost seem to indicate an earlier date for this gallery than that of the occupation of the buildings around its entrance, the inhabitants of which contributed to the midden of ashes and rubbish. It is of course possible that after the conquest of Seistan Timur ordered the demolition of all the strongholds of the country and Trākun was included in the general destruction, and that it was re-inhabited afterwards and the houses restored and rendered habitable. The complete destruction of the gateway and of the projecting tower in the centre of the northern walls certainly tends to render this supposition probable, as their destruction rendered the place of no value as a fortress, and the demolition seems to have been systematic and carried out with that end in view.

Description of the wall and buildings inside.

The walls of Trākun are defended by no towers, and are merely pierced with large embrasures or windows, and loopholed. A series of the latter extend along the summit of the walls, and inside a narrow berm was constructed to give the defenders standing room. In order to provide a cross fire the loopholes are arranged in sets of three; the centre loophole facing the front, and those on the left hand and on the right facing obliquely in those directions. The ramparts are very substantial and a narrow vaulted gallery constructed in the thickness of the walls communicating with various chambers afforded means of access to portions of the town adjoining the walls to the north and south. Owing to its position Trākun forms a prominent landmark visible for many miles in all directions, and it is quite the type of a feudal stronghold of romance. It is utterly deserted now, owing to the lack of water; the landscape generally is of a most melancholy description as the neighbouring bluffs are crowned with cemeteries and mausolea in every stage of decay. As far as the eye can reach towards the west groups of domed buildings containing tombs stand on all the headlands of the dasht, relieved against the pale blue colours of the distant peaks of the Palang Koh range that forms the background to this scene of utter desolation. In pre-Islamitic times, according to traditions still existing, but which are fast dying out, there was a famous pyrœum in Trākun which was destroyed in course of time after the Arabs obtained the mastery over the country.

Description of the defences.

Old Arbāb Seif-ud-din gave me an account of the fire temple and the manner in which the priests kept up the sacred flame, which agrees almost word for word with the description of the author Kasvini who wrote in 1275 A.D. It is not possible that Seif-ud-din had obtained his knowledge from books, as his literary attainments are of a very modest nature—and books are not to be had in his country. His information has been derived from oral traditions alone. To begin with, he said the wood of the Tāgaz, the variety of the tamarisk which grows and thrives only in the waterless tracts, was used alone for maintaining the sacred fire. Tāgaz fuel burns well giving a clear flame with a minimum of smoke, and burns into a clean ash which can easily be removed. Tamarisk wood on the other hand has a marked tendency to smoulder, and gives forth a great deal of smoke.

Account of the Fire Temple here, preserved and related by Arbāb Seif-ud-din, fuel used to maintain the fire.

The attendant priests, according to Seif-ud-din, knelt at a respectful distance from the altar when on duty, veiling their mouths and nostrils, and from time to time placed small pieces of Tāgaz wood on the altar with long silver tongs, just sufficient to maintain a steady blaze. At Trākun was a fire temple second only to that at Kārku Shah, and these were the chief fanes in the country prior to the conquest by the Arabs when both the shrines were probably destroyed and the sacred fires quenched by the invaders; other minor fire temples may have been allowed to exist, but the destruction of the principal Pyrœa was probably considered to be necessary in order to emphasize the supremacy of Islam.

Method of keeping the sacred flame alight.

CHAPTER XIV.

Description of Kala Fath.

A description of Kala Fath[1] will be of interest. Its citadel is a very prominent feature in the landscape, and being constructed after the fall of Zāhidān, it is a good specimen of the style of buildings erected in Seistan during mediæval times. The citadel is said to be the work of Malik Kutb-ud-din, and in order to render it secure, he built it upon an isolated block of Kim, some 30 feet above the plain. A deep gorge probably either cut, or enlarged artificially, separates it from the lower features of the Dasht-i-Meski to the east. This gorge is a continuation of the old river-bed and the later canal flowed through this past the town, towards the north. The citadel is a lofty pile of pisé work or sundried bricks with few towers, none of the latter possessing much relief owing to the restricted area on the summit of the block of Kim. The interior of the citadel is divided into two huge piles of buildings, both palaces, which are known as the east and west palaces. In one the reigning Prince took up his abode; in the other the members of his family—dependants, kinsmen and others who had claims upon the bounty of the Prince. The usual galleries and chambers line the walls. Inside the courtyard there is a great well with a masonry shaft, the water of which in olden times used to be lifted by means of a Persian wheel worked by a camel. Some few years ago the well was cleaned out, but the water after long disuse proved to be brackish. A tower higher than the rest of the building as in the case of the palace inside Sār-o-Tār must have afforded a very extensive view of the country on all sides, owing to its height. It was no doubt also used both as a watch tower in times of war, and a place where the banner of the Prince was hoisted.

Position of Kala Fath, and the Citadel Palace.

Around the base of the citadel and a short distance away from it there exists a second line of defence to act as a covered way and to prevent an enemy approaching the foot of the mound on which the citadel is placed; where, owing to the great height of the walls and the inadequate relief of the towers, there must exist a large area of dead ground.

Defences of the Citadel.

Far in advance of this covered way was placed the city wall. This formed an irregular square, the eastern side being shorter than the other three. Each of the latter it is said was originally defended by 26 towers, while the eastern wall had only 16 towers. The town was a flourishing place as late as 1049 A.H., 1639 A.D., but now it is in ruins.

---

[1] Kala Fath is mentioned by name as the capital of Seistan by the author of the Bādshāh Nāmah, an Indian chronicle of the reign of Shah Jahān, the Moghul Emperor of Delhi—17th century. Malik Hamza, the Prince of Seistan at this time, is also mentioned by name in that record.

Vestiges of old buildings.

There are remains of reservoirs and hummāms (baths) still visible where the river has not carried away all traces of its former splendour, or where the sand has not concealed them. There is still one hummām in the town which is huddled away between the second line of defences and the front of the citadel. Another hummām is still existing inside the citadel. But the glory of Kala-i-Fath, the proud and unconquered fort, has long since departed. This name was probably given to it by Malik Kutb-ud-din who was for some time in a condition of insubordination to his Suzerain and benefactor, Shah Rukh, and held out in this place successfully against the latter.

Walls and towers of Kala Fath.

The town of Kala-i-Fath was girdled with an outer wall defended by 94 towers in all, and if on an average a space of 200 feet be assumed to have separated the towers one from another, the perimeter of the walls alone must have been fully 3 miles. Beyond these outer walls there were suburbs and gardens, and these were all nourished by canals. The latter probably were local works and had their origin below and distinct from the great canal which distributed the water below Kala-i-Fath. The outer wall and the defences of Kala-i-Fath were the handiwork no doubt of Malik Muiz-ud-din Husen (killed in 859 H.), but the gardens round them must have grown up in course of time as the country was restored to a condition of prosperity. There seems to be no reason to doubt the story that is told of the gardens and hamlets having extended as far as the gravelly plateau to the west.

Description of Gumbaz-i-Surkh. The State aided College of Seistan.

Beyond the wall of Kala-i-Fath, to the south-west of the citadel, there stand the ruins of a college which is said to have been endowed by Malik Hamza. It is now in ruins and the dome of the central building has fallen in, and because it is built entirely with baked brick, it is called now the Gumbaz-i-Surkh or the red domed-building. On either side of the central building there extended two wings containing apartments and a colonnade, which were built to house the professors and their pupils, some of whom coming from a distance probably lived there. It is said that a staff of 80 mullas were maintained, who, besides fees from the parents of the scholars, received 100 Kharwars of grain and 200 tomans in money. The measures of grain was according to the Tabrizi Kharwar.[1] The actual building of the college is attributed to the urgency of the Mulla Shāhi, who was the Mujtahid of Kala-i-Fath in the days of Malik Hamza, and when it was finished the latter endowed it to the extent already mentioned. The descendants of this person, the head of the established religion, those times in Seistan, are now living in somewhat straitened circumstances in Persian territory, in the modern villages of Bunjar and Gauri. Both the college and its staff have long ago ceased to exist. The final removal of the descendants of the former head of this college into Persian territory took place about thirty years ago. This group of buildings

---

[1] About 100,000 lbs. in all English.

occupies a commanding position upon the brow of a low plateau, and it can be seen from a distance; the reddish colour of the baked brick of which it was built attracts attention, as it is not usual to meet with the ruins of such buildings in Seistan.

Description of Gumbaz-i-Yakdast.

Further to the south of this ruin there is another domed-building. Its origin and name is lost, but a story exists that the architect lost his right hand, which was struck off after he had built Gumbaz i-Surkh in order that he might never again construct a similar work, thereby causing the former to remain without a rival. The Gumbaz-i-Yakdast, or the domed-building of the one handed architect, is older than the Gumbaz-i-Surkh. The fact of its origin not being known proves that. It is not improbable that it may contain the tombs or tomb of some previous ruler of this country, or possibly of several members of that family. It may even be the place where Malik Kutb-ud-din was buried. Like the College this building stands upon a low plateau, but almost upon the very edge of the northern cliff.

Gumbar-i-Surkh compared with the ruins of Chahardari.

The architecture of the college is remarkable for the way in which the arches of the central building had been constructed. Instead of the bricks radiating from a centre, or even laid on edge as is sometimes met with in buildings in this country, the arches of the building in question are formed by the horizontal courses of the bricks overlapping one another, the massive walls giving solidity to this peculiar method of forming such openings. In one other case has such an arrangement of the bricks forming an arch been met with. This is in ruins called Chahardari about 6 or 7 miles to the south-west of Kārku Shah. This also strangely enough is a building constructed with baked bricks. This method of building was probably considered to be unsafe when any other less durable medium was employed. The Chahardari ruin was a mausoleum, the four sides of which, duly oriented in the direction of the cardinal points of the compass, are open archways, the angles of the four walls forming narrow piers. In their case the openings were constructed by the overlapping of the horizontal courses of the bricks which formed the piers or supports. This building also was covered with a dome covering a grave; it was also built of backed bricks. Tradition also states, with regard to the college, that when Malik Hamza Khan died he was buried within the central building, which, as is generally the case in all Islamitic religious and educational foundations, was also used as a Masjid and built for this purpose.

15th Century A.D. Architectural details. Older buildings undecorated.

Kala-i-Fath dates from the 9th century of the Hegira. And the citadel is a very good example of the way in which the Seistani was able to build with sundried bricks and pise. The lofty walls are pierced here and there with windows or large embrasures. The outer face of the walls are plain with the exception of an occasional course of herring bone ornamentation on a small scale, which does not obtrude its existence on the spectator. The outer walls of Zāhidān are absolutely plain. Not a moulding exists to break the surface of the plaster which covers the brick and pisé work. The buildings of the age of Zāhidān all show this absence of outward decoration. The excellence of the work is however very striking, and such older remains, when, as in the case of the fort at Rāmrod, they have been included in modern work, can be at once picked out, so great is the difference between the old and the later work. Arches that still exist in the ruins with which the citadel is surrounded are built of square bricks laid edgeways. The thin laminæ of clay met with in Sār-o-Tār, and the ruins on the Koh-i-Khwaja, and in some ruins on the dasht terrace to the south of the Rud-i-Biyaban, which were used to construct arches, seem to have belonged to an earlier age. But the arch of the Darwaza-i-Bakhtiari at Zāhidān, a fragment of which alone remains standing, shows exactly the same arrangement of this lamina. This no doubt had a lining of masonry in which baked brick could have alone been used. It seems to be the general rule that the older buildings in Seistan were but little adorned without and within; whereas the architecture of succeeding periods shows a very florid taste in such designs; in the buildings of the period of Malik Jalla-l-uddin or Malik Hamza these details are carried out skilfully. The lines are perpendicular, and those intended to be horizontal are actually so. In later buildings these details are, as a rule, found to be completely absent. The result is that the general effect is both tawdry and displeasing. The masonry of sundried brick set in clay of the later buildings also shows signs of an absence of care and skill.

Varieties in the construction of arches—exemplified in the older buildings in Seistan.

There is a place some two miles below, or to the north of Kala-i-Fath, where the waters of the canal that took off above the Band-i-Bulbaka were distributed. It is still called Ab-Baksh or the dividing of the waters. From this place a main canal followed the alignment of the old Zorkan canal, following the ancient channel fairly closely. This tailed off at or close to the Ziarat of Amran, and by means of it the country round that place and along the banks of the canal was rendered fertile. The distributaries of this channel can still be seen in the vicinity of the ruin of Kala Gāwak. The area under cultivation was, however, largest close to the capital; and no attempt was made to turn to account the lands around Ghulghula or Sār-o-Tār. These districts, it is said, were then in very much the same condition as they are now, covered with barkhans of loose sand moving onwards every year under the impelling force of the wind of 120 days. It will be seen from this that the area which benefited from the efforts of Malik Mahmud and his successors was probably less than had been reclaimed by Malik Kutb-ud-din and his immediate successors. The date on the memorial tablet found not far from the ruins of Ghulghula proves that district to have been inhabited. The desolation wrought by Amir Khalil Hindukah had given the final impulse under which the prosperity of Seistan had commenced to decline, following

Extent of Malik Hamza's area of cultivation.

Yak Gumbaz, near Kala Fath.

(Part III to face page 249).

as it did not very long after the losses that took place during Timur's invasion; and the expiry of 74 years would barely have proved long enough to allow of the restoration of the country being placed on a firm basis. And when again a member of the ancient family of the Maliks was allowed to return and govern the country of his forefathers, it was necessary to cause orders to be issued that all the neighbouring districts should contribute their share of colonists and make up 1,000 families, who were forced to migrate to Seistan and settle there, forming the nucleus of the population and assuring a supply of labour with which to commence the task of restoring the prosperity of the country and its population.

From the dividing of the waters to the north of Kala-i-Fath, a wisp of canals trended towards the north-east upon which depended the existence of the districts in that direction which are now so thickly covered with ruins. These districts and the ruins it contains are worthy of description. The barrier between the northern delta and the districts of Ghulghula and Sār-o-Tār has already been described, but to the east of it there is another and with the exception of one or two small outcrops of dasht, the space between them is a strip of alluvial deposit some 5 miles wide, extending northwards for a great distance, covered now by the sandhills in this direction. The southern end of this eastern dasht is an isolated block, separated by a narrow space full of broken clay mounds and alluvial soil forming the under features or Talus that descends from the cliffs of the Dasht-i-Meski. This isolated block of dasht is some 50 feet in height above the plain at its foot, and it is rendered still more prominent by a ruined building which stands on its northern brow, overlooking the plain below. The Baluch and other inhabitants have placed within the ruin a ziarat dedicated to Sheikh Husen. To the north of this isolated block of dasht a narrow strip of alluvial soil separates it from a plateau of dasht, which a little further to the north attains to a height of 30 or 40 feet, forming well marked though low plateaux which slope comparatively abruptly towards the west, but which shade off gently into an extensive and undulating gravel covered plain which descends gradually towards the east and south-east. The canal that turned to the east under the ruins of Sargah-i-Seistan passed through the gap to the north of the Ziarat; and the spoil banks of the later canal which dates possibly from the period of Malik Hamza can be also traced almost as far as the ruins of Paisai about 4 miles to the east of the Ziarat-i-Sheikh Husen. The older canal probably watered the lands around Tikāla and may have also nourished the outlying lands of Sār-o-Tār itself. This gravel plateau to the north of the Sheikh Husen Ziarat trends away in a north-easterly direction. On it stands the conspicuous mound called Dik-i-Dalil by the Baluchis, because it is the landmark by which the Dagal Gardis, or explorers who visit the ruins in search

Malik Hamza Khan's canal system.

of antiques, direct their course to Sār-o-Tār. The plateau increases in height further to the north, as in that direction there is a chain of very lofty sandhills which shut out the view for several miles to the north-west of the Sār-o-Tār ruins, and which undoubtedly rests upon a continuous chain of detached plateau. To the north of the mound of Dik-i-Dalil it is not possible to speak with any degree of certainty as to the disposition of these blocks of dasht. But as the canals that used to water Sār-o-Tār and the lands to the north at an earlier period entered that district evidently some 5 miles to the north-east of the Dik-i-Dalil mound, the only inference that can be drawn is that the plateaux on which the sand now rests, as upon a foundation, are separated from each other by narrow strips of alluvial soil, in exactly the same way as the embouchures of the Rud-i-Biyabān wind in and out towards the Hamun through the sloping Talus of dasht. The ancient canal systems that nourished these districts took advantage of these natural outlets, or where to do so would have entailed a circuitous course they were probably cut boldly through the dashts, as the Zarkan canal was constructed through the plateau to the south-east of the Gāwak ruins.

<small>Dik-i-Dalil mound.</small>

The restoration of these were, however, beyond the resources and skill at the disposal of Malik Hamza, who was content to see the lands up to the edge of the sandhills placed under cultivation. His canals are as yet quite recognisable.

<small>Ruins known as Palangi.</small>

In this tract of country in the vicinity of the capital of those days were placed the manor houses of the leading personages of the day, and these form the ruins around Palangi. These are so numerous, and lofty in some instances, as to induce the casual observer to regard them as the ruins of a city. Of all these ruins, that which is called Palangi is in the best state of preservation. It is called by this name because on one of its walls there is picked out by an arrangement of small square holes in the plaster the representation of a leopard, or panther; whether this was done with any object, and was the cognisance of the owner of the mansion, or whether it was merely a freak on some one's part, it is not possible to say. But it is interesting to note that devices not unlike coats-of-arms were evidently once used in Seistan by quite ordinary persons who lived a long time ago in this country.

The ruin known as Palangi is a very good example of the manor house of the period. Fortified to a certain point so as to resist the attack of a private enemy, it was intended to serve primarily as a residence. In plan it is a square, each side of which is 200 feet in length. The angles are oriented and one side faces the direction of the prevailing wind during the summer. The interior of the square is divided into two equal parts, the northern half in full of dwellings of an ordinary type; the domed roofs of these have fallen in, and the interior of the buildings are now choked with sand. Along the north wall there were two tiers of such dwellings, the roofs of which served as a

<small>Plan and construction of the Palangi Ruin.</small>

platform, if it was necessary ever to man the walls against the attack of an enemy. The southern half contained the dwelling of the landholder, or owner of the building, and here also the apartments were arranged on two floors. On each floor a large hall occupied the centre, the other apartments being arranged around the halls. The interiors were handsomely finished in lime mortar with which the walls were plastered and the inside of the domes were divided into small lozenges, the dividing lines of the pattern having been made with stucco and the whole plastered over and whitewashed. Each of the halls was 30 feet long by 20 wide, and at each end an arched entrance gave access to smaller vaulted chambers. The floor of the upper apartments having collapsed and the roof as well, the plan of the lower story alone can be traced, the rooms at either end of the hall being still intact, though filled up to half their height with sand and débris. The apartments of the upper floor were ventilated with large windows. These openings were arched, and at the point where the curve of the arch springs there is a horizontal piece of masonry,—a very flat arch—dividing the opening into two unequal portions, the lower one being rectangular and the upper nearly a half circle. This seems to have always been the method of forming such openings. A carpet was probably hung before the rectangular larger openings, while the upper acted as a clerestory window and admitted light and air. The chambers on the ground floor were ventilated, and to a small extent lighted also by narrow slits or loopholes which in times of emergency could be used in the defence of the building. At each angle of the wall which enclosed the buildings there stood a round tower, partly for purposes of defence and partly built to complete the design and add to the appearance of the building which they certainly enhanced. Towards the northern angle of the northern half of the building there is the ruin of a windmill, in which the grain raised in the surrounding lands was ground, and there was also no doubt a well within the walls, probably inside one of the smaller houses, to secure the inhabitants against being cut off from water. Beyond the north-west face or curtain there were projecting walls built at an angle with the curtain, and also built in a curve, all of which were undoubtedly intended to act as wind-sails to conduct the wind not only to the windmill, but also for purposes of ventilation of the interior. In many of the manor houses which contained a windmill on the premises there is evidence to show that the latter served a double purpose : to grind wheat and also to act as a thermantidote to ventilate and cool the inner apartments.

Windmill also probably used to ventilate and cool interior of building.

Bathrooms and other offices were placed on the roof, and the places in the walls where drains had been constructed can still be seen. The masonry of the latter have disappeared, leaving deep scars to mark their position in the face of the walls. In the north-western face to the south of the opening of the windmill there is a curious semi-circular wall curving away from the latter which extends from the ground to the full height of the building; its purpose is not at all evident, unless it was intended to prevent all chances of contaminating matter being introduced to the interior of the mill, and was therefore built as a guard to the windmill. In this face of the building there are no large windows, and the openings that look out into the small space between the semi-circular wall and that of the building are small, little larger than loopholes, and may have been used as shoots to throw sweepings and other rubbish out of apartments or offices above. At present the entrance is by a gap in the walls, and as the original gate was not especially fortified, it is not possible to locate its position; but it probably existed in the south-east wall of the menials' quarters; and the absence of protective works to the entrance shows that the building could never have been intended to offer serious resistance or to withstand an organised and determined attack; the towers, loopholes, and crenelations on the wall were added probably for decorative purposes alone.

Architectural details.

This building stands on a plinth of excellent pisé work, upon which the walls have been raised. The plinth itself is about 6 feet high, and the walls rise to another 25 feet above it; the outside of the walls were decorated in panels; the latter included in a moulded course of baked brick, and the general effect of these breaking the otherwise plain surface of the walls is very pleasing. Altogether Palangi is as good a specimen of a country gentleman's house during the period of Malik Hamza which is to be seen anywhere in the neighbourhood. In many respects it differs from its neighbours and displays an originality of design that is very striking. To the east, west and north the country is covered with the remains of older or perhaps only less skilfully constructed buildings—mere formless ruins; and these perhaps may date from the time of Muiz-ud-din Husen and the Amir Khalil. The buildings of which they are the remains appear to have been much older than the remains of Palangi and some of the numerous ruins that cover the surface of the ground so thickly to the south-west of the latter.

The cistern of Hau-za Khan.

Next, in a southerly direction from the buildings just described, there is a reservoir which originally had been covered in with a dome; the cistern is still clearly visible and the drain which admitted water as well as that at the other end through which it escaped. The stream of flowing water in this way kept the contents of the reservoir pure. This is called the cistern or reservoir of Malik Hamza, and it is said that he used to hold assemblies inside the building. The space between the edge of the cistern and the walls of the building was covered with carpets, and there in the cool shade of the lofty dome by the side of the flowing water the notables of the district were wont to congregate and pass the hours of a summer afternoon with kalians and music. At these gatherings probably a good deal of business was carried on in a desultory way, and the efforts of literary men of the country submitted to the criticism of the assembly. The canals that fed the reservoir are still traceable without much difficulty. The domed-building was surrounded by smaller apartments, in which the attendants of the persons of quality were able to refresh themselves.

Further to the south-west there are extensive ruins of manor houses and stately residences; some in an advanced condition of decay, others in comparatively good repair. The majority of these had the apartments of the gentry arranged in two floors forming a great block which stood in the north-west face of an open courtyard, with quarters around the three other sides. Among these ruins there are several large windmills. The most celebrated of these is one, the side walls of which are profusely decorated with diamond shaped and cruciform studs made in high relief with stucco or plaster. This particular windmill stood in its own premises and was on a very large scale. The lower portion of the building is a plinth several feet in height above which there rose lofty walls built of sundried bricks. The buildings, of which these are the remains, had gardens attached to them and the land between was cultivated and full of gardens. The style of the houses and the general appearance of the country shows that these houses were occupied at a time of perfect peace, internal as well with reference to the relations of the country, as with neighbouring powers.[1]

Description of other ruins near Palang.

This was characteristic of the reign of Malik Hamza. Seistan being under the protection of the Persian Empire, he enjoyed immunity from all outside attack. The Uzbegs had subsided quietly beyond the Oxus, and the Indian Empire of the Moghuls was too far away to trouble itself with the affairs of Seistan. The dry rot that gradually sapped the strength of both the empires of the Suffavi Monarchs of Persia, and of the descendants of Baber, had at yet not made itself evident; and the glamour of the prowess of the founders of both dynasties still clung to their descendants.

Peaceful reign of Malik Hamza Khan.

The Kaiānis of Seistan have always modelled their buildings on the traditionary accounts of the palaces of the ancient Kings of Persia. The buildings generally in Seistan followed the fashion thus set by the rulers and lofty arched adits and halls are a most common feature in all old buildings that still preserve their form and design in Seistan. In the buildings of the Kala-i-Timur to the north of the ruins of Zāhidān, which date from a period far beyond that of Timur, the public apartments are great halls covered with a vaulted roof; while the approach from outside was under a tall arch that rose to the level of the roof. The lofty halls of the Khasraus, their ancestors,

The Kaiāni buildings in Seistan modelled on the traditional accounts of the palaces of the Kings of Persia.

---

[1] These ruins are called Poolgee by Christie. Pulg is a Seistani word for fine sand or dust. Pulgi or Poolgee may be a corruption of Palangi, or this tract may in Christie's time (1810) have been covered with drifts of loose sand that have since moved off under the impulsion of the wind.

seemed always to have been in the minds of this family when building for themselves in Seistan; and every ruin in that country contains the remains of these noble apartments.

Description of Kala-i-Gāwak.

At the site called Kala-i-Gāwak[1] there is a good example of this style of architecture. It was a castellated mansion in its days surrounded by an outer wall. The main building is very much dilapidated and the outer wall is in heaps, but the interior is still intelligible. It is in the shape of a Latin cross, the four equal arms of which are lofty adits communicating with apartments on either side, the former being open to the roof which was arched, while on either side the apartments were arranged in two stories. The courtyard was therefore square and open to the sky.

This site is believed to be the scene of the celebrated combat in which eventually Rustam proved to be victorious. The champions were roused by the song of the larks every morning and prepared themselves for the impending struggle. Hence the place is known as the fort of the larks, Kh being in Seistan sounded like a hard G. The present ruins are said to date from the time of Malik Hamza.[2]

Description of Chigini near Deh Meno.

The decorations in many of the ruins are very well carried out. The best instance of any are to be found in some ruins called Chigini by the Baluchis. This word means adorned or decorated. These ruins are about similar to the east of the modern hamlet of Meno, not far from the south end of the Chung-i-Darazgu in the Ashkin lands near Chakansur.

Lancet shaped windows, heavily moulded with plaster, are the principal items in the architectural details of old buildings in Seistan. The ruins at Chigini are great piles of apartments one above the other occupying the windward side of an open courtyard. In the centre a lofty arched adit gives access to the apartments on either hand, while a small arched doorway forms the exit opposite the lofty entrance. The detail of ornamentation is clearly preserved on the sides away from the wind, as the material of sundried brick is very easily worn by friction of the dust-laden winds. In this part of Seistan the difference between the highly decorated buildings of later date and the plain unornamented buildings of an earlier period is very plainly contrasted.

The Ziarat of Amrān.

About six miles from Chigini is the Ziarat of Amrān; around the shrine which is housed in a domed building of evidently recent date there are some undoubtedly ancient remains, and the latter are studiously plain and the only decorative features are simple mouldings in the walls and round arches.

Thirteen or fourteen miles to the north of Kala-i Fath.

[2] A find of gold coins struck by this ruler is said to have been discovered. None of his coins have been discovered by me, and it is doubtful if he coined any money at all. His father did—of copper.

Ancient shrine of Amrān, S. of chakānsur. Curious octagonal shaft of minaret in ruins.

(Part III to face page 254.)

THE RUINS IN SEISTAN.

To the north of the ziarat there is a great pile of buildings called Tāk-i-Amrān or the Palace of Amrān. This was in its day a noble building. It is placed with one front towards the direction of the wind, and the side walls of the building were continued in this direction and enclosed a garden, from which a lofty adit gave access to the interior. In this respect the building resembles the palace to the north of Zāhidān. The feature in this building is the size of its apartments. On either hand of the adit there are ordinary rooms, but on the west there is a great hall 60 feet long by 20 feet wide, and about 30 feet high, evidently a room where the owner held his levées. The roof has fallen in to a great extent, but the disposition of the rooms is quite clear. An elaborate system of double walls with very narrow passages between and shafts for ventilation is also a great feature in this building. This building may probably be coeval with that of the palaces to the north of Zāhidān, and the similarity in the entrance seems to connect the Tāk-i-Amrān with the Kala-i-Timur as to age and period of construction. The Chigini ruins are said to have been inhabited during the time of Malik Hamza, but not so the Tāk-i-Amrān. This building is also not as profusely ornamented as those at Chigini. The former is a very prominent feature in the landscape; the great height of the ruins is seen to full advantage in the open plain in which it stands. The great pile of buildings at Tāk-i-Amrān stands to windward of an open court around which were arranged the dwellings of retainers, servants and the following that accompanied the Prince who dwelt there when he moved from place to place. The gateway was in the south-eastern face of the courtyard. This great pile of buildings was in all probability a residence of one of the earlier Maliks of Seistan or of some great personage, and from its appearance it is possible that it was built and occupied before the destruction of Zāhidān by Timur. It is said to have been the palace of Khwāja Amrān. But this is only because it stands not far from the shrine dedicated to that holy person.

Description of Tāk-i-Amrān.

The presence of the Zorkan and Zarkan canals close to the ruin of Tāk-i-Amrān makes it probable that the place may have been inhabited when those ancient canals were in working order. This would put the date of its existence very far back, and it is not by any means impossible that this huge building is actually so old. The situation is such that it has been saved from the direct action of water, and the river has never attacked it. The country around has never been seriously cultivated since the invasion of Timur, and the massive walls have therefore had to resist merely the action of the wind deprived of the assistance of damp, its most potent auxiliary, as well as the ravages of human beings.

Probable date of this building; coeval with the Zarkan, and Zorkan canals.

The ancient buildings in Seistan belonging to the period of Malik Hamza Khan or his father, or to the period before the invasion of Timur, all show a very peculiar method of ventilation. The domes in some instances evidently

General character on the buildings of Malik Hamza Khan.

were crowned by a louvre which allowed ventilation of the apartment below, but the inner rooms were also ventilated and protected from the force of the sun's rays by double walls. The walls which separate room from room on the ground floor were solid and massively built. Those above were double and included a passage same 2 feet wide which were arched over a few feet above the floor beyond which the walls continued solid to the point whence the groining of the domes sprung. In some of the older ruins to the north of Zāhidān inner rooms on the ground floor had a series of small openings ascending towards and communicating with such passages in the walls above. In the lower room these openings were placed just below the springing of the domes and the openings were well finished and combined a useful purpose with a certain decorative effect which broke the monotony of a blank wall. This system of ventilation is met with in the ruins around Sār-o-Tār, in the large palace within the inner fort at that place, and even in many of the buildings in the vicinity of the Palangi ruins near Kala-i-Fath which are obviously not older than the period of Malik Hamza, or of his father the Malik Jallaludin. In these buildings of a past age, and even of the present day, there is to be found no doubt the same general plan and method of construction that prevailed in the days of the Sassanian Kings of Persia. The clay well worked is most tenacious after it has dried, and walls built carefully of pisé are as durable as those of brick and probably more so, as the pisé work carefully carried out consolidates into a homogeneous mass, and to destroy buildings made of it is by no means an easy task. In Seistan the older buildings are a fine example of the results than can be attained with merely sundried bricks and clay. Judging from the accounts of recent explorations in the site of the great city of Babylon, these materials were as well handled and as largely employed in those very remote times in which the great piles of masonry were raised, the remains of which now form the great mounds marking that ancient site.

Number of cultivators in the time of Malik Hamza Khan.

The Chigini ruins mark the furthest extent of the cultivation that was carried on by means of the Helmand canals in the time of Malik Hamza; it is said that 2,000 pagos or gangs of labourers were needed for the operations of agriculture and the maintenance of the canals and watercourses between the capital and that place. The lands in the direction of Post-i-Gau and to the north of that ruined town, in the direction of the site called Khwāja Surju, required another 1,000 pagos to carry on the task of cultivation, the lands they tilled being watered from the Khash Rud.

Modern Persian Seistan a waste tract in time of Malik Hamza Khan.

That part of Seistan now in the hands of the Persians in the northern delta was, however, a waste tract. Up to about the position of old Malik Haidari there may have been some little attempt made to cultivate the land in good years. But the remainder was destitute of water, save after rain, and probably here and there wells may have been sunk, around which, in the spring, flocks of sheep, goats, and camels may have been pastured. Zāhidān lay in ruins and the country round it was a wilderness.

Those tracts of land, now a desert, around Trākun, Rāmrod and Hauzdar, on the other hand, were at that time cultivated and populated. The Rud-i-Biyaban discharged the water in separate outlets, and one of these flowed into the deep bay to the south of the Puza-i-Surh Dagal, into which its course can yet be easily traced. These outlets could only have been very full during the season of floods, when the water escaped over the weir of Mashi. During the winter months the volume of water must have been considerably reduced, and the task of utilising and controlling it was therefore rendered much easier. *Hauzdar tract was cultivated.*

It is said that there were in those days from 1,000 to 1,500 pagos engaged in agriculture in the districts from Trākun westwards. These figures are of course not to be taken as being absolutely correct, but at any rate in the absence of all other information they are too valuable to be lost by neglect or a hypersensitive disregard of information that cannot be tested thoroughly. While such was the condition of the outlying districts in Malik Hamza's lifetime, the lands near the capital needed the labours of 1,000 pagos or associations of cultivators, consisting of seven men each; while the lands along the Helmand from Kala-i-Fath to the district of Khānishin gave employment to another 1,500 such associations of agriculturists. *Number of cultivators in the southern delta in the time of Malik Hanza, according to a very precise tradition.*

The Hamun area towards the south when the Helmand occupied the Rud-i-Biyaban differed considerably from its present outline. The northern of all the outlets of that channel enters the bay which lies to the south of Puz-i-Surh Dagal, and at that time it must have, on occasions, converted that bay, and the alluvial plain that intervenes between the sites of Hauzdar (and Kundar) and Rāmrod, into a branch of the Hamun; or at all events have flooded it with water and rendered it impossible for days. Owing to this, in order to keep up communications, a route crossed the dasht from Trākun, and traversing the head of that bay, and the other to the north of the Surh Dagal headland, it passed through the western end of the Sana Rud valley to the site on which modern Sehkoha is built. It is not now easy to follow up this old road, but that it was a thoroughfare is proved by the existence, at one or two places, of permanent marks indicating the positions of passes by which the ascent or descent of the cliffs which form the dasht could be easily accomplished. One of these marks consisted of a low platform of clay in the centre of which an upright stick of the desert tamarisk had been set. The decayed remains of the butt of this piece of wood was found inside the hole in which it had originally stood. These marks must have been set up to render any mistake impossible, as the cliffs do not everywhere allow of a descent (or ascent) being safely accomplished, as the streams that cut back into the *Description of an ancient route across the dasht from Trakun to Sehkoha.*

plateau often disappear underground in a tangle of narrow, deep cut, and unpracticable ravines, amid sharp ridges and knolls of clay. This track had been well used and was a recognised means of communication between Trākun and Sehkoha, when time was a consideration, as by it the distance to be travelled is much shorter than if a traveller proceeded to the southern delta to Rāmrod and thence by Hauzdar to Sehkoha. Also in the season of a high river, the delta of the Rud-i-Biyaban must have frequently been under water for days or weeks at a time. The desert route between these two places must have been in existence at a time when both the northern delta and Trākun also was inhabited; these conditions are known to have prevailed at a period when Malik Kutb-ud-din occupied the throne of Seistan as a Ruling Prince, and when Timur invaded this country. It is probable that after the destruction of the Band-i-Rustam, when the northern delta was deprived of water, this desert track must have at once been given up as a through route except during the winter, when alone, after rain, water was procurable in the northern delta.

Description of Ziarat of Sheikh Husen.

While, however, the outlying districts were in a very fairly prosperous condition, the lands nearer the capital would derive great advantage from their position. In these lands also the aristocracy of the country would naturally be found to dwell. Therefore it is not surprising that from a point some eight miles below the modern village of Chahārburjak to the south down to Kala Gāwak on the north the country is a great mass of ruins which differ in character very greatly from those which are to be found in the outlying districts, both in style of architecture and size. The near relations of the ruling chief probably occupied the majority of these mansions, and it is said that a large portion of the lands to the north of Kala-i-Fath, in the direction of the Palangi ruins, was assigned to Abu Tāhir, the son of the elder sister of Mali Hamza. This youth died in the 22nd year of his age, and it is said he was buried in the cemetery on the isolated block of dasht which is now known as the Ziarat of Sheikh Husen. The later shrine itself being placed over the actual burial-place of the young man. His sorrowing mother raised the mausoleum now in ruins over the grave of her only son placing a tablet to his memory over the tomb itself. This mausoleum was built on a heavy plinth of pisé, above which the domed-building was raised, being entirely built of baked bricks. Close to it are great square blocks of graves which it is possible may have been the burial-place of members of the Ka'ānis. There are several of these blocks of tombs, evidently those of separate families. The tombs are built above ground. The upper surface of the graves is a platform or terrace, and it is only where in parts this roof has fallen in that it is possible to understand that underneath it lie the mouldering remains of human beings. The tomb of Abu Tāhir was rifled by Afghans in 1872 when the latter took possession of the share of Seistan (to which they became entitled by the award of the British Commissioner in 1872). The inscription on the tablet was, it is said, taken by them to denote the existence of treasure, and their greedy natures thus aroused impelled them to this act of desecration. The Baluchis in course of a few years put in a shrine inside the ruined mausoleum, and dedicated it to Sheikh Husen. The tablet erected by the mother of the young man was broken into two pieces ; one of these now placed in the ziarat bears the name Tāhir, and the other portion is said to exist in a small hamlet to the south of Kala-i-Fath, the ignorant possessors believe that the inscription relates to a great buried treasure, and the badly executed Arabic characters are regarded by them as ancient Persian. The inscription to the memory of Abu Tāhir was cut in a slab of the stone from which mill stones are fashioned, the letters being upright in a heavily formed Arabic script, which is not nearly as well executed as those which are now to be found at the shrine inside the ruins of Zāhidān. There are also, in the Ziarat of Sheikh Husen, associated with the broken memorial to the young Kaiāni prince, fragments of another tablet, which was carved in a slab of travertine or alabaster. The inscription on this is in an indifferently executed and cursive modern Persian script One of these fragments bears the inscription "the date of His Highness' (or Holiness') death was the 7th Zil Haj 623 (or 923) A. H." The word Hazrat may refer to either a temporal or spiritual dignitary. There is a doubt as to whether the figure denoting the century is actually a six or the fragment of a nine, as the latter in a partially mutilated form might be read as a six. The difference in the script employed in the memorials shows them to belong to two distinct tablets, and as fragments of inscribed slabs are collected and often brought from great distances to be deposited as *ex voto* offerings at the shrines of saints, the alabaster tablet may have been brought from some place far from that where it now rests.

CHAPTER XV.

The later capitals and towns of Seistan.

Troops of Indian Emperor Shah Jahan invade Seistan and besiege the Capital—Autumn of 1639.

Kala-i-Fath had been besieged for a very brief period, or held to ransom the year before the death of Malik Hamza, and at the same time the Band-i-Bulbaka had been destroyed by a column of Indian troops which had marched down the valley of the Helmand. The details of this inroad has been given in the historical section. Its success shows on what an insecure foundation the prosperity of Seistan rested, and that it was probably not as flourishing as traditions and the scanty information contained in the Shijrat-ul-Muluk would lead one to suppose.

Period of prosperity and decline of Kala-i-Fath.

Tradition states that the period of prosperity of Kala-i-Fath lasted for about 230 years, while its decay set in about 240 years ago. These figures do not agree very closely with the dates which are to be found in history. There is, however, only a difference of 26 years in defect, and from historical data it appears that the two periods of prosperity and decadence were probably almost equal, making a total of 496 years. The period of its gradual descent in the scale of prosperity had now come about and in the time of Fath Ali Khan the Helmand changed its course from the Rud-i-Biyaban. The great change occurred, if tradition be correct, in his reign, but the river had no doubt for some time previously shown its liability to effect a change of course. According to an exceedingly precise and consistent tradition, the year when this occurred was a season of very great flood. The Helmand came down in its *greatest* strength. The waters, it is said, swept away the weir known as the Band-i-Bulbaka, and all other (training) embankments also melted away before the rush of the furious torrent.

The fate that befell Kala-i-Fath was one that has always hung over the capital of Seistan.

Reason for removing the capital from Kala-i-Fath to Kundarak.

The change of Government from Kala-i-Fath to Kundarak was rendered necessary once the Helmand reverted to the northern delta, both on account of the ravages of floods, and more so because the population must have migrated into the more open country again rendered fertile by the return of the river to that tract. The lands around Kala-i-Fath must have been to a great extent abandoned by its inhabitants, and the Government had to follow the emigration northwards. Kala-i-Fath thenceforward fell into decay, and was never again the capital, though it continued for several generations to be the nominal headquarters of the family of the Maliks, members of which no doubt occupied the palaces.

Description of Kundark.

Kundarak continued to be the capital for a generation after Malik Fath Ali Khan's death, and a desperate struggle was maintained between the

Ruined tower, defences of Kundrak.

(Part III to face page 260.)

people and the river which was inclining towards it. The embankments, to which allusion has been made, date from this period, and were raised to protect the capital from the inroads of the river.

This town is the last serious attempt made to found a capital, and its construction bears traces of the decadence of Seistan, in the crude and slovenly way in which the building has been carried out. In this respect it is only a little better than Jallalabad. The plan of Kundarak is that which has been in vogue probably since the days when the earliest fortress was built. Two outer lines of defences enclose a fortified palace which forms the citadel, the inner of the two lines of walls enclosing the town. Between it and the outermost walls the space was taken up with a few large buildings set in the midst of gardens and cultivation. In this particular instance the trace of the walls is rectangular; occupying nearly a square. The sides of the enclosures are oriented and in this respect it differs from Zāhidān. The gardens and cultivated lands must have formed a pleasant suburb for the small town that was packed away behind the inner walls. The latter was a collection of mean hovels, built of sundried bricks, with domed roofs. A street joining the east to west gates divided the inner fort into two equal parts, and this street was almost straight. It passed under the south wall of the palace, a lofty pile of buildings, which occupied the western side of a courtyard enclosed by high walls, along the inside of which there were quarters for the retainers and servants of the Prince. This palace and its precincts was fortified to a certain extent, but not very strongly. The town lay on the east and south sides of the palace, and on the opposite sides between the latter and the walls there were evidently only a few large sized buildings. The latter are now in ruins, but the town is in better repair than the palace and the houses inside probably continued to be inhabited when the palace had been abandoned. All the buildings and the works are built of sundried bricks. The inner walls, though ruined, can be traced, but the outermost wall has fallen completely into ruin. In both the inner and outer walls there was a gate in each face, that of the latter facing the south was defended by a detached work now in an advanced state of decay which looks as if it might have been a fortified palace, or merely a strong redoubt; it was connected by means of a wall with the curtain of the outer wall of the town. To the west of Kundarak there is a very conspicuous ruin of a great windmill, which was built by Kāzi Abdullah of Kundarak, and is called As-i-Gāzi[1] (the Kāzi's windmill) throughout the country.

The ruined Madrasah also, which has been alluded to in describing the Mahal of Gulistan, was built by Malik Fath Ali, and the principal of this college was the head of the family of the Mulla Shahi of Kala-i-Fath.

The Madrasah, or Government College.

Also called As-i-Ghāzi.

It is doubtful whether the ruins in the vicinity of the villages of Jalai and Gauri belong to the period of Kundarak, or whether they belong to an earlier period. The inroads of floods have worn them down to heaps of white clay; but the older remains, which now are merely heaps of clay, probably belong to the period of Zāhidān. Those others of the ruins which still present fragments of walls to view are very probably referable to the period of Kundarak.

Incidents in the reign of Mahmud and Malik Fath Ali Khan the Second.

In the end this town succumbed to the fate which sooner or later has befallen every capital (except Zāhidān) of Seistan. It, however, lasted through the period of Nādir Shah.

From it set forth the young Prince Mahmud, who with a boldness and enterprise worthy of complete success seized the Province of Khurassan, over which he ruled as an independent monarch for some time: finally succumbing to the superior military skill of that great chieftain who freed his country from the oppressive yoke of the Afghans. Malik Fath Ali Khan the Second was put to death in 1160 A. H., according to the Shijrat-ul-Muluk, and his death was marked by a period of confusion in the history of this country.

1747 A.D.

The capitals subsequent to Kundarak only villages.

Kundarak probably was not abandoned, but it came to this nevertheless, and with its end closes the period of the revival of prosperity; though in truth this revival was probably well on the downward path before Kundarak was ever built.

After Kundarak was given up, the succeeding capitals degenerated into mere villages such as the chief town is at present. The pretence of fortifying it was maintained, but the defences were of the flimsiest nature, and the walls and bastions mere shells. Centuries of turmoils, massacre, added to changes in the river's course due to want of control, produced by those disasters which periodically appeared to overtake this country, had driven the greater part of the ancient population out of Seistan, while the remnant that were left had their strength, their courage, and their faith in themselves destroyed and sapped, and they were also more or less out of hand, and not amenable to their rulers who were without the means of compelling obedience.

Allahābād-miyān-i-Shela built.

In the meantime the river had been pressing down in the direction of Kundarak, and it at last had got the better of the resistance against its inroads offered by the people of the country. Kundarak experienced the fate of Kala-i-Fath, and the seat of Government was placed at Allahābād-miyān-i-Shela, a new village founded after Kundarak had become untenable. The site of this new capital between the Shelas, or old beds of the Helmand, was peculiarly unhappy. Not only was it threatened with extinction every time the Helmand rose, but the waters of the Hamun impelled by the strong wind of 120 days were driven towards the east and submerged the lands right up to the walls of the new capital. It shows to what a condition of

Ruins of Kundrak.

(Part III to face page 262.)

ineptitude the persons had fallen who were responsible for the choice of this site, the disadvantages of which must have been obvious, even though the site had been examined during those months when the height of the water both in the river, and in the Hamun as well, was very low.

The Maliks of Seistan had been granted lands in the Kaināt. There was a branch of the family settled in Tun; and Ahmad Shah had added the districts of Khiābād and Khusf to their possessions. It was these possessions which, so to speak, nailed the seat of their Government to the neighbourhood of the Hamun, where the road from Seistan to Kain and Birjand crossed the lake by the Kucha-i-Afzalābād. Allahābād-miyān-i-Shela is about 6 miles to the north-west of the present capital.

Allahābād-miyān-i-Shela is rectangular in plan; its greatest length is from north to south and covers an area of perhaps 800 feet, by about 500 feet wide. The interior is divided into four quarters by streets which connect the north and south and the eastern and western gates, and within these blocks is a mass of dwellings meaner and more squalid than those which form the town of Kundarak. There is no palace within the walls, or if one had even existed, it has completely disappeared. The walls that protect the town are largely built of baked bricks, but notwithstanding this they are in a very advanced state of dilapidation. The outer walls some 200 or 300 feet in advance of the inner defences were protected by a ditch, the trace of which can be still followed. The country in the immediate vicinity of the town is full of ruins of manor houses, with windmills, and fragments of garden walls : all, however, greatly decayed. Allahābād-miyān-i-Shela enjoyed but a brief existence. Malik Suleman Khan is said to have lived in the palace at Kundarak for some time, and it is possible that it is due to this that no palace or official residence was built inside the newer town. Traditions attributed the desertion of Allahābād to the inroads of the water from the Hamun which under certain conditions used to inundate the lands and even encroach on the walls of the town. The outer walls certainly bear this out, but there can be no doubt that the spill water from the too older branches of the Helmand had some share as well in the destruction of this town. The Helmand at this period was pressing towards the southern edge of the northern delta, and the country to the south of the present capital is full of old beds which are the scars left by the river as it swung towards the south, and it was owing to these changes that Kundarak had at last to be abandoned.

To the west of the present capital about 4 miles distant there are ruins, consisting of castellated manor houses, detached residence, all of which were surrounded by gardens, grouped round a fortified dwelling. These ruins are called Ghulam Shah Khan, and it was the abode of the Resident or Intendant of either Ahmad Shah, or his son Timur Shah, of Kabul, who represented the Suzerain Power at the Court of the Malik of Seistan, who had

A representative of the Amir of Cabul lived in Seistan.

become a vassal of the dynasty founded by Ahmad Shah Durrani. The Intendant represented and watched over the interests of his master, and he was also present to support the local prince in his dealings with refractory subjects.

Description of Hauzdar.

Hauzdar is a very modern fort, enclosing within its walls a small town. A gate to the south and one to the north afforded means of egress, and it was surrounded by a ditch some 50 feet in width. To the left of the entrance by the northern gateway within the walls there is a huge pile of pisé buildings, which was the residence of the Chief. Inside the ditch, which is now merely a shallow depression, there are the marks of two or three wells which supplied the town with water when the canals were not running, and even when they were full, as the watercourses were further away from the walls. To the north of the fort there are some broken enclosures which mark the positions of gardens. To the south of the fort there is an extensive cemetery, and beyond the latter is the site of the City of Rustam, with only a crumbling ruin of a small fortalice and an ancient tower of silence on the end of an isolated block of Kim, about a mile to the south of the former.

Description of Kundar.

Kundar was never more than a village enclosed by a wall and surrounded by a ditch. The latter, as in the case of Hauzdar, was probably intended more as a protection against floods rather than an enemy, as both Kundar, Hauzdar and the City of Rustam are on a hard level plain of clay.

Some of the inscriptions in the Machi ruins were dated. No date earlier than 1130 A. H. could be deciphered. In one the words " Mir Ja'afir Khan walad (illegible) Khan dar Sal 1130 " (1717 A.D.).

CHAPTER XVI.

Description of the City of Kakha and Ruins on the Koh-i-Khwaja.

The city of the Kakhas has been described by recent authors who have referred to Seistan in their narratives. There is not much to add to their descriptions of the ruins themselves. Some doubt exists as to the origin of the name. Christie (in 1810) is probably the authority on whose information Kinneir based the notice of Seistan contained in his Geographical Memoir of Persia. He calls the city "Kookhozerd." Jird is the old Persian termination for a stronghold, and Kookho is the corrupted form of the word Kakha, the Seistanis turning the letter "a" into "u" in conversation. Kakhajird would therefore be represented by the name with which Kinneir was supplied either by Christie or some one else. The Kakhas are still a well-known section or tribe of the modern population of Seistan. And this ancient fortress was built and held by the tribe in the days when it was both an important and powerful section of the population. Name Kakhajird mentioned by Kinneir.

This town was not by any means large. It is built on the slope of the Koh-i-Khwaja below the south scarp of the plateau, and from its situation it could have been a terrible place to live in during the summer. Of course when it was built the land around was a cultivated and well populated tract. There is yet a tradition to this effect lingering in Seistan. When in course of time changes in the Helmand converted this part of the lake into Naizar and the country was constantly under water, an Arbab of the Seiād population built a small fort on a spit of dasht which projected towards the south from the foot of the plateau. The city itself was strongly fortified and defended by a double line of walls, the outer one having fallen into ruins forms a line of mounds some distance in advance of the inner line of walls which enclose the town and palace. The outer wall is a rough semi-circle with both its flanks resting on the slopes of the hillsides on which the city is built. Baked brick seems to have been very sparingly used, and its place was taken by stone of which there was an abundant supply at hand. The lower courses of the buildings are all composed of large blocks of stone set in clay mortar, and the buildings above this are altogether composed of pisé. Sundried brick was largely used in building the palace, and string courses of stone are also set in the walls for decorative purposes as baked bricks are elsewhere used. Position of the town.

On the edge of the plateau above is a ruined fort or palace called Kala-i-Kuk, built of sundried brick and pisé. The southern walls of this ancient palace in places rest upon revetments of stone built up from the scarped hill side to form a platform on which the fort was built. It speaks well for the Kala-i-Kuk.

Kakhas of ancient times that they had the energy and skill to raise such piles of mud walls on a site which at all times must have been far removed from water. Water seems to have always been a difficulty before the Hamun became established where it now is to be met with. In every watercourse on the slopes of the plateau there are dams of stones, the earth between which has long since disappeared. These could only have been built to retain water that flowed down the ravines after heavy rain had fallen.

Water-supply. There must necessarily have been wells in the town or within the outer walls and water must have been carried up to the top on donkeys, a wide road having been built to the summit of the plateau. The revetment of stones upon which it rested has fallen down in very many places, but there is a small section as yet in fair order which gives a very good idea of the kind of work it was when it was in good repair. The upper fort is at an elevation of 400 feet above the Hamun, and the upper part of the town on the slope about 200 feet above the lake. The hillsides immediately round the town are covered with graves built above ground.

The shrine. There is a shrine dedicated to Khwāja Ghaltan on the brow of the northern scarp whence a fine view over the lake towards the north can be obtained. Owing to the existence of the shrine there are a great number of modern graves upon the plateau near it.

The Darrah-i-Sokhta. The Darrah-i-Sokhta is a deep valley formed by ravines which have cut back into the plateau of the Koh-i-Khwaja, and up this valley there is a good path by means of which it is possible to ride up to the shrine.

Chahil Dukhtarān. Upon a sheer cliff overlooking this valley and the wide expanse of the Hamun towards the south and west there stands the ruins of a small but ancient building called Chahil Dukhtarān. It was fortified, and the remains of one of the towers that defended the entrance, which faced the east, show that there were two vaulted chambers in each tower, loopholed in the same way as those of Sār-o-Tār and Chahilburj. The arched entrance also shows exactly the same method of construction as the arches of the outer palace at Sār-o-Tār, having been formed with the same laminæ of thin sundried clay. This method of building is also to be met with in some ruins, which are undoubtedly most ancient, situated on the gravel terrace to the south of the Rud-i-Biyaban, among the vestiges of ancient canals that had once irrigated the lands around those ruins. This ruined building of Chahil Dukhtaran stood on a plinth of large stones laid in clay, and as there was a line of loopholes just above the plinth, the place was well protected from attack. An enclosure and huts built for stone and mud lie about 30 yards to the north of this ruin.

Legend about Chahil Dukhtarān. It is said that in bygone ages here lived 40 maidens whose voices and laughter could be distinctly heard by members of their family, who lived in

City of the Kak-hás, Koh-i-Khwaja--from the west.

an ancient fort which occupied the same site upon which modern Sehkoha was afterwards built. A distance of 25 miles separates the two places.

The city of Kakha is said to have been built in the days before Rustam, and to have been the residence of a chief who was at feud with the family of that hero. It was in the assault and capture of Kakha that the latter gave evidence of his future prowess. It is, however, not mentioned in history until the 15th century A.D., 9th and 10th century of the Hejira. The author of the Description of Herat, whose account of the fort of Tāk has been alluded to, mentions, with reference to Seistan, that it possessed a stronghold in an island in the Hamun. The unfortunate Malik, Muiz-ud-din Husen, Prince of Seistan, took refuge in it in 859 A. H., and maintained himself there for a short time until he was eventually forced to abandon the country by his own subjects, who by this means made peace with the Governor of Babar Mirza, the Timuride Prince of Herat, against whom the Prince of Seistan had rebelled. The same author also mentions that the stronghold was called the Fort of Rustam, a name that is still applied to it. After the death of Malik Husen, the fort and town were evidently abandoned, as the same author mentions it as being in a deserted condition when he wrote, forty years after the death of that ill-fated Prince. Later on, it seems to have been again re-peopled and to have served as a refuge in times of trouble when invasion was imminent. In these later times its position in the Hamun would render the island fairly secure from attack on all sides but the eastern, where the water that separated it from the mainland was both narrow, as well as not of great depth. This face of the island was defended by small redoubts loopholed for musketry or for arrows; these still exist and are undoubtedly of recent date. Traditional and historical references to Kakha.

Sehkoha is said to be an ancient site. The modern fort is very imposing, but in a condition of decay, only the citadel being repaired to some extent. It was acquired by the Sarbandi Chief some 100 or 150 years ago, from which all the present works date. This site was probably that of the ancient fortress of Rāskak. No trace of the latter exists, and it would be visible had it not been re-occupied and re-built. The modern fort is not mentioned in history until the 19th century. Description of Sehkoha.

NOTE.—The existence of dams in the ravines on the Koh-i-Khwaja, proves that when the city was built and inhabited, the rainfall in Seistan must have been greater than it is at the present day. The present scanty rainfall could not have filled the gorges or ravines above the dams. If this had been the case at that early period, no one would have been at pains to construct dams that were never likely to be of use. G. P. T.

CHAPTER XVII.

Description of the Mil-i-Kasamābād.

This interesting relic of the early prosperity of Seistan has been so often mentioned in preceding sections, that a detailed account of it has become necessary, and it is placed at the end of this section, as the ruin is itself quite distinct in type from others in the country.

Detailed description of the minaret and its site.

The Mil-i-Kāsamābād is so called because the village of Kāsamābād is closer to the ruined minaret than any other village in Seistan. The minaret has been broken down at its summit, and it is therefore impossible to say what its original height may have been. On the west side a great rift in the solid masonry extends for some 20 feet below the broken summit. The lower courses of brick as far as a man can reach have been picked out for fully a quarter of the thickness of the wall. The entrance also is now merely a hole, the arched doorway having been defaced by the wanton destruction that this building has been exposed to at the hands of the Seistanis. This great landmark stands upon the low ridge or Lurg on which Zāhidān was built, and it is four and a half miles to the north-west of the northern wall of the ruined city.

Subsidiary buildings.

As far as it is possible to make anything of the ruins which surround it, it appears to have stood at the southern angle of a courtyard with chambers or small apartments around it. These also extended along the western side of the courtyard. The orientation of the whole of these buildings is the same as that of the city of Zāhidān. The north-west face of the courtyard was occupied by a building of considerably greater size than the apartments which cluster round the base of the minaret. All these subsidiary buildings were, however, constructed with either sundried brick or " pisé," baked bricks having been sparingly used for purposes of ornamentation, mouldings and other architectural details. Even the arches which communicated between one dwelling and another were formed with unbaked bricks radiating from a centre, and the lower courses only of the walls of these dwellings had been built with baked brick; but the ground round the bases of the ruins and the minaret is so heaped up with the dissolved material of the buildings that the lower portions of the walls cannot be easily examined without excavating. A wall shut off the minaret and surrounding chambers from the courtyard. There seems to have been many buildings of small size all round this ruin, and in the days when it was built the intervening lands between the minaret and the city was probably a succession of houses amid cultivation and gardens, grouped on the banks of the canals that brought water from the Helmand to this tract of country.

To the north of the ruins around the minaret, which was also very thickly populated, the surface of the ground is covered with baked brick and pottery, and traces of ancient dwellings are everywhere visible. A mile distant from the minaret is a mound, which bears a little north of west of the former, formed by the ruins of a fortified dwelling, a manor house probably, held by some family of rank and wealth. The village of Kasamābād is situated a mile beyond this mound on the same bearing as that of the latter from the minaret. The residence of which the mound is formed occupied the north-western side of an open courtyard, and round the interior of the latter there ran a series of out-offices and quarters for the servants and dependants of the owner who lived with his family in the buildings that stood on the windward side of the court. These were two stories high, and beyond them again about 20 or 30 feet away an outer wall was built as a further protection, forming a covered way which probably was continued all round the walls of courtyard. The whole of these premises occupied an outside area of about 4,000 square feet. In the vicinity of this mound there are exposed plints of foundations, all of baked brick, which mark the positions of other dwellings which existed close to and surrounded the manor house. *Buildings in the neighbourhood.*

The highest fragment of the ruined minaret is 75 feet above the present ground level. Unlike the minaret inside the ruins of the inner city of Bina-i-Kai, the Mil-i-Kasamābād is almost a cylindrical tower, standing on a plinth 18 feet square, the shaft apparently tapering gradually towards the summit, the whole diameter of the circular tower at the bottom being 18 feet. The plinth is now only a foot or so above the heap of débris which surrounds this building and the adjoining ruins and which forms a mound several feet high around them. The bricks of the plinth are laid upright and form an ornamental course, which probably was carried round on the four sides to break the plain effect of the ordinary masonry. The entrance faced the north, and from the right of the opening a spiral and narrow staircase ascends the inside of the tower, making two complete turns in a height of about 60 feet. At the bottom a solid pillar once stood, but above this support which did not extend more than 10 feet above the ground, the stairs were built out of the wall. It has been destroyed and only a few inches of brickwork project in parts from the wall. *Dimensions of the minaret.*

On the outside the shaft is devoid of all ornamentation, except a broad band containing an inscription in Arabic characters which runs completely round the shaft between two lines of mouldings. The letters of the inscription are formed of baked bricks, especially moulded, the height of the letters being about 1½ feet. Above this the shaft rises with but little attempt at ornamentation, and close to the summit there is a second and smaller band of inscription, in Arabic characters, above which the minaret was richly decorated; the details are handsome, and although somewhat florid as to *Inscriptions on the minaret.*

design, are very artistic, and well executed in brick. Baked brick of a very excellent quality alone has been used. They are laid in headers and stretchers and the cement is the famous saruj, in this case of most excellent quality, the thin layers of cement between the bricks being harder than the bricks themselves.

The bricks which are used for the inscription and the details of ornamentation, with the exception of courses of plain mouldings, were evidently shaped when soft and carefully dried, and afterwards equally carefully baked. The portions of the Arabic letters having been separately moulded were put together by the architect who probably took an active share in the actual work. The general effect of the studied simplicity with merely a crown of ornamentation is very fine, and the artistic sense of the designer was evidently very well developed, and probably an inherited gift. In a work where decoration might easily have been carried to excess, the studied simplicity of the column is very remarkable and enhances by its contrast the rich effect of the decorative work near the summit.

Action of the weather on the minaret.

The action of the weather is very well exemplified in the state of the inscriptions and architectural detail which encircle the minaret. The portion exposed to the wind of 120 days is in much better order than the portion on the opposite side of the column. The wind has wrought much less damage to this portion than the others have suffered from being exposed on the east and south to the heat of the sun which alternating with the cold of winter has disintegrated to some extent the lettering and architectural detail.

The upper part of the minaret also seems to have been less affected by the grinding action of the wind-borne sand which has smoothed the surface of the building below a certain height; and in this case, as also where other lofty buildings exist, there seems to be indications that the sand or dust does not attain to a height of more than about a few feet above ground level even when impelled by the strongest wind, while the grits and coarse sand that are such an unpleasant feature in the periods of strongest wind probably do not affect any object more than 10 or 15 feet at the very outside above ground level. The people of the country say that the "strength of the wind is greatest close to the surface."

Translation of the inscriptions in the minaret by A. G. Ellis, Esq., of the British Museum.

The inscriptions contain the names of two of the former Maliks of Seistan. The following remarks have been taken from a note on the inscriptions by A. G. Ellis, Esq., of the British Museum, to whose courtesy the author of this memoir has been greatly indebted for translation of such inscriptions as have hitherto been discovered in Seistan :—" The lower inscription on the minaret bears the name of Táj-ud-din, Abu'l Fazl-i-Nasr, and the upper that of his great-grandson Táj-ud-din Harab. The elder Táj-ud-din presumably died leaving his minaret unfinished. According to the Arab historial Ibn-al-Athir his death took place in A. H. 559." The elder Táj-ud-din reigned 80

Mîl-i-Kasimābād (minaret) materials baked brick & "sārūj" mortar (11th century A.D.)

(Part III to face page 270.)

THE RUINS IN SEISTAN.

years; and owing to the downfall of his Suzerain, the Saljuk Sultan Sanjar, having occurred later in his reign, it is possible he commenced to build this minaret towards the close of his life and reign. His great-grandson Táj-ud-din Harab died in 612 A. H. But as this period was one of great unrest and as the affairs of Seistan were in a very unsettled and confused state it seems wonderful that the younger Táj-ud-din could have completed any great work during his lifetime or reign.

This minaret, therefore, dates from about the middle period of the 6th century of the Hejira or about the last quarter of the 12th century of the Christian era. It cannot in any case be referred to any period later than the first half of the following century.

The minaret was evidently built as a pious work and it must have formed part of a religious establishment founded in the ages preceding these dates by some well-known spiritual guide. The smaller chambers were probably occupied by the priests, who managed the affairs of the foundation and who formed a college where a religious and general education was afforded. The premises included a school, and the largest of the mounds at the north-western end of the courtyard probably marks the position of a Masjid used for prayer and for instruction also. *The object of the minaret.*

Compared with the Takht-i-Pul bridge, the minaret shows a great advance in engineering skill. The walls of the latter at the base are not more than $3\frac{1}{2}$ feet thick as far as it is possible to measure them owing to the destruction wrought by human hands. This is attributed to the people of the country who were attracted by the excellent material used in its construction. *Comparison of the minaret with the Takht-i-Pul.*

Compared with the minaret, the bridge appears to have been a much older structure, completed at a time when knowledge in respect to building was in a more elementary stage.

A very interesting comparison is made in the published account of the labours of the Mission of 1872 between the Mil-i-Kasamábád and a similar building in the country to the north of Seistan. "Five miles from Sabzawar stands the minar of Khasru-gird already alluded to, a very remarkable round tower about 120 feet high, built of baked brick with a flight of interior steps leading to the summit only, wide enough to admit one man. Round its exterior the bricks are arranged at intervals so as to form a Kufic inscription. It is in excellent repair though of considerable antiquity and stands on a square foundation still prefectly sound, and which is now (1871-72) exposed to a depth of about 6 feet. The bricks of which it is constructed are joined together with gach (mortar) and in appearance it reminded us much of the tower we had seen at Kasimabad in Seistan (Eastern Persia), Volume 1, page 374." It is doubtful, however, whether the minaret of Kasamábád could ever have attained to that height of 120 feet. One hundred feet must have been at the outside the height of the building in Seistan. *This minaret compared with that on Sabzawar.*

CALCUTTA
SUPERINTENDENT GOVERNMENT PRINTING, INDIA
8, HASTINGS STREET

Charon, the Mission-camp Ferryman and his craft.

End of Part III.

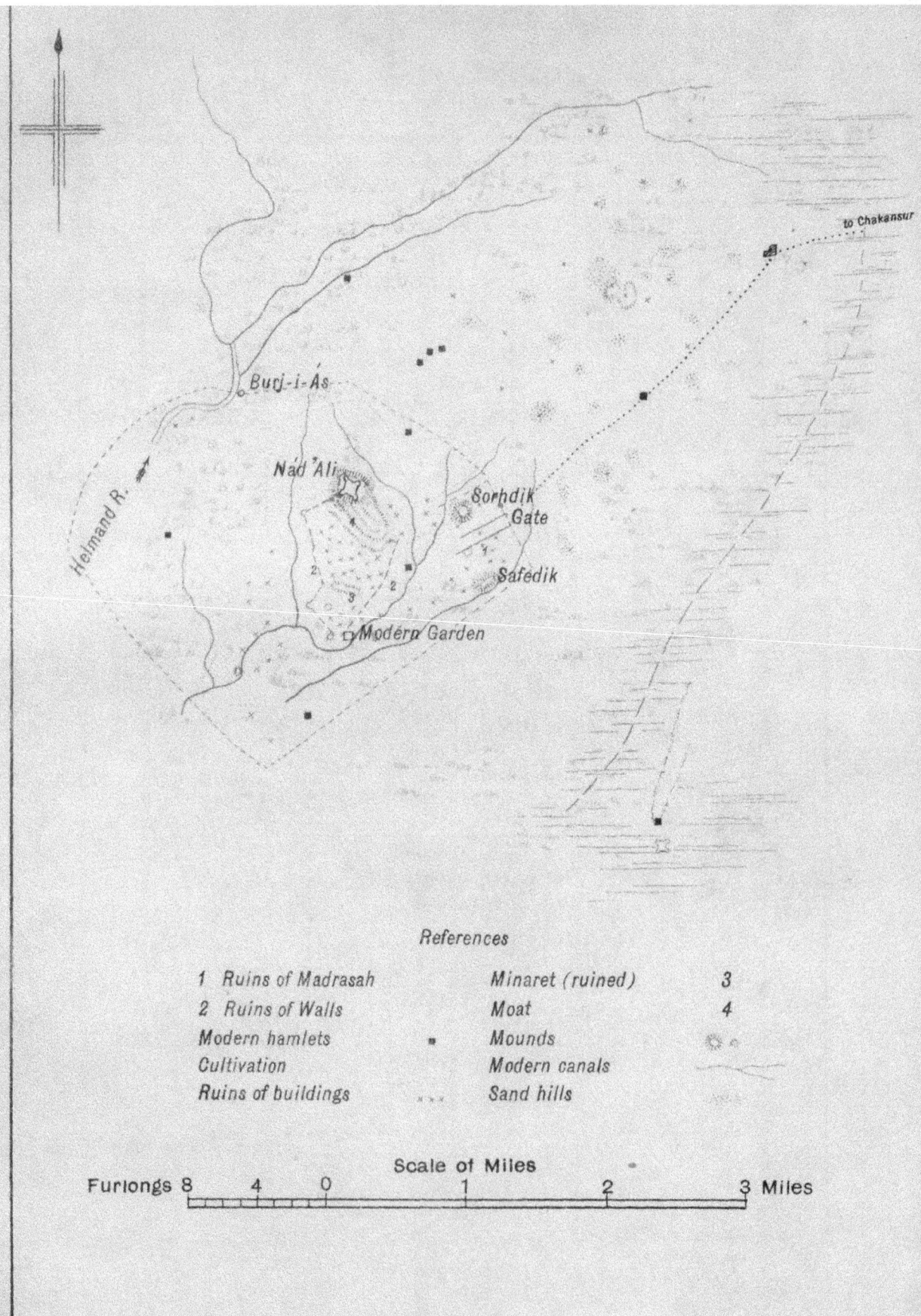

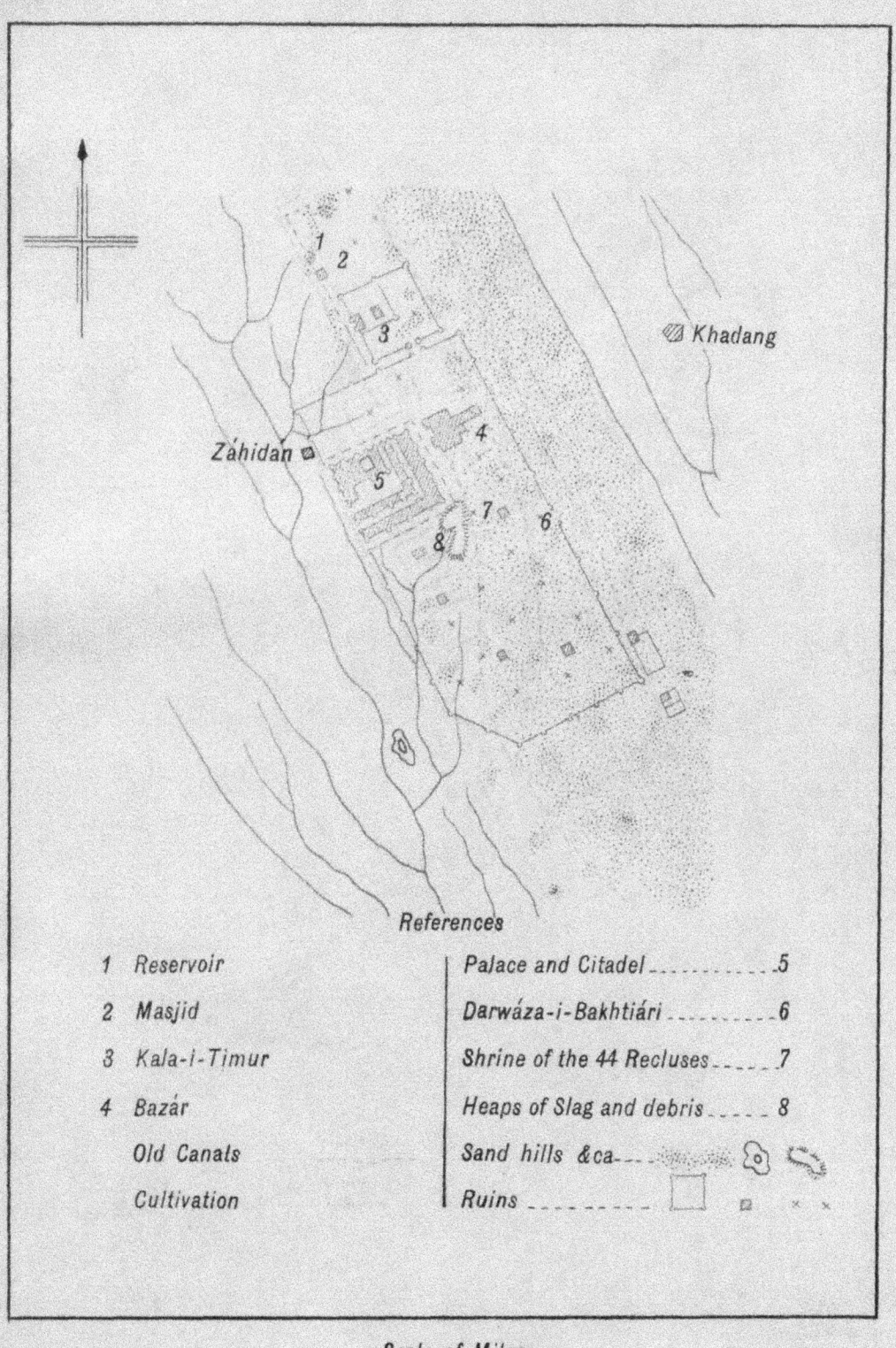# PLAN OF ZÁHIDÁN

References

1. Reservoir
2. Masjid
3. Kala-i-Timur
4. Bazár
   Old Canats
   Cultivation

Palace and Citadel 5
Darwáza-i-Bakhtiári 6
Shrine of the 44 Recluses 7
Heaps of Slag and debris 8
Sand hills &ca.
Ruins

Scale of Miles

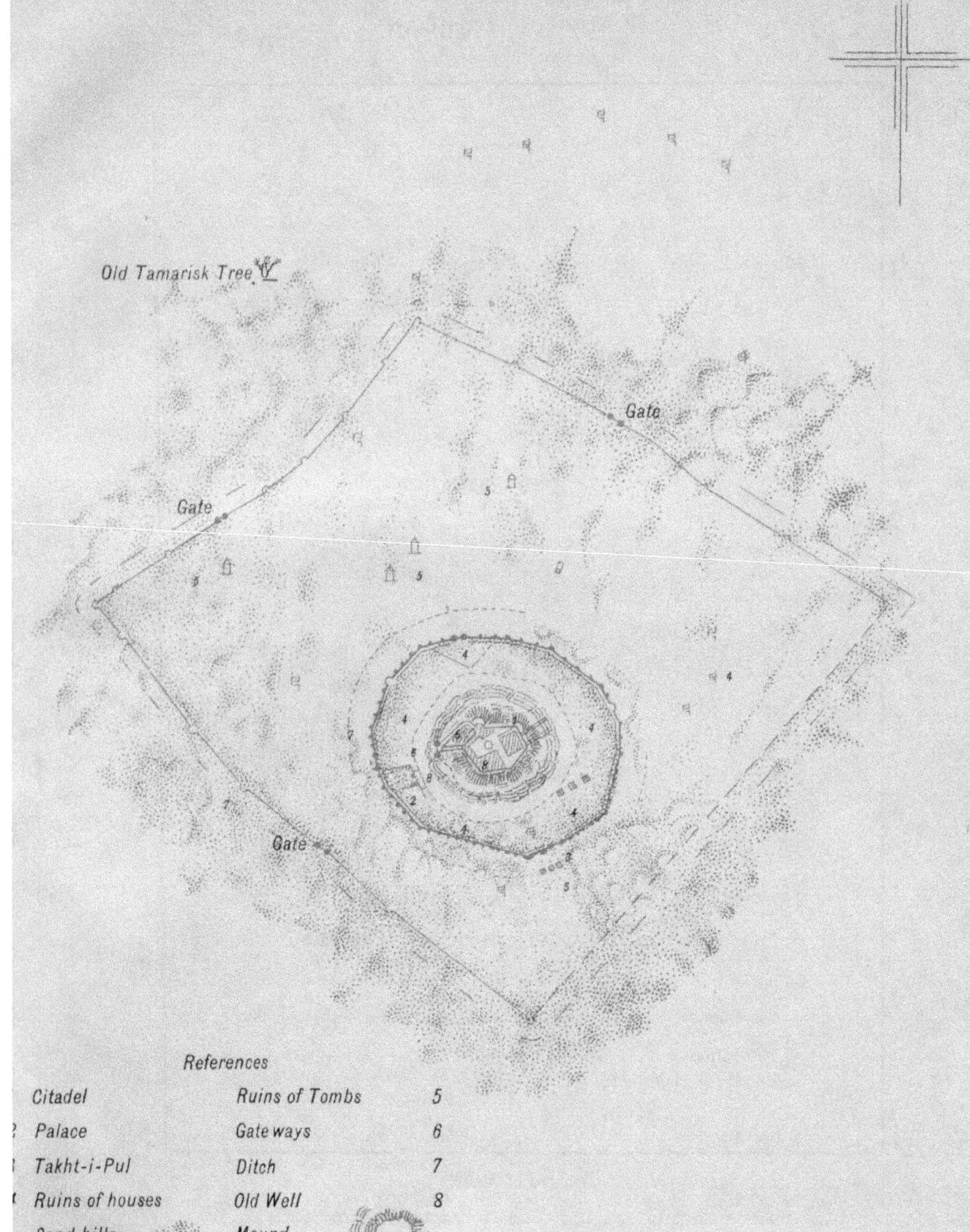

References

1 Citadel
2 Palace
3 Takht-i-Pul
4 Ruins of houses
   Sand hills

5 Ruins of Tombs
6 Gateways
7 Ditch
8 Old Well
   Mound

SEISTAN

A MEMOIR ON THE HISTORY, TOPOGRAPHY, RUINS, AND PEOPLE OF THE COUNTRY

Part IV

SEISTAN

A MEMOIR ON THE HISTORY, TOPOGRAPHY, RUINS, AND
PEOPLE OF THE COUNTRY

IN FOUR PARTS

PART IV

THE PEOPLE OF SEISTAN

AGENTS FOR THE SALE OF BOOKS

PUBLISHED BY THE

Superintendent of Government Printing, India, Calcutta.

IN ENGLAND.

Constable & Co., 10, Orange Street, Leicester Square, W. C.

Kegan Paul, Trench, Trübner & Co., 68-74, Carter Lane, E. C.

Bernard Quaritch, 11, Grafton Street, New Bond Street, W.

P. S. King & Son, 2 & 4, Great Smith Street, Westminster.

H. S. King & Co., 65, Cornhill, and 9, Pall Mall, London.

Grindlay & Co., 54, Parliament Street, London, S. W.

T. Fisher Unwin, 1, Adelphi Terrace, London, W. C.

W. Thacker & Co., 2, Creed Lane, London, E. C.

B. H. Blackwell, 50 & 51, Broad Street, Oxford.

Deighton, Bell & Co., Cambridge.

Luzac & Co., 46, Great Russell Street, London, W. C.

ON THE CONTINENT.

Otto Harrassowitz, Leipzig.

R. Friedlander & Sohn, 11, Carlstrasse, Berlin, W. N.

Karl W. Hiersemann, Leipzig.

Ernest Leroux, 28, Rue Bonaparte, Paris.

Martinus Nijhoff, The Hague, Holland.

IN INDIA.

Thacker, Spink & Co., Calcutta and Simla.

Newman & Co., Calcutta.

R. Cambray & Co., Calcutta.

S. K. Lahiri & Co., Calcutta.

B. Banerjee & Co., Calcutta.

The Calcutta School Book and Useful Literature Society, 1, Wellington Square, Calcutta.

Butterworth & Co. (India), Limited, Calcutta.

The Weldon Library, 18-5, Chowringhee Road, Calcutta.

Higginbotham & Co., Madras.

V. Kalyanarama Aiyar & Co., Madras.

G. A. Natesan & Co., Madras.

S. Murthy & Co., Madras.

Thompson & Co., Madras.

Temple & Co., Madras.

Combridge & Co., Madras.

P. R. Rama Iyer & Co., Madras.

Thacker & Co., Ld., Bombay.

A. J. Combridge & Co., Bombay.

D. B. Taraporevala, Sons & Co., Bombay.

Radhabai Atmaram Sagoon, Bombay.

Sunder Pandurang, Bombay.

Gopal Narayan & Co., Bombay.

Ram Chandra Govind & Son, Kalbadevi, Bombay.

Superintendent, American Baptist Mission Press, Rangoon.

Rai Sahib M. Gulab Singh & Sons, Mufid-i-Am Press, Lahore and Calcutta.

N. B. Mathur, Superintendent, Nazir Kanun Hind Press, Allahabad.

A. Chand & Co., Lahore, Punjab.

A. M. & J. Ferguson, Ceylon.

S. C. Talukdar, Proprietor, Students and Company, Cooch Behar.

Manager, Educational Book Depôts, Nagpur and Jubbulpore.*

Manager, Imperial Book Depôt, 63, Chandney Chauk Street, Delhi.*

Manager, *East Coast News*, Vizagapatam.*

Manager, "The Agra Medical Hall and Co-operative Association, Limited" (Successors to A. John & Co., Agra).*

T. K. Seetharama Aiyar, Kumbakonam.*

Superintendent, Basel Mission Book and Tract Depository, Mangalore.*

P. Varadachary & Co., Madras.*

H. Liddell, Printer, etc., 7, South Road, Allahabad.*

D. C. Anand & Sons, Peshawar.*

* Agents for sale of the Legislative Department publications.

SEISTAN

A MEMOIR ON THE HISTORY, TOPOGRAPHY, RUINS, AND PEOPLE OF THE COUNTRY

IN FOUR PARTS

By Mr. G. P. TATE, M.R.A.S., F.R.G.S.
SURVEY OF INDIA

Author of
Kalat : a Memoir of the Country and Family of the
Ahmadzai Khans of Kalat

PART IV

THE PEOPLE OF SEISTAN

CALCUTTA
SUPERINTENDENT GOVERNMENT PRINTING, INDIA
1912

Part IV

THE PEOPLE OF SEISTAN

TAJIK, JAT, ? GUJAR, AND ? AHIR

PREFACE

SINCE this part has been in the press, I have obtained Professor Olufsen's recent work entitled the Emir of Bokhara and his Country, which contains (with other information of very great value) a most instructive account of that ancient Iranian race, the Tajik, which he found occupying the valleys of the eastern and mountainous districts of Bokhara as well as the open country in the western portion: I have taken the liberty of including the Professor's account of the Tajiks in Appendix III.

I regret that I have been unable to procure a copy of M. Ujfalvy's work Les Aryans au nord au Sud de l'Hindou Kusch, which would have been invaluable for reference.

G. P. TATE.

SEISTAN:

A Memoir on the History, Topography, Ruins, and People of the Country.

ERRATA.

PART I.

Page 2—Note, 3rd line from top, after *Dr. Gerard* insert a comma.
" 3—13th line from bottom, after *Afrasiyab*, delete *and*.
" 4—18th line from bottom, for *Rustom* read *Rustam*.
" 5—Note, 3rd para., 5th line from bottom, after *where* read *a*.
" 8—5th line from top, for *was* read *war*.
" 10—2nd para., 1st line, for *Ardeshar* read *Ardeshir*.
" 11—3rd para., 12th line from top, for *latter* read *later*.
" 12—11th line from bottom, for *Khuspast* read *Khuspas*.
" "—Note, bottom line, delete *in*.
" 13—16th line from top, insert a comma after *Yazdigerd*.
" 15—18th line from top, delete *a* after *which*.
" " —22nd line from top, delete second *a* in *manager*.
" 16—6th line from top, for *may be* read *may have been*.
" " —15th line from bottom, for *Memo* read *Meno*.
" 18—12th line from top, after *time* read *a*.
" 21—25th line from top, for *the acts of Khalaf* read *the early acts*, etc.
" " —13th line from bottom, delete brackets.
" 22—13th line from bottom, for *building* read *buildings*.
" 23—3rd line from bottom, for *Political stage* read *political stage*.
" " —2nd line from bottom, for *Mahamud* read *Mahmud*.
" 25—4th para., 4th line from bottom, for *factions* read *factious*.
" " —3rd line from bottom, for *five* read *four*.
" 26—12th line from bottom, for *Saljueks* read *Saljuks*.
" 27—1st line, delete *semi-colon* after *Kirman*.
" " —4th line from bottom of text, insert *a* before *conspiracy*.
" 28—20th line from top, delete *semi-colon* after *Mono-Machus*.

Page 29—Note, last para, but one, for (9) read (11), for *nine districts* read *eleven*, etc.; delete comma after *Zerkuh*.
" 31—19th line from bottom, delete comma after *Nasirud-din*.
" 34—5th line from bottom, delete *the* before *Salzawār*.
" 49—13th line from top, delete comma after *Shah*.
" 53—6th line from top, delete *the* before *faggots*.
" 59—Wherever occurring, for *Amir Zādah* read *Amirzada*.
" 60—15th line from bottom, for *Samark* read *Samarkand*.
" 61—10th line from top, for *Mazzaffar* read *Muzaffar*.
" 66—8th line from bottom, for *Shāks* read *Shāhs*.
" 68—15th line from bottom, for *olion harp* read *aeolian harp*.
" 73—13th line from bottom, for *Malik Zadāhs* read *Malikzadāhs*.
" 78—13th line from top, for *the followers* read *their followers*.
" 79—Note, 2nd line from top, for *Kilij Khan* read *Khilij Khan*.
" " —Note, 14th line from top, for *Khānsi* read *Khānshi*.
" " —Note, 6th line from bottom, for *Musrat Khan* read *Nusrat Khan*.
" 80—For *Chapter IV* read *Chapter V*.
" 87—2nd line from bottom, for *Maemud* read *Mahmud*.
" 88—For *Bira Ma'ali Khan*, read *Biram Ali Khan*.
" " —4th line from bottom, for *Zi-i-Haj* read *Zil-Haj*.
" 89—10th line from top, for *differs* read *differ*.
" 90—2nd line from top, delete *semi-colon* after *adjusted*.
" 91—9th line from top, delete *semi-colon* after *person*.
" 93—Note, last line, for *Shaharkis* read *Shahrakis*.
" 95—17th line from top, for *note* read *Part*.
" " —15th line from bottom, for *Calif* read *Caliph*.
" 96—9th line from bottom, delete *semi-colon* after *ostentation*.

PART II.

Page 107—12th line from bottom, delete *as* after *country*.
" 109—18th line from top, for *deepest channel* read *deep cut*.
" 110—3rd line from top, after *further away* read *the*.
" " —10th line from top, for *divided* read *divides*.
" 111—17th line from bottom, for *coarse* read *coarser*.
" " —15th line from bottom, for *each* read *beach*.
" 122—17th line from bottom, delete *were* before *wrote*.
" 123—19th line from bottom, for *the preceding alternative* read *an*.

Page 129—2nd line from top, after *plateau* read *which*.
" 134—9th line from bottom, for *Deh Khālkdād* read *Deh Khālikdād*.
" " —last line of page, for *up* after *plain* read *to*.
" 139—19th line from bottom, for *summit* read *summits*.
" 141—5th line from top, for *skeleton* read *skeletons*.
" 142—1st line of page, for *hypothesis*, read *hypotheses*.
" 144—last line of page, for *feature* read *features*.
" 145—15th line from top, for *This* after *Sena Rud* read *Then*.

PART II—contd.

Page 148—last line of page, for *Sona Rud* read *Sena Rud*.
" " —Note, for *Bina-i-kair* read *Bina-i-Kai*.
" 153—20th line from bottom, after *ruins* read *or not of*.
" 156—Marginal reference, instead of *A. D. 1385* read *A. D. 1383-84*.
" 157—19th line from bottom, for *narrowed* after *bed* read *narrows*.
" 159—12th line from top, for *Seistani* read *Seistants*.
" 160—22nd line from bottom, for *the district* read *this district*.

Page 162—2nd line from bottom, for *foundations* read *foundation*.
" 163—10th line from top, for *right of* read *right or*.
" 165—4th line from bottom, for *Nasirabad* read *Nastrabad*.
" 172—8th line from top, for "*Pooljee*" read "*Poolgee*."
" 173—19th line from top, for *Baluch* read *Kashâni*.
" 175—1st line of page, for *east* read *west*.
" 177—Note, last line, insert *in* before *1845*.

PART III.

Page 183—15th line from top, after *they* read *also*.
" 184—15th line from top, for *Dasht-i-Zirreh* read *Dasht-i-Zireh*.
" 188—19th line from bottom, for *other Indian people* read *another Indian people*.
" 192—5th line from top, for *annalei* read *annali*.
" 195—5th line from top, for *except* read *besides*.
" 196—17th line from top, for *Zarang* read *Zaranj*.
" 207—8th line from top, for *course* read *courses*.
" 209—2nd line from top, after *of* read *a*.
" 211—1st line of page, delete *also*.
" 214—2nd para., 4th line from end, after *that* read *dynasty came to an end;* and for *had been* read *was*.
" " —12th line from bottom of page, read *the* before *darkness*.

Page 217—3rd line from bottom, after *by* read *a*.
" 220—18th line from top, for *palace* read *palaces*.
" 222—12th line from bottom, for *dependent* read *dependants*.
" 223—5th line from bottom, for *or* read *of* after *traditions*.
" 232—6th line from bottom, for *1,720* read *1,702*.
" 239—18th line from top, delete *all* before *round*.
" 244—3rd line from top, for *berm*, substitute *banquette*.
" 247—11th line from bottom, delete *also* following *Tradition*.
" 253—19th line from bottom, insert *as* after *well;* and delete *as* following *country*.
" 254—2nd para., 4th line from top, for *Latin* read *Greek*.
" 260—4th line from bottom, instead of *for* before *stone* read *of*.

"The Old Arbab —Seif-ud-din.

(Frontispiece Part IV.)

THE PEOPLE OF SEISTAN.

CHAPTER I.

INTRODUCTORY.

IT would have been very interesting if, during the residence of the Seistan Mission from 1903-1905 in that country, it had been practicable to undertake and record anthropometrical measurements even on a very limited scale. Extensive researches in this direction assuredly would have given opportunities to interested and ill-disposed persons to create a panic among the people : but measurements of even a few selected individual types would have been valuable, forming a link between researches carried on in India and in Central Asia.

The value of anthropometrical observations in Seistan.

In drawing up this brief account of the people of Seistan, the legends collected by me during many years of travel and residence among the tribes dealt with here have been placed on record, and such conclusions as these legends admit of and which are reasonable have been drawn from the information recorded. These conclusions are perhaps not less securely founded than they would have been if based on anthropometry alone.[1]

I venture to give in this place two instances of the light which tribal legends sometimes cast on the origin of the tribes by whom they have been preserved. It is very many years ago that I travelled on duty from Ajmir

---

[1] The usually accepted belief that the form of the head is " an extremely constant and persistent character, which resists the influence of climate and physical surroundings " (The People of India. Sir H. Risley, 1908, p. 26) appears to be disproved by the researches of Franz Boas, Professor of Anthropology in Columbia University. In Maclure's Magazine, Volume XXXV : May 1910, there appears an article entitled " The skulls of our immigrants, " It gives an account of the researches of the Professor and his assistants in a popular form, and the results are summarised in these words—" Short-headed Jews becoming long-headed, and long-headed Sicilians becoming short-headed. Fundamental changes in physical type." The proportions of the human skull appear to alter as the other proportions of the human frame are seen to do under the influence of environment.

The spread of Islam in Asia broke down the barriers, if any ever had existed in ancient times, to intermarriage on an extensive scale between the races inhabiting the regions in which it has become the religion of the people, and has undoubtedly brought about a fusion of type in the present-day population, the distinctions between the various sections or parts of which are now more political and occupational than racial.

274 THE PEOPLE OF SEISTAN.

Proposed identification of the Or or Oḍ with the ancient Oritai.

across the southern part of the Mārwār (Jodhpore) State, to the borders of Sind—the Tharr and Parkar District. In the Sanchor District of Mārwār I encountered several very large groups of a wandering tribe named Or or Oḍ.[1] These persons understood the vernacular of the country in which they lived though possibly speaking their own peculiar language among themselves, and in reply to inquiries as to their place of origin the headmen said that once upon a time they had been a "Rāj" in the country in which Hinglāz is situated. Rāj is a word used to denote possession of the soil and political influence; and Hinglāz is the celebrated shrine, a place of pilgrimage for Hindus at the present day. This shrine is on the right bank of the Hingol river, inside a defile through which its waters pass out of the last range of mountains just before reaching the Sea of Oman. The name Or survives, at the present day, in the names of Ormāra, a sea-side town or village, near the mouth of the Hingol, and in Hor Kalat,[2] a village in the Kolwa valley about 50 miles north-west of Ormāra. This is the tract of country in which, according to Arrian, Alexander encountered the Oritai. Are the Or or Oḍ, then, the modern representatives of that people? Hinglāz is about 100 miles by road, from the western boundary of Sind and in Las Bela territory. The locality at one time occupied by the Or or Oḍ is clearly designated and the tract of country at one time held by them extends to the borders of the Kej District: the identification of the modern Or or Oḍ with the Oritai rests on a better foundation than that of a similarity of names alone.

The legend of Khwāja Amrān in Seistan also throws considerable light on the origin of the Kashānis, a tribe, portions of which are spread over the country from Seistan to Kalat, and from the Panjgur district to Kandahar in Southern Afghanistan. Amrān is said to have been the son of Hamza (Uncle of Muhammad, the founder of Islam) and granddaughter of Naushirwān. Adopting the life of a religious teacher Amrān wandered over many lands, but settled at last in Seistan where he built a Rabāt. His neighbours were an infidel race called the Ashg-ka-Putra, the seat of whose chief

---

[1] Oḍ—a wandering tribe whose proper home appears to be in Western Hindustan * * * wandering about with their families in search of employment on earthwork. They will not as a rule take petty jobs, but prefer small contracts on roads, canals, railways, and the like, or will build a house of adobe and dig a tank or even a well * * * . They eat anything and everything, and though not unfrequently Mussalmans, especially in the West, are always outcast. They have a speech of their own called Oḍki of which I know nothing, but which is very probably nothing more than the ordinary dialect of their place of origin. They wear woollen clothes, or at least one woollen garment. They claim descent from one Bhagīrat who vowed never to drink twice out of the same well, and so dug a fresh one every day till one day he dug down and down and never came up again. It is in mourning for him that they wear wool, and in imitation of him they bury their dead even when Hindu, though they marry by the Hindu ceremony. Till the reappearance of Bhagīrat they will, they say, remain outcasts. They are said to claim Rajput, or Kshatriya, and to come from Marwar. They worship Rama and Siva. Punjab Ethnography, 1883, Chapter VI, § 573.

[2] Hor Kalat, the Fort of Hor, or the Hor (? the Or or Oḍ).

was Sār-o-Tar; but the chief being a minor his uncle acted as regent and dwelt in the fort of Chahilburj, not far from Amrān's Rabāt. There was war between the latter and his infidel neighbours; and one day they surprised the holy man while he was engaged in prayer with his sister and his slave, and the three perished at the hands of the infidels. The shrine of Khwāja Amrān in Seistan is carefully avoided at the present day by the Kashānis: while all the other inhabitants of Seistan pray to Amrān, no Kashāni dares to approach the shrine lest some dreadful misfortune befall him. The reason is this: the Kashānis are the direct descendants of the Ashg-ka-putras who slew the holy Amrān, and the impiety and sacrilege of their ancestors for ever debar the Kashānis from participating in the good offices of the martyr.

The story of Amrān casts a light on the Origin of the Kashānis.

Ashg-ka-Putra is an Aryan form of the term Bani Ashg, a name which Muhammadan chroniclers apply to the Parthians, and we may therefore infer from this legend—which is firmly believed by all the people of Seistan, the Kashānis included—that the latter are the descendants of the Parthians (or Indo-Parthians), and that they were still powerful in Seistan at so late a date as the early years of Islām.

With regard to the possibility of Hinduism having been professed at any time in Seistan, it should be remarked that no legend other than that of Shispāl was obtained in that country on which to base a conclusion. On the site of Sār-o-Tār, however, I picked up a seal of small size on which two Indian humped cattle and two characters of an Indian (? Sanscrit) script resembling Nāgari, were incised. I also saw more than one seal similar to but larger than that which I myself found, which, it was said, had been obtained in the ruins of Sār-o-Tār. But this place had been inhabited down to the end of the 14th century, and the seals may have been the property of Indian traders or others resident there.

The Hindu Religion in Seistan doubtful.

Of Buddhism no remains have been discovered in Seistan, in the country of Panjgur, or in Kej. Among the ruins near Sār-o-Tār certain ruins viewed at a distance appeared to resemble stupas. They were, however, not large. One which was examined was built with kiln-burnt bricks, but Arbāb Seif-ud-din said it had been a granary filled through an opening on the top; as excavations could not be made, no proof of this could be obtained. In the country adjoining Seistan there are, however, certain localities to which legends are attached, or which have names that would almost suggest that they were connected with the legends of Nāgas—deities of springs—which are mentioned so frequently in the translations of the records of the famous Chinese Pilgrims who visited India in the 5th and 7th century A.D. In two places, at Spintizha near Gulistan in the Peshin District, and

Buddhist remains and legends.

at Hulmargh to the east of Khārān, legends of a great serpent were discovered, and at each place there is a famous perennial spring. In the Panjgur and Kej Districts and in the Bolida valley between the two, there are localities named Nāg, at each of which there are strong perennial springs which have never been known to fail. One of these localities is about 80 miles to the east of Panjgur, the other about 40 miles to the east of Kej; and the third at the foot of the Zāmrān hills about 22 miles to the north-west of the fort of Chib in the Bolida valley. No other localities bearing this name exist in those districts, and these are not the only springs in the country the waters of which do not fail.

Super-terrene method of sepulture. Super-terrene interment of the dead is a custom that was once prevalent in Seistan but which has been discontinued recently. In it perhaps may be discerned the lingering influence of the Zoroastrian religion.[1] The sepulchres of the wealthier classes or families used in more remote times to be constructed with kiln-baked brick and mortar. A platform often of considerable dimensions was built, and on it the corpses were laid and enclosed with walls and roofs of the same material. The tops of the graves thus built up are undecorated and form a level platform about 2½ feet above the lower platform on which corpses reposed. The larger collections of super-terrene graves are open to the sky, but small groups of tombs were usually placed inside a mausoleum covered with a domed roof.

Still practised among an Afghan tribe. The custom of super-terrene sepulture is said to be followed still by some tribes of the Kakar Afghans of the Zhob. A hole is left by them in the tomb next to the feet of the corpse, and it is said that on certain days the bereaved members of the family assemble to mourn the dead. In a detached masonry tomb at Chaharshahr a similar opening, about 8 inches square was found to have been left in the masonry wall nearest to the feet of the corpse. The use of masonry for such sepulchres appears to have ceased when this material was no longer in common use in Seistan, probably about 500 years ago. The masonry sepulchres at Chaharshahr are very probably more than 500 years old; dating from a period anterior to the sack of Zahidān (January 1384). Close to these sepulchres are several wells lined with masonry. The more recent super-terrene sepulchres are constructed with sun-dried brick and clay mortar; both exposed to the sky and also within domed mausolea. The former are of course very liable to destruction; the more exposed sepulchres have been eroded away in the course of time, and the skeletons they once concealed are now exposed to view, as in the ruins of Ghulghula.[2]

---

[1] To prevent contact of the unclean corpse with the earth?

[2] I opened several of the masonry tombs but in every case I found only dust and a few small crumbling fragments of bones, conclusive proof of the antiquity of this class of tomb.

The adobe tombs always contained skeletons, some quite complete and in some cases fragments of the bier were recognisable.

The method of burial was to place the bier in position and to build up the tomb enclosing the bier and corpse.

A Seistani Potter.

(Part IV to face Page 277.)

The discontinuance of this method of interment is probably due to the influx of immigrants; but also to the fact that it is far easier to dig a hole in the ground and to put away a corpse inside it and then to fill in the hole, than it would be to erect a tomb above ground. The last case of super-terrene sepulchre took place in 1903; when Malik Gulzár Khan died and was buried in such a tomb. *Possible reason for its discontinuance.*

In respect to the orientation of the super-terrene tombs the custom enjoined by Islam is followed.

In the ancient cemetery at the back of the ruined city of the Kak-has on the slope of the Kuh-i-Khwaja, the super-terrene sepulchres have been built up with stones, which were kept in place by clay mortar. This method of disposing of the dead was at one time generally practised, and was not confined to the higher classes. *Super-terrene sepulchres on Koh-Khurja.*

CHAPTER II.

Tajik or East Iranian Stock.

THE Tajik wherever he is found in Khurassan is regarded as the original owner of the soil and as the representative at the present day of the original inhabitants of that great province. In the Tajik population we perhaps may find the descendants of that East-Iranian, or Aryan race, which was known to the Chinese as the Ta-hia, and which occupied those tracts where agriculture was possible, and formed a dense population in the country on both banks of the Oxus, and throughout the whole of Khurassan, up to the time of the inroads of the hordes of Chingiz Khan, in the first quarter of the 13th century A.D.

"From the annals of Chang Kien we learn that the Ta-hia or Bactrians were very like the other tribes between Ferghana and An-si (Parthia). These people all spoke various dialects, but all understood one another; they were agricultural, treated their wives with exaggerated respect, and allowed them great liberty, and were all distinguished by deep-set eyes and thick beards. They were bad and cowardly soldiers, and only fond of trade."[1]

Appearance and habits.

Devotion to a settled life in village communities and peaceful occupations have always been the leading characteristic of this race; and this as well as their handsome physiognomy noticed by the Chinese envoy more than two thousand years ago, have also attracted the attention of a recent traveller.[2]

"I remember hearing a Russian say that it was the preponderance of Tajik blood in Bokhara which led that Khanate to submit to the Czar without a struggle."[3]

And again:

"The Tajik carries the palm for good looks, at least according to our ideas of beauty. He has the dark, expressive eye and the regular features of his Persian ancestors."[4]

Tajik an uncomplimentary term.

The predilection of the Tajik for a life of peaceful occupations has always placed him on the side of law and order, and has rendered him easy to govern. It has, however, made him a bad soldier; and in oriental chronicles the word Tajik is used in an uncomplimentary sense to denote a man of peace; a mere civilian—a *Pékin*.

---

[1] Bactria from the earliest times to the extinction of Bactrio-Greek Rule in the Punjab. The Hare University Prize Essay, 1908; by H. G. Rawlinson, M.A. Also Early History of India, Vincent Smith, London 1908, 2nd Edition, pages 234 and 258. See Appendix III, p. 373.

Chang Kien was an envoy from the Chinese Court to the Yuch-Chi. He returned to his native land after various adventures in about 125 B.C.—Early History of India.

[2] In Russian Turkestan; a garden of Asia and its people, by Annette M. B. Meakin, author of "A Ribbon of Iron." Fellow of the Anthropological Institute of Great Britain and Ireland, London, 1903.

Also see the description of the Tajiks in the Valley of the Oxus (Badakhshan) by Captain John Wood in his mission to discover the sources of the Oxus.

[3] *Ibid*, page 9.

[4] *Ibid*, page 10.

Photo. by Ganga Singh. Photo. Engraved & printed at the Offices of the Survey of India, Calcutta, 1912.
(1) (2)
Muhammad, Dadi (1) and his coadjutor (2).

(Part IV to face page 279.)

Notwithstanding this love of peace few oriental races have proved more enduring than the Tajik. Wherever there is land which can be cultivated, and where water can be brought to it, the Tajik has clung to the soil which his forefathers have tilled. Bad government, or the absence of any sort of government, has failed to utterly exterminate this people, or to drive them from the land. They have bowed to the inroads of Scythian and Turkish tribes; the Greek and Arab conquerors to whom the Tajik has been subject have lost their identity and have become absorbed into the mass of the population of the countries they subdued, but the Tajik remains a distinct race still.[1]

Enduring character of this race.

The operations of agriculture and the science of irrigation were matters in which the Tajik specialised. The desert-born Arab conquerors, without experience of these matters, were glad to leave such affairs, and the revenue administration of the subdued countries, in the hands of the unwarlike Tajik, while retaining in their more practised hands the conduct of military operations, and the control of political relations. The Greek soldiers perhaps may have done so; but the rude Turkish conquerors, and later the Mongols, certainly did so. The Tajik, therefore, was at all times a most useful person, and the most abandoned oriental government would hesitate from pushing oppression to a point which would drive the long-suffering and peaceful Tajik from the soil.

Value of the Tajik.

The various masters to which this race has been subjected have left an impress, in a greater or lesser degree, upon it. But while the physique and the features of this ancient Iranian race may have been affected, they have preserved their character and their language practically unchanged through the vicissitudes of time. To-day their mother-tongue is Persian. Whether they be called Deh-kān, Dehwār, Arbāb, Tajik, Tāt or Sart[2] they are practically unchanged and are Farsiwān—Persian men—as distinguished from the nomad tribes of Turk, Mongol, or "Afghan" origin to whom they are subject. The Tajik is of course conversant with the languages of his overlords. In addition to a knowledge of agriculture, this race possesses a very considerable aptitude for trade, and affairs generally. A hereditary acuteness of intellect elevates the Tajik above the mental plane

Modifications in type due to admixture of alien blood.

---

[1] The Greek military colonists must have intermarried with the races by which they were surrounded and among which they were stationed as soon as they occupied their posts. The deviation in the features of the later Bactrian Kings, figured on their coins, from the pure Greek type may be due to this admixture of indigenous oriental blood.

The early Arab conquests in Asia were purely military operations. The Arab garrisons in the Rabāts or posts, which were established to maintain the supremacy of Islam, must at once have taken wives from the Tajik and other races among which they were stationed. The migration of tribes *en masse* from Arabia into Khurassan took place later and was restricted to certain districts.

[2] In Russian Turkestan, the Sart apparently is a race of mixed Uzbeg and Tajik descent.

of his ruder neighbours; and though these may profess to despise the Tajik, they cannot do without the latter as their subjects or their agents.[1]

Tajiks skilful Engineers.

The author referred to praises in glowing terms the skill displayed by the Sarts in the construction of irrigation canals and channels, and describes the wonderful system of canals in Turkestan constructed in past ages by this industrious race. Her description of the method employed in aligning the course of these canals ere the soil is turned is very interesting, and it agrees word for word with the method described to me by Muhammad, the Dādi, in 1903 and 1904 as being followed by him in laying out canals in Seistan. It is a method which must be as old as the earliest dawn of civilization in Asia; and therefore it is worthy of mention and record here:—

"But how, we naturally ask, does a Sart manage without these instruments which to European engineers would be essential."

Method of aligning canals.

"The answer is simple: where we should use a level, a Sart uses his eye. If he wants to know whether a canal can be carried to a certain part of his field, he throws himself on his back, and with his chin in the air, looks over his forehead towards the point in question. If he can see it with his head in that position he knows that water will flow to it."[2]

A rude form of water-level.

This is exactly the way in which Muhammad, the Dādi, told me that he carried out his trial levels. Only in the description given by the author quoted she reverses the sequence of ideas. If a man in the position she describes can see a point behind him, the latter must be higher than that on which he is lying. For further refinements in levelling canals while they are under construction, a shallow dish of brass or iron, filled with water almost to the brim, is used. I have seen this used both in the Pishin District, and also among the Bhils in Mewar (Rajputana), where irrigation channels have to be carried for considerable distances round spurs or undulations in the ground.

The Kaiānis the type of the East Iranian Race.

In Seistan the Kaiānis belong to the ancient race of the Kings of Iran, and therefore may be taken as types of the Eastern Iranian or Aryan race which has been described in the foregoing pages. With regard to the Kaiānis little doubt exists that they preserve to a considerable extent the characteristics of that race, or what are regarded as such at the present day. Malik Azim Khan, the eldest living representative of this ancient family (in 1905), had inherited a share of the good looks of his father, the

---

[1] Whenever the Arabs conquered a town or province of Persia, they called the Deh-kāns, asked them what taxes had been paid under the Khosraws, and confirmed generally the ancient regulations. En Nowairi (MS. of Leyden N. 2. D,) gives us in the History of the Sassanians, an account of their regulations of the land tax, which agrees literally with what Abu Yūsof considers as law under the Abasside Khalifs. And as the Sassanians had been the restorers of the ancient order of things to what they were before Alexander, we may trace the same institutions to the ancient Persians—Sprenger's El Masudi, Volume I, pages XLIII—IV—note.

[2] In Russian Turkestan—pages 12—13.

worthless Malik Jallāl-ud-din. In Malik Azim Khan's appearance the air of breeding which was to be expected from his ancient lineage was combined with regular, aquiline features, full eyes set in well marked orbits, and a well proportioned skull; a handsome and full beard; sinewy hands and when young a well proportioned, though small frame, now bent with age. In the younger members of the family, especially in the nephews and kinsmen of Malik Azim Khan, there was unfortunately only too evident that air of degeneracy characteristic of the urban population of Bokhara.

There are two other families named the Jamāli and Kamāli, dependants or clients of the family of the Maliks, who with the latter are regarded as of the ancient Iranian race; and from these two families (Jamāli and Kamāli) it is said that the Maliks of bygone days chose their personal attendants. No spurious descendants of the Kaiāni Maliks have been found to exist as a caste or tribe of the population, as was the case in the family of the Maliks of Bāmpur and among the Gichki Sardars' family of Panjgur and Kej. There these spurious descendants of the Chiefs were known as the "Tolag" or "Tolagen" Maliks or Gichkis as the case might be—the "jackal" Maliks or Gichkis are still well known, and the family of the Maliks of Bampur is now represented only by their spurious descendants. Among the Kaiānis the son of the handmaid or concubine of inferior race inherits his mother's disabilities and inferior status.

The families of the Jamāli and Kamāli.

Another tribe belonging to the ancient race is the Kak-hā, to which everyone in Seistan concedes an old and illustrious origin. The custodians of the Sacred Fire, which was maintained in the fanes at Karku and at Trākun, were recruited, it is said, from this tribe. Coming down to recent times, the architect of the famous barrage the Band-i-Yakau—better known as the Band-i-Rustam—is believed to have been a member of this tribe. Then again it is believed that the later weir—the Band-i-Bulbaka—was constructed by a Kak-hā. Some 55 years ago, when it became necessary to construct the Band-i-Seistan (to guard which the Kuhak Fort was built), it was a Kak-hā, the Kadkhuda Shāh Beg, father of Kadkhuda Ghulām Raza, Kak-hā, whom Tāj Muhammad, the Sarbandi, placed in charge of the work.

In the ages before the Arabs conquered Khurassān, there seems to have been a Tajik family predominant over their fellow countrymen in the district round Kandahār. When the first Arabs entered that country they found representatives of this family pre-eminent therein, and these were probably intrusted with Revenue affairs and other matters appertaining to the civil side of the administration. It is in this way that the family

The Arbābs of Kandahār, Khāsh and the Helmand valley.

2 o

acquired their distinctive title of Arbāb—Lords. In course of time branches of this family separated from the parent stem, one of which gained a pre-eminence similar to those enjoyed by their kinsmen in Kandahar, in the district of Khāsh, and another branch in the valley of the Helmand.

The Arbābs of Kala Fath represent the last named.

In Seistan, the latter—now represented by the Arbābs of Kala Fath—were the family from which the officials of the Kaiāni Princes were recruited, and as lately as the time of Nādir Shah and of the first Durāni King of Afghanistan, a member of this family was a supervisor of the revenue collections along the Helmand. At the present day, only the head of the Arbāb family of Khāsh retains any vestige of their ancient authority. He is the responsible official in that small district; but the hand of the Governor of Kandahar lies heavy on his head, and the Afghan inhabitants of the towns or villages within his jurisdiction pay him scanty respect as a Tajik.

In physiognomy, physique and general appearance the Arbāb closely resembles the Kaiāni and some of the former possess traces of the same air of breeding which characterises the latter. This is the case with the older members of the communities who have known better days. The younger members show the effects of repression beneath the heel of the Afghan; they are uncouth, boorish, and at the same time servile in their manners.

The Pahlawān.

Another tribe now represented in Seistan and which is said to belong to the ancient Iranian stock is the Pahlawān. Members of this tribe possess the same aquiline features and well proportioned skull which characterise the Kaiānis and Arbābs; and which, therefore, we may with some degree of confidence regard as the type of the ancient Iranian stock.

Tribal names among the Tajiks.

This race is divided into many tribes each of which are known by a separate designation; some of these names, such as Kunda, Diwāna, Dādī and others, are in use as the tribal designation of parts of the agricultural population of Seistan, and these tribes are also to be found in other places in Khurassan. It appears to be the case that, when the knowledge has disappeared as to the particular tribe to which a family or group of families have originally belonged, but where the general knowledge is preserved that it (or they) are descended from the ancient allodial population, the general term Tajik is used.

The Tajik had his use in ancient military operations.

Though the Tajik was a bad soldier, he had his uses in warlike operations. His athletic frame inured to, and hardened by labour, skill in the use of spade and mattock, and accustomed to excavating canals and earthwork, won for him a place in oriental armies. His value lay in the construction and repair of fortifications, and in siege operations. Strong contingents of Tajiks equipped with spades and mattocks accompanied oriental armies, and took the place of the modern corps of sappers. It was the Tajiks who were employed in driving the galleries of mines directed against the defences of a besieged stronghold; or who were set to work to cut channels to drain the water from the wet moats which protected the walls from the approach of enemies.

The Tajiks were in not very remote times distributed widely over the districts adjoining Seistan, which are now in a semi-desert condition, and occupied by roaming communities who call themselves Baluch. In the Dizak valley (Bāmpūr District of the Kirmān Province of Persia) there is a large Tajik population which style themselves Dehwār. Situated as they are, among a mixture of tribes calling themselves Baluch (among which the "Rind" element is strong), the difference between the two is apparent at a glance. The Dehwār are dwellers in villages composed of substantial tenements built of pisé, grouped together, and surrounded by fields; whereas their neighbours are nomads dwelling in tents, or in collections of squalid blanket-tents or mat-huts, situated among the groves of date palms, or upon the talus of the hills beyond the limit of permanent cultivation. The difference in physique and physiognomy is also equally marked. Kādir Bakhsh who in 1889 was the chief man of the Dehwārs was able to place a comparatively strong force of matchlock men into the field, and although old Dilāwar Khan, a so-called "Baluch," was the chief man in the district in 1890, he was unable to take any action whatever, unless he was supported by the Dehwār headman. But the Dehwārs of Dizak dwelt in a country surrounded by a turbulent Baluch population, where outbreaks against the oppression of the Persian Government were frequent, and as they had also to contend against the exactions of the local officials, they possessed a retreat in the neighbouring hills to which the whole Dehwār population used to resort with their moveable property and the approaches to which could be defended by the fighting men of this race, whenever the exactions of the local officials became outrageous and unbearable, leaving their empty villages and bare fields to the mercy of their enemies. The Dehwārs of Dizāk said that they were the remnant of the settled Tajik population, which at one time occupied the Khārān District; and a small tract of country along the south edge of the Māshkel Hāmūn is still called Dehwār after this race. When the conditions became such that the Tajik population were no longer able to continue in the low country now known as the Khārān District they withdrew to the hills, to Dizak and to Mastung.

Distribution of the Race in Baluchistan.

Traditions of the Dehwārs of Dizak.

The abandonment of their lands by the Dehwār or Tajik population was due not altogether to political causes, to bad government, or to the oppression of their turbulent neighbours, but most probably to climatic changes.

Probable reason for the Tajiks abandoning Khārān.

When a prolonged cycle of scanty rainfall lowered the level of subsoil water, and springs and streams failed, the Tajik population could no longer make a living from the produce of their lands, after satisfying the demands of more powerful neighbours, or overlords, who regarded the Tajik as their prey; and as these exactions would naturally be enforced by violence, the agricultural population had the alternative of either starving in their ancestral possessions, or of abandoning their lands and moving elsewhere.

Influence of environment on the Tajik character.

The influence of their environment in the Dizak valley on the Dehwārs is apparent in their movement into the hills when driven to desperation; but with this exception they are a fixed population settled in houses among nomadic and shepherd neighbours, and the distinction between the two is marked to a degree which is not so apparent in other localities. But if the circumstances prevailing at any period were such as to render agriculture impossible (and such periods in the history of the country have been only too frequent) the Tajiks as a body, or sections of them, would be forced in self-defence to adopt a nomadic life in order to live. In the course of a very few generations Tajiks who had degenerated to the condition of nomads would come to regard themselves as a part of those who had followed this mode of life from earlier periods, and be regarded by the latter as part of their own tribal or political association, and be classed as "Baluch" or as "Brahui" whichever term was applied by the nomads of the locality to their associations.

In Seistan, on the other hand, a reversal of this process has been in operation. In the delta of the Helmand, where arable soil and water has always been plentiful, immigrants have assimilated themselves to the mode of life of the Tajiks. The tribes of acknowledged Arab origin such as the Sarbandi, Shahraki, the Mirs of Iskil and of Chakānsur, and others of Baluch origin are now indistinguishable from their neighbours, who are of confessedly Tajik origin. This has been the case elsewhere than in Seistan, wherever soil and water have been abundant.

"M. Nalivkin, in his history of Fergana, divides the Uzbegs into three classes: nomads, semi-nomads, and nomads who have become sedentary, that is to say, those who conquered the Tajiks, and settling down among them, gradually adopted their manners, their customs, and their agricultural pursuits."[1]

Intermarriage between Uzbegs and Tajiks—their descendants the Sarts.

From the Uzbegs, who became in all respects Tajiks and who must have intermarried with Tajiks, is descended the people who call themselves Sarts, and this mixed race preserves a great many Uzbeg features in their appearance owing to the recent admixture of Uzbeg blood with that of the older Iranian race. In this way the Arab conquerors of Khurassan have in the course of centuries been absorbed into the Tajik or Iranian population whom they subjugated. The Arab remains a distinct type only in those tracts in which the conditions were most favourable to a pastoral, nomadic

---

[1] In Russian Turkestan, pages 227 and 228.

Farsiwán Kadkhudas of Seistan.

(Part IV to face page 285.)

Tajiks of Kandahar.

(Part IV to face page 255.)

and predatory mode of life. The predominance of the Arab in Khurassan ceased with the downfall of the House of Omeya, and the policy of the first Caliphs of the Abassides in discouraging the use of Arabic by the descendants of Arabs who remained in Khurassan after the downfall of the House of Omeya, rendered the absorption of the Arab element into the mass of the Iranian population easy and rapid.

"The Eastern Iranians are considered by modern anthropologists to be what is generally, for want of a better name, called the Aryan race, and to be strongly affected by that branch of the Caucasian race which has been named *Homo Alpinus*, which extends through central Europe and Asia Minor to the highlands of the Hindu Kush. One of the most consistent features of this race is its consistent brachycephaly, and its purest examples are found among the Tajiks of Turkestan and the Galchas of the Hindu Kush."[1]

Homo Alpinus.

The broad head combined with "the characteristic eagle nose[2] of the true Iranian" is the type of the Tajik wherever the race is to be found, except in a few cases where a recent admixture of Mongol blood has modified the ancient type. In Wakhan, the outpost of the ancient Iranian race, the features and complexions of the people who speak "a remarkably conservative descendant of the ancient tongue of Eastern Iran"[3] distinguished the immigrants of their race whom the adventurous traveller met in Hunza. The "peaceful character of the Wakhis is curiously symbolised by the implement which every respectable householder carries about with him on State occasions. It is a long staff with a small heart-shaped shovel of wood at the end, used for opening and damming up the irrigation courses, that bring fertility to the laboriously cleared terraced lands."[4] The comparatively fair complexion is also a heritage of the Tajiks which distinguishes them in Seistan and elsewhere, and at once attracts attention among the darker-visaged Baluch of the same tract or country. Individuals show the admixture of alien blood by variations in physique, features, and complexion. In Seistan the offspring of Tajik and Baluch parents present curious deviations, being much taller than the usual stature of the races to which their parents belong, and while preserving the brachycephaly of their Tajik parent with frequently the same prominent "eagle nose," the darker complexion is that of the Baluch parent. Round Chakānsur there seems to have been considerable intermarriage of Tajik and Baluch, and a Chakānsuri (man of Chakānsur) can always be easily detected in Seistan in a crowd composed of Tajik (Farsiwān) and Baluch by reason of his tall stature, bony gaunt frame, and complexion.

Anthropometrical characteristics of the East Iranian Race.

Variations of type in offspring of unions between Tajik and Baluch.

---

[1] (The Baluch Race, by M. Longworth Dames As. Soc. Monographs, Volume IV, London, 1904, page 10 taken from Les Aryans au nord et au Sud de l'Hindou Kusch. Ujfalvy.)

[2] Sand-buried ruins of Khotan, A. Stein, London, 1903, page 46. See also Appendix III.

[3] *Ibid*, page 45.

[4] *Ibid*. page 47.

THE PEOPLE OF SEISTAN.

"The Tajiks of different parts of the Iranian plateau have an index ranging from 81 to 84, the Darwazis 81·4 and the Ghalchas 85. The index of the Bombay Parsis, who have kept distinct amid their Indian neighbours, is 82·3."[1]

Anthropometrical measurements.

In 1901, the Dehwārs in the Kalat State (who are principally located in the fertile valleys in the vicinity of Kalat itself, and of the town of Mastung), numbered 6,727 souls; besides these there were 273 in the Quetta-Pishin District, and 18 in the Chagai District. The average anthropometrical measurements of the Dehwārs in the Kalat State were as follows:—

Average cephalic index	81·7
,, nasal ,,	74·3
,, stature	164·2
,, orbits-nasal	118·

They also present the other characteristics of the Tajik race: they live in villages, are purely agricultural, and do not migrate to the low country in the winter. The headman of the Dehwārs is styled Arbāb.[2]

Difference in the photograph of Tajiks of Seistan and Kandahar explained.

The photographs of the Farsiwāns (or Tajiks) of Seistan and of Kandahar do not show many points of resemblance between the individuals composing the groups. But this is due to the great difference between the costumes of their respective countries. There can be no doubt that the Afghan costume follows the ancient fashion. The beard also is untrimmed and allowed to attain the proportions permitted by nature; and the general effect is far more dignified than is produced by the frowsy "Sardāri," or frock-coat and over-worn and ill-fitting trousers, which is the modern costume Persia has borrowed from Europe. In Seistan the beard is usually trimmed except in the case of very old men and the priesthood, and this renders the appearance of the Farsiwāns of that country different from that of their fellows in Kandahar, who follow the fashion, in this respect, prevalent in Afghanistan.

---

[1] The Baluch Race, page 11.

[2] Baluchistan Gazetteer Series, Volume VI, 1907, page 63.

The tribes of the Mastung Valley are undoubtedly of Tajik origin, though in recent times they have been joined by Afghāns, Baloch, and Brahuis. A small section, particularly good cultivators, are known as Kashmirzai, and are said to have come from Kashmir. They all speak Persian. The nucleus of the Dehwārs—the most ancient of the present inhabitants—is said to have migrated here from Balkh.

In Appendix III will be found an interesting and valuable account of the Tajiks of Bokhara taken from Chapter 6 of the Emir of Bokhara and his country. O. Olufsen: London William Henemann, 1911.

CHAPTER III.

THE early oriental Muhammadan authors, whose works have survived, write of Seistan as Sijistan, and of the people as the Sigzis, but in later chronicles there seems to be a distinction made between the Sigzis and the Seistanis. In the first quarter of the 13th century, the Sigzis are mentioned in connection with the fortress of Uk,[1] which seems to have been their headquarters. That this fortress is that of Lāsh is established by the notice of it in the Matla-us-Saadein of Abdur Razzak (1408 A.D.). I venture to suggest that in the Sakzīs or Sagzīs whose headquarters are even now in the ancient district of Uk, which is now called Juwein or Lāsh-Juwein,[2] we find a remnant of the Sigzis of early oriental (Muhammadan) authors and in all probability of the race known at a still earlier period as the Sakas.

Early notices of the Sigzis.

The fortress of Uk was besieged by the Mongol troops for nineteen months (or two years according to some authors); and again in 1408, Shāh Rukh, the son of the famous Timur (Tamerlane) laid siege to this place, which was resolutely defended by the Sigzis with aid from the Seistanis (the author of the Matla-us-Saadein mentions the Sigzis and also speaks of the inhabitants of the delta, subjects of Malik Kutb-ud-din, as Seistanis). At this period the Sigzis occupied the district of Farah and were intermixed with other tribes in that district. Farah succumbed to Shāh Rukh, who then marched against the fort of Uk, that is Lāsh, which also eventually was surrendered by its defenders. The Sakis are now regarded (and even by themselves) as "Afghan" and they are supposed to be descended from one Ishak, a descendant of Kais. Hence this tribe is usually spoken of (and written of) as the Ishakzais. Ishak (Isaac), son of Abraham, would naturally commend itself to a Muhammadan genealogist as an illustrious name for the eponymous ancestor of this powerful tribe; but in their headquarters in Lāsh-Juwein, this people call themselves the Sakzī or Sagzī (but never Ishakzai) which is practically the name to be found in early Arab writers when treating of the country and people of Sijistan.

Proposed identification of modern Sakzīs (Ishakzais) with the Sigzis and the Sakas.

The late Major Raverty indeed derived the name Sigzi or Sijzi from Sijistan (on the analogy of Rawizi for an inhabitant of Rei); but the authority for the derivation of the name Sakastāna from the Sakas (and consequently of Sijistān or Sajastān from the Sigzis) cannot be disputed. Although the headquarters of the Sakzī is in the district of Uk (where

Origin of the name Sigzi. Distribution of the modern Sakzīs.

---

[1] See Part I, pages 31 and 32.
[2] And also called now-a-days Hokāt.

it has been located certainly since the 13th century and probably from time immemorial), the tribe is spread over a great tract of country in Southern Afghanistan; almost up to Herat on the north, and into the valley of the Arghasān river to the east of Kandahar. The seat of the chieftains, however, has always been the fortress of Lāsh and the fort of Juwein. Of the former they held possession as late as the middle of the last century. Afterwards the ruler of Afghanistan took possession of the place and planted a garrison in it of his own troops and the fort has been held as an outpost, after it was evacuated by the Persians in 1857 or 1872.

Their mode of life. In their mode of life the Sakzis are pastoral and their lands in the Hokat, or Lāsh-Juwein, are tilled by tenants, or metayers, most of whom belong to the Farsiwān race settled from time immemorial in the Hokat. The Tajiks of this district are called Aukāti or Hokāti. The Sakzi are also Gaudārs—cattleowners—and they have their stations in the reed beds of the Hamun-i-Puza, and along the northern edge of the Hāmun. Unlike the Gaudārs of Seistan, the Sakzis are also shepherds, but this is probably due to the fact that only sheep and goats can thrive, or exist, on the Dasht or barren steppes over which the greater part of the tribe is scattered.

Influence of environment. The Sakzis have always displayed a predilection for a life of rapine, and the conditions under which they have existed for centuries on the borders of Persia and Afghanistan has enabled them to indulge their leanings in this direction. One of their chiefs, Musa Khan, is still remembered by his sobriquet of "Dungī," or the freebooter.[1]

The Sajiti of Panjgur probably an offshoot of the Sakzis. Far to the south of Lāsh Juwein, in the district of Panjgur, there is a tribe called the Sājiti: which may also, perhaps, be representatives of the ancient Sākas. At the foot of the Kalat plateau, overlooking the sandy plains of the wide Khārān valley, and about 100 miles to the north-east of Panjgur, is a small valley named Dārdān near a better known locality named Gresha, which lies at the foot of the hills. In this valley of Dārdān is the headquarters of the Sājiti. This tribe is divided into two portions, one of which, the Sangur, extends into Kej, the hills between the Kolwa valley and the sea, and also in the direction of Ormāra. They are nomads, owning flocks of sheep and goats, and breed camels. The Sājiti are found higher up than the Sangur, and the latter may be of a separate origin than the Sājiti, but it is generally regarded as a branch of the latter. The clan of the Sājiti chief, or head man, is called Sākazai (? Sakzai-Sakzī, or Sagzi) and they say that they emigrated from Seistan about 20 generations ago; or say, about 450 years ago.[2] They at first settled in the valley immediately

---

[1] Dung is a well known term for a raiding expedition.

[2] This is accepting the statement as being correct. This is, however, very doubtful. The Sājiti are illiterate, have no records, and the number of generations is probably only a guess, and equivalent to saying that their migration from Seistan took place a very long time ago.

to the south of Panjgur, where they built a fort (which still exists), and this settlement still bears the name of Sakai Kalat or Saka Kalat—the Fort of the Sakas. In the census of 1901, the Sajitis numbered 6,063 souls and the Sangurs 4,385 souls. To complicate matters the latter assert that they are Jat as to origin, and claim affinity with the Jokhias of Sind. Now, if we allow 22 years on an average for a generation, the migration of the Sakas from Seistan took place about 1461 A.D., and the years following the sack of Zahidān up to the end of this century was a very disturbed period in the history of Seistan,[1] when such an emigration would not have been surprising. In the Panjgur District and elsewhere the Sājiti have relapsed into a nomadic mode of life; any cultivation in which they may engage is quite insignificant and their wealth consists in their live-stock. In Seistan there is a very small group of agriculturists belonging to a tribe named Sāj: and it has been suggested that perhaps the Sajiti broke off from the Sāj, and that the latter are the remnant which clung to the soil. There is, however, more similitude as to mode of life between the Sakzī of Lāsh-Juwein, and the Sājiti (or Saka)[2] of Panjgur and Kej, in their manner of life, and possibly the latter were originally a portion of the better known tribe whose headquarters are in Juwein.

While neither the Sakzi nor the Sājiti preserve any knowledge regarding their ancient location beyond the Oxus, there is a tribe which still remembers the fact that they migrated thence, the Mingal or Mengal tribe, whose headquarters are at Nushki. A section of this tribe are also settled in the Jahlawān division of the Kalat State, where their headquarters are at Wad, about 100 miles to the south of Kalat.

Neither preserve any knowledge of their origin.

The Mingals or Mengals of Nushki call themselves Zughar or Zaghar Mingals, to distinguish themselves from the Jahlawān section which is known as the Shāhizai. The Zaghar Mingals say that their distinguishing appellation is taken from Zughd near Samarkand, from whence their ancestors emigrated. This is one of the several provinces mentioned in the first chapter of the Venidad: in Zend Sughda, and in old Persian Suguda from which the Greek Soghdiana may have been derived. This form of the ancient name survives, for Soghd still is the name of the district in which Samarkand is situated.[3]

The Zaghar Mingals of Nushki-tradition respecting their origin.

---

[1] Part I, page 65, et seq.

[2] Sāka still exist on the borders of the Caspian—Baluchistan Gazetteer: Volume VI-B, page 98.

[3] It would appear that the memory of the Greek conquest still survives here; for in Russian Turkestan, at page 249, the author states that "near the lake named Iskander or Alexander, there is a mountain village called Anzob, the inhabitants of which are said to be direct descendants of some of the Greek soldiers who accompanied Alexander the Great on his conquering journey from Macedon to Soghdiana." The lake Iskander is situated in the higher valley of the Zarafshān River, a long way above Samarkand, on the left bank of the river. One of the tributaries of the Zarafshān is also named Iskander for the reason given above.

Established in their present locale before the Arab Conquest, according to their tradition.

This district then was the home of the Zaghar Mingal tribe of Nushki, who have been domiciled for very many centuries in the country round Nushki. Compared with their arrival, the Arab conquest of the country was a recent event. At the point where the Khaesār river emerges from the hills above Nushki itself, on the right bank of the stream, and at the end of the outer range of hills, there was a rectangular enclosure with stone walls—built of rough stones without cement of any kind—which was pointed out as an Arab camp; and which was called so. There is only one tribe in the neighbourhood which, the Mingals told me many years ago, had been settled in the country longer than they had, and this is the people who hold the arable lands watered by the Karezes of Ahmadwāl, a few miles south of Nushki. The so-called Brahui tribes are regarded as absolutely new comers by the Mingals of Nushki. The people of Ahmadwāl are called Rakshānis, and although regarded as Brahui, they are probably a remnant of the original Tajik population of the district. It is said that they were once upon a time the occupants of all the land west of Nushki. A large section of the Mingals of Nushki occupy the desert between Nushki and the eastern elbow of the Helmund river. After the delimitation of the boundary between Baluchistan and Afghanistan (1896), this portion of the tribe (about 4,000 families it is said) became subjects of the Amir, and have remained such since that time. Under the leadership of Mahmud they completely separated from the rest of the tribe domiciled in Nushki. At this place, however, the Sardar of the Zaghar Mingals continues to reside. The Zaghar Mingals have lost their influence and prestige now-a-days, and are outnumbered by the Mingals of Jahlawān.

The Mingals of Jahlawān a composite tribe.

The latter numbered (in 1901) 62,136 souls and are of mixed origin. The predominant subdivision—the Shāhizai—claim a Persian origin. The Muhammadzais and Bārānzais are of Afghan Tarin origin. The Raisānis are collaterals of the Sarawān Raisanis,[1] also of Afghan Tarin origin—the Spin Tarin section. The Mardoi section are Bulfat Jadgals (Jats) descended from Jām Arī, progenitor of the Baprāni, Hamalāni, and Lohārāni Jāms of Thāna Bhula Khan and Tawang in the Karachi District of Sind. They were tributary to the Mengal Chief, but within the last twenty years they have been regarded as part and parcel of the Mingal or Mengal tribes. Feroz, one of their leaders, is believed to have turned out of Khuzdār the Mongol Intendant Malik Chap. Pahlawānzai section also claim a Persian

---

[1] The following anthropological measurements are given for the Mengals of Jahlawan :—

Ceph. Index	82·8
Nasal ,,	59·5
Orbito-nasal Index	120·6

The People of India : Calcutta, 1908, App. IV.

descent (the Pahlawān is still a well-known Farsiwān section of the population of Seistan).[1]

In the 17th century the Indian Moghul Emperor Shāh Jahān annexed Balkh and held the country up to the Oxus for about two years. Indian troops also occupied one or two posts on the further bank to control the principal ferries over that river. Abdul Aziz Khan, ruler of Samarkand, mustered his fighting men and overran the country held by the Indian troops. Among the tribes which answered the summons of the Khan of Samarkand was one named the Meng or Ming.[2] *The Ming or Meng, a tribe of Trans-Oxiana, in the 17th Century.*

In the Balochi language, plurals of substantives and collective nouns are formed, generally, by adding the suffix *gal* to the noun itself, and hence all over Baluchistan the word Jadgal is used to denote the Jat population at large, and also individuals—Jadgal a single individual, and also the Jat element as a whole in the population. So that the term Mengal (Meng-gal,) merely denotes the Meng (Ming, or Men, or Min) tribe. The well-known ancient city of Minnagar[3] in Sind (town of the Mins) appears to have been so named from this tribe, a part of which still retains its distinctive name though no longer a power for good or ill. *The name Mingal explained.*

While the connection of the Sakzis and the Sājitis with the country beyond the Oxus is conjectural, there is some evidence, not amounting perhaps to absolute proof, which connects the Mingals of Nushki with that tract of country in which Samarkand[4] is situated. The fact of the former having lost the knowledge of their origin, while the Mengals still preserve a tradition, is almost a proof that the latter were a part of a later horde, or migration, from beyond the Oxus. It is possible that when the bulk of the Mins (or Mings) passed on to the valley of the Indus, where in course of time they founded the city of Minnagar, a remnant may have been left behind in the country now occupied by the Mengals of Nushki, where *The Mingals a remnant of the Min tribe of Sind.*

---

[1] Baluchistan Gazetteer series, Volume VI-B, page 83.

[2] Badshāhnāmah Bibliotheca Indica.

[3] The author of the Periplus of the Erythraean Sea (McCrindle's translation: the date of this work has been much debated. Mr. McCrindle places it between 80 and 89 A.D., M. Renand, 246 or 247 A.D., while the author of the Early History of India States—p. 218 note—that "it may be dated with some confidence between 77 and 105 A.D.") in the 1st or 2nd century A.D. calls the valley of the Lower Indus, known at the present day as Lower Sind, Scythia, and describes it as being under the government of Parthian Chiefs who were at war with one another. The capital at that time was Minnagar, and the principal port of the country was named Babarikon. The capital lay at some distance up the country. The changes of the river in its lower course and the building up of the coast by the silt brought down by its waters has rendered it impossible to identify these towns, and it is impossible as yet to penetrate the obscurity in which the topography of this country, at that period, is enveloped.

[4] The foundation of Samarkand is attributed to Kaus of Kobad, of the Kaiānian Dynasty of Persia, and its completion to his son Siavakhsh. The name is supposed to have been given to this city from Samar, the general of the Yemenite King Toba Abu Karib or Toba-al-Akbar, and thus to be the relic of a very early Arab conquest of the country beyond the Oxus. The Cities of Iron—by Jivanji Jamshedji Modi, B.A., Bombay (1899), page 133.

they have continued to dwell as a pastoral tribe and have preserved their identity. They are now counted among the "Brahui" tribes.[1]

The story of the origin of the Kashānis from the Ashg-ka-putras has been already mentioned.[2] It shows that the "Parthians, or Indo-Parthians," who are known to have ruled over Seistan and Arachosia are yet represented in the first-named country, and in the adjoining districts once included under the name of Arachosia, which comprised the districts of Pishin, Quetta, Kalat, Khuzdar, and the country between them and the Helmand on the west, including Kandahar, up to Karabāgh, on the north, and as far south as the watershed separating the streams that flow into the sea of Oman from those falling into the arid plains of Kharān. On the north of this watershed at various places in this area, groups of Kashānis are yet to be found. In the Panjgur District the headquarters of the Kashānis is at Shāhbāz Kalat. In the Panjgur District, where they numbered 350 souls, they say that they are an offshoot of the Shahwānis of Iskalku near Kalat, and that their forefathers owing to a quarrel, to the number of 700 families, migrated to Panjgur, in the time of the Maliks of Panjgur. The name Kashāni or Kishāni[3] is still the designation of one of the clans of the Shahwāni tribe. "Owing to quarrels with the Gichkis most of them migrated in the course of time to Chakānsur in the Helmand valley."[4] The Kashānis of Panjgur are flockowners and camel-breeders, but they also possess dry-crop cultivation in the district of Shāhbāz. The Shahwānis of the Sarawān Division of Kalat (with whom the Kashānis of Panjgur maintain communications) are, like all other clans of so-called Brahuis, composed of a variety of tribes. "The nucleus of the tribe, the Ramadānzai and Alizai sections, is said to be of Baluch or Afghān origin, while another story is to the effect that they came from Sharwān in the neighbourhood of the Caspian."[5] "All the remaining sections are of alien origin."[6] The Shahwānis (who numbered 6,318 souls in Kalat) occupied the foremost position among the Sarawān Brahuis, until in course of time, probably subsequent to 1839, this position was acquired by the Raisānis.[7]

---

[1] The Mingals of Jahlāwān were possibly fragments of various races which attached themselves to the Mingals of Nushki originally as dependants or followers, when the chief of the latter possessed a great deal of influence and power. This they possessed as late as the time of Nasir Khan I of Kalat who died in the spring of 1794, and afterwards in the course of time the former called themselves Mingals, which they have continued to do ever since.

[2] Chapter I, pages 273 and 274.

[3] Baluchistan Gazetteer, Volume VII, pages 103, 104. Bunyād Khan Kashani mentioned in Part II, page 173, was chief of this tribe in Seistan; he was killed by the Afghans in about 1898, at Shāhgul on the Helmand, trying to escape to Persian soil. A fine of 50,000 krans had been imposed on him and the Notāni headman for some cause not generally known but said to have been their revolt against Afghan oppression.

[4] Ibid, page 104.

[5] Baluchistan Gazetteer, Volume VI, page 52.

[6] Viz.:—Zaghar Mengals of Nushki, Mirwāris, Mengals from Nushki. The Shahwānis are regarded as Brahui.

[7] See Pottinger's account of the Kalat State. Travels in Baluchistan and Sinde, London, 1816.

THE PEOPLE OF SEISTAN.

From the foregoing paragraphs it would seem as if the account, in the Gazetteer quoted above, contradicts the story obtained in Seistan as to the origin of the Kashānis. The story of Khwaja Amrān, and the Ashg-ka-putras; of the descent of the Kashānis from that people; and of the reason for the avoidance of the Ziarat of Amrān, by the Kashānis, are all genuine traditions, clearly delivered, and firmly credited by the people of Seistan. The refusal of two of the leading men of this tribe who were with me to approach the shrine, led me to search for the reason which prompted such a strange procedure in a Pir-ridden country like Seistan. The Shahwānis of Kalat have not yet lost all idea of the original location of their remote ancestors, and Shirwān is still the name of a small district in the Province of Daghestan (Georgia), on the west coast of the Caspian. This was one of the provinces of the ancient Kingdom of Armenia which was annexed in A.D. 34, by Artabanus, the Parthian Monarch, on the death of Artaxias III, the nominee of Germanicus. The throne of Armenia was bestowed on Arsaces (the eldest son of Artabanus), the first of a line of Parthian Kings of Armenia, and Parthian influence became all-powerful in that country. The legend preserved by the Shahwānis of Kalat merely carries the story of their origin to a period much earlier than that referred to in the legend of Khwaja Amrān, when the Ashg-ka-putra were still possessed of authority over a part, at least, of Seistan.[1]

Discrepancy between legends in Seistan and Kalat regarding origin of the Kashānis explained.

Among the "Brahui" and "Baloch" tribes there are fragments of ancient, and at one time powerful tribes, whose original seats in times of antiquity were very remote to those in which their impoverished descendants are now to be found. Among the barren hills of the Palangān Range in Seistan there are a few scattered families of a Brahui tribe named Sarparra. The headquarters of this tribe is in the Kalat State, the localities known as Kardagāp and Gurgina; where, in 1901, they numbered 885 souls. These localities are in the Sarawān Division of the Kalat State. The Chief Imam Baksh Khan (in 1889) explained the name Sarparra to mean decapitators, owing to the warlike propensities of his tribesmen. "They are notorious for quarrelling among themselves, and it is said that they will fight each other over a dog or a cat. The Murrais, who are dominant in Gurgina, are the most turbulent of all the clans."[2]

The Sarparra Chief's interpretation of the name.

Owing to the proximity to the border between Afghanistan and Kalat this tribe occupies an important position, and in former times were

---

[1] In 1904 the Kashānis in Seistan numbered about 2,553 souls. Of these about 2,374 were settled in Afghan territory. Of this number about 632 souls were cultivators holding about 4,500 acres of land at Erindas to the east of Chakansur. The greater part of this land is dependant on rain for cultivation, and cannot be cultivated, in all probability, oftener than once in three years.

There were about 180 souls, Kashānis, cultivating land, on the Persian side of the boundary.

[2] Baluchistan District Gazetteer, Volume VI, page 65.

294   THE PEOPLE OF SEISTAN.

Proposed identification with the Saraparœ of Strabo.

constantly at feud with the Barechis of Shorāwak. The tribe is partly of "Baluch" and partly of "Afghan" stock. It is interesting to note that a tribe of almost identical name with an identical meaning was in ancient times dwelling much further to the west. "Some tribes of Thracians, surnamed Saraparœ or decapitators, are said to live above Armenia, near the Gouranii and Medes. They are a savage people, intractable mountaineers, and scalp and decapitate strangers, for such is the meaning of the term Saraparœ."[1]

Sarparra are not migratory.

Unlike other Brahui tribes the Sarparra does not migrate periodically to the plains. Their principal occupation is agriculture, but two of the clans possess large flocks of sheep and goats.[2]

Original and present locale of this tribe.

The position assigned by Strabo to the Saraparœ makes it appear that they were neighbours of the tribes now known as the Kurds and dwelt between those tribes and the Caspian Sea; and in the Kalat State, at no distance from the Sarparra, there is a fragment of the Kurds, now regarded as "Baloch" or "Brahui," who are to be found throughout the State at the head of the Bolan Pass (their headquarters); at Bāghwāna in the Jhalawān Division; and a small group of Kurds is also to be found in the Las Bela State.[3]

Only a rough classification of the modern population of Seistan is possible.

It is only possible to divide the population of Seistan into two classes— those whose mode of life is pastoral and the remainder who are agriculturists and who style themselves Farsiwān. Among the latter, however, it is possible to pick out a few sections of the population who, though called Farsiwān, were clearly not of the old East Iranian stock. The Shahrakis and Sarbandis[4] claim to be descendants of Arabs. The former are probably the remnant of the Kharijis who were once predominant in Kirmān and Seistan, who were driven by the orthodox Muhammadans to the eastern fringe of the empire of the Khalifs of Bagdad. A feature that attracted attention[5] was the occupation of the Kharijis (in Seistan at least), who were

---

[1] Strabo, Geography, Bk. XI, Chapter XIV, § 14—Falconer's translation.

[2] The Rodenis, another tribe from Kardagāp in the Sarawan Division of the Kalat State which numbered (in 1901) 1,978, are to be found in Seistan where they numbered about 946 souls. The clans of Sumalzais and Zahrozais are represented in Seistan.

[3] There were Kurds settled in the Kirmān Province of Persia. Rāhbur, a district to the south of Kirmān itself, was their headquarters, and here the Kurd Chief dwelt. The Kurds were overpowered by the Ghuz tribes in the 12th century, and their influence was destroyed, but there are Kurds still to be found at various places in that Province at the present day. For the Kurds of Rahbur see Md. Ibrahim's History of the Saljuks of Kirman, an author who wrote in the 17th century, but who based his work on earlier records. (Md. Ibrahim's History was edited by M. Th. Houtsma, and published by E. J. Brill, Leyden, 1886.)

[4] Traditionally the Shahrakis came into Seistan 900 and the Sarbandis 300 years ago. The former name, I think, should not contain a second h. It would then be derivable from Shark, the East. The Kharijis and other Schismatics being driven in that direction, or rising up there, were also known as Sharkis, or the Eastern (heretics), the western dominions of the Khalifs being (nominally) orthodox.

[5] In the 10th century the Arab Geographers who treat of Seistan allude to communities of Khariji weavers—see Part III, page 209.

Seiād Dwellings.

(Part IV to face page 295.)

weavers of cloth. Weaving a coarse cotton fabric is still exclusively the work of men in Seistan, and it is carried on principally in Shahraki villages by those people. This attracted the attention of a traveller in the 19th century (as it does at the present day)—Doctor Frederick Forbes, H.E., I.C.S., who was murdered in Seistan. "The weavers here" (Seistan) "struck me very much as resembling a class of operatives in Scotland, now fast disappearing—the hand-loom weavers, as similarity of habits, no doubt, beget similarity of disposition to some extent. They all appeared intelligent, given to politics, disputations, and possessed of a quaint independent humour very different from the generality of Persians."[1] Doctor Forbes also remarked the weavers of the village of Deluwi of Gunābād in the Kuhistan to the north-west of Seistan. The characteristics which attracted his attention to the weavers of Seistan were exactly those of the Khariji Schismatics of Seistan of the earlier days of Islam.[2] At one time the Shahrakis were a very important section of the population of Seistan; in 1904, however, they numbered only about 2,300 souls. The Sarbandis numbered about 1,800 souls, but the chief of this section of the population possesses influence, above all others, in Seistan. In addition there are about 1,000 Sarbandis in the district of Chakānsur in Afghan territory; while the Shahrakis are all Persian subjects. The family of the Mirs of Seistan is also of acknowledged Arab origin, but they are a family and not a tribe. With the exception of the Farsiwāns, who are regarded as the remnant of the original ancient Iranian population of Seistan—the Kaiānis, Arbābs, Jamālis, Kamālis, Pahlawāns, and Kak-hās, the rest of the Farsiwān population, with exceptions which will be noted, cannot be placed with any degree of certainty. They bear names derived in most cases from their original seats. Thus there are the Dilārāmi from Dilārām, to the west of Girishk, Dalkhakis from Dalkhak, a stage to the west of Dilārām on the Kandahar-Herat road, Gurgs from Gurg to the south-east of Fahraj near Bam, Shurgazi from Shurgaz near Gurg, Khāra Kuhis, from Khāra Kuh on the Helmand above Landi Muhammad Amin Khan, and so on. Among these are a few, such as the Pate Pashm, Pilpili Sanādgul, Shekh Weisi and Mir Weisi (both to be found round Kandahar); Sanchuli (also sometimes called Sangchuli), Joteghs, and others who are called and who call themselves Farsiwān, but whose origin is no longer certain. Both the Sanchuli and the Joteghs, however, recognise their own headmen and the heads of both these sections use the title of Dahbāshi. The Joteghs, however, believe that

Other tribes in Seistan.

---

[1] Jour. Royal Geogr. Soc., No. X, Vol. 14.

[2] From the deposition of Forbes' Persian servant by Rawlinson in Kandahar some time after his master's murder, it seems that Forbes' zeal, and the obtrusively open way in which he prosecuted his researches, had excited much unfriendly criticism in the country. The capture of Kalat also appeared to have thoroughly alarmed the people of Makran and Seistan. *Ibid.*

296   THE PEOPLE OF SEISTAN.

The Joteghs.

in the times of the ancient Maliks the tribe emigrated from the Jabal Barīz to Seistan and were soldiers of the Maliks, and that their leader (Dahbāshi) was the hereditary standard-bearer of the Seistani Maliks.[1] The Jabal Barīz (a corruption of Jabal Barīd—the "cold mountains") is the lofty range of mountains overlooking the fertile plains of Narmashir. These mountains were a natural fortress which provided retreats probably from the earliest times for the ancient inhabitants of the country previous to the Arab conquest, and after that to Khariji and other malcontents. It is impossible to say to which of these the Joteghs originally belonged—probably, however, owing to their physiognomy, physique, and to their original habitats the Joteghs are referrible to the Kharijis, and therefore to Arab forefathers who probably married into the indigenous population. The Kharijis were by no means always pure Arabs. The Sanchuli do not preserve any legends (none at any rate were discovered) as to their origin, but possibly their ancestors may have accompanied the Joteghs into Seistan as soldiers of the Maliks of ancient times, and hence the fact of their headman still retaining the title of Dah-bāshi. Most of the Joteghs I saw were small men and the heads

Physical difference among sections of the population.

of some of them appeared to be noticeably narrow. The Kakhās among the Farsiwāns are famous for their physique and stature. The Shahrakis are, generally, a fine race: some of them would have attracted attention anywhere owing to their athletic frames. The Shahrakis are also of darker complexion as a race than their fellow-countrymen, and occasionally among individuals of the latter tribe I noticed the narrow head of the Semitic race.

The Jats are also styled Farsiwān.

Then among the Farsiwāns are included the Jats and other sections of the population allied to them, and other tribes which show a marked affinity to the Gujar (and allied tribes) of India. These will be described separately.

Population in Afghan Seistan.

Across the Helmand in Afghan territory the acknowledged Farsiwān element is insignificant compared with the "Afghan" and "Baluch;" except in the Chakānsur District, which immediately adjoins Persian territory. In the Kang sub-division also are settled the 1,000 Sarbandis.

The "Afghan" element is strong in the Kang division, probably placed here to prevent encroachments on the part of the Persians. Among the Afghans the Ghilzais and Tarins are most numerous:

"Afghans" are predominant.

numerically they are almost equal. Next come the Alizais, followed by the Sakzī and Seiads. The Ghilzais numbered (1904) about 1,827: the

---

[1] The peaceful nature of the Farsiwāns must have led the Maliks to favour the introduction of more warlike races. There was always a very strong "Peace Party" in Seistan which in times of invasion seriously hampered the defence of the country and caused the spirited foreign policy of the Princes to end in disaster.

Tarins about 1871. None of the Tarins[1] are nomads, and only about 80 Ghilzais follow a pastoral life. The Alizais numbered about 1,372, with only 25 families who were non-agricultural. There were about 611 Sakzis, all agriculturists.

Among the tribes other than Afghan in this District the Rakshānis[2] predominated with 1,836 souls, agriculturists: only some 400 being pastoral.

In the Chakānsur subdivision the population was "Baluch" with a large admixture of "Farsiwāns," 2,614 souls, all agriculturists. Here, however, the Dalkhaki, who in Persian territory were agriculturists, numbered about 4,667, all of whom were either "Gaudārs," cattle owners, or pastoral, only four families being returned as agricultural.

Population of the Chakānsur District.

Other sections of the population of Seistan, not yet noticed in the foregoing paragraphs, are the Seiāds and the Kūls. The former, as their name indicates, depend as a means of livelihood on fishing and snaring wild fowl on the lake of Seistan, and in addition they construct the "tutins" or rafts which are so necessary in the country. They live in "Shacks"—huts made of bundles of reeds and bulrushes—along the shore of the lake. In the Shahristān to the west of the Pariun, there are no Seiāds among the village communities which are exclusively agricultural: but in the jungle-clad district of the Miān Kangi, there were (in 1904-1905) Seiāds settled in the villages of Deh Seiād ("the Seiād village") not far from the left bank of the Siksar, of which the Kad Khuda, Jāni, was himself a Seiād, and which contained about 482 souls, all belonging to this tribe. A proportion of the population of Siādak were Seiāds. This village is close to the right bank of the Pariun, and the Seiāds maintain the ferries across that branch of the Helmand, and keep up the tutins used to ferry people over. Here the Seiāds might have numbered 80 souls. In the village of Safar, also close to the right bank of the Pariun, there were a few Seiād families, probably not more than 4 or 5. The ferrymen at the Pariun combine fishing with their other duties. The latter are performed by the able-bodied men; while boys and old men devote themselves to fishing to make a livelihood. The Seiād community in the Mian Kangi district was (in 1904-1905) probably under 600; and there were probably not more than 1,500 souls forming this community. In addition to their other occupations the Seiāds supply the villages, and shepherds domiciled in the neighbourhood of the villages, with

Seiāds and Kūls described.

---

[1] The cephalic index (average) of the Tarins is 82·8; nasal index (average) 67·8, orbito-nasal index (average) 116·4. There is a close correspondence between the cephalic index of the Tarin and of the Parsis of Bombay and of the Tajik. The Tarins are agricultural and traders as a tribe, which is significant when taken into consideration with the close agreement of their average cephalic index with those of the Parsis and Tajiks.

[2] See page 289 for the Rakshānis of Ahmad wāl.

298   THE PEOPLE OF SEISTAN.

mats¹ which are a necessity in this part of the country; and this important manufacture adds very considerably to their livelihood. Mats are woven from the leaves of bulrushes, and are manufactured by the women, old men, girls, and boys who are not old enough to fish or to man tutins.² I noticed that the Seiāds used a large proportion of Arabic words in their speech, and were acquainted with Arabic words for objects, for which colloquially they used ordinary Persian or Baluchi words. The Seiāds also, I noticed, were much less conversant with Baluchi, or even with Persian, than the Farsiwān population of the villages. Their traditions point to an Arab origin, and this is borne out by their cast of features and the shape of their skulls which (as far as I could judge by mere observation unaided by measurements) appeared to be narrower than that of the Farsiwāns. I am inclined to believe that the forefathers of the Seiāds migrated from the district of Kufa, where in the marshes of the Euphrates they acquired the semi-aquatic habits of life which the Seiāds in Seistan display.³ The Seiād huts are grouped in small communities, each of which is ruled by a headman called Kad-Khuda. The waters and swamps of the Hāmūn are parcelled out among these communities, the members of which pursue their vocations within those limits, and for this they pay a cash assessment collected by the Kad-Khudas. It is owing to the presence of the Seiād and Gaudār communities, which derive their support from the waters and reed-bed of the submerged area, that the various parts of the lake bear names to distinguish each of them.

Seiāds probably of Arab descent.

Kūls or helots probably descendants of slaves. Taj Muhammud Kūl their headman.

The *Kūls*, or helots, form a class distinct from the rest of the inhabitants. From their very inferior social standing it seems to be highly probable that they are the descendants of slaves either bought or captured in war; who were compelled to labour on the lands of their owners. The Kūls are agricultural in their mode of life. Their headman (in 1903-1905) was Tāj

---

¹ A man takes a bundle of yellow stems, cuts them to the same length, about 6 feet or more, lays them on the ground, and stamps on them till they split up. Then he picks out the long small fibres, strips off the leaf sheaths, and plaits them into mats in a moment. Sven Hedin, Overland to India, Volume II, pages 265, 599.

² When I wished to obtain mats to roof my hut in Mission camp, and to spread on the floor under my rugs, I had to send to the shores of the Hāmūn and order them from one of the Seiād communities. The mats are of two kinds and qualities, one called Sar-i-khāna, and the other Pusht-i-khāna. The former is a heavy quality, made up in long strips or large squares and is used in roofing huts and to make the walls as well. The latter are for use inside the huts, and are of a lighter make, and usually about the size of a prayer carpet. These mats are used by the people in the agricultural area of Seistan, in place of rugs, to spread on the floors of houses or mat-huts.

The word Haṣīr, a mat, is an Arabic word, used on the shores of the Persian Gulf, where the mats are woven from the leaves of the Pish or palmetto. Haṣīr was not in use nor understood by the people of Seistan.

³ There were great risings of the Khariji in the district and city of Kufa, and these zealots "separated themselves" from the orthodox followers of Islam, and after the reverses they sustained at the hands of the latter, they departed into Kirmān and Khurassān where they formed strong communities and became formidable disturbers of the peace and harassing their rulers by sudden revolts which deluged the country with blood ere they could be put down.

Muhammad, who owing to being a facile tool in the hand of the governor was used by him to humiliate the Kaiānis, by compelling the late Malik Gulzār Kaiān to give a daughter in marriage to Tāj Muhammad Kūl—a blow to his pride which broke the old Malik's heart.[1] To his credit be it said, that Tāj Muhammad is a capable and energetic man who has risen to the necessities of his responsible position, and was a most efficient mayor, the circles under his order being well administered from the government point of view. Unpopular with his fellow Kad-Khudas, who regarded him as an upstart, Tāj Muhammad of necessity had to be very amenable to his patron's wishes and orders; but he seems to have been a man who deserved his good fortune, and his wife is much better off as far as worldly circumstances are concerned, as the wife of a prosperous Kad-Khuda or mayor, than she would have been if she had married any one of her impoverished opium-eating cousins. Tāj Muhammad's sons, by this wife at least, will probably call themselves Kaiānis.

In the Shahristān, the Kūls inhabited one portion of the villages known as Deh Kūl; here they numbered about 387 souls. In the other part the Kūls shared the village with Aukāti's (Farsiwāns from the Hokāt) and probably numbered about 300 or 350 souls. In one of the Deh Gurg villages the Kūls numbered (in 1904) about 172 souls. The small village of Khan Muhammad contained about 200 Kūls. In Deh Akbar Shah Nazar there were about 86 Kūls; this was a Kūl village. The important village of Jazinak contained a population of about 928, out of which probably half were Kūls. In the Miān Kangi, the village of Khāmak (population of over 800) contained the bulk of the Kūls who probably numbered 400; and a few were to be found in the smaller villages and hamlets. The Kūls or helots (in 1904) probably numbered altogether between 2,000 to 2,500 souls. *Distribution of the Kūls.*

According to the testimony of Malik Azim Khan and Arbāb Seif-ud-din the tribes of Bakhtiāri[2] and the Jamshīdis inhabited Seistan down *Bakhtiāri and Jamshidi Tribes once dwelt in Seistan.*

---

[1] Malik Gulzār Khan had an altercation with Tāj Muhammad's father; and the Kūl, taking advantage of the Malik's fallen estate, is said to have grossly affronted him. Enraged beyond all bounds and losing his self-control, the Malik unslung his gun and shot the Kūl dead—a proceeding which in the days of his ancestors would not perhaps have even provoked unfriendly criticism, for was not the victim a Kūl who had so far forgotten his inferiority as to offend his Prince? The Hashmat-ul-Mulk, the Governor and Chief of Kain, had been refused a daughter of the Kaiānis in marriage, on the grounds that his mother was only the daughter of the Kad-Khuda of Duruh, and therefore as her son he had inherited his mother's inferior position. Tāj Muhammad was egged on to apply for redress to the Hashmat-ul-Mulk, who happened to be in residence at Nasratabad. Seizing the opportunity, the Governor expressed great indignation at the lawless act of the Kaiāni, condemned him to pay a fine in money to the State whose peace he had disturbed, and forced him to give a daughter in marriage to Tāj Muhammad for his father's blood to put an end to the blood feud. Such a feud can only exist between equals. An inferior cannot "demand satisfaction." Since then the governor has supported Tāj Muhammad and made him a Kad-huKda, greatly to the sorrow and disgust of this class; who resented but were unable to object to it, or to show their ill-will actively.

[2] Hence the Dawāza-i-Bakhtiāri, a gate of Zāhidān.

300   THE PEOPLE OF SEISTAN.

to the destruction of Zahidān by Timur (December 1383—January 1384). These warlike tribes probably inhabited the mountains and Dashts round the delta of the Helmand in which their chiefs may have held lands in return for military service. Timur is said to have transported them from Seistan to their present habitations. When the Agha (head chief) of the Jamshīdis incurred the enmity of the late Amir of Afghanistan, he fled to Seistan with his family, hoping to find a refuge and allies in his ancient country. Seeing that this country was unable to afford either, he returned to his own country and submitted to the Amir Abd-ur-Rahman and was sent for to Kabul. Such was the story related by the Arbāb. The cephalic index of the Bakhtiāris given by M. Ujfalvy is 88 * * although his researches among them "are based on too small a number of observations to be altogether trustworthy."[1] Both the Bakhtiāri and Jamshīdi tribes were undoubtedly pastoral and they may have formed a part of the Nikudari filibusters, whose headquarters (according to the author of the Rauzat-us-Safa) was situated within the boundaries of Seistan, and from here they extended their forays up to Yazd. Evidence (not amounting to absolute proof perhaps) will be presented in a subsequent chapter that the Nikudari headquarters was probably in Dehwār (or Degwār) the district adjoining the Māshkel Hāmūn, which in the 14th and preceding centuries were within the boundaries of Seistan.

Depopulation of Seistan.

Seistan was nearly depopulated in the century following the destruction of the capital by Timur; and the influx of immigrants, attracted thither by the waters of the Helmand and a fertile soil, took place towards the close of the 15th and commencement of the 16th centuries, and has gone on since those times. The man who showed me over the ruins of Zāhidān did not use a figure of speech when he said that the life-blood of his countrymen had been drained, and had left them apathetic and inert.[2]

---

[1] The Baloch Race, page 11.
[2] The rough analysis of the population of Seistan contained in the foregoing pages proves how very useful it would have been if any anthropometrical measurements could have been made in Seistan.

Seistani labourers at work on the Band-i-Seistan.

(Part IV to face page 301.)

CHAPTER IV.

THE JAT, GUJAR AND AHIRS IN SEISTAN.

THERE seems to be an agreement among those who have studied the subject that the ancestors of the Jats and Gujars were members of a pastoral horde, which migrated from the country beyond the Oxus, closely associated with and possibly allied in blood to the White Huns,[1] and that while the Jats are recognised universally to be akin to the Gujars it is impossible to define the relationship.[2] The original seats of their remote ancestors is unknown, but their Central Asian, or "Scythian" origin[3] was first suggested by Colonel Todd; who regarded them as probably representing the "Scythian" Getœ[4] of classical authors. Recently this opinion has received a certain acceptance, and although it is impossible to bring forward evidence in support of this opinion, still it is worthy of notice that a tract of country beyond the Sihun, the Jaxartes of classical authors, and the modern Syr Darya, was known by the name of Jatah, or Jitah, as late as the 14th century of our era; and the earlier editions of the Map of Turkestan perpetuated this name.[5] In the 14th century the famous Timur led several expeditions in person into the Jatah. Marching from Samarkand his troops crossed the Sihun, also called very frequently the River (Āb) of Khujand (modern Khujent) probably because the troops appear to have always made use of the ferry at this place. Tashkent was usually visited and appears to have lain on the most frequented route. Beyond the Jatah lay the Dasht-i-Kipchāk, and Moghūlistān, and on one occasion the armies of Timur crossed the Artish (Irtish) river by swimming. The operations were carried on in the country towards the Asikul (Issykkul) and the strength of the country is alluded to very pointedly.[6] In those days the Jatah was overrun by Moghul tribes, and Qamar-ud-din, the Doghlāt chief, was Timur's most inveterate opponent.

Origin of the Gujar and Jats.

This is the position beyond the Jaxartes which classical authors assign to the Scythian Massa Getœ. Another curious name appears in the account

---

[1] Early History of India, V. A. Smith, 1908, second edition, page 303.

[2] *Ibid*, page 377.

[3] "No one any longer doubts that the Scythians of Europe and Asia were merely the outer, uncivilized belt of the Iranian family, and * * * the close relation of the Scythian dialects to the Zend and Persian is beyond dispute." Jour. R. A. S., January 1906, page 198.

[4] Massa-Getœ: Massa = the modern Balochi word Mazan, *i.e.*, great. The name therefore meant the great Jits or Jats?

[5] In the most recent editions of the map, Russian names of places, and of districts, have displaced the ancient names which only are to be found existing when these names belong to well-known towns that have been in existence for ages, previous to the Russian conquest of Central Asia.

[6] The various expeditions are noticed in the Zafar-nāmah of Ali Yezdi. Pers. text. Bibliotheca Indica, Calcutta, 1887.

THE PEOPLE OF SEISTAN.

Traces of their names beyond the Oxus and Sihān.

of the first hostile contact between Timur and the troops of Jatah. The former was prosecuting his conquests on the left bank of the Oxus when he was forced to recross that river to repel an invasion from the Jatah. After putting a body of the enemy to flight, Timur halted in the *Maidān-i-Gujrāt* or *Gujarāt*.[1] From thence he advanced to Kesh, the enemy, under the Dārogha (superintendent or governor) of Jatah, retiring before his advance. This name—the Plain of the Gujars (Maidān-i-Gujarāt) is curious in view of the association that existed at a very much earlier period between the Gujars and the White Huns, the latter being clearly recognised as having occupied the country in the valley of the Oxus.

Traditions lost in India.

In India the Gujars have lost all traditions with regard to their original habitations. The Jats also are nearly in the same predicament, but among the Jats in the Punjab some traditions exist as to the last move made by them into India. These will be noticed later on. It is not surprising if the Jats and the Gujars migrated from Central Asia a century and probably more than a century previous to the Christian era, that, being illiterate and depending on oral traditions alone, they should have forgotten everything that might have connected them with the country beyond the Sihun in the case of the Jats, and the Oxus in that of the Gujars.

Seistan a link between these tribes and their original seats.

A link between these countries and India was found to exist in Seistan, and it will be possible to suggest a probable connection between a portion of the population of Seistan with the important Jat and Gujar sections of the population of Upper India. It will be better to describe this part of the Seistan population, and then to show the reasons for connecting them with the Indian tribes alluded to ; lastly, the traditions of the Indian Jats will be dealt with.

Discovery of the Jat in Seistan.

During the course of survey operations in connection with the Seistan Mission, it came to my notice that the Baraj Jats formed a part of the inhabitants. This led me to devote considerable time to collecting information regarding the population ; hoping that further light would be cast on the extent to which the Jat element was present.

The Jats who preserve their name and other tribes or sections of the population, probably of this race

In 1904 the Jats formed the village community of Deh Nawāb and the Kad Khuda-Dād-was a Jat. The villages of Kaud and Warmāl contained the rest of the Jat element of the population, which numbered about 700 souls. These called themselves Jat. But it is probable that other sections of the population, whose origin is unknown, belong to this race ; such as the Kalavi (or Kuloi) Pate Pashm, Nuri, Mahakaki (who call

---

[1] Zafar-nāmah, page 86.

Photo. by Ganga Singh.

Gaudar Dwellings.

(Part IV to face page 303.)

themselves Baloch), Sanādgul, Bāruni, Panjika, Sheikh Weisi and Mir Weisi (who also are to be found in the country round Kandahar), Tillar Shahriāri, Piri, Safed-khāki, Siahsar (who call themselves Baluch but who are cultivators), Belar, Khammar, Zaur, Karut-Khar, Khalil, Pudna, Katlok, Bazi, Darni, Sheikh Nuri, Jur, Aladau, Rahdār, Karim Kushta, Awāzi, Sufi, Khizri and Rahāz. The resemblance in appearance between the agriculturists of Seistan and of parts of the Punjab probably is not accidental, but is due to their being of the same original stock.[1] Of the tribes just enumerated there seems to be little doubt in the case of the Kalavi, also called Galavi, that they are Jats. The Maha-Kakki probably migrated to the country south-west of Nushki, where the ruins of a small village crowded on a low rocky hillock still bears their name. The tribes just enumerated are industrious agriculturists and form the bulk of the labouring class in Seistan.

The Jats are regarded as and call themselves Farsiwān. They speak Persian, and this is the case also with the other tribes, who may probably be Jats.

The Gaudārs or cattle owners, are the Dahmarda, Saruni, Kalb-Ali, Abils, and Dalkhaki (that is from Dalkhak, a place to the west of Dilārām and one stage from the latter, on the Kandahar-Herat Trade Route). The Saruni are also called Sarwini in the country on the Persian side of the boundary. To a very small extent the "Gaudār" tribes cultivate land, and on the Persian side, here and there, the Dah-mardas are agriculturists; but the wealth of the tribe consists in the herds of cattle which they pasture in the reed-beds of the Hāmūn. Those who engage in agriculture have their cattle stations in the Naizār of the Hāmūn, which are placed in charge of their slaves or hired servants; as a rule the cultivating Gaudārs are those who do not own many head of cattle. *The Gaudār tribes.*

These live in habitations which are permanent, but those whose sole livelihood consists in their cattle have no fixed dwellings. They dwell in huts constructed with mats, rendered windproof by the addition of great bundles of reeds which more often than not conceal the mat roofs and walls, and give the huts an appearance of being made from bundles of reeds alone. During the season when the Helmand is in flood, and as long as the level of water in the Hāmūn is maintained, the Gaudārs place their huts just above the highest water-mark. As the water recedes, owing to the dessication of the lake, the Gaudārs follow it till their winter dwellings are situated well within the flood area of the Hāmūn. In order to protect their cattle, *Their mode of life.*

---

[1] This resemblance was noticed and commented upon by my Punjabi followers. The Seistanis, however, usually wear the felt cap, which gives them a distinctive appearance of their own.

and their own huts, against an accidental and temporary increase of water, they surround their huts with a low embankment of earth, the ditch caused by the removal of the soil encloses the embankment on the outside. Sufficient space is left in front of the dwellings to allow of cattle resting on dry ground during the night, and occasionally separate cattle pens are similarly protected with an embankment close to the enclosure within which the huts are located. The area of the Naizār is portioned out among the Gaudār communities, each of which confines itself within these limits. The sites occupied by their summer and winter quarters, and in the intermediate season, are occupied year after year, and this is attested by the condition of the embankments, which are grass-grown. The reeds, which eke out the matting of which the huts are composed, are carefully stacked for use in the following year (when a Gaudār community is forced to move its dwellings) within the enclosures formed by the embankment.

Their dwellings.

The mats are stretched over large hoops formed by tamarisk boughs and stems, both ends of which are firmly embedded in the ground. As the huts are sometimes as much as 12 to 13 feet long and about 5 or 6 feet high and as the mats are usually strips about 10 feet by 4 feet, they are stretched over the hoops and securely fastened to them. The hut resembles the tilt of a waggon placed on the ground. The open end or entrance faces the south, and the opposite end is filled with matting, and in the winter the whole is surrounded with bundles of tall reeds, and bundles are placed across these to give additional protection to the roof of mats. The huts are placed close together to afford mutual support in a gale; but still more to provide shelter from the cutting blasts from the north and north-west, to the cattle which couch on the lee side of the huts at night. Weakly or especially valuable animals, milch-cows as a rule, are covered at night with ragged quarter-pieces of worn-out felts, blanketing, or other stuff, roughly stitched together, and several folds thick.[1]

Seistani Cattle are highly prized.

These coverings are removed before the cattle are turned out into the Naizar after "milking time," that is between the hours of 8 and 9 A.M. The cattle are of the usual Persian type, with very little hump, and some of the larger and finer animals, in shape, are not unlike English cattle. They are black as a rule, and sometimes dark brown in colour and occasionally dappled black and white. The Seistan cattle are much prized in the country round, and before the restrictions on trade were placed by the

---

[1] In the valley of the Helmand cattle, which are not very plentiful, donkeys, and ponies are housed below ground during the nights in winter. A square hole several yards in dimension is excavated and roofed with tamarisk boughs, admission is obtained by a sloping cutting at the lower end of which tamarisk boughs and trunks are placed across from side to side, the ends being inserted in sockets made in the sides of the cutting, closing the exit from the pen.

Afghan Government and duties imposed, a considerable trade was carried on with Kandahar, Herat and Meshed. Whenever the country was moderately quiet, large droves of cattle, guarded by parties of 40 or 50 matchlock men, used to be driven by regular stages destined for those places, while a brisk local trade was also carried on in the course of the journey. Now a languid trade is carried on with Meshed, which is about a month's journey from Seistan. The cattle sell at very nearly the same price as that which prevailed in 1839 when Conolly visited Seistan, about 30 Tomans. The bulk of the trade has fallen off since that time principally on account of the diminution of cattle. Cattle disease in the winter of 1902-1903 following on a famine, was said to have caused the loss of seventy-five to eighty per cent. of the cattle and sheep in Seistan, and it would need some years before this loss could be made good. Only "salted" cattle can thrive in Seistan. Buffalos were introduced, it is said, many years ago, but they died off before they became acclimatized.

Types of Gaudārs. — The Gaudār huts are squalid to a degree. The furniture necessary for a family consists usually of a spinning wheel, heavy wooden cradle (evidently heirlooms) and a hand-mill or quern for grinding grain. These articles are usually seen placed outside the huts. On the floor inside are mats and heaps of frowsy unhealthy-looking coverlets and rugs, judging from appearances heirlooms of great age and liveliness. A long matchlock may be seen occasionally leant against the wall of a hut or suspended from the framework of the dwelling. The appearance of the people is equally squalid with their dwellings. The women appear to age very rapidly, though young women possess considerable beauty of a purely sensual type, large lustrous eyes, regular features, thick lips often with down on the upper lip and the hair at the temples extending down towards the cheek, plenty of hair and stalwart forms. They are unveiled and are not shy when alone; a sack-like garment dyed blue, or red, reaching below the knee in various stages of disrepair and dirt; some tawdry ornaments round the neck and a coloured fillet round their heads. In complexion they are brown, but the natural colouring is toned by neglect of cleanliness. The men wear a long coat with a belt round the waist, a turban, and trowsers of a white cotton material, that is, those who can afford these garments. The dress of their poorer brethren is a cotton smock girdled at the waist and reaching to the knee.

Although the conditions under which the wealthier members of this community live are sufficiently squalid, the conditions which prevail in the small outlying cattle stations which are managed by hirelings and slaves are inconceivably dreadful. The following description from personal observation of the station situated upon the Tapa-i-Kohlak mound in the Chung-i-Beringak (in 1905) will give an idea of the conditions prevailing in such places. A *corral* of tamarisk boughs, some 40 or 50 feet in diameter, had been made to house the cattle at night. On the windward side of this was a screen about 10 feet high extending on both sides of the *corral* to the water's edge, and it provided shelter from the wind for the cattle, and for the caretakers also. The latter—three men and three women—were dressed in rags; barely sufficing for decency. No roof sheltered them from the sun by day, or from the dew at night. A few ragged mats were their beds; and they evidently must have huddled together for warmth, in the lee of the screen, without any other covering but their ragged clothes. A waterlogged tutin enabled them to carry milk and butter to the villages where the cattle owners themselves lived (who in this case cultivated lands in the Miân Kangi). The day on which I had visited the mound the wretched caretakers had allowed their fire to die out. The nearest village was about 3 miles distant, from which fire might have been brought with the very greatest care. They begged me to give them a box of matches, and I was able to give them a full box of sulphur-matches, for which their gratitude was something wonderful. Fuel was plentiful for the mound was covered with dung, which was fully a foot deep inside the *corral*. In the larger encampments the space before the huts is in the same condition, though here the dung is dried and stacked for use. A camp fire smoulders day and night before the huts, and supplies the households with fire for cooking, or for their Kaliâns. A few pans for warming milk, cooking-pots and other humble household utensils (all lacking attention to cleanliness) complete the outfit of a Gaudâr homestead. The milk converted into Ghi (roghan) is sold to dealers on the mainland, or bartered for commodities which the Gaudâr does not raise.

In 1904, the Dahmardas in Afghan territory numbered 863 families, Gaudârs, and 170 cultivating lands who possibly may have owned cattle also. the Dalkhakis 1,318 families, cattle owners pure and simple, and 4 families who were engaged in agriculture. Sarunis numbered 219 families all cattle owners and 20 cultivating the soil; Kalbalis, 618 families owning cattle, and 55 families who tilled the soil; Abils about 541 families cattle owners, and 94 engaged in agriculture. These figures do not include sections of these tribes residing on Persian soil in villages, who were enumerated with other tribes forming the village communities, and it is not possible to separate them. The total Gaudâr families, cattle owners pure and simple, numbered (in 1904) about 3,411. If ten head of cattle be allowed as a very moderate average number owned by each of these families, these must have been fully 34,110 head of cattle

THE PEOPLE OF SEISTAN. 307

owned by them; putting aside any cattle which the cultivating sections of these tribes may have owned. A year or two later Sir Sven Hedin mentions that some of the Gaudār households, which he met with after crossing the Lake of Seistan, must have owned fully 100 head of cattle. The Sakzī Gaudārs, also, have not been included in this estimate, and the cattle owned by them must have numbered at least another thousand.[1]

<small>Probable number of cattle in Seistan in 1904.</small>

The cattle graze in the reed beds during the day and in water which frequently reaches to their bellies; and as the afternoon wears on they gradually work their way back towards the dry spots where they pass the night. The caretakers and herdsmen pole their tutins through the reeds, and collect stragglers and hasten the progress of their charges homewards. The Gaudārs of Seistan reminded me very strongly of the Jat communities who graze their herds of cattle on the low-lying alluvial flats in the delta of the Indus (between the Uchto and Haidari mouths of that river), below Keti Bandar. All over this tract there are cattle stations placed at considerable distances from each other. The dwellings of the cattle owners in this tract are surrounded by high and strong embankments to keep out the water, for at high tides the alluvial flats are submerged, and the cattle pens are similarly protected. At high tides the groups of huts, from a distance, appear to be standing in water, and every group of dwellings forming these settlements possesses a boat to allow them to communicate with one another, for the country is intersected by a network of tidal creeks of varying width and depth, which even at low water are never dry. The alluvial flats are covered with *dhub* grass and the cattle graze on this even when the land is submerged. The Jats in this tract keep buffalos as well, and while the oxen keep to the shallower portions at high tide, the buffalos wander further on into comparatively deep water. It is a common sight to see these animals with only their backs just appearing above the water, dipping their heads below the surface to reach the submerged grass, and raising their heads above water as they chew each mouthful.

<small>Resemblance between conditions of life in the Hāmūn of Seistan and in the Delta of the Indus.</small>

The tribes of the Gaudārs in Seistan, although distinguished by various names (which is the case also among the Jats and Gujars of India), are clearly related (as those tribes are in India) and are practically one people dwelling in close proximity to one another, and are distinct from the

---

[1] The Sakzis living in villages also owned a great number of cattle and grazed them on dry land. Sir Sven Hedin seems to have been struck by the number of animals he saw grazing in the Naizar, adjoining the Shahristan. Overland to India, Volume II, page 265, *et, seq.*

The great bulk of the cattle are, however, to be found in the Mian Kangi and the Chakānsur districts where they graze in the Naizar of the Hāmūn and Hāmūn-i-Puza. Only a small part feed so low down as the Naizar near Afzalabad, where the famous traveller crossed the Lake of Seistan.

308   THE PEOPLE OF SEISTAN.

The Gaudārs are practically one people. Resemblance between them and Gujars of certain districts in the United Provinces, India.

agricultural population, the difference being very marked. While the agriculturists speak Persian and are comparatively civilized, the Gaudārs understand Persian very indifferently, excepting those who are mixed with the agriculturists in village communities. The graziers appeared to have a dialect peculiar to themselves ; not to understand Baluchi very well ; and generally they belong to a lower plane of civilization than the " Farsiwān " agriculturists of the mainland. The Gaudār households resemble very closely, in appearance and mode of life, the Gujar communities to be met with in the submontane tracts of the United Provinces of India ; and it will, I think, be possible to show that this resemblance is not accidental. In physique, too, the Gaudār differs from the agricultural classes. The former are taller, with bony frames, and slighter in build than the latter.

The Numrias of Sind and their legend.

In the Kohistan district in Sind the country is inhabited by a race called the Numrias. This is a corruption of Nuh-mardi or Noh-mardi by which they were known as late as the 17th century and by which they are mentioned in the Institutes of Akbar, compiled by Abul Fazl. The Numrias at one time were a predatory race, but now they have settled down to a peaceful mode of life as camel-breeders, shepherds, and in the Kotri district as agriculturists. In this respect they resemble the Gujars of the Punjab and India. Some years ago, I found a very faint tradition existing among the Numrias of Thana Bhula Khan (in the Karachi district) to the effect that they once formed part of a horde which migrated into " Persia " and afterwards towards India. This horde was composed of two sections, the Nuh-mardi and Dah-mardi, and while the former moved into India, the latter, the Dah-mardi, did not do so. The conclusion does not seem to be unreasonable that in the Dahmarda of Seistan we have found the Dah-mardi of the Numria tradition ; and that at one time—in ages far remote—they formed one people or horde ; and that the Dahmarda of Seistan are ethnologically of the same original race as the Numrias of Sind.

Connection between the Numrias of Sind and the Dahmardas of Seistan.

The connection between the two depends on this tradition alone, but the Numrias continued, that before they moved into Sind, another division of their people took place, and a part of them remained behind in Baluchistan, and that these form a numerous section of the so-called " Brahui " tribes of the Jahlawān Division of the Kalat State.[1] The connection between the Dahmardas of Seistan and the Nuh-mardi or Numrias of Sind would have been established without very much room for doubt if it could have been confirmed by the Dah-mardi of Seistan. It was, however, quite impossible to get so closely into touch with the latter as to make any enquiries as to their legends and traditions. They are very exclusive and shy ; and not understanding either Persian or Baluchi sufficiently to make that

---

[1] This is correct—see Baluchistan Gazetteer series, Volume VI-B, Jhalawan, pages 82 and 83 and elsewhere.

language and dialect a means of communication, researches in this direction received a severe check. The Gaudārs also, who form the bulk of this tribe, dwell in Afghan territory, and consequently free access to their settlements was impossible, it was quite impossible to break down the barriers raised by their ignorance and retiring dispositions, and, therefore, dependence can only be placed on the information obtained in Sind; and the connection between the Dahmardas of Seistan and the Numrias of Sind rests only upon a faint tradition which I discovered lingering among the latter.

Judging from a similarity between the latter and the Gujars of the Punjab and other parts of India in their mode of life in the past and also at present—when a lawless, predatory existence can no longer be pursued with impunity, it appears not unreasonable to believe that the Numrias of Sind formed part of that horde of Gurjaras or Gujars, which overflowed into India, and part of which in course of time acquired considerable political influence in Rajputana and Gujerat over which they ruled for centuries, and whose early capital was Bhīlmāl (Bhīnmāl, Śrīmāl) situated some 50 miles to the north-west of Mount Abu (Bhīnmāl is now a town of only secondary importance in the Jodhpore State),[1] and who are the origin of many of the Rajput clans of the present day, as well as less aristocratic castes.[2]

_{Numrias probably a relic of the Gujar immigration into Sind.}

"Nobody could think of doubting the identity of the modern caste-name Gujar with Gūjara (Ku-che-lo of Hiuen Tsang), the spoken form of Gurjara. The Gūjars are a well-known and powerful caste, numerous in Rajputana, parts of the Punjab, the northern district of the United Provinces, and Central India. They are primarily a pastoral people with a strong tendency to a life of rapine; but of course in modern times have been obliged to devote their attention largely to agriculture. They are closely allied to the Jats or Jāts, from whom they are almost indistinguishable in physique and are also connected with the Āhirs and Golas. A proverb is current to the effect that "the Jat, the Gujar, Āhir and Golas are all four hail-fellows well met."

_{Connection between the Gujar, Jat, Ahir and Gola.}

I also offer the suggestion that in the Ābīls (Hābhīl and Ābhīl are variants of the name; this is evidently, in Seistan, a very ancient race, and which has given its name to the terraces above the Hāmūn, Dasht-i-Habīl, and who are closely associated with the other "Gaudārs" of Seistan), we have found a fragment of the race which gave their name Abhiria to the northern coast of the Arabian sea, and who were the progenitors of the third race mentioned in the proverb quoted in the foregoing paragraph—the Āhir of India.[3]

_{Proposed identification of the Abīl with the Ahir of India.}

---

[1] Journal R. A. Society, January 1909: III the Gurjaras of Rajputana and Kanauj, by V. A. Smith, page 53.

[2] *Ibid.* page 64.

[3] The west coast of India and Gujarat would appear to be their ancient homes * * * and at one time there was an Āhir dynasty in Nepal. Outlines of Punjab Ethnography, page 271.

"All observers (except Sir H. Risley) are agreed that the Gújars and Jats seem to be the descendants of foreign immigrants, and the peculiarities of the Gújars indicate that their ancestors were members of a pastoral horde. Ample justification, therefore, exists for the belief that the Gurjaras were originally pastoral nomads from the steppes of Central Asia, who entered India during the sixth century, probably subsequent to the defeat of the Hunas or Huns."

Probable strong Jat and Gújar element in the "Afghan" and "Baloch" tribes.

The fact that Jats exist in Seistan and the probability of an actual connection between the Gaudārs of Seistan and the Gujars of India is an interesting and valuable link in the chain of evidence which would connect the Indian Jats and Gujars with Central Asia—the Jatah, and the country between the Oxus and Syr Daria. There are Gújars in the Zamindāwar country to the west of the Helmand and north of Girishk. There are Gujars also in the former eastern district of Afghanistan in the valley of the Indus, now under British influence. The Jats also occupied the country now known as Baluchistan, and in the Kej district they were once powerful, and are yet represented in that district as well as in the Bāhū and Dashtiāri districts of Persia on the coast of the Persian Gulf, adjoining the boundary between Persia and Kalat. And an analysis of the tribes now calling themselves "Baluch" and "Brahui" shows a very great and acknowledged admixture of Jats in the composition of those tribes.

It is probable that some of the "Afghan" tribes of Southern Afghanistan may be also of Jat origin.

Migration of the Gujars towards the Caspian Sea.

But India was not the only direction in which these tribes moved from Seistan. There is a class in the population of Ashraff in Mazenderān on the Caspian Sea who are called Godars (Gaudar, or a corruption of Gūjar). They are, however, regarded as pariahs.[1] Judging from the proverbs extant in India referring to the Gūjars, the latter were unwelcomed intruders in India. "A desert is better than a Gūjar;" "wherever you see a Gūjar hit him;" and lastly, "when all other castes are dead make friends with a Gūjar"—to select a few quoted by the late Sir Denzil Ibbetson[2] is a sufficient indication of the estimate in which this people were held in India, where their numbers saved them from repression; while the Godars of Ashraf being few compared to the rest of the population, it would be possible for them to have been reduced to the level of pariahs. The Jats have been associated for many centuries with the tribe of the Meds. The Zat (Jat) and Meds[3] are mentioned in the 9th and 10th centuries as settled on the coast of the Persian Gulf—Makran. They are there at this time. It is said that

---

[1] Encyclo. Brit., 10th edition, Vol. VIII, page 543.
Punjab Ethnography.
Average cephalic index ... 82
„ nasal index ... 68·1
Orbito-nasal index ... 127·3

Baluch types, adults and children.

(Part IV to face page 510.)

THE PEOPLE OF SEISTAN.   311

there are Meds now living in the province or district of Milan on the Caspian.

But the Jats appear to have penetrated still further to the west, for in the historical work of Zenobius,[1] a Syrian Bishop and Primate of the Convent of Innaknian who flourished in the early part of the century from 300 to 400 A.D., there is an account of a Hindu colony in Armenia:—

> "This people had a most extraordinary appearance. They were black, long-haired, ugly and unpleasant to the sight. The story of the idols worshipped by them is simply this: Demeter and Keisaney were brothers, and both Indian Princes. They were found guilty of a plot formed against their king, Dinaskey, who sent troops after them, with instructions either to put them to death or to banish them from the country. The felons, having narrowly escaped the pursuit, took shelter in the dominions of the king of Valarsaces, who has bestowed on them the principality of the country of Taron. Here a city was founded by the emigrants, who called it Vishap or the Dragon. Fifteen years after their settlement in the country both the brothers were put to death by the king. He, however, conferred the principality on their three sons, named Kuar, Meghti, and Horain. After a certain time these three persons changed their abode and settled on the mountain named Karki, a pleasant locality abounding in all things necessary to existence combined with a delightful climate. Here they built temples and set up two idols dedicated to Keisaney and Demeter, in honour of whom attendants were appointed of their own race. Keisaney had long flowing hair, in imitation of which his priests allowed the hair of their heads to grow, which custom was afterwards prohibited by authority. This class of people after being converted to Christianity were not deeply rooted in their faith. They durst not, however, openly profess the religion of their Pagan ancestors. They continued, therefore, dissemblingly to allow their children to wear plaited hair on the crown of their heads in remembrance of their idolatrous abominations."

Possible immigration of a section of the Jats into Armenia.

Eventually, in the month of July (about) 300 A.D., this community was finally subdued, being disastrously overthrown in battle by the Christians. The idolators put 6,946 men in the field, of whom 1,038 men with their Chief Priest Arzan (? Arjun) fell on the field of battle.

> "The tribes of Bhular, Her, and Man regard themselves as the pure or true Jats, and claim to have sprung from the matted" (? plaited) "locks of Mahadeo, whose name is Bhula-Mahadeo."[2]

Jat also is the vernacular word for hair. To the comparatively fair-complexioned Armenians, the swarthy, long-haired immigrants must necessarily have appeared ugly and repulsive; and the fact of the long hair would seem to establish the identity of these emigrants from the east with the Jats. If the migration took place from Seistan, the route followed would have probably been through the valley in which Meshed was afterwards

---

[1] Published by the Mechitharistic Society of Venice in 1832 having been carefully collected with five Manuscripts of this work, copied at different periods. Translated by Johannes Avdal. Jour. As. Soc. Bengal, Vol. V, page 331, Calcutta, 1836. The account which follows has been condensed.

[2] Punjab Ethnography, Ibbetson, page 435.

built, and along the Attrek to the Caspian, as indicated by the existence of the Meds on its shores.

Period of this immigration into Armenia.

Valarsaces or Wagharashag was a member of the Parthian Royal Family under whose leadership Armenia threw off the Syrian yoke; between (about) 151 and 128 B.C.[1] The settlement of this Colony in Armenia was about the usually accepted date of the Saka inroad into Sakstana or Seistan[2] in the 1st century B.C.; though the mention of the Sakas, coupled with the Makas[3] in the Inscription of Darius at Behistun, would appear to be conclusive evidence in favour of the Saka occupation of this part of Khurassān at a very much earlier date.

The Jats in Afghanistan and in Makran and Kalat.

Reverting to the Jat occupation of Baluchistan and Afghanistan, there is evidence which may be noticed with advantage before concluding this chapter. The movement of the Jats into the Kej district may have thrust the Or or Oḍ further east into India, or the latter may have accompanied the bulk of the Jats when they moved eastwards.

Evidences in Kalat.

The capital of the Kalat State, in the 17th century and until the family of the present rulers attained to independence, was officially known as Kalat-i Nichara.[4] Nichāra is now the largest permanent village in the Jhalawān country, and consists of some 400 houses situated below the southern slopes of the great Ragh hill of the Harboi Range, at an elevation of about 9,000 feet. When the Jats occupied the country, the great man, or chief, of Nichāra was one Hamir, a Jat, from whom the present inhabitants are supposed to have wrested the lands which they now occupy. The Nicharis, according to their tradition, are Alakozai "Afghans," and their eponym Alako migrated with his flocks to Nichara in the lifetime of Hamir the Jat. Alako's tomb is in this place.[5]

According to the ballad of Sassi and Punu, which probably dates from the early years of the Arab conquest of Sind, the hero, Punu, was a Jat, the son of the Jām or ruler of Kej. In one of his journeys to Sind for the

---

[1] A reign of 22 years is assigned to this monarch, whose kingdom is declared to have extended from the Caucasus to Nisibis, and from the Caspian to the Mediterranean. Parthia, by George Rawlinson, page 125.

[2] In Gilān, on the Caspian, there are curious points of resemblance between the people there and in India. The diet of the people is fish and rice. The cows of Gilān and Mazenderān are small in size and resemble the lesser breeds of these animals in India. They have small humps, but those of the bulls are larger, differing in these respects from the cattle of Upper Persia. The sheep also are small and of the long-tailed variety (as in India). The "dumba" or fat-tailed sheep is not indigenous to this district; and the people carry loads slung on either end of a stick placed across the shoulders (the Indian *Banghi*). Gazetteer of Persia.

[3] Jour. R. A. Soc., January 1906. The ancient race inhabiting Makran.

[4] Kalat is a contraction of this name, but the foundation of this (now the capital) place dates from recent times. Under the Ghaznivide Sovereigns Khuzdār was the principal town both commercially and from a military point of view. It was a garrison town (Tarikh-i-Baihaki, Bib. Indica) to overawe the rulers of Makran who were feudatories of Ghazni and to maintain authority in the southern portion of Ar-rukhaj.

[5] Baluchistan Gazetteer series, Volume VI-B, page 221.

purposes of trade he saw the fair Sassi, and then befell all the misfortunes to both which are elaborated in the ballad. The ruins of the Miri in Kej mark the position of the ancient capital, the residence of Jām Āri, Punu's father. The ancient name of this place was Fatehpur. In the 13th century when Marco Polo sailed up the Persian Gulf on his return from China, he was informed that the country of Kes-Macoran (Kej-Makrān) was inhabited by idolators and Saracens—Hindus and Muhammadans. This agrees with the local tradition discovered by me in 1891, according to which the country of Kej at one time was in possession of the Jad-gal, the Jats. The country of Kej was bounded on the west by the Dashtiāri river and in the opposite direction by Las Bela (the Armān Bela of the Chachnāma). On the north the watershed was the boundary of Kej and the Sea of Oman formed the southern limit. *Evidence of the popular ballad of Sassi and Punu.*

A reference to the volumes of the Baluchistan Gazetteer series will show how very strong is the Jat element in the "Brahui" tribes of Jhalawān and in Kej-Makran.

The traditions preserved by the Jats of the Punjab are few in number, and very indistinct. These traditions merely record the fact that some of them originally came from Herat, and in some cases from Ghazni, and it is not improbable that these were the last places from which their ancestors migrated to India. The fame of Mahmud, the Sultan of Gazni, has undoubtedly led to the tradition that the Jats who emigrated from Ghazni were brought to India by that famous sovereign. There was a great admixture of races in the armies of Ghazni. Indian (Hindu) troops together with Turcomans and Khurassanis garrisoned Kirmān in the reign of Sultan Masaud, and took part in the wars waged in other directions by him, participating in the final defeat of that monarch by the Saljuks at Dandankad, two marches from Merve, on the 9th of Ramzan 431 (23rd May 1040 A.D.). Turcomans were employed in the Punjab, where the Governor Nialtigin rebelled against Masaud. The expedition despatched to subdue him was led by Tilak, a Hindu, and the son of a barber, who had risen to a high position in the Ghaznivide service. The troops composing this expedition were Indian, especially selected for this purpose by the leader. At this time the Satlej river formed the boundary of the Indian dominions of the Sultan of Ghazni; and although the Jats on the near side of the river are alluded to, the independent Jats beyond the river are especially mentioned, for Tilak[1] addressed letters to them to seize Nialtigin if he escaped to them, and by them he was seized. The bulk of the Jat *Traditions preserved by the Jats of India regarding Mahmud of Ghazni.*

---

[1] Was he a Jat himself? It is not improbable that he was. From the narrative he appears to have been confident that his letters would have the desired effect.

population of the Punjab had been long established in that country by the 11th century.

The most distinct tradition relating to their origin is that preserved by the Varaich tribe of Jats in the Punjab.

Probable connection between the Varaich Jats of India, Seistan, and the Barech "Afghans."

"The Varaich is one of the largest Jat tribes in the Province. In Akbar's time they held two-thirds of the Gujrāt district, though on less favourable terms than those allowed to the Gujars who held the remainder; and they still hold 170 villages in that district * * * * They do not always even pretend to be Rajputs, but say that their ancestor Dhudi was a Jat who came into India with Mahmud Ghaznavi, and settled in Gujrat, when the tribe grew powerful and partly dispossessed the original Gujar lords of the soil. Another story is that their ancestor was a descendant of Raja Karan who went from the City of Kisrah to Delhi and was settled by Jalal-ud-din Feroze Shah in Hissar, whence the tribe moved some five centuries ago to Gujrānwāla. They are almost all Muhammadan, but retain many of their Hindu customs. They appear as Chung or Varaich indifferently in the Lahore district. They intermarry with all the best local tribes."[1]

The traditions of this tribe not only connect them with Ghazni (that is the district in which that town is situated) but refer them back to Seistan. For the "City of Kisrah" can be identified, as it is practically the name given by the modern Seistanis to the ancient capital of that country, the site of which has been identified with the ruins named (at the present day) Nād Ali. According to this tradition, then, the Varaich appear to have been settled, once upon a time, in the country round that city, close to which the Jats of the township of Deh Nawāb are still to be found. In addition the name Varaich is practically the same as that of a widespread "Afghan" tribe—the Barech. There are still Barech Afghans to be found in the Chakānsur district of the Afghan portion of the delta of the Helmand, not far from Nād Ali, but the seat of this tribe in more recent time has been

---

[1] Outlines of Punjab Ethnography. Ibbetson, paragraph 2432, page 27.

Incidentally the author of the Tarikh-i-Baihāki drew a most vivid picture of the state of society in Khurassān and Persia in the 11th century A.D. These countries were densely populated, and the greater part of them supported a civilized population, commercial and agricultural in their instincts, which had attained to a high level of refinement. Even such tribes as the Khalaj, which had wandered into Khurassān from Central Asia, had settled down into good citizens and had become highly civilized. They were mainly located round Kala-i-Bist, on the Helmand. The arable lands were highly cultivated while the mountain-sides supported flocks of sheep, etc. The population was mainly of Iranian or East Iranian stock but among them the Jats may have found a place. The Ruling Family of Ghazni was also of the Iranian Race and traced their descent through Sabaktakin to the Ancient Royal Race of Persia. The aristocracy was, however, military and Turkish. The Turks held command of the forces of the Empire, most of the leaders having been the mamelukes of the Sultans, who had advanced them to high command by virtue of their qualities as soldiers first, and then as leaders. Turks and Turcomans were largely recruited.

There was a complete division between the civil and military branches of the administration. The Turki leaders in the King's Council dealt only with questions affecting their profession. The Tajik or Iranian officials who had the civil administration in their control advised their Sovereign on matters connected with Revenue, the Policy of the Empire, and on all questions relating to the Civil Administration. The Vazier was always a member of the Tajik or East Iranian Race.

The Indian troops were led by Indian officers, and in Council they apparently followed the lead of the Turkish Commanders who had seats in the Council.

(1)

Baluch—Safar Khan (1) and his son.

(Part IV to face page 315.)

the valley of the Helmand, where Landī-Barechi, Pulālak and other lands are still occupied by them. From this place they spread into the Shorāwak district, which they occupy with the Shirānis. The Barechis are to be found in the district of Khāsh and in the country round Kandahar. They are mainly an agricultural tribe, and as such are equal to the Tajik in industry and knowledge; and their predilection for agriculture has lowered the Barech almost to the level of the Tajik in the eyes of the pastoral tribes in Afghanistan. In Shorāwak and the Helmand also the Barech are breeders of camels, and the animals raised in those districts were famous for endurance in the old raiding days in Baluchistan. In 1886-1887 I was told in Shorāwak that the Barech had migrated into it from the west very long ago. Although an agriculturist from choice, the Barech is by no means averse from taking part in raids. The Barech from the Helmand and from Shorāwak always sent a contingent to swell the numbers of old Azad Khan's Lashkars, or forces, and shared in the plunder collected. But the Barech is never altogether a nomad, nor do they as a tribe depend altogether for a livelihood on flocks of sheep and goats.

<small>Character of the Barech Afghans favours the foregoing conclusion.</small>

The identity as to place of origin of the Varaich Jat of the Punjab and the Baraich or Barech of Southern Afghanistan, and also between their names and mode of life, and habits, renders it by no means impossible that at one time (very long ago) they were one tribe. Nor is it unreasonable to assume that, while a part of this tribe migrated from the City of the Kisrah in Seistan, to Ghazni, and subsequently into India, another part elected to remain behind, and have continued to dwell in the country in which their forefathers had lived, after their migration from the Jatah.

NOTE.—For the presence of Jats in Mesopotamia, the adjoining country and Syria see Appendix IV.

CHAPTER V.

Migration of Jats from Kej and Baluchistan.

THE final and latest migration of the Jats from Kej and Baluchistan was probably due to a variety of causes, but the chief of these was likely to have been a very long continued and progressive dessication of the country, a condition to which the depopulation of many regions of Asia has been attributed. In Kej and Baluchistan springs probably continued to fail and at length ceased to flow. Karezes provided a steadily diminishing supply of water and agriculture became progressively less profitable. As years went on and the rainfall diminished the supply of fodder also would become precarious, and in course of time the conditions prevailing in the country brought the struggle for existence between the Jats and the "Brahui" immigrants to a crisis as the country progressively became less able to support the population. The Jats migrated eastwards into Sind, and only a remnant stayed behind who in course of time became incorporated among the so-called "Baluch" and "Brahui" immigrants, forming in many cases important sections of these tribes; and a reference to the volumes of the Baluchistan Gazetteer series will demonstrate this very clearly.

Ballad describing the war between the Jats and Brahuis.

The Ballad which commemorates the strife between the "Brahuis" and Jadgals (Jats) clearly proves that the former were not invaders and not a migrating horde, but that they had been settled for some time in Baluchistan. The mother of Mir Bijjar, the "Brahui" hero, was a woman of Khwaja-Khels of Mastung. The Jats of Las Bela and the Kachhi are alluded to as the opponents of the "Brahui," and it is only to be expected that they should have afforded assistance to the Jats of Kalat and Kej in their struggle for supremacy with the "Brahui" tribes. This was a protracted struggle as is indicated from evidence afforded by the Ballad, which like all of its class of literature condenses in a poetical narrative the events and rivalries of many generations which may have at last come to a head and have resulted in a pitched battle.

Probable dessication of these districts from evidence of abandoned Karezes.

It can be demonstrated (short of actual proof perhaps) from historical and other sources that as recently as the 11th and 12th centuries the condition of the country of Kej and the adjoining districts of Panjgur and Khārān were very different to what they are at present, and that the country was capable of supporting a large, fixed, and agricultural population; intermixed, no doubt, with a pastoral and semi-nomadic alien element. In Kej itself, the country along the bank of the Dasht river is irrigated now by means of ancient Karezes, which derive their flow of water from the river and are not dependent on subsoil water other than that which exists in the bed of that river—the catchment area of which is very great. Similarly the Karezes which nourish the cultivation round the townships of Panjgur are supplied from the water in the bed of the Rakshān stream. Elsewhere in the districts adjoining Kej and Panjgur there are numerous Karezes out of use, abandoned because the water has either completely failed, or is so scanty that it is not worth while to clean and restore the shafts and galleries. When these Karezes were made—at considerable cost of money and labour—they must have provided water for cultivation; and the subsoil springs on which these works depended must have been perennial.

The Khārān district is situated to the north of Panjgur, and the Rās Koh mountains separate it from the Chagai district, which lies to the north of Khārān. Khārān is now to all intents and purposes a desert. Cultivation is now only possible in certain localities after rain. This district was drained by the Bado stream, the deeply cut channel of which can be followed till it disappears in the lowlying tract into which the Mashkel river discharges its floods, and the bed must have been excavated by flowing water. This stream in its lower course now only contains water when there has been very heavy rain, and snow in the hills in which it rises. Then, too, the flood water just suffices for the cultivation round Khārān itself. But the plain of Khārān abounds with the long-ruined sites of villages which were at one time composed of permanent dwellings which at that time sheltered an agricultural (and possibly, too, a Jat) population. Among the narrow valleys in the Rās Koh mountains there are terraced fields, the retaining walls of which are composed of huge natural blocks of stones and boulders, almost cyclopean in character. No people would have incurred the labour of constructing these works unless they had reason to expect a good return. The only intelligible inscriptions discovered in Baluchistan exist in a gorge above the fort of Jālwar and in Kalag in the Rās Koh mountains. They are extensive inscriptions, cut on the face of the rock, in Arabic character. From dates copied from these inscriptions they are referrible to the 10th and 11th centuries of our era, and prove that a certain standard of civilization and education prevailed at that time in the country. All indications point to more favourable climatic conditions than those which now prevail, to a time when the rainfall was greater, and cultivation was probably extensive. The sandhills which now cover the greater part of this district are composed of material eroded from the surface of the soil—a sandy loam—which under the influence of long-continued drought is rendered

The terraced fields known as Gaurbastas, further evidence on this point.

moveable by the wind. At that period Khārān was probably an outlying district of the territory governed by the Maadanite Rulers of Makran.[1]

The Tarikh-i-Baihāki contains the following incidental allusion to this family, which also throws considerable light on the condition of the country they held in the time of the famous Sultan Mahmud of Ghazni and his son Sultan Mas'aud. "When Maadan (Wali of Makran) died, his two sons, Isa and Abul 'Askar, quarrelled over their inheritance. But as the fighting men and agricultural classes were in favour of Isa, Abul 'Askar fled from the country." This was in 412 A.H. (which began on Monday 17th April 1021 and ended Friday 6th April 1022 A.D.). Abul 'Askar made his way to Seistan where he was honourably received by Khwaja Bu Nasr, Khāfi (apparently the Intendant of Sultan Mahmud who was on his expedition to Somnath). Here he remained for some time. After Sultan Mahmud returned from Somnath he summoned the fugitive to Ghazni, when the latter was retained at court. Isa was greatly troubled and he sent a deputation, headed by the Kazi of Makrān, accompanied by the Reis,[2] representatives of the learned and religious classes, and the principal men of the agricultural classes, to the court of his Suzerain. A letter was sent with the deputation, setting forth that he, Isa, was the heir of his father, and that if his brother had not been treacherous and hostile, his share of the inheritance would not have been denied him; offering also if he, Isa, was confirmed as Ruler, to discharge any tribute that might be imposed on him. The request was granted and the Makran Embassy was allowed to return, 'Askar being detained at court.

After Mahmud's death, when his son Mas'aud was absent on an expedition towards Rei, some dissatisfaction made itself apparent among the governors and feudatories of the Empire: Isa-ibn-i-Maadan among the number. It was decided to remove him and to place Abul 'Askar on the seat of authority in Makrān. Matters of greater importance caused this affair to be postponed for a time.

At last an expedition was despatched for this purpose to Makran and a strong reinforcement to Khuzdār in support of the movement. Isa, on hearing of the movements of troops, prepared for war and collected his fighting-men from all directions, raising 20,000 foot soldiers from the Kechis, Rekis, and Makrānis, and also 6,000 horsemen. On the day of battle the Jāmah-dār,[3] commanding the Ghaznivide troops, placed 2,000 chosen horse-

---

[1] Bibliotheca India, Calcutta, 1862. Persian text.

[2] A very powerful section of the present population of Kej, and formerly in the country of Sarhad, north and east of Bampur. Here they are now, however, the offspring of Ghuz who married into the Reis tribes.

[3] Master of the Royal Wardrobe.

Tomb of the Nikūdar Chief Guachig.

(Part IV to face page 319.)

THE PEOPLE OF SEISTAN. 319

men (Sultani, or regulars—Turkish horse) in ambush among the date groves. The Makrāni advanced to the attack with his men arrayed for battle, riding on an elephant, with ten elephants trained for war. The invaders were on the point of succumbing to the onset of the local forces, when the Jāmah-dār rallied his disordered troops, and the men lying in ambush declared themselves. The Makrāni forces were finally routed and their leader was caught in a defile, his head was cut off and carried away. Numbers of his adherents were slain. For four days his city and the surrounding districts were plundered, and much booty and plenty of animals collected. Abul 'Askar was declared Ruler, and the Jāmah-dār and Imperial troops remained till his authority was established, after which they withdrew, and Makrān remained in the hands of Abul' Askar till he died.[1]

Those who know the country as it is—its scanty population, and impoverished and dry condition—will be able to contrast the conditions prevailing there in the 11th and present century.

The country then and now.

---

[1] It is not possible to locate with any certainty the exact site of this battle. Bampur (written Ban-fal in the Alam Ara-i-'Abbasi, 17th century A.D.) had been the capital of the Maliks of Kej and Makran for very many generations before their possessions were absorbed into Persian Territory, after which, and under the blighting influence of Persian Rule, this ancient family declined and died out.

Fahraj or Pahra, about 4 miles from Bampur itself, is a very ancient site and is the Poura of Arrian. Here there is a very fine grove of date-palms, but there were similar groves round the old fort of Bampur which have almost disappeared. Fahraj or Pahra may well have been the battlefield on which Isa-ibn-i-Maadan was defeated, and in this case the Ghaznivide troops must have advanced through Seistan, then subject to Ghazni (see Part I, Chapter II, page 21, *et seq.*). The reinforcements sent to Khuzdār may have been despatched to prevent a general rising against the Ghaznivide Ruler, and also to support the Jāmah-dār should he have been confronted by a great coalition of the surrounding tribes of the western districts of Makran.

" In 1023 H. (began Tuesday, 1st February 1614, ended Friday, 20th January 1615) Ganj Ali Khan, Zik Kurd, Governor of Kirman, laid siege to Bampur, and Malik Shams-ud-din, son of Malik Dinār, was compelled to surrender the fort, and with his sons and members of his family was deported to Ispahan. Shams-ud-din died 1027 (1617-1618). Tomb at Jalk (Sykes, 10,000 miles in Persia, pages 233—234). "

Malik Dinār is mentioned as having been the Ruler of the whole country of Kej and Makran. He is eulogised as a wise and great man.

"In 1030 H. (began Thursday, 16th November 1620, ended on the 5th November 1621), Malik Mirza visited the Court of Shah 'Abbas I. His country had been dependent on India, attached to the Provinces of Tatta and Sind, and he had been subject to the Rulers of Hindustan. But owing to the distance from Agra and Delhi, the Rulers of that Empire were content with a very nominal tribute (from Makran), while the arm of the Sovereign could not conveniently reach the Rulers of Kej and Makrān." (Alam Ara-i-'Abbāsi).

"Malik Mirza was the greatest of all the Maliks (local families of Panjgur and Kej) and of all men of that country * * *. With a small following he presented himself at Isfahān, where he was accorded an interview, and his protestation of helplessness and submission were graciously accepted." (*Ibid.*)

Malik Mirza probably died very soon after, for we read further on of "the arrival (at Court) of Malik Ikktiār-ud-din from Ban Fahal (*sic* in original) of Kej and Makran. He was one of the great men of that country. Led by his good fortune to the foot of the throne, he was accorded an interview, and rewarded as fitting a devoted subject." In 1033 H. (began Wednesday, 15th October 1623, ended Sunday, 3rd October 1624 A.D.).

"The district of Ban Fahal was assigned to him, while the presents that were bestowed on him exceeded the ordinary (or usual) scale. He served under the Royal Standard in the second campaign against Baghdad 1035 H. (began Friday, 23rd September 1625, ended Monday, 11th September 1626 A.D.), at the head of a contingent of Matchlock-men of that district (of Ban Fahal), when he rendered good service." (*Ibid.*)

Previously in the 15th century (1441—42 A.D.), Abdur Razzak, the author of the Matla-us-Saadam, was sent on an embassy to India by Shah Rokh (son of Timur). He arrived in Kirman, but found the governor absent on an expedition against Kej-Makran (Bampur).

320   THE PEOPLE OF SEISTAN.

Date of the Ballad of the Jadgal War.

The date of the Brahui-Jadgal war, described in the ballad given in Volume VI-B of the Baluchistan series, can be fixed with reasonable accuracy as having taken place either in the very last years of the 14th or in the early years of the following century. It will be shown as conclusively as can be expected at this distance of time that the circumstances prevailing in the country at that time were such as to render probable a struggle for the possession of the tracts over which the Jats had been predominant, on the part of the so-called Brahui tribes—that is, the nomads who hitherto had been the neighbours of the Jats.

The Nikūdaris.

The inroads of the hordes of Chingiz Khan not only overthrew the fabric of society and politics in the Middle East, but let loose on the countries that had been devasted in the course of the great invasion prowling bands of Turkish and Mongol tribes that supported themselves by rapine. Such were the bands of the Nikūdaris and Karunas mentioned by Marco Polo as infesting the country through which he travelled from Kirmān.

Degenerate into banditti.

These were, in all probability at the outset distinct tribes of Turks; but as time went on they were joined by all to whom a life of rapine appealed, and eventually became mere organised bands of robbers—broken men, and smaller associations of brigands, some of whom may have been descendants of Arabs, the Mamasenis, perhaps Tajiks also, who had given up their peaceful calling, and even Jats to whom a life of rapine would offer strong temptations. The Nikūdaris of a later day had probably become a very mongrel race, and the name merely another term for a robber or brigand.[1]

First appearance in Khurassān and headquarters in the 14th century.

Their first appearance in Khurassān was in 1298-99[2] and they very soon became notorious. By the middle of the 14th century a band of Nikūdaris had taken up their abode within the boundaries of Seistan; they were nomadic in their mode of life, and seemed to have been in the habit of spending part of the year encamped on the banks of the Helmand. Timur, after his first expedition into Seistan, rested in their tents to recover from the wound he had received. (Part I, page 49.) The famous well of Chah Amir, on the road connecting the burial-place and the headquarters of this tribe at Gwachig near Galugah, with the valley of the Helmand, was probably dug by the order of a Nikūdari Amir, as it is almost half-way across the intervening desert between the two places.

Their power broken.

From Seistan territory the Nikūdari bands extended their raids up to Yazd and Fars and were a terror to the inhabitants of the countries between. Their aggressions first received a serious check by successive defeats inflicted on them by the founder of the family known to history

---

[1] Kazāki and Nikūdari became technical terms for a predatory warfare carried on by horsemen.
[2] Part I, page 42.

as the Muzaffaride, who received the government of Yazd which in course of time he converted into an independent principality. He fought very many engagements with the Nikûdaris and in one of these the free-booting chief himself, the Amir Naushirwân, received wounds from the effect of which he died and the depredations ceased. This reverse was followed early in 1384 (after the sack of Zahidân) by the slaughter of the Nikûdari chief and his followers by order of Timur. This chief, prompted no doubt by an uneasy conscience (owing to his loyalty to the Kaiâni Princes of Seistan), was preparing to move off with his tribe into Kej and Makran from Karan, a locality to the south of the Helmand, from whence Timur's selected troops reached it in a night and a day, travelling rapidly. The Julgah of Karan may have been either the Mâshkel district to the west of Khârân or Chagai, but the probabilities are greatly in favour of Mâshkel and that the route used was by the way of Chah Amir.

In the winter of 1888-1889 I found a valley in the hills near the village of Sinukân, to the west of Jalk, named Nokodar, and a short time after I visited the "Tombs of the Maliks" at Guachig near Galugah, which I found situated in a great cemetery. Here, among weather-worn super-terrene tombs, there were nine very remarkable mausolea standing on hollow plinths, the latter also being full of human bones in various states of preservation, while on the floor of the chambers above (which were covered by domes) there were graves built up above the floor—also containing human remains. The majority of these tombs had been rifled by the Baluchis who, of course, could not tell me anything about the people who were buried there or to what tribe they had belonged—"they were Maliks" was all the information which I could obtain from them. *Their tribal cemetery at Guachig, west of Kharan.*

The most curious feature of the mausolea—which had been built of kiln-burnt brick set with clay mortar, and the lower portion of which were plain courses of brickwork was the outer decoration of part of the walls of the upper storey supporting the dome. Baked tiles about two feet square were set in a kind of concrete plaster which covered the brickwork of the walls. There were several courses of these tiles. On them while yet soft, rude figures of men, mounted on animals intended to represent camels and horses, armed with bows and swords and evidently the representations of warriors, had been engraved in low relief and the tiles had then been baked. On others there were the representations of peacocks with snakes in their bills, and of deer with hunters on foot, and on one was a crude representation of a one-masted boat or vessel. On some of the tiles nearest the entrance to the upper floor (reached by steps, the surfaces of each of these having been paved with brick), were representations of bangles and of human footprints such as would be left *Mausolea described*

2 T

on sand by a foot shod with sandals of the Las Bela pattern. These last appeared to correspond roughly with the number of graves inside the chamber. On one of the decorative tiles was the representation of a man ploughing with a yoke of oxen, all in the roughest and crudest manner possible, short of being unintelligible. Although the representations of animals, horses, camels with their colts, bullocks and leopards, and mounted warriors were the most frequent, household implements such as hand mills were also represented, with rough imitations of human hands, the fingers spread out.

Evidence afforded by the adornment of these buildings.

The scenes were taken, as might be expected, from the daily life of a semi-nomadic uncultured people, who were warriors and hunters; and in respect of the decorations, the tombs in the (Gwachig) cemetery near Galugah resembled the Palija or Kalmatti graves near the Railway Station of Jangshāhi (the Royal Battlefield) in Sind. In the latter, tombs of men are adorned with the representation (cut on stone slabs and not on baked tiles) of weapons and sandal prints; those decorated with figures of bangles and other feminine ornaments were said to have been women's graves. In the graves near Galugah other purely ornamental designs occur on the decorative tiles with those already described.

I spent a whole day in 1889 examining these tombs and provided Sir Thomas Holdich with the result of my examination and with a rough sketch of one of these mausolea, copied from my notes—still in my possession.

"Tomb of the Nikūdar (Chief)."

One of these buildings is still known as the Gumbad (Gumbaz or dome, *i.e.*, mausoleum) of Naushirwān, and upon a decorative tile on it was engraved the inscription Mazār-i-Nikūdar—the tomb of the Nikūdar (chieftain).[1] In view of the historical fact that Amir Naushirwān was the Nikūdari chief mortally wounded in a battle by the Amir Muzaffar in the district of Yazd, this name of the mausoleum, coupled with the inscription on it—"tomb of the Nikūdar (chieftain)"—would prove that his corpse was carried off, as is said to have been the case, and eventually buried by his followers in the tribal cemetery near Galugah in Māshkel, and that the other mausolea were in all likelihood the graves in which his forefathers or other earlier chieftains of this tribe had been interred.

The interments in the tombs in the upper chambers were probably ceremonial (as is the case in China); and when a fresh interment in the family tomb had to be made, the bones of a previous corpse were removed to

---

[1] Mazar, a tomb; used to describe the last resting-place of a holy man or illustrious layman. The proper name Mazar is from a different root.

Carpet-making by Baluch women.

(Part IV to face page 323.)

the vaults below the chamber.¹ This is the custom in China, where, however, the bones are placed in earthen pots after removal from the sepulchre and covered up, the covers luted with cement to keep the jars securely closed. The latter are arranged outside the family sepulchres, which are then ready to receive a fresh corpse. Mausolea built of kiln-burnt bricks bearing the names of various "Maliks" or petty chiefs are met with at several places in the Khārān district, and still remembered as the burial-places of certain personages who were probably the men of influence in Khārān at various dates; "the tombs in the Shimshan—with Sālām bek *Niābat*" (of Kharan) "bear the names of the brothers Hāla and Tūho and their sister Bibi Basso, the first two of whom are famous in Brahui ballads as having taken part in the great Brāhui-Jadgal war in the Jhalawān country."² The old fort at Wāshuk (foot of the hills about 85 miles south-west of Khārān) was probably the headquarters of the chief himself, though his tribesmen most certainly must have spread themselves (in the Baluch and Brahui fashion) over the whole district, dividing the lands among themselves and each ruled by its petty chief.

^[margin] Super-terrene sepulchre in Kharan in Mediæval times.

The assumption is not unreasonable that the Nikūdari tribes known to have been settled within the limits of Seistan had their headquarters in the present Khārān district, and that the eponym of the Naushirwāni family (the chief of which rules the country), and who is called by them Mir Naushirwān, was the famous freebooting chief Amir Naushirwān, who died of wounds received in battle in the district of Yazd, and whose descendants may have been Malik Dosten, and his son Malik Dinār, who figure as the heroes in the war between the Mirwāris (leading the Brahuis) and the Jadgals (Jats).³

The severe check inflicted by the Amir Muzaffar near Yazd on the predatory Nikūdaris, followed by the death of their chief and the slaughter of his followers a short tim afterwards by Timur's expeditionary force, in all probability cut off the family of the chiefs and the leading men of his followers. But it was the spread of Timur's authority which rendered it impossible to carry out those organised raids which had yielded a rich spoil in the past. Just as recently the spread of British authority over Baluchistan put a stop to the restless activity of old Azad Khan, the Naushirwāni, a true descendant of the freebooters of an earlier age. Under these circumstances it is not to be wondered at that the miscellaneous nomadic tribes who had been in the habit of forming the lower rank and file of the followers of the Nikūdari chiefs, should have turned a covetous eye on the comparatively rich country held by their Jat neighbours; rich, that is, in comparison with Khārān, and worth fighting for.

Azad Khan a probable descendant of the Nikudari Chief Naushirwan.

---

¹ This would account for the vaults below being filled with heaps of disjointed bones, not complete skeletons, which might be expected if these vaults also were used as sepulchres.

² Baluchistan Gazetter series, Volume VII A, page 49.

³ *Ibid*, page 33.

324   THE PEOPLE OF SEISTAN.

The present condition also of the Khārān district may be attributed to the progressive failure of moisture which began to make itself felt in the next few years after the final overthrow of the Nikūdari chief in 1384 and has gone on ever since.[1]

The date of the Brahui-Jadgal war may therefore be assigned to either the very end of the 14th or to a very early date in the next century.

The corpses discovered in the tombs at Gwachig are probably the last interments that were made in those mausolea following the slaughter made in 1384. The humbler graves in the cemetery, which surround the more pretentious burial-places of the chiefs, are also super-terrene.

The Nikūdari chiefs are known to have been allies of the Maliks of Seistan, and were probably also on friendly terms with the Maliks of Bampur, between whose territories these freebooters had their headquarters.

Influence of trade with India and the coast.

The peacock is not found in this country and its representation proves an Indian influence. The Nikūdari chiefs probably traded with Sind, where the slaves and other more valuable booty would have obtained good prices, and the ship was due to a similar cause—trade with the coast.[2]

---

[1] The gradual desiccation of the country accounts for the absence of jungles of tamarisk. If the condition now prevailing had been due to political causes alone, and if subsoil moisture and rainfall had not gone on decreasing, the rapidly growing tamarisk would have overrun the deserted tracts in a very few years and the country would have been clothed with a dense growth of this species of tree. The rapidity with which tamarisk grows in places where water and moisture is close to the surface has been described in the description of Seistan in Parts II and III.

[2] The orientation of the graves inside the mausolea at Gnāchig, and of others round them, show that the Nikūdaris professed Islam. But the mode in which the corpses were prepared for burial is peculiar, and proves that they were brought from a distance for burial (at least in the case of those who were interred in the upper chambers of the mausolea).

" Local accounts state that the corpses were in good preservation in the early part of the last century * * * The skeletons are further said to have been lying on bedding and carpets, and to have been clothed in brocade and silks, which were removed by the people. Much damage is alleged to have been done to the contents of the tombs, and many beads, jewels and valuables to have been removed by an Afghan *fakir* several years back, his example being afterwards followed by the local Rakis. Bangles worn by one of the corpses have been obtained and also some pieces of ragged cloth, which were presumably used as shrouds."

" No. 5, a vault 21 ft. square, is particularly interesting as it contains a well-preserved corpse in the upper storey which appears to be that of a woman. From the top of the head to the toe the body measures 5 feet. Excepting the nose and the parts below the navel, the remainder still bears the dried skin, all the fingers and one of the ears being quite undecayed. A blue thread has been passed through the right ear. The skeleton is quite naked. The local people have moved it from time to time placing it sometimes upright and sometimes in a recumbent position. In doing so a good deal of uncrushed barley is said to have fallen from the stomach." Bal. Gazetteer series, Volume VII-A, pages 47—48.

Evidently the viscera must have been removed prior to burial and replaced with fine bhusa or chaff in which the grains of barley were included, or with grain alone. In the very dry climate of Māshkel a very slight knowledge of the art of embalming would suffice to preserve the corpse thus treated for centuries. There would have been no special object in treating a corpse in this manner unless it had been brought from a distance for burial in this mausoleum—evidently therefore a family tomb.

In 1889, the Rekis of Māshkel told me that the corpses in the mausolea had been wrapped, and dressed, for burial in coloured cloth or clothes.

The name Nakodar appears in the Punjab, where one township at least was found by me to bear this name.

After the inroads of the Mongols, India seemed to have been the direction in which fugitives from Seistan sought their fortunes. The Sultan Gheiāth-ud-din Balban, Ruler of Delhi, was accompanied by a body-guard of Seistani Champions (Pahlwānān) when he rode abroad, who marched with their swords drawn (Sultan Balban reigned from early in 664 H. to 686 H., or from 1265-66 up to 1287-88 A.D.). Tarikh-i-Firuz Shahi of Zia-ud-din, Barani, Bib. Indica, p. 30.

Agriculturists—Seistan.

(Part IV to face page 325.)

CHAPTER VI.

The Village Communities and Population in Seistan.

THE Seistani village is a collection of squalid adobe hovels grouped round the Kad-Khuda's residence, or that of a deputy mayor. The outlines of the domed beehive-shaped roofs are broken by the cowls of the ventilators, which admit air and let out smoke, on the apex of the dome. The entrances are all on the south and south-west side; the aspect of a village from the north or north-west is that provided by blank walls, pierced with small square holes to admit air, and most of these are plugged with clay in the winter. *A village in Seistan*

Rarely is a village so poor that it does not possess one garden on its outskirts. It is generally the property of the Kad-Khuda, or of a Saiad, or some member of a family of priests who resides at the place—and as such it is out of reach of the exactions of the government. At a distance no one would recognise the existence of a garden, owing to the high prison-like walls that are necessary to protect the trees within from the ravages of the wind, and it is only as the wayfarer rides through the village that he obtains a glimpse of what is inside—a carefully-tended garden, verdant with beds of lucerne, and gay with the white and purple blooms of the poppy which, with the glossy foliage of rose bushes, of pomegranate shrubs and vines, and in a corner the tall feathery sprays of a clump of cultivated reeds which supplies the owner with his pens, make a charming contrast to the dreary expanses of dilapidated walls and a saline-encrusted plain that form the usual setting of the picture. *Gardens.*

The water supply of the villages is derived from the canals, but when these are not close at hand, the inhabitants have recourse to the village pond (a cesspool too often), the water in which is very frequently too filthy for description. When the canals are dry, wells are sunk inside them by the side of the ford, and form very dangerous traps for the unwary traveller when the canal is full of water. *Water supply.*

The country is divided into circles each of which is under a Kad-Khuda. This person is not elected by the inhabitants, nor is the office strictly hereditary. The Kad-Khuda is only a sub-contractor under the Governor of Seistan, who is in turn the sub-contractor under the Prince Governor of Meshed. The last-mentioned purchases his government and is a farmer of the taxes. He squeezes the governors under him, so that the Governor of *Revenue administration.*

Seistan in his turn squeezes the Kad-Khuda; who continues the process, and extracts all he can from the agriculturist; and the latter tries to get as much as he can out of the land, without paying any heed to the necessity of nourishing the soil. Anyone, therefore, can become a Kad-Khuda, at the annual sale of circles held by the governor, by out-bidding his rivals. But a man whose fathers before him have held this office possesses the necessary funds to purchase a circle and commands respect which is denied the "new man" or upstart. The Kad-Khudas obtain a rebate on the revenue which they collect on behalf of the government, and also are given other privileges.

The Pāgo.

The agricultural community in a village organises itself into groups of partners who take up land for cultivation. These groups are called Pāgos. The number of these is regulated by the amount of land which the Kad-Khuda decides to cultivate. The numbers of Pāgos in each township, circle, and in the country at large, varies from year to year.

Derivation of this term.

There can be no doubt that this system is of very great antiquity. It would seem highly probable that the name Pāgo is from the primæval root which occurs in the Latin Pagani and the Early-English Pagi (adopted from the Latin) which was the sub-division of a hundred. The rural outlying communities, from which our word Pagan is believed to have been derived, were probably groups of cultivating people who occupied lands at a distance from the parent township, which was a centre of civilization and refinement, just as in the Miān Kangi the Pagani (Pāgos) who dwell in rude huts on the land they till, in very many cases belong to the larger townships of the Shahristān, where are to be found such refinement and civilization as exist in Seistan.

Two kinds of Pāgos and their respective corvées.

Pāgos are of two kinds—Ghami, *i.e.*, subject to public, laborious or vexatious (Gham) corvées—and Tahwil. The former have to work on any land they may be allotted and wherever it is situated. The latter, who work for the Kad-Khuda, usually are favoured as to the quality of the soil, and are usually kept within easy reach of their village, as they discharge the corvées, for which they are liable, to him, repairs to his residence, work in his garden or opium patch, etc. The corvées to which their less favoured brethren are liable are usually the construction and maintenance of canals, or the governor's residence in the capital town, and the annual construction of the Band-i-Seistan in the Helmand. While thus occupied the labourers provide their own food and live in the spot as best they can till the work for which they have been selected is completed. The strength of an ordinary or Ghami Pāgo is fixed at 6 men. Tahwil Pāgos vary from 6 to 10, but the greater number of these consist of 7 men

When the partners contribute equal shares in the outlay necessary to put the lands allotted to them under cultivation, they divide equally the portion of the yield which is left after satisfying all demands.

The custom of the "Dead-man."

In the Afghan portion of Seistan the partners in each of the associations set apart one man to be on the spot in the village to discharge the corvées for which they are liable. This man takes no share in the work in the fields, and is called the "*dead-man*" or *mard-i-murda* in the vernacular. The other partners are able to devote themselves uninterruptedly to agriculture.

Fees exacted for allotments of land unfairly worked, village officials the Kad-Khuda and irrigation engineer.

The land is the property of the State, no one has any right to it. Each Pāgo has to pay a fee, which is supposed not to exceed 60 krans, before it receives an allotment of land. The allotments are made annually, and the Ghami Pāgos have no idea where the land may be situated. In this respect the members of such a Pāgo are absolutely at the mercy of the Kad-Khuda, and do not know beforehand whether they will have to cultivate lands in the Shahristān or be called on to move to more remote allotments into the Miān Kangi. The distribution of lands is delayed till just before it is time to commence operations, and having paid their fee the members of a Ghami Pāgo are not in a position to refuse to go. The allotment and personnel of the Tahwil Pāgos cause a great deal of cavilling, and a certain amount of this would be inevitable almost, even if the system was worked with scrupulous impartiality. Those, however, who know the East, know that from China to Turkey, however excellent the Laws of the Land may be, scrupulous impartiality in administering them does not exist in any oriental country. The administration of rules and regulations depends on the rapacity of those who are supposed to administer them. The most important official under the Kad-Khuda or Mayor, is the irrigation engineer. Not infrequently the latter has to look after the canals of more than one village, but where a village is important and the area under crops is considerable the irrigation engineer has his time fully occupied with the care of the irrigation channels and the distribution of water to the cultivators. His duties are to align canals or distributaries, and when these have been established, it is his duty to see that they are maintained in working order, and regularly cleaned; to acquaint the Kad-Khuda whenever it is necessary to repair embankments, both of the canals and those which have to be maintained to prevent the overflow of water from the Hāmūn or the river; and to summon the gangs of able-bodied labourers (Hashr) for this purpose. The distribution of water enables the irrigation engineer to add very considerably to his income, which (like the other village officials) is a dole of grain from each Pāgo, the amount of which has been fixed from time immemorial, and represents his legal emoluments; but his goodwill can always be purchased by a timely gratification.

THE PEOPLE OF SEISTAN.

The latter found wherever irrigation has existed.

This useful member of the village community has been in existence as long as irrigation has been practised; and he is found to exist wherever irrigation channels or canals have been found to be necessary. The native irrigation engineer was found by the Russians carrying on his work in the fertile tracts in Turkestan, where canal irrigation was in existence, just as he was found to exist by the Arab and other conquerors when they overran the countries occupied by the East-Iranian race, where canal irrigation was practised. It was found "that with all their ignorance and want of technical skill, the natives, simply following the custom of their forefathers, and an inherited understanding of the wants of the soil, were more successful than Europeans in whose hands the management of the canals had been placed as an experiment with the object of doing away with the post of Arik-Aksakal,"[1] the name by which the native irrigation official or engineer is known in the country round Samarkand. Mir-āb (water-master) is the name used elsewhere than in Seistan, where the term Paukār, and sometimes Jhar-Chin, is usually employed, and in the Helmand valley Galba. Under the Russian Government the Arik-Aksakal (or Mir-āb) is paid in proportion to each year's harvest, but there, as elsewhere (and in Seistan), this official makes his money not from his recognised emoluments but from the bribes which he receives. Men of this class in bygone times have not infrequently risen to high office, for in addition to their training continued for innumerable generations, the office has always been most lucrative. Muhammad Taki Khan who, in the time of Nādir Shah, rose to become the Governor of Fars and the Kuh Geiluyeh, began life as Mir-āb of Shirāz.

The Kalgir.

In addition to the Pāgo there is the Kalgir. This term is applied to grants of land free of revenue. In Seistan, it was estimated that such grants comprised an area which 100 Pāgos could cultivate, three or four Kalgirs being regarded as equivalent to the area which one Pāgo could cultivate. The number of families which enjoy these grants was estimated at 800. These are in the possession of the holders and are managed and cultivated by their households. These grants are made as a rule to Mullas and Mujtahids; but can be a reward for good service generally. These have been included in the Tahwīl Pāgos.

Opium.

Opium is cultivated for local consumption, and it was estimated that fully eighty per cent. of the population use this drug.

In return for Tahwīl grants, the Kad-Khudas are liable for military service. They maintain horses or ponies (and in the Miān Kangi "jambāz" camels) on which they mount their kinsmen and dependants, who form the ordinary militia or police of the country. In 1904 this levy was made,

---
[1] Russian Turkestan, page 16.

Threshing Floor in Seistan.

(Part IV to face page 329.)

probably to enforce the obligation, when it was reported that 450 men assembled under arms. Their firearms are antiquated and useless as an armament. The levy *en masse* of Seistan is theoretically "10,000 matchlocks or muskets," and the last occasion on which they mustered was when Azad Khan of Khārān threatened Seistan, but wisely decided not to entangle his mounted followers among the canals, and swept by Chakānsur into the Helmand valley. The number of Pāgos will give the strength of the able-bodied men in the population of Seistan, which would be about 13,720 (in 1904-05) for the Shahristān and Miān Kangi, but even antiquated firearms for this number would not be forthcoming.

Kad-Kudas liable for military service. Fighting strength of population.

The revenue is collected in kind, and the demand for the use of the land is one-third; but in addition a further demand of one-tenth on the remainder, called locally *dahnima*, which brings the total demand up to two-fifths of the total outturn of the lands cultivated by each Ghami Pāgo. Each Tahwīl Pāgo is assessed at about half of the yield of the land cultivated by them. In point of the revenue-demand the Tahwīl Pāgo is not better off than the Ghami Pāgo, but it is better off in respect to tenure, quality of soil, and situation; careful agriculturists being naturally favoured as the cultivators of Tahwīl lands.

Revenues.

In addition the Kad-Khuda takes from each Pāgo 30 *mans* Seistani measure of grain. In ancient times this was 50 mans. These form a part of the Kad-Khuda's emoluments.

Kad-Kuda's perquisites.

The collection of revenue is by actual division of the grain, which is the produce of the lands held by each Pāgo, on the threshing floor, or Batai as it is usually called in Afghanistan and known to British administrators. The system is condemned on obvious grounds; but in a country like Persia, or anywhere in the East, the abuses which arise from it are very great, and it provides opportunities for illicit gains on the part of the village officials. Each of the latter is entitled to a proportion of the produce from each Pāgo as his wage on each crop.

Collection of the revenue in kind.

Then in addition there are those most useful members of the village community who are non-agricultural and represent the professional and learned classes of more favoured countries. Each of these has a fixed scale according to which every Pāgo remunerates them with doles of grain—the barber-surgeon 5 mans, the blacksmith 20 mans. Mullas (or priests) who officiate at births, deaths and marriages, and have charge of education, also receive their doles.

Other village officials receive doles.

If plough oxen are hired, about a third of the nett yield in grain is paid for their hire. After discharging all their legal and other obligations the

Hiring of plough oxen.

members of a Ghami Pāgo may, perhaps, divide up about a fifth of the grain or produce they raise.

Cash assessments or payment and area cultivated by each Pāgo.

The only cash payments are the fee to the Kad-Khuda on taking up land, which is called Sar Naskhi, and the hire (when this is necessary) of cattle for treading out wheat and barley from the ear; this is paid for by contract by a small cash payment. It was estimated that each Pāgo tills on an average about 70 acres of land.

Exhaustion of the soil.

And sources of manure available.

Under the system described in the foregoing pages, agriculture in Seistan is carried on with the view of getting as much as possible out of the land under cultivation. Except on lands in the immediate vicinity of villages manure is unknown. Shepherds are encouraged to camp on fallow land and the dung of cattle, sheep and goats forms a most valuable addition to the very scanty farmyard manure, and to the sweepings of households which are the usual resources of cultivators whose allotments are conveniently situated with respect to their homes. In the Shahristān and the Miān Kangi, about 159,560 acres are annually under crop, or about 248 square miles. Deducting the area of land which cannot be cultivated owing to extreme poverty of soil, or being situated above the reach of water, covered with sand-dunes and ruins, or rendered useless by wind erosion, and last but not least river-beds—the Pariun and its channels alone covers about thirty square miles of country with its flood waters—less than a third of the whole area of the Shahristān and the Miān Kangi is under crop in any year, and it is possible for lands which have been cultivated to lie fallow for two years. Then again the deposit of silt, either from canal irrigation or floods, contributes to restore vigour to soil that has been recklessly cultivated, and thus the progressive impoverishment of the soil is checked.

Scientific management of the water would give very great results.

A barrage across the Helmand and scientific irrigation by means of canals would result in about 5,000 square miles of land being placed within the reach of water, and therefore rendered available for cultivation. The existence of a barrage—the Band-i-Rustam—previous to its destruction by Timur is a proof of the civilized condition of Seistan previous to that catastrophe, and of the existence of a scientific irrigation system, the value of which must have been clearly perceived by some of the early rulers of the country. The construction of such a work to a great extent must have minimized the occasional failure of the Helmand: for when no water reached the Delta in 1902 (the date of the last failure of water in the Helmand), there was water in the river-bed as low down as Chaharburjak.

In Afghan Seistan, in the Kang District, there are regular villages which are inhabited chiefly by Afghan cultivators. The Ghilzais are represented among the latter, and their presence in Seistan probably dates from the time of Mir Weis, who, after he wrested Kandahar from the Persians, overran Seistan just before his death. In this district also the lands are irrigated, whereas in the district round Chakānsur, where the Afghan Governor resides, the cultivation depends principally on natural moisture. In the latter district it was estimated that about 40,000 acres had fallen out of cultivation during the six or seven years preceding 1904-1905. This, however, was chiefly due to the policy of the Government in inducing Baluchis to migrate into the Bādghīs District to the north of Herat where lands were given to the immigrants. The reason for this was said to be the desire of the Amir to establish a Sunni population in Bādghīs (and the Baluch is always a Sunni) in the midst of the Hazaras, who are Shias. Afghan Seistan described.

In the Shahristān it was not possible to obtain the number of circles into which the land was divided for administrative purposes. Here we were too close to the seat of Government. Across the Pariun, however, the people were more communicative: the Miān Kangi District is divided into circles which are farmed to contractors, who pay a sum of money to the Governor for the right to collect revenue. Circles in the Shahristān omitted.

In this district the Siadak Circle was (in 1904-1905) farmed by Sardar Khan Jahān Khan, Sanjarani, and this circle was assessed in kind at 400 *kharwārs* of grain, wheat and barley, in equal shares; and in addition a cash assessment of 12,000 krans per annum. The Sardar was allowed a rebate of 60 kharwārs; and the three bailiffs who worked under his orders received each a rebate of 10 kharwārs on the grain collected by them individually. In this circle the produce of the *Kalgirs* was divided into five shares. The Sardar took two shares and the cultivators three, out of which they defrayed the allowance due to Kad-Khudas, village officials and menials. Circles in the Miān Kanji.

Deh Dost Muhammad: This circle was assessed in kind at 1,000 kharwārs of wheat and barley in equal shares, and 20,000 krans in cash, annually. Dost Muhammad, Saruni (but who calls himself a Kazilbāsh, as he has risen in the social scale), the sub-contractor under the Government, receives a rebate of 93½ kharwārs of grain per annum, in return for which he has to maintain two horsemen and one Jambāz (camel-rider). Each of the former receives 10 kharwārs of grain and the latter 5 kharwārs per annum.[1] In addition Dost Muhammad contracted for the right to collect grazing dues throughout the Miān Kangi. Deh Dost Muhammad.

Burj-i-Mir Gul: Assessed annually at 560 kharwārs of wheat and barley in equal proportions, and 5,000 krans in cash. The farmer of the revenue receives 40 kharwārs as his rebate. Burj-i-Mir Gul.

---

[1] The proportion of 2 to 1 represents the consideration shown to a horseman over his comrade who is mounted on a camel. This has been established by ancient custom, and the loot collected by a band or raiding force of brigands is divided in these proportions between mounted men.

This held good in the raids made by the late Azad Khan, a bandit on foot getting only half a share.

Jhānābād.	Jhānābād: Assessed at 400 kharwārs of wheat and barley equally, and 3,000 krans in cash, annually.
Pulgi.	Pulgi: Assessed annually at 260 kharwārs of wheat and barley equally, and 6,000 krans in cash. The farmer is also assessed at 3½ horsemen, and two Jambāz, or camel-riders. He received a rebate of 70 kharwārs of grain.
Gurguri.	Gurguri: This circle's annual assessment is only 60 kharwārs of wheat and barley in equal proportions, and 800 krans in cash. Two horsemen were maintained. The rebate was 20 kharwārs.
Padai.	Padai: Dur Muhammad, Saruni, and Mir Haji, Khammar, divide the farm of this circle between them and are equally responsible for it. The annual assessment was 200 kharwārs of wheat and barley in equal proportions, and 2,000 krans in money.
Daulatābād with Khāmak.	Daulatābād with Khāmak: Annual assessment was 1,080 krans and 350 kharwārs of wheat and barley in equal parts. Taj Muhammad, Kūl, who had farmed a number of villages in the Miān Kangi, for his own convenience divided them into two portions, placing one-third under Daulatābād and the remainder under Khāmak. The annual assessment was probably divided into similar proportions.
Work on canals.	Work on the canals being a state corvée, the men employed on this work do not receive any remuneration and provide their own food. Each Págo has to detail one man for this work.
Incidence of villages in Persian territory.	In the Persian share of the Delta there were 386 villages including the Miān Kangi, where, however, the majority of the villages do not deserve this title and are hamlets both as regards the number of family tenements they contain, and the nature of these dwellings—which are of a very temporary character. Of this number, only three had an estimated population of over five hundred; two contained a population of (about) from three to five hundred families. The remainder were little better than hamlets.
In Afghan territory.	Across the boundary in Afghan territory there were permanent villages only in the Kang sub-division; and with the exception of the town of Chakānsur, where the Governor resides, the cultivators reside in collections of very squalid temporary dwellings, among which are to be found a few small adobe huts of a more permanent character.
Incidence of village to area.	On the Persian side of the boundary the average area of land occupied by a village community is less than three square miles. In the Kang sub-division it is about the same, but in the Chakānsur District an average would give a very erroneous idea, as in this district there are very large areas covered with ruins, and which could only be cultivated in years of abundant

Photo by T. R. J. Ward, Esq., C.I.E., M.V.O.   Photo-Engraved & printed at the Offices of the Survey of India, Calcutta, 1912.

The long suffering Persian Ass.

(Part IV to face page 333.)

THE PEOPLE OF SEISTAN.

rain and snow-fall—a condition which does not often recur in Seistan. The ruins round Sär-o-Tär alone cover an area of over 500 square miles, in which human beings cannot live.

The enumeration of the population of both the Persian and Afghan portions of the Delta of the Helmand was made five or six times, and the mean results have been entered in the Tables. These are as accurate as it is possible for such information to be, as the rigorous methods in use in census operations in more advanced countries could (for obvious reasons) not be adopted in a foreign country. *Population—how enumerated.*

As far as possible the agency employed was the subordinate staff of the Survey Party attached to the Mission. Alphabetical lists of villages, and note books with numbered pages were issued to the Surveyors, who were ordered to push enquiries just short of the point of the investigations being brought to the notice of the Persian and Afghan authorities. An interval was allowed to elapse and a redistribution of villages was made, each enumerator being given a different set of villages (and books) each time regarding which the information was required. The final results were collated by me. This method was employed in collecting the information on the Afghan side of the boundary, but here the services of local Mullas were utilized for this purpose. *The agency available for this purpose.*

As an individual and detailed enumeration was out of the question, an enumeration of "families" was substituted, the investigation of the average number of souls being conducted by me personally. In the village communities of the Farsiwāns, principally on the Persian side of the boundaries, and in the Kang sub-division of the Chakānsur District, which was inhabited by Afghans and where there were regular villages, an enumeration of the number of houses in each village was made. These villages are composed of tenements—separate *family dwellings*, each of which comprises in itself the dwelling of the household, and, in an enclosed yard attached to it, the stalls for livestock owned by the household, its provision of fuel, fodder, and the implements and necessaries of life for man and beast. *Enumeration made by families.*

The Persian word "*Khānah*" is used indifferently for such tenements as well as for the family of the householder in ordinary colloquial. The number of houses or tenements in any village therefore represents, within reasonable limits of error, the number of families composing the village community.

A small floating population of shepherd and pastoral families are usually to be found attached to most of the villages. These, however, dwell in blanket tents or in mat huts on the outskirts of the villages and are easily enumerated. Here also each family has its separate tent or hut. *The floating population.*

THE PEOPLE OF SEISTAN.

The rule appears to be that as soon as a man (Farsiwān or pastoral) marries he sets up as a householder, and his parents, where there are many sons, generally take up their abode with one of the latter. Daughters marry into other families and leave their own family.

Average number of souls in a "family."

The average number of souls in a family was found to be 4·3, the result derived from 40 to 50 observations.[1] This has been taken as a general average for the country. It is very probably correct, as in the higher classes, the use of opium by both sexes, and their stagnant lives and sensuality, result in very small families. The observations in this direction were made from the agricultural labouring classes, which in Seistan, as elsewhere, are probably more prolific than the classes above them in the social scale.

Numbers of families in Persian and Afghan territory.

From the results obtained the population expressed in families of Seistan in 1904-05 was made up as follows :—

	Agricultural.	Pastoral.
Persian Territory—		
Shahristān	13,787	1,835
Miān Kangi	5,541	232
	19,328	2,067
Afghan Territory—		
Kang District	3,620	1,884
Chakānsur	2,380	3,150
Total	25,328	7,101

making a grand total of 32,429 families located in the Delta of the Helmand ; or the total number of persons to be 139,294.

Incidence in persons per square mile.

The incidence on the Persian side of the boundary (in 1904-05) was about twenty-six families, or 111 persons, to the square mile ; while on Afghan territory the incidence was about sixteen families, or about 69 persons, to the square mile.

Total population of Seistan.

To obtain the total population of Seistan it will be necessary to add the estimated number of inhabitants in the southern delta of Persian territory and in Kala Fath and Chaharburjak (Afghan) districts, in which the total population (agricultural and pastoral—principally the latter), was about 5,012 families ; or the number of persons to be about 21,552 persons ; making the whole population of Seistan as it stood in 1904-05 to have been about 169,846.[2]

---

[1] In Baluchistan, at the census of 1901, the incidence per house (a family) was found to be 4·5.

[2] In the Frontiers of Baluchistan, page 224, this is stated (erroneously) to have been the population of the Delta alone.

In the actual Delta of the Helmand the distribution of the population was, on the Persian side of the boundary, 91,998 persons; and in Afghan territory—in the Kang and Chakānsur Districts alone—about 47,296 persons.

Distribution population.

Appendices I and II contain the figures of population, village by village, in Persian Territory, and an abstract of the estimated strength in families of the tribes composing the agricultural and pastoral sections of the population for the Afghan share of the Delta of the Helmand.

Final remarks.

These results are, of course, not to be regarded as absolutely correct. Care was not spared to make them as accurate as the nature of the enquiry, and the circumstances under which it was prosecuted, would permit. They are, however, the conclusions arrived at after a very careful and independent enquiry, and are, therefore, entitled to respect on these grounds, in comparison with other researches in this direction carried out under the same conditions.

Results are approximate.

There can be no doubt that great fluctuations have taken place in the population of Seistan at different periods of its history. The decrease in the population has always been attributed (by chroniclers) to the anarchy that has prevailed in that country since the conquest by Timur in 1384. From the beginning of the 16th to the middle of the 18th century, under the rule of the Kaiāni Maliks as feudatories of Persia, the country enjoyed peace from outside enemies, and the population accordingly must have increased both naturally and by the influx of immigrants. On the decline of Persia and the rapid downfall of the family of the Maliks, the country suffered, until in 1872, the late Sir Frederick Goldsmidt estimated the population occupying the delta at only 45,000 souls.

Variations in the population.

Judging from the ruins of all descriptions and from traditions collected in the country, I estimated that previous to the invasion of Seistan by Timur (1383-1384) the population must have numbered at least a quarter of a million, and probably had been twice as great as it was in 1904-1905.

Population of Seistan prior to invasion by Timur.

APPENDIX I.

(A)

Abstract of the village population, and Pāgos, of the Shahristān, and Miān Kangi Districts, of Seistan.

PERSIAN TERRITORY.

1904-05.

THE PEOPLE OF SEISTAN.

SHAHRISTĀN.

No.	Name of village.	PĀGOS.		NUMBER OF FAMILIES.		Kadkhuda.	Tribes of the inhabitants.
		Ghami	Tahwil	A*	B†		
1	Akbar Abbās	12	2	88	24	Purdil Khan, Sarbandi	Andi, Sanchuli.‡
	Abbās Kor	3	1	24	15	Sultan, Shahraki	Tribes of Gurg and Safed Khāki.
	,, Khān	3	1	40	...	Muhammad Amir, Jamāl-zai.	Tribes of Mir Shikār and Safi.
	Adimi	21	1½	310	...	Mir Kasim (Mir)	Pudna, Sanchli and Dilārāmi. Four Kalgirs no Tahwils.
5	Afzalābād	10	2	76	15	Mulla Husen, Arbāb	Arbābs.
	Aghai	5	3	74	...	Kad. Aghai, Arbāb	Arbāb and Gadāh.
	Akbarābād	6	2	52	22	,, Fakir, Mir Shikār	Mir Shikār, Zaur and Panjak.
	Akbar Jāfir	4	1	40	...	,, Muhammad Amir, Sarbandi.	Sarbandi and Zaur.
	Akbar Shāh Nazar	2	...	20	...	,, Mirza Haidar, Kāini.	Kul.
10	Akhund, Mulla Ghulām.	2	2	25	...	,, Mir Beg, Sarbandi	The Tahwils granted to Muhammad K a k h a. The Ghami pāgo under Mir Beg. Gurg, and Mulla Ali.
	Aliabad, No. 1 (Saiyad).	21	9	198	50	,, Saiad Ali	—
	Aliabad, No. 2 (Zāhidān).	9	3	76	...	,, Mir Kasim	Sheikh, Tillar, Sanchli.‡
	Ali Akbar No. 1	3	1	27	...	,, Ibrahim Dabāshi, Jotegh.	Jotegh and Khidri.
	,, ,, ,, 3	1	...	8	...	,, under Chilling	Mir Shikār.
15	,, ,, ,, 2	3	3	40	24	,, Purdil Khān, Sarbandi.	Gurg, Shahriāri, Raház.
	Aliāri	2	1	9	...	,, Muhammad Haidar, Kharrāt.	Mulla Shāhi. Some inhabitants live in blanket tents.
	Allahi	5	1	32	...	,, Ghulam, Shahriāri	Shahriāri and Zaur.
	Ala Sufi No. 1	3	1	26	6	,, under Chilling	Khizri, Mir Shikār.
	,, ,, 2	...	5	34	...	,, Muhammad Māhdi, Kakha.	Zauri, Belar, Kamāli, Ala Sufi.
20	Allahābād	8	2	64	20	,, Arbāb Haidar	Kakha and Raház.
	Ali Jafir	4	...	...	...	,, under Jazinak	Cultivated from Jazinak.
	Ās	4	1	60	...	,, Ghulam Tamarabadi, Misgar.	Rahdār, Galavi.§
	Carried over	131	42½	1,323	176		

* A Agriculturists. † B Shepherds, graziers, etc. ‡ شَپُو or سَنْچولي. § گلوي or گلوي

SHAHRISTĀN—continued.

No.	Name of village.	Pāgos. Ghami.	Pāgos. Tahwil	Number of Families. A*	Number of Families. B†	Kadkhuda.	Tribes of the inhabitants.
	Brought forward	131	42½	1,323	176		
	Ās-i-Kāzi	3	...	18	6	Kad. Tāj Muhammad, Piri	Piri.
	Awāz	3	...	24	...	„ Fakir Muhammad, Khammar.	Awāzi.
25	Bachadur	3	...	35	...	Nawab Khān, Gorgej, Haidar Ali, Nahrūi.	One pāgo under Haidar Ali Sharifābād Rākahāni, Gazma (Baluchis).
	Baghak	6	1	44	5	Muhammad, Kakāh	Zaur.
	Bahrāmābād	24	...	144	36	Tāj Muhammad, Kūl	Sargazi, Kūl, half produce goes to Kad Khuda who maintains sowars, for service, half to Government.
	Bakhtai	6	...	94	...	Haidar Ali Khan, Nāhrui	Bakhlāi, Zaur, Dilārāmi.
	Bālākhānā	10	2	76	30	Muhammad Mehdi, Kakah.	Sargazi and Kaka.
30	Bolai	12	3	160	...	Aghai, Mir Weis	Mir Weis, Saiad, Jur, Abwil.
	Bazi	3	3	60	...	Khani, Jotegh	Bazi.
	Bunjār	30	10	524	...	Mir Amir, S. of Mir Abbas.	Khammar, Sanādgul, Gadah and Mir.
	Burj-i-Afghān	8	3	112	...	Sher Ali Khān, Sanjarāni.	Haji Rus, Mir Ghilzai.
	Burj-i-Muhammad Khān.	2	...	14	...	Tāj Muhammad, Kūl	Karim Kushta, Haidari, Zaur.
35	Burj-i-Sarband	4	...	24	14	Muhammad Hasan, Khan, Shahraki.	Shahraki.
	Chāh-i-Nima	6	1	18	5	Safar, Baluch	Baluch. Five pāgos belong to Parsiwan and only three pāgos actually reside in this village, the others live at Kaftargi.
	Chār Khāmi	2	...	12	8	Under Husenābād, Pilpili	Pilpili.
	Chilling	3	4	200	...	Darwesh, Mir Shikār	Mir Shikar, Rahdār Sarbandi.
	Chung-i-Marghun	3	...	32	...	Ghul. Shāh, Sharaki	Sharaki, Pudna.
40	Daragi	2	2	200	...	Dād Shāh, Arbāb	Panjika, Arbāb, the inhabitants cultivate at Shaitan and Deh Mirza Ghulam, as the lands are not well commanded by the canals.
	Carried over	261	71½	2,114	280		

* A Agriculturists.   † B Shepherds, graziers, etc.

THE PEOPLE OF SEISTAN.

SHAHRISTĀN—*continued.*

No.	Name of village.	PĀGOS.		NUMBER OF FAMILIES.		Kadkhuda.	Tribes of the inhabitants.
		Ghami.	Tahwil.	A*	B†		
	Brought forward	261	71½	3,114	280		
	Dandi	20	10	260	64	Fakir, Khammar	Karūt-khār, Khammar, merchants, shopkeepers and coppersmiths.
	Daulatābād	...	30	240	100	Purdil Khan, Sarbandi	Sarbandi—Jāgir.
	Deh Amir	3	...	18	5	Under Ibrahimabad	Nuri and Piri.
	„ Askari	6	...	86	...	Haidar Ali Khan, Nahrui	Gazma, Nahraui (Baluchis Askari).
45	„ Arbāt	15	5	210	...	Ali Akbar Arbāb Askari	Mir and Arbāb.
	„ Darrani	1	...	12	...	Sardar Said Khan Nawab	Nahrui Karimdādzai (Bal.).
	Dah Bāshi Deh	4	1	62	...	Under Saddaki	Shahriāri, Ghilzai.
	Darwesh (Deh)	...	3	26	...	Saiad Hāji	Saiad, (under Gauri) and Mir.
	Dashtak	6	2	50	...	...	Mostly ruined. Shahraki.
50	Deh Gazma	1	...	9	...	Under Sharifābād	Gazma.
	„ Gurg. No. 1	4	...	40	...	Mirza Haidar, Kāini	Kūl, K.
	„ „ „ 2	2	...	9	...	Gurg Ali, Gurg	Gurg.
	„ Hāji	...	15	110	...	Ali Akbar, Sarawini	Sārawini, Dahmarda.
	„ Khān (1)	3	...	18	8	Muhammad, Kakah	Rahdār, Gadah.
55	„ „ (2)	3½	1	42	...	Sadulla, Mir Shikār	Zaur, Mir Shikār.
	„ Khidri	3	1	26	9	Under Chilling	Khidri, Mir Shikār.
	„ Kākar	1	...	9	...	„ Khwāja Ahmad	Zardazai (Afghān?) Kākar.
	„ Karri	4	...	21	...	„ Bunjār	Urmāgai (Khurmagai?).
	„ Khālikdād	8	6	84	32	Seiad Ali	...
60	„ Kūl, S. W.	15	...	90	35	Taj Muhammad, Kūl	Kūl (S. W. of Nasratābād). K.
	„ „ N. E.	11	2	100	...	Muhammad Mehdi, Kākah.	Kūl. Aokāti. K.
	„ Khān Muhammad	4	...	28	...	Taj Muhammad, Kūl	Under Jallālābād. K.
	„ Kundil	3	...	30	...	Under Khwaja Ahmad	Rakshāni, Kashāni, Gorgej.
	„ Ibrahim	2	1	16	...	Purdil Khan, Sarbandi	Sarbandi.
65	„ Piran	5	2	64	...	Muhammad Mehdi, Kakha	Zauri, Belar, Kamah, and Ala-Sufi.
	Carried over	385½	150½	4,774	533		

* A Agriculturists.   † B Shepherds, graziers, etc.

SHAHRISTĀN—continued.

No.	Name of village.	Pāgos. Ghami.	Pāgos. Tahwil	Number of Families. A*	Number of Families. B†	Kadkhuda.	Tribes of the inhabitants.
	Brought forward	385½	150½	4,774	533		
	Deh Pudna	3	...	18	...	Purdil Khan, Sarbandi	Pudna.
	,, Mashadi Saring	2	...	22	...	Amir Dahbashi, Jotegh	Sheikh.
	,, Naū	2	...	10	...	Muhammad Haidar, Siāksar.	Siāhsar.
	,, Mirza	3	...	18	5	Tāj Muhammad, Kūl	Mirza.
70	,, Nawāb Khān	9	3	80	...	Nawab Khān, Gorgej	Gorgej, Shahristāni, Rashki.
	,, Jafari	1	1	14	6	Ghulam Saddaki	Shahriāri, Sanādgul.
	Diwāna (1)	4	1	32	9	Muhammad, Kakha	Diwāna and Sarhadi (Bal.).
	Deh Rasul	2	...	12	4	Ghulam, Shahriāri	Rasulzai (Baluchi or Brahui?).
	,, Sheikh (1)	3	...	18	9	Fakir, Khammar	Sheikh.
75	Diwāna (2)	3	1	26	6	Ghulam Haidar, Jamalzai.	Diwāna.
	Deh Sheikh (2)	2	1	22	...	Under Daūdi	Khammar, Sheikh Weisi.
	,, Siāhsar (1)	3	1	26	9	Ghulam-i-Shahbāz, Khammar.	,, Siāhsar.
	,, ,, (2)	3	1	30	...	Ahmad Khān, Notāni	Mulla Shāhi, Piri.
	Fathulla	5	...	30	8	Muhammad Haidar, Kharrāt.	Siāhsar, Sargazi.
80	Ganri (1)	12	5	102	56	Amir Dahbāshi, Jotegh	Jotegh and Saiad.
	,, (2)	...	17	102	...	Saiad Hāji	,, ,,
	Gaz-i-bár	9	3	75	...	Ali Murad, Bandāni	Dahmarda, Sheik Weisi, Bandānis.
	Ghulām Ali	4	1	52	...	Mir Murteza, Arab	Arab, Dilarāmi.
	,, Khān	3	...	46	...	Under Sharifabad	Gorgej, Idozai, (Mammasenni).
85	Hamzābād	3	...	18	6	Under Sekoha	Same as Sekoha.
	Husenābādi	4	1	30	9	Under Wasilān	Same as Wasilān.
	Husen Abdullah	1	...	16	...	Sadulla, Mir Shikár	Mir Shikár.
	Husenābād Pilpili	6	2	48	28	Murādi, Pilpili	Pilpili, Sārūni.
	,, (City)	40	14	500	...	Muhammad Mehdi, Kakha and Muhammad Haidar, Kharrāt.	Kharrāt, Kakha, Siāhsar, Sargazi, Hatla, (? Jat).
90	Husena	7	...	66	...	Husena, Sarhadi Baluch	Zaur, Sarhadi.
	Carried over	519½	202½	6,187	688		

* A Agriculturists. † B Shepherds, graziers, etc.

SHAHRISTĀN—continued.

No.	Name of village.	PĀGOS. Ghami.	PĀGOS. Tahwil	NUMBER OF FAMILIES. A*	NUMBER OF FAMILIES. B†	Kadkhuda.	Tribes of the inhabitants.
	Brought forward	519½	202½	6,187	688		
	Husen Rais	3	...	26	...	Purdil, Khān, Sarbandi	Gadāh.
	Hasan Jāfar	3	1	26	7	Ghulām Misgar, Tamarābādi.	Rahdār.
	Husen Bākar	1½	...	19	...	Muhammad, Kakha	Shahriāri, Rahdār.
	Husenkhān	...	2	13	...	Said Khan, Nāhrūi	Zardazai (Afghāns?).
95	Husen Mashadi	3	...	26	...	Sadulla, Mir Shikār	Mir Shikār, Rahdār.
	Husen Muhammad	2	...	20	...	Given to Nāzir of Governor.	Gorgej.
	Ibrahimābād	8	1	54	40	Saif Ali Khān, Sarbandi	Nuri and Piri.
	Ibrahim Kuchāl	1	1	14	...	Under Chilling	Barechi (Afghān).
	Ismail, Khanwar	7	3	66	18	Ali, Shahriāri	Rahdār, Shahriāri.
100	Ibrahim Muhammadi	2	...	18	...	Hāji Dān, Kāini	Muhammadi.
	Isa	6	...	72	...	Muhammad Akram, Sākzai-Afghan.	Rāz, Panjika.
	Iskil	...	25	205	...	Mir Amir	Galavi (Jat) Tākar, Panjika, Mir.
	Izat	2	...	14	...	Sardar Said Khān Nawāb	Gorgej, Aladaū.
	Jabbar (1)	5	1	33	...	Mir, Amir, Mir	Sanādgul, Zauri.
105	Jahāngir (1)	4	1	24	...	,, ,, ,,	Panjika, Ahangar.
	Janai (2)	5	4	116	...	Amir Jahāngir, Bāmiri	Bāmiri (Bal.), Dilarāmi.
	Jalai	7	...	42	10	Muhammad Ali, Siāhsar	Karrūtkhār, Alāri, Jotegh, Siāhsar.
	Jallālābād	...	...	8	...	...	Karim Kushta, Haidari Zauri.
	Jamalābād	8	2	64	16	Ali Akbar, Galavi	Rahdār, Galavi.
110	Jotegh	...	4	24	8	Muhammad Mehdi, Jotegh.	Siāhsar, Jotegh.
	Ju Baksh	...	8	48	30	Nāzir to Governor of Seistan.	Gadāh, Shahriari, Mir Shikar.
	Juma	1	...	5	...	Under Bazi	Bazi.
	Jazinak	21	15	216	80	Tāj Muhammad, Kūl	Ramredi Rais) Shahnak, Kūl
115	Kala Baz (Kand). (Tandurak included)	9	2	66	...	Alimurad, Siāhsar	Siāhsar and Baruch.
	Kala Kuhna	30	10	240	70	Seiad Ali.	
	Carried over	648	282½	7,646	967		

* A Agriculturists. † B Shepherds, graziers, etc.

SHAHRISTĀN—continued.

No.	Name of village.	PĀGOS.		NUMBER OF FAMILIES.		Kadkhuda.	Tribes of the inhabitants.
		Ghami.	Tabwil	A*	B†		
	Brought forward	648	282½	7,646	967		
	Kala Naū	25	8	300	...	Saiad Muhammad.	
	Kala Naū (new and old).	13	2	160	...	Muhammad Mehdi, Kakha.	Towards Gazbar and Bolai—Sanādgul, Kakha, Panjika.
	Khadang (new and old).	14	1	130	...	Sultān Mir Husen, Arab.	Arab, Bārūni, Piri, Safedkhāki.
120	Khāmak	12	5	102	45	Mehdi Khan, Kazāk.	Siahsar, Sharaki, Kūl, Piri.
	Khammar (Farari)	10	1	68	18	Murādi, Khammar.	Sheikh Weisi, Khammar.
	Kachiān	17	1	260	...	Darwesh Khān, Kaiāni.	Sargazi, Dilarāmi.
	Khwāja Ahmad	5	4	80	...	Said Khān Nawāb Sardar.	Nahrui Rāshki.
	Khudādād	1	...	12	2	Mir Jafir Khān, Sarbandi.	Shahriāri Tillar, Sarbandi.
125	Kang	8	1	54	20	Under Jazinak	Bauri, Khalil.
	Kosha (Sheb)	14	6	120	80	Mir Jafir, Sarbandi.	Shahriāri, Tillar, Sarbandi.
	„ (Bala)	8	2	60	45	Sher Muhammad Khān, Shibzai.	Sargazi, Ghilzai.
	Kapolak	5	...	30	...	Under Kala Kuhna.	...
	Karbalāi Husen	3	...	18	5	Haji Muhammad Ali, Siāhsar.	Siāhsar.
130	Karbalāi	4	...	24	8	Mir Beg, Sarbandi.	Sarbandi, Karim Kāshta.
	Karbāsak	4	2	36	5	Sheikh Razu, Kakha.	Siāhsar, Kakhā.
	Karami	3	...	18	6	Ali, Shahriāri	Shahriāri.
	Kāsamābād	12	5	180	...	Mir Kasim	Mulla, Mir, Panjika.
	Kalukhi	4	...	30	...	Jahāngir Khān, Murād Kuli.	Murād Kuli.
135	Kaud	10	7	175	...	Mir Beg, Khammar	Pati Pashm (? Jat), Sheikh Nuri, Piri.
	Kalbali	4	2	58	...	Jān Muhammad, Pati Pashm.	Kalbali, Pati Pashm.
	Kimmak	11	1	200	60	Muhammad Jān Khān, Kazāk.	...
	Karbalāi Asghar	6	2	54	...	Mir Kāsim	Belar, Murād Kuli.
	Kaftārgi	4	1	34	...	Nur Muhammad, Sheikh Huseni.	Sheikh Huseni, (Baluch) Parsiwāns.
	Carried over	845	333½	9,849	1,261		

* A Agriculturists.   † B Shepherds, graziers, etc.

THE PEOPLE OF SEISTAN.

SHAHRISTĀN—continued.

No.	Name of village.	Pāgos. Ghami	Pāgos. Tahwil	Number of Families. A*	Number of Families. B†	Kadkhuda.	Tribes of the inhabitants.
	Brought forward	845	333½	9,849	1,261		
140	Kamāli	10	1	68	22	Mahdi, Bandāni	Jur Kamāli, Bandāni.
	Lalu	...	...	...	...		Deserted.
	Lup	6	4	48	22	Under Daūdi	Shadād, Khammar, Karut Khār.
	Lutak	7	2	56	34	Purdil Khān, Sarbandi	Piri, Khalil, Siāhsar.
	Lutfullah	7	1	18	...	Under Husena (Deh)	Sarhadi, Zaur.
145	Malik Haidari	2	7	72	...	Mir Sher, Mir	Sheik Nuri, Mir, Jotegh.
	Mansuri	5	2	84	...	Murādi, Pilpili	Rāhdāo, Pudna, Zauri.
	Masti Khān	4	2	70	...	Ali Murād, Jotegh	Jotegh, Sheikh.
	Mirza Ghūlām	10	3	75	...	Mirza Urh, Aukāti	Ankāti, Sulemāni.
	Muhammadabad	16	...	96	44	Mir Darwesh, Saind	Sargazi, Nuri, Piri.
150	Muhammad Azam	4	1	52	11	Muhammad Azim, Mir Shikar.	Galavi, (Jat).
	Muhammad Dādi	2	0	18	...	Mir Kāsim, Mir	Jotegh.
	Muhammad Khān	5	1	50	...	Muhammad Khān, Sheikh Husein.	Sheikh Husein, Gazma Gorgej (Baluchis).
	Muhammad Safar	10	2	80	...	Muhammad Amir Khān, Jamālzai.	Jamālzai (Bal.) Gadāh.
	Muhammad Shāh Akram.	5	1	107	...	Under Sharifābād	Askari, Gazma, Nahrūi (Baluchis).
155	Mulla Abdulla	3	0	32	...	Mullā Abdulla, Sheikh	Mullā, Sheikh, Sanādgul.
	Mulla Ali	8	2	70	...	Ghulām-i-Mullā Ali	Galavi, (? Jat) Sanādgul.
	Mulla Rashid	2	...	20	...	Mullā Rashid, Kashāni	Kashāni, Idozai, (Baluchis).
	Mulla Rustam	...	1	8	...	Mullā Rustam, Dilārāmi	Dilārāmi.
	Muhammad Akram	...	...	22	...	Muhammad Akram, Sākzai Afghan.	Sākzai.
160	Naigard	3	...	50	...	Darwesh, Zaur	Zaur, Mir Shikār.
	Nasirābād, Khoja	10	2	76	25	Khoja, Pudna	Pudna, Darni.
	,, Seiad	5	2	42	14	Mir Muhammad, Seiad	Siāhsar, Sanchli.
	Niāz Beg	7	...	52	...	Mir Sher, Mir	Jotegh, Kurd, Murad kuli.
	Nur Muhammad Kohi	3	...	27	...	Under Sharifābād	Rākshāni, Baluch.
165	Nohar	4	...	35	...	Ghulam Ali, Ahangar	Sharaki, Ahangar.
	Nur Muhammad	1	...	10	...	Nur Muhammad, Kāini	W. of Nasratibād.
	Nawāb	4	2	64	...	Dād, Jat	JAT (Baraj).
	Carried over	988	369½	11,251	1,433		

*A Agriculturists. †B Shepherds, graziers, etc.

SHAHRISTĀN—continued.

No.	Name of village.	Pāgos. Ghami.	Pāgos. Tahwil.	Number of Families. A*	Number of Families. B†	Kadkhuda.	Tribes of the inhabitant.
	Brought forward	988	369½	11,251	1,433		
	Pirdād	...	1	40	...	Nawāb Khān, Gorgej	One pāgo cultivator, rest gandārs.
	Pulgi (Sheb)	7	1	50	11	Seiad Ali	Shāraki.
170	„ Bālā	8	...	48	16	„	...
	Pusht-i-dasht	6	2	52	22	Muhammad-i-Ghulām Ali Khan.	Kakha, Pilpili.
	Rāhdār	12	1	86	...	Hamza, Rāhdār	Rāhdār, Kamāli.
	Rustamāni	3	1	50	...	Agha Jān Dahbashi	Sanchli, Dahbāshi.
	Sadaki	6	2	52	32	Ghulam, Shahriāri	Shahriari, Ghilzai Afghān.
175	Shahriāri	4	1	36	...	Hāji Dān Kāini Peshkar.	Shahriari, Rāhdār.
	Shamsābād	6	...	6	...	Under Aliabad	...
	Shahristān	7	...	94	...	Akbar Khan, Gorgej	Kiyāl (? Jat) Rāshki, Dahmarda.
	Shāhrukh	1	...	12	...	Under Chilling	Mir Shikār, etc.
	Shāhhān	3	...	14	...	Muhammad Haidar, Kharrāt	Mulla Shāhi.
180	Sharifābād	12	5	260	...	Haidar Ali, Nahrui	Sanādgul, Gazma (Bal.). Mir Shikār and Pati Pashm.
	Shāhgul	2	1	34	...	Under Sharifābād	Barechi (Afghān).
	Shāhrak	5	1	80	...	Under Jazinak	Shāraki, Ramrodi, etc.
	Safar	2	...	14	...	„ Pusht-i-Dasht	Kakha, Pilpili.
	Sadulla	2	1	12	...	Muradi, Pilpili	Pilpili.
185	Sehkala	5	2	54	...	Abbas-i-Jahāngir; Bāmri	Murād Kuli, Bāmri.
	Sehkoha	14	6	132	80	Purdil Khan, Sarbandi	Siākhar, Khalil.
	Siāhkhān	2	...	30	...	Siahkhān, Nahrūi	Kāshāni and Nahrūi.
	Siāhmard	2	...	7	...	Siāhmard, Sarbadi (Bal.)	Sarbadi (Baluch).
	Sanchli	9	3	78	24	Saiad Reza	Sanchli, Nuri.
190	Sherdil or Zainul	4	...	24	8	Sherdil, Sarbadi	Rāhdār, Sarbadi, Baluch.
	Sūfi	3	...	35	...	Muhammad Amin Jamālzai.	Sūfi.
	Suleman	1	...	20	...	Suleman Nahrui	Nahrui (Baluch).
	Carried over	1,114	397½	12,571	1,626		

*A Agriculturists. †B Shepherds, graziers, etc.

SHAHRISTĀN—concluded.

No.	Name of village.	PĀGOS.		NUMBER OF FAMILIES.		Kadkhuda.	Tribes of the inhabitants.
		Ghami.	Tahwil.	A*	B†		
	Brought forward	1,114	397½	12,571	1,626		
	Sokhta	10	4	84	18	Seiad Ali	......
	Shaitan	4	2	45	...	Mir Jafri, Sarbandi	Arbāb, Khara Kui.
195	Safdar	4	1	32	6	Muhammad Haidar, Kharrāt.	Mir.
	Taki	5	1	38	6	Muhammad Tuti, Kakhā	Kakha, Taki.
	Tāghazi	8	2	64	20	Muhammad Mehdi ,,	,, Sargazi.
	Tāj Muhammad Nūri	...	5	30	...	Under Jazinak	Kūl, Shahraki, Kamrodi.
	Tillar	3	1	36	...	Purdil Khān, Sarbandi	Tillar.
200	Tilfak	3	...	25	...	Darwesh, Khammar	Barūni, Khammar.
	Tūti	15	5	210	...	Muhammad, Kakha	Kakhā, Rāhdār, Zam.
	Tamarābād	10	2	78	28	Ghulām, Misgār	Karrūtkhār, Rahdār Katlok.
	Wasilān	20	10	180	40	Jahāngir Khān	Piri, Kazak, Shahraki, Siahu, etc.
	Warmāl	20	5	160	72	Muhammad-i-Ghulām Ali, Kakhā.	Kakha, JAT, Shahriāri.
205	Yār Muhammad	4	2	36	5	Sheikh Raza, Siahsar	Siāhsar.
	Zāhidān	3	2	65	...	Muhammad Shrif Khan, Notāni	Panjika, Notāni.
	Zainul Dādi	3	1	26	...	Under Ismail, Khammar	Rāhdār, Mir Shikrar.
	Zainulkāsām	1	1	14	6	Seiad Daud, Seiad	Bazi.
	Ziāratgāh	2	0	12	4	Mir Mehdi, Kazak	Jotegh.
210	Zulfikari	3	0	18	4	......	......
	Zabardast Khān	1	...	13	...	Zabardast Khan, Gorgej	Gorgej.
	Zamān Khān	1	...	20	...	Nawab Khan, Gorgej	Gorgej, Shahristāni.
	Ziārat-i-Bibi Dost	...	3	30	...	Mir Kāsam	Wakf lands for the Ziārat.
	GRAND TOTAL	1,234	444½	13,787	1,835		

*A Agriculturists.   † B Shepherds, graziers, etc.

MÍAN KANGÍ.

No.	Names of villages.	Circles.	Ploos. Ghami.	Talwil.	Kalgir.	Families. A	B	Kadkhoda.	Tribes.
	'Abbās Jafr	Pulgi	1	...	1	18	...	'Abbās Jafr, Karat-Khar.	Karat-Khar, and Sārawīnī (?Sārunī)
	'Abbās Rāmradi	Burj Mirgul	9	...	4	92	...	Sherdil Sāruni	Pudoa and Rāmradi (Reis).
	Agha Jān	Siādak	1	...	1	11	...	Agha Jān Sharaki	Sharahis and Galabacha (?Balueh).
	Akhund	,,	2	1	...	25	...	Muhammad Hassan Pahlawān.	Pahlawān (Farsiwān).
5	Akbar Sauhar	Deh Dost Muhammad	14	...	1	13	...	Akbar Sauhar, Siāhak	Jotegh, Siāhak.
	Aliān	Jahānābād	1	...	...	12	...	Aliān, Bajjani	Bajjzai (?Baluch).
	Aladan	...			Deserted.				
	Ali	Jahānābād	1	...	3	18	...	Kadkhod of Jahānābād	Arab, and Gazma (Farsiwān).
	Ali Khān	Deh Dost Muhammad	1	1	2	20	...	Yusuf Jelām, Bareoh	Sāruni, Malamdozai (?Bareoh), and Bahmurda.
10	Ali-Isa (Luch)	,,	1	...	...	7	...	Under Deh Dost Muhammad.	Rakshāmi.
	Ali Jān	Jahānābād	3	...	2	32	...	Ali Jān, Khamsar	Khamsar, and Sharaki (Farsiwān).
	Ali Jangi	...			Deserted.				
	Ali Mardān	Nur Muhammad	1	...	2	16	6	Nur Muhammad Sāruni	Kāshāni, Zahrozai (Baluch).
	Amir	Deh Dost Muhammad	1	...	2	16	...	Under Deh Dost Muhammad.	Mir Shokār, and Khūgāri (?Baluch).
15	Amir Gurga	Jahānābād	2	...	1	25	8	Amir Gurgh	Dahmarda.
	Amir Siāhgul	Siādak	2	1	9	72	...	Amir, Ghilzai	Ghilzai (Afghan) Seīād and Sāruni
	Asghar	,,	1	...	1	9	...	Asghar Sanidgul	Sanidgul (Farsiwān).
	Ata Muhammad	,,	1	...	2	19	...	Ata Bahmadi	Bahmadi (Bannri Baluch) Siāhsar (Farsiwān).
	Azād	Deh Dost Muhammad	1	...	3	12	...	Azād, Dahzari Dāhzari	Dāhzari (?Baluch).
20	Azro	Jahānābād	1	...	1	8	...	Azro, Noiāni	Noiāni (Baluch).
	Burj-i-Mir Gul	Burj-i-Mir Gul	40	8	40	250	10	Sherdil, Sāruni	Sāruni, Arjuni (?Arjuni, Jat) Buzi, Gurg (Farsiwāns)

THE PEOPLE OF SEISTAN.

No.	Name	Deh						Headman	Tribe, &c.
	Buzi 1	...	5	...	2	66	2	...	Buzi (Parsiwān).
	Buzi 2	,,			Deserted.				
	Chakul, or Karimkushta	,,	2	1	...	32	...	...	Karim-Kusha (Parsiwān).
25	Chāri	Jahānābād	2	...	3	11	...	Jān Muhammad, Sanduli	Chāri (Parsiwān).
	Deh Dost Muhammad	...	14	12	10	676	20	Dost Muhammad Sāroni	Includes Kandu, and Deh Mukhtár. Population very mixed.
	Daulatābād with	...	6	1	2	64	20	Tāj Muhammad Kūl	8 families of Kaiānis, remainder Kūl and Pudna (Parsiwān).
	Shekh Weisi (old)	...	...	...	...	16	3	...	About 160 yards from Daulatābād, Kūl and Shekh Weisi (Parsiwāns).
	Darwesh Muhammad	Pudai	1	...	...	28	...	Kadkhuda of Khatámak	Shekh and Sarawini.
30	Fakira	Jahānābād	5	1	1	65	...	Jān Muhammad Pakira	Dahmarda, Pakira (Parsiwān), Mesh-mast (?Jat).
	Fakir	Deh Dost Muhammad	1	...	1	10	5	Under Deh Dost Muhammad.	Sāruni.
	Fakirān	Burj-i-Mir Gul	3	1	1	35	3	Under Burj-i-Mir Gul	Fakirān (Parsiwān).
	Fakir Muhammad	Deh Dost Muhammad	...	2	...	26	...	,, Deh Dost Muhammad.	Pudna (Parsiwān).
	Fakira	,,	1	...	2	22	...	Mashadi Ali	Fakira (Parsiwān).
31	Gajar	Pulgi	1	...	2	13	...	Under Pulgi	Hori (?Baluch or Jat).
	Gazna	Jahānābād	3	...	2	16	...	Ghulām Shāh, Jotegh	Jotegh and Gazna (Parsiwāns).
	Gazna Burji	Pokak	1	1	...	38	...	Aliābād Saiads	Zauri (?Jat) Murād Kuli (Farsiwāns).
	,, Zairal	,,	2	...	1	24	...	?Saiad Ali	Gazna (Farsiwāns).
	Ganguzār	...			Deserted				
40	Ghulām Didi (Dashti)	Jahānābād	3	...	4	24	...	Ghulām Dādi Dashti	Buzi, Jotegh, and Gazna (Parsiwāns).
	Gulzer Agra	Nur Muhammad	2	...	2	19	2	Nur Muhammad (Contractor).	Rakshāni (Baluch) and Sāruni.
	Gurguri	Gurguri	8	...	6	85	...	Agha Khān, Sarbandi	Sāduar, Buzi, Jotegh and Sarbandi (Farsi).
	Ghulām Kifān 1	Siādak	...	...	...	16	...	Shāh Gul, Sharaki	Sharaki, grant to Shams-ud-din, Sharaki.
	,, 2	Deh Dost Muhammad	1	1	1	11	5	Under Deh Dost Muhammad.	Property of the wife of Dost Muhammad Sāruni.
	Carried over	...	132½	82	108	1,972	93		

A Agriculturists.   B Pastoral, graziers, etc.

MIÁN KANGI—continued.

No.	Names of villages.	Circles.	Págos. Ghamí.	Tahwíl.	Kalgír.	Families. A	B	Kadkhudá.	Tribes.
	Brought forward		132½	32	108	1,972	93		
15	Gul Beg	Jahánábád	1	1	1	20	...	Gul Beg, Sajarzai	Sajarzai (Safarzai) and Sarhadi (Baluch).
	Gul Sháh	Deh Dost Muhammad	1	...	2	18	...	Gul Sháh, Nahruí	Nahruí (Baluch), Sherzai (Baluch), Aladau (Parsiwán).
	Gul Muhammad	Pulai	1	...	1	20	...	Gul Muhammad, Shekh	Shekh (?Jat) called Farsiwán.
	Hájí	Hájí	10	3	4	104	...	Ali Akbar, Bunjári	Shekh (?Jat ,, ,,).
	Hájí Khannar 1	Deh Dost Muhammad	10	2	3	80	5	Hájí, Khannar	Nahruí, Sherzai (Baluch), Aladah.
50	„ „ 2	„			Deserted				
	Hájí Karim	Khanak	2	...	...	30	...	Hájí Karim, Ali Ahmad	Ali Ahmad (Farsiwán) includes 17 or 18 Gaudár families.
	Hasan-Husen	Jahánábád	1	...	1	13	...	Hasan, Gazna	Village is also known Nisár Ahmad; Gazna (Farsiwán).
	Hasan-Ibrahím	Siádak	2	...	3	24	...	Hasan, Khásbí	Khásbí (Farsiwán).
	Husen Dilawar	„	1	1	...	16	3	Husen-i-Dilāwar, Jotegh	Jotegh (Farsiwán), Falahachea (Baluch).
55	Husen Rahmán	„			Deserted				
	Hájí	Deh Dost Muhammad	1	1	...	40	...	Hájí, Khannar	Sarani, Chetband (?Parsiwán).
	Husen Ali Khán	Siádak	1	...	1	20	...	Husen Ali Khán	Headman, Khurram, inhabitants Khurram (Parsiwán).
	Ibrahim Muhammadi	Gurguri	1	...	3	14	...	Under Gurguri	Bazi, Jolegh (Parsiwán).
	Ibrahim Fakír	Deh Dost Muhammad	1	...	2	9	...	Ibrahim-i-Fakír	Headman Sárani inhabitants Morai (?Baluch).
60	Ido 1	Siádak	1	1	3	22	...	Under Siádak	Rakshání (Baluch).
	„ 2	Jahánábád	...	...	...	8	...	Ido, Kut-Khel	Kut-Khel, also are Gandárs.
	Isa Khán	Siádak	1	...	4	9	...	Isa Khán, Pahlawán	Pahlawán (Farsiwán).
	Ibrahim	Deh Dost Muhammad	1	...	3	18	13	Ibrahim, Borakzai	Rakshání and Borakzai (?Baluch).
	Isa-Lijjai	Siádak	1	...	...	8	...	Isa-Lijjai	Lijjai (from near Chagai (?Tajik).
65	Jahánábád	Jahánábád	8	5	10	125	...	Ali Akbar, Ankáti	Arab, Khanmar (Ankáti (Parsiwáns), Arjin (?Arjuni, Jat).

THE PEOPLE OF SEISTAN.

#	Name	Location	A		Deserted	B	Headman	Tribe/Notes
	,, old	,,	2	...	...	12	Jahángir, Reki	Khári (Farsiwán) Reki (Baluch).
	Jahángirkhán	Siádak	2	...	3	12	Jahángir, Reki	Khári (Farsiwán) Reki (Baluch).
	Jangi Khán	,,	1	...	1	14	Jangi Khán, Siáhak	Sharaki, Siáhak (Farsiwáns).
	Ján Beg	Pokak	4	...	1	35	Ján Beg, Pahlawán	Pahlawán (Farsiwán) Saiad Ali's.
70	Ján Muhammad	,,	...	...	Deserted	...		
	Jamálndín	Siádak	3	...	...	22	Jamáluddín Ghulám Kadag	Ghulám Kadag (?).
	Juma	Deh Dost Muhammad	1	...	7	25	Juma Khán	Sur Ghilzai (Farsiwán) Zahrozai (Baluch).
	Juma, Zainal Musa	,,	3	...	2	35	Zainal Musa	Sherzai, inhabitants Sherzai (?Baluch).
	Juma Gul	Shekh Weisi	3	...	2	24	Mir Darwesh, Shekh Weisi	Mir Shikár, Karit-Khár (Farsiwán).
75	Karoz	,,	...	...	Deserted	...		
	Kám Khan	Siádak	1	2	1	11	Kám Khan	Karimdádzai, inhabitants Karimdádzai (Baluch).
	Khánsúri 1	Pulgi	1	...	1	18	Under Pulgi	Khánsúri (Farsiwán).
	,, 2	Burj-i-Mir Gul	1	...	...	9	,, Burj-i-Mir Gul	
	Khának	Daulatábád	10	11	5	200	Mír Ali Akbar	Deputy of Táj Muhammad Kúl; Kúls and Khamnar (Farsiwáns).
80	Karbalai Gulzár	Siádak	...	...	...	11	Karbalai Gulzár	Formed in 1904-05 to take up cultivation.
	Karam	Daulatábád	1	...	2	14	Under Daulatábád	Sherzai Karimdádzai (?Baluch).
	Karim Kushta	Deh Dost Muhammad	7	1	2	84	Under Deh Dost Muhammad	Karim-Kushta, Arbábs (Farsiwán).
	Karri	,,	...	...	Deserted	...		
	Katának	Padai	5	...	2	28	4	Dur Muhammad, Sárurí	Gurg (Farsiwán) Sárurí.
85	Kundil 1	Bunjár	2	1	1	34	Hájí Ali Akbar (Bunjár)	Jur, Kárút-Khár.
	,, 2	Jahánábád	1	...	2	13	Kundil, Rodíní	Rodini (Baluch).
	Kurbán Ali (Reg Bazár)	,,	1	...	2	11	Kurbán Ali, Saparzai	Síaraki (Farsiwán) Saparzi (Safarzai, ? Baluch).
	Kurki	Khának	2	1	...	40	Musa-i-Alam, Nahruí	Nahruí (Baluch) Farsiwáns not known.
	Lalla	Siádak	2	...	3	22	Lalla, Mallukzai	Mallukzai (?) Shekh Husein (Baluch).
90	Lashkarán 1	,,	1	...	2	12	Lashkar Khán	Rodini i inhabitants Rodini (Baluch).
	Carried over		230½	60	188	3,244	128		

A Agriculturists.   B Pastoral, graziers, etc.

MIÁN KANGI—continued.

No.	Names of villages.	Circles.	Págos. Ghami.	Tahwil.	Kalgir.	Families. A	B	Kadkhuda.	Tribes.
	Brought forward		230+	60	188	3,244	128		
	Laškarán 2	Padui	1	...	2	13	...	Under Padai	Mír Shikár (Farsiwáns) Sáruni.
	Luch, with Muhammad Karímdád and Pahlawán 2.	Deh Dost Muhammad	2	...	4	23	...	Under Deh Dost Muhammad	Mír Shikár (Farsiwán) Sáruni, Pahlawán (Farsiwán) Mahakaki (? Jat).
			...	...	3	8	...		
	Lutfi	Jahánábád	1	...	...	22	...	Lutfi, Dahmarda	Dahmarda (Farsiwán).
	Malaki	Malaki	2	...	1	9	...	Abdulla, Janoálzai	Janoálzai (? Baluch) Pahlawán (Farsiwáns).
95	Mardán	Shekh Weisi	2	...	...	13	...	Ibrahim, Shekh Weisi	Kakah, Shekh Weisi (Farsiwán).
	Márgo 1	Pulgi	2	...	3	12	...	Under Pulgi	Sargzi (Farsiwán) Arjúni (? Arjúni, Jat).
	„ 2	„	2	...	2	20	...	„	Sanádgul, Dilarúni (Farsiwáns).
			2	...	1	30	6		
	Mílak		...	...	Deserted.				
	Mírán (Mulla Abdulla)	Deh Dost Muhammad	3	...	1	28	5	Under Deh Dost Muhammad	Shekh (Farsiwán).
100	Mirza Khán	Jahánábád	4	...	1	30	...	Mirza khán, Murád Kuli	Murád Kuli, Buzi (Farsiwán).
	Muhammad Abdullah	„	3	...	2	14	...	Abdulla, Karím-Kushta	Karím-Kushta (Farsiwán).
	Muhammad (Deh)	Pulgi	1	...	1	16	1	Mohammad, Gurg	Gurg (Farsiwán).
	„ Reza	Deh Dost Muhammad	1	...	3	14	3	Muhammad Reza, Sasoli	Mahakaki (? Jat) Sasoli (Baluch or Brahui).
	„ Kaaim	Jahánábád	1	1	1	20	...	Under Jahánábád	Sanádgul, Mohammad Kaaim (Farsiwáns).
105	„ Sikandar	Deh Dost Muhammad	1	...	...	18	4	Muhammad Sikandar, Rodini	Rodini and Reki (Baluch).
	„ Jangi	„	...	...	Deserted.				
	Mulla Husen	Mulla Husen	2	1	2	15	16	Ghulam, Sárwini	Kakah, Buzi (Farsiwán) Sáruni (Sárwini).
	„ Haji	„	6	2	6	50	...	Mulla Husen, Kakla	Karút Khár, Mír Shikar.

THE PEOPLE OF SEISTAN.

No.	Village	Belongs to					Headman	Tribe
110	Mulla Dur Muhammad	Nur Muhammad	1	...	...	8	...	Nur Muhammad	Sāruni.
	Mokhtār	Shekh Weisi	2	...	...	14	...	Ibrahim, Shekh Weisi	Galavi, Aladāu (Parsiwān, Jat).
	Murādi	...		Deserted.					
	Muri	Gurguri	1	...	2	8	...	Under Gurguri	Ankāki (Farsiwāns from the Hokāt).
	Mansur Khān	Siādak	1	...	...	15	...	Mansur Khān	Kharoti Ghilzai (Afghāns).
	Muhammad Khān Kalandar	...	2	...	2	15	...	Muhammad Khān, Kalandar.	Rakshāni (Baloch).
115	Mehrāb (Deh)	...		Deserted.					
	Mir Beg	Mir Beg	3	2	1	3	...	Ghafār, Kāini	Seiād, Khāmmar, Tahwil of Mir Ghafār Kāini.
	Najaf	Burj-i-Mir Gul	1	...	1	9	...	Under Burj-i-Mir Gul	Khānsuri; (Farsiwāns).
	Nauroz	Pulgi	2	1	...	25	...	Nauroz, Ghīlzai	Ghilzai and other Afghans from Farah.
	Nur Muhammad 1	Dh. Dost Muhammad.	1	...	2	12	...	Nur Muhammad, Malakaki.	Malakaki (? Jat).
120	" " 2	Nur Muhammad	9	3	3	84	4	Nur Muhammad, Sāruni	Shekh (Farsiwān) Mahmudi (?) Sāruni;
	Nek Muhammad	Siādak	1	...	...	9	...	Nek Muhammad, Isazai	Isazai (? Balteh).
	Padai	Padai	9	3	5	115	...	Dur Muhammad, Sāruni	Seiād, Gazna. Buzi (Farsiwān) Sāruni.
	Pahlwān 1	Pulgi	2	1	1	33	...	Under Pulgi	Pahlwān (Farsiwān).
	Pasand Khān	Siādak	2	...	1	22	...	Pasand Khān, Malakaki	Mahakaki (? Jat).
125	Piāu	Padai	10	4	3	96	4	Dur Muhammad, Sāruni, and Abbas Pudina.	Pudna (? Jat) Sāruni: 2 Tahwils each.
	Pudna	Deh Dost Muhammad.	3	3	4	62	...	Amir Sāruni	Pudna (Farsi) Sāruni.
	Pulgi	Pulgi	10	5	6	130	15	Muhammad Sharif, Sāruni	Karri, Sharaki, Shek Nur, Sheikh (Parsiwāns) Sāruni.
	Rahindā 1	Deh Dost Muhammad	2	6	2	56	...	Rahindād, Sāruni	Saparzai (? Baluch Sufarzai) Arjuni (? Arjuni Jat) Sāruni.
	Rasul Khān	Jahānābād	1	1	1	18	...	Rasul Khān, Belar	Belar (? Jat).
130	Rustam	Siādak	1	...	...	11	1	Alim, Dalmarda	Karim Kushta (Farsiwān) Dalmarda.
	Safar-Murād	"	2	...	...	27	...	Safar-i-Murād	Walidādzai: inhabitants Walidādza (?).
	Carried over		328½	93	257	4,380	187		

A Agriculturists.   B Pastoral, graziers, etc.

MIÁN KANGI—concluded.

No.	Names of villages.	Circles.	PÁGOS.			FAMILIES.		Kadkhuda.	Tribes.
			Ghaui.	Talwil.	Kalgir.	A	B		
	Brought forward		328½	93	257	4,380	187		
	Saparzai	Jahánábád	3	...	2	28	...	Nur Muhammad, Saparzai	Saparzai (Safarzai ? Baluch).
	Safar (Deh)	Daulatáo	1	...	3	16	...	Under Daulatábád	Saṅdágui, Seiád (Farsiwán).
	Seiád	Siádak	11	...	6	112	...	Jáni, Seiád	Seiád (Farsiwáns).
135	Siádak	,,	9	5	10	105	...	Khan Jahán Khán	Sanjaráni, Rakshani (Baluch) Dahmarda.
	Seiad Ali Shah	,,	1	...	2	14	...	Seiad Ali Shah	Kháshi : inhabitants Kháshi (Farsiwán).
	Sikandar (Deh)	Burj-i-Mir Gul	2	1	...	24	...	Under Burj-i-Mir Gul	Pahlawán (Farsiwán).
	Shaláh Khan	...		Deserted.					
	Sahib Khan 1	Deh Dost Muhammad	1	...	...	8	...	Sahib Khán, Nahrui	Nahrui (Baluch).
140	,, ,, 2	Siádak	3	...	...	32	...	Sahib Khán	Pahlawán : inhabitant Pahlawán (Farsiwán).
	Sháh Dost	Deh Dost Muhammad	1	1	1	20	...	Shah Dost, Duari	Duaris (? Duwari-from Zamindáwar) Saruni.
	Shah Dost Alim	,, ,,	2	...	1	9	...	Shah Dost-i-Alim	Sáruui : Dahmarda and Sáruni.
	Shah Gul	Burj-i-Mir Gul	...	2	2	20	35	Shah Gul, Murad Kuli	Shazrai (? Baluch) Murád Kuli (Farsiwán).
	Shah Rakh	Jahánábád	1	...	1	9	...	Shah Rukh, Sharaki	Murad Kuli, Sharaki (Farsiwán).
145	Shams-ud-din	Siádak	11	...	3	194	...	Shams-ud-din Khán	Sarjaráni : Pahlawán, Mir (Farsiwán).
	Sargazi	,, ,,	2	1	...	26	...	Ali Akbar, Sargazi	Sargazi (?) Arjini (? Arjuni Jat).
	Shah Murad	,, ,,	2	...	2	18	...	Shah Murád	Alam-Khel : inhabitants Alam-Khel(?) Galavi (? Jat).
	Siúhraki (Deh)	Palgi	6	1	3	78	...	Maulán, Sharaki	Sharaki, Buri (Farsiwán).
	Sharif 1	Daulatábád	1	...	1	10	...	Sharif, Dázdarí	Dázdarí (Farsiwán).
150	,, ,, 2	...		Deserted.					
	Sáruni 1	Jahánábád	1	...	2	22	...	Huseu Muhammad, Sheikh	Sheikh (Farsiwán) Sáruni.
	,, ,, 2	Deh Dost Muhammad	2	...	3	18	...	Ghulam, Sáruni	Sáruni.
	Sauádgui	...		Deserted.					

THE PEOPLE OF SEISTAN.

No.	Name	Deh						Headman	Tribe / Remarks
	Shekh Weis	Shekh Weisi	7	2	...	1	4	Ibrahim, Shekh Weisi	Shekh Weisi: 4 families of Gaudārs.
155	Shekh (Deh)	...			Deserted.				
	Sher Muhammad 1	Pulgi	1	...	1	37	1	Sher Muhammad, Gamshādzai	Gamshādzais (from Sarhad, Baluch).
	Singo 1	Ali Akbar Burjāri	1	...	2	19	...	Alam, Karri	Karri (Farsiwān).
	„ 2				Deserted.				
	Sohrāb 1	Deh Dost Muhammad	1	...	2	15	...	Sohrāb Khan	Ijbāri; inhabitants Ijbāri (Baluch? Māmaseni).
160	„ 2	Siādak	1	...	1	12	...	Karimdād, Maiādādzai	Sajurzai (Safarzai, ? Baluch) Maiādādzai (?).
	Surkh (Deh)	...			Deserted.				
	Shāhsawār	Daulatābād	2	...	...	20	4	Shāh Sawar	Mir Shikār, Burzi and Mir Shikār (Farsiwāns).
	Sher Muhammad 2	Burj-i-Afghan	1	...	2	15	...	Sher Muhammad, Sauchuli	Sauchuli (Farsiwān), Arjīni (Jat).
	Sarfarāz Khan	„	1	...	2	20	2	Sarfaraz Khān, Sharaki	Pahlawān and Sharakis (Farsiwān).
165	Sadaki	Khamak	1	...	1	18	...	Taj Muhammad, Sāruni	Sāruni.
	Taj Muhammad-i-Dāru 1	Deh Dost Muhammad	3	1	...	70	...	Under Dost Muhammad	Sargazi (Farsiwān) Sāruni.
	Taj Muhammad 2	„	1	...	2	11	...	Taj Muhammad, Sāruni	Sastli, Rakshāni (Baluch).
	Tafis	„			Deserted.				
	Yār Muhammad 1	Siūdak	8	...	9	92	...	Yār Muhammad, Dāzdari	Dāzdari, Musezai (? Baluch), Seiād.
170	„ 2	Jahānābād	1	...	...	8	...	Yār Muhammad, Dalmarda	Dalmardas.
	Yusuf (Deh) 1	„			Deserted.				
	„ 2	Jahānābād	1	...	...	8	...	Yusuf, Rodini	Rodini (Baluch).
	Wali (Deh)	Daulatābād	2	...	1	20	...	Under Daulatābād	Aladau (Jat).
	Total for Miān Kangi		410½	105	322	5,541	232		
	Add for Shahristān		1,234	444½	...	13,787	1,835		
	(Tahwil Pāgos include the Kalgirs)								
	GRAND TOTAL FOR PERSIAN TERRITORY		1,644½	549½	322	19,328	2,067		

Area (approximate) of cultivation represented by 2,194 full pāgos = 153,580 acres.
„ „ „ „ „ 322 „ „
„ „ „ „ „ kalgirs = 5,000 „

Total approximate area = 158,580 „ or 247·8 miles.

Under crops in 1904-05.

A Agriculturists.   B Pastoral, graziers, etc.

APPENDIX I.

(B)

Abstract of the Population in the Districts of Kang and of Chakansur of Seistan.

AFGHAN TERRITORY.

1904-05.

ABSTRACT OF THE POPULATION (IN FAMILIES) IN THE KANG DISTRICT.

Afghán Tribes.

	Barakzai		Achakzai		Isakzai (Sahzi)		Nurzai		Dabbashi		Baroch		Alizai		Ghilzai		Khugári		Tarin		Babi		Farahi?		Saiads		Total	
	A	B	A	B	A	B	A	B	A	B	A	B	A	B	A	B	A	B	A	B	A	B	A	B	A	B
	20	...	56	...	265	...	96	...	15	...	40	15	310	25	425	20	34	...	435	...	130	...	40	...	188	9	2,063	69

Other Tribes.

	Dahmarda		Mahabaki		Sanjarani		Saparzai		Sarguzai		Gathbacha		Bakhshani		Sundzai		Shorzai		Zahtozai		Saidzai		Kashani		Sarimi		Musazai		Total	
	A	B	A	B	A	B	A	B	A	B	A	B	A	B	A	B	A	B	A	B	A	B	A	B	A	B
	...	515	35	...	...	...	...	258	...	15	...	65	427	104	10	...	265	...	50	10	50	...	204	21	...	210	...	26	1,041	1,253

	Baluzai		Notani		Belar		Sarbandi		Bodlai		Ibari		Isakzai		Kutzbhi		Kundahi		Kiral		Abdis		Rekis		Banarti		Total	
	A	B	A	B	A	B	A	B	A	B	A	B	A	B	A	B	A	B	A	B	A	B	A	B	A	B
	...	20	60	125	...	13	225	...	...	22	34	...	...	5	...	18	...	10	...	15	96	315	35	10	60	...	516	562

Total for Kang District . 3,620 1,884

Number of Pigas held by—
Afghans, Ghami . . . 179
Baluch 35
Farsiwans . . . 91
Saiads 15
Total . . 314

Tahsil . . . 83
. . . 36
. . . 35
. . . 8
. . . 162

A Agriculturists.
B Pastoral, graziers, etc.

360 THE PEOPLE OF SEISTAN.

ABSTRACT OF THE POPULATION (IN FAMILIES) IN THE CHAKANSUR DISTRICT.

	Kashani		Notani		Tajik		Kaibali		Dahmarda		Dalbaki		Abdi		Mahbaki		Nahrui		Baskhuti		Halashi		Gorgej		Musazai		Ibshi		Gulabcoba		Isozai		Baroch		Total
	A.	B.	A.	B.	A.	B.	A.	B.	A.	B.	A.	B.	A.	B.	A.	B.	A.	B.	A.	B.	A.	B.	A.	B.	A.	B.	A.	B.	A.	B.	A.	B.	A.	B.	A.	B.
	158	139	194	106	608	...	55	618	170	348	4	1,319	94	226	120	10	42	75	58	30	...	40	60	4	75	...	60	...	12	...	55	60	10	...	1,837	3,007

	Ibari		Gulbizai		Gwarh		Gudkhel		Sarani		Zahrozai		"Brahui,"		"Baloch,"		Shahozai		Kundah		Karimdadzai		Uzbaksai		Mallazazai		Shekh Weisi		Shauhari		Lijjai		Total
	A.	B.	A.	B.	A.	B.	A.	B.	A.	B.	A.	B.	A.	B.	A.	B.	A.	B.	A.	B.	A.	B.	A.	B.	A.	B.	A.	B.	A.	B.	A.	B.	A.	B.
	10	70	20	20	10	...	24	...	20	...	70	...	10	...	12	...	12	...	57	...	55	15	140	...	30	5	12	...	21	...	40	32	543	143

Number of Pagao in the Chakansur District:
- Ghami: 254
- Tahsil: 119
- 414
- 162

Add.—Total for Kang District: 281

Grand Total: 668

Total for Chakansur District: 2,380 / 3,150
Total Kang District: 3,620 / 1,884
Grand Total for Afghan Territory: 6,000 / 5,034

A Agriculturists.
B Pastoral, graziers, etc.

Representing an approximate area under cultivation of 66,430 acres or 103¾ sq. miles (in 1904-05).

APPENDIX II.

"BALOCH" AND "BRAHUI."

APPENDIX II.

"BALOCH" AND "BRAHUI."

IN the preceding chapters the terms "Baluch" and "Brahui" have so frequently been used that it may be as well to attempt to solve the riddle—what are the Baluch and the Brahuis? This is a question which cannot be finally disposed of now, as both the terms "Baluch" and "Brahui" in course of time have lost any ethnological significance that originally may have attached itself to these terms.

It will be as well to consider first the Baluch, as the Baluchis are universally (in Baluchistan) believed to have arrived before the Brahuis; and also to state what conclusions have been drawn, firstly in the volumes of the Baluchistan Gazetteer Series, and in the "Baluch Race," both being the work of authors who have studied the subject diligently; but before doing this it will be as well to see what light is thrown on the subject by chronicles dealing with the countries which are known to have been originally the habitat of these tribes.

The dialect spoken by the tribes which are named Baloch or Baluch is called after them Baluchi. It is technically described as belonging to the Iranian branch of the Aryan sub-family of the Indo-European family. It has been called Balochi or Baluchi merely from the fact of its being the dialect which these tribes speak, and it is probably quite wrong to distinguish this descendant from an ancient language by this name. Baluchi is universally spoken and understood by the Farsiwān population of Seistan, and a careful search would probably establish the fact of its being spoken, or understood, by most of the tribes in modern Persia. The Baluchi dialect is a relic of the widespread Empire of the ancient Persian Dynasties whose authority extended over a vast tract of country, before and after the commencement of the Christian era. The western limit of this dialect is unknown, but its eastern limit has been the watershed of the Indus, which coincides very well with the frontier in this direction of the ancient Persian Empires. The Baluchi dialect has been carried into the valley of the Indus and the Punjab by the tribes who use it, when they migrated eastwards. In this direction the Baluchi dialect has become so corrupted with local tongues, Jad-gali and Sindi for instance, as to be very nearly quite unintelligible to natives of Kej and Makran who speak a more correct version of the ancient dialect.[1]

The fact that all Balochis speak and understand either the corrupt eastern or purer western variations is not in itself evidence in favour of an Iranian origin for the tribes who speak it.

The Baluch tribes seem to have been a floating population of equestrian and pastoral tribes ranging over the Kingdom of Persia from very early times. The inclusion of

---

[1] Some few years ago the eastern and corrupt form of Baluchi was studied by all who were desired to qualify by the Higher Standard for the certificate and the reward for passing in this dialect. In those days no matter how well versed a candidate might have been in the purer western dialect, he could not hope to satisfy the examiners that he knew Baluchi or was speaking it. There was a very striking instance of how unintelligible the eastern dialect was to a native of Western Baluchistan. In 1891 the Officer Commanding the troops in Panjgur (he had been the President of the Board of Examiners in Baluchi, in Karachi) asked the author to arrange an interview with the Gichki Sardar of Panjgur. On that occasion, the officer mentioned addressed to Muhammad Ali Khan Gichki a long speech in the very best quality Baluchi as spoken on the Sind Frontier. The Gichki turned to the author who was present and folding his hands, he whispered to the latter—"tell me, Sahib, what may this Lord be saying to me?" and Captain's ***** speech had to be translated into the western dialect by the author.

the Baluch (under the designation of Kuch wa Baluch) in the armies of the Khasraus, by Firdausi in his great epic the Shāhnāmah probably embodied a tradition to this effect that existed on the 11th century A.D., which at that time was regarded as being ancient, and as preserving a historical fact. The authorities on which this famous work was based are known in part, but it is not unlikely that other materials which were in existence in Firdausi's age and to which he had access, now have been lost. In addition Firdausi probably used well-established and current traditions regarding the past which were in existence in his day, and which have been destroyed in the overwhelming catastrophe of the Mongol inroad in the first quarter of the 13th century.

The organisation of the Baloch (or Baluch) tribes has always been the same as that which prevailed among the tribes called "Scythian" by classical authors, which were spread over a vast tract of Western Asia and had even penetrated into Eastern Europe. It is considered now that these tribes were only the outer and less civilized fringe of the Aryan or East Iranian race, and the modern Baluch is, therefore, a descendant from this ancient stock, a relationship which is suggested by the anthropometrical measurements of selected types taken from the Baluchis settled in the Dera Ghazi and Dera Ismail districts to the west of the Indus. A comparison between the cephalic measurements of 60 Tajiks given by M. Ujfalvy with those of the Baluchis alluded to, shows a very striking correspondence, the highest index in each case being the remarkable figure 95 or 96. The nasal index for the same Baluchis is 68·8. It is clear, therefore, that as far as the shape of the head is concerned the Balochis must be classed with the brachycephalic Iranians and not with the dolichocephalic Arabs or Indians.[1]

The composition of a Baluch (or Baloch) tribe is very suggestive of the manner in which these nomads in the course of countless generations have picked up and included among them fragments of other races:—

"The constitution of a Baloch tribe resembles that of the Brahuis.[2]

"It may be briefly explained here that a Brahui tribe is based primarily not upon agnatic kinship like an Afghan tribe, but upon common good and ill; in other words, it is cemented together by the obligations arising from the blood-feud, and heterogeneity, rather than homogeneity, is the striking feature of its composition. Round a nucleus several groups of diverse origin, including Afgān, * * * , Jat, and even sometimes freed slaves, gathered together in time of emergency and ultimately became consolidated into a tribe. * * * All comers gained easy admission to the tribe. As soon as a man joined the tribe, he permanently became a participator in its fortunes both good and ill. Then, having shown his worth, he was given a vested interest in the tribal welfare by acquiring a portion of the tribal land, in return for which he was bound to share all tribal responsibilities. Admission was then sealed with blood by women from the tribe being given to him or his sons in marriage."[3]

In the course of ages broken men and even families, whom the stress of circumstance had separated from their original tribes, Kurds, Lurs, Turks, Jat, Arabs (and possibly Mongols) and Tajiks joined themselves to the nomadic Baloch Tribes who were located, or were prowling in their neighbourhood, and in a very short time these recruits were admitted to full membership with them. Whatever ethnological

---

[1] The Baloch Race. As. Soc. Monographs, Vol. IV, by Longworth Dames, London, 1904, pp. 11 and 12.
[2] Baluchistan Gazetteer Series, Vol. VI-A, p. 32.
[3] Ibid, Vol. VI. B, pp. 71 and 72.

significance may have been attached at one time to the term Baluch disappeared and the name at last came to mean merely nomads of mixed blood.

The term Kuch wa Baluch, *i.e.*, nomads, has been in use for a very long period of time. Firdausí uses it with reference to the nomadic and floating section of the population of Persia. In the 10th century A.D., the population of the Kirmān Province (conquered 65 years after the death of Naushirwān) was composed of Kurds, Baluch, Jat, and the tribes named Qufs or Qufas. The Jat element very soon lost its distinctive features and was merged into the bulk of the agricultural population on the one side and possibly into the Kuch wa Baluch on the other. The Kurds and the Qufs, however, continued to remain separate from each other and from the agricultural population. Muhammad Ibrahim in his Chronicle of the Saljuk Rulers of Kirmān brings this out very clearly, and from his narrative it is clear that both tribes were confined to certain distinct portions of the Kirmān Province.[1]

The Qufs, or Qufas, held the country from Jiruft southward including the Makran districts (Makrān-āt) to the coasts of the sea. They were a savage race who extended their forays to Khurassān on the north, and up to the confines of Fars on the west. Numerous and warlike, they had for a long time maintained their independence against the members of the Dilemite family who had held possession of Kirmān, and had defeated M'uin-ud-din Abul Khair, the Dilemi, in the passes and defiles of Darfārid and Sarpazan, in which the latter lost a hand in the conflict.

Malik Kāward, the Saljuk, after the acquisition of Kirmān (about 1045 A.D.), lulled the fears of this people by making over to them the country between those passes and the Sea of Oman. Finally as the resources of the upland districts of Kirmān proved insufficient to maintain his followers, Kāward formed a plan to overpower the Qufas who at this time were concentrated in the hilly country of Bārjān. He surprised the leaders and their followers who had assembled for a wedding festival at Jiruft, drawn together from all the districts to the coast of the Sea of Oman. The whole of the assembled tribesmen were slain—not even a single child was left alive; and the whole of the Garmsir or lower districts of Kirmān were taken possession of by Kāward the Saljuk.

No mention of the Qufs and Qufas again occurs in this chronicle.[2]

Later on appear the Kuch wa Baluch. At page 154 they are alluded by the name of Kuj wa Baluch (evidently a mistake on the part of a copyist for Kuch wa Baluch). They were located in the Garmsir of Kirmān. The fort of Rāsukhān apparently was in their possession: after this place was reduced by Malik Dinār, the Ghaz Ruler of Kirmān, he proceeded to Minujān. The Kuch wa Baluch of the Garmsir are mentioned as being allied to the Ruler of Hurmuz. The Kuch wa Baluch are mentioned as occupying the northern portion of the country (in the vicinity of Jiruft) which had been in the possession of the Qufs and Qufas in the time of Kāward Shah, Saljuk; and it seems not improbable that the Kuch wa Baluch of later times may have included among them a part of the dispersed Qufs and Qufas of an earlier period; and after the Ghaz

---

[1] History of the Saljuks of Kirmān: by Muhammad Ibrahim published by M. Th. Houtoma, Leyden E. J. Brill, 1886. Although Muhammad Ibrahim wrote in the 17th century, he used information obtained from the earlier chronicle of Afzal Kermān who wrote at the close of the 12th century during the reign of Malik Dinar, the Ghuz chieftain who had gained possession of the Province and capital city of Kermān.

[2] Their descendants may be possibly the present inhabitants of the Bashakird district and the Khafajai of the Rafsinjan district.

had overrun the province and laid it waste, fragments of other races, such as the Kurds and very possibly the descendants of the ancient Arab, Jat and Tajik races, may have been compelled to descend to a lower plane of existence and in self-defence to join the "nomadic tribes" (Kuch wa Baluch) who were able, owing to their tribal organisation and fluid mode of life, to either protect themselves against, or to evade, the Ghaz who had taken possession of the country.

The inroads of the Ghaz preceded by a short period the more terrible visitation of the hordes of Chingiz Khan; and the Baluch, who were by this time a very mixed race, had to move into those districts further to the east—Lāshār, Magas, Sib, Sorān, Bug, Dombak around Bāmpur, and the western districts of Kej—Buleda, and others. From these districts they migrated again into Sind at a subsequent period, but the fact that the tribes had by this time lost their ancient names, and were known only by those taken from the districts which they occupied, is proof that they were a very mixed race, which it was impossible to refer to any one common stock, and who had become known merely as "the nomads" or "wanderers,"—the Kuch wa Baluch of those districts.

The Ghaz element itself still lingers in Sarhad, the most eastern district or fringe of the Kirmān Province; where the Yār Ahmadzais, Gamshādzais, and others which together are nowadays styled the Dāmuni (border) tribes are undoubtedly the representatives of the Ghaz, and they exhibit the same lawless, predatory, and rapacious instincts, combined with the low standard of civilization which distinguished their Ghaz progenitors. In 1889 when I was in Dizak I was informed by men from Khwāsh to the north-west of that place, that the Sarhadis "were all Ghazz." The Reis who were once upon a time a widely spread powerful tribe, which is still represented in Kej and in Seistan, and where they retain very many of the Iranian characteristics in their physiognomy, in Sarhad call themselves indifferently Ghazz and Reis. The Dāmuni tribes in common with the Nahruis who (claim to be descendants of Arabs from Nahrwān in the vicinity of Baghdād), are also classed as Baloch or Baluch.[1]

The allusions to Syria and to Turkish warriors contained in the ballads or of this people preserve undoubtedly the memory that some part of the tribes known as Baluch were recruited from Arab Kharijis, from the descendants of the adherents of 'Ali, and from the remnants of the Army of Yazid bin Muhalab's who fled by sea to the Kirmān Coast after the death of their leader in battle (24th August 720 A.D.) or of accessions of strength gained later on by Ghaz recruits,[2] or from contact with them.

The so-called Rind section of the Baluch tribes which migrated into India were possibly descendants of the old separatists (Kharijis). But another derivation was obtained by me for the term Rind in Panjgur and Jalk. There it was said that those Baloch tribes who agreed together to abandon their lands owing to the oppression of their Turkish overlords (*Rindi Kutha* in Baluchi) were the actual Rinds. The Rekis of Jalk and Māshkel having formed a part of these separatists account themselves as a section of the "Rinds;"[3] thus Rind had merely a political significance.

---

[1] The repression of the Ghaz in Kirmān was effected by the Atabek of Fars Sád-ibn-Zangi, but they continued to lead the life of robbers (as the Dāmuni tribes do), till an army from Khwarazm under Razi-ud-din, Malik of Zauzan, took possession of Kirmān, and in a few years afterwards the minor troubles of the Province were swallowed up in the terrible castastrophe of the Mongol Invasion.

[2] See pages 7 and 8 of Kalat, by G. P. Tate, Calcutta, 1896.

[3] *Ranūd wa aubāsh*, *i.e.*, turbulent, abandoned or lawless folk, is a well-known compound noun in Persian. *Rind* or *Rand*, the root of the first member, is the root of the vulgar Hindustani word, *randi*, an abandoned woman—a prostitute. See also Kalat, Calcutta, 1896. The word Rind signifies the "irreconcilables" merely, and has not an ethnological meaning.

The Turkish oppressors may have been the Ghaz, the Khwarazm troops, the Mongols, the successors of Timur, or lastly the Kāra Koinlu Turkomans who occupied Kirmān from the middle of the 15th to the early years of the 16th century. The arrival of the Baluch tribes in Sind according to their own traditions took place in the lifetime of Jām Nizām-ud-din, Samah, who succeeded Jām Sanjar, on the 29th November 1461, and died sometime in 1498-99.

But the Baluch ranged over a wide area in Khurassān, and were not confined to the Kirmān Province. They formed a numerous and nomadic section of the population (in the 13th and 14th century) of the country to the north of Herat in the direction of Badghīs, according to the author of the *Rauzat ul Jannat-fi-l-ausāf-i-Madinati-l-Herat*. At the present time there is a not unimportant Baluch element in the population of the Zanindāwar district of Afghanistan. In the Khāsh district also the Baluch and Brahui were not inconsiderable in 1904-05. Part of them were settled in the villages of Razai and Shishāwa which were occupied by the Kirais, and "Baluch" (Uzbakzais), respectively. The headman of the Karai part of Razai, was Shāh Nizar Khan—and of the Uzbakzais of Shishāwa the headman was one Akbar. The pastoral tribes (Māldār) of Khāsh in 1904-05, included the following groups: Bahramzai "Brahui" (106 families), Shāhakzai (37 families); Kirais "Brahui" (185 families), Liwārzais (45 families), Ishākzais (47 families) and the Nuk Baluch (37 families), or 1,955 souls.

It was said that the "Brahui" tribes enumerated above all belonged to sub-tribes of the widespread Mamasenni tribe, the head-quarters of which are in Jebri to the south-east of Panjgur.

A very curious variant of the word or term "*Brahui*" is in use in the Khāsh district and applied to the tribes enumerated as such. They are called *Brahoki*.

While it is possible to assign an origin to the tribes who are known as the Baluch, the "Brahui" is an insoluble riddle. They are without doubt comparatively recent immigrants into the country in which they are now to be found; but the language they speak has been classed by Dr. Grierson as one of the Dravidian languages.

The Brahui has been described as of middle size, square-built, and sinewy, with a sharp face, high cheek bones and long narrow eyes. His nose is thin and pointed. His manner is frank and open; though active, hardy, and roving he is incomparable with the Baluch as a warrior, but he makes a good scout. * *. With a few exceptions the Brahui is mean, parsimonious, and avaricious, and he is exceedingly idle. He is predatory but not a pilferer, vindictive, but not treacherous, and generally free from religious bigotry. His extreme ignorance is proverbial in the countryside. "If you have never seen ignorant hobgoblins and mountain-imps come and look at the Brahui."[1]

They claim to have "come from Seistan" and the low standard of civilization prevailing among them would almost be a sure indication that they are a remnant of the Ghaz tribes, who overflowed into Kirmān and into Afghanistan, after they were pushed out of Central Asia. To give an account of the ravages committed by the Ghaz in the Province of Kirmān would necessitate a translation of the latter part of Muhammad Ibrahim's History of the Saljuks. Kirmān was devastated and the agricultural population, unable to endure the oppression of the barbarous shepherd-invaders, abandoned their lands and fled into the neighbouring countries which possessed governments too strong to be overthrown by these barbarians.

---

[1] Baluchistan Gazetteer Series, Vol. VI-B, p. 102.

Most of the tribes now classed as "Brahui" are confessedly of other well-known and ancient origins such as the Mamasseni, who are Lurs (called Muhammad Hasnis in Baluchistan); the Mirwāris who claim descent from Arab ancestors who originally came from Oman, or they consist of a variety of races drawn together and forming tribes by the obligations entailed by the blood feud. The Mengals of Jahlāwan are an example of the operation of this obligation. They are of acknowledged Persian, Afghan and Jadgal (Jat) origin. The Mardoi clan are Bulfat Jadgal descended from Jām Bhādin, fourth son of Jām Ari progenitor of the Baprāni, Hamalāni, and Lohārāni Jams of Thana Bhula Khan and Tawang, in the Karachi District, who call themselves Numrias.

The tribes whose origin cannot be referred to some well-known races such as those already mentioned, may perhaps be regarded as the original "Brahui" nucleus, such as part of the Zahri tribes in Jhalawān; and the Rodeni in the Sarāwan country. The "Brahui" tribes[1] of this division of the Kalat State can clearly be referred to other origins and are not "*Brahui*" using this word in an Ethnological sense.

If however this term is used in a Political sense alone, meaning a combination of the tribes and their chiefs, of the hill country, then the meaning suggested for the word Brahui, as signifying a hill man, or mountaineer, seems to be feasible. In Sind Barohi is generally used for the people of the hilly country of Kalat, and this probably suggested an explanation of the term or name, *Brahui*.

How a people which regard themselves as emigrants from the West, have come to speak a language sprung "from the same source as the Dravidian language group," but which has "freely absorbed the alien vocabulary of the Persian, Baluchi, Sindhi, and other neighbouring languages, but in spite of their inroads its grammatical system has preserved a sturdy existence"[2]—is a problem of which a solution seems to be impossible, at least for the present.

---

[1] See the list of "Brahui" tribes given in Vol. VI of the Baluchistan Gazetteer Series; and in the *People of India*, by the late Sir Herbert Risley.

[2] Baluchistan Gazetteer Series, Vol. VI, p. 49. If these immigrants learned the Brahui language in their present abodes, it would solve the difficulty. It is barely possible this may be the solution, but there are obvious objections to it which do not appear to be capable of explanation, in the existing state of knowledge of the subject. *Brahui* seems to be used in the same sense as the earlier word *Rind* was; to signify a coalition of the tribes of the hilly country for political purposes, and their own protection. The Brahui language is known as *Kurd-gāli*.

NOTE.—The "Brahui" tribes of Sarawān are (1) Raisani, (2) Shahwāni, (3) Bangulzai, (4) Muhammad Shāhi, (5) Sarparra, (6) Kūrd, (7) Lahri, (8) Lāngav, (9) Dehwār. Of these the nucleus of (1) are Spīn Tarin Afghans of Ahmadun, in the Sibi District. (2) Shahwanis (see pp. 292 and 293); nucleus of this tribe, Baloch and Afghan origin. (4) according to local accounts are some of the oldest inhabitants of the Sarawān District. The nucleus of the tribe are all descended from an eponymous ancestor Muhammad Shāh, to whom other fragments of Baluch tribes have allied themselves. (5) see pp. 293, 294. (6) These are an off-shoot of the Kurds of Persia. (7) The nucleus of this tribe belong to the Dombki stock of the Baluch; with whom other fragments of Baluch and Rind tribes have joined themselves. (8) Have always been looked on as a subject race, and are of Jat origin, *i.e.*, the Langahs of Multan. Their main occupation is agriculture. (9) Tajiks to whom fragments of other tribes have joined themselves (Bal. Gazetteer, Vol. VI, p. 49 *et seq.*).

The term "Brahui" applied to these tribes is clearly used in a political sense, and it has no ethnological significance.—G. P. T.

APPENDIX III.

THE TAJIKS OF BOKHARA.

APPENDIX III.

THE TAJIKS OF BOKHARA.

"THE Tajiks are the original inhabitants in all the towns of Central Asia. This sentence appears in all books of travel and geographical works on Bokhara and its neighbouring countries. The fact is, however, that we do not know anything about it. As mentioned in the chapter on religion[1] it is not only probable, but unquestionable that the Tajiks have superseded another people from Bokhara and most likely a Tartar-Mongolian people. If the Tajiks have proceeded from the west, probably over Khorassān, they have expelled the Tartars towards the east and north-east beyond the Syr. Darya and Tshu towards the Altai mountains, and from here the Tartars (Usbegs) reappeared when a favourable opportunity, caused by internal decay in the Tajik dominion, made the conquest of their former territories possible. For long before Islam made its way here in the 7th century, the Usbegs were the masters of the country and this they are even now."

"The Tajiks are, however, the oldest historical agriculturists in Bokhara who have influenced and still influence the culture in spite of their being now in subjection. To them is due—at any rate according to the legend which is here certainly true—the irrigation of the oases and the regular agriculture which was holy in the Avesta faith like cattle breeding. They represent and represented the intelligence of Bokhara, and even now they look upon themselves as the original inhabitants of Bokhara and upon the Usbegs as usurpers who have overrun the oasis of Bokhara from the country towards the north-east round the Altai mountains and from Turkestan over Samarkand and Shahr-sebbs (Shahar-i-Sebbs) have forced the Tajiks towards the east into Karategin and the Pamir valleys south of this region which are now practically inhabited by Tajiks. This is,

---

[1] "By the oldest population of Bokhara are generally meant the Iranians, the present Tadjiks, whose purest types are seen in the Bokharan Pamir valleys. According to Chinese sources, Khiva, Bokhara and Turkestan had formerly an Aryan population, and the Tartarth-Mongolian race did not immigrate until a comparatively late time. But the fact that the Tartar-Mongolian people, now the rulers in Central Asia, met with Aryan tribes does not preclude the possibility that the Aryans on their arrival here met with Tartar aborigines who on the Tartar-Mongolian invasion had long ago become swallowed up by the ruling Aryans, the bearers of culture. The possibility that a non-Aryan population existed alongside of the Aryan is not excluded, but even proved in Avesta where non-Aryans are dealt with several times. The non-Aryan countries are fought by the Aryans by the help of Zarathustra, and this shows clearly that a war between races has taken place, here the Aryans got the upper hand, but this war is in Avesta removed to a very distant time."

"In Bokhara the Parsee religion was closely pressed by two other religions, namely, Buddism and Christianity. In the 1st century Buddism gained several adherents here, and even for a long time after the invasion of Islam Buddhistic idols are said to have been sold in the bazars of Bokhara, and on their arrival the Arabs found rich temples with idols in gold and silver and temple doors carved with mythical figures. Before Islam the Christian doctrine had gained access in Mid-Asia, thus we know that in the year of 420 there was a Christian Archbishop in Merve, 503—520, a Bishop in Samarkhand, in the circuit of which town large Christian congregations are said to have existed which did not disappear totally until the end of the 13th century."

"Before the arrival of the Arabs and the conversion of the Aryans to Islam, the latter had already lost the government of Bokhara, as Turkish (heathen, Buddistic or Shamanitic) nomads had forced their way from the north into the countries on the Oxus and Jaxarts. They destroyed Balkh in the second century, and in the 6th and 7th centuries they have immigrated in so great numbers into Bokhara and Turkestan as to completely deprive the Aryans of their influence. The Arabs who marched into Bokhara in the year 666 under Rebi-Ibn-ul-Harith, spreading the doctrine of Mohammad with fire and sword, found the country under Turkish rule." The Emir of Bokhara and his Country. O. Olufsen, London: William Heinemann, 1911, pages 365, *et seq*.

indeed, consistent with the fact that Tajiks live in great numbers in Afghanistan and Baluchistan. It is well known that the Turks destroyed Balkh in the second century, and if this invasion has been efficient, it is probable that Tajiks owing to a strong pressure from the Turks, have been forced into the narrow and poor valleys in west Pamir to which no agriculturist resorts if not obliged to do so, and the Arabian invasion during which Islam was spread over Central Asia has caused a further expulsion of the Tajik towards the east. They adhered, however, to the old Avesta faith, the fire-and-light-religion, which they sought to maintain in the narrow valleys in Pamir fortified by nature."[1]

"The Tajik is in Bokhara proud of his nationality, and even now he recalls the frontiers of his former country, the old Khorassán (Khor means in old Persian sun and sun region, *i.e.*, the region of the sun or the east). The Tajiks have produced the most renowned teachers, the first statesmen and officials; nearly all the mullahs are Tajiks, and all intellectual culture is with the Tajiks, but at the same time also the greatest vices. In the oasis of Bokhara itself the Tajiks are in the majority; then they live in great numbers on the middle course of the Serafshan; in Karategin, one of the best mountain provinces of Bokhara, the Tajiks are the main population, and they inhabit the provinces of Darvas, Roshan, Shugnan, Garan and Vakhan, further they live more collectively in the oasis of Shirabad, wheras the Usbegs are the main population in Hisar, Karshi, Shahrsebbs, Kasan, Husar, Kerki, Charjui, Chiraktshi, Kulab, etc. The number of Tajiks in Bokhara may be estimated at one-fourth part of the whole population."

"The word Tajik may mean Arab,[2] and some natives themselves say they are descended from Babylon.[2] It is, indeed correct that during the persecutions of which the family of the Prophet were the object under Haijai in the last 25 years of the 1st century after Hedshra, many members of the latter fled to the regions beyond the Oxus, and there they became mixed up with the native population, and therefore it is possible that a few Tajiks have a right to carry their pedigree up to these and consequently to the Prophet on account of which they receive the title of Saïd or Saït; but much more cannot be ascribed to this. In Afghanistan the Tajik often goes by the name of Dihkan (farmer) or Dihvâr (inhabitant of a town), but in Bokhara these designations are not reserved to Tajiks alone, but are used of all cultivators of the soil or those belonging to the sedentary class."

"If we refer, however, all inhabitants of Iranian descent to the Tajiks which is justified by the fact that every Iranian in Bokhara calls himself by this name, it is necessary to divide the Bokharan Tajiks into two classes, namely, the mountain Tajiks in the East Bokharan mountains and Pamir valleys, the purest races of the original old Iranians, because they have avoided intermixture with the Usbegs into whose

---

[1] "The valley of the Gund river is exclusively inhabited by mountain Tajiks or Galtshas, as it has been the fashion to call them; among the numerous mountain Tajiks I have spoken with, I have never met one who knew the word Galtsha." Page 22.

[2] "The Arabs. The few Arabs who live in Bokhara are descendants of the first conquerors who brought Islam into the country or of those immigrated under Timur. They live in the valley of the Serafshan near Samarkand and in Katta Kurgan near Vardausi in Bokhara and near Eldjik on the Amu Darya. Formerly they always lived in their tents in the old Arab way, but now they live in houses like the other natives especially engaged in carpet weaving, cattle-breeding and horse dealing. They still speak a sort of Arabic and are easily recognised owing to their almost pitch black faces and black hair." *Ibid,* page ?

families they do not marry, even if there might be occasion in some places, and the Tajiks of in the oasis of Bokhara and in the level country who are much intermixed with the Turks, and the numerous slaves introduced from Persia; although they are Iranians, the latter have received many foreign elements." * * * * *

"Although it is commonly said that there are but few of the original Tajiks left in the oasis of Bokhara, still the Usbegs know how to distinguish those considered as Tajiks and those thought to be Persian." * * * * * * *

"The mountain Tajik (he is sometimes called Galtsha) very much resembles the present Persians with their oval faces, sharp, beautiful features with large straight nose, which is sometimes, however, apt to assume a Jewish form, dark hair and rich growth of beard; but the features are coarser than in the present Persians. The difficult conditions of life in the mountains have rendered him agile, strong and persevering, and his isolation from the centres of the world have kept him free from the many vices and disagreeable qualities which are characteristic of the Tajiks of the low lands. The mountain Tajiks are very peaceful peasants, half-nomads if this is necessary, but elsewhere they prefer to live exclusively on agriculture; they are very hospitable and ready to help, and every large house-owner, generally Kasis ' (Qazi) ' or Aksakal, has a special room ' Mehemân-Khanâh ' (room for guests), where he receives the newly arrived strangers. Some authors state that slavery has never existed with them; certainly this is not correct, as the word kul (slave) is very well known here, but is probable that it has not existed to such an extent as elsewhere in Bokhara where, in spite of the Koran, slavery flourished under Islam until the Russians conquered Central Asia. The mountain Tajiks have rarely more than one wife which is partly due to the fact that they cannot afford more; the women are not veiled, they are not strict Mohammedans, and especially here the customs of the Avesta religion hold their own.[1]

"The Tajiks on the plains are like their fellows in the mountains, well-grown people; they are long skulled, have black hair and eyes. Nose, mouth and eyes are beautifully formed, the first rarely curved, but as a rule straight and much more prominent than in the Usbegs. The mouth is large, the same is the case with eyes and feet, and they are very hairy all over the body. The Iranian race is in the low lands intermixed with foreign elements, especially Turkish, but the Iranian characteristics are nevertheless so well marked that the Tajik and the Usbeg are easily distinguished, the former being more elegant than the latter. He is polite, complimentary, more

---

[1] "We know with certainty that the old Iranian fire-and-light-religion had its main seats here (Bokhara), ' and that Zoroaster, Zara Thustra, the beaming, had his first adherents on the banks of the river Serafshan after being ejected from his presumable home, Atrapatenal (the present Asserbaijan or Adarbaigan, guarding the fire).' * * * * * * * *

"Among Parsee customs still in practice in Bokhara may be mentioned the celebrating of the spring festival and the new years festival (Naurus!), and the crowning of the isolated pillars on which the flat roof rests with wreaths of ears of corn; the latter custom still prevails in the Pamir valleys. Further that on a certain day in the year, Tshârshumbéh-Sunni fires are lighted which people leap over, whilst pots are broken at the same time; and all this is to drive away the evil spirits and to be purified from sin and illness. The latter custom, however, only continues in remote regions, being energetically counteracted by the ecclesiastics, but when a Bokhara man is asked whether he knows of it, he smilingly says: Oh! no! in such a way that the custom seems to be maintained secretly. The mountain Tadjiks unwillingly blow out a candle, but extinguish it with earth in order not to pollute the holy flame with their breath; the sick are led round the fire, or a lighted candle is held up before their face. On a child being born a candle burns for 40 days at its cradle to keep off evil spirits. Candles are also lighted at holy tombs, etc., * * * and finally Bokhara is still haunted by practically all the innumerable spirits and demons of the Parsee religion." *Ibid,* pages 365, 367.

discreet than the Usbeg, but on the other hand shrewd and untrustworthy. He is very diplomatic and adorns his speech with a torrent of empty phrases to avoid the matter which he does not want discussed, and it is not pleasant to have to do with him in money affairs."

* * * * * *

"The Tajik on the plain has no proper country, and the Mountain Tajiks do not consider Bokhara as their country. They call themselves Karateginians, Darvasians, Shugnans, etc., but the connection between these regions and Bokhara has not until lately become more intimate. In the level country the language of the Tajiks is a Persian dialect differing no more from the present Persian than that by means of this language one may after a short time learn the language of the Tajiks; the latter is, however, greatly intermixed with Usbegic elements. Their language is the official language, that of the clergy and the cultivated, whereas Usbegic is more the language of the lower classes and the merchants in Bokhara. The farther south one gets from Karategin into the Pamir provinces, the more old Persian is the language. In Shugnan and Vakhan entirely old Persian languages are spoken which it is even difficult for the cultivated Tajik from Bokhara to understand. Practically not the least tribal tradition exist among the Tajiks; in genealogy they take very little interest."

"Domestic life with the Tajiks is more sympathetic than with the Usbegs. The man often spoils his wives[1] to such an extent that they become quite articles of luxury, whereas among the Usbegs they must generally work hard. The children are brought up to show great modesty in their conduct towards their parents, but an Usbegic boy often scolds his father most terribly, which I have witnessed even with the Beg of Roshan and Shugnan, an Usbeg despatched from Bokhara by the E m. The Tajik is very fond of argument, of making long speeches, of negotiating; scolding frequently takes place, but they rarely come to blows, and murders and violent attacks are seldom heard of among the Tajiks."

"Their women are among the most beautiful in Bokhara; as with the Usbegs, their stature is always much smaller than that of the men; they have round faces, almond shaped, large, black eyes, coal black hair, their complexion is pale because they always stay within doors or wear a veil before the face, and they soon become stout like the Persian women. Many mountain Tajik women are with their fine features real beauties. In Bokhara the Shugnan women pass for the ideal of beauty and not unjustly, especially from a Bokharan point of view."

"The Emir of Bokhara and his Country. O. Olufsen: London, William Heinemann, 1911, Chapter 5."

---

[1] See page 278.

APPENDIX IV.

THE JATS IN MESOPOTAMIA AND SYRIA.

APPENDIX IV.

THE JATS IN MESOPOTAMIA AND SYRIA.

THE well-known orientalist, M. J. de Goeje, has collected from the works of Muhammadan authors some very curious and interesting information regarding the Jats (called Zott in the works consulted); in his "Contribution to the History of the Gypsies" in the "Koninklijke Akademie van Wetenschapper" of Amsterdam, 1875.

In A.D. 768 in the reign of the Khalif al-Mansur, Med pirates penetrated into the Red Sea, and captured Jeddah, the Port of Mecca. There was a settlement of Jats (Zotts) in Bahrein, at al-Khatt, a town on the sea coast. Biláduri mentions another Indian tribe, named Sayábija who were established before the beginning of Islam on the sea coasts; while the Zotts (Jats) pastured their cattle in the Tofuf, the bottom lands of the Euphrates, in the neighbourhood of Babylon. An old canal in the Batiha (marshes of the Euphrates) near Babylon was known, even for a long time after that, as the "Canal of the Zotts." There was a colony of these people in Khuzistan. Biláduri mentions the "Territory of the Zotts" as among the districts which were conquered in the reign of Omar (A.D. 635—644). This territory was situated between Rámhormuz and Arraján and retained this name long after the inhabitants were no longer recognized as Zotts. Istakhri and Ibn Haukal mention it as being extensive, populous and rich.

Biláduri relates that the Khalif Moawia in A.D. 669 or 670 transferred several families of the Zotts and Sayábija from Basra to Antioch on the Orontes, and other sea board towns of Syria. In the third century of the Muhammadan era, there was a quarter in Antioch known as "the quarter of the Zotts;" and descendants of this people were living in Búka. A second colony, and afterwards a third, was sent into Syria by Walid I and Yazid II.

During the state of semi-anarchy which was caused by the war between the sons of Hárún ar-Rashid, al-Emin and al-Mámún, the Zotts (Jats) of the Kaskar lowlands had obtained the mastery throughout the regions of the Lower Tigris. They took possession of the highways—by land and water—plundered ships and caravans, and sacked the granaries of Kaskar. In A.D. 820, matters had reached such a pass that people no longer dared to cross their territory, and ships destined from Basra to Baghdad with provisions remained lying at Basra.

In 820 and 821 A.D. expeditions sent against the Zotts were altogether unsuccessful and the prestige of the Khalif suffered greatly therefrom. This state of things lasted till 834 A.D., when the successor of al-Mámún resolved to grapple with the difficulty in earnest. After nine months were spent in the operations among the marshes, in the end of 834 A.D., the outlaws finally surrendered on the condition that neither their lives nor their possessions were to be forfeited. They are reported to have numbered 27,000 persons, of whom 12,000 were men capable of bearing arms. They were deported, first to Khanikin, and from there to Ainzarba (Anazarba) on the northern frontier of Syria.

Bilāduri states that fully the greatest number were taken to the Ainzarba; but that a part remained in Khanikin, and a few were placed in other parts of the Syrian frontier.

In the year 855 A.D. (according to Tabari and Ibn-l-Athir) when the Byzantines attacked Ainzarba, they captured all the Zott prisoners in that town; and carried them off to their own country, along with their women, children, buffaloes and cattle.

In Sind—Bilāduri speaks of "the Zott of al-Bodha." They dwelt to the west of the Indus and lived by camel-rearing. They brought their produce to market at the town of Kandabil—the modern Gandava. The Meds inhabited the country on the banks of the Indus, from the borders of Multan to the sea. They differed little from the Zotts. The inland Meds supported themselves by sheep-rearing, but their brethren who dwelt along the coast lived by piracy. They were known as Kork (or Kerk) and they were a sea-faring people.

The Arabs corrupted Jat into Zott. In the Arabic Dictionary *al-Kāmūs* this entry occurs: "*Zott* arabicized from *Jatt*, a people of Indian origin. The word might be pronounced *Zatt* with equal correctness." In the lexicon *Mohit* we read: "*Zott*, a race from India, arabicized from *Jatt*." Vullers in his Persian Dictionary quotes this from a native Persian Dictionary: "Djat nomen tribus segregetæ infimæ sortis et deserta habitantis in Hindustan."

"The Gypsies of India." David MacRitchie. Kegan Paul, Trench and Company, London, 1886.

INDEX

TO

NAMES OF PERSONS, TOWNS, TRIBES, RIVERS, RUINS, LOCALITIES, etc.

PARTS I TO IV.

A

	Pages.
Abaka Khan	40
Abar Koh	61
Abarwīzh	15
Abassides	285
Ab-Baksh	248
Abbas	18, 19, 189
Abbasid Caliphs	36
'Abbas Khan	89, 92
Abbott, Major	94
Abdālis	79, 81, 82, 83
Abdul Aziz Khan	291
Abdul Khair	77
Abdullah-ibn-ul Amir	13
Abdullah Jarim	13
Abdullah Khan II.	77
Abdul Latif	64
Abdur Rahman	19, 46, 300
Abdur Rahman Ghairāni	33
Ab-i-Istādah	184
Abīls	188, 303, 306, 309
Abir	188
Abivard	13, 46, 83, 84, 85, 86
Abu Anf	217
Abu Ibrahim	21
Abu Ishak	10, 25
Abu-l'Abbas	24
Abul 'Askar	318, 319
Abu-l-Fazl Allami	183, 184, 308
Abu'l Fazl-i-Nasr	270
Abu-l-Hasan-i-Nasr	21
Abu-l-Hifs	3
Abu Muslim	19
Abu Said-i-Ispahbad ("Ghuri Bacha")	52, 53, 61

	Pages.
Abu Said Sultan	44, 45, 47, 48, 49
Abu Tāhir	258, 259
Abu-Yūsof	280
Adarbaigan	373
Adil Shah	91
Adira	164
Adraskan	5, 184
Afrasiyab	3, 7, 52
Afshārs	71, 75, 76, 84, 85, 86
Afzalābād	169, 307
Aga Muhammad Khan Kajar	93
Aghāzādah	67
Agriaspœ (or Ariaspœ)	6
Ahmad	21, 89
Ahmad Shah	92, 94, 179, 263, 264
Ahmadwāl	290
Ahirs	301, 309
Ahwaz	20
Ainzarba (Anazarba)	377, 378
Ajmir	273
Akbar	170, 314
Akbarābād	151
Akhœmenean Dynasty	2
Akhundzada	180
Ak Timur Bahadur	54
Aladau	303
Alam Khan	64, 192, 202
Alamut	29
Ala-ud-din	40, 42
Alb Arsalan	24
Alb-i-Ghazi	5
Aleli	211
Alexander	4, 7, 9, 10, 183, 188, 274, 289
Aliābād	96, 133, 134, 135, 142, 143, 144, 169, 17, 176,

INDEX.

	Pages.
Ali Akbar Khan	93
Āl-i-Buwiah	36
Ali Beg	53
Ali Khan	95, 96, 98, 175, 200,
Ali Kuh Khān Shamlu	82
Al-i-Kurt	36, 37, 38
Ali Mardan Khan	79
Al-i-Muzaffar	47
Alinjān	37
Al Istakhrī	10, 17, 122, 123, 124, 126, 127, 145, 146, 147, 148, 149, 150, 151, 155, 156, 193, 195, 196, 198, 199, 203, 204, 205, 208, 210, 212, 215, 217, 223, 224, 377.
Alizais	296, 297
Al-Khatt	377
Al-Māmūn	377
Allahābād-miyan-i-Shola	164, 165, 262, 263
Altai	371
Aman Koh	42, 43, 51, 52
Amir Ak Bughā	53
Amir Ali Khat-tai	44
Amir Aweis, Tarkhān	65, 66, 67
Amir Aziz	50
Amir Chah	113
Amir Ghuri	53
Amir Hajī Seif-ud-din	53
Amir Husen	45, 48, 49, 240
Amir Husen Jāndār	65, 66
Amir-i-Nikudar	42
Amir Iqbal Sabiq	47
Amir Khalil Hindukah	64, 65, 66, 70, 208, 252
Amir Kutlugh	41
Amir Mansur	21
Amir Mubāriz	61
Amir Muhammad Khwājah	51
Amir Muzaffar	322
Amir Nauroz	41, 43
Amir Naushirwān	321, 322, 323
Amir Seif-ud-din	91
Amir Shahinshah	24, 25
Amir Shams-ud-din	58
Amir Sheikh Haji	67
Amir Sitalmish	51
Amir Sultan Arghūn	79
Amir Timur Gurgān	233
Amir Wajih-ud-din	46
Amir Wali	54
Amir Zādah Ali	59
Amir Zādah Mirānshah	62
Amru	123, 165, 204, 231
Andijan	53
Andikhud	46, 50
Anjil	37, 51, 56
An-si	278
Antioch	377
Anushirwan the Just	11, 12
Aoba	4, 34
Arachosia	292

	Page.
Aral	107
Arbāb Dost Muhammad	139, 147, 233
Arbāb Seif-ud-din	62, 177, 179, 180, 181, 244, 275, 299.
Arbābs	12, 67, 72, 167, 179, 181, 218, 282, 295
Ardashar-i-Babak	10, 11, 12, 232
Ardavan	232
Ardeshir	232
Arg	31, 32
Arghand Āb	73, 127
Arghasān	288
Arghūns	71
Arlat	46
Arrajān	377
Arrian	274
Arrokhaj	16, 145
Arsalan	38
Artabanus	293
Artish	301
Arzan	311
Asadullah Khān	79, 80, 81
Asghar	174
Ashg	10, 232
Ashg-ka-Putra	210, 232, 274, 275, 292, 293
Āshkin	117, 140, 173, 175, 176, 177
Ashkinak	16, 210
Ashraf	89
Ashtarpi	85
Az-i-Ghāzi	237, 261
Aserbaijan	373
Atishkada	144, 192, 193
"Aughan"	61
Auk	122
Aukat	32
Aukatir	122
Avdal, Johannes	311
Avesta	184
Awāzi	303
Ayajī	41
Azab	35
Azad Khan	81, 315, 323, 329, 331
Azarbaijan	84

B

Bābākudrat	86
Babār Mirza, Prince	64, 67
Babylon	377
Bactria	11
Bad arābād	54
Badghis	12, 64, 331
Badi-uz-Zamān Mirza	71, 73
Bāgh-ak	237
Baghdad	5, 20, 89, 122, 189, 366, 377
Bāghwāna	294

	Pages
Bahadur Tair	32
Bahar	4
Baha-ud-Daulah Tahir bin Nasr, bin Ahmad	24
Bahman	2, 4, 208
Bahrāmābād	176, 237, 238
Bahram Chubin	36
Bahram Gur	11, 36
Bahram Khan	92, 93
Bahrein	377
Baihak	46
Baisanghar Mirza	64
Bakar	40
Bakhārz	38, 44
Bakhtar Zamin	2, 48
Bakhtiāri	299, 300
Bak Tuzun	22
Bakwa	12
Balkh	1, 2, 4, 11, 20, 22, 27, 36, 46, 50, 70, 291, 372
Balochāp	108
Baluchis	363, 364, 365, 367, 368
Bām	93, 110, 196, 214, 215, 295
Bampur	17, 94, 281, 283, 318, 319, 324, 366
Banādir	81
Bandān	108, 109
Bandar	128, 129, 224
Bandar-i-Kamal Khan	127, 128, 129, 131, 132, 136, 148, 149, 157, 240
Band-i-Bul'baka	159, 161, 163, 248, 260, 281
Band-i-Bulghān	159
Band-i-Chash-Makā	155
Bandik	135, 144
Band-i-Koshk	153
Band-i-Raskak	159
Band-i-Rustam	60, 155, 156, 157, 258, 281, 326
Band-i-Seistan	159, 281, 326
Band-i-Shahr	159
Band-i-Yakau	157, 281
Bāni Ommeya	9
Baprāui Jams	290, 368
Bārakzai	95
Bārānzais	290, 367
Barandak	69
Barechis	294, 315
Barka Khan	40
Bāruni	303
Basher	198, 205, 216, 217
Basrah	13, 377
Basrig	12
Basta	67
Batu Khan	37, 39
Bāyāu	365
Bazi	302
Beglar Begi of Merv	82
Beglar Begi of Meshed	80, 81, 82
Behar	86
Behistan	312
Beladheri	199
Belar	303

	Pages
Belkis	4, 5
Bellew	216
Beshbaligh	37
Bessus	7
Bhislar	311
Bibi Basso	323
Bilādurī	377, 378
Bina-i-Kai	17, 25, 98, 148, 165, 177, 194, 196, 198, 202, 205, 218, 219, 222, 223, 225, 226, 269
Biram Ali Khan	88
Birāt Khwājah	58
Birjand	108, 263
Birj-i-Mir Alam Khan	94
Bist	16, 30, 145, 211, 212, 218
Biyats	74, 84
Boaz, Franz	273
Bokhara	21, 52, 77, 90, 278, 371, 372, 373, 374
Bolai	177, 221, 235
Bolida	276
Brahui-Jadgal War	320, 323, 324
Brahuis	27, 363, 364, 367, 368
Bug	366
Bughrajak	23
Bujae	43
Būka	377
Bu Kamij	85
Buleda	366
Bulfat Jadgals	290, 368
Bulgha, Prince	39
Bunjar	15, 150, 152, 164, 167, 246
Bunyād Khan	173
Burak Hajib	31, 37, 61
Burj-i-Afghan	235
Burj-i-Alam	96
Burj-i-Ās	202, 204
Burj-i-Asp	201
Burj-i-Ilamdar	176
Burj-i-Lar	192, 213
Burj-i-Mirgul	124, 206, 331
Burj-i-Sarband	169, 172
Burnes	2
Burri	167
Bushish	29

C

	Pages
Caspian	107
Chagai	62, 98, 210, 286, 317, 321
Chagatai	37
Chah Amir	320, 321
Chahārburjak	136, 145, 147, 148, 157, 226, 241, 258, 330, 334
Chahārdari	151, 235, 247
Chaharshahr	276

INDEX.

	Pages.
Chahilburj	136, 146, 229, 231, 232, 239, 266, 275
Chahil Dukhtārān	266
Chahilimirez	148, 241
Chahil Khana	236
Chah Nima	142, 143, 144, 150
Chakānsur	24, 30, 76, 94, 147, 160, 175, 176, 180, 187, 200, 210, 212, 213, 218, 254, 284, 285, 293, 295, 296, 297, 307, 314, 329, 331, 332, 333, 335.
Chang Kien	278
Chap	76
Chapu	187, 188, 192, 212, 213
Chargewak	47, 76
Charjui	372
Charkh	177
Chārūnak (or Jārūnak)	74, 75, 76
Chato	27
Chib	276
Chigini	160, 254, 255, 256
Chilling	172, 174, 175
Chin	67
Chingiz Khan	7, 32, 33, 34, 35, 36, 37, 38, 45, 47, 48, 50, 52, 53, 69, 158, 180, 215, 278, 320.
Chiustia Nimroz	184
Chiraktshi	372
Christie, Capt.	169, 170, 171, 172, 235, 253, 265
Chung-i-Aruna	125
Chung-i-Beringak	306
Chung-i-Chahārshahr	209
Chung-i-Chori	175
Chung-i-Darāzgu	117, 148, 254
Chung-i-Khargoshki	176
Chung-i-Marghun	237
Chung-i-Reg-i-Zaruni	125
Connolly	4, 5, 95, 96, 172, 173, 177, 211, 215
Cyrus	8, 9

D

	Pages.
Dād	302
Daghestan	293
Dahana	147
Dahmarda	303, 306, 308, 309
Dāītī	188
Dakhmas	191, 192
Daki	39
Dak-i-Tir	173, 176
Daikhak	89, 303
Daikhakis	295, 297, 303, 306
Damb-i-Kalān	146
Damb-i-Rustam	138, 145
Dam Damah	201
Dames, M. Longworth	285
Dandankad	313

	Pages.
Danishmand Bahadur	43
Dantanu	148, 149
Darah-i-Juz	84, 88
Darband-i-Bāku	49
Darband-i-Nādiri	214
Darband-i-Seistan	214
Dārdān	288
Darek	195, 196
Darfārid	365
Darg	118, 121, 188, 189, 190
Darius	7, 9, 312
Darni	303
Darra-i-Sokhta	266
Darun	85, 86
Darvas	372, 374
Darwaza-i-Bakhtīāri	248
Darwazis	286
Darya	371, 372
Daryā-i-Singi	108, 184
Dashāk	171, 175
Dasht	109, 111, 316
Dashtak	97, 169
Dasht-i-Bíaz	29
Dasht-i-Katrān	26
Dasht-i-Kipchāk	301
Dasht-i-Margo	128, 130, 131, 132, 138, 140, 141, 225
Dasht-i-Meski	128, 225, 245, 249
Dasht-i-Zireh	133, 184
Dashtīāri	313
Date wor	145
Daud Beg	24
Daulatabad	170, 172, 332
Dāwar	16
Dehak	211
Deh Akbar Shah Nazar	299
Deh 'Ali	75
Deh Bahlol	175
Deh Ghulām Haidar	136
Deh Gul Muhammad	202
Deh Gul Shah	175
Deh Ido	175
Deh Jahāngir	175
Deh Karimdād	173
Deh Khālikdād	134
Deh Khoja	202
Deh Kūl	299
Deh Lueh	175
Deh Meno	254
Deh Mirak	63
Deh Nawāb	302, 314
Deh Niaz Khan	148
Deh Surkh	206
Dehwārs	283, 284, 286, 300
Dela's Peak	135
Deluwi	295
Dera Ghazi	364
Dera Ismail	364
Deshu	128

Dik-i-Dalil	249, 250
Dik-i-Dela	135, 136, 137, 138, 142, 154
Dik-i-Shah	174
Dik-i-Surh	210
Dilarām	81, 89, 109, 295, 303
Dilāwar Khan	283
Dilem	36
Diwālak	173, 177
Dizak	35, 283, 284, 366
Dombak	366
Dooshāk	170, 235
Dor	147
Dost Muhammad	95, 331
Dost Muhammad Sāruni	176
Drangiana	8, 183
Dua, Prince	41
Dur Muhammad	332
Dushāk	167, 168, 169, 170, 171, 175

E

Eldjik	372
Ellis, A. G.	49, 181, 222, 270
Energetœ	8, 9
Euphrates	18, 377

F

Fahraz	295, 319
Fanakat	27
Farah	5, 6, 31, 32, 35, 36, 37, 38, 42, 44, 45, 54, 60, 63, 66, 67, 69, 74, 75, 76, 81, 82, 83, 89, 90, 91, 108, 110, 116, 117, 184, 212, 287
Farah Rud	68, 108, 109, 111, 116, 117, 118, 119, 120, 121, 134, 139, 158, 160, 216
Faridun	3, 8, 83
Farmakān	54
Fars	20, 35, 61, 63, 122, 184, 204, 320, 365
Farsiwan	8, 10, 36, 180, 286, 291, 294, 295, 296, 297, 298, 303, 333, 334
Faryab	38
Fasharud	29
Fatehpur	313
Fath Ali Khān	82, 85, 87, 88, 90, 161, 163, 165, 260, 261, 262
Ferghana	278
Feroz	290
Ferrier, M.	6, 176, 177
Firdausi	7, 204, 363, 365
Firuzabad	33, 43, 70
Firuzkuh	33, 38
Forbes, Dr. Frederick	98, 175, 295
Forij	15
Foshanj	21, 23, 32, 51
Frazdān	184

G

Gabrs	186
Galavi	303
Galugah	320, 321, 322
Gamshadzais	27, 366
Gandava	378
Garan	372
Garmsir	44, 54, 72, 91, 365
Gaudārs	303, 304, 305, 306, 307, 308, 309
Gaud-i-Gaz	198
Gaud-i-Zireh	74, 108, 109, 127, 129, 131, 132, 157, 161, 183, 184, 240.
Gauri	246, 262
Gāwak	149, 250
Gerard, Dr.	2
Ghalchas	286
Gharjistan	38, 41
Ghazan Khan	41, 42, 43
Ghazni	27, 34, 36, 184, 313, 315, 318
Ghazz	214, 365, 366
Gheiath-ud-din	5, 27, 28, 34, 38, 63
Ghilzais	79, 81, 296, 297, 330
Ghulams	99, 147
Ghulām Shah	174, 263
Ghulghula	16, 140, 146, 147, 160, 225, 238, 239, 240, 248, 249, 276.
Ghur	3, 42, 43, 52, 53, 109, 145
Ghuris	7, 28, 51, 61
Ghuz	8, 27
Gina	163, 167, 242
Girdi Kalat	240, 241
Girishk	89, 110, 147, 295, 310
Goeje, M. de	211, 377
Golas	309
Goldsmidt, Sir Frederik	68, 95, 98, 99, 171, 202, 335
Gresha	288
Grierson, Dr.	372
Gudar	211
Gudar-i-Shah	161
Gudarz	61
Gujars	296, 301, 302, 307, 308, 309, 310, 314
Gulistān	193, 237, 275
Gumbaz-i-Baluch	30
Gumbaz-i-Surkh	78, 246, 247
Gumbaz-i-Yakdast	247
Gunābād	295
Gund	372
Gurg	63, 295
Gurgina	293
Gurguri	282
Gushtasp	1–4
Guthrie	2
Guzar-i-Khāsh	211
Gwachig	320, 321, 322, 324

H

	Pages.
Hadali	168
Haftār Kund	148, 149, 153
Haidari	307
Haji	8
Haji Turab	84
Halā	323
Halkato	40
Hamalāni Jams	290, 368
Hamdin	80
Hamir	312
Hamun	10, 31, 70, 108, 109, 110, 111, 113, 114, 115, 119, 120, 123, 124, 125, 127, 129, 132, 134, 140, 143, 151, 156, 157, 160, 161, 164, 165, 169, 170, 171, 172, 183, 188, 198, 206, 208, 209, 216, 217, 236, 238, 250, 257, 262, 263, 266, 267, 288, 290, 298, 303, 307, 327.
Hāmun-i-Puza	107, 118, 121, 174, 176, 199, 288, 307
Hamun-i-Sāwari	107, 119, 120, 156, 217
Hamun-i-Seistan	107, 109, 122, 358
Hamzabad	95, 167
Hamza Beg	73, 74, 75
Haruri	211
Hārut Rud	109
Hasan-i-Sabah	29
Hashmat-ul-Mulk	97, 99
Hashnu	30
Hauzdar	8, 137, 160, 167, 168, 196, 257, 258, 264
Hazārājat	78
Hazaras	61, 331
Helmand	1, 8, 12, 16, 17, 50, 60, 62, 63, 74, 76, 78, 79, 97, 98, 108, 109, 110, 111, 112, 114, 115, 116, 117, 118, 119, 120, 123, 124, 126, 127, 128, 129, 130, 131, 133, 134, 135, 136, 137, 138, 139, 140, 141, 142, 143, 144, 146, 147, 148, 149, 152, 153, 155, 156, 158, 159, 160, 161, 162, 163, 164, 165, 166, 167, 169, 172, 173, 174, 176, 177, 179, 180, 181, 182, 183, 185, 191, 195, 196, 198, 199, 202, 212, 214, 219, 222, 223, 224, 225, 226, 233, 236, 237, 238, 240, 256, 257, 260, 262, 263, 265, 268, 281, 282, 284, 292, 295, 296, 300, 303, 304, 310, 314, 315, 320, 321, 326, 330, 333, 334, 335.
Her	311
Herat	1, 4, 6, 10, 12, 13, 19, 21, 26, 27, 33, 34, 35, 37, 38, 39, 40, 42, 43, 48, 50, 51, 52, 53, 54, 56, 61, 63, 67, 70, 71, 75, 81, 82, 91, 92, 94, 110, 159, 170, 173, 184, 195, 205, 214, 215, 216, 288, 305, 331.
Heri	4
Hindmend	15, 16, 122, 145, 198, 199
Hindu Kush	285
Hinglāz	274
Hingol	274
Hirmend	3, 29, 72, 77
Hisanik	15, 123, 198, 199, 209
Hisham, Caliph	19
Hissar	314, 372
Hisun	15, 16, 198
Hokat	32, 71, 122, 160, 188, 215, 216, 217, 288
Holdich, Sir Thomas	322
Homo Alpinus	285
Hor Kalat	274
Hormuz	214
Hormuz the Fourth	12, 36
Houtsun-Schindler, Gen	189
Hulmargh	276
Hurmuk	123
Hurmuz III	11
Husar	372
Husenābād	165
Husan 'Ali Beg	86, 87
Husen Khan	89
Husen Khan-i-Sani	91
Husenki	152, 167, 169
Husen Shahid	64
Husen Sultan	88, 89

I

	Pages.
Ibbetson, Sir Denzil	310
Ibn-Haukal	212, 224, 377
Ibn-i-Rusteh	15, 17, 122, 123, 193, 196, 198, 199, 205, 209, 215, 216, 217.
Ibn-i-Samurah	16, 17
Ibn-I-Athir	378
Ibn-ul-Husen, Prince	71
Ibrahimābād	175, 176
Ibrahim Khan	87, 98, 99
Ibrahim Khan Sanjārāni	94, 166, 175, 176
Ikhtiyār-ud-din	43, 52, 53
Ilagh Beg	64
Ilak Khan	23
Ilamdar	16, 149, 169, 170, 172, 175, 176, 177
Iliyats	83
Iljikdae Nuyin	33, 34
Ilkhan, Court of	39, 40, 41
Imam Kuli	83
Imam Reza	88
Imam Zeid	68
Indus	11, 307, 378
Iraj	3
Irak	20, 32, 40, 41, 42, 69, 70, 97
Iran	2, 3, 6, 46
Irindās	211
Irtish	301
Isa	318, 319

INDEX.

	Pages.
Isfahan	77, 79, 81, 82, 88, 89
Isfandiyar	1, 208
Isfarain	86
Isfirar	4, 5, 31, 35, 36, 38, 42, 43, 44, 54, 110, 184
Ishakzai	10, 217, 287, 367
Iskander	289
Iskil	284
Ismail Khan, Ghulam	82
Ispahan	20, 26
Ispakalacheh	42
Issykkul	301
Istājlū	71
Istakhr	10
Izat Khan	79
Izz-ud-din Maraghāni	28, 37, 38, 49
Izz-ul-Muluk	27

J

	Pages.
Jabal Bariz	296
Jadgal	291, 363
Jafir Khan	89, 91, 92
Jafir Sultan	72, 81
Jahānābād	98, 170, 175, 176, 332
Jaihun	3
Ja-i-surkh	150
Jaj	27
Jājurm	86
Jalai	164, 176, 262
Jālawān	289, 290, 292, 294, 308, 313, 323, 368
Jālk	128, 321, 366
Jallālābād	148, 150, 167, 169, 171, 172, 175, 210, 261
Jallaluddin Khan	171, 181
Jalwar	367
Jām	38, 51, 70, 88
Jamālis	281, 295
Jamal-ud-din Muhammed Sam	43
Jamalzai	98
Jam Aū	290, 368
Jām Bhādin	368
Jām Nizām-ud-din	367
Jām Sanjar	367
Jamshid	153, 154, 156, 157, 299, 300
Janābad	29, 86
Jan Beg	98, 210
Jandi Shahpur	30
Jangshāhi	322
Jān Muhammad	168, 202
Jatah or Jitah	301, 302
Jats	10, 289, 290, 291, 296, 301, 302, 303, 307, 309, 310, 311, 312, 316, 320, 364, 365, 366, 377, 378.
Jaxartes	301, 371
Jaziuak	237
Jazruan	42
Jeddah	377
"Jehanam" or "Hell"	140
Jharoki	173, 199

	Pages.
Jiruft	214, 365
Jizah	212
Jokhias	289
Jotegh	237, 295, 296
Jui Gershap	148
Jui Hamdār	167, 168, 170, 174
Jui Kohneh	16, 155
Jui Malāni	37
Julgah of Karan	321
Jun Ghurbānis	53
Jur	303
Jurg	69
Juwein	10, 17, 76, 80, 86, 108, 118, 122, 170, 188, 198, 199, 209, 215, 216, 217, 287, 288, 289
Juzdez	23
Juzjanān	23

K

	Pages.
Kabul	2, 3, 4, 8, 18, 38, 65, 67, 68, 173, 263, 300
Kacha Koh	109, 132
Kachiān	152, 167, 181
Kachhi	316
Kadah	160, 187, 212, 218
Kadamgāh	85
Kadir Bakhsh	283
Kadkhuda Ghulām Raza	281
Kadkhuda Shāh Beg	281
Kad Khuda, Taj Muhammad	99
Kad Khudas	298, 299, 302, 327, 328, 329, 330, 331
Kāfir Kal'a	82
Kaiānis	1, 2, 6, 8, 9, 12, 13, 14, 20, 22, 23, 24, 26, 36, 37, 45, 48, 49, 54, 57, 60, 65, 71, 76, 80, 81, 83, 85, 86, 87, 91, 92, 95, 98, 99, 136, 157, 159, 164, 166, 170, 179, 181, 253, 258, 280, 281, 282, 295, 299, 335.
Kai Kasrau	83, 198, 199
Kaikhasrau	13, 14
Kaikubad I	3
Kain	29, 88, 89, 92, 217, 263
Kaināt	29, 31, 110, 263
Kairābād	121
Kājārs	87, 93, 94
Kakh	92
Kakha	158, 159, 243, 265, 267, 277, 296
Kakhajird	265
Kakhās	265, 266, 281, 295
Kalag	317
Kala-i-Bālān	187
Kala-i-Bist	17, 60, 62, 79, 80, 110, 127, 179, 184, 205, 210, 314.
Kala-i-Surkh	62
Kala-i-Dukhtar	5
Kala-i-Fath	63, 64, 72, 76, 77, 78, 79, 128, 136, 137, 138, 139, 140, 146, 156, 158, 159, 160, 161, 162, 163, 165, 177, 179, 245, 246, 247, 248, 249, 254, 256, 257, 258, 259, 260, 261, 262, 282, 334.

INDEX.

	Pages.
Kala-i-Gāwak	140, 146, 248, 254, 258
Kala-i-Kah	10, 31, 37, 67, 68, 69, 90, 110, 190
Kala-i-Kakah	62
Kala-i-Kang	176, 199, 210
Kala-i-Khārān	241
Kala-i-Kohna	94, 96, 169
Kala-i-Kuk	265
Kala-i-Mahmud	148
Kala-i-Maksud	161, 240, 241
Kala-i-Mir	63
Kala-i-Nan	15, 94, 96, 135, 144, 169, 191, 192
Kala-i-Sam	6, 169, 238
Kala-i-Taimur	223, 253, 255
Kala-i-Ziro	237
Kalāntars	91
Kalat	52, 53, 74, 83, 84, 85, 86, 88, 274, 292, 293, 294, 295, 308, 310, 312, 316, 368.
Kalat State	35, 286, 288, 289
Kala Tapa	207
Kalavi	302, 303
Kalb 'Ali	89, 306
Kalgirs	328
Kaliyun	33, 35, 38
Kalukhi	169, 174, 175
Kamal Khan	128
Kamālis	281, 295
Kanaz	13
Kandabil	378
Kandahar	2, 6, 12, 17, 40, 48, 50, 65, 71, 73, 75, 78, 79, 81, 89, 92, 95, 98, 110, 159, 179, 214, 215, 274, 281, 282, 286, 288, 292, 295, 303, 305, 315, 331.
Kang	296, 330, 332, 333, 335
Kankulis	36
Kānsu	184
Karabāgh	292
Karacha	34, 35
Karachi	290, 368
Karak	145
Kara Khitais	26, 52
Karamania	9
Karan	62
Karategin	371, 372, 374
Karbala	94, 218
Kardagāp	293
Kariyetein	211, 212
Karim Kushta	303
Kārku	150, 151, 156, 176
Kārku Shāh	192, 206, 207, 208, 244, 247
Karkuyieh	15, 198, 208, 209
Karlugh	37
Karnein	15, 16, 211, 212
Karshasp	3
Karshi	372
Karunas	320
Karut Khar	330

	Pages.
Kārzargah	19
Kasan	372
Kash	302
Kāshān	91
Kashānis	274, 275, 292, 293
Kashghār	50
Kasimābād	15, 150, 152, 271
Kaskar	377
Kussamābād. See Kasimābād.	
Kasvini	208
Katbuga Nuyin	39
Katlok	303
Katta Kurgan	372
Kaud	169, 302
Kaud-i-Gaz	176
Kaward Shāh	26, 214, 215
Kazi Abdullah	261
Kazvin	81
Kech	17, 48
Kej	12, 17, 62, 65, 274, 275, 276, 281, 289, 310, 312, 313, 316, 317, 321, 363, 366.
Kej Makrān	313
Kemāri	137
Kerki	372
Keti Bandar	307
Khabushān	83
Khadang	56
Khaesār	38, 40, 43, 46, 290
Khāf	88, 110
Khaibān	82
Khāia Kuh	295
Khakan	36
Khalaf-ibn-i-Ahmed	223, 224, 231
Khalaj	314
Khalan	21, 22, 23, 24, 25
Khalif-al-Mansur	377
Khalif Moawia	377
Khalil	303
Khāwak	176, 332
Khandan	27
Khan Jahān Khan	92, 98, 99
Khan of Kalat	169
Khanikin	377, 378
Khānishin	257
Khānshi (Khānishin)	79
Khārān	16, 120, 216, 276, 283, 286, 292, 316, 317, 318, 321, 323, 324, 329.
Kharijis	18, 19, 25, 31, 97, 191, 209, 216, 294, 295, 296, 366.
Khar Kushta	176
Khāsh	10, 12, 17, 30, 50, 76, 108, 109, 110, 116, 117, 147, 160, 192, 199, 205, 211, 212, 218, 225, 281, 282, 315, 367.
Khash Khak	61
Khāsh Rud	12, 17, 80, 108, 109, 117, 141, 147, 160, 187, 199, 256

	Pages.
Khasrau I.	11, 145
Khasrau Parvez	12, 13
Khasrau II.	13
Khasraús	253, 280, 364
Khasru-gird	271
Khazars	12
Kheshk-i-Dukhtar	202
Khiábád	80, 92, 263
Khiaban	4, 53
Khiaban Alia	84
Khisht	12, 17, 50, 199, 218, 225
Khiva	371
Khizri	303
Khubanduz	4
Khudabanda	42, 43
Khujand	301
Khurassan	2, 3, 4, 5, 6, 7, 9, 10 11, 18, 19, 20, 23, 26, 27, 28, 32, 33, 36, 38, 39, 40, 41, 43, 44, 45, 46, 47, 54, 61, 62, 69, 71, 72, 75, 77, 78, 81, 83, 84, 85, 89, 189, 191, 224, 225, 262, 278, 281, 282, 284, 285, 298, 312, 313, 314, 320, 365, 367, 371, 372
Khusf	92, 263
Khush	70
Khuspas Rud	12, 109
Khutlan	27
Khuzdâr	290, 292, 318
Khuzistan	377
Khwábgáh	16, 111, 128, 129, 130, 135, 140, 142, 143, 148, 149, 150, 153, 172, 194
Khwajah 'Ali Mu'wid	54
Khwaja Ali	79, 127, 128
Khwájahs (or Khojas)	68
Khwajah Ahmad	97, 149, 173
Khwájah Amírán	232
Khwája Amran	274, 275, 293
Khwaja Bu Nasr	318
Khwaja-Kels	316
Khwajah Rabi	87
Khwajah Rabat	175, 176
Khwajah Siah-posh	187
Khwaja Surju	160, 256
Khwarazam, Empire of	26, 32, 36, 52
Khwash	366
Khyber Pass	90
Kilich Khan	83
Kimak	144, 192
Kimmak. See Kimak.	
Kinneir	170, 171, 465
Kipak, Prince	45
Kipchak	36
Kirais	367
Kirmâns	13, 14, 15, 17, 18, 20, 26, 27, 31, 37, 47, 61, 63, 77, 80, 81, 92, 93, 94, 97, 122, 123, 195, 196, 214, 215, 283, 294, 298, 320, 365, 366, 367.
Kirmiz	48
Kish	16, 17, 155, 199, 224, 225
Kishmar	188, 189
Kisrah	314, 315

	Pages.
Khilij Khan	79
Kizzilbashes	74, 78, 81
Kohat	89
Koh-i-Chako	113
Koh-i-Khwajah	65, 107, 108, 113, 116, 158, 169, 184, 238, 243, 248, 265, 266, 267, 277
Koh-i-Sangin	86
Koh-i-Sultan	109, 110, 113
Kohlak	151, 164, 167, 236, 241
Kolmarut	119, 216, 217
Kolwa	274, 288
Koshk	153
Koshk-i-Mahdi	86
Krateras	
Kubilai Khan	158
Kucha-i-Afzalábád	108, 263
Kuch wa Baluch	365, 366
Kuchan	83, 84, 85, 86, 87
Kufa	298
Kuhak	149, 150, 152, 173, 281
Kuhdastan	50
Kuhistan	13, 18, 34, 42, 46, 89, 110, 295, 308
Kuh-Khwaja. See Koh-i-Khwajah.	
Kuhpura	39
Kuhsuieh	38, 51
Kulab	372
Küls	297, 298, 299
Kundar	168, 257, 264
Kundarak	79, 163, 165, 237, 260, 261, 262, 263
Kundrak. See Kundarak.	
Kurdo	146, 147, 160, 239, 240
Kurds	83, 84, 85, 86, 87, 88, 294, 364, 365, 366
Kuring	122, 123, 198, 205, 216, 217
Kurki	167, 176
Kurun	123, 209, 216
Kurung	199
Kushans	11
Kushishtan	122
Kutlugh Turkán Agha	54
Kutluk	55
Kyánsih	184
Kyaxares	52

L

	Pages.
Láftán	118, 217
Lake of Zirreh	145
Lalue	80
Landi Barechi	315
Landi Muhammad Amin Khan	79, 295
Landi Wali Muhammad	127
Las Bela	274, 294, 316, 322
Lash	10, 31, 80, 118, 175, 215, 216, 287, 288
Láshár	366

Lash-Juwein	287, 288, 289
Leis, House of	122, 123, 165, 204, 211
Lestrange, Guy	199
Liwārzais	367
Lohārāni Jāms	290, 368
Lora	107
Lorasp	4
Lovett, Capt.	68
Lurg	236
Lurs	364, 368
Lutf Ali Khān	82, 88

M

Maadan	318
Macedon	289
Machi	137, 168, 196, 264
MacRitchie, David	378
Magas	366
Mahakaki	302, 303
Mahdi	84
Mahmud	22, 23
Mahmud Ghaznawi	36
Mahmud Ghilzai	81, 82
Mahmud Khuarazm Shah	31
Maidān-i-Gujarāt	302
Makran	17, 35, 62, 65, 89, 90, 110, 128, 308, 310, 319, 363, 365.
Mala Khān	128
Malik Abdullah	76
Malik Abu Bakr Marjaki	33
Malik Ali	76
Malik Ali-i-Mas'ud	39
Malik Asadullah Khan	88, 89
Malik Azim Khan	238, 280, 281
Malik Bahā-ud-din (or Ma-ud-din)	67
Malik Bahrām Khan	96, 98, 136, 167, 168, 169, 170, 171, 172, 181, 196
Malik Bakr	45, 51
Malik Daud	61
Malik Dinār	27, 323, 365
Malik Dosten	323
Malik Fakhr-ud-din	41, 42, 43, 52, 66
Malik Fath Ali Khan	79, 80, 90, 91, 95
Malik Gheiath-ud-din (Amir-i-Ghuri)	52
Malik Gheiath-ud-din Muhammad	72, 222
Malik Gheiath-ud-din Pir Ali	51, 52, 53, 61
Malik Gheiath-u]-Hak'-wa-ud-din	43, 44, 45
Malik Gulzar Khan	99, 277, 299
Malik Hafiz	45
Malik Haidari	160, 162, 164, 176
Malik Hamza Khan	78, 79, 93, 94, 96, 160, 161, 181, 245, 246, 247, 248, 249, 250, 252, 253, 254, 255, 256, 257, 258, 260.
Malik Hisam-ud-din	41, 42
Malik Husain Ghuri	47
Malik Husen Khan	89, 91
Malik Husen Kurt	47, 48, 50, 51, 52, 61, 71
Malik Ishāk	84, 85, 86, 88, 89
Malik Izzat	75
Malik Izz-ud-din	43
Malik Jafar Kaiāni	79
Malik J'afir Khan	79
Malik Jallaludin	41, 48, 49, 54, 63, 71, 73, 74, 75, 76, 77, 78, 173, 281.
Malik Jallaludin Mahmud	240
Malik Kalb 'Ali	88
Malik Kāward	365
Malik Khasrau	44
Malik Kutb-ud-din	44, 45, 47, 48, 50, 57, 58, 61, 63, 66, 155, 156, 158, 159, 181, 216, 237, 238, 245, 246, 247, 248, 258.
Malik Lutf 'Ali	89, 90, 93, 94, 95
Malik Mahmud	72, 73, 74, 75, 76, 77, 80, 81, 82, 83, 85, 86, 87, 88, 89, 91, 92, 248, 262.
Malik Mahmud Khan Kaiāni	171
Malik Mamakatu	62
Malik Miran Shah	40
Malik Mubāriz-ud-din	33
Malik Muhammad (Amir-i-Khurd)	51, 53, 61
Malik Muhammad Azim Khan	99
Malik Muhammad Jallal-ud-din Khan	93, 94, 95, 98, 181, 248, 256.
Malik Muiz-ud-din	45, 46, 50, 51, 246, 267
Malik Mu'i'z-ud-din Husen	64, 65
Malik Mujd-ud-din-Kaliyuni	37, 38
Malik Nasr-ud-din	74, 75, 76
Malik Nasr-ud-din Khan	92
Malik Nizam-ud-din Yāhyāh	70
Malik Nusrat Khan	79
Malik Nusrat-ud-din	31, 33
Malik Qutb-ud-din bin Shah Rukn	46, 47
Malik Rukn-ud-din	31, 32, 33, 38, 40, 42, 43
Malik Rustam	89
Malik Shah	21, 24, 26, 30, 31, 32
Malik Shāh Husen	76
Malik Shams-ud-din	27, 29, 37, 39, 40, 41, 43, 45
Malik Shihab-ud-din Mahmud	31
Malik Sulemān Khan	91, 92, 95, 263
Malik Taj-ud-din	24, 26, 27, 28, 29, 31
Malik Taj-ud-din Khar	40, 167
Malik Taj-ud-din Mal Tigin	31, 32, 35, 37, 41, 43
Malik ul Ashtar	95
Malik-ul-Sais	27, 28, 30
Malik Zainalo (Zain-ul'Abidin)	67
Malik Zarif	76
Mamasenni	367, 368
Man	311
Mangu Khan	38
Marco Polo	313, 320
Mardoi	368

Märgo	151, 210
Maruchak	38
Mārwār	274
Masaud	184
Mashi	149, 161, 257
Māshkal Hamun	283
Māshkel	62, 107, 184, 317, 321, 322, 366
Masita	29
Masjidak	216
Mask	29
Mastung	39, 283, 286, 316
Maulānā Muhammad Shah of Farah	66, 67
Maulānā Nizām-ud-din	52
Mazenderan	39, 54, 69, 70
McCrindle, Mr.	291
Meakin, Annette M. B.	278
Meds	310, 311, 312, 377, 378
Meno	16, 140, 173, 199, 254
Merv	19, 27, 71, 86, 88, 313
Meshed	71, 75, 82, 84, 85, 86, 87, 88, 91, 99, 108, 119, 305, 325.
Meski	136, 138, 139, 146, 225, 226
Mewar	280
Mjān Kangi	123, 164, 206, 210, 297, 306, 307, 326, 328, 330, 331, 332, 334.
Mihrab Shah	3, 7
Milak	30
Milan	311
Mili	145, 152
Mil-i-Kasamābād	152, 182, 205, 268, 269, 271
Ming, or Meng, or Min	291
Mingals or Mengals	289, 290, 291, 368
Minhaj-i-Saraj	30
Minhaj-us-Saraj	218
Minnagar	291
Minuchihr	36
Minujan	365
Mirabad	63
Mir Abbas	55, 58, 210
Mirak	63
Mir Alam Khan	172, 181
Mir-Ali	72
Mir'Ali Amuyiah	87
Mirān Mir Abd-Allah	63
Mirān Shāh, Prince	53
Mir Barid	55
Mir Bijjar	316
Mir Haji	332
Mir-i-'Arab	24
Mir Ikbāl	216
Mir-Ismailee	29
Mirkahrez	84
Mir Kambar	91, 95
Mir Khan	96
Mir Mehrab	94
Mir Masum Khan	96
Mir Weisi	79, 295, 303, 331
Mirs	68, 72, 75
Mirza Da'ud	81
Modhar	19
Modi, Jivanji Jamshedji	291
Moghols	31, 32, 33, 34, 35, 36, 38, 40, 42, 43, 44, 52, 304
Moghūlistān	301
Momīnābād	29
Moorcroft	2
Moses of Chorene	9, 184
Mubids	10
Muhammad	82, 89
Muhammad Ali	88
Muhammad Āli Khan	97
Muhammad Beg	75, 88
Muhammad Dādi	180, 280
Muhammad of Ghazni	184, 313
Muhammad Husen Beg	87
Muhammad Husen Khan	80, 92
Muhammad-Ibn-i-Kāsam	16
Muhammad Ibrahim	365
Muhammad Khān	73, 84, 85
Muhammad Khan Chulah	88
Muhammad Nasir Khan	92, 93, 165
Muhammad Raza Khan Sarbandi	8
Muhammad Reza Khan	91, 95, 96
Muhammad Shaibani Khān	77
Muhammad Sultan	58
Muhammad Taki Khan	328
Muhammadzais	290
Muhammedabad	169
Muin	98
M'uin-ud-din-Abul Khair	365
Muiz-ud-din	27, 45, 252
Mulahidah	29, 30
Mulla Khasrau	22, 167
Mulla Muhammad Rafi-ai	84
Mulla Muin	4, 5, 6, 10
Multan	378
Murghab	38, 54
Murrais	293
Musa Khan	288
Mutawakkal	189
Muzafar Husan, Prince	78
Muzaffar Koh	5
Muzaffar-ud-daulah	177, 181

N

Nād Ali	98, 111, 139, 148, 156, 173, 177, 194, 196, 198, 199, 200, 201, 202, 210, 211, 213, 218, 226, 314.
Nadir	82, 85, 86, 87
Nadir Kuli	83, 85, 86, 87, 88, 89, 90
Nadir Shah	91, 93, 95, 96, 166, 201, 215, 262, 282, 328
Nadir Shah's Tower	217
Naharjān	29

	Pages.
Nāhruis	27, 94, 95, 96, 97, 98, 166, 192
Nahrwān	366
Naizār	124, 303, 304, 307
Najaf	92
Nakhe	80, 92, 93
Nakodar	321, 324
Nalivkin, M.	284
Nariman	3
Nar-Tu	33, 34, 35, 38
Nash Rud	15, 145, 148
Nasirabad	25, 63, 164, 165
Nasir Khan Kaiani	165
Nasir-ud-din Uttman	28, 29, 41
Nāsr	23
Nasratabad	165, 184, 191
Naushirwān, Dam of	150, 155, 188
Naushirwān the Just	135, 146, 150, 155, 156, 157, 274, 365
Nauzād	29
Neh	10, 30, 31, 217
Neti	113
Nial Tigin	31, 37, 43, 44, 45, 218, 313
Nichara	312
Nikudaris	43, 46, 54, 62, 300, 320, 321, 322, 323, 324
Nimroz	46, 61, 77, 110, 153, 154
Nimroz, Malik of	26
Nimruz, Satrap of	12
Nisa	86
Nishapur	10, 13, 19, 22, 27, 29, 31, 33, 34, 35, 51, 84, 85, 86, 184
Nishk	145, 146, 160, 198, 199, 212, 218
Noken Kalat	239
Nuh-Mardi	308
Nuk	15
Nuk-Baluch	367
Numrias	308, 309, 368
Nushki	169, 289, 290, 291, 308
Nuri	302

O

Oba'd Ibn Ziyad	16, 17, 155, 199
Omar, Caliph	19, 377
Ommeya, House of	18, 19, 285
Or or Od	274, 312
Oritai	274
Ormāra	274, 288
Orontes	377
Otrār	158
Oxus	7, 9, 10, 11, 18, 20, 27, 32, 36, 38, 45, 46, 48, 51, 52, 64, 66, 69, 77, 253, 278, 289, 291, 301, 302, 371

P

Padai	332
Pāgos	326, 327, 329, 330

	Pages.
Pahlawāns	282, 291, 295
Pahlawānzai	290
Paisai	139, 146
Pā Kash-i-Rustam	196
Palangān	109, 113, 293
Palangi	169, 170, 250, 252, 253, 256, 258
Palang Koh	244
Pamir	371, 372, 374
Panjdeh (Paudi)	47, 53
Panjgur	35, 274, 275, 276, 281, 288, 289, 292, 316, 317, 366, 367
Panjika	303
Pā Pālu	83
Pariun	98, 111, 151, 177, 190, 236, 297, 330
Parkar	274
Parshat-Gau	188
Parsis	297
Parthians	10
Parwān	33, 68
Pasargadæ	2, 10
Pate Pashm	295, 302
Pedro Texeira	206
Peshāwarān	121, 170, 198, 216, 236
Peshin	275
Pilpili	295
Piri	39
Pir Khizr	110
Pir Muhammad	80, 86, 87, 88
Pir Sultan	110
Piruz	11
Pishin	280, 292
Poolgee	169, 170, 172, 253
Post-i-Gau	160, 187, 188, 192, 212, 213, 256
Pottinger, Lieut.	169
Pudai. See Dor.	
Pudna	302
Pulālak	315
Pulchota	110
Pulgi	176, 237, 253, 332
Pumpelly, Mr. Raphael	53
Pusht-i-Koh	68
Pusht-i-Zawah	77
Puza-i-Surh Dagāl	133, 161, 257
Puz-i-Māshi	132, 159, 225

Q

Qamar-ud-din	301
Quetta	290
Quetta-Pishin	286
Qufs or Qufas	365

R

Rabi	15, 16, 198
Rādkān	85

Rabaz	303
Rahbur	294
Rahdār	303
Raisānis	290
Rakshān	317
Rakshānis	290, 297
Ramadthan Ghaibi	110
Rāmhormuz	377
Rāmrod	8, 74, 160, 167, 168, 196, 240, 241, 248, 257, 258.
Rāmrodis	8
Ram Shahristān	30, 155, 163, 192, 193, 194, 195, 196, 198, 199, 225, 238.
Rasak	195, 196
Rasālik	74, 147
Rāshak	193, 196, 238
Rāskak	267
Rās Koh	317
Rāsukhān	365
Raverty, Major	5, 24, 27, 28, 223, 287
Rawlinson, George	312
Rawlinson, Sir Henry	7, 15, 16, 123, 145, 155, 195, 196, 198, 203, 205, 208, 209, 210, 211, 212, 223, 224, 295.
Razai	367
Regān	214
Rei	318
Reis	8, 9, 366
Reis Akbar	8
Reis Ghulam Muhammad	8
Reis Hasan	8
Reis Husena	8
Reis Muhammad	8
Reis Muhammad Ali	8
Reis Nakh Muhammad Ali	8
Rekis	366
Renand, M.	291
Reza Kuli Khan	84
Rinda or Rindān	235, 236, 241
Rinds	89
Robah	42
Rodeni	368
Rosban	372, 374
Ross, Principal E. Denison	52
Rūāmrod	74
Rudbār	16, 17, 127, 169
Rud-i-Biyabān	129, 130, 132, 133, 137, 147, 148, 154, 156, 157, 158, 160, 161, 163, 164, 167, 196, 238, 240, 241, 242, 248, 250, 257, 258, 260.
Rud-i-Pojzghanan	5
Rud-i-Naseru	164, 165, 172, 177
Rud-i-Nasru	148
Rud-i-Seistan	97, 142, 149, 150, 192, 195, 237
Rud-i-Sina	128, 136, 154
Rud-i-Taj Muhammad	176
Rud Māhi	177
Rusht	15
Rustam	3, 4, 6, 7, 9, 15, 112, 168, 182, 187, 191, 196, 201, 204, 208, 211, 242, 254, 264, 267.
Rustam Khan	91, 92, 200
Rustam Mirza	73, 74, 75, 76, 77, 78

S

Sabzawār	4, 5, 6, 7, 10, 34, 44, 54, 66, 83, 110, 184, 271.
Sabz Kūh	134, 135
Sadozais	166
Safar	297
Safedik	139, 177, 200, 201, 203
Safed-khāki	303
Safed Koh	31
Safed Rud	17
Saffārides	20
Saffavis, Empire of	71, 81, 211, 212
Sagastan	184, 188
Said Khan	97
Saif-ud-din	67
Saiyad Ahmad	81
Saj	67, 289
Saji	39
Sajitis	288, 289, 291
Sakai Kalat or Saka Kalat	289
Sakas	10, 12, 287, 288, 289, 312
Sakasaran	8
Sakastana	9, 183, 312
Sakzis	10, 217, 287, 288, 289, 291, 296, 297, 307
Salihan	118, 121
Saljuks	23, 26, 36, 313
Sam	3, 4, 6, 8
Sāmān, House of	20, 21, 36
Samarkand	1, 26, 52, 53, 60, 61, 158, 289, 291, 301, 328, 371, 372.
Samarrā	189
Sam Beg Vakil	87
Sam-Kuh	113
Sanadgul	295, 303
Sana Rud	128, 133, 134, 135, 136, 137, 142, 257
Sanchor	274
Sanchuli	295, 296
Sangun	189
Sangur	288
Sani Beg Sultan	77
Sanjarānis	95, 97, 98, 128, 173, 175, 200
Sanjaris	46
Sarai-i-Siasati	223
Sarai-i-Tahiri	57
Sarakhs	27
Saraparœ	294

INDEX.

	Pages
Sarawan	292
Sarayān (or Saraban)	77
Sarbadāris	51, 54
Sarbandis	91, 94, 95, 97, 98, 166, 173, 284, 294, 295, 296
Sarbaz	89, 90
Sardar Azād Khan	16
Sardar Khan Jahān Khan	331
Sargāh	138, 139, 140, 146, 147
Sargāh-i-Seistan	138, 145, 249
Sarhad	8, 27, 128, 189, 318
Sarhadis	6
Sār-o-Tār	7, 10, 16, 111, 140, 146, 147, 185, 224, 225, 226, 227, 228, 231, 232, 233, 234, 239, 240, 245, 248, 249, 250, 256, 266, 275, 333
Sarparra	293, 294
Sartor	78
Sarts	279, 280, 284
Sarunis	118, 303, 306
Sarwini	303
Sassanian Dynasty	11, 36, 156, 232
Sassanide Dynasty	11
Sassi and Punu	312, 313
Satlej	313
Sawari	108, 109, 115
Sāwari Shah	151, 156, 208, 209, 236
Sayabija	377
Sea of Oman	274, 365
Sehkoha	8, 94, 95, 96, 195, 196, 238, 257, 258, 267
Seiads	75, 124, 125, 166, 296, 297, 298
Seistan, Delta of	1
Sena Rud	15, 16, 17, 145, 148, 149, 154, 155, 173, 199
Serafshan	372
Serat	198
Sha'abeh	149, 150, 155
Shabeh	145
Shab-i-Āb	149, 238
Shab-i-Koh	68
Shadyak	35
Shafilan	35
Shah Abbās the Great	81
Shahr-i-Sabz	52
Shāhakzais	367
Shah Ali	222
Shāhbāz Kalat	292
Shahduz	30
Shah Husen	65
Shah Husen Saffavi	80, 81, 84
Shahi Beg Khān, Kabuli	78
Shah-i-Meshed	83
Shahin Shahi	30
Shah-i-Shāhān	55, 60, 61
Shāh Ismāil Saffavi	71
Shahizai	290
Shah Jahān	245, 260, 291
Shah Kamrān	173, 174, 181
Shah Kutb-ud-din	55, 59, 60, 61, 63, 65
Shah Nusrat	46

	Pages
Shāhrakis	91, 92, 94, 95, 97, 98, 284, 294, 295, 296
Shahriāri	303
Shahr-i-Kalan	239
Shahristan	4, 7, 31, 111, 142, 297, 299, 307, 326, 329, 330, 331, 334
Shahr-sebba	371, 372
Shahristān-i-Belkis	6
Shahrud-i-Bustam	86
Shah Rud	71
Shah Rukh	60, 61, 62, 63, 64, 67, 69, 287
Shah Rukh Mirza	91, 159, 215, 246
Shah Sikandar	66
Shah Sikandar Niāl Tigin	67
Shah Thamasp	84, 85, 86, 87, 88
Shahwānis	292
Shah Yāhyāh	69
Shaibāni Khān	2, 71
Shakan	44
Shakhim	29
Shamiran	4
Shamsābād	134, 135
Shams-ud-din Lachin	38
Shand	147
Shapur	10
Sharafud-i-Din Ali	158
Shārak	174
Shāraki	167, 169, 176
Sharifabad	98
Sharif Khan	96, 97
Shash	27
Sheikh Daud	54
Sheikh Husen	110, 249
Sheikh Mahmud	68, 69
Sheikh Nuri	303
Shekh Weisi	295, 303
Shela	15, 16, 70, 109, 123, 132, 158, 161, 164, 184, 196
Shela-i-Ghulām Shah	125
Shela-i-Inglisi	175
Shela-i-Kafiri	169
Shela-i-Meshkushi	125
Shela-i-Rud-Gashta	175
Shela-i-Shamshiri	175
Shibargan	46
Shihab-ud-din (Ghuri)	5, 32, 36, 38
Shijrat-ul-Muluk	91
Shimir	218
Shirwadh	15
Shirabad	372
Shirānis	315
Shiraz	22
Shishāwa	367
Shorāwak	294, 315
Shoru	96
Shugnan	372, 374
Shujā Beg	71
Shurgaz	295
Shustar	2
Siahsar	303

INDEX.

	Pages.
Sib	366
Sigzis	287
Sihun	301, 302
Sijistan	3, 15, 16, 38, 42, 122, 145, 184, 195, 199, 210, 287
Siksar	177, 297
Sikur	34, 37
Sinā Rud	212
Sind	3, 18, 20
Sinnkan	321
Siraf	214
Sirjan	15, 61
Sish Pal	232
Smith, V. A.	301
Sogdiana	289
Sohren Kalat	237
Somnath	318
Soran	366
Spintizha	275
Sufi Kuli Khan Turkman Oghli	82
Sufi	303
Suleman	82
Sultan Husen Baikara	70, 71
Sultan Husen Mirza	73, 74, 75
Sultan Jallaludin Khwarazm Shah	33, 34, 35
Sultan Mahmud bin Shah	49
Sultan Mahmud-i-Sabak Tigin	224
Sultan Mahmud of Ghazni	223, 224, 318
Sultan Masud Ghaznawi	54, 313, 318
Sultan Muhammad of Khwārazm	32, 38, 52
Sultan Muhammad (Khar Sawār)	81
Sultan Said	69, 70
Sultan Sanjar	26, 27, 37, 271
Sumalzais	294
Surh Dagāl	133, 134
Surhdik	200, 201, 203
Suruwar	210, 211, 212
Sven Hedin, Sir	307
Sykes, Col. P. M.	189
Syr	371
Syr Darya	301

T

	Pages.
Tābān Bahādur	54
Tabar Kan Pass	217, 218
Tabari	377, 378
Tabas	29, 89, 99
Tabasain	218
Tadjiks	371, 372, 373, 374
Ta-hia	278
Tahir	21, 23, 24, 25, 231, 259
Tahiri Maliks	36
Tahlab	184
Tāhzūn (or Tāhazwun)	74

	Pages.
Tair Bahadur	38
Tajiks	6, 12, 33, 36, 68, 69, 180, 364
Taj Muhammad	96, 98
Taj Muhammad Kūl	299, 332
Taj Muhammad Sarbandi	176, 281
Taj-ud-din Harab	271
Taj-ud-din Seistani	55, 270
Tāk	23, 60, 158, 224, 225, 234, 267
Takht-i-Pul	198, 205, 206, 217, 228, 231, 271
Takht-i-Rustam	199
Takht-i-Shāh	124, 176, 198
Tak-i-Amrān	255
Takish	26
Takyan	38
Talus	109, 112
Tamerlane	215
Tamurchi	7
Tapa-i-Khūrān	124
Tapa-i-Mari	202
Tapa-i-Safed	237
Tapa-i-Shagālak	216
Tappa-i-Beringak	151
Tappa-i-Daulatābād	170
Tappa-i-Kohlak	151, 171, 235, 306
Tarins	297
Tashkand	27
Tashkent	301
Tāt	279
Tawang	290
Te'am	145, 146, 147, 203
Teheran	96, 97
Tells	187
Thāna Bhula Khan	290
Tharr	274
Tigris	18, 377
Tikāla	146, 249
Tilak	313
Tilgkoh	154
Timur	15, 48, 49, 51, 52, 53, 54, 55, 56, 57, 58, 59, 60, 61, 62, 63, 64, 67, 69, 80, 155, 156, 157, 158, 159, 193, 219, 222, 223, 225, 234, 236, 240, 243, 249, 253, 255, 258, 300, 301, 302, 320, 321, 323, 330, 335, 366, 372.
Timur Khan	71
Timur Shah	92, 93, 263
Tirah	38
Tirkoh	136, 137, 154
Tirmid	32
Tirmiz	26
Tiz	214
Todd, Col.	301
Tokharistan	11
Topāl Othmān	89
Tora	188
Trākun	74, 129, 130, 132, 154, 159, 160, 161, 167, 192, 240, 242, 243, 244, 257, 258.
Trebeck	2
Trushpap	108

	Pages.
Tshu	371
Tughan	34
Tuho	323
Tulak	31, 35
Tuli Khan	33
Tun	29, 79, 80, 81, 86, 263
Turkan Khatun	26
Turshiz	52, 189
Turuk	86
Tus	13, 34, 84

U

	Pages.
Ubād Sultan	72
Uchto	307
Ujfalvy, M	300, 364
Uk	25, 32, 54, 80, 90, 122, 215, 287
Uktāe	37
Ulema	60
Uljaitu Sultan	43, 44
Umad	43
Umr-i-Maraghāni	28
Umro	20, 23
Urak	127
Usbegs	71, 75, 77, 78, 253, 279, 284, 371, 372, 373, 374.
Uthman	31
Uthman-i-Taj-ud-din Harab	31
Uzbakzais	367

V

	Pages.
Vakhan	372, 373, 374
Valarsaces	312
Varaich Jats	314, 315
Vardausi	372
Vishtaspa	188
Vredenburgh, E	113
Vullers	378

W

	Pages.
Wad	289
Wadi Abras	199
Wagharashag	312
Wakhan	285
Wakhis	285
Walid I	377
Warmal	15, 129, 150, 169, 238, 302
Wāshuk	323
White Huns	301, 302
Wood, Capt. John	278

Y

	Pages.
Yakan Khān	75
Yakan	157
Yak Gumbad	167, 168
Yakub	204
Yakub-ibn-ul Leith	10, 20, 21, 36
Yakut	212, 216
Yaminiah Dynasty	36
Yār Ahmadzais	27
Yasir, Prince	44, 45
Yate, Col.	5, 6, 237
Yazd	75, 81, 158, 214, 217, 300, 320, 321, 322
Yazdigird III	11, 13, 36
Yazid II	377
Yemen	19
Yumurgh	50

Z

	Pages.
Zābil	16
Zabri	368
Zabul (or Zawul)	3, 4, 5, 7
Zābulistan	65
Zahak	118, 121
Zāhidān	21, 22, 25, 30, 55, 56, 57, 58, 60, 61, 63, 71, 151, 155, 156, 160, 162, 163, 164, 181, 195, 218, 219, 220, 221, 222, 225, 226, 233, 235, 236, 237, 241, 243, 245, 248, 253, 255, 256, 257, 259, 261, 262, 268, 276, 289, 299, 300, 321.
Zahrozais	294
Zainulabad	217
Zain-ul-Millat Wa-ud-din	63
Zal	3, 4
Zalik	15, 16, 145, 150, 151
Zamān Khān	81, 82
Zamindāwar	310
Zamin-i-Dawar	27, 71, 73, 76, 77, 78, 109, 127
Zāmrān	276
Zarafshān	289
Zaraha	184
Zaranj	3, 4, 8, 15, 16, 17, 20, 21, 24, 25, 115, 183, 184, 195, 196, 198, 199, 203, 205, 209, 210, 212, 213, 214, 215, 216, 218, 223, 224, 225.
Zari	183
Zarkan	146, 147, 154, 155, 160, 187, 238, 250, 255
Zarnigār	168
Zaro	184
Zaur	303
Zends	93
Zenobius	311
Zerkuh	29
Zhob	276

INDEX

	Pages
Ziarat-i-Khwajah Rabāt	167
Ziarat-i-Murtaza Ali	144
Ziarat-i-Sheikh Husen	249, 258, 259
Ziarat of Amirān the Zorkan	146, 147
Ziarat of Amran	248, 254, 293
Ziarat of Shah-i-Mardān	161
Ziarat of Shah Ismail	206
Zirah	74
Zireh	122, 131, 183, 184
Zirreh	54, 55, 57, 73, 74, 76, 77
Zorkan	146, 147, 154, 155, 160, 187, 238, 248, 255
Zoroaster	186, 188, 189, 190, 191, 276, 373
Zotts	377
Zughar or Zaghar Mingals	289, 290, 292
Zuhak the Tazi	3, 7, 36
Zulnun Beg	71

APPENDIX I.

	Pages
Genealogy of the Kaiani Princes of Seistan from Original Sources, 1904.	191—106

APPENDIX I (A).

	Pages
Abstract of the Village Population, and Pāgos, of the Shahristān and Miān Kangi Districts of Seistan, Persian Territory, 1904-05	339—355

APPENDIX I (B).

	Pages
Abstract of the Population in the Districts of Kang and of Chakansur of Seistan, Afghan Territory, 1904-05	359—360

APPENDIX II.

	Pages
"Baloch" and "Brahui"	363—368

APPENDIX III.

	Pages
The Tajiks of Bokhara	371—374

APPENDIX IV.

	Pages
The Jats in Mesopotamia and Syria	377—378

www.ingramcontent.com/pod-product-compliance
Lightning Source LLC
Chambersburg PA
CBHW080233170426
43192CB00014BA/2453